# WORK
*over*
# WELFARE

# WORK over WELFARE

## The Inside Story of the 1996 Welfare Reform Law

Ron Haskins

BROOKINGS INSTITUTION PRESS
*Washington, D.C.*

*Library of Congress Cataloging-in-Publication data*
Haskins, Ron.
  Work over welfare : the inside story of the 1996 Welfare Reform Act / Ron Haskins.
    p.  cm.
  Includes bibliographical references and index.
  ISBN-13: 978-0-8157-3508-3 (cloth : alk. paper)
  ISBN-10: 0-8157-3508-1 (cloth : alk. paper)
  1. Public welfare—United States. 2. United States. Personal Responsibility and Work Opportunity Reconciliation Act of 1996. 3. Welfare recipients—Employment—United States. 4. United States—Social policy—1993- I. Title.
  HV95.H34 2006
  362.5'840973--dc22                                                      2006021494

2 4 6 8 9 7 5 3 1

The paper used in this publication meets minimum requirements of the American National Standard for Information Sciences—Permanence of Paper for Printed Library Materials: ANSI Z39.48-1992.

Typeset in Minion

Composition by OSP, Inc.
Arlington, Virginia

Printed by R. R. Donnelley
Harrisonburg, Virginia

TO

SUSANN *for love*

HEATHER, SETH, MEGAN, AND LUKE *for joy*

DOROTHY *for ambition*

HARRIET *for standards*

CLAY *for opportunity*

# Contents

Preface                                                                          ix

CHAPTER ONE
Building the American Welfare State                                                1

CHAPTER TWO
Laying the Groundwork                                                             20

CHAPTER THREE
House Republicans Unite behind Radical Reforms                                    37

CHAPTER FOUR
The Contract with America                                                         59

CHAPTER FIVE
The House Initiates the Revolution                                                82

CHAPTER SIX
The Battle in the House, Part I: Hearings                                        106

CHAPTER SEVEN
The Battle in the House, Part II: Markups                                        135

CHAPTER EIGHT
The Battle in the House, Part III: The Floor                                     165

CHAPTER NINE
The Senate Joins the Revolution                                                  194

CHAPTER TEN
Budget Issues Trump Welfare Reform                                               227

CHAPTER ELEVEN
Clinton Vetoes Welfare Reform, Again 254

CHAPTER TWELVE
The Governors Revive the Revolution 268

CHAPTER THIRTEEN
The Revolution Threatened 288

CHAPTER FOURTEEN
Triumph: Clinton Signs 314

CHAPTER FIFTEEN
Ten Years Later: The Triumph of Work 332

APPENDIX
The Welfare Reform Law That
Reshaped American Social Policy 364

Notes 377

Index 429

# Preface

This is my account of how major welfare reform legislation was passed by Congress and signed by President Clinton in 1996. Churchill famously said that democracy is the worst form of government—except all the others. This book lays bare the messiness, complexity, unpredictability, excitement, sordidness, and beauty of American democracy in action. I regret that so many Americans lack the knowledge and understanding of how their federal government works to make big decisions about the future of the nation. By exposing every side in one of the bitterest congressional debates in recent memory, my story shows how members of Congress, members of the Clinton administration, and advocates for a cacophony of views on social policy fought alongside or against each other to create a spectacular piece of legislation that fundamentally changed the direction of social policy in America. Sure, the quality of debate was uneven, and some of the partisans on every side went a step or ten too far. But the uniquely American system of federal democracy all but assured the right outcome. It is a glorious and exciting story and more Americans—especially younger Americans—should know about it.

In addition to telling the story of how the law was written and passed, I believe that the tenth anniversary of its passage is a good time to examine its effects. Having participated in writing the welfare reform law and having some modest skill in understanding research and evaluation, I thought I could look at the evidence in a dispassionate way and draw sound judgments about the law's effects

While I am a Republican, I have strained to be fair to all sides. On the whole, the predictions of the right about the effects of the welfare reform law have been more accurate than the predictions of the left. As noted in chapter 15, scholars have been surprised by the magnitude of the decline in welfare rolls, the unprecedented increase in female employment and income, and the remarkable drop in child poverty associated with the implementation of welfare reform. But the legislation has not been a panacea. Poverty is still a major problem in America, and there have been some unfortunate outcomes that can be reasonably ascribed to welfare reform. More to the point, establishing policies to encourage opportunity and reduce poverty is still a top item on the nation's domestic agenda. And the policies Republicans advanced to fight nonmarital births—a significant factor leading to our most difficult domestic problems—have certainly not yet produced major changes in marriage rates or illegitimacy. If demography is destiny, we are still flirting with disaster.

I did seek to defend Republicans against the attacks leveled at our welfare reform legislation during the colorful debate of 1995 and 1996. The invective directed against the bill on the floor of the House and on the nation's editorial pages is a matter of record, as this book will show. To some extent, I believe the extreme partisanship that now afflicts the nation's capital finds at least some of its roots in the welfare reform debate of a decade ago.

Although most of the thirty or so people who have read all or part of the book have reassured me that it is not overly partisan, I have a lingering concern that some who read it will think I am unfair to Democrats. So be it. The fact is that President Clinton created a political opportunity, Republicans seized it and expanded it, and, despite the divisiveness of the debate, in the end the law passed with a huge bipartisan majority and was signed by a Democratic president. There is credit enough for everyone—and more than enough work left for both Republicans and Democrats to undertake. To prepare, they could do worse than ponder the lessons of 1996.

Debts pile up when you write a book. The people who commented on parts of the manuscript include Henry Aaron, Ken Apfel, Richard Bavier, Randy Capps, Sharon Daly, Bill Dickens, Elizabeth Donahue, Brian Gaston, Peter Germanis, Meg Haynes, Mike Hershey, Jack Howard, Kerry Knott, Ed Kutler, Mike Laracy, Jack Lew, Larry Mead, Phil Moseley, Wendell Primus, Robert Rector, Bruce Reed, Alice Rivlin, Senator Rick Santorum, Isabel Sawhill, Judy Schneider, Peter Schuck, Representative Clay Shaw, Melissa Skolfield, Mark Strand, Don Wolfensberger, and Sheila Zedlewski. Fortunately, I have several friends who are not above acts of masochism as indicated by their willingness to read the entire book and make extensive written comments, many of which I followed. These included Matt Weidinger, Vee Burke, Mark Greenberg, and Howard Rolston. The four of them sum up much of my two decades in Washington: they are hypercompetent and work tirelessly in their respective provinces for the public good, Matt as a conservative, Mark as a liberal, and Howard and Vee as persons of unknown and undetectable political persuasion.

Equal indebtedness goes to those who gave me documents or information that proved useful in writing the book. These generous individuals include Gina Adams, Gordon Berlin, Doug Besharov, Cassie Bevan, Richard Billmire, Becky Blank, Helen Blank, Randy Brandt, Gary Burtless, Howard Cohen, Sheila Dacey, Jason DeParle, Gene Falk, Don Fierce, Susan Golonka, Harry Holzer, Wade Horn, Kate Houston, Andrea Kane, Leighton Ku, Jason LaFond, Paul Legler, Bob Lerman, Irene Lurie, Steve Martin, Sara McLanahan, Ron Mincy, Martha Moorehouse, Zoe Neuberger, Don Oellerich, Sharon Parrott, Jonathan Rauch, Karen Spar, Stephanie Ventura, Kent Weaver, Celeste West, Don Winstead, Barbara Wolanin, Robert Wood, and Marty Zaslow. I especially thank Bruce Reed for telling me the story of the July 31, 1996, meetings in the Cabinet Room and the Oval Office during which President Clinton discussed whether to sign the welfare reform bill with his top advisers. I also have immense gratitude for Diane Kirkland who helped me arrange to study several volumes of documents on welfare reform that she had collected, catalogued, and arranged for binding for the House Ways and Means Committee.

The people at Brookings Institution Press have been terrific. They answered all my questions and always made me feel they were giving my book special attention. The editor, Diane Hammond, made the book shorter and easier to read and worked quickly. What more could anyone want from an editor? Eric Haven fact checked the book as if it were his own and saved me from an embarrassing number of errors. Janet Walker, Bob Faherty, and Chris Kelaher have given me strong support on this and other book projects. Sarah Chilton of the Brookings library helped us obtain numerous documents. I am immensely grateful to all of them.

During the time I wrote this book our Center on Children and Families (previously the Welfare Reform and Beyond initiative) at Brookings was supported by grants from the Annie E. Casey Foundation, the Ford Foundation, the Foundation for Child Development, the Joyce Foundation, the John D. and Catherine T. MacArthur Foundation, the David and Lucile Packard Foundation, the Harry and Jeanette Weinberg Foundation, and the Charles Stewart Mott Foundation. All supported my work during this period; all have my gratitude; none is responsible for my views or conclusions.

It was a great honor and a great opportunity to work for the House Ways and Means Committee during the heady days of welfare reform in 1995 and 1996. During the years I directed the staff of the Human Resources Subcommittee, I worked for four Republicans who headed the subcommittee, Hank Brown, Rick Santorum, Clay Shaw, and Nancy Johnson, as well as with Bill Archer, who chaired the full committee from 1995 until his retirement in 2000. I have the deepest possible admiration for all of them. Similarly, the Republicans on the subcommittee were among the best, the most persistent, and the hardest working members I have been privileged to work with. Clay Shaw and Bill Archer, especially, were not only an inspiration to know, but treated me with dignity— something that does not always characterize the relationship between members of Congress and their staff. I also have great respect for many of the Democrats with whom I had the good fortune to work, especially Ben Cardin, Tom Carper, and Charlie Stenholm.

Helping develop, draft, and guide the welfare reform bill through Congress was one of the most exhilarating experiences of my life, not least because I worked closely with thirty or more staff members who combined understanding of congressional procedure with knowledge about specific areas of public policy with such competence that I was always proud to be part of the Republican team. The most competent and driven of all was my assistant Matt Weidinger. The truth is that I often was given credit for pulling off feats that were due in large part to his knowledge, skill, and commitment to duty. Ditto for Phil Moseley, the always steady, always persistent, always calm chief of staff of Ways and Means.

By 2000 I had worked in Congress for fourteen years and was ready to return to my roots as a scholar. The Brookings Institution, not exactly a major store- house for aging Republicans, offered me a wonderful position, primarily because of the actions of Isabel Sawhill. For the past six years, Belle has been a trusted col- league and a constant source of intellectual challenge and friendship. Other Brookings scholars have likewise been exceptional colleagues and friends. I am especially indebted to Alice Rivlin, a scholar and government official who stood as my ideal public intellectual many years before I actually met her. She read four chapters in this book and gave me excellent and insightful comments, nearly all of which I incorporated and a few of which I integrated into my understand- ing of how Washington works—or should work. When I needed succor from an ideological soul mate, Bill Frenzel, a former Republican member of the Ways and Means Committee, was always available. All of the ideals of public service and intellectual achievement that I so greatly admire are embodied in Alice and Bill, two of the great public servants of our time.

Over the years my staff at Brookings, including Matt Pennington, Megan Yaple, Joe Johnston, Katie Lambert, and Rob Wooley, have obtained documents, searched the Internet, performed calculations, checked my work, typed and retyped the manuscript, and provided any assistance I required. I was lucky to have them.

The one person who has done the most to help me with the book is my assis- tant and project manager, Julie Clover. A woman of immense organizational ability and intelligence, Julie handled all the administrative details of our Cen- ter while she researched, typed, edited, and harassed me about my book. She was amazing at finding documents and discovering even the most obscure quote or source. Without her, this would have been a very different book—and would likely have been completed in time for the twentieth anniversary of welfare reform rather than its tenth.

During the entire period I was writing this book I also worked as a senior consultant at the Annie E. Casey Foundation. Casey gave me a desk, a word processor, and a printer at their beautiful offices in Baltimore, where for one day a week for five years I was able to devote much of my time to thinking and writing in silence often bordering on reverie. My Baltimore office gave me a kind of psychological separation from the sound and fury of the nation's capital. The contributions of these quiet days to my book are beyond calculating. My respect and admiration for the commitment and optimism of the gifted Casey staff extends especially to its two top leaders, Doug Nelson and Ralph Smith, who tolerated my views and provided sound advice and valuable help at every turn.

My wife, Susann, and members of my family put up with my frequent and often lengthy disappearances into my study or abrupt departure from family events to work on this book. Given the somewhat stately pace at which my work progressed, their tolerance has been spread over nearly six years. Susann especially was patient on numerous trips and vacations when I turned on a light early in the morning to work on the manuscript. She observed that this ritual gave her a new understanding of "I'll leave the light on for you." In exchange for this understanding and her frequent encouragement, I punished her by begging her to proofread the entire manuscript. The inevitable result was that she saved me from many silly errors and inconsistencies. And while I am on the subject of my family, my ability to be a good husband and father was severely compromised during the welfare battle of 1995 and 1996. Here too Susann had to fix my errors—especially the errors of omission.

Given the level and quality of help I have received, it would not be surprising if this book were free of errors. But it is not, and I accept responsibility.

## CHAPTER ONE

# Building
# the American
# Welfare State

Until the congressional elections of 1994, Democrats had dominated the formation of American social policy since the Great Depression. This dominance had been so complete that even one of the most important Republicans between the end of World War II and the Republican takeover of Congress in 1995, President Richard Nixon, was a protoliberal in most matters of domestic policy. In neat Hegelian fashion, this dominance by Democrats produced a reaction against federal social programs that culminated in a revolution in federal social policy following the Republican sweep of Congress in 1994.

This book is the story of how Republicans, with ample support from Democrats and President Bill Clinton, enacted legislation in 1996 that caused this revolution by eliminating Aid to Families with Dependent Children (AFDC), a New Deal program that provided cash welfare to poor parents who in the main did not work and many of whom had children outside marriage. The AFDC program was replaced with a new program, Temporary Assistance for Needy Families (TANF) that required work, penalized states that did not require welfare recipients to work and individuals who refused to work, rewarded states that helped parents leave welfare for work, and set a time limit on the duration individuals could receive welfare. Although the fight over AFDC got most of the attention, the revolution extended far beyond AFDC to eliminate or severely restrict welfare for drug addicts and alcoholics, noncitizens, and mildly disabled children. Moreover, the new law constituted the first broad attack on the nation's exploding problem with illegitimate births by restricting welfare for teenage mothers, giving states new options for reducing or eliminating financial incentives for nonmarital births, strengthening the nation's laws on paternity establishment and child support enforcement, giving cash bonuses to states that reduced their nonmarital birth rates, making it easier for churches and other faith-based organizations to accept government dollars to fight poverty, dependency, and degradation, and establishing a national network of programs to teach abstinence to teens. Taken together, these reforms constitute the most fundamental change in American social policy since the Social Security Act of 1935.

The reaction represented by this revolution was prompted, in part, by the failure of many social programs to achieve their goals. As the noted program evaluator Peter Rossi of the University of Massachusetts in Amherst would have it, if predictions are based on what is known from scientific evaluations, the expected net impact of any new social intervention is zero.[1] The problems with American social policy, however, run much deeper than the mere failure of a few programs. The American people appear to have rejected some of the most fundamental tenets of liberal social policy, if indeed they ever agreed with them. Consider the following dichotomy. On one side are social programs that provide benefits to people who are not expected by the American public to work. The Social Security programs, which provide cash for the elderly and disabled and their dependents and survivors, lead the list of these popular programs. On the other side are welfare programs for the able-bodied, such as the now defunct AFDC program. These programs are suspect because American taxpayers expect able-bodied adults to support themselves and their families.[2]

The welfare system as it existed on the eve of the Republican takeover of Congress in 1995 provided many benefits to many people, especially single mothers and their children. In doing so, however, it violated the instincts and values of the American public by providing generous benefits to millions of able-bodied adults. In this chapter I review the arguments put forth by Democrats and Republicans as they struggled to change a welfare system that virtually everyone regarded as deeply flawed. I review the emergence of the American version of the welfare state between 1935 and 1972, examine several weaknesses in the programs that portended difficulty, assess the underlying factors that shaped the welfare debate of 1993–96, and then examine the goals of Democrats and Republicans as they shaped the reform legislation President Clinton signed into law on August 22, 1996.

Democrats, often with support from Republicans, constructed the American version of the welfare state, especially after 1965, without heeding the distinction between social programs that were acceptable to Americans and those that were not. Eventually, most Americans came to believe that welfare programs encouraged nonwork and induced other behavioral problems such as nonmarital births and crime among the poor. Research evidence that welfare actually does reduce work is overwhelming, while evidence on the connection between welfare and nonmarital births is moderate.[3] Evidence on whether welfare leads to crime and other unfortunate behaviors is weak to nonexistent. Popular beliefs do not always rest on empirical data. Even so, the American public viewed welfare and dependency on welfare as the root of many social ills, including ones for which the evidence was shaky.[4] But political decisions often are based on beliefs and values and not on social science evidence. For a mix of evidence-based and value-based reasons, welfare was destined to be unpopular with the American public.

Democrats began their long campaign to increase the "social security" of Americans by creating insurance programs designed to help people not expected to work. In fact, most of the benefits accrued to people who had a long record of previous work but who could no longer work because of illness, injury, old age, or involuntary unemployment. The centerpiece of this agenda, and indeed the centerpiece of American social policy, is the Social Security Act. Signed into law by President Franklin D. Roosevelt in 1935, Social Security firmly established the principle that the federal government would provide guaranteed (or in federal jargon, "entitlement") benefits to various groups of qualified citizens. Many of the programs contained in the original act were based at least in part on insurance principles because Americans paid taxes on a routine basis to finance the benefits. In 1995, on the eve of the great debate that led to the 1996 welfare revolution, 37.4 million retired workers, wives and husbands of retired workers, widowed mothers and fathers, and various dependents received Social Security benefits of nearly $292 billion.[5]

The Social Security legislation of 1935 also contained the Unemployment Compensation program, which provided entitlement benefits to qualified unemployed workers. The Unemployment Compensation program was also based primarily on insurance principles and, except during recessions, has been financed entirely by a flat percentage tax paid by employers on behalf of their employees. In 1995 almost 8 million workers received benefits equaling $21 billion.[6]

The Social Security Act is the greatest piece of social legislation ever enacted in America. It provides entitlement benefits to the elderly, the unemployed, and many of their dependents. These programs are universal or nearly universal, are financed by taxes paid into reserved accounts, and are somewhat redistributive. They were built to be popular and, therefore, to last. So far, both goals have been achieved, and the popularity of the programs has lasted for more than seven decades.

So popular were these programs, in fact, that Congress significantly expanded them during the 1950s and 1960s.[7] Specifically, a series of legislative actions beginning in 1956 created the Disability Insurance program, which provides cash to workers who become disabled and are no longer able to engage in work. By 1995 nearly 5.9 million disabled workers and their spouses and children received benefits totaling close to $41 billion. Then, in 1965, Congress created Medicare, the fourth entitlement program in this parade of vital and popular programs that form the backbone of American social policy. Medicare, supported in part by a dedicated tax, provides health benefits to the qualified elderly and disabled. In 1995 Medicare provided health benefits that cost $160 billion to more than 8 million beneficiaries.

Four universal programs with redistributive features, four programs with dedicated taxes and accompanying trust funds, four programs directly connected to work, four programs that continue to enjoy huge support from the American public. Taken together, these four programs are the high-water mark of liberalism in America. Although Social Security and Medicare face uncertain futures because of grave financing problems,[8] only a cynic or a grumpy conservative could doubt that the American public is deeply indebted to Democrats for creating these four pillars of American social policy.

But these insurance-based programs have not been the only items on the Democrats' social policy agenda. Since the Great Depression, and more particularly since the 1960s, Democrats—sometimes joined by Republicans—have tried to provide guaranteed benefits to many groups of Americans, not just to those who worked or were in families with workers. Indeed, among the fondest goals of many Democrats was the redistribution of income. Few Democrats have adopted the socialist goal of redistributing the nation's wealth based strictly on individual or family need, but a major component of the liberal soul is a willingness to tax middle-class and wealthy Americans to provide benefits to poor and low-income Americans (and, as it turned out, to resident noncitizens). As Martin Gilens of Yale University has shown, the American public is quite willing to help the poor, perhaps in part because of our tradition as a religious nation.[9] Whatever the reason, for Democrats the very definition of fairness became the willingness to support the poor through income redistribution.

Thus nestled among the seedling Social Security and unemployment programs in the Social Security Act of 1935 was the little welfare acorn called Aid to Dependent Children (later called Aid to Families with Dependent Children). This tiny and inconspicuous program—designed originally to support widows with minor children—grew into the towering oak that is the huge array of federal and federal-state social programs designed to provide benefits and services to the poor. Beginning with President Lyndon Johnson's War on Poverty during the mid-1960s, new social programs and spending on social programs grew dramatically. The three most important new programs were Medicaid, which provides health insurance to the poor; the Food Stamp program, which provides food vouchers to the poor; and the Supplemental Security Income (SSI) program, which provides cash to the elderly and disabled who are also poor, including the families of disabled children.

By the mid-1970s the broad outlines of American social policy were more or less settled. The outline might be thought of as consisting of three tiers. On the top tier were the insurance programs providing universal benefits: Social Security, Medicare, Disability Insurance, and Unemployment Compensation. On the second tier were the large entitlement programs for poor Americans: AFDC, Medicaid, Food Stamps, SSI, and a few others. Finally, the third tier consisted of a few hundred programs for poor and low-income individuals and families. Most of these programs were small, and most of them competed with one another for annual congressional appropriations.

This overview would not be complete without a numerical accounting of the second and third tiers. At the beginning of the welfare debate in 1995, House Republicans asked the Congressional Research Service (CRS) and the General Accounting Office (GAO, now the Government Accountability Office) to estimate the number of federal social programs. CRS and GAO counted 336 social programs divided into eight domains; no domain contained fewer than eight programs (cash welfare), and one domain (employment and training) had over 150 programs.[10] Spending on these means-tested programs rose consistently between 1950 and 1995 in constant dollars, from less than $1 billion to more than $375 billion.[11] Spending on these two tiers, combined with spending on the social insurance programs in tier 1, brought total spending on social programs to nearly $900 billion in 1995. There was, in short, a blizzard of social programs and a flood of spending.

Between enactment of the SSI program in 1972 and enactment of welfare reform in 1996, there was a curious stability in American social policy. Existing programs were expanded somewhat and new ones added, but they were small and of little consequence. Nixon's Family Assistance Plan (FAP), which failed in 1971, would have revolutionized American social policy by providing every family with a guaranteed minimum income.[12] Even able-bodied adults who did not work would be "entitled" to receive cash payments from the federal government. Similarly, the Mondale-Brademas child care legislation, which would have established the federal government as a major funder of child care and child development programs throughout the nation, was vetoed by Nixon in 1971.[13] The FAP and the Mondale-Brademas bills were among the last serious attempts to significantly expand the second tier of the welfare state. As surprising as it now seems, the major leadership for the FAP, by far the more radical of the two bills, was provided by a Republican president who was defeated in his efforts by liberals in the Senate who wanted a higher guaranteed benefit level.[14] Thus the central defeat of liberal social policy in America until 1996 was self-administered.

There were also attempts to reform welfare under President Jimmy Carter, but these attempts came to naught.[15] President Ronald Reagan, too, began his presidency with a welfare reform agenda, much of which he actually managed to pass in the budget act of 1981.[16] However, these reforms did not change welfare programs in any permanent way, although they did reduce spending on employment and training programs while simultaneously initiating a series of large-scale demonstration programs that soon began to show some success in promoting work.[17] The most significant reform tightened the AFDC rules that governed how much welfare money people could keep when they went to work. The effect of this change was to reduce the financial gain from work (because welfare benefits fell quickly as earnings rose) and to force many families that were combining welfare benefits with earnings to leave the rolls. These so-called disregard rules, which stipulated how much of a person's earnings could be ignored ("disregarded"), were later eased so that even this modest Reagan reform was watered down before the end of his presidency.

Despite these modest reforms in welfare law, there were nonetheless portentous developments that set the stage for the big changes of 1996. Throughout this period, one of the two or three welfare issues about which liberals and conservatives argued the most was whether welfare programs induced dependency.

Not surprisingly, given the lack of systematic data, the debate about how public aid affects the motivation to work raged for centuries.[18] However, modern social science has produced strong and consistent evidence that public welfare does reduce work. A thorough 1981 review of these studies by the prominent social scientists Sheldon Danziger, Robert Haveman, and Robert Plotnick confirms that AFDC reduced the hours of work by single mothers.[19]

Evidence on hours worked by welfare recipients, however, is only half of the story. The other half is evidence on whether recipients use welfare as a temporary crutch to overcome a life crisis, such as divorce or sudden unemployment, or whether recipients adopt welfare as a way of life and remain on the rolls for long periods of time. This question was answered definitively by Mary Jo Bane and David Ellwood of Harvard in 1983.[20] Using sophisticated statistical techniques, Bane and Ellwood found that of the recipients on welfare at any given moment, 65 percent would eventually be on the rolls for eight years or more. At its peak in the spring of 1994, the AFDC caseload totaled about 5.4 million families. Bane and Ellwood's results showed that, in 1994, on the eve of the great welfare debate, about 3.5 million adults were in the middle of stays on welfare that had already or would eventually exceed eight years.

Not surprisingly, the Bane and Ellwood study was popular among conservatives and Republicans. E. Clay Shaw Jr. from Florida, the leader of the Republican forces in the congressional battle that led to the 1996 reforms, used a pie chart—with the huge piece depicting the 65 percent on welfare for eight years or more shown in bright red—that graphically depicted Bane and Ellwood results during debates on the House floor. A table based on Bane and Ellwood's research was placed in the House Committee on Ways and Means *Green Book*,[21] a 1,600-page encyclopedia of social programs that is read avidly by congressional staff and other Washington policy wonks and even, it is rumored, by a few members of Congress. In addition, House Republican members frequently used Shaw's figure in discussions with constituents at town meetings, and several members used the chart during the welfare debate of 1995–96.

Caseload dynamics are not easy to grasp. This fact, combined with the fervid desire of partisans on both sides to make the data fit their view of reality, led to no end of mischief with caseload data. In the end, however, having watched the use of these numbers by politicians since the mid-1980s, I think Bane and Ellwood's finding that 65 percent of recipients were on welfare for eight years or more astounded almost everyone and was the clear winner in the battle for people's understanding of whether dependency was a serious problem. The Bane and Ellwood study is one of the most influential scholarly studies used in a major congressional debate on social policy in the last twenty years or so. Ironically for university scholars, who are mostly left of center, one of their most creative and definitive products was used by Republicans to drive home the point that welfare dependency was real—and as a primary argument in the debate that led to the demise of a major New Deal program. I doubt this outcome is what Bane and Ellwood had in mind when they initiated their study, but like the principled scholars they are, they published their results anyway.

In addition to welfare dependency, another social problem that provoked debate leading to the sweeping changes of 1996 was illegitimacy. Births outside marriage rivaled welfare dependency in the Republican hierarchy of social ills. By 1995 the nation had been subjected to an avalanche of illegitimate births. Led by the ideas of Charles Murray of the American Enterprise Institute and many others, conservatives were intent on making illegitimacy a central issue of the welfare debate.[22] The essence of the conservative position was that the guarantee of welfare benefits—not only cash but also Food Stamps, Medicaid, housing, and many other programs—helped lead young men and women to a reduced state of vigilance in avoiding pregnancy before marriage. There is, of course, a substantial research literature on whether AFDC contributed to illegitimacy, but as might be expected, Democrats interpreted the literature as supporting the position that welfare did not cause illegitimacy,[23] while conservatives interpreted the same evidence as demonstrating that AFDC was clearly related to increased rates of illegitimacy.[24] In my view, primarily because the empirical studies are weak and somewhat inconsistent, the results provide only moderate evidence that welfare is linked with illegitimacy. Of course, conservatives did not allow the lack of strong consensus in the social science literature to dull their claims about welfare and illegitimacy. The argument that guaranteed welfare benefits contributed to increased illegitimacy rates makes sense to most Americans. Coupled with the widely accepted view that illegitimacy has negative effects on mothers and children,[25] the public's agreement that welfare contributed to illegitimacy rates was justification enough for conservatives to label illegitimacy the nation's gravest social problem and welfare its major cause.

As in the case of work and welfare, the value issue was central. Republicans, as well as important Democrats such as President Bill Clinton, discovered that voters responded to the argument that AFDC directly violated the moral precept that only married adults who can provide for the economic and emotional needs of their children should have babies. The fact that traditional rules of marriage and sexuality were being challenged throughout the period does not vitiate the fact that the majority of Americans remained traditional in their judgments about illegitimacy, especially when they saw their tax dollars supporting a system that subverted their values.[26]

There is little doubt that many Democrats also deplored illegitimacy. A classic claim by conservatives is that, beginning in the 1960s, liberals argued that everyone should be allowed to create their own set of values, to do their own thing.[27] Whatever the truth about this claim, it is certain that by 1995 few members of Congress thought illegitimacy was simply a matter of individual expression. On the contrary, both Democrats and Republicans were greatly concerned about the causes and consequences of illegitimacy. In fact, President Clinton had been more outspoken than any other president about the tragedy of illegitimacy; he was even given to stating flatly that it was "wrong" for young people to have children outside of marriage whom they could not support. Speaking to the National Baptist Convention in 1994, Clinton said, "[too many] babies will be born where there was never a marriage. That is a disaster. It is wrong. And someone has to say, again, it is simply not right. You shouldn't have a baby before you're ready, and you shouldn't have a baby when you're not married. You just have to stop it. We've got to turn it around."[28]

Thus, although conservatives were successful in making illegitimacy a major part of the welfare reform debate, at least part of their success was attributable to the fact that many Democrats were in substantial agreement that illegitimacy was a major problem and that the consequences were bad for both the mother and the child. Democrats, however, were less willing than Republicans to single out welfare programs as a major cause of illegitimacy, let alone use illegitimacy as the rationale for major changes in welfare programs.

A minor problem in the conservative rhetoric about illegitimacy was that no one knew of any policies that had been shown by solid evidence to increase abstinence, reduce pregnancy among single women, or promote marriage.[29] Even the studies on attempts to reduce second pregnancies were discouraging.[30] Undaunted, Republicans argued that the best approach was to do everything possible to attack the problem, especially by rewarding states that tried new approaches and even by cutting off some or most of the welfare benefits of unmarried teens who had babies. So great was the problem, and so serious the consequences, that conservatives insisted on trying as many approaches as possible to reduce illegitimacy, including policies that could and would be portrayed by Democrats as cruel.

The Republican focus on illegitimacy was a great irony. The first scholar to bring national attention to the problem of mother-headed families and the growing crisis of nonmarital births was Daniel Patrick Moynihan, who later was elected as a Democratic Senator for New York.[31] In 1965, while an obscure official in the Department of Labor, Moynihan had written an incendiary report arguing that the major reason black Americans were not making more economic and social progress was the weakness of the black family. Too many black children were being reared in female-headed families, with devastating consequences for their development. Moynihan's report carefully reviewed the evidence on the rapidly growing incidence of nonmarital births among blacks and deplored the trend in unequivocal terms. Blacks were thus not ready to seize the opportunities then being presented by the recently enacted civil rights legislation.[32] Nor, according to Moynihan's thesis, would blacks be prepared to make the most of their chances until illegitimacy declined and two-parent families became the norm.

The reaction to the Moynihan report was explosive.[33] The report was debated inside the White House and Congress, on the nation's editorial pages, in the nation's leading journals, and among scholars. But little was actually done to address the problem of single-parent families. In 1969 Congress passed a law intended to slow the rise in unwed motherhood. The measure imposed a freeze on federal funding for the share of children in a state who received AFDC because of illegitimacy or desertion. Highly controversial, the freeze never took effect. By contrast, in the years following the Moynihan report, there was an outpouring of spending and a proliferation of social programs as the nation attempted to fight poverty through government spending. The federal government created education and training programs, nutrition programs, health programs, housing subsidies, community development programs, and a host of other programs designed to reduce poverty. The government tried everything, in short, except creating programs to reduce illegitimacy and promote marriage. But in 1995 Republicans began attempting to establish programs to address family composition, the very problem identified three decades earlier by Moynihan as the nation's leading social problem. At the time of Moynihan's report, about 25 percent of blacks were born outside marriage; by 1995 the figure was pressing 70 percent and the figure for whites was nearly the same as the figure for blacks in 1965. If a black illegitimacy rate of 25 percent is a crisis, what is the word for 70 percent? Clearly, it was undeniable that the problem identified by Moynihan as critical had grown much worse by 1995.[34] And yet Moynihan became perhaps the leading opponent of the Republican welfare reform legislation.

Another underlying factor of the gathering movement to reform welfare was a remarkable increase in attention to welfare and related issues by conservatives. Charles Murray's revolutionary book *Losing Ground*, published in 1984, caused a huge stir during this period, but his shocking recommendation to end welfare programs cold turkey was never pursued as a serious policy option, even by conservative Republicans.[35] Even so, Murray became relentless in arguing that welfare, far from helping the poor, actually caused them all sorts of problems, including illegitimacy. In 1993 Murray published a long op-ed piece in the *Wall Street Journal* in which he linked welfare to the rise of illegitimacy among both blacks and whites and specifically labeled illegitimacy as "the single most important social problem of our times."[36] Murray accorded this dubious honor to illegitimacy because it was, he claimed, a prime cause of all the major social problems faced by the nation including "crime, drugs, poverty, illiteracy, welfare, [and] homelessness." This article had an electrifying and energizing effect on Republican politicians in Washington, especially in the House of Representatives. Murray's work was to create huge fights among Republican welfare reformers over the issue of strong, indeed unprecedented, policies to attack illegitimacy. These intraparty fights became so raucous that they threatened to split the Republican coalition and kill welfare reform. More broadly, Murray's work and the reaction to it created the view among conservatives—and even a number of moderates and liberals—that something was fundamentally wrong with welfare. Murray's work also had a stimulant effect on conservative thinkers and activists. In the long run, his most important contribution may have been to bring renewed respectability to conservative thinking about the causes of poverty and the effects of welfare programs and to stimulate other conservatives to think and write about welfare.

A good example, although not as colorful as Murray's controversial book, is Larry Mead's *Beyond Entitlement*, published in 1986.[37] Mead, a professor of political science at New York University, proposed a solution to welfare dependency that was to have immense influence. Mead argued that the poor needed aggressively administered and authoritative welfare programs to force them to adopt appropriate behaviors. The most important such behavior, of course, was work. Mead argued, while cleverly marshalling empirical data to support his claims, that welfare-to-work programs with clearly stated requirements backed by tight administration and quick sanctions would help many recipients enter the workforce and reduce their dependency on welfare. Policies like this that provided welfare recipients with punishments or inducements to meet certain standards of behavior came to be called the "new paternalism."[38]

Work became the cannonball of the Republican welfare reform agenda, blasting straight ahead through all obstacles. As other issues—time limits, block grants, illegitimacy, child care—developed, work remained the central issue of the debate. Beginning as early as the 1960s, Republicans extolled the virtues of work as the antidote to welfare dependency. In doing so, Republicans were squarely within a tradition of welfare reform going back at least as far as Victorian England, in which conservatives held that work was redemptive. Work required consistency, schedules, alarm clocks, routines, cooperation, self-discipline—all the traits, in short, that conservatives believed would rescue welfare recipients from the companions of sloth, including booze, idleness, illicit sex, and hanging out.[39] Moreover, in the modern American context, conservatives argued that work was easily available and would inevitably—especially when combined with government programs designed to provide support to low-income working families—lift the poor out of poverty.[40]

This agenda was greatly strengthened by the high-quality studies on welfare-to-work programs conducted by scholars and by large research organizations that began to make their appearance during this era. One of the most impressive organizations of this type was the Manpower Demonstration Research Corporation (now named MDRC).[41] In setting the standard for policy research, MDRC's studies incorporated all of the hallmarks of scientific evaluations: random assignment to an experimental and control group, large sample sizes, experiments conducted under field conditions, multiple outcome measures, and benefit-cost analyses.[42] The basic results were unequivocal. Exactly as Mead had predicted, welfare-to-work programs that emphasized job search and were tightly administered produced significant increases in employment and earnings and decreases in welfare rolls, although they had only modest impacts on total family income. The impacts may not have been huge, but they were consistent. Such programs were also generally cost beneficial; that is, they saved more money than they cost to run.[43]

Seldom has social science presented a clearer case to policymakers: aggressively conducted work programs produce clear effects on caseloads, employment, and spending. This consistent result gave a strong impetus to mandatory work programs for mothers on welfare, an impetus that was reinforced by the increasing labor force participation of mothers who were not on welfare. Beginning with the debate on the Family Support Act of 1988, conservatives adopted the mantra "What works is work." Here was a message that resonated with both policymakers and the American public.

That the details of work programs were vital is amply demonstrated by the welfare reform debate of 1987–88, which led to passage of the Family Support Act in 1988. Democrats were forced by the research showing that work programs were effective, and also by the popularity of work with the American public, to support the need to encourage work. Republicans believed, however, that the Democrats' commitment to work was paper-thin, as shown by the history of federal welfare reform legislation "requiring" work. The Work Incentive (WIN) program, established in 1967, was a typical example. The original WIN law said that states must require "appropriate" AFDC mothers to register at labor department job centers. But program regulations stated that unwilling mothers could not be required to work ahead of several other categories of workers. The 1967 law also provided work incentives to mothers who worked by ensuring that they did not lose a dollar of benefits for each dollar they earned. In 1971 Congress replaced the "appropriate person" rule with a requirement that most AFDC mothers register for work when their youngest child reached age six. However, so many AFDC recipients were exempt and so few recipients were penalized for ignoring the requirement that most welfare offices continued the routine operation of determining eligibility and writing checks; the WIN program barely had an impact. By 1987, WIN funding had declined to $110 million from its peak of $365 million in 1981.[44]

Although Republicans attempted to make work the centerpiece of welfare reform in 1988, Democrats expanded welfare benefits, particularly by requiring all states to provide AFDC coverage to two-parent families in which a parent was unemployed.[45] Republicans were not united against expanding welfare to two-parent families, but in my experience more Republicans opposed than supported the policy because it expanded welfare, even though providing welfare to one-parent but not two-parent families could be portrayed as antimarriage. After two years of rancorous debate, especially in the House, Congress settled on a compromise bill that Republicans believed leaned distinctly to the left. More specifically, there were no work requirements imposed on single parents, who constituted about 95 percent of the AFDC caseload.[46] Rather, the legislation established the Job Opportunities and Basic Skills Training program (JOBS), which provided states with around $1 billion a year to help adults leave welfare by joining the workforce. States were given mandatory participation standards, but "participation" was broadly defined to include education, training, and job search. To illustrate just how insignificant the work requirements were, by 1994, six years after enactment of the JOBS program, about 36,000 of the 5 million adults on AFDC—less than 1 percent of the caseload—were in work or job search programs.[47] On the other hand, the 1988 law did allow states to require mothers with preschool children as young as three years old to participate and gave states leeway to impose strong work requirements. Yet few governors, including few Republican governors, did so.

In the end, the Family Support Act did not provide a resounding victory for the principles being pursued by either Democrats or Republicans. Because all of the major programs remained intact and were actually expanded somewhat, because about half of the AFDC caseload was exempt from any participation requirement, because virtually no one was required to actually work, and because day care and Medicaid were guaranteed for adults on AFDC who participated in jobs programs and, for a transitional period, for those who left the rolls, Democrats should be accorded an edge on the partisan tally sheet. For Republicans, the bill at least had participation standards that required states to involve mothers in some type of constructive activity, even if the activity was preparation for work rather than work itself. The idea that states should be required to involve a specific percentage of their caseload in some activity turned out to be the model for federal provisions that could dictate the way states dealt with their caseload. Moreover, the 1988 law required states to place an increasing percentage of their two-parent caseload in an actual work program for a minimum of sixteen hours a week, but states did not need to implement this requirement for five years. Even so, these modest changes in AFDC law, accomplished under a Democratic House and Senate, showed that the ice was beginning to crack. Personal responsibility was beginning to make inroads on the claim that able-bodied recipients who did not work had an entitlement to welfare benefits.

These inroads on entitlement welfare were expanded by a series of reports issued by several influential groups during the mid- to late-1980s. In 1986, under the sponsorship of the Bradley and Olin Foundations, Michael Novak and Doug Besharov of the American Enterprise Institute in Washington organized a group of twenty policy intellectuals, including several with government experience, to examine welfare programs and make recommendations for reforming welfare. Called the Working Seminar, the group was composed of left-of-center policy experts such as Robert Reischauer, Alice Rivlin, Barbara Blum, and Franklin Raines as well as right-of-center figures such as John Cogan, Charles Murray, Larry Mead, and Glenn Loury. After approximately a year of discussions, commissioned background papers, and several meetings, the seminar recommended substantial, even radical, reform of welfare programs, especially the AFDC program.[48] In fact the recommendations uncannily anticipated several major provisions of the 1996 reform legislation.

The seminar's report began by emphasizing the importance of welfare dependency and other behavioral dysfunctions. Although no government program could by itself solve these problems, the report argued, federal, state, and local governments had been assigned fundamental tasks that, although limited, were indispensable to the common good.[49] Clearly, because some of the nation's leading conservatives were members of the Working Seminar, this endorsement of government's role in helping poor people find work and of supplementing their income showed that many leading conservatives recognized the important role government must play in welfare reform. In part, perhaps, conservatives agreed to this definitive statement of government responsibility because the report also emphasized the role that the private sector, including religious organizations, should play in emphasizing personal responsibility as an antidote to behavioral dysfunction. The report went on to recommend mandatory work requirements, sanctions for not fulfilling work requirements, and time limits on cash welfare benefits. The report strongly recommended that more authority be shifted to the state and local levels and that states continue to experiment with innovative programs. Every one of these recommendations became central features of the 1996 welfare revolution.

One of the most important and interesting sections of the report compared the Working Seminar's approach and conclusions on welfare reform with the approach and conclusions of reports that had been issued during the previous year by four other commissions: the American Public Welfare Association; the Project on the Welfare of Families, co-chaired by Governor Bruce Babbitt of Arizona and former Republican secretary of the Department of Health, Education, and Welfare Arthur Flemming; the Task Force on Poverty and Welfare appointed by Governor Mario Cuomo of New York; and President Reagan's Low Income Opportunity Board.[50] Each of these reports focused on welfare dependency as a primary problem, stressed the connection between welfare benefits and reciprocal obligations by recipients, emphasized policies to strengthen personal responsibility and self-reliance, and examined ways to make AFDC temporary.

The report from the Working Seminar, as well as the reports from other groups representing several points along the political spectrum, shows that the big issues, including mandatory work and time limits, were clearly on the table almost a decade before the welfare reform debate of 1995–96. Moreover, a prestigious group of conservative and liberal policy intellectuals endorsed the major policy proposals that were to create such havoc in Congress and between liberals and moderates within the Democratic Party nearly a decade later. Perhaps it is too much to claim, as the Working Seminar report did, that there was "consensus" on welfare reform provisions such as time-limited benefits, mandatory work with sanctions, and major devolution of responsibility to states. It does seem fair, however, to conclude that both liberal and conservative policy intellectuals were convinced that welfare dependency and other behavioral problems were the major issues that had to be addressed by welfare reform. At the very least, there was a willingness to seriously consider radical reforms.

For those who doubt this formulation, consider four examples of liberal and centrist Democrats who were well aware of how far federal social policy had departed from American values and how radical the reforms might become. The first example is President Bill Clinton—or rather, presidential candidate Bill Clinton—who saw clearly that several liberal policies were alienating voters. During the presidential campaign of 1992, Clinton put this knowledge to good use in developing campaign themes, particularly regarding welfare. One of the most popular themes of his campaign was "ending welfare as we know it."[51] That a prominent Democratic presidential candidate would use this theme is surprising. Even more surprising is the fact that a Democratic politician realized the political effectiveness of abandoning positions long held by liberals and even the advantages of attacking those same positions. For liberals who wanted to defend or expand the means-tested pillar of the welfare state, candidate Clinton and then President Clinton was a dangerous man. His historic mission seemed to be to reposition the Democratic Party as centrist or even somewhat right of center on vital issues like welfare reform, trade, and spending.

David Ellwood's ground-breaking book *Poor Support* is a second indication that many liberals were aware that the welfare state was flawed and needed reform.[52] Although Ellwood would be pilloried by the left for his scholarly work on welfare reform, as well as the leading role he played in the Clinton administration's welfare reform efforts,[53] *Poor Support* was a serious and creative attempt to transform AFDC into a program that could provide entitlement benefits while simultaneously addressing the problem of dependency. Ellwood came under fire from the left because he was one of the first liberals to recommend time limits on AFDC.[54] Of course, Ellwood also insisted that time limits would only be appropriate if accompanied by a federal guarantee of a job for recipients who reached the time limit. Another of the major items on the Ellwood agenda, subsequently adopted by President Clinton, was "making work pay." For Ellwood, the cornerstone of making work pay was significant expansion of the Earned Income Tax Credit (EITC), a program that gave cash to low-income workers with children through the tax system.[55] Unlike his liberal critics, Ellwood played a major role in both providing the intellectual justification for an EITC increase and then helping President Clinton to propose, and members of Congress to support, the increase, which they did by enacting a major expansion in 1993. Ellwood must be given a share of the credit for putting the tidy sum of nearly $15 billion a year in cash into the pockets of poor and low-income working Americans (compared with the pre-1993 EITC law).[56]

A third example is provided by Christopher Jencks of Harvard, one of the most widely respected of the liberal scholars who study social policy. As early as 1992, Jencks would write: "Until liberals transform AFDC, so that it reinforces rather than subverts American ideals about work and marriage, our efforts to build a humane welfare state will never succeed."[57] Jencks went on to argue, like Ellwood, that an important part of the solution to welfare was to make work pay, a proposition that came to play an important role in the welfare debate. Jencks's writing about the cultural contradictions of AFDC cut right to the heart of the matter: AFDC was un-American. In this understanding, Jencks was eventually joined by a host of state and federal Democratic policymakers. When the moment of truth arrived in 1995, AFDC had few defenders.

The fourth indication of the growing perception among liberals that AFDC was a failure was freelance writer Mickey Kaus's seminal book *The End of Equality*.[58] Kaus's subject was considerably more than welfare, but his welfare chapters touched on and accepted, at least in part, nearly all the claims about welfare that were standard fare for conservatives. In particular, Kaus granted that welfare played an important, though by no means exclusive, role in the breakdown of the family and the rise of illegitimacy, in the creation of the "ghetto underclass," and in the decline of work in the underclass.

Kaus's radical solution was to condition not just AFDC, but Food Stamps as well, on work. Under Kaus's system, all able-bodied adults would either work or lose most of their welfare benefits. If they could not find their own job, government would give them one. The larger issue addressed by Kaus was that of social inequality and its growth in America. Because he viewed the growth of social inequality as the most important issue of our times, Kaus's book is a search for the policies that would promote social equality. Work is one of the experiences that all classes in society should share. Moreover, Americans place a high value on adults who work hard to support themselves and their children. As a result, any group that becomes known for nonwork is, by definition, unequal to working Americans. Government support for nonwork exacerbates the problem of social inequality both because it encourages nonwork and because productive citizens resent being forced to support those who so conspicuously flout the value Americans place on work and self-support. Promoting work by welfare-dependent adults would, in Kaus's view, strike a major blow against social inequality.

Next to Murray's proposal to end welfare altogether, Kaus's was the most radical welfare reform idea put forth by any major figure. It would have ended much more than merely the AFDC entitlement. Liberals ferociously attacked Kaus's proposal because it would virtually end welfare for anyone who refused to work.[59] Conservatives cited the proposal incessantly because they were only too happy to argue that "even liberals" admit that AFDC must be abandoned and that mandatory work is the best replacement. Because most conservatives rejected the idea of big government guaranteeing jobs, however, they were reluctant to fully support Kaus's proposal.

Besides adding to the building momentum for reform, Kaus's break with the traditional liberal agenda represented an important symbolic victory for the conservative reform movement. Kaus had served as a senior writer for the *New Republic*, the leading intellectual and cultural journal of the left for most of the century. Indeed, one of the founders of the *New Republic* was Herbert Croly, a dominant liberal thinker during the Progressive Era and the author of *The Promise of American Life*, a prime document of American liberalism.[60] Despite this background, the editors of the *New Republic* supported Kaus and endorsed his radical reform proposal, which first appeared in its pages in 1986.[61] Later, in July 1996, as the crucial welfare votes in Congress approached, the *New Republic* urged both Congress and President Clinton to support the Republican welfare reform legislation.[62] It would be impossible to think of more striking evidence that important elements of the American left recognized the serious problems of AFDC and the need for a change in the entitlement mentality that had been almost the sine qua non of American liberalism. Some disillusioned liberals must have thought that Herbert Croly turned over in his grave the day the *New Republic* endorsed the end of entitlement and the beginning of mandatory work.

In his State of the Union message to Congress in 1935, the year he signed the Social Security Act, President Roosevelt stated flatly that welfare was a "narcotic" and "a subtle destroyer of the human spirit" that "induces a spiritual and moral disintegration fundamentally destructive to the national fibre." "Work must be found for able-bodied but destitute workers," he said.[63] He went on to say that the nation "must and shall quit this business of relief." Simply put, Roosevelt knew that welfare created the moral hazards that can induce nonwork among its recipients. What he probably did not know was that something very much like a culture could and would grow up around lives based on permanent welfare and fatherless families.[64] For over half a century, American policy for helping the poor ignored Roosevelt's injunction to quit the business of relief. Indeed, the nation did quite the opposite by building a large means-tested welfare state. Worse, until recently, the nation's welfare programs required almost nothing from their beneficiaries except nonwork and continued destitution. As Kate O'Beirne, now with *National Review,* was to put it in testimony before the Ways and Means Committee during the great welfare reform debate of 1995, "Spend more and demand less."[65] O'Beirne's pithy statement could serve as both the watchword and the epitaph for the liberal welfare state that was about to implode.

By 1996, most Americans, nearly all elected Republicans, and many (if not a majority) of elected Democrats came to believe that Roosevelt's fears and predictions had been proven correct. As a result, Congress and the president took a giant step in the direction of forcing adults to behave more responsibly by making welfare contingent on preparing for, seeking, and actually entering employment. National policymakers also put the force of the federal government behind a movement to encourage more responsible sexual behavior and sent a much clearer message than in the past that it was wrong to have children outside marriage whom single parents could support neither emotionally nor financially.

Why did the nation ignore Roosevelt's precautions for so many years and why did the nation make a complete U-turn in 1996? That the nation had created a massive welfare state that annually provided hundreds of billions of dollars in benefits to millions of poor and low-income Americans, often on an entitlement basis, is beyond dispute.[66] That the nation was spending more and more money on these programs without adequate compensating benefits is very likely. Although the programs had, over the years, helped millions of Americans survive a personal crisis and even in many cases get back on their feet following unfortunate life events, the programs also reduced work among young parents, subsidized a shocking increase in the number of illegitimate births, promoted intergenerational dependency on welfare,[67] contributed to the rearing of a huge and growing proportion of the nation's children in fatherless families, and stifled the development of children growing up in welfare-dependent and fatherless families.

Democrats, usually with help from Republicans, created welfare programs in the name of compassion for the unfortunate and because of the tradition of noblesse oblige. To some extent, Democrats gained politically from being the party of welfare, but the rewards for being the party of social insurance were much greater. Further, when it seemed to become a liability to support welfare entitlements, many Democrats continued their quest not just to defend, but actually to expand, them. They continued their support right up to and even after the turning point of 1996. This record suggests that Democrats were motivated primarily by the desire to protect people, especially children, from the ravages of poverty, even if the poverty was often of the parents' own making.

Chance played an important role in the history that I have traced. In 1935 Roosevelt may have been one of the few people who believed that "relief" posed a moral hazard. The typical welfare beneficiary at the time was a widow, and the incipient AFDC program was small. But two demographic events left the growing program exposed as a cultural outlier. First, the years after 1960 produced a relentless increase in the number of mothers entering the workforce. That working mothers, millions of them single, should work to pay taxes so that other single mothers could stay home with their children proved to be a highly unstable political situation. Second, every uptick in the number of mothers entering the workforce was matched by an increase in the number of illegitimate births. For many Americans, that mothers who failed to work were also violating fundamental American values about responsible sex and responsible parenting further jeopardized programs widely perceived to support both nonwork and irresponsible parenthood.

These trends inevitably produced a moment of reckoning. Why this moment came in 1996 is impossible to explain fully, but the coincidence of six conditions played an important role. The first was the apparent failure of the 1988 Family Support Act, signaled so clearly by a rapid expansion of the welfare rolls in the years immediately following the enactment of the new law that would, as Democrats argued, put welfare mothers to work. The second was a Democratic president who supported serious reform and indeed was the most effective politician of his time in publicizing both the problems of welfare and potential solutions. Third, just as the Democratic president was giving credibility to traditional conservative claims about the defects of welfare and proposing solutions no national Democrat had ever proposed, Republicans seized control of both chambers of Congress for the first time in forty years. Fourth, when Republicans took over Congress in 1995, members on the most important committees of jurisdiction over welfare programs in the House of Representatives had a comprehensive welfare reform bill ready to introduce. Fifth, in something of a turnaround for the Republican Party, a group of Republican members in the House, all of whom had been working together for a year and several of whom had been working together for three years, had both the expertise and the determination to push the bill through the legislative process. Sixth, Republican control of Congress was matched by Republican control of the nation's governorships. Several of these Republican governors were devoted to and experienced in welfare reform and worked tirelessly to support the Republican bill in Congress. These conditions ensured that President Clinton would have the opportunity to sign a major reform bill. As it turned out, he had three opportunities, the last one of which he grabbed. The days of tireless tinkering with welfare were over; the nation was set on a course of deep reform, the results of which are still being determined.

Let us now trace this history in detail.

## CHAPTER TWO

# Laying the Groundwork

On January 4, 1995, E. Clay Shaw Jr. of Florida, from the Committee on Ways and Means, Jim Talent of Missouri, from the Economic and Educational Opportunities Committee, and more than a hundred other Republicans in the U.S. House of Representatives introduced HR 4, the most radical welfare reform bill ever introduced in Congress until that time.[1] Although Shaw's bill would go through substantial changes in both name and substance, this bill served as the basic text for all subsequent Republican welfare reform legislation in the House and Senate during the great welfare debate of 1995–96. More important, many of its basic provisions, including nearly all of the most radical, were signed into law by President Bill Clinton on August 22, 1996. In both its original and final forms, this bill constituted a revolution in American social policy for the poor, with ramifications that would project far into the future. Where did this bill come from? Who wrote it? What are the origins of the ideas it embodied? The answers to these questions are explored in this chapter.

There are many paths legislation follows to become law. Most legislation fails to become law, or even to have anyone take notice except the member of Congress who wanted the bill and the congressional staffers who wasted their time drafting it. During each two-year session of Congress, between 5,000 and 6,000 bills are introduced, but fewer than 500 are typically enacted into law.[2] For those lucky 500, the obstacle course to completion can be as varied as the subjects addressed by the legislation.

The full obstacle course involves bill development, bill drafting, bill introduction, hearings, committee markups, floor action, repeating each of these steps in the house of Congress that did not initiate the bill, a House-Senate conference committee to eliminate all differences between the bills passed by the two houses, final passage of identical bills by both houses of Congress, and presidential approval. In most cases the administration attempts to influence the bill as it moves through Congress, especially once the bill conquers the first few hurdles and shows that it is gathering steam and might become law. In the case of major legislation that is a priority for the administration in power at that moment, negotiators for the administration often constitute a force at least the equal of House and Senate negotiators. Thus the bargaining often takes place among three powerful forces, although if the president's party holds a majority in either house, that house will often—but by no means always—support the administration.

Nor does this accounting yet include the often exceptionally powerful forces impinging directly or indirectly on the legislation. There is virtually no such thing as legislating de novo. Most bills enacted by Congress amend an existing law by dropping or modifying previous provisions, adding new ones, or both. All of American domestic policy is composed of statutory continents, some big like Asia, some small like Australia. The biggest are the tax code and the Social Security Act. If God governs the seven earthly continents and allows them to move only at a glacial pace, a combination of forces inside and outside Congress watches over the statutory continents and tries to ensure either that their basic contours remain fixed or that changes meet with their approval. Washington is fundamentally a city of elected federal officials who create the continents, federal bureaucrats who tend the continents, and nonelected interest groups and lobbyists who guard or disrupt the continents. In the case of the welfare statutes, the National Governors Association, the American Public Human Services Association, the Children's Defense Fund, the Center on Budget and Policy Priorities, the Center for Law and Social Policy, the Heritage Foundation, Empower America, the National Conference of State Legislatures, the U.S. Chamber of Commerce, the Christian Coalition, Focus on the Family, Concerned Women for America, and a host of other organizations vie for influence, often by stepping over each other—with perhaps a kick or two on the way.

My story is about how Republicans, seizing an opportunity created by President Clinton and joined by President Clinton at the critical moment at the end of the legislative trail, managed to overcome these inherent checks and enact controversial legislation that fundamentally changed the terrain of American social policy. They even created a new continent. Both in watching the chapters of the story unfold in 1995 and 1996 and now in recounting the tale, I have often felt like students of genetics must feel. The more they study genetics, the more amazing and spectacular the entire process seems. It's so amazing, in fact, that it seems a wonder that either organisms or legislation is ever produced.

This chapter traces how Republicans developed many of the ideas that provided raw material for the bill that eventually was introduced, amid great fanfare, by Clay Shaw and Jim Talent in January 1995 as HR 4. This is an obscure subplot but essential to the bigger story nonetheless, for at least three reasons. First, HR 4 did not spring full-blown from the imagination of those wild-eyed Republicans who seized control of the House after the November 1994 elections. Many reporters, aided and abetted no doubt by those rascal Democrats, made it seem that HR 4 was a mishmash of reactionary ideas and prejudices thrown together at the last minute by Republican radicals. False. Every major provision in the bill had appeared in previous Republican bills and many had been carefully developed over the years by Republicans working together in task forces and other quasi-legislative groups. All had been developed in close cooperation with or direct participation by House Republican leaders and by individuals and conservative lobbying organizations outside Congress, especially the Republican Governors Association, the Heritage Foundation, and Empower America.

The second reason to examine this obscure part of the HR 4 story is that good legislation requires knowledgeable and aggressive members of Congress and staffers willing and able to lead the fight that is necessary to push the bill through the congressional maze. As a sports junkie, I often thought of legislative fights as a peculiar form of American sporting event. The parallels are arresting. They include the necessity of thorough preparation, the need for teamwork, a willingness to expose oneself to public combat during which the chance of embarrassment is constantly present, the self-discipline needed to stand up to competition even when the adversary has superior forces, the physical and mental strain of days and months of long hours of work, and the near certainty that on far too many occasions great effort will be rewarded by losing the game.

Just as a solid sports team needs good players, so too behind most solid legislation lies a small band of smart, aggressive, and prepared members of Congress. To say that members are prepared means, at a minimum, that they must know the statutes and programs that already exist; they must know the often complex details of the policy problem they are trying to solve; they must understand the politics of the issue; and they must understand and have experience with the many procedural requirements of enacting legislation. The great masters of the congressional universe and the statutory continents like Everett Dirksen, Lyndon Johnson, Gerald Ford, Sam Rayburn, Newt Gingrich, Tip O'Neill, and Bob Dole had learned to assemble the forces inside and outside Congress so that a critical mass of them pulled in the same direction. All these men spent a good part of their lives thinking about legislation, devising strategy, and most of all schmoozing with other members of Congress, members of whatever administration happened to be in power, and those powerful outside lobbyists. Few jobs in America require as much intellectual commitment and investment of time as being an effective leader in the United States Congress.

And behind every great member of Congress is a great staff. It is useful to think of three categories of congressional staff: staff that work directly for members in their personal office, staff that work for congressional committees, and staff that work for congressional leadership—especially the Speaker, majority and minority leaders, and the whips. There is generally a clear line of demarcation between personal staff on the one hand and committee and leadership staff on the other. Personal staff members tend to be relatively young, many having recently graduated from college. Senior members of Congress often have a few experienced staff members, especially in the crucial positions of chief of staff, legislative director, and office manager. These are often people who have been with the members for a decade or more. Before joining the member's staff they may have held other staff positions or positions in state government, sometimes positions in which their current member was also their boss. If their member retires or is defeated in a bid for reelection, they often take senior staff positions with younger members who need their experience and savvy.

Committee and leadership staff are older and far more experienced than most staff who serve in members' offices. A large majority of committee and leadership staff are exceptionally competent individuals. They have survived years of partisan warfare, election campaigns, and legislative battles. More to the point, they have gained experience by surviving, in true Darwinian fashion, the inevitable crises that afflict anyone who has worked in Congress for many years. It is not unusual for senior committee staffers and leadership staffers to make all manner of legislative decisions without consulting their member beforehand, on the grounds that they know precisely what their member would decide.

A third reason for carefully tracing the welfare bill's development is that it will be difficult for future students of social policy to believe either that Republicans were able to dream up the seminal ideas found in the 1996 reform legislation or that they exerted the considerable energy and doggedness necessary to push the legislation through Congress and onto President Clinton's desk—once, and again, and yet again. It would be a serious error to regard the 1996 legislation as some quirk of legislative history created by a strange and accidental intersection of random forces, although chance certainly played the same important role it often plays in human affairs. Nor is it correct to view the bill as the result of a bunch of Republicans stomping their feet and shouting out their rejection of programs for the poor. True, God put Republicans on earth to fight against high taxes and big government, to balance budgets (at least until recently), to establish free trade, to maintain a strong national defense, and generally to fight for legislation that helps business and against legislation that hurts business, especially small business. The system of rewards within the Republican Party, and indeed the most basic reasons people join the Republican Party, has a lot more to do with taxes, trade, and business than with social policy. All the more reason that it is important to know the true story of how Republican members of Congress carefully thought through the social policies embodied in the 1996 law and were accompanied throughout the process by Republican (and a few Democratic) governors—who, if anything, knew even more about social policy because they had not only thought hard about the issues but had practical experience actually running social programs.

As our story begins in the early 1990s, House Republicans were a somewhat pitiful force for influencing legislation. Although Republicans more than held their own at the presidential level after the end of the Harry Truman administration in 1952, and actually controlled the Senate on a few occasions, the House of Representatives was owned in its entirety by Democrats. So Republicans learned to find ways to oppose legislation and, when lucky, to amend Democratic bills so that their views would at least have some—usually modest—impact on lawmaking.

Another thing House Republicans did to survive permanent minority status was to form work groups and write reports, a tactic that was usually ineffective except in providing the underemployed Republican members and staff with something to do while Democrats made law. On January 5, 1991, I received a phone call from a House staffer named Ed Kutler. Kutler, whom I barely knew, was the staff director of one of those Republican work groups known, for the day it typically met, as the House Wednesday Group. The Wednesday Group was composed of about fifty, mostly moderate, Republicans. From the perspective of other House Republicans, "moderate" was a misnomer; there were many liberal Republican members of the Wednesday Group, in a day when liberal Republicans were not yet an almost extinct species. To counteract the image of being too liberal and to appeal to a wider cross section of House Republicans, in 1990 the leaders of the Wednesday Group decided to ask Vin Weber of Minnesota, perhaps the leading young conservative in the House and a member of the House Republican leadership, to serve as their co-chair. The other co-chair was the distinctly moderate but widely respected Bill Gradison of Ohio, who was also a senior member of both the Ways and Means Committee and the Budget Committee.

Weber and Gradison, after extensive discussions with other Wednesday Group members, had decided to make poverty a major focus of Wednesday Group activities for 1991. As staff director of the group, Kutler was calling to ask if I would be willing to give some advice on the project.

Ordinarily a staff member working for the Ways and Means Committee needs to be wary of entanglements with outside Republican groups, because members of the committee expect—and receive—complete staff loyalty. However, because Gradison was a senior member of Ways and Means, and because I was just being asked to read an outline of a project, I agreed to do so. I asked Kutler to clear my involvement with Gradison and then send me their outline. Having received the outline within a day or two, I gave Kutler several constructive comments. The original outline was somewhat unconnected to the welfare reform policies then being considered by Republicans on the Ways and Means Committee and by conservatives outside Congress. So I simply made some comments about causes of poverty from a Republican perspective and the types of policies that might be used to address those causes. I also recommended that the project be broadened to include information on taxes and government spending to provide the necessary background for making welfare recommendations—and not so incidentally to defend Republican tax policy against charges of favoring the rich. As usual, Republicans were being pilloried, not least by the former Republican Kevin Phillips and his 1990 book *The Politics of Rich and Poor,* for the spillover effects of the 1980s in supposedly enriching the rich and further impoverishing the poor.[3]

In short order, Kutler called me on the phone and asked if I would write the paper for them. Pretty surprising. Most congressional staffers consider themselves to be in a contest to get the attention of members. Writing a paper like this for one of the most respected House Republican organizations could result in lots of members knowing your name and, perhaps, liking your work. But Kutler, as I came to learn over the next decade and more, didn't see things that way. He was close with both Gradison and Weber (Weber later hired him as a senior manager with the major Washington lobbying firm Clark and Weinstock) and didn't care who got credit. He just wanted a good report.

I began by revising the outline along the lines I had earlier suggested to Kutler and then set to work writing the report. The Wednesday Group report showed that, in inflation-adjusted dollars, spending on benefit programs for poor and low-income Americans increased substantially during the 1980s.[4] Spending on income support, nutrition, social services, education and training, health, and housing programs had increased from about $104 billion in 1981 to $123 billion in 1989, an 18 percent increase in inflation-adjusted dollars. Spending on many individual programs such as the Earned Income Tax Credit (EITC), child support enforcement, foster care, and housing had increased by between 60 percent and well over 100 percent in just eight years. Even more important, the Congressional Budget Office was projecting that spending on important social programs either created from scratch or expanded by legislation in the 1980s would dramatically increase during the 1991–95 period. Spending on the major program designed to help mothers leave welfare for work (called the JOBS program), Medicaid, the EITC, child care, and homeless programs was projected to increase from more than $9 billion to nearly $23 billion, thereby showing that legislative actions taken during the 1980s were providing substantial new resources for the poor, especially the working poor.[5]

After 1965, Democrats had constructed a series of programs—often on a bipartisan basis—designed to provide cash and in-kind benefits to the poor. According to Democrats and to many scholars outside Congress, poverty was difficult to reduce because not enough money was spent on these programs. On the face of it, this argument had serious problems. Between 1965 and 1995, federal and state spending on programs for the poor in the form of cash assistance, education, health, food, housing, and others had increased from around $50 billion to nearly $350 billion in inflation-adjusted dollars.[6] Yet child poverty drifted upward during this period. If more spending would solve poverty, how could the nation increase its spending on social programs by a factor of seven and still see child poverty drifting upward?

The Wednesday Group report provided two answers: young people, especially minorities, had babies outside marriage and many young parents did not work.[7] Here was the intellectual heart of the welfare debate, which was to be so dramatically intensified by the introduction of HR 4 in January 1995. The lack of a work incentive and the absence of work requirements in welfare law had always been a Republican issue, but the 1991 Wednesday Group report is perhaps the first document sponsored by members of Congress that put the issue of family formation, especially illegitimate births, alongside work at the forefront of the debate.

Of course, it is hardly surprising that Republicans would focus on illegitimacy. Republicans are the party of modest government and therefore the party of individual responsibility. Moral behavior taught and regulated by families, local institutions (especially churches), and civil society in general reduces the need for government; the breakdown of morality increases the need for government authority. The historic increases in illegitimacy and the appearance of dangerous neighborhoods in which a high percentage of families were headed by women represented for Republicans a breakdown in moral discipline. Even more important, it destroyed the natural order of child rearing. Charles Murray, one of the few social scientists conservative Republicans admire, had placed illegitimacy at the center of his diagnosis of the problems induced by the welfare state in his seminal 1984 book *Losing Ground*.[8] The Wednesday Group report provided detail, similar in many respects to Murray's analysis, to show that illegitimate births were the Fifth Horseman of the Apocalypse. Illegitimacy had been increasing rapidly since the mid-1960s, and even earlier for minority groups, with the result that more and more children, especially minority children, were being reared in single-parent families. These children were more likely than average to live in poverty, live in dangerous neighborhoods, attend bad schools, be supported by welfare, drop out of school, commit crimes, have an illegitimate birth themselves, remain jobless, and so forth.[9] The Wednesday Group report demonstrates that, as early as 1991, even moderate Republicans believed that illegitimacy was a major public policy problem. This willingness to ground reform in the call to individual responsibility was one of the most fundamental of the differences between Republicans and Democrats that shaped the welfare debate.

In deciding on the policy recommendations for the report, Republicans were, as always, cognizant of their minority status in the House. Because the Wednesday Group was composed largely of practical and moderate politicians, they were more interested in having an impact on welfare legislation than in making partisan debating points. This choice between practical positions that might influence legislation as opposed to stentorian claims designed to sharpen differences with Democrats and rally support from the Republican Party's base is one that is faced by any congressional minority party on a regular basis. Because its members wanted primarily to influence policy, the recommendations of the Wednesday Group were a mixture of bold new ideas and practical recommendations. By far the boldest policy idea, and one that was to play a major role in all subsequent welfare reform debates, was that welfare should be time-limited. From the day the Wednesday Group report was issued in October 1991 until the fundamental reforms of 1996 were signed by President Clinton, almost every Republican bill contained some version of time limits.

It would be difficult to exaggerate the importance of this idea. The proposal is straightforward enough: able-bodied adults signing up for welfare are given a maximum number of years of eligibility that cannot be exceeded. After the eligibility period has expired, cash welfare is permanently terminated. Three aspects of this policy account for its power and for the partisan, sometimes vicious, debate that accompanied it as the welfare reform war developed. First, one of the most basic features of the Aid to Families with Dependent Children (AFDC) cash welfare program—as well as other welfare programs such as Medicaid and Food Stamps—is that of entitlement. Entitlement is a legal concept, developed at least as much through the courts as through legislative policy, that provides individuals and families with a legal right to receive a benefit if they meet the qualifications for that benefit.[10] In congressional jargon, entitlement programs contrast with discretionary programs, which are funded annually at a fixed level and provide their benefits on a first-come, first-served basis. Whereas every family that met its state's requirements for the AFDC program had to be given the cash, qualified families were given housing benefits only as long as the money lasted. There were no waiting lists for AFDC, but families might wait years before getting a place in public housing. As Republicans viewed the world, the entitlement approach to welfare was precisely wrong, primarily because entitlement made it difficult to make benefits contingent on behavior.

The second reason the concept of time limits was so important can be stated simply: time limits send the clear message that welfare is temporary. Instead of aiding and abetting the dependency of unlimited welfare duration associated with entitlement, time limits send the unmistakable message that cash welfare is limited to a maximum period of time. Poor adults would need to plan their lives so that some option of supporting themselves and their children other than welfare would be forthcoming, and soon. Given a program in which 65 percent of those receiving the benefit at any given moment would eventually use the benefit for eight years or more, a time limit of even five years would have dramatic impact over the long run.[11]

Yet a third reason time limits were so important is that they demonstrated how far Republicans were willing to go to move the able-bodied from welfare to work. As Republicans viewed the world, the secret of American affluence and power is free economic markets. A defining characteristic of free markets is risk. Individuals who enter the market must have the education, knowledge, habits, and attitudes required by the job at hand. And regardless of the skill level required for specific jobs, individuals must be willing to show up on time every day, get along with co-workers, follow orders, and be responsive to customers. These are the rules, and everyone's decisions are disciplined by the natural forces of the market, including destitution for individuals who fail. But if an outside force steps in, such as government, and for reasons of its own disrupts the market discipline imposed by risk, the market no longer works and inefficiencies begin to appear.

Government social programs can encourage inefficient, even counterproductive, behavior. Welfare allows people to make all sorts of fundamental mistakes—such as having children outside marriage, dropping out of school, and refusing to work—and yet be guaranteed a living (below the poverty line, to be sure, but a living nonetheless). Worse, having survived these bad personal decisions, young people on welfare serve as a model for others in their community. Worse still, at some point, when a high enough fraction of people in a community shows that serious personal mistakes do not have such bad consequences after all, a tipping point is reached and the discipline normally imposed by natural forces evaporates. Chaos is the result. By the early 1990s many Republicans were joining the apocalyptic view advanced by Charles Murray and declaring that the welfare entitlement was already causing chaos in the inner city.[12]

Lest it be thought that Republicans were the only perpetrators of scary visions of the chaos that results from bad personal decisions, here is Daniel Patrick Moynihan, writing in 1965 on the long-term effects of rising illegitimacy rates:

> From the wild Irish slums of the 19th-century Eastern seaboard, to the riot-torn suburbs of Los Angeles, there is one unmistakable lesson in American history: a community that allows a large number of young men to grow up in broken families, dominated by women, never acquiring any stable relationship to male authority, never acquiring any set of rational expectations about the future—that community asks for and gets chaos. Crime, violence, unrest, disorder—most particularly the furious, unrestrained lashing out at the whole social structure—that is not only to be expected; it is very near to inevitable. And it is richly deserved.[13]

The human psychology at play here among the poor is more subtle than it might at first appear and definitely more subtle than many Republicans knew or cared to admit. The values held by most poor people are not different from the values held by the middle class.[14] Specifically, the poor believe in work and marriage. To know the right thing in the case of the poor (and perhaps one or two of the rest of us) is not necessarily to do the right thing. It takes discipline—and a long-term vision doesn't hurt—to rise above poverty and decide to stay in school, get a job, and resist sex and cohabitation until marriage. Many poor people do not have this discipline, especially given that official government policy before 1996, plain to all, was to rescue young people from the worst consequences of their mistakes.

It gets even worse. Perhaps one of the most unfair aspects of being poor is that bad personal choices have great consequences for long-term well-being. Rich kids can make lots of mistakes, even serious mistakes, and their parents' influence, money, and commitment can help them recover. But the poor often do not have these advantages. They often have only one hard-pressed parent, and that parent often lacks the personal and material resources to promote recovery. Unfair as it might be, dropping out of school, having a baby outside marriage, not working, or committing a crime can put a poor adolescent or young adult on a path leading to more of the same for themselves and even for the next generation, which begins making its appearance all too soon. There are few second chances among America's poor.

To some extent Democrats agreed with this view. However, they focused much more than Republicans on the downsides of the policies that Republicans were developing to address dependency. In the implicit cost-benefit analysis of creating a welfare system, Democrats believed that the minimum living provided to the poor by welfare benefits more than balanced the damage those very benefits might cause to education, work, and marriage incentives. Besides, argued Democrats, how can a just society deny benefits to babies? Can a just nation stand by and watch poor mothers and babies wind up on the streets?

But Republicans argued that the inevitable trade-offs imposed by welfare were such that, in attempting to rescue poor mothers and children, the nation was producing more of them. In the dark calculus of Republican reasoning, the sum of human misery was increased by entitlement because an inevitable consequence of entitlement was more poor, uneducated, welfare-dependent, nonworking young adults. Although Republicans were understandably reluctant to state the case quite so boldly, the implication of their analysis was that the risk of exposure to time limits and other measures designed to restore work and marriage incentives would result in some families being worse off than they were on welfare. But a time limit would leave at least part of the discipline of natural forces intact and thereby limit the number of young people who were lured into a life of dependency while rearing children who would have a high likelihood of repeating the cycle. Republicans were willing to tolerate a few more people in deep poverty, at least temporarily, as a reasonable price to pay for having fewer young adults dependent on welfare in the long term. Most Democrats weren't.

Besides, Republicans intended to subject only the cash benefit to this new system of risk. Families would retain their entitlement to Medicaid and Food Stamps under most circumstances. This combination of contingent cash benefits and entitlement food and health benefits, despite the elevated risk, struck nearly all Republicans as reasonable reform. Democrats, by contrast, were willing to stand a lot more welfare dependency in order to avoid more risk.

A word about evidence is in order here. In the political world, it is often nearly impossible to separate fact from fancy. This is especially true of the core beliefs of the Republican and Democratic political parties. A study or two is not going to persuade a Democrat that taxes on the rich are too high nor a Republican that they're too low. In policy debates, assumptions and values usually trump data—and often reason as well. Even so, over the long run, evidence can play an important role in changing the views of policymakers, even when it bears on fundamental political assumptions. In the case at hand, there is strong evidence that if government provides people with welfare payments, they work less.[15] Here is a case in which common sense and social science evidence are entirely consistent. The upshot is that, in the long run, Republicans have an advantage in the debate over work requirements because most American voters believe, and the research evidence strongly supports their view, that the nation's welfare programs are responsible, at least in part, for nonwork among the poor. This advantage enjoyed by Republicans will play a major role as our story of welfare reform unfolds.

The Republicans of the Wednesday Group were generally pleased with the report and with its reception.[16] For his part, Weber decided that the best way to follow up the report was to write legislation embodying some of its conservative ideas. He and Shaw worked simultaneously on two bills, both of which were introduced in 1992. Weber, teaming up with Shaw and others, including Gradison, introduced his bill in June.[17] The bill embodied several of the ideas Republicans had developed in the Wednesday Group report: a mandatory work requirement, specification of a minimum number of hours of work, and mandatory sanctions for those who did not work all remained central elements in the Republican definition of what it meant to require work. Weber and Shaw's was probably the first congressional bill to impose a time limit on welfare. Among other provisions, the bill would also reduce the marriage penalty inherent in the AFDC program by allowing mothers who married to retain their welfare benefits for two years.

The Weber-Shaw bill was everything Shaw had hoped to achieve from the Wednesday Group project. Even Newt Gingrich, at that time the Republican whip in the House, agreed to put his name on the bill as a cosponsor. Now, two powerful members of the Republican leadership (Weber and Gingrich) were supporting a bill with strong work requirements, mandatory sanctions, parental responsibility, a marriage initiative, and time limits. Even better, and a factor that Shaw had not expected, Gingrich was just starting to heat up the kettle that was to brew a set of ideas for reform of many federal programs and budget and tax policy and to spread these ideas among many Republicans in the House—and even more important, among Republican candidates for Congress. Gingrich's primary genius was leadership, not simply in the sense of inspiring people but in an even more fundamental sense of thinking up a million ways to surround his acolytes with his ideas and convince them that with these ideas they could conquer the world—or at least break the Democrats' stranglehold on the House. The various strands in the Gingrich megaoperation now began to focus on welfare reform, which would lead eventually to the inclusion of welfare reform on his list of major Republican goals.

In addition to working with Weber and Gingrich on the Weber-Shaw bill, Shaw—joined by Nancy Johnson of Connecticut and Fred Grandy of Iowa, who were members both of the Wednesday Group and of Shaw's Ways and Means Subcommittee on Human Resources—decided to write a second report, focusing specifically on the poverty issues and on additional legislative proposals. The second report, released in June 1992, was an early indication that a group of senior Republicans on a congressional committee with major jurisdiction over welfare understood and aimed to improve the nation's system of supporting low-income working families. The major claim made by Shaw and his coauthors was that the goal of Republican welfare policy was to "insure that families willing to work will be better off financially once they leave welfare and to achieve this goal, not by cutting welfare benefits, but by subsidizing work."[18] President Clinton was to make this goal famous during the 1992 presidential campaign against President Bush with his catchy campaign promise to "make work pay."[19]

An important point about this report is that a group of senior and influential Republicans wanted to help poor families both by insisting on work, even at low wages, and by using public dollars to supplement their income. This Republican policy has two parts: work and work support. At the time of the Shaw report in 1992, the nation was slowly moving to establish both. Most Republicans thought that, of the two, the work agenda was getting far too little attention. That is why every Republican welfare reform bill emphasized mandatory work. In fact, the Shaw report contained a table showing that the combination of low-wage work and work supports, primarily through the EITC and Food Stamp programs, was already producing a clear financial advantage for low-wage work compared with welfare. More specifically, a mother in the typical state working at $5 an hour and receiving the EITC and Food Stamps had a total income of nearly $1,200 a month, as opposed to $625 on welfare. Even after deducting around $370 a month for work expenses and taxes, the working mother was still better off by nearly $300 a month. The problem, according to most Republicans, was that too few mothers worked. Cracking dependency was the issue; the Shaw report showed Republicans groping their way to a solution.

On October 1 and 2, 1992, just weeks before Clinton was elected president—in part based on his promise to reform welfare—the Shaw-Johnson-Grandy team introduced three welfare reform bills, all of which had support from the Republican leadership.[20] The most important goal of these bills was to expand state authority to conduct reform experiments and to give some direction to the experiments. The legislation would have provided states with more money to spend on welfare-to-work programs and would have established a federal office with its own budget to promote these demonstration programs. The goals of the demonstrations were to help poor and low-income families achieve self-support and independence, strengthen family relationships, and improve their living conditions. States were given authority to conduct demonstrations involving seventy social programs. Introduced near the end of the congressional session, these bills simply died without receiving any attention. But most of the ideas in the bills survived to rise another day.

During this period of the run-up to the nominating conventions and the final battles of the 1992 presidential campaign, welfare became an issue of growing importance and a target of considerable coverage in the media. All of this public attention helped to set the stage for the appearance of radical reform bills from stage right. As far as Shaw and his colleagues were concerned, opening night was just around the corner and they were determined to keep Republicans in either a lead or at least a major supporting role. Though operating from their low perch in the House as the seemingly permanent minority, Shaw and other Republicans on the Ways and Means Committee believed they could influence the impending welfare reform debate by teaming up with moderate Democrats. For the time being, as the interest in welfare reform grew, Shaw and his Republican allies began a game of moving as far to the right as they could while still taking positions that some Democrats could support. As always for the minority, the trick was keeping all or nearly all your own forces in line while attracting as many moderates from the majority party as possible. This moderation is the classic affliction of minority parties and one of the glories of democratically elected legislative bodies.

Besides the interest generated by the presidential race, another major cause of the growing interest in welfare reform was the rapid expansion of the welfare caseload after 1989. The numbers tell an interesting story. Trends in the rolls between the end of World War II and 1995 are easily summarized. During the two-decade-long period ending in the mid-1960s, there was a gentle rise in the caseload almost every year. Between 1950 and 1966, for example, the number of adults and children on AFDC gradually increased from 2.2 million to about 4.5

million, an increase from about 1.5 percent to 2.3 percent of the U.S. population over sixteen years. By contrast, over the decade after 1966 the number of adults and children on the welfare rolls exploded from 4.5 million to 11.4 million, or from 2.3 percent to 5.2 percent of the U.S. population. The caseload then entered a period of relative stability until another explosion began in 1989. Over the next four years the number of adults and children on welfare reached well over 14 million, an increase of nearly 30 percent.[21]

The causes of the remarkable caseload growth between 1989 and 1993 have never been well understood. Studies by both the Congressional Budget Office and the Congressional Research Service found that the most important single factor was the rapid increase in nonmarital births.[22] Previous work by the Congressional Budget Office had shown that most mothers who have a birth outside marriage wind up on welfare within a few years and that their average length of stay on welfare is much longer than the average stay for divorced mothers.[23] So it was no surprise that illegitimacy would play some role in caseload increases. But nonmarital births, which had been increasing since 1950 and increasing rapidly since about 1965, accounted for only part of the growth. A fuller and more satisfactory explanation of the underlying causes of the explosive growth in the rolls between 1989 and 1993 is still needed.

The timing of this rapid growth was especially unfortunate for the reputation of the bipartisan Family Support Act. Signed by President Reagan in October 1988, the act was implemented just as the AFDC caseload began its historic and surprising growth. The heralded bill that was supposed to at last promote work among welfare recipients seemed to be a bust. Many conservatives argued that the Family Support Act was a major cause of the caseload increase because it did not do enough to emphasize work. But regardless of whether the act actually played a direct role in caseload increases, it was certainly apparent that simply giving money to states to pay for job search, work programs, education, training, and child care would not necessarily lead to increased employment and caseload reduction. The dispiriting caseload explosion after 1989 turned up the volume on the calls for welfare reform—and especially for tougher work requirements.

Besides the apparent failure of the Family Support Act and the rising welfare caseload, another vital factor in the growing reform movement was the rapidly rising desire by states to have more control over welfare programs and to conduct demonstration programs to show the results they could produce if they were given more control. Since the second Reagan administration and the aggressive marketing of state welfare reform demonstrations by a special presidential assistant named Chuck Hobbs, states had been experimenting with a wide variety of reforms, especially those involving mandatory work. Although Hobbs had remained with the first Bush administration for a few months, by 1992 he was working on state-level welfare reform for a private lobbying group in Oregon. But the effects of his actions in the Reagan and Bush administrations were now bearing fruit. It was Hobbs who had persuaded Reagan to place such an emphasis on state experimentation by forming the Low-Income Opportunities Board and by encouraging states to submit waiver requests.[24] Hobbs had also worked directly with states, encouraging them to initiate welfare reform experiments.

Two states—Wisconsin and New Jersey—were leading the way on welfare reform and what was called the new paternalism. In 1979 the Wisconsin legislature appointed a committee, led by an accomplished scholar from the University of Wisconsin named Robert Haveman, to make recommendations on welfare reform. Based on the committee's recommendations, two important reforms were enacted in the early 1980s.[25] The first was a state earned income tax credit, which provided an income supplement to low-wage workers, thereby providing an incentive for adults to leave welfare for work. Unfortunately, the welfare rolls increased substantially during the early 1980s in Wisconsin, suggesting that convincing people to work requires more than providing cash incentives. Based on the work of Irwin Garfinkel, another University of Wisconsin scholar, the state legislature also enacted several important changes in its child support enforcement laws, including mandatory withholding of income (similar to tax withholding) from the paychecks of fathers who owe child support and a new approach to establishing how much child support fathers owe. Judicial judgment in establishing the size of child support orders was replaced by a percentage-of-income standard, which increased with the number of children. These and other reforms soon gave Wisconsin one of the nation's most effective child support enforcement programs and one that has been copied by many states and even by federal policymakers when the nation's child support system was reformed in 1984 and 1988.

Despite these reforms, the Wisconsin welfare rolls continued to rise. By 1986 more than 100,000 Wisconsin families were on welfare, the highest ever. In response to this rise in the rolls, the Democratic state legislature enacted reforms that emphasized work and preparation for work. Called Work Experience and Job Training, the new program emphasized intensive case management as well as education and training. But the most innovative and portentous feature of the program was that it required recipients who failed to find jobs to participate in a mandatory work program. The requirement of mandatory work became a fixture of Wisconsin welfare reform and played an increasingly important role in future reforms under Wisconsin governor Tommy Thompson.[26]

Legislative action to reform welfare in New Jersey was also strong, surprisingly so, given that the leadership was provided by liberal Democrats. Indeed, the major mover in welfare reform in New Jersey was a black Democrat named Wayne Bryant from Camden, one of the poorest cities in the nation. In January 1992, after skilled parliamentary maneuvering and pointed speeches by Bryant, the Democratic legislature enacted and sent to the Democratic governor Jim

Florio a series of welfare reforms that was, on paper at least, even more revolutionary than Wisconsin's. The reform package, in a harbinger of the federal
reform debate three years later, was strongly opposed by church groups such as
the Lutheran Office of Government Ministries, elements of the Roman Catholic
church, and the New Jersey Council of Churches as well as by traditional liberal
groups such as the American Civil Liberties Union and the National Organization for Women. The ink was hardly dry on the governor's signature before the
legislation was challenged in court.

And no wonder. In addition to a work mandate backed by sanctions, the
reforms reflected New Jersey lawmakers' desire to stop paying additional benefits for mothers already on welfare who had additional children. Families working for private companies do not get a raise when they have more children, so
why should families on welfare? Again in a harbinger of the federal debate still
three years away, New Jersey became the first state in the union to stop paying
additional benefits for children born to mothers already on welfare, a provision
that came to be known as the family cap. In addition to the work requirement
and the family cap, a third remarkable provision created a marriage incentive by
allowing mothers who married to retain their entire welfare benefit as long as
combined family income from earnings and welfare did not exceed 150 percent
of the poverty level.[27]

Republicans in the House working on welfare reform were amazed by the
actions in both Wisconsin and New Jersey. Governor Tommy Thompson, a
Republican, was the undisputed leader of welfare reform in Wisconsin, but his
reforms were enacted by legislative bodies controlled by Democrats; in some
instances Democrats proposed reforms that were as radical as Thompson's and,
in any case, predated Thompson's reign as governor. If Wisconsin, a predomi-
nantly liberal state with a well-deserved reputation for progressive government,
was enacting radical welfare reforms aimed at changing the behavior of welfare
recipients, how could any observer fail to conclude that the stars were coming
into alignment for groundbreaking national reform? And if New Jersey, a state
governed by liberal Democrats at every level and with a substantial welfare population, could enact reforms that were well to the right of anything Democrats
in the nation's capital would support, how much more would an observer be justified in concluding that deep proreform forces were afoot in the nation?

Clearly, states were in the lead on welfare reform. Even before Bill Clinton
made welfare reform one of his central campaign issues, before Clinton was
elected and appointed a task force that finally produced recommendations after
Clinton had been in office for eighteen months, and as House Republicans were
doing everything possible to bring attention to their radical reform proposals and
clothing them in legislative packages that included moderate reforms, a few states
were already enacting and then implementing reforms that were equally as rad-

ical as—or even more radical than—the reforms that did not yet enjoy majority support in the U.S. Congress. The experience and knowledge possessed by state-level Democrats like Governor Florio and assemblyman Bryant that made them so different from most Democrats in Washington is difficult to even imagine. In February 1992 when Senator Moynihan brought Bryant to Washington to explain his reforms to the Senate Finance Committee, a Martian could not have represented thinking that was more different from the thinking that befuddled the perception of Chairman Moynihan and his fellow Democratic senators.[28] As congressional Democrats began to understand the arguments being advanced by reforming states such as Wisconsin and New Jersey, as Governor Bill Clinton, first as a candidate and then as president, continued to bring serious public attention to "ending welfare as we know it," and above all as House Republicans developed and popularized their radical reform ideas and proposals, the moment for historic welfare reform was taking shape. The forces were gathering.

## CHAPTER THREE

# House Republicans Unite behind Radical Reforms

The problem with campaign promises is that after the election many people remember the promises and actually expect the newly elected candidate to deliver. So it was with President Clinton. After repeatedly promising to "end welfare as we know it" during the campaign, he had to have an initiative on welfare reform—and many of us hoped and believed that he truly wanted to pass legislation reforming welfare. On February 2, 1993, at the annual Washington meeting of the National Governors Association, the newly inaugurated president announced that he would appoint a task force to draft his welfare reform legislation. But as the months ticked by, Clinton did not appoint a task force. In fact, he did not appoint one until summer. By then it had long been obvious that the administration would emphasize health care reform and move more deliberately on welfare reform.

Although health care reform was to dominate the headlines throughout the first two years of the Clinton administration, welfare had become too big—in no small part because of Clinton's campaign rhetoric—to just ignore. Clinton's optimistic statement to the governors about his intentions on welfare reform brought even more attention to the issue. And Chairman Moynihan of the Senate Finance Committee was to be a constant prod to the president to get moving on welfare reform, sometimes in terms that bordered on derision.

But the president's task force was a problem from the beginning. Before it finally materialized more than six months into the administration, the media asked, Where's the president's task force? Once the task force was formed and began to meet, the question became, Why isn't the task force making more progress? And if Moynihan's machinations, the media's focus on Clinton's campaign promises to reform welfare, and the public and private activities of Clinton's task force when it was finally appointed were not enough to keep the welfare story in the news, the *New York Times*'s Jason DeParle was. Arguably the most aggressive, relentless, and gifted welfare reporter in the nation, DeParle offered nonstop coverage of the task force and its progress, or lack thereof. His stories, which were numerous, provocative, and often based on leaks from the task force, frequently appeared on the front page of the *New York Times*. So intriguing and detailed were DeParle's stories that I often wondered whether he had bugged the rooms in which the task force met.[1]

If IQ meant anything, Clinton's task force could have written a new Constitution as well as a measly little proposal on welfare. David Ellwood and Mary Jo Bane, two of the task force leaders, were brilliant professors from Harvard who came to Washington to serve in Donna Shalala's Department of Health and Human Services. They knew as much about welfare as anyone in the country. Bruce Reed, a mere Rhodes Scholar and Clinton's top thinker on welfare, was the third leader of the troika that directed the task force. Reed, the author of the powerful phrase, "End welfare as we know it," was a true believer in welfare reform and a highly competent political operative. Even better from the perspective of congressional Republicans, he seemed to be advising Clinton to cut a deal with Republicans and in the end was a very strong voice within the administration for Clinton to sign our bill.

Ellwood and Bane were squishier. My impression, based on knowing both of them as individuals and as scholars, was that they knew welfare had bad effects on its recipients and needed to be reformed. Both were also capable of reading the polls, and both were well aware of Clinton's campaign promises on reform, which undoubtedly led them to understand that Clinton was under great pressure to actually require welfare mothers to work. But Ellwood and Bane were sincerely worried that, given the pressure from Republicans, Clinton might wind up signing a bill that put welfare mothers and their children at great risk. They were both repelled by all versions of the Charles Murray proposal to end welfare benefits, even if the question was on the comparatively mild version being pushed by House Republicans in which "only" mothers under age eighteen would lose "only" cash welfare. When Bane met with Ways and Means Committee Chairman Bill Archer of Texas shortly after the beginning of the 104th Congress, he asked her directly if she supported time limits, tough sanctions on mothers who refused to participate in work programs, and welfare cutoffs for minor mothers who had children outside marriage. She hemmed and hawed a bit, then said that on some issues she was "a marshmallow." Not surprisingly, she left the administration shortly after Clinton signed the welfare reform bill, to join Ellwood—who had left the administration more than a year earlier—in the safer confines of Harvard Yard, where the influence of the Republican hordes was minimal, to say the least.

But knowledge and excellent leadership alone could not rescue the Clinton task force. For openers, the task force, which eventually grew to thirty-two members representing several cabinet-level departments and the White House, accurately reflected the huge range of views on welfare within the Democratic Party. If Reed was a true believer and Ellwood and Bane were the moderates, other factions on the task force were equally divided. In the end, they produced a proposal, but only after lots of infighting and disarray. And the final product, the most shocking welfare reform proposal ever put forth by a Democratic administration, was doomed from the beginning.

Clinton's real problem was that there was no single proposal that could unite Democrats. As Clay Shaw presciently told *USA Today,* Clinton needed Republicans to pass welfare reform because liberal Democrats simply would not support the kind of bill Clinton and his task force were brewing up.[2] Republicans and the public demanded mandatory work, sanctions, and a time limit, all of which split the Democratic Party, especially in the House of Representatives.

Unwieldy and divided against itself, operating against a backdrop of constant leaks and front-page stories in the *New York Times,* and with no unifying proposal in sight, the task force suffered from yet another problem: money. Welfare reform was expensive. In March 1994, when Clinton invited the task force leaders to a cabinet meeting to present their proposals, they offered three options, with costs ranging from $10 billion to $18 billion a year. Where would the money be found? Republicans had no problem with money because our proposals included the termination of benefits for most noncitizens and a nutrition block grant, both of which saved enough money to cover costs, and then some. But Clinton could not support anything close to the elimination of welfare for all noncitizens, because low-income families and minorities were a major part of the Democratic coalition. Besides, cutting off immigrants would subvert the Democratic Party's tradition of helping the poor and downtrodden. The task force scrounged around in the federal budget and came up with several proposals to finance its work program: reduce veterans' benefits, impose a sin tax on gambling, cap the mortgage deduction, cap the tax break on interest on annuities, and even tax the poor's welfare benefits. All of these caused immediate reactions from one or more territories on the political landscape, seismic disturbances measuring at least 6 on the Richter scale.

As it became clear that Clinton would not move quickly on welfare reform, Clay Shaw decided that the administration's inaction created an opening for Republicans. At the beginning of the administration, Shaw—still the leading House Republican on welfare reform—had high hopes that the president would follow through on his campaign promise to reform welfare. Shaw had even written an op-ed piece in *Roll Call* (the local newspaper of Capitol Hill avidly read by members of Congress, staffers, lobbyists, and reporters who cover Congress) that Clinton's promises during the campaign were compatible with the very proposals that House Republicans had been developing.[3] Shaw went so far as to suggest that Clinton's best chance of passing serious reform was to form a coalition of Republicans and moderate Democrats in Congress. Although Shaw's public utterances emphasized our common ground with Clinton on the importance of work and of limiting benefits and his confidence that the president was serious about welfare reform, he and other Republicans were unsure whether Clinton really intended to propose serious reforms or to follow through if he did make a proposal.

As Republicans were trying to decide whether Clinton was serious about welfare reform, the administration officially proposed delaying one of the most important features of the 1988 Family Support Act. In testimony before Ways and Means on May 4, 1993, Wendell Primus, a senior official at the Department of Health and Human Services and a former senior Democratic staffer on Ways and Means (and who will come to play an important role in our story), requested that the sixteen-hour workweek requirement for two-parent families in the Aid to Families with Dependent Children (AFDC) program be delayed for two years.[4] This provision was the only true work requirement in the 1988 law and served as a symbol for Republicans of a requirement that all welfare adults should meet—and soon would, if Republicans got their way. Thus when the administration asked to delay implementation of the provision, many of us took it as a very bad sign. Primus told the committee that both because the welfare rolls had expanded so rapidly in the late 1980s and early 1990s and because the recession of the early 1990s had played havoc with state budgets, states could not afford the programs that were "required" to help welfare recipients get the education and training necessary to qualify for a job. But this argument further annoyed Shaw and other Republicans. Work requirements were not about education, they were about work. Another bad sign.

Even after this unfortunate episode, however, Shaw was reluctant to believe that Clinton's campaign promises were bogus. But other Republicans took the administration request to delay work as proof that Clinton did not intend to sponsor serious reforms. Many Republican congressmen and staffers—probably a majority—believed that Clinton was bluffing and that we should avoid working with him on welfare reform. At the very least, the trust quotient Republicans granted to Clinton took a big hit.

Given the uncertainties, Shaw decided that he and other Republicans on the Ways and Means Committee needed to make welfare reform an important issue for as many House Republicans as possible. No matter what Clinton did, our only chance to be effective in the pending welfare debate was to present a united Republican front. Most issues before Congress remain central to only a few members, usually senior members on the committee that has jurisdiction over the legislation. Typically, they toil away in semiobscurity, developing the legislation and bringing it through committee. Only when the legislation goes to the House or

Senate floors do other members take notice. This notice typically lasts about as long as the floor debate—a few hours. But for major issues like welfare reform, for which members are likely to be lobbied by constituents at home and by interest groups in Washington, many members develop their own views, even if they are not on committees of jurisdiction and even if they are not working directly on legislation.

But old views on welfare were rapidly changing. There was no doubt that almost all Republicans would support strong work requirements now, even for mothers of very young children. But the particulars of the plan to promote work were subject to sharp disagreements, even among Republicans. Moreover, a new and vitally important factor that was to cause immense strife among Republicans was beginning to rear its head. Many conservatives, especially conservative intellectuals outside Congress, began to minimize the importance of work while emphasizing that "true" welfare reform consisted of measures to fight illegitimacy. During the first two years of Clinton's presidency, conservatives outside Congress were in the initial stages of both formulating this view and beginning to sell their ideas to conservative members inside Congress. Over this period, the media would be flooded with stories and editorials about the evil consequences of illegitimacy and policies to reduce the number of illegitimate births. Top conservative thinkers, including Charles Murray, William Bennett, George Will, Charles Krauthammer, Ben Wattenberg, and Michael Barone, would take up the cause.[5] Even the brilliant moderate editorial writer Robert Samuelson joined the fray.[6] Worst of all, many of these editorials virtually ignored or even dismissed the importance of work. A huge substantive and political problem for Republican welfare reformers was growing out of control. Illegitimacy was fighting work for the welfare reform spotlight on the Republican stage.

Whether House Republicans would join forces with Clinton to enact sweeping reforms or oppose a less-than-radical bill that Clinton might develop once the relatively liberal congressional Democrats worked their influence on him mattered less at this point than keeping House Republicans united. As early as February 1993, Shaw was stewing about the course we should take. A new factor that might make our position especially difficult was that Shaw had decided to temporarily step down from his post as the ranking Republican on the Ways and Means Committee's Human Resources Subcommittee. At the beginning of each Congress, Ways and Means Republicans meet to decide their subcommittee assignments and to determine who would be the ranking member on each subcommittee (at that time, the Ways and Means subcommittees were Social Security, Trade, Oversight, Health, Human Resources, and Special Tax, each of which had a ranking Republican member). Because of the needs of his district, Shaw had been waiting for the opportunity to join the Trade Subcommittee. Given the particulars of the committee's selection rules, Shaw might have to give up his position as ranking member of the Human Resources Subcommittee in order to take a position on the Trade Subcommittee.

Staff could not attend the selection meeting, so during the first week of January 1993 I anxiously awaited word on whether Shaw would have to step down and, if so, who would be our new ranking member. Of course, I was greatly concerned about the prospect of Shaw leaving. I was even disappointed in him for sacrificing his ranking membership just to join the Trade Subcommittee. Who cared about his district or his next election? The long-awaited opportunity to reform welfare was at hand, and Shaw was the acknowledged leader of House Republicans on welfare. He was smart, amiable, very knowledgeable about welfare, and he and I had an excellent working relationship. Now at the critical moment he might be gone.

Late in the afternoon of the subcommittee selection day, I went by the chief of staff's office in Room 1102 of the Longworth Building. Just as I had feared, when Shaw selected the Trade Subcommittee and his ranking membership on Human Resources came open, Rick Santorum, a new member of Ways and Means from Pennsylvania, had seized it. I knew Santorum only by reputation. Elected to the House in 1990 at the ripe old age of thirty-two, primarily by conducting an old-fashioned campaign of knocking on doors, the word was that he was smart and very aggressive. Several people even told me that he was a little mercurial.[7]

So now I could start again to educate a new ranking member of the subcommittee on the glories of welfare reform. Santorum would be the third ranking member I had worked with in just six years as the Republican staffer on the Human Resources Subcommittee. Hank Brown of Colorado and Clay Shaw had proven themselves to be spectacular leaders of subcommittee Republicans and had turned into students of welfare and of welfare reform. More important, both had fought for Republican reforms of the system. They believed that AFDC and the blizzard of other welfare programs were serious policy mistakes, which harmed nearly all they touched. Would Santorum follow in the Brown-Shaw mold? Would Santorum devote the time needed to learn about the programs, learn about and take a strong stance on reforms, and lobby other members to bring them over to his views? And equally important, would Santorum and Shaw get along with each other? Shaw was bound to regard Santorum as simply a placeholder until committee rules permitted him to resume his leadership of the subcommittee in two years. And Santorum, brash and ambitious, might resent Shaw's avuncular influence on members of Ways and Means and House Republicans in general.

As it turned out, all my concern was wasted. Santorum and Shaw respected each other and worked together without a single conflict over the two crucial years that Santorum headed the subcommittee and Shaw continued to serve as a member. Not only did Santorum respect Shaw's years of work on welfare reform, but Santorum himself became a serious student of welfare programs and a forceful leader of not just the subcommittee but also House Republicans in general. Santorum recognized that Shaw and I had a close relationship and that, in all likelihood, Shaw would soon be the ranking member again. He himself consulted frequently with Shaw and encouraged me to do the same. Santorum's general approach was simply to pick up where Shaw had left off and continue figuring out ways to keep Republicans in the thick of things on welfare reform and to be ready to either support or oppose a presidential initiative, depending on whether the president proposed serious reforms. It probably didn't hurt that during much of this period, Santorum had his eyes on a prize other than ranking member of the Human Resources Subcommittee; namely, being elected to the U.S. Senate.

A clear benefit of having Santorum as the new ranking member was that he was widely seen as more conservative than Shaw. It is not too much of an exaggeration to say that from the introduction of the first Shaw welfare reform bill in February 1993[8] until President Clinton signed the final welfare reform bill in August 1996, the single greatest threat to the Republican welfare reform machine was internal division. By the winter of 1993 it was becoming increasingly clear that many Republicans outside Congress wanted to push Republicans toward the most conservative possible position. Many Republicans were still smarting from Clinton's theft of an issue that had always worked to our advantage. But for some Republicans, the way to recapture the issue was to push Republican ideas and legislative proposals as far to the right as possible and thereby maximize the differences with Clinton and the Democrats.

The emerging disarray among Republicans was a sign that our ideas on welfare were in flux. As a participant in the process of thinking about new ideas, talking—and often arguing—with Republicans inside and outside Congress about them, trying to build support for them among House Republicans, and then drafting specific legislative provisions, I undoubtedly carry a heavy bias in believing that Shaw, Santorum, and the other members of the Human Resources Subcommittee were the major source of Republican wisdom on welfare reform. Shaw's (and now Santorum's) Human Resources Subcommittee actually was, along with the presidency of Bill Clinton, the most important institutional force behind welfare reform. Unlike radical Republicans outside Congress and even a few Republicans in the House and Senate who wanted to maximize their differences with the president in order to score political points, Republicans on our subcommittee wanted to reach agreement with Clinton and change the law. During the initial phases of developing our proposals, we were in the minority in the House. Thus we wanted to develop reforms that could be accepted by moderate Democrats on the Ways and Means Committee in particular and in the House in general. We also wanted to work with Clinton, who seemed to be very close to us on the issues. We had managed to move things somewhat in our direction with the work requirement that covered two-parent families and the participation standards that applied to everyone on the welfare caseload in the 1988 Family Support Act, and many Republicans inside Congress (as long as we were in the minority) were willing to compromise again to move the law another step or two in our direction. By working with Clinton and other moderate Democrats, perhaps we could achieve a real work requirement for the entire caseload. Clinton's rhetoric argued that we could. But we had to neutralize, join, or overcome the conservatives outside Congress, who would rather show a clear difference with Clinton and not reform the laws than compromise with Clinton and share the credit.

As conservatives outside Congress began to criticize the subcommittee Republicans' "pallid" provisions to promote work and our support of waivers and demonstrations on liberal ideas like guaranteed child support benefits, Santorum and Shaw became increasingly concerned that we would have trouble keeping House Republicans united. During February and March of 1993, we solicited the views of House Republicans, conservative Republicans outside Congress, the Republican National Committee, and Senate Republicans on how best to promote Republican unity on welfare reform. Then on March 10 an event occurred that was to have major impacts on both our current efforts to unite House Republicans and the central features of the welfare reform policy that House Republicans would eventually support. Jan Meyers, a forceful and determined Republican member from Kansas, introduced a bill to change AFDC from an entitlement program into a block grant and to cut off aid to unwed teen mothers. This remarkable bill brought the internal conflicts among Republicans into the open. Because of Robert Rector of the Heritage Foundation, whom Meyers had worked with, we now had some markers for what it meant to be truly conservative on welfare reform. Of course, as we would soon find out, the goalposts would change several times over the 1993–96 period, but these two markers— block grants and cutting aid to unwed mothers—remained central. Republicans love block grants. The most important characteristic of block grants is that they greatly increase state and local, as opposed to federal, control of social programs. Part of the birthright of Republicans is wariness about big government. Measured in terms of taxation, spending, and ownership of physical capital, the federal government is the richest, most powerful entity in history. All the more reason for Republicans to look for ways to subtract power and authority from the federal government and give it to state and local government. So Jan Meyers's proposal to convert AFDC to a block grant, precisely because it could appeal to many Republicans, was a major threat to us.

Again, Santorum and Shaw were trying to keep Republicans, stuck in the minority in both houses of Congress, in the game of determining the characteristics of a welfare reform bill that could pass a Democratic Congress and be signed by a Democratic president. Rhetoric about block grants was fine—we loved them as much as or more than other Republicans—but as long as Democrats controlled the House, the Senate, and the presidency, the idea of an AFDC block grant was a nonstarter. We needed a proposal that could attract moderate Democrats, and then we would be not only in the game but possibly in control. Our greatest advantage was that any proposal from Clinton with real work requirements and time limits would split the Democrats. But Republican support for a block grant would destroy any possibility of a coalition between Republicans and moderate Democrats or with the president.[9]

The second major feature of Meyers's proposal was equally radical. She proposed to simply eliminate cash benefits for unwed teen moms. We took to calling this proposal "Murray Light," a reference to the proposal by Charles Murray in this 1984 book *Losing Ground* to completely end all welfare benefits.[10] Rather than end welfare completely as Murray had recommended, the Meyers proposal—and many like it that were to emerge over the next two years—would "only" end some welfare benefits for some mothers. Again, it seemed good to have this proposal out in the open. Shaw and Santorum were not opposed to all versions of this proposal on its merits, but they were afraid that moderate Republicans and nearly all Democrats would hate it. We were also concerned about being pummeled in the press for supporting a policy that "starved children."[11] This policy, above all others, played into the perception that Republicans were indifferent to the well-being of the poor. Thus the Murray Light proposal, like the block grant, was something we found attractive, but supporting it would destroy any chance of working with Democrats.

During this period, I had any number of discussions about strategy with Phil Moseley, the chief of staff for Republicans on Ways and Means. Phil and I were close friends, and although he was not a welfare expert, few people I knew understood House politics better than Phil. A big burly guy, Phil had been working with Bill Archer, the senior Republican on Ways and Means, for twenty years. In a story that was not unusual in Congress, as Phil became more expert in programs under Ways and Means jurisdiction, especially taxes, and learned more about the often obscure ways of the House, Archer accumulated seniority and Phil, as his chief staffer, became more and more influential. In 1992, after twenty years in Congress, Archer became the ranking member on Ways and Means and brought Phil from his personal staff to head the committee staff. Phil quickly showed that he would be a terrific staff director. He was knowledgeable, practical, friendly, firm, and decisive. And despite these formidable abilities, he was without question the most modest senior staffer I ever met in fourteen years of work in the House. He never seemed to be trying out for the next highest position. Phil was a good old boy from Texas, and he was truly proud to be chief of staff for Republicans on

Ways and Means. And as usually happens in these cases, he was totally committed to protecting and advancing the interests of Bill Archer.

As Phil and I discussed the rapidly changing situation on welfare reform, we gradually came to believe that, after talking with Santorum and Shaw, we should approach Archer and get him to propose to the leadership that House Republicans develop a reform bill that all or nearly all House Republicans would support. Santorum and Shaw, both of whom agreed that we needed to reach out to other House Republicans, were concerned about how difficult it might be to keep our forces unified because of the conservative agitation on illegitimacy and now perhaps on the block grant issue.

By May 1993 there was general agreement that the Republican leadership should appoint a work group on welfare reform, that a member of the leadership should co-chair the work group along with a member from the Ways and Means Committee, and that a broad representation from House Committees with jurisdiction over welfare programs should be members of the work group. The work group was duly appointed under the co-chairmanship of Tom DeLay of Texas, then the secretary of the House Republican Conference, and Rick Santorum, the new ranking member on our subcommittee. There were nine other members of the work group: Clay Shaw of Florida, Nancy Johnson of Connecticut, Fred Grandy of Iowa, and Dave Camp of Michigan representing the Ways and Means Committee; along with Jan Meyers of Kansas, Chris Shays of Connecticut, Mike Castle of Delaware, Bill Paxon of New York, and Gary Franks of Connecticut representing the Budget, Education,[12] and Commerce Committees. Shays, Paxon, and Franks were included in the work group because they had demonstrated a direct interest in welfare reform by introducing their own legislation. Meyers not only had introduced her own legislation but also was aggressively lobbying Bill Archer and other members of the Republican leadership to adopt the central provisions of her bill. Everyone knew that Meyers would be a difficult member of the work group, but an old Lyndon Johnson adage guided the decision to include her: "It's probably better to have [dissenters] inside the tent pissing out than outside the tent pissing in."[13] Between June and November 1993 this group was to meet on at least ten occasions and to develop a truly radical and expansive Republican bill supported by almost all House Republicans. Although the bill enacted into law in August 1996 was even broader, many of its concepts and even specific provisions were developed by this Republican work group.

After we had been meeting for a month or so, a second small group of members from the Budget Committee, led by Jim Kolbe of Arizona and Wally Herger of California, joined the work group. With technical help from a staff team led by Laurie Felton from Kolbe's office and Roger Mahan from Herger's office, the smaller group had been working on a nutrition block grant that would combine funds from the Food Stamp program and several child nutrition programs, control the growth of spending in the block grant, and save money over the long run while greatly increasing state flexibility. Mahan had gotten the idea for a nutrition block grant from a paper on ways to cut federal welfare spending written by Peter Germanis in 1990 for the Heritage Foundation.[14] The assumption underlying the block grant, which was consistent with Republican thinking about block grants, was that states could realize savings if they could administer one big grant program rather than twelve or thirteen smaller grant programs. After consulting with analysts at the Congressional Budget Office (CBO), Roger recommended that 5 percent be cut from each program put in the block grant as a reasonable approximation of potential administrative savings. In addition to saving money, like all block grants, the nutrition block grant gave states lots of flexibility. States that wanted to expand their popular Special Supplemental Nutrition program for Women, Infants, and Children (WIC), for example, could do so in a cost-neutral way by eliminating the subsidy for families above the income cutoff in the school lunch program and shifting the savings to the WIC program. Everyone on the work group agreed that the nutrition block grant was a very worthy addition to the bill.

We all thought that welfare reform could be an important issue in the 1994 congressional elections. The goal of the work group was to develop a bill that, precisely because it had been written by a group of Republicans representing a breadth of committees and viewpoints, would be acceptable to nearly all House Republicans. The bill would then go through the normal institutional procedures followed when House Republicans wanted to create a bill that enjoyed official support of the House Republicans. Specifically, once the work group had reached agreement on a bill, it would first have to be approved by the Republican Policy Committee, chaired by the rotund, grey-maned orator from Illinois, Henry Hyde. Then, after incorporating changes required by the Policy Committee, the bill would come before the House Republican Conference, composed of all House Republicans and chaired by Dick Armey of Texas, for a final vote. It was also agreed that the work group, and Santorum in particular, would maintain contact with offices of several Republican governors who were beginning to emerge as leaders on welfare reform in their own states.

At the first work group meeting in early June 1993, Santorum, after discussions with other members of Ways and Means, handed out a document summarizing where he thought the work group should begin. Santorum's document outlined five proposals he wanted to include in the bill produced by the work group: mandatory work after two years for welfare mothers, a set of rewards and sanctions for appropriate parenting (primarily taking children for immunizations and ensuring school attendance), more state flexibility to encourage experimentation, incentives within the AFDC program for marriage, and stronger child support enforcement. All of these elements were present in varying degrees in all subsequent Republican bills, but the work group also developed new proposals.

As with all our bills, the heart of Santorum's welfare reform agenda was the work requirement. His provision on work grew from the previous bills introduced by Shaw and other Republicans. The work requirement would create a two-tier AFDC program. Parents joining AFDC would enter the first tier of the program, known as work preparation. While in the work preparation tier, they would engage in education, training, and job search for a maximum of two years. At the end of that time, if they did not have a job they would be placed in a mandatory work program. Certain parents, such as those who just had a baby and those caring for an incapacitated child, would be exempt. Parents who failed to maintain satisfactory participation would have their benefit reduced, and would eventually lose their entire benefit. A major problem with a program of this type, as both the House Republican work group and the Clinton task force were discovering, was cost. In a back-of-the-envelope estimate, based on previous estimates of other proposals by the Congressional Budget Office (CBO), I guessed that this work proposal would cost at least $3 billion or even $4 billion a year when fully implemented. Given that the program was to be gradually implemented over five years, the costs for the first five years would probably be on the order of $7 billion to $8 billion. But after the first five years, the full cost of as much as $4 billion every year would begin.[15]

Santorum's documents also included a list of the criteria by which the adequacy of President Clinton's bill would be judged, a long list of quotations from Clinton speeches that we advised members to use in holding Clinton's feet to the fire on welfare reform, and two charts, which were to play a major role in all the subsequent debates.

Surprisingly, a good chart can be useful in a congressional debate. Because members deal with so many policy problems, they do not have time to become expert on every issue on which they vote. Members and staff who work directly on legislation find it to their advantage to summarize major arguments, generalizations from research, or other vital facts on charts and in terse, usually bulleted, talking points. Members then show these charts and talking points to each other, include them in their newsletters, place them in the *Congressional Record*, and if they're useful enough, have them blown up to poster size for use in committee hearings and markups and in floor debates. In the case at hand, there were two arguments about welfare that virtually all Republicans already believed but that could be beautifully summarized in simple charts. The first dripped with irony. Harvard professors Mary Jo Bane and David Ellwood, both of whom were now—as we have seen—senior Department of Health and Human Services officials in the Clinton administration with major responsibility for welfare reform, had conducted sophisticated research on the average duration of welfare spells.[16] Ellwood and Bane used statistical estimation techniques to determine, for everyone on the rolls at a given moment, how much time they would eventually spend on welfare, including future spells.

There is a complexity to the problem of understanding welfare duration that few members of Congress understood. Think of welfare as a one-room house with a front door and a backdoor. Applicants come through the front door and enter the room once they are accepted onto the welfare rolls. They then stay in the room for varying periods of time ("spells") and leave through the backdoor. If you want to know something about the dynamics of welfare use, there are two basic approaches you could take. First, you could count everyone who came through the front door and compute the average amount of time they had been in the room before leaving, including the time they spent in the room on return visits. Second, you could look just at the people in the room at any given moment and determine the average length of time they had been in the room. As it turns out, these two approaches provide very different answers to the question of how long the typical recipient stays on welfare. The reason is that some people have short spells and some have long spells. If we include everyone who ever joined the rolls, the average duration of spells in the room is relatively short because the group being considered includes all those with short spells. But if we look just at the group of people on the welfare rolls at a particular moment—only those inside the room in our analogy—the average duration of spells is much longer because people with long spells are more likely to be in the room (on the welfare rolls) at any given moment. By contrast, those with short spells are less likely to be in the room at any given moment. Bane and Ellwood found that for those on welfare (in the room) at any given moment, about 65 percent would eventually be on the rolls for eight years or more (including repeat spells).

Liberals could fairly respond that the 65 percent figure was misleading because it provided only part of the picture. What about all the people who had already left the room? But politicians use the products of social science to advance a political agenda. And whereas social scientists start with a question and follow strict rules to arrive at an answer, politicians usually start with the answer and use the results of social science—selectively if necessary—to support their predetermined answer. There is an entire continuum of ways to manipulate social science data. As Mark Twain said, first get your facts straight; then you can mangle 'em any way you want to. But using facts correctly that do not provide the entire story is not regarded as particularly heinous in politics. So we made a wonderful pie chart, with a big red slice showing that 65 percent of welfare cases would eventually be on the rolls eight years or more. This fact, true but selective, was impressive to Republican members. By late 1993 about 5 million families were on welfare. Based on Bane and Ellwood's research, we could estimate that more than 3 million of them would be on the rolls for eight years or more. During that time, each family could easily consume $90,000 or even $100,000 worth of welfare benefits if the value of cash, Food Stamps, and Medicaid were included in the estimate. If housing, school lunch, and other benefits (which are not received by all AFDC families), were included, the total cost could be well over $150,000. These numbers were red meat for Republicans, and the pie chart handed out by Santorum to the work group in June 1993 became a major component of the Republican argument about the tragedy of welfare dependency. Eventually, Republicans could be seen hauling around big poster board charts of pies with a piece equal to 65 percent of the pie marked in red and labeled "long-term dependency."

Santorum's second chart compared income from welfare with income from low-wage work. A major theme of the Democratic response to the Republican demand for work was that welfare moms could not qualify for "good" jobs that paid a reasonable wage. Indeed, Harold Ford of Tennessee, the chairman of the Ways and Means Human Resources Subcommittee, would soon be arguing publicly that no welfare mother should be required to work for less than $9 an hour.[17] Under Ford's vision, millions of low-wage workers would pay taxes so that millions of mothers, many of them high-school dropouts with illegitimate children, could collect welfare benefits because the mean capitalists would not just give them a job for $9 an hour.

But regardless of Ford's musings, the heart of welfare reform for Republican was work, not wages. Wages were simply another device by which liberals like Ford would try to avoid requiring welfare recipients to work. Rather than compare the actual wage that welfare mothers could earn to the fictitious wage commanded by a modern version of King Canute like Chairman Ford, Republicans wanted to focus everyone's attention on the total income package of a mom working at low wages with the total income of the same mother on welfare.

In what was to become a main point of debate for Republicans, since roughly the mid-1980s, the federal government had created new programs and modified old programs so that low-income working families would retain a sizable package of earnings and benefits when they went to work. Santorum's chart showed that the welfare package in the average state provided a low-income mother and two children with about $6,000 in cash and Food Stamps in addition to Medicaid health insurance worth about $4,000. As compared with this total package of $10,000, if a mother took a low-wage job at minimum wage she could earn about $10,000 working full time. In addition, she would qualify for about $2,000 in Food Stamps and around $3,000 from the Earned Income Tax Credit (EITC), which had been expanded in both 1986 and 1990 (and would be increased again by tax legislation enacted in 1993). Moreover, primarily because of a series of bipartisan legislative initiatives pushed through Congress by Henry Waxman of California, and provisions in the 1988 Family Support Act, a mother leaving welfare would have a year of Medicaid coverage and her children would have coverage as long as she had low earnings. And finally, the mother would qualify for a child care subsidy for at least one year after leaving welfare. So the Republican chart showed the mother with total income of $10,000 plus Medicaid when she was on welfare and $15,000 ($10,000 in earnings, $3,000 in EITC cash income, $2,000 in Food Stamps) plus Medicaid if she left welfare.[18] As with the pie chart on welfare dependency, Republicans would turn again and again to charts like this one to advance the argument for welfare reform.[19]

A day or two before the first meeting of the work group, several of us had attended a breakfast meeting sponsored by the House Republican Research Committee. Committee member Chris Shays asked Doug Besharov of the American Enterprise Institute to come and talk about welfare reform. The topic of welfare for noncitizens had come up at that meeting, although it was clear that no one knew the precise policies governing welfare participation by noncitizens nor did anyone know the magnitude of their participation. But in both the Shays meeting and the Santorum-DeLay meeting, many Republicans were surprised to learn that noncitizens were even allowed to receive welfare benefits. Here again, the Republican gene for conservative social policy came into play. My consistent experience was that most Republicans immediately believed that it was wrong—not just bad policy, but wrong—for noncitizens to receive welfare benefits. The first meeting of the work group was also notable because it marked the initial discussion of the possibility of restricting the welfare benefits of noncitizens.

After the June 1993 meeting of the Santorum-DeLay work group, I immediately began research on the rules governing noncitizen eligibility for welfare, the extent of noncitizen participation in specific welfare programs, and the cost to taxpayers of such participation. When members read the staff report and realized the magnitude of the problem, they were amazed. Data showing that noncitizens were even more likely than citizens to receive welfare benefits really got Republican juices flowing. Against all the claims of Republican cruelty toward noncitizens on welfare by Democrats and many pontificators in the media, I offer the simple observation that most Republicans believed that it is a privilege to come to America because of the opportunities it offered to everyone lucky enough to land here. To give welfare to people who were supposed to be here for opportunity was a fundamental violation of logic and principle. Moreover, since Congress first passed legislation about welfare for immigrants in the 1880s, serious restrictions had been placed on welfare receipt.[20] In any case, greatly reducing the eligibility of noncitizens for welfare benefits became a feature of every major Republican bill after it was included in the bill written by the Santorum-DeLay work group.

At a very long work group meeting on July 1, 1993, attended at least in part by nearly every member, a wide variety of issues were discussed and some decisions were made. The group always worked from an agenda, usually circulated before the meeting. Both DeLay and Santorum, who tended to co-chair the meetings, ran a tight ship, so the meetings moved right along. However, members of Congress love discussion, and we had lots of interesting and controversial issues to discuss. Decisions were made by consensus, and nearly every member stood by the group's decisions. At the July 1 meeting, the first decision was one that showed how important the agitation by outside conservatives had been. It was agreed that, instead of emphasizing just work, the two leading themes of our bill and the publicity on the bill would be increasing work and reducing illegitimacy. There was also extensive discussion of provisions we could adopt to strengthen the paternity-establishment requirement in current AFDC law. Mandatory work by fathers, caps on total federal welfare spending, welfare fraud, benefits for noncitizens, and Supplemental Security Income benefits for adults who qualified on the basis of drug addiction and alcoholism were also discussed, some at considerable length.

But the most remarkable aspect of the discussion was the agreement that illegitimacy had to be a focus of our bill. There is no question that if Robert Rector and other conservatives outside Congress had not been lobbying for several months on the importance of illegitimacy, the work group would have simply adopted mandatory work as the bill's major goal and relegated illegitimacy to a backseat. Even though the work group emphasized the importance of illegitimacy from the time of its first meeting, and included a host of provisions addressed to illegitimacy in the bill, conservatives were never satisfied with the provisions. The internal fight among Republicans on illegitimacy showed no signs of abating. The essence of the disagreement was that conservatives wanted a mandatory provision that ended AFDC benefits for at least some unmarried mothers; some conservative members eventually wanted to go so far as to permanently ban both cash welfare and Food Stamps for the illegitimate children of mothers under the age of twenty-five. But the furthest the work group was willing to go was to make a partial cutoff for some mothers a state option.

At another lengthy meeting, on July 14, Santorum and DeLay pursued ways to incorporate the major provisions of bills previously introduced by Jan Meyers, Gary Franks, Chris Shays, and Bill Paxon.[21] Based on discussions with DeLay, with Ways and Means Republicans on the work group, and with the authors of the bills, Santorum had developed a list showing how the main provision from each of the bills could be incorporated into the text of the work group bill. The provisions on Santorum's list that were adopted by the work group included requiring states to set up hospital-based paternity establishment programs and requiring states to grant AFDC eligibility only to children whose paternity had been established; extending Medicaid eligibility and income disregards for moms leaving welfare and increasing the limit on assets she could have and still qualify for

AFDC; improving marriage incentives for mothers on welfare; and removing the incentive for interstate migration to maximize welfare benefits by allowing a state to apply the eligibility test and benefit amount of the state left by a new arrival.

The two major reforms supported by Jan Meyers were the most difficult to accommodate: converting AFDC to a block grant and prohibiting AFDC payments to unwed teen mothers. Everyone on the work group wanted to make recommendations that could be supported by all House Republicans, and these two provisions were still too controversial. There were innumerable discussions between Meyers and other members of the work group, both during and between meetings. An interesting aspect of the discussions was that they did not concern whether either the block grant or Murray Light provisions were worthy policies in their own right. Nearly everyone on the work group agreed that they were. But they were also a step too far that would make it impossible to unite Republicans and to form a coalition with moderate Democrats. In addition, these provisions would be seen as too radical by the media, once again reinforcing the notion that Republicans supported welfare reform primarily to save money at the expense of the poor. So members of the work group decided to compromise by including both provisions in the bill only as state options: states could adopt them if they wanted to but were not required to do so.

But Meyers strongly disagreed with this decision. She was worried that too few states would adopt the options, and she wanted to see similar impacts across the country in order to truly change the nature of welfare. Though persistent, even to the point of driving DeLay, Santorum, and Shaw nuts, Meyers knew how to conduct a debate within the family. She determined that she could not accept the decision of the work group and told us immediately that she was going to write to Henry Hyde and request that consideration of the work group bill by the Policy Committee be delayed.

On July 16, 1993, she sent a very thoughtful four-page letter to Hyde describing her reasons for wanting to slow down the process. Surprisingly, her major argument was not that Republicans should be emphasizing illegitimacy or block grants. Rather, she argued that welfare reform was an election issue (the 1994 elections were at this point about sixteen months away) and that the work group bill, like the Shaw bill before it, was too much like the bill that Clinton was likely to produce, especially in its emphasis on work after two years. She argued that what Clinton was really up to was the enactment of "sham" reform, just like the Family Support Act that Democrats had passed in 1988 (with very substantial bipartisan support, a fact that she didn't mention). Moreover, with his rhetorical emphasis on work, Clinton was trying to establish a basis for creating a "national day care system." Unfortunately, according to Meyers, the work group bill simply mimicked the Clinton bill and did not draw the sharp contrast Republicans needed both to defeat any sham Clinton bill and to use welfare reform as an election issue. For all these reasons, House Republicans needed to slow down and "reconsider our basic approach to the welfare debate."[22] Fortunately, Hyde ignored her recommendations and the Policy Committee's consideration of welfare reform went ahead as planned.

Here again is the basic problem that confronts the minority party in Congress. Choose your poison: seek compromises with the majority and share credit while achieving only part of your agenda; or separate yourself from the majority as conspicuously as possible, sacrifice all chance for compromise, and take the issue to the voters. Many members of the work group believed, based on the reports about Clinton's welfare reform task force, that his proposals would be downright radical, far to the right of anything ever proposed by a Democratic president in the past—or by a Republican president, for that matter. Many of us with years of experience trying to reform welfare saw the 1988 legislation that Meyers and conservatives dismissed so readily as a step in the right direction, especially because it put participation standards and sanctions in the statute. Now a Democrat was apparently proposing to strengthen the system and to actually require work by all or most welfare mothers. In response, some conservatives wanted to virtually abandon the work agenda and focus on illegitimacy. For Shaw, Santorum, Johnson, Camp, Phil English of Pennsylvania, Jennifer Dunn of Washington, and other members of the Ways and Means Committee, the major goal of welfare reform was still to require work. True, illegitimacy was a major cause of poverty in America, but no solutions were obvious. Our members certainly did not object to having provisions designed to attack illegitimacy, and indeed had been advocating such policies for years, but there was little reason to think these provisions would work. By contrast, group members believed with good reason that mandatory work and the end of cash entitlement would end the dependency of millions of mothers on welfare. On this agenda, Republicans were doing the bidding of the American people by fighting for provisions that huge majorities of the public supported.[23] Now at last Democrats seemed to be on the ropes because one of their own had joined us and many more were willing to join. So much the better, if the goal was to change the nation's welfare system and not to start a brawl. But many conservatives wanted the brawl and not the legislation. The crack among Republicans over illegitimacy was growing into a chasm and threatening to swallow our coalition.

An interesting aspect of the work group's task was the degree to which members constantly tried to convince other Republicans outside the work group that our bill had the provisions all Republicans could support. Santorum and Shaw frequently talked with other members of Ways and Means, especially at the regular Wednesday lunch meeting that Ways and Means Republicans had been having for many years. These attempts to ensure the support of other members were informal at first, but as the vote in the Republican Policy Committee and then the

Republican Conference approached, work group members made elaborate plans on how other members would be contacted. In this task, we were helped immensely by Bob Okun and Karen Buttaro from Republican leader Bob Michel's office. They were used to communicating with the entire caucus of House Republicans. Among other things, they had computer lists of the members' offices and even of the staff members who handled specific issues. We put these lists to good use.

Although somewhat mundane, our lobbying activities to rally Republican support for our bill were vital. Especially in a situation in which there are ongoing conflicts within the party, the side that does the best job getting out its message usually wins. "Educational" activities are necessary at both the staff and member levels, but member-to-member contacts are much more important in rallying support for a bill. As members of the Santorum-DeLay work group lobbied other members, Santorum worked especially closely with the Ways and Means members on the work group because they knew the issues so well. He asked them to concentrate their efforts on members who seemed the least likely to support our bill. To this end, Santorum had me compile the names of members who had cosponsored the Meyers bill and divide up the names among the Ways and Means members, including himself, so we were assured not only that they would be lobbied directly but that they would be lobbied by someone who knew the arguments and was highly motivated to persuade them to support the work group's compromise with Meyers.

At the same time as we were drafting a bill that we hoped would enjoy general support among Republicans we were also working with the National Republican Congressional Committee (NRCC) and with governors' offices. Richard Billmire from the NRCC continued to attend work group meetings. We hoped to achieve two goals by coordinating our activities with Billmire and the NRCC. First, working with campaign staffers is always useful because they have their finger on the pulse of Republican candidates around the country. Not only do they work with candidates on a regular basis, but they also do lots of polling and focus group testing. In fact, Billmire gave reports at our meetings about what candidates were thinking and what the NRCC polls were showing. Two messages that he consistently gave the work group were that strong work requirements enjoyed overwhelming public support and support among our candidates and that reducing the welfare benefits of noncitizens also enjoyed very substantial support. He also emphasized that our bill should not increase spending.

Both Santorum and Shaw also wanted us to talk regularly with governors. As early as the work group meeting of June 18, members wanted to know what states thought about the Murray Light provision and about the block grant idea. In finding out, we were greatly assisted by the fact that almost every state government has an office in Washington. The big states often have several people in their

Washington office, one of whom usually focuses exclusively or primarily on social policy issues. Because states administer many of the big welfare programs—including AFDC, Food Stamps, and Medicaid—and spend considerable sums of their own money on these and similar programs, they have a direct interest in social policy legislation in Washington. It was while contacting state offices to get their reaction to our various proposals that I first met and began to work with a young staffer in the Michigan office named LeAnne Redick. LeAnne was close to Michigan governor John Engler and would come to be one of the most important state staffers in the development and final passage of welfare reform. Santorum himself called Governor Tommy Thompson of Wisconsin, the leading welfare reformer among all the nation's governors, to tell him about the work group and especially to discuss the Murray Light provision. Thompson and his fellow Republican governors opposed the Murray Light provision, although they supported the block grant. In addition to getting their reaction to specific provisions in our bill, we wanted governors to feel they had been consulted. We were planning ahead for the time when we would release the bill at a fancy press event that would feature not simply members of our work group but also Republican governors, who would actually implement whatever welfare reform might pass Congress.

All of the lobbying proved effective, because the Policy Committee approved our bill at a July 1993 meeting with only a few recommendations for changes, the most important of which was a cap on spending on five major social programs (AFDC, Supplemental Security Income, the Food Stamp program, and two housing programs), offered as an amendment to our bill by Tim Hutchinson of Arkansas. This spending cap (which had originated with Robert Rector of the Heritage Foundation, who had apparently convinced Hutchinson of its value) was an exceptionally radical proposal: it would have ended the entitlement to every program under the cap and cut spending by perhaps $25 billion over five years.[24] Although most members of the work group opposed the spending cap, we regarded it as a small price to pay for getting the bill through the Policy Committee. Approval by the Policy Committee was a major victory, but we knew we faced an even more important hurdle in the upcoming vote in the Republican Conference. So once again we set to work perfecting the provisions in our bill and lobbying other Republicans to support our bill and oppose the Meyers bill.

In lobbying members, this time we devised a plan to contact all 160-plus House Republicans who were not members of the work group. Again we approached every office at both the member and staff levels. Again, Santorum had me devise a plan for member-to-member contact that reserved all of the Republicans supporting Meyers for our Ways and Means members. We counted fifty-one members who had either added their name as sponsors of the Meyers bill or who we believed were likely to support Meyers. Every one of these members received a personal contact from Santorum, Shaw, Johnson, Grandy, or Camp. In addition, the staff or members of the work group were to call me if anyone on their list of member contacts seemed either to support Meyers or to be leaning in her direction. These reluctant members were also contacted by one of the Ways and Means members, usually either Santorum or Shaw. We also sent a long letter to all House Republicans pointing out the virtues of the work group bill and urging members to vote against the impractical bill being sponsored by Jan Meyers. The letter argued that the work group had been toiling all year with a diverse group of Republicans from several House committees with jurisdiction over welfare programs to produce the splendid bill that would be brought before the Republican Conference for a final vote. In addition to being based on broad representation from House Republicans, the work group bill benefited from input from both Republican governors and the National Republican Congressional Committee. Now was not the time to abandon a bill that defined welfare reform "as more work, less spending, more flexibility for states, and no welfare for aliens"[25] in favor of a bill that did not even require work and focused almost exclusively on fighting illegitimacy.

On September 29, 1993, Dick Armey, the head of the Republican Conference, sent a memo informing members that the conference debate and vote on welfare reform would take place on October 13.[26] When the conference met, all of our preparation paid off. The debate and voting was structured so that there would be an immediate showdown between the work group bill and the Meyers bill. Both sides had ten minutes to present their case, and both sides did a good job of showing how their bill was the key to the future while the other bill was inadequate. I thought—and there could not possibly be any bias in my view!—that Santorum was especially persuasive in arguing that our bill had strong provisions on both work and illegitimacy and that it would save around $19 billion over five years because of the provision eliminating most benefits for noncitizens and the block grant on nutrition spending (we were still working out the details of the Hutchinson cap and did not yet have a good cost estimate). In the vote that followed, our bill prevailed easily. The conference also endorsed putting in the Hutchinson spending cap, which had been approved in concept at the meeting of the Policy Committee, and a minor amendment strengthening our provision requiring mothers on welfare to take their children for regular medical checkups and to follow the appropriate schedule for immunizations. After the defeat of the Meyers bill and the approval of these two amendments, the conference unanimously endorsed the bill.

Following the conference meeting, Santorum organized yet another campaign, this time to get as many cosponsors to sign the bill as possible. By the time we introduced the bill on November 10, 160 of the 176 Republicans in the House and the entire Republican leadership had agreed to cosponsor. It was certainly satisfying to have such broad support among Republicans for the bill, which was given the designation HR 3500, but those of us who had worked so hard on it knew that conservatives were far from satisfied and were circling the bill like so many buzzards. HR 3500 was to enjoy only a brief and shining moment of Republican unity before exploding.

## CHAPTER FOUR

# The Contract
# with America

For members of Congress, an election year means that every speech, every bill, every thought has to pass through the crucible of whether the action will gain votes or lose votes. This means that strategy for passing a particular bill might give way to strategy for winning the election if the two should conflict. For those like me who had the luxury of watching rather than running in elections, it was easy to determine that, whether in the minority or majority after the 1994 elections, House Republicans would not be able to pass a good welfare reform bill unless they were united.

Thus the welfare reform negotiations among Republicans in the lead-up to the 1994 elections were extremely important. The period of interest here is roughly the eleven months between the introduction of HR 3500 in November 1993 and the big election rally for Republican candidates for the House on the steps of the U.S. Capitol on September 27, 1994, just before the elections. For Clay Shaw, Rick Santorum, and other Republicans on Ways and Means, three considerations dominated this period. First and foremost, could Republicans develop a powerful bill that maintained unity among House Republicans yet held promise for attracting support from Senate Republicans and the Republican governors as well? Second, could Republicans find policies on illegitimacy that were strong enough to satisfy conservative Republicans but reasonable enough to avoid a schism with the moderates? And third, because Republicans seemed nearly certain to be in the minority after the elections, could we develop a bill that satisfied nearly all Republicans while giving us grounds to compromise with moderate Democrats and President Clinton? This eleven-month period was vital in developing both the provisions of legislation that would maintain Republican unity and the personal relationships of trust and confidence that would be needed in the great legislative battle that was to take place after the 1994 elections.

Begin with the governors. Sad to say, until 1993 or 1994 the main repository of ideas about and understanding of welfare policy among Republicans resided with governors. One of the accomplishments of the Santorum-DeLay work group was that it developed a team of well-informed Republican leaders on welfare reform. Even so, Republican governors in general, and Tommy Thompson of Wisconsin and John Engler of Michigan in particular, were the real experts because their administrations had designed and implemented serious reforms of AFDC and other welfare programs.

Given our success in uniting (or so we thought) House Republicans behind HR 3500, we wanted to solidify our relations with Republican governors. The governors, and especially Governor Engler's Washington office, headed by LeAnne Redick, had worked with us at the staff level on HR 3500. Although the governors strongly supported the general idea of welfare reform, and even most provisions of HR 3500, they seemed to have some doubts about the bill. With the blessing of Santorum and Shaw, a few other House staffers and I met with Redick and the Washington staffers of nine other states having Republican governors on January 14, 1994, in Room B-318 of the Rayburn House Office Building. The meeting confirmed that the governors had several concerns with the bill. As usual, their major problem was with any reduction in the amount of money states would receive from Washington or any reduction in their authority. Their biggest objection—about which in fact they were livid—was the Hutchinson spending cap. They believed the cap was unworkable and would lead to a lot more paperwork and bureaucratic decisions about eligibility. Worse, the cap touched the spot guaranteed to send any governor, Republican or Democrat, off the cliff—namely, cutting federal dollars. When the cap kicked in to control spending, the people who would previously have qualified for benefits under federal and state statutes would still need the benefit. Who would pay? The obvious answer was that, since the individuals who lost benefits would still live in a particular state and a particular city, there would be lots of political pressure for state and local governments to pick up the tab.

Similarly, the proposal to cut welfare benefits for noncitizens (including seniors on Supplemental Security Income who had in many cases resided in the United States for years) was unpopular with many governors. In most states, immigrant households were more likely to receive at least one welfare benefit than households composed exclusively of citizens.[1] If welfare benefits for noncitizens were actually ended, states would wind up with the entire responsibility for several million additional households previously on welfare. States also strongly argued against any provision that required them to opt out of a federal mandate. Their reasoning was that opting out gave the appearance, but not the substance, of flexibility.

One outcome of the January meeting with governors' staffers was that we made arrangements for Santorum to meet with the Republican governors. On

Saturday, January 29, Republican governors were meeting at the Ritz-Carlton in Pentagon City, Virginia, and they invited Santorum to join them for a discussion of welfare reform. Governor John McKernan of Maine, the head of the Republican Governors Association, gave Santorum a nice introduction to the assembled governors. Santorum then had, as they say, a "frank exchange of views" with the governors. Despite his reputation as something of a rabble-rouser, Santorum was superb in summarizing HR 3500 for the governors and in listening intently and sympathetically to their concerns about the bill. He was equally adept at bringing the governors to understand the powerful forces on the right that were insisting on some of the provisions that troubled them, especially "Murray Light," the family cap, and the spending cap.[2]

Following these two January meetings, I maintained our contacts with the staffers of Republican governors, but there were no more big meetings involving governors and members about welfare reform until after the 1994 elections. The major purpose of the January staff and member meetings was to show governors that we were serious about working with them and to demonstrate that we understood their concerns. And not so incidentally, the personal relationships established between our members and the governors as well as the staff relationships turned out to be very important in the long run.

Regardless of the status of our work with governors, far more important was the status of our work to keep congressional Republicans united. The struggle continued among House Republicans to find policies to reduce illegitimacy. The shadow of Charles Murray hovered as Republicans fought each other to shape policy on illegitimate births. Although no one seriously argued that Republicans should adopt the Murray approach by ending all welfare programs, several policies that used sanctions to impose behavioral requirements on young mothers had been agreed upon by House Republicans. These policies included requiring teen mothers to live at home in order to be eligible for AFDC, requiring teen mothers to stay in school in order to be eligible for AFDC, and greatly strengthening paternity establishment requirements in the child support program. These provisions not only were liked by nearly all Republicans but enjoyed considerable support among Democrats as well. Even the family cap policy of eliminating the automatic increase in AFDC when a mother already on welfare had another baby enjoyed widespread support among House Republicans, among a surprising number of governors, and even among some Democrats. Indeed, as we have seen, Wayne Bryant from the New Jersey state legislature had fought to have the family cap established in New Jersey several years before the Washington debate got under way. To say that not many Democrats in Washington followed him is an understatement. Ironically, the major Republican opposition to the family cap came from the right, because some anti-abortion activists feared that ending additional payments for additional children would induce poor mothers to have abortions.

Murray had predicted that if Congress terminated welfare, illegitimacy rates would fall dramatically.[3] Although it was possible to believe that Murray was correct, three questions presented themselves: Would Republicans support achieving the highly desirable goal of illegitimacy reduction by means of at least some increase in human misery in the short run? Second, was it possible to build a majority in Congress for such a cold calculus? And third, would the harshness of the Murray cutoff cause a political reaction against Republicans? The power of Murray's idea to drive Republican policy in the face of these serious potential downsides is remarkable, especially in view of the fact that there was only modest evidence that ending or reducing welfare would actually reduce illegitimacy. The logic was solid, and the notion that society had an obligation to pay for illegitimacy was, to say the least, shaky. But in the face of the certain misery that ending welfare cold turkey would cause to some young mothers and babies, one (especially if the "one" happened to be a Democrat) might require strong evidence that the increase in misery would produce offsetting benefits. But only modest evidence was forthcoming.

Shaw, Santorum, and most of the Ways and Means Republicans who wrote HR 3500 agreed entirely with Murray's view that illegitimacy was a huge problem. They willingly adopted a host of policies addressed to illegitimacy but wished to avoid the difficult issues raised by the cold turkey cutoff of benefits. Even in the early days of our work with Vin Weber and the Wednesday Group, we had been concerned about illegitimacy. From the beginning of the Santorum-DeLay work group there was considerable agreement on policies that, before Murray's ideas took hold, were considered radical. These policies included mandatory home residence and mandatory school attendance for teen mothers as well as greatly toughened paternity establishment requirements. Under our proposals, young mothers who did not adhere to these requirements would lose their entire cash benefit. Shaw and his colleagues had been open to the need for stirring a national debate on illegitimacy by including strong provisions in their bill. The arguments presented by Jim Talent of Missouri, Jan Meyers of Kansas, and conservatives outside of Congress had produced important changes in HR 3500 as it worked its way through the Republican Policy Committee and the Republican Conference, including the state option to impose a Murray Light provision designed by the state and the state option to impose a family cap. When more than 90 percent of House Republicans, including the entire leadership, officially endorsed HR 3500, Shaw thought we had achieved Republican unity on illegitimacy policy.

Unfortunately, the hope that we had quelled the illegitimacy uprising was wrong. Before the ink was dry on the endorsement of HR 3500 by the Republican Conference, agitation for stronger illegitimacy provisions and work requirements began. Robert Rector of the Heritage Foundation called me on several occasions warning that our moderates had plagues and serpents in their future if the illegitimacy provisions were not strengthened. Equally important, I was told repeatedly by both Newt Gingrich's staff and Dick Armey's staff that there was constant agitation by outside conservatives and their organizations. Primarily as a result of this pressure from Rector and others, Gingrich spoke with Santorum about reconstituting the work group, adding additional conservatives to the group, and further strengthening the provisions on reducing illegitimacy. By this time, however, Santorum had decided to run for the Senate and was too busy making campaign trips and raising money to continue his role as head of the welfare reform work group. So for the time being the issue of appointing a new work group was put on hold.

But the pressure among conservatives for stronger illegitimacy provisions continued to grow among Republicans in both the House and the Senate. Senator Lauch Faircloth of North Carolina had been working with Rector since the summer of 1993 on legislation that would eventually feature stronger illegitimacy provisions than those in HR 3500. Speaking to a nearly empty Senate chamber on November 20, 1993, Faircloth had revealed the first fruits of his work with Rector. Evidently, Faircloth was not yet a complete convert to the preeminent place of illegitimacy in Republican welfare reform because he clearly gave first place in his thinking to the need to reduce the number of programs and spending. The "first step in reforming the system," he said, "is to draw a line in the sand ... [and] place a cap on the growth of welfare entitlement spending."[4] He then announced that when Congress returned in January 1994 he would introduce a bill fashioned around several principles: spending caps, mandatory work requirements, reduced welfare for unwed mothers, strong requirements for paternity establishment, reduction of the marriage penalty in welfare programs, and a new emphasis on abstinence education. Other than rhetoric, there was not much difference between the November 1993 version of the Faircloth-Rector bill and HR 3500.

Nonetheless, agitation against HR 3500 in the House continued to grow after the members returned for the second session of the 103rd Congress in January 1994. On March 9, Ron Brownstein of the *Los Angeles Times* wrote about the fighting among House Republicans over illegitimacy provisions.[5] He knew, perhaps on the basis of a personal interview, that Gingrich had asked the work group to incorporate "sterner measures" to discourage nonmarital births. Brownstein had talked with Jim Talent from Missouri and reported that Talent was working on a bill with stronger provisions on illegitimacy and work than HR 3500. Talent apparently told Brownstein that his bill would end most welfare benefits for unmarried mothers under age twenty-one. Talent was careful in his remarks to the press, saying in effect that HR 3500 was a good bill but that it was necessary to go much further on illegitimacy. Talent was quoted by Brownstein as saying that the "possibilities are open-ended now," apparently meaning that public opinion had solidified against the old welfare system and that Congress could make radical changes without offending the public. As we will see, this view turned out to be questionable. But Talent and Faircloth, with the urging of Robert Rector, now had our pants' leg firmly between their teeth, and they were not about to let go. Later in March, Talent, along with Congressmen Tim Hutchinson from Arkansas and Charles Canady from Florida, sent a letter to House Republicans saying that they would soon introduce a bill that would "truly revolutionize welfare."

For those of us who had worked to create HR 3500, the month of April 1994 was one long nightmare. We were by now well aware that many conservatives were hostile to our bill, but the depth of hostility became ever more apparent. By the end of April, I felt that our careful work to develop the provisions in HR 3500 and to maintain Republican unity was in tatters. Many conservatives now believed that the main goal of welfare reform was not to actually change the law but to draw sharp distinctions between President Clinton and the Democrats, on the one hand, and Republicans, on the other, about how welfare should be reformed. These conservatives believed that Republicans should move to the right of HR 3500. To put daylight between Republicans and the welfare reform proposals now being sponsored by moderate Democrats like Clinton would require that our already radical welfare reform bill become even more radical.[6]

At Santorum and Shaw's urging, the work group took a number of counter-measures to offset the forces gathering against our bill. Two are especially notable. First, we prepared a thirteen-page written document that refuted the charges being cast against the bill by the right.[7] This document, the initial drafts of which I wrote and revised with lots of comments from Santorum and Shaw, and which was then reviewed and further revised by members and staff from the work group, refuted ten charges then being made against the bill. Perhaps the most fundamental charge, made by both Bill Bennett, the former secretary of Education in the Bush I administration, and the conservative columnist Tom Bethell in the *American Spectator*, was that promoting work should no longer be the central goal of welfare reform. According to Bennett, mandatory work proposals "miss the essential point of welfare reform" because they fail to address illegitimacy; in Bethell's view, the work agenda made "no sense."[8]

We were amazed. Work simply could not be dismissed as the major antidote to welfare dependency. We could cite President Ronald Reagan, the ultimate arbiter among Republicans of all doctrinal conflicts, who said in a radio address, "Any [welfare reform] bill not built around work is not true welfare reform."[9] For those who preferred policies justified by research evidence and reasoning, the argument for work was overwhelming. In the early 1990s about 2.5 million mothers left welfare every year (but even more joined the rolls). Research showed that about half of them left because either they or someone in their household got a job or worked more hours.[10] Work was already the main route to breaking welfare dependency, so why not promote it? Further, numerous studies that met the highest standards of scientific rigor showed that welfare-to-work programs could increase employment, reduce the welfare rolls, and save government money.[11] Moreover, one of the strongest arguments for work was that millions of young mothers wasted away on welfare at the very time that other young women were developing their human capital either by getting additional education or by working and developing their experience and job skills. Not only was increased work among welfare mothers good for government and society, it was good for the mothers themselves—and perhaps for their children as well. Few policies can make the claim that they produce such a broad and vital set of benefits.

Another charge against the HR 3500 mentality, stated clearly by Charles Murray, was that many "country-club Republicans" would refuse to support strong welfare reform provisions because they "don't want to be accused of being nasty."[12] This charge gets to the bottom of a dynamic that often pervades the debate between moderate and conservative Republicans. A major weapon in the conservative arsenal is the claim that moderates are too timid or lack the fortitude to adopt tough policies. A number of moderates, especially those from states in the Northeast and in other left-leaning states, must not appear to be too conservative lest they get whacked by voters in the next election. But support for radical reform by Republican moderates had been firmly established by that first Wednesday Group report back in 1991 and by the legislation introduced in 1992 by moderates led by Clay Shaw. The work group that produced HR 3500 included Fred Grandy of Iowa, Nancy Johnson of Connecticut, Dave Camp of Michigan, Gary Franks of Connecticut, and Mike Castle of Michigan, all widely viewed as moderates. And yet they not only endorsed but directly participated in writing the most radical welfare reform bill ever introduced in the House up to that time. When fully implemented, the bill would require thirty-five hours a week of work by 2.1 million mothers on welfare (including mothers of young children), subject recipients to serious sanctions, fine states that did not meet work requirements, create a huge block grant of federal nutrition programs, greatly reduce welfare for noncitizens, allow states to end cash payments to unmarried mothers under age eighteen, cap spending on several major welfare programs, allow states to replace Aid to Families with Dependent Children (AFDC) with a block grant, allow states to stop raising the cash benefit of mothers who had babies while on welfare, and cut welfare spending by billions of dollars. These provisions are not on the agenda of "country-club Republicans." Surprisingly, Murray himself agreed that our work provisions were extremely tough, and we were able to prevail on him to send us a letter endorsing our bill.[13]

The second action we took in our efforts to fend off the Talent-Faircloth-

Rector-Bennett forces was to have Santorum offer to have our HR 3500 work group meet with conservative groups, including the Heritage Foundation, the Family Research Council, the Christian Coalition, Concerned Women for America, and the Eagle Forum. The meeting was set for Room 1129 of the Longworth House Office Building on April 13, 1994. That morning I received a phone call from Ed Kutler, who was now a senior aide to Gingrich, asking if I knew about the Empower America memo on HR 3500.

What a shock! Signed by William Bennett, Jack Kemp, and our close colleague Vin Weber, the memo was a five-page, all-out attack on HR 3500 as pusillanimous. Full of high-tone rhetoric (by supporting HR 3500, House Republicans "will squander a defining moment in our national life," and "it should be our goal to build a coalition of conscience that will inspire both economic and moral hope"), the fatwa identified three reasons the bill should be killed. Specifically, the bill made "no serious attempt to curtail out of wedlock births," its work requirements were weak, and its hidden costs were "exorbitant." Offering states the option to impose the family cap and Murray Light—not to mention the option to convert AFDC to a block grant—did not amount to a "serious attempt" to fight illegitimacy.[14] In other words, the compromise we had reached with Talent and the conservative forces was already too weak.

Although there were some modest problems in our work requirement, our work standards were the strongest ever introduced in Congress. But under the Congressional Budget Office's (CBO) scoring rules, it was expensive to increase work requirements because states had to spend additional money for work programs for every percentage point by which we raised the work requirements. CBO estimated that putting one welfare recipient in a work program cost $6,000 a year. Given a caseload of about five million, each percentage point increase in the work requirement would cost us about $225 million.[15] Clinton's welfare reform task force was caught by this same cost dilemma and was considering previously unheard of policies for Democrats—such as modest reductions in welfare for noncitizens—to pay for their work requirements. But memo writers don't need to worry about silly rules concerning the cost of legislative provisions, especially when they are showing the way to a defining moment in our national life. Indeed, while ignoring the cost dilemma, Bennett and his colleagues actually took the license to criticize our bill for its "hidden costs." They did not, however, mention that the bill included the spending cap, the nutrition block grant, and the ban on welfare for noncitizens. Taken together, these provisions saved at least $40 billion over five years. It was a little galling to be criticized for the costs of a bill that saved more money than any major welfare bill ever introduced in Congress. Between its tone, its half-truths, and its omissions, the memo was infuriating.

It was especially surprising that Vin Weber had signed the memo. Weber was a widely respected member of the House until his retirement in 1992—and, if possible, even more respected afterward. He was both a sponsor and a strong supporter of several of the early welfare reform bills that Shaw and other Ways and Means Republicans had introduced. Indeed, Weber had himself introduced the first bill that placed a time limit on welfare benefits.[16] But now he and his colleagues at Empower America were publicly attacking HR 3500 and supporting the Talent bill even before its details had been made public.

The Kemp-Bennett-Weber group had obviously shared an advance copy of their memo with the media, because on the morning of April 14 there was an editorial in the *Washington Times* by Ralph Hallow about the episode. The Hallow editorial was not as bad as it might have been. Hallow presented a pretty balanced overview of the fight among Republicans over the Murray provision, but the main point of his editorial was that the entire Empower America undertaking was an attempt to advance Kemp's presidential bid. He quoted Weber as saying that the memo directed against the "moderate" House welfare reform bill showed that Kemp "was not out of step with conservatives."[17] Nowhere in the editorial did Hallow say that HR 3500 was actually "moderate" or that it lacked provisions addressed to illegitimacy. Even so, it was now impossible to cover up the fact that Republicans were having a family feud.

On April 22, Jason DeParle, the welfare reporter for the *New York Times* who was one of the most relentless welfare reporters in the country, published a long story on Charles Murray and the power of his cold-turkey welfare reform proposal.[18] DeParle focused carefully on how Murray's ideas had been adopted by Empower America. He pointed out that if Murray's proposal were to become law, poor mothers would face what I call the cold calculus of the termination of cash benefits. Specifically, mothers could put their baby up for adoption, place the baby in an orphanage, marry, or seek charity. He did not, but could have, mentioned the other difficult options such as going to work and trying to support the baby, trying to get more money from friends and family, and having an abortion. The point of DeParle's article was to get people to see exactly what position young women would be placed in by the Murray proposal. DeParle did not say so explicitly, but the reason Murray and others believed that going off welfare cold turkey would have such profound effects on young women is precisely the stark choice set the policy imposed on them. Of course, it is possible to argue that these young mothers deserve their fate—they made their choice to have a baby, or at least to have sex, and let the chips fall where they may. In these circumstances, most Americans would probably agree that the public does not have an affirmative responsibility to rescue them from their choice. This argument can be granted, but it nonetheless raises what for many Republicans was a more serious underlying issue: Would voters accept Murray's proposal and the difficult choice it forced on young mothers and their babies?

And finally, none of the media stories raised the main concern of Shaw, Santorum, and other members of the HR 3500 work group: Would it be possible to unite Republicans behind stronger versions of the provisions in HR 3500? It is one thing for an elected member of Congress to put her name on a bill, but it is quite another to vote for the bill in public when it comes to the floor of the House or Senate. The attention of the media and the public is then focused on the bill, especially if the bill turns out to be controversial. Our main concern about Murray Light and the family cap was always that they might split our Republican coalition. In the spring and summer of 1994, as these fears were coming true, I would say that at least 75 percent of House Republicans had not thought through the illegitimacy issue. And Senate Republicans, considerably to the left of House Republicans on most issues, were a big question mark on both the illegitimacy and work provisions. But if the past was any guide, it would be exceptionally difficult to get many Senate Republicans to support any version of Murray's proposal.

And yet House members were already being pushed beyond the tough provisions of HR 3500 and indeed were being confronted with the charge of being moderate—a truly dreaded term to many Republicans—if they failed to understand the necessity of ending welfare payments to a few million young mothers and their babies. On April 24, Bennett, Kemp, and Weber published an op-ed piece in the *Washington Times* that made the assault on "moderation" very clear. The editorial consisted of two major arguments. First, President Clinton was in a fix because he had not delivered on his election promise to end welfare as we know it. It would be "irresponsible and politically unwise," the Empower America group argued, "for Republicans to assist the president in perpetuating fraudulent welfare reform." They also pointed out that it was "not the duty of House Republicans to rescue Bill Clinton from problems of his own making."[19] If only House Republicans had thought of that. Apparently, the Empower America group's understanding of HR 3500 led them to fear that a Republican Party unified behind a bill that actually did end welfare as we know it would force Clinton to deliver on his campaign promise. As we will see, this aspect of the politics of welfare reform never changed: Republicans forced, cajoled, or encouraged (depending on your politics) Clinton to live up to his promise. True, in 1993 Clinton made a strategic decision to reform health care before welfare, but there was little evidence that he was lying when he promised to "end welfare as we know it." In fact, there was lots of evidence emanating from the president's welfare reform task force that, whatever else might be said about the president's reforms, they were serious. In fact, they promised to be more conservative than anything proposed by previous presidents, including Republican presidents. To call Clinton's proposals "fraudulent" was simply unfair.

The second major claim of the Empower America group's op-ed piece was that Murray's proposal to end welfare for young mothers was "sensible, compassionate, incentive-oriented welfare reform" and that HR 3500 lacked sufficient strength on the illegitimacy front. Never mind that the bill contained a host of illegitimacy provisions, including versions of Murray Light and the family cap. Bennett and company wanted a complete end to welfare payments for young mothers, period. Anything less was "tepid" and, by implication, deserving of support only from moderates. The word "compassionate" has done a lot of work in recent years, but even in 1994 it was unlikely that a room full of dictionary writers would include any form of Murray's plan under the label of compassionate reform.

An important issue clarified by the editorial was that conservatives were willing to publicly criticize their colleagues, especially by accusing them of being moderates, in order to move them further to the right. This strategy is a major part of how conservative organizations like the Heritage Foundation operate. Three steps are required. First, as demonstrated by the Empower America editorial, the policy favored by mainstream Republicans is publicly attacked as moderate. It is not necessary to adopt the superior tone taken by Bennett and his colleagues, but the message must be that the moderate position is flawed because what is needed is real change, not the tepid bowl of porridge being served up by those lousy moderates. Second, conservatives outside Congress, in the typical role played by lobbyists, work with selected members of Congress to embody "true reform" in a bill that is drafted and officially submitted by several members. This bill then becomes the conservative standard against which other bills are measured and the instrument for driving mainstream bills to the right. The third step is to write editorials, go on television, meet with members of Congress, and take other public and behind-the-scenes actions to reduce political support for the moderate bill and rally support for the conservative bill.

Perhaps the most important anti–HR 3500 event occurred on April 28. Conservative forces inside and outside Congress appeared at a press event to discuss the bill they were preparing to introduce in both houses of Congress. Talent, Faircloth, and Bennett were featured speakers at the press event, which was well attended and resulted in reports in several major newspapers.[20] Dubbed the "Real Welfare Reform Bill" by its authors, and referred to as "courageous" by Bennett, the bill exceeded the strong provisions Faircloth had promised in his November speech on the Senate floor. In addition to the cap on welfare spending and strong work requirements, the bill contained a much stronger version of Murray Light than promised by Faircloth in his Senate speech. Specifically, one year after enactment, unmarried women under the age of twenty-one who had babies would not be eligible for either cash welfare or Food Stamps. After four years, the age of the cutoff would be increased to twenty-five years and under. The toughest part of the Murray-type policy now being supported by the conservative groups was that children born to these young mothers would never be eligible for welfare benefits, unless the mother married and her husband adopted the child. Even when the mother turned twenty-one (or twenty-five) their children would not be eligible. The money saved by this provision would be given to the state in which the ineligible mothers resided and could be used for adoption, orphanages, supervised group homes, or other programs designed to reduce illegitimacy or provide care for children born outside marriage but not residing with their parents. This was not the full welfare cutoff recommended by Murray, but my term Murray Light somehow seemed inappropriate for this provision.

As the momentum against HR 3500 continued to build, Santorum and Shaw came to realize that Republican unity could be maintained only by making another accommodation with conservatives. As summer replaced spring, Newt Gingrich and Dick Armey came to our rescue. Gingrich had decided that Republicans should attempt to nationalize the 1994 congressional elections, by which he meant that the Republican leadership in Washington should create issues that would be important throughout the nation and not in just a certain state or region. Elections for House seats usually turn primarily on local issues, but by developing a set of national issues that could provide Republicans with campaign themes, Gingrich hoped to have an impact on a number of congressional races. Working primarily with Armey, Gingrich developed a set of ten legislative proposals that, taken together, would constitute what he called a "revolution" in federal policy. Dubbed the "Contract with America," the initiative ultimately became a set of ten bills that Gingrich believed would appeal to voters across the nation.[21]

Whether the specific provisions of the "contract" had the effect of capturing votes for Republican candidates may be doubtful, but the contract did have at least two effects that advanced the Republican cause.[22] The first was that it gave candidates something specific to stand for. Part of the Gingrich strategy was to supply candidates with talking points and other materials on each of the ten bills in the contract. Many candidates used this material, often in combination with local and state issues, in the conduct of their campaigns. Even if voters did not know much about the Contract with America, they could certainly recognize a candidate who stated clearly what he intended to do once he got to Washington. The second indirect effect of the contract was that it provided informed voters with a vision of a political party that stood for something. Especially in a time when voters were showing high levels of dissatisfaction with politicians, even the term Contract with America had the tone of something serious and ethical. Republicans offered to enter into a deal with voters: You elect us and here are the ten returns we provide in the bargain. No matter what those ten legislative items were, the entire approach may well have influenced some voters.

Regardless of the contract's effects on voters, it certainly became a focus of attention and a repository of many thousands of hours of work by House members and staffers, both before and after the election. Drafting ten pieces of legislation, especially when the bills were intended to represent consensus among House Republicans, was a major undertaking. Throughout the summer and late into September 1994, in many cases up until the event on the Capitol steps on September 27, staff and members were hard at work drafting the legislation.

I doubt that any of the ten were as divisive or difficult to write as the welfare reform bill. Some of the members of the work group that had produced HR 3500 resented having to work on another bill. After nearly a year of intense effort and of lobbying their colleagues, especially as the bill ran the gauntlet of the Republican Policy Committee and then the Republican Conference, the work group had produced a bill that enjoyed—at least for a nanosecond—nearly universal support among House Republicans. Further, we had produced a bill that served as a concrete definition of "ending welfare as we know it" and that would have a major impact not just on the bill produced by the president's task force but on the legislative debate in the House. If the president's bill was even close to ending welfare as we know it, the president would lose at least 90 or 100 House liberals and would not be able to pass a bill without working with us. We were in the catbird seat for a minority party; the majority needed us to pass a bill. And yet we were now being forced to draft another bill to replace HR 3500.

On the other hand, Santorum and Shaw saw the Contract with America as an opportunity to heal the growing rift in Republican ranks. The majority of members had not yet begun to focus on welfare reform, so it was impossible to determine whether they would stick with HR 3500 in the face of the increasing agitation from the right over illegitimate births. Most probably would, but we could easily lose fifty or sixty Republicans, thereby greatly weakening our position. Nor were Gingrich and Armey necessarily with us. Gingrich had supported us when our bill was seriously criticized during the April meeting with the conservative groups, but Armey was more conservative than any of us and so was his staff. So we doubted the continuing support of our leaders.

Losing our unity on welfare reform was the greatest hazard we faced. The press treatment of the president's welfare reform task force—whose every move was reported on the front page of the *New York Times* and every difference in views within the task force reported as impending disaster for consensus within the administration—served as an example of our fate if we could not produce a bill that nearly all Republicans supported.[23] The lesson could not have been clearer: be unified or lose your power to influence events. Fortunately, we were enjoying the advantage of working out our problems in relative obscurity. Bennett, Kemp, and Weber had attempted to stir up press coverage by attacking HR 3500, but that strategy, even though a credible presidential candidate was involved, did not capture the interest of the media for long. The story that some Republicans were toying with radical reforms along the lines proposed by Charles Murray was also a story with some legs, but these articles had already been written.[24] As long as Republicans were in the minority, especially with an election pending and Clinton's health care effort dominating news coverage, we would have lots of privacy to work out our differences. As we toiled to produce a new bill throughout the summer and early fall of 1994, with the relentless media attention to the president's task force fresh in my mind, I often thought of how fortunate we were to be out of the spotlight. If we could come up with a bill that conservatives could support, and if we won either house of Congress, we would be united and major parts of our bill might become law.

The upshot of Gingrich's decision to put Armey in charge of the Contract with America was that Armey and his staff would oversee the day-to-day drafting of the ten bills. In the case of the welfare reform bill, it also meant that Armey and his staff would have the opportunity to take sides, thereby adding another layer of complexity to our task. From the outset it was clear that producing a consensus bill would be difficult and could be made even more difficult by the personalities involved. There is a tired adage that two things people with delicate stomachs should never watch being made are sausage and legislation. The adage is a slander on sausage making. The process of writing a bill and working to amass political support for the bill often brings out the worst in people. I was continuously concerned that personal conflicts among members and among the staffs on the new work group would greatly complicate the goal of producing a consensus bill. In the worst case, it might prove impossible for members to work together effectively, thereby requiring the leadership to step in and make final decisions about the bill. Certainly, there was no reason to doubt that Armey and his staff would take over writing the bill if the work group became deadlocked.

The personalities that guided the new work group were quite a mix. A great deal hinged on Jim Talent, a junior member of Congress, serving only his second term in the House. He quickly became the leading figure on the right in the House for welfare reform. Talent was brilliant, hardworking, and aggressive. Like the lawyer that he was, he always appeared to believe completely in whatever position he took. In the case of welfare, he was a complete convert to Murrayism and to the predominance of the illegitimacy issue. Talent also had a smart and effective staff, led by Reid Cavnar and Kiki Kless. Santorum was like Talent in every respect. He was equally brilliant, equally hardworking, and equally relentless in support of his views. Like Talent, he also had a terrific staff, led by Mike Hershey, who covered welfare issues for him. Nancy Johnson was also bound to play a major role in the negotiations, and she was nothing short of a force of nature. As I had learned working with her for many years, she was at least as relentless as Talent and Santorum. Perhaps being a pro-choice Republican woman having to stand up for her position against Republicans who thought abortion was evil, she had developed an aggressive and tough approach.

Balancing these true believers were several members with a more conciliatory approach. Clay Shaw, the senior leader of House Republicans on all things welfare, was the most important of the moderating influences. But Dave Camp of Michigan, another member of Ways and Means and someone who had not played a major role in the formulation of HR 3500, also became an important figure, both in the new work group and in the subsequent fight to pass welfare reform in 1995 and 1996. Camp was a lawyer and had done pro bono work for families with child protection cases pending in his home state of Michigan, so he had a good grasp of the issues and well-formulated views about welfare programs. He was moderate and listened to arguments from all sides. Like Shaw, he tended to be conciliatory in working with other members, both Republicans and Democrats, to formulate legislation. Tim Hutchinson turned out to be a surprise. A very conservative Republican from Arkansas, who would also later be elected to the Senate, Hutchinson was just plain nice. I never could tell how strongly he subscribed to the Murray-Bennett-Kemp text on illegitimacy, but he managed to maintain the full confidence of conservatives inside and outside Congress while appearing moderate and reasonable in negotiations with Shaw, Johnson, Camp, and others in the work group. Like Shaw and Camp, his role was to keep things civil and to push for compromises.

The work group began meeting in June and met at the staff or member level on more than ten occasions over the next four months. The first meeting took place in the ornate Rayburn Room, just off the House floor, in early June. Talent, Camp, Shaw, and a few others, plus staff, were present. Camp, who had been asked by the leadership to serve as convener of the group because of Santorum's Senate race and their belief that Shaw would be too polarizing to lead a group intended to reach compromise, wanted to begin by establishing some ground rules and determining the major changes in HR 3500 that the Talent forces hoped to achieve. Camp and Shaw, who had talked at length before the meeting, did not want to explicitly discuss whether HR 3500 would be the base bill and who would be responsible for drafting the Contract with America bill. Rather, they wanted to proceed on the assumption that HR 3500 would be the base bill and that Ways and Means staff would be responsible for the drafting. Their thinking was that HR 3500 already had lots of support and that the approach of the work group should be simply to modify—or from Talent's perspective, strengthen—the provisions that conservatives thought were weak.

That first meeting in the Rayburn Room had a tone distinctly different than meetings of the work group that produced HR 3500. The members did not exchange the normal banter, and the good spirit that pervades most meetings of House Republicans and had been such a notable feature of the Santorum-DeLay work group was missing. The members were tense and serious. But one advantage of having staff is that members can leave the testosterone-induced tactics to them. Although this first members' meeting and one or two meetings that occurred near the September deadline for a final bill were tense, neither in this meeting nor any of the others did members exchange sharp words. Shaw and I often discussed how important this was, and Shaw and Camp both realized that we would need to continue to work with the Talent forces after the election—when, whether we were in the majority or minority, the chips would really be down.

Given the sound and fury about deficiencies of HR 3500, and the various threats from conservative groups that they would revolt if HR 3500 were included in the Contract with America, it would be reasonable to expect that the Talent forces would try to make huge changes in HR 3500. But surprisingly, by September, when the final welfare reform bill was completed by the Contract with America work group, the changes agreed to by the authors of HR 3500 were important but not radical. Going back to that first meeting in the Rayburn Room, the major tension had always been over the illegitimacy provisions. Talent's opening bid was to suggest that we include the provision from his bill; namely, that mothers under age twenty-one (phased in after several years to age twenty-five) who have babies outside marriage be ineligible for both cash (AFDC) and Food Stamps and that their babies be permanently ineligible. There had been agreement among members of the original work group that strong measures on illegitimacy were good policy but also very strong feelings that the Talent proposal was too harsh. By adopting it, Republicans would be opening themselves to the typical accusations: Republicans are indifferent to the poor, Republicans are mean, and Republicans are engaging in class warfare. In Shaw's view—as well as that of all of the Ways and Means Republicans—we were jeopardizing the popular work agenda to bring to prominence an illegitimacy policy that was, no matter what your politics, exceptionally tough and not supported by the American public.[25]

I confess to bias on this point. In politics, as in other professions, bias drives lots of behavior. After participating in years of academic research and reading, and working on legislation to promote work among adults on welfare, I believed that a historic moment had arrived. For at least twenty years I had believed that mandatory work backed by sanctions and a time limit on welfare benefits would have a huge impact on the welfare caseload, on the income of previously welfare-dependent families, and on the life prospects of young mothers (and perhaps their children). With luck, a combination of strong child support enforcement and strong work policy might even have an impact on young males. But Democrats, because of their commitment to entitlement welfare, did not enact a serious work requirement while they controlled Congress. They understood that the essence of Republican policy was to end the entitlement to cash welfare and subject mothers on welfare to the same market risk that disciplines other Americans. We had made modest progress on this agenda in the 1988 Family Support Act by making participation standards part of the AFDC statute and by instituting an actual work requirement for two-parent families receiving welfare. Now a work-oriented Democrat was in the White House, and he had opened a new round in the welfare debate with the slogan "End welfare as we know it." Here was a wonderful slogan, one that we would have used if we had thought of it first. And if by some miracle we could seize control of the House and Senate, the moment for fundamental changes in welfare policy would be at hand. But now a fairly small band of conservatives had appeared to announce that the Republican work agenda was old-fashioned. Shaw was determined that we would not jeopardize our pending revolution in American social policy in order to test a new, albeit provocative, theory of how to contain the epidemic of illegitimate births. But for now, the Talent and Rector forces had the upper hand, and we would have to bide our time.

Given this mounting cry for stronger illegitimacy provisions, my greatest fear during the months of negotiations was that the Talent forces would not be willing to compromise. But after the June meeting in the Rayburn Room, it became clear that Talent and Hutchinson were willing to modify their goals for the sake of Republican unity. One reason was that they too subscribed to the vital importance of the work agenda. Both had seats on the Education Committee, which shared jurisdiction over work requirements in the AFDC program, and both were knowledgeable about work programs. Our mutual agreement that mandatory work was important and that we had an opportunity to deeply reform AFDC was clearly a uniting force. After two or three weeks of discussion among staff and members, it emerged that all could agree on the rather simple expedient of converting HR 3500's state option to adopt Murray Light and the family cap into a requirement that states adopt both provisions. In addition, states were given the option to expand Murray Light to other programs and beyond age eighteen, roughly in accord with the mandatory provisions that were phased in under the bill. The final Contract with America bill, then, prohibited states from using federal AFDC funds to provide cash benefits to mothers under age eighteen. The mother would never be able to claim a cash benefit for herself or any baby born when she was under age eighteen unless the mother married the biological father or another male who legally adopted the child.

States were also given the option to expand this prohibition to babies born outside marriage to mothers under twenty-one years of age at the time of the birth and to prohibit housing benefits as well as cash welfare. There were several other less central changes as well. The most symbolic was that, against Shaw's true desire, we agreed to demote our work program to Title II of the bill and to give illegitimacy reduction the honored place as Title I of the bill. Once we reached agreement on the illegitimacy provisions, it seemed that the work group's assignment was nearly completed and that the major job left was to draft the agreements to everyone's satisfaction. By late August we had drafts of these provisions that seemed to be acceptable.

But Murray Light and the family cap were not the only items on the agenda of Republicans who wanted to modify HR 3500. An underlying dynamic of the Contract with America was that Gingrich had ruled out several of the issues that were red meat to conservatives, including policies to reduce the number of abortions, to encourage school choice, to allow school prayer, and to outlaw flag burning. Gingrich's thinking was that he wanted only issues that were not divisive because he intended to use the contract to appeal to as many voters as possible. An assumption underlying this decision—and an assumption that turned out to be correct—was that the conservative base of the Republican Party would stick with us because, once in the majority, we could address abortion, school choice, school prayer, and other issues that were so important to them but were proscribed from the contract because of their divisiveness. Besides, the contract did contain a few big issues important to conservatives, such as welfare reform and a big tax credit for all families with children. Even so, as members and staff worked under Armey's guidance on the lucky ten issues to be included in the contract, there was a general understanding that those of us working on the ten bills would accommodate conservatives as much as possible because most of their favorite issues had been left out.[26]

For their part, the conservative groups did not hesitate to make their wishes known and to lobby aggressively, especially on the welfare bill. As part of their campaign to influence the welfare bill, they requested and were granted a meeting with Armey that was scheduled by Armey's staff for August 25, during the summer congressional break. My family had rented a beach house in North Carolina for our summer vacation, which was supposed to begin on August 20 and end on August 27. Unfortunately for domestic tranquility in my household, the demands of writing the Contract with America welfare reform bill caused me to postpone the vacation for one day, then another. On August 19 I heard about the meeting scheduled for August 25. My choice was simple: attend the meeting or continue my marriage. So I went to the beach and missed the meeting, but I didn't enjoy the beach very much on August 25.

Based on the accounts of several of those in attendance at the August 25 meeting, upon returning I wrote a memo summarizing three agreements that Armey had reached with the conservative groups. First, Armey agreed to insert language at the beginning of the bill, written by Robert Rector and called "sense of the Congress" language, which listed several findings about the ill effects of illegitimacy on society, the central role of marriage in providing the optimum environment for rearing children, and the evils of fatherless child rearing. The second agreement was to include a provision that would give states a financial incentive to require working-age adults who did not have children to enroll in a Food Stamp work program. The third agreement was to include a $1,000 tax credit for married couples with at least one full-time worker. These provisions came straight from the Talent-Hutchinson bill.

These agreements were not egregious, and indeed the language on the threats from illegitimacy and the importance of marriage actually formed a nice preamble to our bill. We modified them slightly and then included them in every subsequent version of the bill. Nor was a Food Stamp work program a bad idea. Like the AFDC program, many Republicans regarded Food Stamps as a giant giveaway, with virtually nothing expected from recipients in return for the benefit. Especially in the case of able-bodied adults with no children, the lack of a work requirement was, for most Republicans, a scandal. The family tax credit was also very popular among Republicans, including moderate Republicans. But the $1,000 credit to which Armey agreed was extremely expensive. The Heritage Foundation estimated the cost at about $2 billion to $3 billion a year. But based on discussions with the Congressional Budget Office, I thought the cost would be closer to $10 billion a year when fully implemented.

Thus the agreements themselves were fine, but the members from Ways and Means resented the way the agreements had been reached. Detached reflection would have shown that Armey was in a tough spot with the conservative groups (Heritage Foundation, Christian Coalition, Empower America, and so on) that he had met with on August 25. Especially given that these groups represented the heart of the Republican coalition and that most of their major issues had been barred from the contract, Armey was working mightily to keep them excited about the upcoming election by giving them as much as he could. From this perspective, the agreements made good sense, especially since they were consistent with Republican philosophy and with the spirit of our entire welfare reform effort. But from the perspective of Ways and Means members, they had already agreed to several of the most important illegitimacy provisions, albeit modified, from the Talent-Hutchinson bill. It seemed to Ways and Means members that the bar was constantly moving: after every compromise, more demands arose. I was reminded of the Tibetan proverb, "After the mountains, more mountains."

During this crucial and furiously hectic final phase of writing the bill, nerves were wearing a little thin. Brian Gaston, a former staffer with Jan Meyers who worked for Armey and whom Armey had appointed to provide liaison between the work group and his leadership office, was necessarily in the middle of the conflicts. It was easy enough to see that he had personally long opposed the positions taken by Ways and Means on welfare reform, first with Jan Meyers, who conducted a running battle with Ways and Means for over a year, and then with Armey, who sided with the Talent-Hutchinson forces. Brian was in one of the most difficult positions a congressional staffer can occupy. He had to represent his boss or he would soon be unemployed. But the Ways and Means members did not agree with some of the specific policies that Talent and Hutchinson, with Armey's support, wanted in the bill. Now Brian, accurately I believe, came to see the struggle over welfare as a kind of acid test that the conservative groups were applying to Armey's ability to represent their interests. Both on substance and politics, Brian saw the importance of Armey winning the struggle with Ways and Means members. These tensions over policy and control were heightened by the rapidly approaching September 27 date for the public event on the Capitol steps unveiling the Contract with America. We were running out of time.

The tensions came to a head in meeting held in Santorum's office on the second floor of the Longworth building on September 13. The purpose of the meeting was to make final decisions about which of the agreements that Armey had reached with the conservative groups would be included in the bill. Neither Talent nor Hutchinson was present at the meeting, leaving Brian in the position of carrying Armey's water. Again, this is a very tough spot for a staffer. Ways and Means members were already upset by the manner in which the agreements had been reached and by, from their perspective, being constantly pushed further and further away from HR 3500. The meeting was not very friendly, and Santorum—by now in the midst of a very tough Senate race in which he was trying to unseat an incumbent—was livid about the entire process to which we were being subjected. Not surprisingly, nothing was resolved at the meeting.

Over the next week, there were lots of discussions at the staff and member levels. Ways and Means members, after extensive discussions with Talent, proposed that we include the preamble language at the beginning of the bill as well as the Food Stamp work program. Leadership had already agreed on a $500 tax credit for families with children (they judged the $1,000 tax credit to be too expensive) and a reduction in the tax code's marriage penalty in another of the ten bills in the contract. Thus the conservative groups would be getting at least part of everything Armey agreed to in their August 25 meeting. This proposal seemed to at last bring closure to our search for a compromise bill.

But alas, another late-breaking issue suddenly appeared. On Friday, September 16, I was sitting in my Longworth office reviewing what I thought was the final draft of the bill when my phone rang. On the other end was none other than Dick Armey, the scourge of Republican moderates, calling from a cell phone in his car. He told me everyone had done a good job in writing the bill but that there was one more provision that had to be inserted. As part of our compromise on the illegitimacy provisions, we had created a block grant for each state of the money saved by denying AFDC benefits to unwed mothers under the age of eighteen. States were to use this money for food, diapers, clothing, housing, or any other needs of the young mothers and their babies. Armey wanted to insert a provision stating that none of the money could be used for abortion or abortion counseling.

I recognized immediately that this provision was a close cousin of the gag rule that, under the Reagan administration, had prevented money in the Title X program that supports health clinics for the poor from being used to pay for abortion or abortion counseling.[27] The biggest controversy over the provision among Republicans was not the bar on abortion but the bar on counseling. Critics of the provision argued that it interfered with a health professional's right to offer the best medical advice in every situation and the patient's right to know all the alternatives. Clinton had killed the gag rule, but it was still a great favorite among most pro-life Republicans. And virtually every pro-choice Republican opposed the gag rule. Without question, the gag rule was an emotional and difficult issue, which split Republicans.[28]

I was not delighted to be placed in this situation by Armey. Gingrich had firmly committed to the view that provisions on abortion and school prayer were going to be omitted from the Contract with America. They were just too divisive, and the major purpose of the contract was to unite Republicans and attract voters. Now Armey was threatening to cause a major split. Nancy Johnson, for example, had fought for abortion rights throughout her political career and would never change. Although she would accept a ban on use of the grant funds for abortion, she would reject out of hand any provision that barred abortion counseling. Agreeing to such a provision not only would be against her conscience but would also put her in political jeopardy during what was already a very tight reelection bid in her liberal and heavily Democratic Connecticut district.[29] Now I was being asked at the eleventh hour to insert an abortion provision that had the potential not just to deeply offend Nancy Johnson and other Republicans who supported abortion or opposed the gag rule but also to alienate almost every member of the welfare reform work group, because the provision was imposed from outside, thereby violating the integrity of the work group decision process. It would also offend many, probably most, Republican members of the Ways and Means Committee because it showed that the leadership could ride roughshod over our jurisdiction.

Thus I simply could not make the change Armey was requesting. When I told him that I would not make the change, he said the change had to be made. I said that was fine, but I would not be the one to make it. He then suggested that someone on his staff go to the Office of Legislative Counsel and make the change. I responded that I would not attempt to prevent his staff from carrying out his wishes, but that I would talk with Shaw, Santorum, and Johnson and that one or more of them might want to call him. In the meantime, I would let Legislative Counsel know that Armey's staff was authorized to make a change in our bill.[30]

Throughout our four- or five-minute conversation, Armey was courteous and even pleasant, but he was clearly determined to make the change in the bill. He had not called to discuss what the consequences of making the change would be.

I assume that he, along with his staff, had thought through the possible consequences and decided that the risks were worth the benefits of having a gag rule
in the bill. Again, the GOP right flank did not have many of their favorite policies in any of the Contract with America bills. With the election just weeks away,
and with Armey and other senior Republicans actually believing that Republicans
could take over the House, less than two months before the voting was not the
time to continue denying the fervent desires of the most important, powerful,
and rich faction of the party—not to mention the most likely to vote on election
day if energized by promises like the gag rule.

Given the attention generated by more than 300 Republican House members
and candidates on the Capitol steps on September 27, it was inevitable that
Democratic staffers and reporters would read the language in the Contract with
America welfare reform bill. The issue of *Newsweek* magazine that appeared the
first week in October reported that Charles Millard, a pro-choice GOP candidate
from New York, found the gag rule language before the signing on the Capitol
steps and refused to sign the contract.[31] Soon there were more media stories
about the gag rule. *Roll Call* reported in its October 13 issue that Democrats
were hoping to use the provision as a wedge issue against Republican candidates. EMILY's List and the National Family Planning and Reproductive Health
Association distributed a memo claiming that "millions of American women
will be banned from receiving complete and honest medical information"
because of the provision.[32] Both the *Washington Post* and the *New York Times*
published editorials condemning the provision and sowing confusion by seeming to imply that the language applied not just to welfare spending but also to the
Title X health clinic program (the legislative language was crystal clear: the provision did not apply to Title X).[33] Several Republican members—including
Nancy Johnson and, ironically, Jan Meyers—were put on the spot by local pro-
choice groups for their support of the contract because it contained gag rule
language.[34] Both pointed out that the contract language did not apply to Title X
and that, in any case, they did not support the language and would have it
removed from the bill.

None of the Republican candidates appeared to be badly hurt by the gag
rule language. But it is difficult to think that the manner in which the language
was inserted represented a model of cooperation among Republicans. Gingrich's press secretary, Armey's press secretary, and Gingrich himself told the
media that the language had been inadvertently included by staff at the last
minute.[35] Regardless of who in the leadership knew exactly what had happened,
the most important lesson of the episode was that the Republican leadership
could take over responsibilities normally reserved for committees and even
overrule the decisions of a work group it had appointed. It was a harbinger of
things to come.

Despite this somewhat unpleasant episode, and indeed despite the entire experience of the last ten months in modifying HR 3500 to mollify the forces so aggressively and effectively represented by Talent, Hutchinson, Faircloth, Rector, Bennett, Kemp, and the conservative groups, we could examine the new compromise bill with a great deal of satisfaction.[36] Above all, House Republicans and a wide range of conservative interest groups were still unified. Despite all the differences in philosophy and the varying motives pushing those fighting to shape the bill, we had created a product that seemed to unify our coalition even better than HR 3500, because now the conservatives were solidly aboard. The simple fact was that now, in late September of 1994, Republicans had moved to the right en masse and the provisions of HR 3500, almost unanimously endorsed less than twelve months previously, no longer represented the thinking of the most important elements of the Republican coalition, either inside or outside Congress. It was like riding a bronco, but as views moved right, so did the bill.

The Republican unity on welfare reform contrasted sharply with the disarray among Democrats. President Clinton had won the 1992 election in part by surprising the electorate. Never before had anyone heard a Democrat talk about ending welfare or requiring work after two years. Clinton was just as powerful and surprising, perhaps more so, in discussing the dramatic problems with teen pregnancy. But he failed utterly to bring his own party along. His bill, nearly eighteen months in coming, arrived in the House in the summer of 1994, too late to produce even hearings or markups let alone House and Senate passage.[37] Not only was the bill late in coming, but the administration had simply not faced up to the deep splits among Democrats. By building a coalition with moderate Democrats and Republicans, the administration might have been able to enact a bill before the congressional elections of 1994.

But the president and his first-rate team of welfare experts bided their time. An honest survey of the welfare landscape on the eve of the November 1994 elections would have revealed a House Republican Party and powerful Republican interest groups united behind a bill that would create a revolution in American social policy. As long as House Republicans were in the minority, their best chance of using the bill to influence congressional consideration of welfare reform was to cast their lot with moderate Democrats and President Clinton. Of course, any bill produced by this coalition would be well left of the radical Contract with America bill that had united Republicans, and the modified bill would split Republicans like a rotten watermelon. However, if a miracle occurred, and Republicans took over the House—let alone the House and Senate—Democrats and the president would be on the bronco. Republicans were united behind a sweeping and detailed welfare reform bill and had an aggressive and well-informed team of expert members and staffers who knew what they wanted and knew how to defend it. Democrats had a lot to worry about as the elections of 1994 approached.

## CHAPTER FIVE

# The House
# Initiates
# the Revolution

Sometime after midnight on November 9, 1994, I fell asleep watching election returns on television. As on so many of these lonely biennial vigils of defeat, I drifted off. For what seemed like only a few minutes, I existed in the hazy world between consciousness and dreaming. Two words circulated in my spinning mind like socks in a clothes dryer: "Speaker Gingrich, Speaker Gingrich, Speaker Gingrich." Surely it was a dream. So again I gave up and fell more or less asleep. At five in the morning. I awoke with the television still on and again the first thing I heard was "Speaker Gingrich." Realizing that I was fully conscious and that in the real world there now was an actual Speaker Gingrich of the U.S. House of Representatives—as well as a Majority Leader Bob Dole of the U.S. Senate—two thoughts immediately rose up from the depths, so long repressed: "Republicans are in charge." And "We're going to pass welfare reform."

Republicans now had an awesome responsibility. The welfare system the nation had constructed over a half century was vulnerable as it never had been before. It might now be possible, given the sudden Republican control of both the House and Senate, and the Republican-like goals of President Bill Clinton and some of his senior advisers like Bruce Reed, to make fundamental changes in the nation's welfare programs. Within thirty minutes I was driving to the Longworth House Office Building on the cold and dark George Washington Parkway. My thoughts were about establishing a tone, a style of decisive but balanced thinking and behavior that would carry me through as long as it might take to enact welfare reform.

As always, the key was to focus attention and effort on the fundamentals. Fundamental one was that Republicans were the majority in the House and Senate. If we could maintain party discipline, as the Democrats had not been able to do, we could enact whatever we wanted to in the House and most of what we wanted to in the Senate. If we were sufficiently clever—meaning primarily that if we did not reach too far—President Clinton would sign welfare reform legislation along the lines of HR 3500 and even most of the Contract with America bill.

Fundamental two was that, as the primary committee of jurisdiction, Ways and Means would be the first among equals in the welfare reform parade. There had long been rumors that if we won the House, Gingrich might make some important changes in House rules, including committee jurisdiction. But surely we would be able to maintain Ways and Means jurisdiction over welfare.

Fundamental three was that we already had a bill. Yes, in Clay Shaw's view and in my own, the Contract with America bill was somewhat flawed, but it contained most of what we wanted.

Fundamental four was that because of the months of conflict during which we wrote the Contract with America welfare reform bill, House Republicans were united behind almost every provision of the sweeping reforms contained in the bill. We had a few disagreements, but given our track record for reaching accord, I was confident we could do so again, especially because all the main players were still in place at both the member and staff levels. Santorum would no longer be with us in the House, but his successful Senate campaign meant that he would bring the seeds of serious welfare reform to the Senate, where he might, given his expertise and aggressiveness, be able to play an important role.

Fundamental five was that Clay Shaw of Florida, now chairman of the Ways and Means Subcommittee that handled welfare, Bill Archer of Texas, now the powerful chairman of the Ways and Means Committee, and the rest of the Republicans on the committee were poised to become the single most important institutional force—except for the administration of Bill Clinton—in the pending battle to reform welfare. Taken together, the fundamentals showed that the possibilities were enormous and that the Ways and Means Committee and Clay Shaw and Bill Archer would be in the eye of the storm, right where they belonged.

After parking my car in a remote parking lot (as part of the impending program of spoils to the victors, my parking privileges were about to take a turn for the better), I walked to my office on the second floor of the Longworth Building. Focusing now on the specific tasks at hand, my first thought was that the Contract with America welfare reform bill should be changed in at least two major ways. First, we needed to find a way to remove the spending cap provision because it would require us to perform surgery on too many popular programs.[1]

Second, block grants were now the order of the day. As the minority, we would not have been able to enact even a state option for a block grant, the provision that was in the Contract with America bill as an attempt to appease Jan Meyers. But given the ascendant Republican majority, block grants became not only a possibility but almost a certainty. Block grant policy decisively separates Republicans and Democrats. As we have seen, for Republicans block grants embody some of the party's most important goals, especially getting power and authority out of Washington and into the states and localities. In addition, by converting entitlements that often grow automatically (without the need for further legislation) into block grants with fixed funding, Congress could achieve much greater control over spending. Finally, Republicans believe that states are the laboratories of democracy and should have the flexibility to try new policy solutions to social problems.

There was yet another argument supporting block grants. Within two days of the election we had asked the Congressional Research Service (CRS) and the General Accounting Office (GAO) to examine eight domains of social policy (cash welfare, nutrition, employment and training, child care, foster care and adoption, social services, housing, medical) and list every federal spending program that fell within each domain and the amount of spending on each program. CRS and GAO found that the federal statutes contained authorizations for 336 social programs that together spent $375 billion in 1994. Within domains, program proliferation ranged from 154 employment and training programs to 6 cash welfare programs.[2] As the CRS and GAO reports began to come in, we prepared a simple table listing the eight domains, the number of programs in each domain, and the spending in each domain.

This table was used extensively by Republicans in speeches, hearings, and debates on the House floor. It was powerful in two respects. First, it energized Republicans because it supported one of the major claims of the Republican critique of the social policy created by liberals: that program proliferation under Democratic stewardship had produced rolls of bureaucratic fat. The War on Poverty and its aftermath had created a blizzard of federal programs that now rivaled kudzu for growth rate. Second, even in a calm and analytic environment, it was impossible to mount a defense of this great, bloated blob of programs. On all the occasions I personally used the table of 336 social programs or saw it used by other Republicans, I never heard anyone defend the blizzard or even offer a rational explanation for how so many programs came into being or were needed.

The big idea that emerges from the table of 336 social programs is that the perfect Republican agenda would be to collapse all these programs into eight large block grants, one for each type of social policy (cash, nutrition, health, education, and so on), and give control of the block grants to states. Some conservatives would like to completely end federal welfare programs and move the entire responsibility for welfare to state and local government and to the private sector. Not only would this reorganization of responsibility meet all the arguments for state control, but it would also greatly reduce the size of the federal government, something that ranks near the top of the conservative agenda.[3] Equally wonderful from the perspective of conservatives, many of the least favored and biggest federal agencies (such as the Department of Health and Human Services, the Department of Education, the Department of Housing and Urban Development, and the Department of Labor) could be greatly reduced or even eliminated.

This movement of power and responsibility to the state level would then open the possibility that was (and still is) the most attractive of all to conservatives. Rather than form block grants and send the responsibility and money from Washington to state capitals, if the federal responsibility for social programs were moved to the state level, why not also move the responsibility for raising the funds to pay for the programs to the state level? If this goal could be accomplished, federal income and corporate tax rates could be slashed and states would be responsible for raising the revenue to conduct social programs. Taken together, these reforms would constitute a complete overthrow of the New Deal and the War on Poverty and a return to a much smaller and less powerful and meddlesome federal government. Few Republicans wanted to go this far in 1995, but some conservatives—I would say a small but influential faction—regarded the block grant agenda of 1995–96 as a step on the road to a true federalist revolution.

As I reflected on the beauties of block grants on that glorious morning of November 9, 1994, I wandered down to the main Republican Ways and Means office on the first floor of the Longworth Building. It now being almost seven o'clock, I might find someone to talk with about the election returns and the now mighty House Republicans. As I walked through the door of the Ways and Means minority office in Room 1104, I immediately saw Phil Moseley, the staff director for the committee, his imposing stature filling the doorway to his office.

In the first of many early morning discussions Phil and I would have over the next two years, we quickly dispensed with gloating over the election. The weight on Phil's shoulders now would be enormous. Five of the ten bills in the Contract with America would have to come through Ways and Means, thereby requiring an immense commitment of time by the members and staff of the committee. But Bill Archer, about to become chairman of the most important committee of Congress, was not particularly interested in any of the bills except the tax cut and welfare reform. Even these drew only half-hearted enthusiasm from Archer. His true desire was to completely reform the tax code: "pull [it] out by the roots and throw it away so it can never grow back," as he was to say.[4] This enterprise, which turned out to be more than Bill Archer and the mighty Republicans could achieve, would nonetheless require many hearings and meetings with members and lobbyists—and would add significantly to Phil's burden. Against the huge responsibilities our committee and Phil as the staff director would be carrying, welfare reform seemed relatively minor.

But Phil didn't think so. Despite the diversity and complexity of his responsibilities, Phil's mind was already focused on welfare reform. Our work together over the years, and especially over the past two years in developing HR 3500 and the contract bill, had convinced him that welfare reform was doable and that passing something close to our bill would be revolutionary and would greatly improve the nation's approach to poverty; and of course it would bring great and lasting credit to the Republican Party, never mind that we would have to share the credit with Bill Clinton. On this remarkable morning and for the next two years, Phil regarded (and more important acted like he regarded) welfare reform as one of the prime goals of the Republican revolution.

I quickly briefed Phil on changes I thought we should make in the bill and the central importance of block grants now that we were in the majority. He agreed. He also agreed that I should meet with Archer and Shaw as soon as possible to see how they felt about these changes and about block grants. I told him that Shaw and I had discussed changes in the bill on many occasions and that he too wanted them. But we would have to proceed with caution; above all, we could not change any of the illegitimacy provisions. We also agreed on getting the information from CRS and GAO on the number of social programs and then developing a short memo to explain the results. Among many other issues we covered that morning, we agreed that the Republican governors would now be central to our agenda. If block grants and state responsibility and flexibility were our agenda, governors would be our prime agents.

We also had a discussion about the perils of changing the bill. We both knew that its welfare provisions represented a shaky compromise between, on the one hand, Shaw and the Republicans on Ways and Means and, on the other hand, the conservative Talent forces inside and the Rector-Bennett forces outside Congress. We also agreed that changes would be even trickier because Armey and others in the House leadership would want to hew close to the Contract with America bills and would be likely to side with the Talent forces if conflicts arose.

The issue of changes in the welfare bill highlighted a problem that was to cause mountains of consternation and conflict among Republicans for the next two years and beyond. Phil and I assumed that everyone would agree that Gingrich was in charge. As events were to demonstrate, Gingrich would indeed be king of the Republican Party and the House for at least the next year, at which point, due in large part to his own personality and several missteps, his power would begin to wane. But even if Gingrich were king, the big question was, What was the division of responsibility and authority under the king? The chairmen of House committees, especially the major committees such as Ways and Means, had historically been at least princes if not kings themselves, with considerable autonomy over their own domains. In the case of Ways and Means, the domain was immense. Some of the programs under Ways and Means jurisdiction were the perennial objects of reforms that were of interest to nearly every member of Congress and to the richest and most powerful lobbying firms in the nation's capital. Especially in a time of ferment and change like the one now dawning, who had the right to determine Republican policy on these programs? Normally it would be Archer, in close cooperation with the Republican leadership. But Gingrich had ideas and plans and so did lots of other important Republicans. In addition, we had committed to lots of policy changes in the Contract with America. Along with everything else it brought with it, the Gingrich revolution and coronation made for uncertain lines of authority, not the least of which was the role of committee chairmen.

The problem of unclear lines of authority was intensified by another factor, demonstrated clearly by Armey, with his September surprise on the gag rule.[5] Apparently, Republican leadership had the power to make fundamental changes in our bill, even changes that were directly and strongly opposed by members of Ways and Means. Such a possibility would have been unthinkable under Democratic Chairman Dan Rostenkowski, but Republicans in the House had been dominated by Gingrich so completely in recent years that the leadership had immense power. Gingrich's power was even greater now that he had led Republicans into the Promised Land. If Gingrich wanted a particular provision in or out of our bill, it would be difficult to resist him. As it turned out, the ability of the members of Ways and Means to outmaneuver Gingrich would be necessary if a final welfare reform bill were to be enacted. But that struggle was more than a year in the future. In the meantime, the great advantage of having a leader as powerful as Gingrich was that, under his leadership, nearly all Republicans could be made to pull in the same direction—gladly or not. Gingrich's immense power was both a curse and an advantage, but it is undeniable that he led Republicans to a host of legislative triumphs during the two years of the 104th Congress.

A more immediate problem loomed in the form of Gingrich's laudable goal of bringing some reason and coherence to the House committee structure and the organization of statutory programs among the committees. Even before the House convened in January 1995, Gingrich appointed David Dreier of California to head a small group of members who would make recommendations to our leadership on streamlining the House's committee structure.[6] The rumor was that the Dreier group was actually considering a new committee that would have jurisdiction over major welfare programs. This rumor was later confirmed by discussions with leadership staff. The programs brought together under the jurisdiction of the new welfare committee might include the Food Stamp program, Medicaid, housing, Aid to Families with Dependent Children (AFDC), and perhaps others. Inevitably, the proposed cross-cutting welfare committee raised big issues: How many and which welfare programs would be included? Who would chair the committee? Who would serve as staff? Would the new committee take over the welfare reform bill?

The possibility of losing jurisdiction over AFDC and perhaps other welfare programs got the attention of Phil, Archer, and Shaw. Based on our contacts at both the member and staff levels, we quickly discovered that the Dreier discussions were real. None of us doubted that Gingrich would support huge changes of this sort and would not hesitate to alter the historic jurisdiction of either the Ways and Means Committee or other House committees. Our concern led very quickly to an episode that taught all of us how being in the majority had changed our lives.

On December 1, 1994, Shaw granted an interview to Elizabeth Shogren of the *Los Angeles Times,* an experienced welfare reporter. At this point, Shaw and I were talking several times a day about how to handle the welfare reform bill and we were meeting regularly with staff of Republican governors and with staff of House committees and House leadership. Everyone working on the bill knew that changes were necessary, especially dropping the spending cap provision and converting the provision on an optional block grant to a mandatory block grant, but we agreed that everyone would be kept well informed of all changes. Nothing would be done in secrecy. We also agreed that I would keep Robert Rector of the Heritage Foundation and a few other conservative leaders outside Congress well informed as we proceeded. We were determined to show conservative forces outside Ways and Means that we were honest brokers of the Contract with America agreements.

Knowing that Shogren had interviewed Shaw and would probably have an article in the paper on December 2, 1994, I made it a point to get a copy of the *Los Angeles Times* first thing in the morning. The headline was "Key Republican Retreats on Welfare Reform."[7] The text informed readers that Shaw would not "support Gingrich's proposal to permanently deny cash benefits to poor women who have children while they are teenagers." It also said that Shaw would not use the Contract with America as his "blueprint in committee deliberations over welfare reform." The conclusion Shogren drew from these statements was that the "retreat" was "unexpected" and that it implied that "the new Republican majority on Capitol Hill is not fully united behind the aggressive legislative agenda promoted by expected House Speaker Newt Gingrich." Given the threat to Ways and Means jurisdiction over welfare represented by the Dreier task force, the *Los Angeles Times* article was a potential disaster.

Of course, the headline alone caused my heart to miss several beats, and the text of Shogren's article did nothing to help me avoid a full-scale heart attack. I especially enjoyed the parts about Shaw having "deep reservations" about "a central element of the GOP's 'Contract with America'" and about Shaw's plans showing that "the new Republican majority on Capitol Hill is not fully united."

By seven-thirty I was in Phil's office engaged in a serious discussion about damage control. I kept thinking, So this is what it's like to be in the majority. Phil was if anything even more concerned than I was about the possible consequences. He immediately decided that we should call Archer and recommend a course of action. After discussing various alternatives for ten minutes or so, we agreed that Archer should talk directly with Shaw and urge him to issue a statement "clarifying" his position. The statement should state flatly that Ways and Means would use the Contract with America welfare reform bill as its blueprint. We still hoped to change the bill by dropping the spending cap, making the block grant mandatory, and incorporating other modest changes that members of the committee and Republican governors wanted and that would, we were certain, be supported by the leadership. In dealing with the Shogren article, we did not want to confirm or deny our plans to change the bill. Terms like "blueprint" or "basis of" that left us with some room for modifications would be desirable for the Shaw statement.

We called Archer and reviewed the situation. Archer, whose major worry was losing Ways and Means jurisdiction, was just as concerned as we were. Fortunately, Archer and Shaw were close personal friends. Further, Shaw was a very even-tempered and reasonable person. If Archer told him that, given the Dreier threat, we all had to be exceptionally careful about changes in the bill, Shaw would understand and be willing to "clarify" his position. And that is exactly what happened. After Archer talked with Shaw, and I talked with both Shaw and his press secretary, Shaw issued a terse press statement headed "House Republicans United on Welfare Reform." The statement did not mention the Shogren article but noted that "there have been recent efforts to drive a wedge between Republicans on several issues included in the Contract." The key statement was simply that "the Contract with America welfare reform legislation will be the basis for our deliberations on welfare reform in the Ways and Means Committee."[8] There must have been something wrong with the Los Angeles Times distribution system that day because I received fewer than ten phone calls about the Shogren article and only one death threat. Perhaps the 500 copies of the December 2, 1994, issue of the Times that Phil and I collected and burned before eight o'clock had something to do with the relatively mild response.

The Shogren episode highlighted our need for an expanded and sophisticated press operation. During our tenure in the minority, Republicans on the committee had conducted a low-key press operation. To tell the truth, no one cared much what Republicans on the committee thought, especially when Democrats controlled the White House. When Reagan was president, House Democrats had to pay at least some attention to House Republicans—and sometimes even let them come to meetings. This had certainly been the case with the 1986 tax reforms and the 1988 Family Support Act. In these and a few similar cases, what House Republicans might do in cooperation with their president was potentially important, and the press might be interested. But under a Democratic president, we were so far underground they had to pipe sunlight to us. And when you live in the dark, there's not much need for a press secretary, especially a high-powered press secretary capable of helping shape important policy messages and plan legislative and media strategy.

But all that changed when we assumed the majority. Phil and Archer had realized immediately after the election that we would need a greatly souped-up press operation and had been looking for an experienced, top-flight press secretary ever since. But when Archer was invited to appear on the NBC news program *Meet the Press* on December 18, 1994, the need for a press secretary took a step up. Archer and Phil had already heard about Ari Fleischer, who had formerly worked for Senator Pete Domenici of New Mexico and who was recommended highly by the senator. As Phil and Archer discussed interviewing Ari, Phil had the idea of conducting the job interview as part of the preparation for Archer's pending appearance on *Meet the Press*. Because Archer might be asked about welfare reform on the program, he and Phil invited me to come to Ari's "job interview" and prep Archer on welfare issues as well as give them my opinions about Ari's performance. So early on Sunday morning, before Archer's TV appearance, I exchanged church for politics and joined the Archer-Phil-Ari trio in Archer's office in the Longworth House Office Building.

I no longer recall the specifics of the meeting, but to say that Ari was impressive would be an understatement. He must have been feeling lots of pressure. Not only was this a live performance, with Archer about to appear on national television and perhaps repeat specific lines that Ari gave him, but landing this job would give a huge boost to Ari's career. If he got the job and performed well, there was no telling what his future might hold. Despite the pressure, Ari was the picture of calm throughout the prep session. Indeed, I would say he dominated the session and was very firm in telling Archer what to say and what not to say. He evidently had prepared thoroughly for the meeting because he was well-versed on the Contract with America and on the bills in the contract that were under Ways and Means jurisdiction. He was especially insistent on the messages Archer should stick by. These included a "failed welfare system" that Republicans "had a plan to fix," overtaxed families that deserved a break, and similar big ideas dressed up in simple language. As I discovered when Ari left and the three of us discussed whether to offer him the job, we were all deeply impressed by his knowledge, his obvious flair for shaping Republican messages, and his self-confidence. We all agreed that he should get the job, a decision that was made even easier after Archer had followed the script we developed during Ari's interview and gave a polished performance on the Sunday morning program.[9]

Ari accepted the job, performed brilliantly, as we will see, and took the next step in a career that eventually carried him to be the press secretary for President George W. Bush and to be the founder of a successful consulting business. I always admired Ari, and his contributions to our adventures in passing the welfare reform bill were vital. But from that first meeting with him I always had a nagging little doubt about his approach to the press.

I had realized since very near the beginning of my career in the nation's capital (I had originally left my research and teaching position at the University of North Carolina to come to Washington on a one-year fellowship and then found it impossible to leave) that in some sense a congressional press operation was the precise opposite of social science. Ideally, social science begins with a question and then uses reason and empirical evidence to reach an answer that may inform policy. But politicians usually begin with the answer and then use their resources, including their press operation, to convert the answer into policy and to defend the policy. It is possible for a social scientist to participate in the political process and maintain the integrity of social science as long as she merely advises. The classic example would be testimony before a committee that calls on social science evidence to advise the committee on how to proceed. A social scientist playing this role, for example, might testify before the education committees during a Head Start reauthorization that research shows that investments in preschool programs produce long-term benefits that justify the program costs. Imagine a ten-point scale about the certainty of evidence that Head Start boosts school readiness and helps poor children perform better when they enter the schools. As a social scientist, I would tell the committee the evidence is about a four (with ten being the highest).

But say I worked for Democrats on the committee, who in all likelihood want to increase Head Start funding; my press release would ignore the four and say something like: "Social science research shows unambiguously that investments in Head Start more than pay for themselves." On the other hand, if I were a press aid working for Republicans, who wanted to hold Head Start spending constant, my press release would say something like: "Based on social science evidence, it is far from certain that children attending Head Start get any boost in school preparation," or even: "Social science evidence shows that Head Start is mostly ineffective in preparing children for school achievement."

Ari was a master at using arguments and evidence to support any position Republicans wanted to adopt. He didn't go for fours; he saw tens, and anyone reading his press release or hearing a politician using talking points he prepared would be completely persuaded that a ten it was. Sad to say, if the stakes were high, I might stand by and let Ari convert a four to a ten and then feel guilty for ten or fifteen seconds.

But this and similar communication issues arose gradually as we began to exert control over the Ways and Means Committee and the House. Of immediate interest was our ability to write welfare reform legislation that could pass in the House. There is a trick to understanding legislation and the exercise of power in Washington. The trick can be stated succinctly: follow the bill.

If following the bill is the key to understanding the development of legislation, who writes the bills? The answer would surprise most Americans. Bills are written by a small group of nonpartisan lawyers who constitute the Office of Legislative Counsel in the House and Senate. The men and women of Legislative Counsel are the keepers of the laws. All the statutes of the United States, more than 50,000 pages in all, are in the domain of the Office of the Legislative Counsel in each house, with particular lawyers responsible for particular statutes (or "zones of law") in which they specialize.[10] If members of Congress want to change the statutes, the typical procedure is to discuss the changes with one or two of their staff members, who then work with the appropriate lawyer at Legislative Counsel to actually write the new law. The House Legislative Counsel Office employs thirty-five attorneys and approximately fifteen staffers whose major job is to draft legislation and to do it in such a way that the organization, logic, and integrity of the federal statutes are maintained.

When I first began to meet with the lawyers in the Office of Legislative Counsel in 1986, I questioned the very bureaucratic and expensive (especially since both the House and the Senate have an Office of Legislative Counsel) system used to write the laws.[11] However, with growing experience in writing legislation, I came to understand that the 50,000 pages and nearly 184 pounds of statutes of the U.S. government are immensely complex and that this complexity makes it very difficult to gain mastery of how a particular statute is organized and how any particular provision of a statute relates to other, similar provisions. Moreover, if a particular statute changes, other statutes may have to be changed because of an underlying relationship between them. Knowing these connections and being able to figure out all the associated changes that are necessitated by changes in a particular statute requires knowledge of all the statutes.[12]

I should not leave this brief overview of Legislative Counsel without mentioning a personal condition that afflicts all congressional staff. Although it would often be difficult to know by simply observing the work behavior of congressional staffers, especially senior staffers, it is rumored that some actually have personal lives. A few even have families they see occasionally. This condition of working for Congress applies with special force to the lawyers at Legislative Counsel. There is no organization in world history that has had worse hours than military units during war and the U.S. Congress near the end of a congressional session. Working for Congress the month or so before the end of a session or the week or so before floor consideration of a big bill is often like being in the theater except that every day is opening night. Stay until midnight or three in the morning, then return in the morning by six or seven and start again. Often, this time is being filled by writing and rewriting complex statutory language as members reach agreement and then modify the agreement again and again. In other words, much of the time is wasted. The late hours, the wasted time, the waiting for members to make a decision, the inevitable personality conflicts that arise in these circumstances make for something approaching the ultimate test of human character, especially patience and fortitude.

The Office of Legislative Counsel is one of the unsung, indeed virtually unknown, heroes of American government. Without Legislative Counsel to impose and maintain order on the laws, the statutes of the United States government would be a complete and hopeless mess.

But members of Congress must invent the substance of the laws, and congressional Republicans were about to get lots of help from Republican governors in reinventing the welfare reform bill. House and Senate Republicans were not the only members of the Republican Party to flourish on the night of November 8, 1994. Republicans running for governor had an equally spectacular night. When all the votes were counted, Republicans controlled the governorship of thirty states, including all the big states except Florida. Even a dark horse in Texas named George W. Bush won his race against a strong incumbent.

The new Republican governors joined a group of Republican governors that already included two of the most welfare-reform-oriented governors ever. Tommy Thompson of Wisconsin and John Engler of Michigan were immensely influential, not least because they both had already implemented major welfare reforms and because they both had big plans for future reforms. Engler in particular played a major role in the welfare reform debate, both because of his reputation as a welfare reformer and because he was co-chairman of the National Governors Association welfare reform task force (a position once occupied by President Clinton). The major goal of governors in the welfare debate was to secure maximum independence from Washington in the conduct of social programs. As Tommy Thompson often put it, he was sick of coming to Washington to "bow and kiss the ring" of the secretary of Health and Human Services in order to obtain some modest increase in flexibility.[13] But he didn't mind accepting those federal dollars.

Engler and many other governors—such as William Weld of Massachusetts, George Allen of Virginia, and Tom Carper of Delaware—were already joining Wisconsin in pursuing reforms aimed at moving welfare recipients from dependency on government cash to self-sufficiency through work in the private sector. To do so, they wanted the maximum amount of flexibility they could obtain from the federal government. Here was something on which both Republican and Democratic governors agreed: flexibility in designing their programs with minimum interference from the federal government. And of course keep those dollars rolling from Washington to the state capitals.

The concept of state flexibility was a major component of the reform fever that swept the capital following the 1994 election. If work promotion and illegitimacy reduction were the central elements of the welfare revolution Republicans were pursuing, devolution of control to state government through block grants was now a third theme of the revolution. Although most programs for the poor were administered by the states, nearly all of the programs had extensive federal statutory and regulatory provisions that governed how the states were to administer them. States had some flexibility, with the specific amount of flexibility varying from program to program, but there was a growing view among governors that states needed more flexibility because they were being hamstrung by federal statutes and regulations. However, Democrats in Washington were reluctant to provide states with much flexibility, primarily because they wanted to ensure that minimum standards of eligibility and benefits were maintained and because they didn't trust the states to adopt policies that truly addressed the needs of the poor. With regard to the racist southern governors and state legislatures that still prevailed in the 1960s and 1970s, Democrats were correct and were wise to maintain considerable control in Washington. But by the 1990s, with official racism greatly diminished, the level of federal control was under severe challenge by both Republican and Democratic governors in the programs that provided cash welfare, child care, nutrition, health, child protection, and even disability payments. Now there was no telling how far down the devolution road Republicans, as the majority party, could travel. But the road would be extremely bumpy and perhaps impassible unless the governors were accompanying Congress on the trip.

The road was now leading to Williamsburg, Virginia. The Republican Governors Association had long planned to hold a meeting in Williamsburg after the 1994 elections. Given the importance of coordination between the newly powerful Republican governors and the triumphant Republicans on Capitol Hill, Haley Barbour, the head of the national Republican Party, and his immensely capable lieutenant Don Fierce, believed it was necessary for Gingrich and Dole to join the governors in Williamsburg for strategy discussions.[14] Dole was not enthusiastic about the Contract with America, so Barbour and Fierce wanted to use the governors to convince Dole to accept and support the policy ideas in the contract. They told the governors they should ask Gingrich and Dole to form task forces that would include governors to write the Medicaid, spending, tax, and welfare legislation that would constitute a major aim of the Republican revolution: moving power and authority out of Washington. The governors agreed with this recommendation, and both Gingrich and Dole agreed to the governors' request. By this stratagem, Barbour and Fierce used Williamsburg to ensure that the House, the Senate, and the Republican governors were united behind an emerging set of policies first laid out in the Contract with America. The strategy was brilliant; best of all, it worked, notably in getting Dole to agree on the importance of major parts of the contract.

But there was a problem. Based on years of experience working with governors and their staffs, I knew that the governors would put lots of pressure on Gingrich and Dole to give states control of welfare reform and every other part of domestic policy they could get their hands on. Unfortunately for the governors, there was simply no way we could turn welfare over to them. The Republican House members who had worked so hard on welfare reform, the conservative intellectuals outside Congress, led by William Bennett, and the conservative groups led by Robert Rector were not going to drop their demands to attack illegitimacy or require strong work standards and turn the whole problem over to governors. If Gingrich allowed the Republican governors to write the welfare reform bill, we wouldn't even be able to get the bill out of committee. As Charles Krauthammer put it in an opinion piece in the *Washington Post:* "Fix first. Then punt."[15]

Just as I had expected and feared, in their opening Williamsburg press conference on November 20 the governors were assertive about gaining control of welfare. In an article that opened, "A host of Republican governors raised objections to the leading House GOP welfare reform plan," John King of the Associated Press quoted Governor Leavitt of Utah as summing up the position of all the governors: "Give us the ball and then get out of the way."[16] Even the moderate Republican Christine Todd Whitman of New Jersey got into the act, declaring that "if we have the flexibility to design the programs . . . we can do it, we can do it smarter, we can do it for less money."[17] There were a number of similar quotes from other governors, including Tommy Thompson's standard line about kissing the secretary's ring (which, ironically, would someday be his).[18]

Such rhetoric was standard fare for governors. Those of us working on welfare reform with their staffs heard it two or three times a meeting or telephone conversation. Much more alarming to me were Gingrich's statements. Gingrich and Dole had a long breakfast with a few of the governors on Tuesday, November 22, and then attended a big meeting with all the Republican governors, in which both Gingrich and Dole gave speeches. Probably still feeling a rush from the spectacular election results, both the governors and Gingrich and Dole may well have been prone to flattering each other and to an exaggerated sense of trust. In a speech interrupted several times by standing ovations, Gingrich, following the Barbour-Fierce script, told the governors they would have much greater control over welfare programs. He said: "We can't be here suggesting the social engineering of the right will be more clear than the social engineering of the left." He also said: "This is the meeting which crystallized the process of getting power out of Washington."[19] Talking to reporters, he even said that everything in the Contract with America was open to change by the governors: "This is all open to negotiation."[20]

I talked with Rector several times as the Williamsburg lovefest was taking place. He was livid. He immediately began telling the press, in his no-holds-barred manner, about how inept the governors were and how they would kill true welfare reform. The provision the governors seemed to like the least was the restriction that a child born to a mother under age eighteen could never receive cash welfare unless the mother married the child's father or another male who legally adopted the child, precisely the provision that Rector and the conservative groups liked the best.[21] Shaw and I were in total agreement with Rector and other conservatives that welfare should not just be turned over to the governors.

One result of the Williamsburg meeting was that it would fall to Ways and Means Republicans to show the governors and their staffs that we intended to continue working with them but that the final bill would contain strong work requirements and illegitimacy provisions—call them social engineering from the right, if you please. In this delicate task, we had the inside track because we controlled the drafting of the bill. We could proceed without them, but they could not proceed without us.

Fortunately, Shaw and Rick Santorum of Pennsylvania had been talking with governors as we developed both HR 3500 and the Contract with America bill, and we had been meeting with governors for months at the staff level as the contract bill was developed. In the several weeks after the election, I spoke by phone and in face-to-face meetings with many staff members representing Republican governors, but especially with Gerry Miller, the director of welfare in Michigan, Gerry Whitburn, the director of welfare in Wisconsin, Mary Kay Mantho, who handled welfare issues for the Wisconsin office in Washington, and of course with Engler's Washington staffer on welfare reform, LeAnne Redick. Primarily because Governor Engler was the co-chair of the welfare committee of the National Governors Association, Republican governors appointed him to head the effort to influence the welfare reform bill as it developed. It followed that Gerry Miller and LeAnne were my major contacts throughout the process. But I also had a personal friendship with Whitburn, and we often talked on the phone as the welfare reform bill worked its way through Congress.

Over the course of several meetings, Shaw and I developed a plan for working with the governors that was blessed by Archer and Phil as well as by Gingrich through his senior staffer for welfare, Jack Howard. On December 2, less than two weeks after the raucous meeting in Williamsburg, I sent a memo to Gerry Miller and Gerry Whitburn proposing a plan of action and providing some preliminary documents on the welfare reform bill we were writing, using the contract bill as the blueprint. We had rough drafts of two block grants, one for the AFDC program and one for child care. In another week or so we would have the draft of a third block grant, this one on child protection programs. The draft bills had been approved by Shaw and Archer and by William Goodling of Pennsylvania, the chairman of the Education Committee. The Education Committee shared jurisdiction with Ways and Means over the Job Opportunities and Basic Skills Training (JOBS) program, the unsuccessful program that had been enacted in

1988 to help adults on AFDC prepare for and find work. Goodling's committee also had jurisdiction over the Child Care and Development Block Grant, the program that we proposed as the basic vehicle for the child care block grant.

We gave the two Gerrys (Miller and Whitburn) several days to consider our drafts and to talk with Engler and Thompson (and with other governors if necessary) and then to meet in Washington to reach agreement on all three of the block grants we were developing. We assumed that staff could work out all but a small number of issues and that Shaw and Goodling and perhaps a few additional members would meet with Engler, Thompson, and whomever else the Republican governors wanted to send to resolve the remaining issues.

The Republican governors came to Washington on Wednesday, December 8, to continue discussions on all the issues raised in the Williamsburg meeting. They devoted one session in their meeting at the Hyatt Hotel to welfare reform. Shaw and I attended, as did Goodling. I had talked previously with Phil and with Jack Howard of Gingrich's staff, and we all agreed that it would be good for Shaw to describe how he planned to write the bill in consultation with the Republican governors. Given the confusion resulting from the Williamsburg meeting about who was going to write the bill, we thought it would be important to let the governors know that we had already started drafting and that we would consult with them on a regular basis throughout the process. We already had told the two Gerrys as much, but telling the governors directly would eliminate any chance for confusion. Following the principle that he who controls drafting controls policy, we intended to make it clear that Ways and Means would control drafting.

I was a little nervous as we waited in the meeting for Shaw's turn to talk. If Governors John Engler of Michigan or Tommy Thompson of Wisconsin wanted to create a showdown and appeal to Gingrich in order to seize control of the drafting, it would be a signal that House Republicans had lost a great deal of power to the governors and would make Republicans on the Ways and Means Committee extremely upset. It would also create an outcry from conservative members of the House and conservatives outside Congress who wanted to ensure that we followed the Contract with America bill as closely as possible. In short, welfare reform would be dead. When Shaw's turn came, he explained how the House planned to take up welfare reform. Each committee would write the legislation that fell within its own jurisdiction. The committees involved would include Ways and Means, Education, Judiciary, Agriculture, and Commerce (for Medicaid). The bills from all the committees would then be put together by the Rules Committee or the Budget Committee to form a single coherent bill and be brought to the floor as HR 4. Shaw also announced that he would introduce the Contract with America version of HR 4, exactly as written, in early January.

But the contract bill was being rewritten, because we were creating an AFDC block grant, a child care block grant, and a child protection block grant—just as the governors wanted us to do. We were also dropping the spending cap (which the governors hated) and making several other more modest changes. This revised bill would be introduced in early February and would be marked up by Shaw's subcommittee in early-to-mid-February. The bill would then be marked up by the full Ways and Means Committee in early March and be on the House floor the second or third week in March. The other committees would follow the same procedure by marking up their own section of the bill and sending the results to the Rules Committee or the Budget Committee. Finally, he explained that we had sent a memo to the state staff group headed by the two Gerrys (both of whom were present) and invited them to a meeting to get the governors' reactions to our initial drafts and to make concrete arrangements to work together until we had a bill that everyone could defend. We would share all our draft bills with the governors, seek their input, and plan additional meetings (including meetings of the principals) if necessary.

This was an important talk. Without offending anyone, Shaw had clarified (actually, changed) Gingrich's message from the Williamsburg meeting by making it clear that each House committee would mark up its own bill and that input would be sought from governors. The message from Williamsburg that governors would write the welfare reform bill was dead the moment Shaw finished his talk. The fact that we were drafting the legislation also made it clear that Ways and Means would be in control of our sections of the bill and that governors would have to work directly with us to influence the bill. Of course, they could do an end run around us and go directly to Gingrich or other members of the leadership—something that in fact Engler often did—but meeting with the Republican leadership would not work very often and involved lots of risks for the governors. If the congressional committees controlled the drafting, governors could not afford to offend us. From this point on, if we kept the governors informed, incorporated as many of their suggestions as we could, and made sure that conflicts were minimized, we could avoid the foolishness and disorder that would result from the Republican leadership constantly intervening with the committees to change the legislation. For the first time, on December 8, I felt that Ways and Means was finally in the driver's seat. We had come a long way in the mere six days since the Shogren article threw us into such disarray.

As Shaw promised, we convened the Republican staff group on December 12 in our subcommittee's hearing room. The House was represented by staff from Ways and Means, Education, Agriculture, Commerce, and the Republican leadership. We also invited staff from the Senate Finance Committee and the Senate Education Committee to participate, since the Senate would be acting on the bill once the House had completed its work. The delegation from the governors was led by LeAnne Redlick, who was joined by Mary Kay Mantho of Wisconsin and several others. LeAnne and Mary Kay had been in constant discussion with their respective governors and the two Gerrys and would take positions favored by Engler, Thompson, and other Republican governors.

A major feature of the meeting was the cordiality among staffers representing Congress and the governors. In retrospect, I think there are four major reasons Republican members, governors, and staffers were able to work together so well despite the extreme pressure and public scrutiny we were under. First, all of us had a wonderful negative example before us. Democrats were notorious for their intraparty fights. Perhaps they had been in the majority so long, and had such low regard for Republicans as an opposition party, that they believed they could run the House with impunity. Democrats showed us that fighting and animosity are the enemies of effective party control of legislation.

The second factor that helps account for Republican unity is that we were under siege almost from the day of our electoral victory on November 8. There is no force more effective in uniting any group than the feeling that its members share a bunker and that outside forces are lobbing in grenades. As we shall see, House Democrats, liberal intellectuals and pundits, and many members of the media were ferocious in their assault on the Republican agenda. Of all the items on our agenda, none was the target of as much over-the-top rhetoric as welfare reform. This external attack drove Republicans together as few other forces could have done.

A third factor contributing to Republican unity was that the committee chairs and senior members had not held power long enough to fully appreciate how autonomous they could be. Over time, Republican committee chairmen in the House would come to dominate their colonies in the manner taught so well by Democratic chairmen like Dan Rostenkowski of Ways and Means and John Dingell of Michigan, the virtual emperor of the Commerce Committee for many years. But in the beginning, Republican chairmen were feeling their way and were quite willing to work across committee lines and even to consider giving up jurisdiction of some programs, a course of action that would never have been considered by the all-powerful Democratic chairs.

Finally, there was a very clear understanding among all of us—members, governors, and staff—that our reforms of welfare programs were of great historic importance. This theme was constantly played up by members and the press. Literally hundreds of articles appeared in the major newspapers and magazines about this or that aspect of the "Republican revolution." We knew that an immense opportunity for Republican reform was at hand and that it was unlikely another opportunity like this would present itself in our lifetimes. I feel that nothing I ever worked on in my life has been as important as welfare reform in 1995 and 1996. During the nearly two years of partisan warfare that followed the elections of 1994, the historic importance of our legislation was a constant motivating factor.

It became apparent in the December 12 meeting that several issues were going to be contentious. Given our previous work with the governors, none of these issues was a surprise. The biggest issue was that governors wanted us to form block grants, set some broad goals, institute a few modest accountability measures, and give them the money. The two phrases that came to summarize this position were "block grant with no strings" and "put the money on a stump in the middle of the night." Because nearly all Republicans were intent on requiring mandatory work programs, and because conservatives were ferocious about provisions to reduce illegitimacy, there was never a chance that we would accept the no-strings approach. LeAnne reminded us several times during the meeting that Gingrich had told the governors at Williamsburg that they could write the welfare reform bill. I told her, with a member of Gingrich's staff present, that if Gingrich called Bill Archer and told him to let governors write the bill, we would follow Gingrich's guidance. But in that case we would not even mark up the bill, because it could never pass the committee, let alone the House. In order to get out of committee and command a majority on the House floor, the final bill simply had to have strong work requirements and tough provisions on illegitimacy. LeAnne, who was a gifted operator in the congressional environment, must have known that I was right.

Another issue was that governors insisted that the block grants be entitlements to states for five years. Although Congress can cut funding for any program, it is more difficult to cut entitlement programs than appropriated programs: the latter depend on an annual appropriation, a complex process during which many programs compete for the same pot of money. By contrast, if the block grant were a five-year entitlement, the money would automatically keep flowing for five years unless Congress passed legislation to stop it. Shaw and the members of the Ways and Means Committee working on welfare reform agreed on entitlement funding for the AFDC block grant, but John Kasich and others were still prevailing on our leadership (not that they needed much encouragement) to keep child care from becoming an entitlement. Because Shaw regarded child care as central to welfare reform, he would bide his time but would try to achieve entitlement funding for child care, and more money if possible, as the legislative process unfolded.

House Republicans and the governors also differed sharply over work standards. Even so, by the December 12 meeting, governors were beginning to accept the inevitability of federal work requirements. Their goal then became to keep the work standards modest. Under the 1988 JOBS program, participation standards were exceptionally weak, and about half the caseload was exempt from any participation requirements at all. States had to have only 20 percent of the remaining cases (about 10 percent of the overall caseload) in a program of some sort.[22] Even worse, the program did not need to involve any actual work. Education, training, job search, and a host of other activities counted as work.

Given this background, House Republicans were determined to have a detailed work requirement so that a specific percentage of the entire caseload was engaged in work activities for a given number of hours a week. No bill that failed to have this level of work specification was acceptable. Unfortunately, because governors eventually agreed to—or at least bowed to the inevitability of—all the elements of the House's definition of work, we made the mistake of agreeing to the very modest work standard that required only about 20 percent of the caseload to work. This puny level left us vulnerable to the ironic charge from Democrats, including the president, that Republicans were "weak on work." Of at least equal importance, it left us open to hostile comments from conservatives inside and outside Congress.

Another problem was that governors wanted to kill our provisions on illegitimacy. Ironically, they were willing to accept a vast set of requirements in the child support program, including those related to illegitimacy such as strong paternity establishment requirements, a hospital paternity establishment program, and the mandatory use of blood tests. But they were adamant in their opposition to the major House provisions on illegitimacy—Murray Light and the family cap—because these provisions would have greatly restricted state control of cash benefits for supporting children born outside marriage. Again, we told the governors that a bill could not pass the House without these two provisions.

After December 12 we did not have another big meeting before February, when the Ways and Means Committee began to take action on the bill. Even so, I was in constant contact with both Gerrys, LeAnne, and a number of other state representatives. On January 28, 1995, as the subcommittee's February markup approached, I sent out a set of summary documents to all the staff and members with whom we were working in the House and governors' offices. The documents described the bill, what changes had already been made in the bill, how it conformed to the governors' proposals, and what issues remained to be decided.

The documents also included an outline, based on the ongoing meetings of staffers from the respective House committees and the Republican leadership, of what the final welfare reform bill would look like when it reached the House floor, including the provisions that were not under Ways and Means jurisdiction. As envisioned by House members and staff by late January, the bill would have seven titles containing eight major sets of provisions. These included the AFDC block grant, the child care block grant, the child protection block grant, a child nutrition block grant (the Food Stamp block grant was still in doubt), Food Stamp program reforms, reforms of Supplemental Security Income for children, limits on benefits for noncitizens, and child support enforcement reforms. This outline was very close to that of the bill that ultimately passed the House and, as amazing as it would have seemed to us in January 1995, the final bill signed into law by President Clinton in August 1996.

An important part of the documents I sent to those working on the bill was a list of the nine major items on which staff had not yet been able to reach agreement. These issues included the work requirement, the time limit, and the illegitimacy provisions. Of course, governors wanted all of these to be weak or nonexistent, and their staff members would not agree to any of them. Governors also opposed the provision to dramatically cut benefits for noncitizens and even the data-reporting requirements. There were also three funding issues about which staff had haggled but failed to agree. These included the House-supported cuts of about 10 percent in each block grant. The governors appeared to be willing to accept, at most, a 5 percent cut. But if they were to absorb a cut of even 5 percent, they wanted virtually no strings, an exchange the House could not accept.

The final issue, and one that would plague the bill throughout the legislative process, was determining the formula by which the money in the block grant would be divided up among the states. Under the AFDC program, states set the benefit level and then the federal government paid them a fixed percentage of total benefits paid. The federal percentage, which varied inversely with state per capita income, was at least 50 in every state and went as high as 78 in low-income states like Mississippi. Thus the biggest factors in how much money states received from the federal government to run their AFDC program were the number of recipients, the generosity of state benefit payment levels, and the federal reimbursement rate. Under this financing arrangement, poor states received proportionately less money because they had historically set their benefit levels so much lower than wealthier states. Because some states like Mississippi and other southern states had such low benefit levels (the benefit level in Mississippi was $120 a month as compared with $636 in Connecticut), they received fewer federal dollars per person than states that had higher benefit levels.[23] As a result, the governors' proposal to give states the same amount they received in 1994 from the AFDC program contained a major flaw: namely, the huge discrepancies in federal payments per poor family under the AFDC financing approach would be frozen into the block grant formula.

As Republicans worked hard, sometimes almost around the clock, to revise the welfare reform bill and other bills in the Contract with America, Democrats were floundering. For many years, the Democratic leadership in the House had been ineffective, first because Jim Wright of Texas was embattled with ethics issues, thanks in part to relentless campaigning by Newt Gingrich, and then because Tom Foley of Washington was not a very aggressive leader. Ironically, part of the problem for House Democrats was President Clinton's success in defining himself as a New Democrat and getting elected president. Clinton showed that Democrats could appeal to the broad American public by becoming more like Republicans on trade, defense, crime, responsible budgeting, and welfare, while maintaining the Democrats' traditional emphasis on universal insurance programs and help for the little guy. But Clinton had opened his presidency with several unfortunate moves. The process of selecting senior officials for his administration looked to the public like a vast exercise in political correctness. Americans believe in both merit and fairness, so any hint of quota-like appointments can be seen as un-American. The media portrayed Clinton's appointment approach as one steeped in giving representation to minority groups, an approach the public associated with traditional Democratic policy on minorities.[24] Within a few days of his inaugural address, Clinton was also mired in controversy over the issue of gays in the military. Again, the media associated him with a traditional Democratic policy of trying to advance the interests of a minority group at the expense of the majority.[25]

But these and similar episodes were minor compared to the huge problems Clinton had with his health legislation. Clinton's election promise to "end welfare as we know it" took a backseat once Clinton was in office. The president and some of his senior aides saw the opportunity to achieve something very close to national health insurance. For any Democrat, especially one who admired Franklin Roosevelt as Clinton did, the temptation would be overwhelming to complete the social security project by achieving passage of universal health insurance to go with universal pensions, disability insurance, and unemployment insurance provided in the Social Security Act. Adding health insurance to this list of Democratic achievements would ensure Clinton a place in the pantheon of liberal Democratic heroes. This temptation to achieve a place in history proved fateful for Clinton.

Clinton's health plan, and indeed his entire approach to creating a plan, soon encountered grave difficulties.[26] The secrecy of the health care task force led by his wife raised questions about what it was up to. Then when the plan was unveiled, Republicans were able to label it an old-fashioned, big government boondoggle with a level of complexity that rivaled rocket engines. Equally important, one of the most important Democrats in Congress, Daniel Patrick Moynihan, who headed the committee that would control the plan's fate in the Senate, went public with his view that health care reform should not be allowed to preempt welfare reform.[27] Largely because Clinton made it a cornerstone of his presidential campaign, by 1993 welfare was a major issue, commanding more media coverage than it had in many years. Despite the sharp conflicts between and within the two parties about specific reforms, nearly everyone agreed that the current system had numerous problems, including constantly rising costs for both federal and state governments.

For the first eighteen months of his administration Clinton pursued health insurance while his welfare reform task force worked at a somewhat stately pace to write his welfare reform bill. Despite urging from liberal editorial page writers like E. J. Dionne of the *Washington Post*,[28] from Chairman Moynihan, and from many members of his own party, including White House staff, it was the summer of 1994 before Clinton had a welfare reform bill ready to send to the Hill. With the 1994 congressional elections bearing down on members of Congress, both the House and Senate Democratic leadership had good reason not to take up the bill so late in the session. In addition to the prospect of running out of time, Democratic leaders in the House did not want to engage in such a tricky and divisive issue and one on which their party was badly divided.

Now, as King Gingrich reigned and House Republicans dramatically changed House rules and began their hundred-day legislative onslaught to enact the Contract with America, Democrats were rudderless.[29] For the first several months of the 104th Congress they failed, with one or two exceptions, to mount effective opposition to Republican initiatives.

Nor were congressional Democrats the only ones trying to figure out how to stop the Republican onslaught. Even President Clinton, clearly one of the best politicians of his era, was struggling to get on top. At one point he even resorted to telling the press that he was not irrelevant.[30] It's easy enough to see why he might have felt irrelevant. His "historic" health care reform turned out to be a fiasco. His 1993 tax increase mobilized Republicans in Washington, Republican candidates, and potential Republican voters. His welfare reform bill arrived on Capitol Hill with a resounding thud. Then, in part because of his 1993 tax increase, in 1994 Democrats were handed one of the most astounding electoral defeats in the nation's history. And thanks to the Contract with America and Gingrich's immense popularity (or notoriety, depending on your politics), Republicans were dominating the media and were marching forward on their legislative agenda. To Clinton and many Democrats, Republicans must have looked like they were conducting a revolution.

Regardless of what the Democrats thought, we believed we were conducting a revolution. In this regard, the importance of the Contract with America cannot be overstated. The ten pieces of legislation that made up the contract immediately involved virtually every committee, every member, and every staffer in the House. Republicans in the House and Senate were hard at work within a day or two of the election (a few might have needed a day off before the onslaught because of excessive celebration on November 8), and for many the work was maintained at a pace between frenzied and ridiculous for more than two years. Above all, the Contract with America brought specific goals and coherence to the turnover in power in the House from Democrats to Republicans. Democrats were left to do little more than observe and say no whenever they could.

No Republican member of the House had ever been in the majority. It followed that none had chaired a committee, written a chairman's markup bill, organized hearings, prepared a majority bill for the floor, or been responsible for controlling activities in the committees or on the House floor. Under ordinary circumstances, new chairmen might have taken their time and eased into their new responsibilities as a majority. They might also have had less than a clear idea of exactly what legislation they wanted to enact. But because of the Contract with America, almost everyone was thrown immediately into a crash course in governing the House. Inevitably, some mistakes were made. Even so, a major advantage of complete immersion was that, from the Speaker to the committee chairs to staffers, we quickly learned how to be a majority.

Nowhere was this steep learning curve more important than in the Republican leadership. The three most important leaders in the House are the Speaker, the majority leader, and the majority whip. On paper their major duties are somewhat clear: the Speaker provides overall direction and makes final decisions on the party legislative agenda; the majority leader is responsible for action on the House floor; and the majority whip is responsible for ensuring sufficient votes to enact the party's legislation. As the leader, Gingrich was a bundle of contradictions. He inspired near adoration and, when necessary, fear among Republicans. Because of his hounding of Speaker Wright, his use of exceptionally partisan and sometimes over-the-top rhetoric against Democrats, his success in leading Republicans to defeat Democrats, and his occasional arrogance, Gingrich inspired near hatred or worse among Democrats. Soon enough, Gingrich's rhetoric and arrogance would get him in major trouble with the media and the public.

Even so, in most cases his leadership style was to inspire and to work for consensus. Although Gingrich could make decisions and enforce them when necessary, he preferred to bring all parties together and use discussion and compromise to lead his forces to legislative victory. And, again because of the Contract with America, the victories in the House began on the first day of Congress and proceeded in an almost unbroken string for the two years of the 104th Congress, thanks in no small part to Dick Armey and his superb staff and the spectacular whip operation run by Tom DeLay. In the long run, the single most important victory would prove to be the welfare revolution. The Committee on Ways and Means and its Subcommittee on Human Resources were about to harness the growing forces supporting welfare reform and begin the orderly process that would produce this revolution.

## CHAPTER SIX

# The Battle
# in the House,
# Part I: Hearings

Few scenes in American politics are more familiar than the hearings of the House Un-American Activities Committee in the 1950s. Witnesses and their lawyers sat at long tables placed in front of members of Congress perched behind long desks on risers. Every seat behind the long desks was filled by a member of Congress. Behind the members were ambitious young staffers, ready to answer furtively whispered questions or supply new information at a moment's notice. And of course, the hearing room was packed with witnesses. This all made for good newsreels, movies, and television reenactments, although it was a minor miracle that the people could see each other through the cigarette smoke.

Most hearings are very different from this dramatic depiction of members of Congress grilling suspected Communists. In a typical year in Congress, its approximately 250 committees and subcommittees may conduct 2,000 or 3,000 hearings.[1] It is not unusual for only two or three average-looking Americans (and no lawyers) to be at the witness table, for only one or two members to be perched at the long desk above the witnesses, and for the hearing room to be mostly empty. In short, most hearings are routine.

Hearings can be roughly divided into two types: oversight and legislative. Oversight hearings are devoted to exploring an issue in detail. Often this type of hearing aims to determine whether a particular program is working or whether a problem in which Congress is interested is serious and getting worse or better. The hearing may lead to legislation, but considering new legislation is not the primary purpose of this type of hearing. Oversight hearings aim to establish facts and to help members and their staffs master the facts as well as provide both parties and interested constituencies and organizations with an opportunity to put their own slant on the facts.

By contrast, legislative hearings are designed to examine the advantages and disadvantages of particular legislative proposals. Nothing captures the attention of the denizens of Washington like the prospect of legislation. Legions of legislators, administration officials, advocates, and lobbyists exist to change legislation or to prevent others from changing it. The real action, then, is trying to open existing statutes so they can be changed or trying to keep existing statutes closed so they can't be changed. I always thought of legislative hearings as occasions when the statute books are slightly open. Legislation is not being written or modified during the hearing, but the hearing signals that the committee is warming up and probably intends to write legislation and may even have drafts of a bill. A legislative problem has been identified, perhaps by oversight hearings, a few members already have a good idea of how they want to change the statute to address the problem, and the parties may already be far along in developing their usually contrasting approaches. The legislative hearing is designed to bring reason, opinion, political arguments, and evidence to bear on legislation that will solve the problem. Both majority and minority parties would also like to use the hearing to get media coverage of their respective legislative solutions to the problem.

The legislative hearing is especially important when the majority party has already made its legislation public and has asked for reactions from the public. In this case, the statute book is open wider, the committee is not only aroused but has clarified in detail what it intends to do, and those on all sides of the issue had better jump into the game. Moreover, depending on how important the issue is perceived to be to the American public, the media may begin to pay attention, and major news outlets might even cover the hearing. Now the stakes have been raised and a hearing vaguely reminiscent of those old House Un-American Activities Committee newsreels could well occur, without the cigarette smoke.

Although hearings are part of the democratic process, they do not necessarily give both the majority and minority parties an equal chance to influence the process. The nature of the rules in both the House and Senate are such that the majority party begins with an advantage. And here, as in so many other cases, the written and unwritten rules are somewhat ambiguous, leaving plenty of room for mischief. In the case of Ways and Means and many other committees, tradition, committee rules, and House rules stipulate that the minority must always have the opportunity to invite at least one witness to a hearing. In practice, especially on our Human Resources Subcommittee of Ways and Means, this tradition has usually been interpreted to mean that the minority can have a witness on each panel during the hearing (hearings are often organized into two or three panels of three to five witnesses each).

With all these considerations in mind, Phil Moseley, staff director for the committee, Chairman Clay Shaw, Chairman Bill Archer, and I spent a lot of time talking about and planning the initial hearings. We were often joined by the knowledgeable and exacting committee counsel, Chris Smith. Chris was the guy who made sure the trains ran on time. He was also the expert in parliamentary procedure, and in this capacity he would rescue us in those moments in which parliamentary procedure would suddenly determine the rights of the majority and the minority and, hence, the manner in which the committee would proceed.

Our team was rounded out by Ari Fleischer, who ran our press operation.[2] Ari quickly established himself as our leading expert on how to deal with the press and the public. Given that our major goal was putting our legislative proposals in the most favorable possible light, Ari was enormously helpful in planning the hearings. He was relentless in forcing us to figure out our major message and to state it in the simplest possible terms. In fact, after about five minutes of work with Ari, I permanently changed my approach to hearings. In the future, I never worked on a hearing without first writing out the one or two headlines that I wanted to come out of the hearing. In addition to helping us select and refine our major messages, Ari bordered on genius in helping us shape the message so that it had the maximum appeal to the media and the public.

Because the initial version of the welfare reform legislation would be written by the subcommittee and then considered and amended by the full committee, we planned to conduct hearings at both the subcommittee and full committee levels. Of course, because five of the ten bills in the Contract with America fell under Ways and Means jurisdiction and because Speaker Newt Gingrich had promised the nation that the House would consider all ten of the contract's bills within a hundred days, the full committee had lots of issues to cover in a short time. Even so, the welfare bill enjoyed a prominent place on the full committee's agenda. The subcommittee hearings, which would then be devoted entirely to welfare issues, would follow.

The major message we wanted to convey in all the hearings was that the welfare system was broken and that Republicans had a plan to fix it. More specifically, we wanted witnesses to emphasize that the welfare system reduced work, reduced marriage, stimulated illegitimacy, lured young mothers into dependency, featured overlapping and inefficient programs, and cost too much money. These outcomes, according to the case we intended to build, were the inevitable result of the nation's entitlement welfare system. Regardless of whatever else they might say, we wanted witnesses invited by Republicans to sing this tune—that welfare hurts the very people it was meant to help and therefore must be radically changed. In addition, we planned to emphasize three supplemental messages: welfare recipients should work, births outside marriage were wrong, and the power to control welfare should be moved out of Washington to the states.

The first Ways and Means hearing would provide a platform for Gingrich to explain the entire Contract with America to the committee as well as give Democrats an opportunity to question him. Because Gingrich was being given the opportunity to present the Republican view of the contract in the first hearing, we invited Richard Gephardt of Missouri, the Democratic leader in the House, to be the lead witness in the second hearing and say whatever he wanted to about the Contract with America. The second hearing would also feature Donna Shalala, secretary of the Department of Health and Human Services (HHS), who was the lead Democrat on social policy in the Clinton administration; and Leslie Samuels, the assistant secretary for tax policy at the Department of Treasury and one of the administration's leading authorities on taxation. We assumed that Gingrich, Gephardt, and Shalala would place substantial emphasis on welfare reform, but in order to be certain that all our messages received lots of attention as full committee action on the contract got under way, we decided to devote considerable attention to welfare in three of the subsequent full committee hearings. Then we would follow up the full committee hearings with a series of eight subcommittee hearings that would explore our legislative proposals in detail while repeatedly emphasizing our messages.

The first day of full committee hearings, January 5, had the atmospherics of a circus.[3] The hearing was conducted in Room 1100 in the Longworth House Office Building, one of the largest and most beautiful rooms on Capitol Hill. The room is more than eighty-five feet long and nearly eighty feet wide, with ceilings nearly thirty feet high. The front third of the room was taken up by members' desks, arranged in two semicircles and located on two levels of platforms that put members above the audience and, more to the point, above the witnesses. There were one or two tables for witnesses, depending on how many were scheduled to testify, directly in front of and below the members. Behind the witness table was a long row of about twenty chairs for staff or other associates of witnesses. When administration officials testified, they often brought eight, or ten, or twenty staffers, who were ready at a moment's notice to provide their boss with answers to questions. Fortunately, no one has ever conducted a benefit-cost study of the practice of cabinet secretaries appearing before a committee with a flock of staffers, who mostly just sit in their chairs and try to stay awake.

Perhaps the characteristic of the room that made it so stately and imposing was the high ceiling, which gave persons entering the room for the first time the impression they were entering a cavernous auditorium. Few auditoriums, however, feature huge American eagles perched in alcoves near the ceiling in all four corners. Nor do auditoriums generally have the entire front of the room covered by 2,000 or so square feet of elegant curtains, which served as a backdrop for members as they occupied their large and soft swivel chairs like so many chief executive officers. The room, in short, is fit for the powerful Ways and Means Committee and its members as they make, year after year, some of the most important and far-reaching laws that guide our nation.

For Ways and Means members it was the first day of the Republican revolution, and every member was present to soak up the intoxicating aroma of power. The only witness was Speaker Gingrich. I happened to be standing near the front door of the Longworth Building when Gingrich walked across Independence Avenue from the Capitol and through the front door. In his wake was an unruly herd of perhaps forty or fifty people, some of them staff, some of them reporters, others not identified. The rear door to the Ways and Means hearing room is directly across the hall from the Longworth front door, and Ways and Means had a staffer weighing in at around 250 pounds standing by the door to make sure that no one entered except members, Ways and Means staff, and guests. Gingrich lost most of his entourage as soon as he cleared the backdoor of our hearing room.

On this particular day there was standing room only in the hearing room. Probably more than 300 congressional staff, lobbyists, scholars, and advocates were squeezed into Room 1100. The lobbyists for tax and trade issues stood out because of their expensive clothes. The children's advocates' clothes probably cost a third as much.

As Gingrich sat down at the witness table, the members took their seats, the audience seated itself and quieted, and Archer began by introducing the new Republican members of the committee, ten in all. Although Archer didn't say so, I doubt that the majority party on Ways and Means had ever previously had ten new members to introduce. After routine announcements, Archer turned to assessing the occasion.[4] "Historic" and "profound" rolled off his tongue, and then, as anyone who knew him could have predicted, he said his job and the committee's job was to represent taxpayers. To Archer, one of the most fiscally conservative members in either house of Congress, this meant cutting taxes and slashing spending or at least holding both to the lowest level possible. As events developed, Archer and his committee would be busily engaged in cutting taxes, eliminating a prominent welfare entitlement, and dramatically reducing spending on several welfare programs. Archer also made a point of emphasizing the importance of fairness and civility in committee proceedings. He invoked one of his personal heroes, Wilbur Mills, a previous Democratic chairman of the committee, who was not only an income tax guru but also, as least in Archer's view, a fair and impartial chairman. Citing a Democratic chairman as his model was a nice touch.

He then turned to a theme that many House Republicans had emphasized in the recent campaign and would continue emphasizing throughout the first several weeks of the 104th Congress. Republicans believed that Democrats lost the election because the American people lost faith in their ability to govern. Archer said that the people were "watching this great and historic committee with very short patience." The American people have heard a lot of promises from Washington in the past, but Republicans are breaking with the past, he asserted.

Republicans have a "contract" with the American people, he further asserted. Half of the bills in the contract had to be passed by the Committee on Ways and Means, and Archer intended to make sure the committee did its part to "cut spending," "cut taxes," and "revolutionize welfare" in order both to honor the contract and to prepare the nation for the twenty-first century.[5]

Near the end of his opening statement, he briefly alluded to the impending welfare debate, declaring that the nation had spent more than $5 trillion on programs for poor and low-income families in the previous thirty years, while child poverty continued to increase. From these facts he drew the conclusion that Congress should no longer measure compassion by "the amount of money the government spends" but by "how much better life becomes." He closed with a crisp statement of his governing philosophy: "We must ask working Americans for the least possible amount of taxes so that government will do only those things that they cannot do for themselves." In his view, the five contract bills under Ways and Means jurisdiction would move the nation in this exact direction.[6]

Even today I can recall the pleasure I took from this opening statement. Given the occasion, almost every politician in Congress—especially if they had been the chair of the mighty Ways and Means Committee—would have waxed eloquent for fifteen or twenty minutes, perhaps more. But the committee had an immense amount of work to accomplish in the next ninety days, and Archer wanted to set brevity as a standard for committee business. He was more than brief, however. He managed to review the basic tenets of his philosophy of government; establish the broad outlines of the committee's agenda for the next several months; characterize and justify the Contract with America in the concrete terms of lower taxes, lower spending, and fundamental changes in welfare; and directly tell the Democrats that he intended to be fair—all in less than eight minutes. It was pure Archer.

After the senior Democrat, Sam Gibbons of Florida, had made a similarly terse opening statement, Archer turned to Gingrich. Given Gingrich's predilections, he wanted to talk in the broadest philosophical terms before discussing the Contract with America. The contrast with Archer's succinct talk could hardly have been greater. Gingrich opened, as members of Congress always do, by thanking everyone in sight. He then observed that "we are at the edge of a potential opportunity of historic proportions." That's the way he often talked; being on the edge of opportunity was not enough—the opportunity had to be "of historic proportions." Moreover, he was encouraged by a meeting between the president and leaders of Congress that had occurred that very morning and that was suffused with a "spirit" of "reconciliation, of trying to work together." And in that spirit, Gingrich wanted to outline "my thoughts as the newly elected Speaker and to give you a framework in which, from my limited perspective, I would hope you would engage over the next ten or twelve months."[7] The word "limited" has seldom been used with less justification.

The framework consisted of four broad points: that America's entry into the information age, as conceived in Alvin Toffler's theory of historical evolution,[8] had important implications for the tax code; that the demands of the world economy required America to cut regulations and taxes to create a hospitable environment for business and job creation; that the welfare state had "failed" because the tax code and programs like welfare and Social Security "punish" people who work and marry; and that the federal government had to balance its budget by 2002.

Next, the Speaker turned to Medicare. In doing so, he launched into one of his favorite topics, the "sick" culture of press, lobbyists, and bureaucrats in Washington. He said these villains wanted Republicans and Democrats to fight each other. But as the new Speaker, he would do his best to ensure that Republicans and Democrats would work together to convert Medicare from a "clunky" big government program to an efficient, market-driven program. The "mind-set" of the Washington culture was that Medicare could play its part in reducing spending to move toward a balanced budget only if recipients were "punished" by program cuts. This mind-set is "sick" and "out of touch," and both Democrats and Republicans must learn to "reach beyond it to the American people and work with them."[9]

With this invocation of bipartisanship in the midst of sickness, the Speaker took up the Contract with America. He began by declaring that speed was of the essence; Republicans had promised to bring all ten bills in the contract to a vote on the House floor within a hundred days, and he intended to be sure the promise was kept. Then he said that the bills in the contract were not written "in stone" (something Shaw and I were certainly glad to hear, because we were modifying the welfare bill every day). And in modifying each of the ten bills, he urged members to listen to witnesses and to each other with an open mind and to become educated on the vital matters of taxing and spending contained in the bills.

It was a solid performance, notable especially for the tone of conciliation. Of course, like nearly all of Gingrich's speeches, it had unfortunate characteristics. Labeling lobbyists, the media, and Washington bureaucrats as "sick" seemed to puncture the spirit he was trying to establish. Moreover, the talk was a little abstract. Why would the new Speaker, talking to the most important committee in Congress and one absolutely vital to his agenda, spend more than half his time presenting his worldview? But these are quibbles. An important goal the Speaker was pursuing was to get the committee moving on the contract's bills, to provide a sense of urgency, and to wrap the urgency in a cloak of bipartisanship if at all possible. Thus challenges to open-mindedness were entirely appropriate. It seemed to me at the time that, at the very least, knowing that many Democrats literally despised him, Gingrich had been wise to hold out an olive branch and establish a tone that would make it difficult for Democrats to be hostile.

As the questioning began, Republicans were exceptionally respectful, even bordering on servile, while Democrats were no more than mildly aggressive. Several Republicans made brief statements and then yielded time so that Democrats would have more time to ask questions (time was limited because Gingrich, controlled by an outrageous schedule, had agreed to stay for only a little over an hour). Given that Republican members knew that the national media were focused on the committee and that they might have a shot to make CNN or even the evening news, yielding time to Democrats was more than just an empty gesture. Even Charlie Rangel of New York, who had been deprived of chairing the committee by the Republican victory, and a man exceptionally clever on his feet and fully capable of giving Gingrich all he could handle, made an eloquent statement emphasizing his hope that Gingrich would continue showing the interest in the poor he had shown in his inaugural address as Speaker of the House the previous day.[10] He closed by saying that he would "look forward" to working with the Speaker to improve the Contract with America and, at least by implication, make it bipartisan.

Pete Stark of California focused his questioning on what he regarded as the inequity of the contract provision that would reduce taxation of Social Security benefits of some recipients. In 1993 Democrats had raised the share of Social Security benefits that were subject to taxation from 50 percent to 85 percent.[11] This tax increase generated about $15 billion in additional revenue for the Social Security Trust Fund. The contract would repeal the 1993 tax increase on Social Security benefits on the grounds that older people should be able to retain more of their Social Security benefit rather than have it taxed away if they continued to work after retirement. But Stark argued that only the 13 percent of beneficiaries at the top of the income distribution receive this benefit while the remaining 87 percent receive nothing. Stark's argument, of course, was the Social Security version of the Democrats' class warfare gambit, of which Stark was a master practitioner: Republicans steal from the poor to enrich the wealthy. Many Democrats believed that class warfare made for good politics. Stark truly believed it was inequitable to, in effect, allow the wealthy elderly to retain more of their earnings.

The Speaker gave one of the patented Republican responses by telling Stark that he could "help me and the country understand" the tax increase Stark was defending by revealing the lowest income at which the tax on Social Security benefits started. Stark replied accurately that the tax started at $44,000 for a family. Stark could have avoided the $44,000 figure by giving the median income of around $90,000 of those hit by the tax, which he later did. But Gingrich leaped on the $44,000, arguing that Stark (and by implication, Democrats in general) believe that at $44,000 "you are now rich enough that since we don't have the courage to directly means test Social Security and take it up front, we will simply steal it from you from the backdoor by raising your taxes." Draw your own conclusion about who won that exchange.[12]

A few minutes and a few softball questions later, Gingrich rose to leave the hearing room and rejoin his herd. He had been in front of the committee for less than ninety minutes. The hearing had been surprisingly cordial, and certainly no Democrat had put even a minor scratch on the new Speaker. Whether because they wanted to appear to be balanced, or because they wanted to give Gingrich a chance to be fair in his governing of the House, or because they were simply overwhelmed by the events that had dashed their political fortunes, Democrats were not sharp in their questioning of the newly powerful speaker. Gingrich had waxed eloquent about everything from his theories of history to Mario Vargas Llosa's introduction to Hernando DeSoto's *The Other Path*, heaped praise on the contract, laid out the basic Republican case for lower taxes and smaller government, and appeared gracious throughout.[13] The effect was electrifying for Republican members of Ways and Means, especially the new members. There had always been plenty of private skepticism about the contract among seasoned House Republicans, but Gingrich's bravura performance the previous day in opening the House and on this day before potentially hostile Democrats made Gingrich and his ideas look formidable, even impregnable. As the Speaker cleared the door of Room 1100, Republican members of the Ways and Means Committee could not wait to do their part to advance the revolution.

The full committee held six more days of hearings over the next two weeks. Not only would the new members learn more about welfare reform through the hearings, but careful selection of witnesses presented us with the opportunity to lay out and defend our proposals on work, illegitimacy, and spending cuts, as well as our major reforms of Supplemental Security Income (SSI), child support, and other welfare programs.

The full committee hearing on January 10 promised to provide the first serious objections to our welfare proposal by Democrats. Both Gephardt and Shalala would appear alone in front of the committee, giving them an opportunity to put all their arguments against Republican welfare reform on the table for the national media to distribute to the nation. I was not comfortable with allowing two Democrats to open the second day of hearings; among other problems, it meant that we would have to rely on the questioners of Gephardt and Shalala to defend our bill.

Surprisingly, Gephardt was quite restrained in his comments on welfare. In yet another sign that welfare was a huge issue, despite all the tax provisions in the contract, Gephardt devoted nearly half of his oral testimony to welfare reform. His major complaint about our bill was that it turned over too much authority to the states. Rather than simply trust the states, he argued that the federal government should set standards and require states to meet them. He was even willing to give states that performed well in meeting the standards additional money.

Sitting on the dais behind Shaw, I could hardly believe that Gephardt had taken such a mild approach. The contract bill presented a dozen or more juicy targets for a liberal Democrat like Gephardt. He could have attacked us for ending the entitlement to cash benefits, for starving the hard-working immigrants who came to America for work, for throwing handicapped children into the streets, for making moms with little babies go to work, for abandoning the poor on a wholesale basis. All these criticisms and more were in the *New York Times* and elsewhere on an almost daily basis. A rookie staffer could spend a morning reviewing just the *New York Times* and the *Washington Post* and have enough material to write talking points that would have made Republicans seem like a bunch of mean old men robbing children. Nor did Gephardt play the class warfare card. After all, the contract did cut taxes on the rich (and the middle class as well, but Gephardt could simply overlook this inconvenient fact) and did reduce welfare spending by an unprecedented amount. With material like this to attack us, I was prepared for a dazzling performance of anti-Republican rhetoric that would rally the Democratic forces against provisions that were truly anathema to all liberals. But Gephardt let this opportunity slip from his grasp.

After a little more than an hour of testimony and questioning by committee members, Gephardt was replaced at the witness table by Secretary Shalala. It is impossible for a fair person not to be impressed by Shalala. She had made it a point during her first two years in Washington to meet individually with influential Republicans and to always return their phone calls. Some members, especially Nancy Johnson, trusted her and admired her greatly. And they had every reason to do so.

Unlike Gephardt, who had a free hand to say anything he wanted to about the work requirements, time limits, and spending cuts being proposed by Republicans, Shalala was restricted in how much she could criticize the major requirements of our bill, some of which were now or might soon be supported by the president. Even so, the media had been full of stories containing quotes from the secretary about flaws in the Republican bill.[14] So though she could not and did not say our work requirements were too tough, she did criticize us for not having enough money for support services such as child care, education, and training. She was also critical of our proposed block grant for child protection and of stopping cash payments for teenage mothers and their babies.

Of the many appealing features of our nation's legislative system, one of the best is the tradition of witnesses from the administration coming before congressional committees to explain and defend administration policy or to criticize the policies of the other party, especially when the opposition party has a majority in one or both houses of Congress. The secretary's testimony presented us with a chance to respond to her criticisms and to put our welfare policies in the best possible light. To do so, thorough preparation was necessary. Once witnesses have been selected, Republican and Democratic staffers of most committees prepare for hearings by taking two actions: writing a brief opening statement to be delivered by the senior member of their party present at the hearing, usually the chair; and preparing a list of questions for each witness that members can use during the hearing. Often, especially in the case of major hearings, committee staffers also meet with the staffers who work for members of the committee, and sometimes even members of the committee themselves, and review the goals for the hearing as well as the list of questions designed to help achieve the goals. Committee staffers also solicit additional questions and try to find out the issues on which each member is likely to concentrate.

Over the years I had used all of these methods to prepare for hearings, but for important hearings, especially those in which we wanted to make specific points with potentially hostile witnesses, I often developed a script for quizzing witnesses. The script contained specific questions followed by the answers the witness would be most likely to give and, in light of these likely responses, possible follow-up questions. The questions were arranged so that they were related and built toward the point we hoped to make.

In most committees, only members can ask questions during a hearing. Often, of course, members have their own questions, but most members are willing to work closely with committee staff to develop probing questions. Shalala's appearance before the full committee under the national spotlight gave us a chance to test our adroitness.

She began by announcing that the president was going to sponsor a big meeting on welfare reform at Blair House. She didn't give much information about the purpose of the meeting nor did she mention anything about the agenda. We were all surprised. Shaw immediately guessed that the president was trying to get back on top of the welfare reform agenda. House and Senate Republicans would be conducting hearings and markups of our welfare bills for the next several months. Clinton's advisers may well have thought it necessary for the president to grab some public and media attention to show that he was still a major player in the welfare reform game.

Secretary Shalala then reviewed the president's record on welfare reform, asserting that he had fulfilled his election pledge to the American people to reform welfare by sending Congress his Work and Responsibility Act during the last Congress. A detail about the president's bill she did not mention was that the leaders of his own party had decided that his bill was too controversial—and had arrived too late in the congressional session—to be considered by the Democratic Congress. Nor was his bill getting any attention in the 104th Congress. She then reviewed the president's work on the 1988 Family Support Act as the National

Governors Association's lead governor on welfare reform as well as the work of his administration in granting welfare reform waivers to twenty-three states. This was indeed a record to be proud of. If she had testified in this manner at the beginning of 1994, the last year Democrats had controlled Congress, and extolled the same virtues of the president's work to reform welfare (and introduced an administration bill), she and the president would truly have been in the lead on welfare reform. But in politics, timing is everything and there was simply no denying the fact that Shalala and the president were behind the curve.

She used the rest of her brief testimony to review the all but irrelevant administration reform plan and to raise several objections to the Republican bill. She argued that the Contract with America bill ended all adult assistance after two years, even if recipients were willing to work. This claim was based on a tendentious reading of the contract bill, but in any case the bill that Shaw would introduce as the chair's initial bill, most of which was already written by the time Shalala testified, would certainly not have this feature. Her second criticism was that the bill did not have strong child support provisions. I expected her to criticize us because we had decided to introduce a separate child support bill—a criticism with which Shaw agreed, as I was soon to find out. We had been working on child support legislation for nearly two years, but I fervently hoped to enact a welfare reform bill and then work on child support because of time pressures. Watching Shaw's reaction when the secretary brought up child support, I knew that my efforts to keep child support separate from the welfare reform bill would fail. It was now just a matter of time before it too would be added to welfare reform. Score one for the secretary.

Having made a mark with her comments on child support, Shalala brought up two criticisms of our provisions on illegitimacy that also promised to rally support among Democrats. The bill's provision on paternity establishment denied benefits to any child for whom paternity had not been established. She argued, logically enough, that even if the mother cooperated with the state in identifying the father but the state failed to find him and, if necessary, test his DNA, the child would still be denied support. This approach was unfair to the mother and child, especially because it made their benefits dependent on actions of the father and the state. Score two for the secretary.

Pressing her advantage, she then broadened her comments to the issue of reducing illegitimacy. Asserting that welfare dependency would be "reduced significantly" if young people delayed sexual activity and childbearing, she held that it deters pregnancy if teen parents know that to receive welfare they had to live at home, stay in school, and identify the child's father so that child support officials could try to collect child support payments (research showed that many of the men who impregnated teenage girls were two or three or more years older).[15] Combined with work requirements and time limits, this approach to nonmarital births "sends a strong message to young people that welfare will never be the same, that it will be a second chance, not a way of life." Warming to the topic, she stated emphatically that "we strongly disagree with the Contract's approach of denying benefits to children born to mothers under 18." The bill "raises the possibility of sending them to orphanages." By contrast, she and the president "believe that the solution to welfare is not to make children go into foster care or into orphanages; it is to make their parents go to work."[16] Watching her deliver this testimony, and even reading her words in the hearing record after all these years, is to be impressed with the strength of her arguments. Score three for the secretary. But her argument about orphanages was about to receive a forceful rebuttal. After a discussion of the importance of ensuring that low-income families, including those leaving welfare, have health insurance, the secretary ended on a conciliatory note, telling Archer that the administration wanted to work with him and the new Congress to reach agreement on welfare reform.

Given the disadvantages of her political situation—the Democrats having just lost control of both Houses of Congress in part because of the administration's failure to deliver on welfare reform—Shalala did an excellent job of justifying the president's record and of identifying parts of our bill that most Democrats were sure to fight. Despite the points of contention, the secretary's testimony showed the areas of agreement that would have been inconceivable between Republican welfare reformers and any other Democratic administration. Clinton accepted strong work requirements, time limits, probably the end of entitlement, and several of our proposals on teen pregnancy.

But Shalala was operating in a forum in which opposition is invited. The issue on which Democrats had gotten the most traction in the media was orphanages.[17] Thus my staff and I had developed scripts that laid out lines of questioning to clarify the role of orphanages under current policy, under the president's policies, and under the conditions that would be created by Republican welfare reform. Although we had worked with Phil Crane of Illinois to sharply question the secretary on orphanages, she effectively parried his questions. Fortunately we had also worked with Chairman Archer and had developed a script for him to force the secretary to make some important clarifications in her somewhat partisan jibes about Republican policy on orphanages. Archer's goal was to get the secretary to admit that the president's own welfare reform proposal would very likely result in children being removed from their families and placed in orphanages. The basic logic here is that any policy that allows the complete termination of cash benefits to families places them in danger of losing their children, and the president's plan allowed the complete termination of benefits for violations of the work requirement. Archer started innocently enough. Referring to the president's welfare reform plan, he asked: "In the event that a welfare recipient does not show up for work and fails to comply with the work requirement, what sanctions do you contemplate?"[18]

After some preliminary verbiage, the secretary said, "They can be cut off of the program."

After a brief exchange, Archer asked her, "You have said, as I understood you, that all welfare benefits would ultimately be taken away from these people. . . . Then what happens to the children?"

Again after some evasiveness, the secretary was surprisingly forthcoming: "If a parent is not prepared to take responsibility, then the child welfare system must move in to take responsibility for those children."

Archer, probably very pleased with the way things were going, now clarified the secretary's answer and took it one crucial step further: "So you contemplate that . . . the children would be taken away from the parent by the State authority and be taken care of, perhaps in an orphanage?"

Now being as evasive as possible, the secretary began to run through the options the states would have after removing the children from their home. After her disquisition, Archer said: "Now let me be certain about this. Your plan does contemplate that where the mother refuses to comply with the work requirement that the children can be taken away from the mother. . . . Under current law and under your proposal [these children] could be put in orphanages. Is that not correct?"

Archer was showing that precisely what the secretary had been criticizing Republicans for doing—creating conditions under which children could be placed in orphanages—was already routine under current law and was a possible outcome under the administration's own welfare reform plan. Realizing her predicament, the secretary avoided using the word "orphanage" or admitting that the president's plan allowed the use of orphanages. She talked about foster care, about what would happen if the children were babies, about what would happen if they were teenagers, and about "residential settings"—anything but orphanages. But Archer was relentless. After each evasive answer, he brought the question back to whether the president's plan contemplated the use of orphanages. Finally, he interrupted her and asked firmly: "Could they be put into orphanages by the State? That is a simple question. Yes or no?"

The secretary replied: "As part of the overall series of options that a state has before it, the answer is yes."

The secretary did everything possible to avoid admitting that the president's plan could lead to increased use of orphanages. She was responsive to the questions but cleverly and gracefully avoided granting Archer's point, just as she had evaded Crane's. But by returning again and again to the main question, by using very few words in his questions, and by demanding a yes or no answer, Archer was able to wear her down and get the answer that Crane failed to get. The policy for which Republicans had been so roundly criticized by Secretary Shalala and other members of the administration was already in place under current law and would be expanded by the president's own welfare reform proposal. Archer, an old pro at questioning witnesses, had gotten the secretary of HHS in the Clinton administration to admit these facts. Archer gets an A, and if he were still chairman and I were still the welfare staff director, this conclusion might do me some good. Unfortunately, Archer's excellent questioning, and the implications of his questioning, were not mentioned the next day in the *Washington Post* or the *New York Times,* both of which had been only too anxious to print stories about Republicans putting children in orphanages.

As could be expected from her strong testimony about those nasty Republican provisions on illegitimacy, many of the Democrats questioned Secretary Shalala about the "Murray Light" provision.[19] Congressman Gerald Kleczka, a moderate-to-conservative Democrat from Wisconsin who supported most of the provisions in the Republican bill, asked especially compelling questions about the consequences of ending assistance for teen mothers. And the secretary was superb in drawing the distinctions between the president's plan and the Republican plan in their treatment of teen mothers. The secretary's points boiled down to this: Does the American public support rendering teen moms and their babies destitute in order to punish the teen mother for a mistake? Polls consistently showed that the answer was no.[20]

Another notable exchange, also based on careful preparation, occurred during the questioning by Jim McCrery of Louisiana, one of the smartest and hardest-working Republicans in Congress. McCrery, who was a member of our subcommittee and who was playing the lead role in developing our reforms of the SSI children's program, had shown himself to be cool under fire. My staff and I always turned to him when we wanted to question a difficult witness about something complex or technical. McCrery was usually willing to sit down with us before a hearing to prepare the questions. Typically, we would write out a script and meet with him to develop and perfect it. McCrery would then flawlessly use the script to skewer a witness.

An issue that we were becoming more and more concerned about was an estimate, made repeatedly by HHS and then repeated by other Democrats, that under the Republican bill millions of families would lose benefits and be cast into destitution. Senator Daniel Patrick Moynihan of New York was already using very colorful language about kids freezing on the streets, so this kind of estimate from HHS would simply provide more ammunition for Moynihan and others opposing the bill.[21] Creating an estimate like this is a typical ploy in Washington. Create an estimate you like, using more or less reasonable methods, and then get it repeated by policy actors and the media. We needed at the very least to know how HHS arrived at its estimate, so we could discredit it.

McCrery asked Secretary Shalala what "methodology" was used to generate the estimate. The secretary did a commendable job of explaining how the study was done. It was based on an annual study of randomly selected cases from the

AFDC caseload and conducted by HHS and the states to determine whether states were computing AFDC benefits accurately. HHS had simply used these data to estimate the number of children who would lose eligibility for AFDC because of five provisions in the contract bill: Murray Light, the family cap, the elimination of benefits for noncitizens, unestablished paternity, and teen mothers not living with their parents.

McCrery then turned to an issue that was bound to undermine the HHS study in the eyes of committee Republicans. He asked her if the study assumed "a change in behavior due to the change in public policy."[22] She answered that it did not. McCrery's point was that the administration had used a static model to estimate the impacts of Republican policy. In effect, their estimate begged the question. The very reason Republicans supported most of these policies was that we assumed they would change people's behavior. If Congress stopped cash benefits for teen moms, made them stay in school, and made them live at home, surely there would be some teens who would take steps to avoid getting pregnant (or, it must be admitted, have an abortion). Even though the number of teenagers who would make this decision was unknown, it is a decision that is rational and is in accord with a modest body of social science research.[23]

Having gotten the secretary to admit that the HHS estimate assumed no changes in teen behavior despite all these tough policies, McCrery emphasized how the secretary's decision to use a static model captured the profound differences between Republicans and Democrats on welfare reform. If a teen mother has a baby she can't support, Democrats want to rush in and give her welfare benefits. But Republicans want to support policies that assume people will be rational and responsible in their decisionmaking. If a young woman knows that if she has a baby outside of marriage and wants welfare she will have to identify the father, will not get cash support, must live at home, and must continue attending school, she may adjust her behavior (by not having sex or using effective birth control). Republicans had long been opposed to tax estimates based on static models that assume people do not change their behavior depending on how they are taxed. Thus our members were sympathetic to McCrery's line of questioning.

McCrery concluded: "We think public policy changes can affect behavior in this country. That is what the welfare reform debate, I think, should be all about: What public policy changes can we make to positively affect behavior in this country, because we think public policy for the last 30 years has affected behavior negatively."[24]

His time to question had expired, but Shalala could not let this pointed conclusion to McCrery's line of questioning stand unchallenged. She quickly agreed that public policy could have powerful effects on behavior, but the issue for the president and Democrats was "to what extent we wish to punish innocent children as part of the process of changing—"

At which point McCrery cut her off with a sharp rebuke: "Madam Secretary, the current system is punishing innocent children every day. If you deny that, you are missing the point."

The secretary responded that both she and McCrery were in "this business" because they wanted to provide opportunity for innocent children. Both Republicans and Democrats, she said, often used powerful incentives in their bills. Democrats, however, were more willing than Republicans to recognize the "point at which . . . the proposals are too punitive, where we can achieve the same result without being overly punitive." McCrery immediately agreed that policies can be too punitive and stated again that he looked forward to working with the administration to craft policies that are not too punitive.

"Fair enough," said the secretary.

This was questioning of witnesses at its best. McCrery had established every point we hoped for; namely, that the HHS model predicting dire consequences from the Republican bill was flawed, that it was good policy to use strong incentives to influence behavior, and that the incentives in current law had produced bad outcomes for children and it was time for a change. For her part, the secretary answered all his questions but by giving as little ground as possible and managed to get in a few shots of her own. They both get an A.

The next full committee hearing, held on January 11, opened with a panel of "real people."[25] Ari convinced us that it would advance our cause with the media and the public if we held a hearing that featured normal, working people explaining how they would be affected by our reforms. But inviting "real people" to testify is tricky. It is necessary to find out a lot more about a potential witness than simply how they feel about the policy on which we want them to testify. At a minimum, witnesses must have the nerve to talk before the committee with a room full of spectators and to answer questions, many of which cannot be predicted beforehand. In a hearing about fathers, we once had a teenage boy appear before our subcommittee who would not talk, even under the friendliest possible questioning. Finally, after repeated prompting from Chairman Shaw, he said something that directly undermined his father's testimony.[26]

Following these principles of witness selection, we wanted either a welfare mother or someone who had worked with welfare mothers to testify in support of our welfare reform policies, especially our Murray Light proposal. I recalled an African American woman named Virginia Kellogg who worked under contract with the state of Maryland to deliver job readiness services to mothers on welfare. Having worked for many years with mothers trying to leave welfare, she was surprisingly conservative in her views. Thinking she might be a good witness to testify about work and teen pregnancy, I called her and we talked at length on the phone. Her views were exactly as I had remembered them. She strongly supported both the policy of ending cash payments for young unwed mothers and the policy of mandatory work, having spent a number of years trying to help young mothers avoid more pregnancies and prepare for and find jobs. In addition, she was exceptionally fluent and came across as a strong personality. I was convinced that she would be an ideal witness.

Kellogg appeared on the first panel on January 11, along with an elderly couple from Kentucky. The couple had been invited to talk about the Social Security earnings test for workers between ages sixty-five and sixty-nine, which we were trying to repeal. A small business owner from Provo, Utah, was also on the panel to talk about capital gains tax reduction. Testifying last, Kellogg was spectacular. She said that welfare had created a "subculture" of dependency: "Over the years, we have learned not to do for ourselves but to be totally dependent on government. This dependency must be redirected."[27] Looking directly at members of the committee, she continued: "Our moral values must be redefined and we must go back to basics. I say we have had enough enslaving handouts." The hair on my neck was standing straight up. But she wasn't finished yet: "When I was growing up . . . families took care of their own. There were fewer unwed mothers. . . . In today's society, unwed mothers get cash benefits for having children. The federal government has seemingly taken away the families' responsibility." She went on to say that she believed that Congress should end welfare completely within five years.

The reaction to this amazing testimony was entirely predictable. Republicans were invigorated and moved by a middle-aged black woman who, based on her years of experience working with welfare mothers, held views nearly identical to our own. Democrats were dismayed. Here was a phenomenon I had seen before. An African American with conservative views is often dismissed by liberals. Ward Connerly, the African American who had led the fight to repeal racial preferences in California, is a prime example.[28] So now here was a successful black businesswoman telling the committee that cash welfare led to unwed motherhood, created a subculture of dependency, and undermined families. She was Charles Murray and Robert Rector in one package. And best of all, her views were based on her personal experiences as a Southern black female, a mother of two children, and a businesswoman.

Not surprisingly, Democrats tried to undermine her testimony. Rangel spent most of his first round of questioning trying to demonstrate that, because she accepted government contracts, she too was dependent on government. On this line of reasoning, all the members of the committee, including Rangel, were dependent on government. But as it turned out, at that time Kellogg did not have a contract with the state of Maryland to work with welfare mothers, so Rangel could not even make the somewhat dubious point he intended to make. Sander Levin of Michigan used a major part of his time to call attention to a factual error in her testimony. She had testified that many blacks from the South came north to get government jobs. Levin, whose home district was in Michigan where many southern blacks had come to work in the automobile industry, asserted that few blacks took government jobs. But Kellogg told him that she wasn't trying to make a point about dependency induced by working for government; rather, her point was that welfare induced dependency because people got money from government without working. Like Rangel, Levin wasted his time trying to make points that did not even touch on the heart of Kellogg's testimony about illegitimacy, welfare dependency, and terminating benefits.

By contrast with Rangel and Levin, the questioning by Gerald Kleczka, the moderate Democrat from Wisconsin, was constructive and informative. As he had when Secretary Shalala appeared before the committee, Kleczka wanted to explore the Murray Light policy. He asked Kellogg, who had testified that she would end welfare altogether, whether she would favor continuing at least some cash payment to support the child. Kleczka favored requiring the teen mother to live at home and to continue in school as the price of receiving benefits, but cutting off cash welfare was going too far in his view. But Kellogg stuck to her guns: "I certainly do not think they should get benefits because I think that encourages them to be . . . 'grown before they are ready,' and they are certainly not ready to parent. . . . We do not want to encourage that."[29]

As sometimes happens during hearings, when everyone has had an opportunity to question the witnesses, the chair will allow a few members on each side of the aisle to ask a second round of questions. Rangel was anxious to question Kellogg again, so he was recognized for additional questioning. This time Rangel drew a grim picture of life in the ghetto. He characterized a young man and a young woman with low self-esteem, "very little hope," and low motivation living amid drug dealers and crime.[30] The young lady probably gets pregnant, and the young man doesn't have any education or training, doesn't care if he gets arrested, and "doesn't mind shooting up a block knowing that someone will come looking for him, so that even the question of life isn't that important to him." Rangel went on in this vein, further describing the despair, disease, and hopelessness in these neighborhoods. Then he asked Kellogg: "So the whole community here is lacking something, isn't it?"

Kellogg responded: "Well, what I am saying is where did we get this community from? We get the community partly from the welfare system. We have been taking welfare for over 40 years, so we have had plenty of time to create this. . . . I know a woman cannot raise a child on her own, so we have created these communities and partly because of welfare."

The first witness on the second panel was Michael Novak, the George Frederick Jewett Chair in Religion and Public Policy at the American Enterprise Institute. As a theologian and scholar, Novak was without peer. He had won nearly every award for religious writing and thinking and was frequently called to the Vatican for advice on theological matters. Not so incidentally, he had also chaired

a group of distinguished scholars and former senior government officials exploring welfare in America and had written the group's report, published in 1987,
which was one of the most closely reasoned, compelling, and elegant reports on
welfare ever written.[31] Many of that report's recommendations had been incorporated into our bill. Novak made one point. About one-third of his five minutes of testimony was a quote from Thomas Jefferson about the advantages
(Jefferson called them "felicities") that providence and effort had bestowed upon
America. Then, asked Jefferson, "What more is necessary to make us a happy and
a prosperous people?"

Answering his own question, Jefferson wrote: "Still one thing more, fellow citizens: a wise and frugal Government." This, said Novak, was the "original contract
between the people of the United States and their government." "We have wandered far from these principles," Novak went on, but "if the debate of the next
weeks leads this Nation to retrace its steps back to the tracks on which it began,
this shall have been a great and historic debate . . . and [we will] regain the road
which alone leads to peace, liberty and safety."[32]

Although the Republican Contract with America was a document of many
parts, its major goal—reflecting perhaps the major difference between the Democratic and Republican parties—was to shrink the size of government. Novak
had, in five minutes, provided the historical context and captured the political
stakes in the huge undertaking that lay ahead.[33] As Novak said: "There is a kind
of covenant . . . whereby those who receive from the public good must also contribute to the public good." Any Republican member who paid careful attention
to Novak and reflected on his words would be infused with the knowledge that
our work was of great historical importance. There would be far too little reflection on first principles during the hectic days that followed, but years from now
students of American government and politics can return to the words of
Michael Novak to understand what the impending fight was about.

After Michael Boskin, professor of economics at Stanford and a senior fellow
at the Hoover Institution, a conservative think tank affiliated with Stanford, had
testified on capital gains taxes, the next witness was Kate O'Beirne, the vice president for government relations of the Heritage Foundation. O'Beirne, who had
been a senior official at HHS during the second Reagan administration and who
went on to be the Washington editor for the conservative journal *National Review*
and a frequent guest on national news and talk shows, was one of the smartest
people in Washington on welfare issues.

She began her testimony by criticizing the 1988 Family Support Act. She said
that the Congressional Budget Office had estimated before its passage that the
Family Support Act would actually lead to an increase in the welfare rolls. "This
passes for welfare reform in Washington," she observed tartly. But now, under
Republican leadership and the Contract with America, Congress might be able

to "truly revolutionize our welfare system and begin to end the cycle of dependency." To do so would require control of costs, reduction of illegitimacy, and imposition of tough work requirements. "All of these things your Contract plainly addresses," she said. She went on to present a hard-hitting critique of the plethora of welfare programs Congress had created or expanded since the beginning of the War on Poverty. She summarized the problem with current welfare programs with the terse judgment that "the theme has been spend more and demand less."[34] She also made pitches for devolving control of welfare programs to the state and local levels and increasing involvement by nongovernmental institutions such as civic associations and churches. In short, she hit every button that would light up Republican members.

O'Beirne's testimony showed yet again the very substantial advantages of being in the majority. The reforms we were pushing were far more radical than any proposed previously by a congressional majority party. Judging by many of the editorials in the media, especially the *Washington Post* and *New York Times*, it was possible to believe that the true intent of Republican reform was to balance the budget on the backs of the poor, throw poor people into the streets, and cast millions of children into poverty.[35] But because we had almost a free hand to plan the hearings, inside Congress where members were directly exposed to information and arguments, we could defend our proposals with some of the most brilliant and politically astute people in the nation. And because many of the hearings were televised, we could take our message directly into the homes of millions of Americans. Best of all, under committee rules, we could often plan the hearings so that we had two witnesses for every one the Democrats invited.

Given that ten of the twenty-one Republican members of the committee were new and were at best only somewhat familiar with welfare programs, the full committee hearings were successful in acquainting them with the major policies in the welfare reform bill and in demonstrating for both new and old members that our diagnosis of the major welfare problems and the policies we had selected to attack these problems were coherent and could be defended. We were off to a good start.

As the full committee hearings were taking place, we were busily planning extensive hearings at the subcommittee level.[36] We would begin subcommittee hearings with the governors, talking about the flaws in the current system and the need for block grants and a greater emphasis on work. We would then devote separate hearings to illegitimacy; welfare-to-work programs; reforms of the SSI programs for drug addicts and alcoholics, for children, and for noncitizens; and reforms of the child support enforcement program. Because of the central importance of child care in our plans, and because of the controversy over ending so many programs and creating a child care block grant, we planned a joint hearing on child care with the Education Committee. During this hearing, we would also take testimony on our sweeping reforms of child protection programs. Given the widespread interest in welfare reform among both Republicans and Democrats in Congress, we decided to issue an open invitation to members and to devote a complete hearing to testimony from members. Similarly, as the hearings proceeded and the subcommittee was inundated by requests from prominent individuals and organizations to testify, Shaw decided to add an eighth day of hearings and to allow anyone who submitted a request to testify.

In eight days of subcommittee hearings between January 13 and February 6, 1995, we heard 180 witnesses; their testimony occupies more than 2,200 pages of hearings transcript. Witnesses included 46 members of Congress, 3 governors, several state and local officials, a small platoon of professors and scholars, and representatives of many organizations that had an interest in programs for children. The groups that testified included Catholic Charities, the American Academy of Pediatrics, the Service Employees International Union, the Rosebud Sioux Tribe, Bread for the World, the Child Welfare League, the National Black Women's Health Project, the Children's Rights Council, the AIDS Project of East Bay (Oakland, Calif.), Community Legal Services, the Coalition to Stop Welfare Cuts, the Center for Community Change, the Heritage Foundation, and the National Welfare Rights and Reform Union. On February 2 the subcommittee heard every person who had requested to testify: 71 witnesses talked and answered questions for more than eight hours. Across the eight days of hearings held over a period of about two and a half weeks, the subcommittee was in session for over forty-three hours.

Several events that took place during the subcommittee hearings stand out. When Robert Rector testified as the lead Republican witness following the governors and Mary Jo Bane of the administration in the January 13 hearing, I was quietly pleased that we were able to turn the tables on Harold Ford of Tennessee, who during a hearing on welfare reform on August 9, 1994, in his status as chairman of the subcommittee, had ordered Rector to be quiet or be removed from the room.[37] At that hearing Rector testified about his study of total spending on means-tested programs since the War on Poverty began.[38] His study was corroborated in almost every detail by Vee Burke's report from the nonpartisan Congressional Research Service.[39] But Ford didn't want to hear it. After accusing Rector of trying to "distort" the facts by making people think the hearing was about billions of dollars in welfare spending and not the comparatively modest sum spent on Aid to Families with Dependent Children (AFDC), and after telling Rector that his employer, the Heritage Foundation, was itself "a welfare program" because it qualified for reduced taxes as a 501(c)(3) organization, Ford cut Rector off, saying, "We're going to end this right now. . . . This Committee will come to order. Mr. Rector, either leave the committee room now or respect the committee. You will not be recognized anymore."[40] Now, just a few months later, with Shaw chairing the subcommittee and Ford sitting silently, Rector was the center of attention and had the floor to say whatever he liked.

Although there were plenty of moments of quiet satisfaction like this one stemming from our newfound power, we also had several very difficult moments. The hearings were interrupted several times by demonstrations. In one case, Chairman Shaw simply stopped the hearing and had the Capitol police remove the demonstrators from the room. On another occasion, the Children's Defense Fund had arranged for children dressed in skeleton costumes to march into the hearing room. In that case, we simply asked them to stand quietly in the back of the room to make their point—that Republican plans involved starving children.[41]

Another interruption happened during the hearing on nonmarital births on January 20, as James Q. Wilson, a noted social scientist appearing before the subcommittee as part of a panel that included two other males, was responding to a question from Republican Jennifer Dunn of Washington. Two women leaped up from the audience, walked toward the front of the hearing room, and began shouting about white males telling women what to do. Shaw told the ladies in a calm voice that they were guests and should be quiet during the proceedings or he would have them removed from the room. Harold Ford chose this moment to express his solidarity with the demonstrators: "Mr. Chairman, they sound pretty good to me. It sounds as if we ought to let them speak and replace these three men."[42]

After Shaw reminded Ford that the "Ranking Member" (meaning Ford) should support the chairman when he was trying to maintain order, Ford said that he wanted to maintain order while simultaneously proposing to abandon order: "Mr. Chairman, I do support you in maintaining order. But I think they have made the point that we have made on this Democratic side of the aisle. We have three males talking about problems that women are faced with in the poor communities of our society. I respect all three of them. . . . I don't think they are that much of an expert."[43] After Jennifer Dunn pointed out that she was a woman and that she was "very interested" in what the witnesses were saying, Shaw, who was silently seething, commented. "We will have a balanced hearing"—two mothers who had been on welfare were on the next panel—"but we are going to proceed in an orderly fashion." After Dunn repeated her question, Wilson began his response by saying: "I apologize, Mr. Chairman, for being male, but it was a matter beyond my control."[44]

Perhaps the most embarrassing moment for us in the hearings was almost entirely our own fault. As we were planning the January 20 hearing on nonmarital births, I contacted William Bennett, who had given us such difficulty during our writing of HR 3500 and also the Contract with America bill. But we now appeared to be on the same side. He had taken a strong public position on illegitimacy as the leading cause of welfare growth and many other domestic problems and was a very forceful speaker. He not only agreed to testify but also volunteered to head a panel of witnesses to testify on illegitimacy. He wanted us to invite Glenn Loury, a black economist from Boston University, and James Q. Wilson, the widely admired social scientist. Senator Moynihan once referred to Wilson as the "smartest man in America."[45] When I told Bennett we would need to add a witness invited by Democrats to the panel, he balked and said he wanted just himself and Loury and Wilson to testify so they could make a coherent case without disruption. I told him I would get back with him.

Shaw and I discussed at length Bennett's request to have three Republican witnesses and no Democratic witnesses on the panel. We both knew that Democrats would strongly object to not having a witness on the panel and would probably protest publicly at the hearing. But Shaw decided that as long as Democrats could invite several of their own witnesses to participate in subsequent panels at the hearing, we would go ahead with Bennett's recommendation.

As expected, at the beginning of the hearing on January 20 in front of another packed house in Room 1100, Ford, Levin, and Rangel protested our decision to refuse to allow a Democratic witness on the panel. Rangel claimed that Democrats had been assured by both Chairman Shaw and staff (meaning me) that they could have one witness on every panel.[46] Rangel was referring to a meeting Shaw and I had held with Ford and Debra Colton, the top Democratic staffer for our subcommittee, in early January, during which both Ford and Debra thought we had told them they could have one witness on every panel. I could not remember exactly what had been said, but Shaw was nearly certain that we guaranteed witnesses at every hearing but not on every panel. Nothing was given in writing, and committee rules did not require that the minority have a witness on every panel. In any case, we opened ourselves to legitimate criticism by allowing Bennett to set the terms of his group's testimony (I doubt that either Loury or Wilson knew anything about these circumstances). I'm still torn today because I was hopeful that the panel would give persuasive testimony and bring credibility to our plans to enact Murray Light and the family cap. But it was yet another good lesson in being the majority: be careful what you say and put everything in writing. I think to this day that we misled the Democrats and that they sincerely thought we were going back on our word.

The Bennett-Loury-Wilson hearing did not turn out as I thought it would. Bennett cannot have been too pleased with the testimony of Wilson and Loury, because both were skeptical about whether Murray Light and the family cap would actually work. They were not against trying them on a limited basis but were clear in saying that there was little evidence that would lead one to expect big impacts. Loury's testimony on this point was superb. He compared ending welfare benefits to reduce nonmarital births to trying to push thread back into a piece of unraveled cloth. Even if pulling the thread would "unravel the garment, pushing on the [thread] will not put the weave back together again." Thus "we must not be too sanguine, almost arrogant, about our ability to push and pull and manipulate and maneuver in order to fix what is a very subtle and complicated problem."[47] I thought at the time, and I still think, that the term "almost arrogant" revealed Loury's personal views about Republican enthusiasm for cutting the welfare benefits of young mothers.

If anything, Wilson was even more frank in his views. As the panel was winding down, Rangel asked the witnesses if they supported cutting off cash welfare for young mothers. Because Rangel's time was up and the next panel was waiting, Shaw asked the panel to respond in writing to Rangel's question. Wilson subsequently sent a letter to the subcommittee saying that he would support "a few carefully controlled and carefully evaluated experiments" but that until experiments had been conducted—and by implication had produced evidence that the cutoffs would reduce illegitimacy—he would "oppose a blanket Federal ban that would deny benefits."[48] In other words, he directly opposed both our Murray Light policy of terminating cash benefits for mothers under age eighteen and our family cap provision of banning states from increasing benefits when mothers already on welfare have a baby, the very provisions he had been invited to support.

Here is a prime example of why social scientists often make indifferent witnesses in a hearing over highly partisan issues. Both Loury and Wilson were social scientists in the single most important sense: they based their positions on policy issues on good evidence. Both were so concerned about illegitimacy and its effect on the nation that they were willing to support tough policies, but both also knew that there was only modest evidence that cutting benefits would reduce illegitimacy, would "reweave the garment." Until such time as stronger evidence existed, they supported limited experiments but no more. Clearly, good social scientists are deeply flawed; they believe in being guided by empirical evidence rather than political philosophy. You just can't trust them.

By contrast, Bennett was gung ho to cut off benefits. His major rationale was the economists' dictum that you get more of whatever you subsidize. He claimed that the endgame of welfare reform was that "sometime soon we want welfare to end." He continued, "We have already lost large parts of an entire generation because of the terrible human wreckage left in its [welfare's] wake. Enough is enough. It is time to pull the plug—for the sake of the children. Let's get to it."[49] This is analysis by outburst and assertion, exactly the techniques that Bennett had used against us when he was supporting the Talent-Faircloth-Rector bill against HR 3500. On balance, if a major purpose of the hearings was to establish the wisdom of our provisions on illegitimacy, I don't think we won many converts.

This is especially the case since the testimony of Rebecca Blank, a professor at Northwestern University, whom we had banished from the first panel, was such a spirited attack on both Murray Light and the family cap.[50] Blank, a former member of Clinton's Council of Economic Advisers who is generally considered to be one of the best labor economists in the nation, completely rejected the idea of cutting benefits to reduce illegitimacy. "Once you control for other variables," she said, the cause of declining marriage and rising illegitimacy is not welfare: "The effects are either small or simply nonexistent."[51] Rather, she argued, illegitimacy has complex roots and is related to women's ability to find jobs, the decline in men's ability to support a family because of low and falling wages, and the decline of social stigma against illegitimacy. If the benefits of Republican policy were uncertain, she argued, cutting or terminating the benefits of young mothers and their babies would have "devastating costs." These would include an increase in abortion, women being forced to live with boyfriends who abused them, and an increase in homelessness. She referred to our policy as a "scorched earth" approach to illegitimacy.[52] Blank concluded by urging the committee to "recognize the complexity of this problem and resist simple, easy, and wrong answers that only increase economic need."[53]

These are the standard arguments against the Murray approach. Although reading both her oral and written testimony is in itself quite persuasive, the full effect could only be achieved by watching her performance before the committee. I suspect that neither of them would approve of the comparison, but Blank reminded me of Kate O'Beirne. Both talk exceptionally fast while conveying an atmosphere of knowledge and aggressive readiness to defend their views. Even members of Congress would be well advised to hesitate before publicly disagreeing with either of them, and indeed the members were noticeably cautious in their questioning of both women.

The Blank arguments against Murray Light and the family cap simply showed that the evidence that welfare caused illegitimacy was circumstantial. But it was still undeniable that young unmarried mothers often received AFDC cash, Food Stamps, Medicaid, and sometimes housing and other benefits. At the very least, welfare enabled them to sustain a lifestyle based on nonwork and nonmarriage. Until policymakers agreed to try cutting off cash welfare to see whether illegitimacy would decline, the real relationship between welfare and illegitimacy could not be known. The clear fact that separated Republicans from Democrats—and Murray from Blank—was that Republicans and Murray were willing to risk increased hardship for young unwed mothers and their children as the cost of finding out whether reducing welfare would reduce the number of such mothers and children. Democrats were not.

The case for Murray Light was perhaps best explained by Jim Talent, the major House sponsor of the provision, in his testimony before our subcommittee on January 30.[54] As the fine lawyer he was, Talent laid out his approach to denying cash benefits to unwed mothers in dispassionate and systematic fashion for the record. First, he pointed out that the provision in the subcommittee bill would apply only to unwed mothers under age eighteen, at most 5 percent of the caseload. Second, the mothers would continue to qualify for Medicaid, school lunch, and Food Stamps on an entitlement basis and many other programs such as housing that relied on annually appropriated funds. Third, states would receive a block grant of the money saved by denying the cash benefit to young mothers in their state. State officials were free to use this money to help the mothers in whatever ways they thought appropriate except by giving them cash. They could use the money to set up group homes for the mothers, to provide in-kind benefits such as child care or job training, or to facilitate adoption.

The point was to force the mothers to confront the fact that living alone, often in "drug- and gang-infested neighborhoods," they would have a very difficult time providing an appropriate rearing environment for their child. Moreover, Talent argued firmly that removing the cash benefits would be a disincentive for unwed births. As a result, over time the number of these births would decline. His conclusion was a nice summary of the entire movement to end welfare's cash incentive for illegitimate births: "Reducing the out of wedlock birthrate must be the highest priority of any welfare reform legislation. Without it, we run the risk of merely making the current system a more efficient destroyer of families. Without it, we will lose our best chance, and maybe our last chance, to attack the problem of illegitimacy, by basing our welfare system on the dignity of work and the power of healthy families."[55]

Perhaps the most astounding testimony presented during the subcommittee hearings came during the February 3 hearing on child care and child protection programs.[56] Based on a tip from Cassie Bevan, a long-time House staffer whom I had known for twenty years and who would join our subcommittee staff in March 1996, I contacted Patrick Murphy, a lawyer who headed the Cook County (Chicago) Public Guardian program. In that capacity, he was the chief lawyer for the City of Chicago charged with protecting abused and neglected children and prosecuting their parents. A self-described "liberal Democrat," Murphy was more scathing about the effects of nonmarital births than any other witness— including Rector and Bennett. In recent years, he said, the circumstances in which these children live had deteriorated so badly that they constitute "a different world." The families were not just poor but actually constituted an "underclass." If something was not done, the problem of child abuse and neglect would "explode, to haunt the rest of us and our children for generations to come." Even worse, "as a society [we] are flushing the lives of many potentially talented human beings right down the toilet." He was forthright in supporting our Murray Light proposal: "Legislation to prevent any person without a high school diploma under the age of eighteen from receiving any kind of AFDC benefits for children born out of wedlock."[57]

As might be expected, Democrats aggressively questioned Murphy, trying to get him to move away from his support for Murray Light. Ford, for example, pressed Murphy repeatedly, emphasizing especially the point that children would suffer. But Murphy refused to budge: "I am very frustrated because everything we have tried has made the problem worse." He recommended setting a date certain for terminating benefits. "I think we have to make it as difficult as possible for children to have children." When an exasperated Ford asked, "What about these kids in the meantime?" Murphy responded, sounding exactly like Jim McCrery during his lively debate with Secretary Shalala: "The kids are suffering now, today. They are coming into court [and] ending up in prison." When Ford cut him off, saying sarcastically: "So there is nothing wrong with more and more kids suffering in the meantime," Murphy shot back, "I think there would be less suffering because I think many girls, because they are girls and not young women, would delay childbearing to a later age. One of the things that we are pushing are the same microeconomic realities that you and I face onto a teenager, and it is hard. It is very hard to say that, but if you sit in court day in and day out and see the shambles of people's lives, I think we have to think hard." Shaw and other Republicans were amazed to hear a Democrat talk this way. In closing the panel, Shaw said, "I have very little opportunity to associate myself with the remarks of a liberal Democrat, but, Mr. Murphy, I think you have a very clear picture of what is going on."[58]

By the time the last witness had testified in the eighth hearing on February 6, we were frantically working to get ready for the subcommittee's markup session, during which Shaw's initial bill would become public. My staff and I were finishing the drafting of the chair's bill, writing Shaw's speech that would accompany the unveiling of his markup bill, writing remarks for my press briefing to explain the bill, preparing the elaborate markup documents that had to be distributed to subcommittee members, and preparing my detailed overview of the bill that would be given at the beginning of the markup. These somewhat frenzied activities prevented us from taking a break to reflect on the hearings for more than a moment. The single most important purpose of the hearings was to expose all our members to the major provisions in the bill and to show them that the provisions could be strongly defended. Once the debates began in earnest during the markup and floor fights, the Republican members would need to know the arguments themselves—perhaps even think of their own arguments—and use them to fend off the criticisms that were certain to come from Democrats and reporters. The hearings had been a tutorial on the issues involved in welfare reform, on the provisions of our bill, and on the arguments being used by both sides. In this sense, the hearings were a great success.

A second goal of the hearings was to show the Democrats, the press, and other critics that every provision in our sweeping bill was a reasonable response to real problems with our welfare system. Although Democrats wanted to define "welfare" as "AFDC," we were determined to look far beyond simply the AFDC program and its tepid work requirements. The hearings established that there were major problems with AFDC and SSI and that there were opportunities to greatly improve child care, child protection, and child support enforcement. In every case, Republicans had carefully thought out solutions, often controversial to be sure, but consistent with Republican philosophy and capable of being strongly defended.

Finally, I think we achieved our goals in a way that showed the Democrats that we would be fair to them. Shaw and Archer had been evenhanded in running the hearings, and Democrats were given almost all the time they wished to pose questions to witnesses. We also invited every witness that Democrats wanted to invite and even invited a number of witnesses ourselves who opposed some of the items on our agenda. We created a problem with the Bennett panel by not allowing a Democratic witness on the panel, but we had the estimable Professor Blank on the next panel. And the fact that we provided a forum for any member of Congress and any member of the public who wanted to testify was an especially powerful statement of how far we were willing to go to be certain that everyone and every point of view was heard.

So the stage was set. The time was at hand to introduce our bill, and the revolution it promised, to the legislative gauntlet.

## CHAPTER SEVEN

# The Battle
# in the House,
# Part II: Markups

If the statute books are slightly open during a legislative hearing, they are wide open during a markup. There are many exciting times during a bill's journey from obscurity to law, but only action on the House floor and the House-Senate conference are more exciting than a markup. Especially when major legislation is at hand, the number of organizations and individuals who try to influence the outcome is enormous. The political parties themselves often have a major interest in the outcome; many members of the committees of jurisdiction and some members outside the committee almost always have specific provisions they want enacted as part of the bill; several categories of lobbyists and special interest groups will be blitzing Congress with e-mails, telephone calls, and as many visits with members and staff as they can arrange; and the public may also express itself directly through e-mails, phone calls, and visits to members or indirectly through lobbying organizations or polls.

Inside this cacophony of interests, those experienced in the legislative process focus first on the chair's markup bill. Some of the players will be fighting to keep their favored provision in the mark as it embarks on its congressional journey, others will be laboring to get their provisions in the bill, and still others will be fighting to remove or change provisions they don't like. All will continue trying to influence the bill at every stage in its congressional odyssey.

A host of rules and traditions are in play that shape the committee markup and how the bill can be formulated and changed. The chair of the committee has the privilege and power to introduce the bill that forms the basis of the markup. It would be difficult to overemphasize how important this first bill is or how important the chair is to writing the mark. In our case, because of the subcommittee structure of Ways and Means, E. Clay Shaw Jr., the chairman of the

Human Resources Subcommittee, would have the privilege and responsibility of writing the first mark.

There is considerable art in assembling a markup bill. The chair will usually talk first with members of her own party on the committee and include as many of the provisions favored by them as possible. If members have their provisions in the bill, they are usually willing to accept provisions they don't particularly like. Even more important, they will help the chair fight to pass the bill. If the members don't have provisions of their own in the bill, they will still usually support the chair because they want his help in the future.

Two forces bind the majority members together and the minority members together, so the chair and the ranking minority member usually can count on substantial support from their respective members. First, there will be many markups, and he who is faithful to the chair and party position can count on support for his provisions in the future. Second, Republicans and Democrats really do see the world differently. The difference in perspective begins with Republicans wanting lower taxes and less government and Democrats generally wanting more government and more taxes to support it. In the case at hand, Republican and Democratic welfare philosophies could hardly have been more distinctive. Republicans were determined to create strong work requirements and strong measures against illegitimacy, to eliminate most benefits for noncitizens, and to cut spending. Many of these were long-standing goals of the Republican Party and, although Republicans generally are less personally invested in social policy than Democrats, most of our subcommittee members were nonetheless highly motivated by their philosophical views.

At crucial times individual members decided their course of action and urged other members to decide theirs based largely on their belief that Republican welfare philosophy was sorely needed by the nation and that the elections of 1994 had given members the only chance they would have in their lifetimes to enact deep reforms and alter the very basis of the nation's social policy. Shaw, Bill Archer, and Newt Gingrich could count on this overarching philosophical energy to help keep Republicans united. And Shaw's markup document contained the provisions that released this pent-up energy which originated in a very deep philosophical well.

In 1995 one other powerful force bound House Republicans together: after forty years in the wilderness, we were now the majority party. Members understood that our fate depended on unity. The logic of lawmaking in the House is that a determined and unified majority can work its will. On vote after vote over the next two years and beyond, House Republicans enjoyed an invisible bond caused by the common understanding that in unity lies power and victory. As events were about to demonstrate, the Subcommittee on Human Resources, the full Committee on Ways and Means, and the entire House of Representatives were populated by Republicans who were determined to fight Democrats and not each other.

Because writing good amendments requires that members and staff understand the bill, the Ways and Means Committee had developed a tradition of preparing elaborate and informative markup documents and delivering them at least twenty-four hours before the markup session. Especially in the case of a big bill—like welfare reform—members and their staffs have to know precisely what is in the bill. Unfortunately, reading legislative language is like reading *Finnegan's Wake*. The first qualification for a lawyer who works in the Office of Legislative Counsel is to have mastered the art of obscure writing. If members and staff were dependent on understanding a bill based on the legislative text, especially after having the text for only a day or two, markups would be equivalent to staggering around in the dark.[1]

The markup document, written in plain language, that we presented to the subcommittee in early February, had five titles.[2] Title I was the repeal of Aid to Families with Dependent Children (AFDC), the creation of the new welfare block grant, the work requirements, the time limit, the provisions on illegitimacy reduction, and the state data-reporting requirements; Title II contained the block grant on child protection; Title III contained our provisions restricting welfare benefits for noncitizens; and Title IV our provisions for ending Supplemental Security Income (SSI) benefits for alcoholics and drug addicts and for reforming the children's SSI program. Title V would contain the child support provisions, but they were not yet completely drafted when the markup began. The markup document for the four titles of the bill presented to the subcommittee was fifty pages long.

Although the markup procedure varies somewhat across committees, Ways and Means follows a regular order of events. The chair begins by welcoming members to the markup session and then gives a brief opening statement about the need for the bill and how perfectly his bill meets that need. He then turns to the senior member of the minority and asks him to make an opening statement. Usually, this member assaults the bill the chairman has placed before the committee.[3]

After these opening statements, the chairman asks the majority staff director to "walk through" the bill by explaining each of the provisions to the members. The walk-through is an important part of the markup for two reasons. First, the staff director, who has worked with the chair and senior members of the committee to develop the bill and has supervised both the drafting of the bill by Legislative Counsel and the preparation of the markup document, is usually the person present at the markup who knows the most about current law and about how the chair's bill amends current law. He is in a good position to, in classic professorial style, instruct the members about every provision in the bill and to answer the questions they raise. Staff directors understand the legislative process, know a lot about the statutes under their committee's jurisdiction, and are often also expert in the subject matter addressed by the statute undergoing revision. If the staff director does not meet one or more of these standards, she could very well find herself embarrassed during a markup.

Once the staff director's walk-through is completed, members ask questions of the staff director. Under Ways and Means tradition, the questions are supposed to address only issues of clarification. The purpose of this procedure is both to ensure that everyone understands the chair's mark before the fighting begins and to keep the staff director from engaging in arguments over the justification of provisions in the bill with members of the minority party. However, there is a hazy line between questions of clarification and rhetorical questions that challenge specific provisions in the bill, thereby often putting the staff director in position to defend the bill, never mind committee traditions or rules.

As we prepared for the markups, there might have been a touch of nervousness among our staff and members, but mostly we wanted to be certain to follow committee and House rules and to be prepared to respond appropriately to any parliamentary situation and to the substantive arguments against our bill that the Democrats were certain to raise. An old aphorism has it that, in court, if you have the facts on your side, you argue the facts; if you have the law on your side, you argue the law; if you have neither, you shout and pound and even dance on the table. In a markup, the minority usually does not have the votes, so they often can't change the bill very much through the amendment process. Thus they use parliamentary rules to confuse and confound the majority or to tie the proceedings in knots. If minority members use the rules to disrupt and delay, it is usually because they know they cannot win but also because they believe their rights have been violated by the majority. For this reason, Clay Shaw intended to scrupulously observe the minority's rights.

To avoid the confusion and delay that might result from mistaken parliamentary procedure and to prevent any of us from looking like rookies during our maiden markups, Ways and Means Committee staff director Phil Moseley decided to give the staff directors of all five Ways and Means subcommittees a refresher course in how to conduct a markup. To fill us with procedural knowledge, Phil invited an expert from the Congressional Research Service, Judy Schneider, to conduct the briefing. In Congress, among both members and staff, Schneider is a legend. In addition to publishing more than a hundred papers on congressional organization and operations, she gives great speeches, is outrageously funny, and seems to know everything that ever happened in a committee markup and on the House and Senate floors. She talked about Jefferson's rules of procedure as if Jefferson had been her friend and adviser—or she his.[4] Best of all, in the ten or so years I had known her, I never had a clue about her politics. The moment we took over Congress, she was meeting with us and taking phone calls by the dozens to give us advice about how to use House and committee rules properly. As far as I could tell, she simultaneously remained on good terms with her former primary clients, the now minority Democrats.

At the time of our meeting in early February, I was so busy that I was not at all interested in meeting with Schneider. But once the meeting started and I heard a few of her stories about how the minority could use the rules against the majority, I knew hers was a life-or-death crash course. This was especially so for the committee counsel Chris Smith, whose function it was to make sure that the committee operated smoothly during hearings, during markups, and when we took a bill to the House floor.

In the meeting, Schneider reviewed House and committee rules on hearings and markups, the documents we should prepare for markups, and the specific procedures we should follow during markups. We also role-played exactly what we would do during the markup and then discussed and role-played various difficult situations that could arise. We also had extensive discussions on how we would handle demonstrations from the public during our hearings and markups. This discussion was primarily for the benefit of our Subcommittee on Human Resources, because feelings were running so high against our welfare reform bill.

In the days leading up to the markup on February 13, my staff and I were consistently putting in fifteen-hour days. Hours like these are the only way known to man in which it is possible to avoid the D.C.-area traffic. Whereas it took an hour or so to drive from my home in Rockville, Maryland, during rush hour, I consistently made it in twenty-three minutes door-to-door during the halcyon days of the Contract with America and the Republican revolution in the House. Unfortunately, when these all-consuming days ended in August 1996, I had to give up my leisurely trips to the office at five in the morning and my equally leisurely return home at ten or eleven at night.

Despite the hours, our merry little band of five intrepid workers on the subcommittee maintained high discipline and spirits. Our offices were located in Room B-317 of the Rayburn House Office building, adjacent to the subcommittee hearing room, B-318, and an entire building away from the main committee offices on the first floor of Longworth. This separation gave both a sense of independence from the main committee and welcome isolation from the general hubbub of committee activities. Margaret Pratt, the office manager, was an old-school secretary who could type well over a hundred words a minute, could take shorthand, rarely made a mistake, and was fanatical about doing her work on time and correctly; Matt Weidinger was the original model for the Energizer Bunny and had the IQ of a graduate of the University of Chicago, which he was; and Jona Turner, our legislative assistant, was new to Congress but smart and talented and willing to take on every needed task, and was highly dependable. We also enjoyed help with every task at hand from Scot Smith, our office assistant.

I tried to arrange our workload so that Margaret and Scot never stayed late and the rest of the staff shared late hours. As markup approached, however, some nights everyone except Margaret stayed until ten or eleven or later. One morning at about two o'clock Matt and I were putting the final touches on a markup document when a question arose about current law. We rummaged through law volumes in the subcommittee library to make sure we had the detail correct. As three o'clock approached, I said to Matt: "This is ridiculous. Here we are at three in the morning looking up some obscure provision of law. Why do we do this?"

Matt, looking at me in utter seriousness, said: "Because we work for the Ways and Means Committee."

We finished the first four titles of the chairman's bill in good order and distributed them to subcommittee members late in the day on February 12, in anticipation of the markup on February 13. But there were two problems. First, given the hours we were putting in, there was no time to prepare two bills and two markup documents, so we were going to be at risk for lots of secondary amendments during the markup.[5] Second, we were not able to complete the drafting of the child support provision, which would become Title V of the bill, before the subcommittee markup began. But because of the commitment to bring all ten Contract with America bills to the floor within a hundred days, we were so wedded to our schedule that we went ahead with the markup on Wednesday, February 13, as planned. We promised to distribute the child support title as soon as it was finished.

The morning of the big day dawned well after I was at my desk. Shaw's plan was to present opening statements (one by each side), conduct the walk-through, answer any questions about the bill, and then complete the amendment process for Title I, the most controversial part of the bill, by the end of the first day. To do so, he called for the markup to begin at noon and was prepared to keep the subcommittee in session until well after midnight if necessary. We would then meet again Thursday and Friday until the amendments to the other three titles were completed and the bill had been passed. Our fear was that the Democrats, hating the bill as they did, would be dilatory so as to disrupt our schedule. Shaw cheerfully put out the word, in plenty of time for members to inform their spouses, that we would work as late Friday night as necessary, and even on Saturday and Sunday if need be, to complete work on the bill before Monday.

Under these strict injunctions, the Subcommittee on Human Resources convened at noon on February 13, 1995, in Room B-318 of the Rayburn House Office Building for its historic markup. The room was packed with over a hundred people, heavily weighted—as B-318 always was—toward liberals and advocates strongly opposed to, even horrified by, the Republican bill. Every member of the subcommittee was in attendance. C-SPAN was televising the proceedings; America could watch Republicans and Democrats engaging in raucous debate while attempting to create a new welfare system. The old days of the House Un-American Activities Committee were here again.

Shaw opened by welcoming everyone and reviewing the schedule, including his intent to work all weekend if necessary to finish the bill. He then presented a somewhat elaborate opening statement that combined the talk we had written for him with several things that apparently were on his mind. He began by emphasizing that Democrats, including those on the subcommittee and many in the Clinton administration, agreed with us on many of the major tenets of our bill. He emphasized points of commonality: there was clear bipartisan agreement that the current system was broken and, he said, Donna Shalala, secretary of the Department of Health and Human Services, told him that the administration was in agreement with us on "probably" 80 percent of our bill.

Shaw then singled out the Murray Light provision, arguing that even after losing the cash these young mothers retained their entitlement to Food Stamps and Medicaid.[6] Withdrawing the cash was necessary to provide a "disincentive . . . to make them think twice before they engage in any self-destructive activities." He then recounted the principles on which our bill was based, including dignity through work, personal responsibility, and state flexibility, each of which he aggressively defended. He ended by again reviewing the subcommittee schedule, including a pointed reference to the possibility of weekend sessions, and by making an appeal for respect and order in the markup. He promised to be fair with Democrats and to give them markup documents at the earliest possible moment, to hold votes when all or most members were present, and to give members plenty of time to explain their amendments and to raise questions of clarification.

Harold Ford of Tennessee, the former chairman of the subcommittee and a liberal Democrat, was not in high spirits. Only a year earlier he had announced that as long as he was chairman of the subcommittee no mother would ever be forced to leave welfare unless she was guaranteed a job paying at least $9 an hour.[7] This dictum struck me at the time as the perfect embodiment of liberal policy on welfare. Never mind a person's qualifications, never mind the market, Congress could just wave its magic wand and a few million high school dropouts with no job experience would suddenly command $9 an hour. Let's see, if we assume half the mothers had left welfare in 1996 for these $9-an-hour jobs, that would be about 2.5 million mothers at a little more than $18,000 a year, or a total of $258 billion in wages. If the mothers can't produce $258 billion in labor value, where does the money come from? Ford was not troubled by calculations of this sort.

The American people, he said, "expect us to protect our children, hold their parents accountable, but don't make children pay for the mistakes of their parents." The language was revealing, especially the reference to "our" children. As the nation's child protection system shows, government is not a good parent. And as the history of AFDC showed all too clearly, unconditional government payments to young, able-bodied parents contributed to dependency in mothers, a rise in female-headed families, and ultimately disorder in entire communities. The major goal of Republican welfare reform was to smash this noncontingent entitlement approach to welfare and to make it clear that individual responsibility meant that the children were the direct responsibility of their parents. In the future, mothers would have to work or prepare for work or they would lose their cash benefit. Fathers would have to pay child support or face a host of penalties, including suspension of their driver's license, seizure of their assets, and incarceration. Government would provide some protection against the consequences of their irresponsible behavior in having children they couldn't support—protection such as temporary cash, child care, health insurance, Food Stamps, education and training, and cash wage supplements in the form of the Earned Income Tax Credit—but the new system would make many of these benefits contingent on work. As Ford was showing, he and many Democrats were not ready to support such a system.

When Ford had finished, Shaw turned to me to begin the walk-through. The events leading up to this historic markup, combined with the pressure and tension of the walk-through and the tough questioning by Democrats that was certain to follow, made this one of the most thrilling moments of my life. The Human Resources Subcommittee had been the source of the ideas and policies that had grown and matured since Shaw and Gingrich's staffer Ed Kutler and I had worked on the Wednesday Group reports and even since Hank Brown—then the ranking Republican of the Human Resources Subcommittee and later a U.S. senator—and I had begun preparing for the debate over the Family Support Act in 1987. Indeed, our initial ideas, expanded by the ideas of many other Republicans, had been transformed into the most radical welfare reform bill ever considered by a congressional committee. Shaw and I had been working together for four years on not just the ideas but also the actual language in what was now, amazingly, his mark.

But in a larger sense, I had been thinking and writing about the idea of individual responsibility since my days as one of the few conservatives at the University of North Carolina at Chapel Hill. My many years of working with and studying poor families had gradually created the belief that most of them were entirely capable of supporting themselves and that only a demanding welfare system would break their dependency on government benefits. Despite the great complexity of the welfare system itself and the hundreds of empirical studies it had generated, at bottom the biggest problem of welfare was simple. Exactly as President Franklin D. Roosevelt had predicted when he inadvertently laid the groundwork for dependency in 1935, the welfare system had broken the spirit of many recipients and had fostered the creation of traditions and habits that were the opposite of those held dear by most Americans and on which the country had been built.

Sitting in that chair before the members of the mighty Ways and Means Committee, I realized that the five Democrats on the subcommittee would mount the first defense of everything we wanted to replace. We had the votes and the discipline, so the outcome in the subcommittee, and probably the full committee too, was preordained. But the real issue for me on this day was the validity of our policies and the ideas that undergirded them. In the weeks and months ahead, as the battle raged, could our members defend the radical Republican policies and show the nation, through media reports, town hall meetings, and speeches, and in a few cases—such as on this very day—through the images of television, that the Republican proposals were consistent with American values and that the old welfare system was not only inconsistent with American values but actually undermined them? All this was at stake, and given committee rules, without ever receiving the vote of a single American citizen, I had the opportunity to explain and defend these ideas at the very beginning of a process that could lead to a revolution in American social policy.

For the next hour I explained the first four titles of Shaw's bill to the members of the subcommittee and the procedures that House Republicans had developed to bring the bill to the floor. After the walk-through was completed, the members asked me questions for about two hours. As Shaw had promised, he allowed as many rounds of questioning as the Democrats wanted. Barbara B. Kennelly (Connecticut), Ford, and Pete Stark of California questioned four times (for up to five minutes each), Sander M. Levin (Michigan) five times, and Charles B. Rangel (New York) six times. Our members questioned many fewer times than Democrats because they wanted to be certain Democrats got every last question answered and would have no basis to complain about subcommittee procedures.[8]

During the questioning, Rangel asked the Clinton administration to send an expert on welfare to the witness table so that Democrats would have someone at the table who could put a Democratic spin on questions and answers. If they could prevent it (and under committee rules they could), Democrats did not want to allow a Republican staffer to be the only person answering questions and providing information to the committee. So the administration sent Wendell Primus to the table. Wendell was a Ph.D. economist, an expert on the budget and congressional budget process, exceptionally knowledgeable about research on social programs, and in firm possession of a deep knowledge of social policy and federal statutes, especially the Social Security Act. He was also a master of spin. The members, both Democrats and Republicans, had a great deal of respect for Wendell, although Republicans were aware that he was a partisan liberal and would favor more social spending and new programs whenever he could.

For the remainder of the markup, Wendell sat alongside me at the table, and the Democrats had their staff voice. But Wendell was not, of course, able to change the substance or direction of the proceedings. A thoroughly Republican bill was before the subcommittee and, as much as Wendell hated the bill (he would resign from the administration when Clinton signed the final bill eighteen months later), as staff director of the subcommittee I was in a strong position to offset anything Wendell said to the subcommittee that might reflect unfavorably on our bill.

Based on the questioning, it became clear that the Democrats' case against our bill consisted of two major arguments. First, as expected, Democrats emphasized that the bill put children at risk. This strand in their approach was clear in Ford's opening statement and remained a major part of their questioning. Second, and somewhat surprisingly, Democrats charged that the bill was weak on work. My first reaction to this charge was that it was hugely, monstrously hypocritical. In 1988 Ways and Means Democrats would not even let Republicans place participation standards in the Family Support Act, let alone actual work requirements. Now, after refusing to create strong work requirements for all the intervening years, Democrats suddenly not only believed in work but attacked our work provisions as too weak.

Unfortunately, Democrats were right. Our work requirements were too weak. Shaw and I understood that, but we were in a negotiating stance with the governors and we agreed to relatively weak work requirements as the price for their promise to support other aspects of the bill, especially flat and even slightly reduced funding in the block grant and provisions they truly detested on fighting illegitimacy. Moreover, for every percentage point by which we raised the work requirement, the Congressional Budget Office would estimate that costs for administration and child care would rise by about $28 million a year. Thus if we raised participation rates by 10 percentage points, the additional cost would be around $1.4 billion over five years. Increasing the work participation rate was expensive.[9]

As Shaw had promised, the subcommittee held to a grueling timetable to complete the markup on schedule. On the three days between February 13 and 15, the subcommittee met for a little over twenty-four hours, with brief time off for members to go to the Capitol to vote. During that time, we conducted the time-consuming welfare walk-through and then an amending process during which we considered forty amendments, thirty-four sponsored by Democrats and six by Republicans. Shaw required the committee to begin with Title I and then proceed through the bill in orderly fashion, closing out each title to additional amendments when all amendments for that title had been considered.

By successfully implementing Shaw's plan of completing the walk-though, questioning, and amendments to Title I on the first day, we got the markup off to a timely start. Title I was the guts of the bill. Before we adjourned the first day of the markup after nearly twelve hours (there were three breaks for members to rush to the floor to vote), the subcommittee had considered sixteen amendments, all but three by Democrats. Although our members defeated all of the important Democratic amendments, these amendments nonetheless raised the major issues that separated the two parties. Perhaps the major goal of liberals like Rangel and Stark was to reestablish the entitlement to cash benefits. Realizing that they did not have the votes for a direct attempt, they offered amendments that would create entitlement-like conditions. Rangel introduced an amendment barring states from reducing recipient benefits. Not only would this reduce state flexibility to establish the level of benefit that various types of recipients might receive, but it would also completely end the use of cash sanctions for failing to meet work requirements.

Ford offered an amendment that was obviously an attempt to arouse the Democrats' hostility to Speaker Newt Gingrich. Ford's amendment would prevent "overzealous" government from removing children from their home. More specifically, states could not remove a child from her home based on the age of the parent or the parent's economic circumstances. This amendment gave the Democrats an opportunity to charge that the Republican policy of ending cash benefits for unmarried teen mothers would result in many children being placed in orphanages. To prevent that from happening, Democrats were willing to severely restrict the flexibility of states in deciding when to remove children from their home, a state right that the federal government had never so directly violated. The Ford amendment seemed to mean that if a young, poor mother were neglecting her child and the state removed the child, the mother could take the state to court and argue that the state, in violation of the Ford provision in federal law, removed a child because the mother was young and poor. This was truly a dangerous amendment and could undermine the entire legal basis of removing endangered children from abusive and neglectful homes, but it gave Ford the chance to charge that Republicans wanted to put poor children in orphanages. Republicans voted down this amendment on another straight party-line vote.

As expected, Democrats attacked the provision denying cash benefits to mothers under the age of eighteen. This amendment, offered by Sander Levin, was notable for the discussion it generated on what was known from research. By 1995 the research on whether welfare causes illegitimacy, and the use of that research, had a long and interesting history. In a somewhat unusual action, Sheldon Danziger of the University of Michigan, working in conjunction with the influential Bob Greenstein of the Center on Budget and Policy Priorities, organized a group of prominent social scientists to sign a statement announcing that research "suggests that welfare programs are not among the primary reasons" for the historical increases in unwed births.[10] The statement was explicitly directed at Charles Murray and his claims that entitlement welfare was responsible for the spectacular rise in illegitimacy and the resulting decline of inner-city neighborhoods. In his influential *Wall Street Journal* editorial in October 1993, Murray had argued that the rising illegitimacy rate among whites was creating white neighborhoods of concentrated poverty and female-headed families.[11] Whites, in short, were following the same devastating path taken by inner-city blacks. Soon millions of white children would be raised in lawless neighborhoods dominated by female-headed families. His article gained widespread and mostly respectful attention, including from President Clinton.[12]

Respectful attention to Murray's claims—as well as the proposals to cut welfare for illegitimate children by Robert Rector of the Heritage Foundation, William Bennett and Jack Kemp of Empower America, and others in Washington that were deeply resonating with Republican lawmakers—was more than the left could stomach. Greenstein and Danziger's memo stated that they were "very concerned about the recent attention Charles Murray and others have received for their views about welfare and out-of-wedlock births."[13] Danziger and Greenstein urged social scientists to sign a public letter attacking Murray's ideas that concluded with a recommendation to policymakers: "*We strongly urge the rejection of any proposal that would eliminate the safety net for poor children born outside of marriage. Such policies will do far more harm than good.*"[14]

This vast left-wing conspiracy against Murray and the Republicans who supported Murray Light culminated in an event at the National Press Club on June 23, 1994. Danziger and Greenstein invited Secretary Shalala to join in the condemnation of Murray and Republican policy. Predictably, she gave a rousing talk about the "surreal" Republican proposal, comparing it to Jonathan Swift's recommendation for hearty eating in "A Modest Proposal."

There is a saying in Washington that there is no such thing as bad publicity. Murray's already considerable notoriety was greatly enhanced by this attack coordinated with the Clinton administration. Republicans, who often have a bunker mentality regarding both professors and the media, were further strengthened in their belief that illegitimacy was the devil incarnate, that Murray was a brilliant social scientist who dared to stand up to the left, and that furthermore he could take a punch. In any case, the *Washington Post*, whose editorial page was a ferocious opponent of Republican welfare policy, carried a story that seemed mildly sympathetic with the left's professorial gambit.[15] But conservatives mounted a strong counterattack, with Jim Talent of Missouri, Rector, and Bennett in the lead.[16] Murray himself issued a statement from his redoubt at the American Enterprise Institute, placing himself above the fray by claiming that he would be satisfied if people "interested in this debate read one or two technical articles I have written on welfare as a cause of illegitimacy."[17] Robert Rector told the Associated Press that the Danziger group was a bunch of "intellectually fatigued liberals engaging in a last-ditch defense of the welfare system."[18]

Matt and I called several reporters to try to get them to use a study that Ways and Means had commissioned from the nonpartisan Congressional Budget

Office (CBO) in 1992. After lots of preliminary discussion with CBO, we had sent a formal letter from Bill Archer, then senior member of the Republican minority on Ways and Means, to Robert Reischauer, the head of CBO, asking him to have his analysts examine the literature on the relationship between welfare and nonmarital births. On September 11, 1992, CBO sent us a six-page summary of the literature, including a two-page table that provided a synopsis of twenty-four studies. In his cover letter accompanying the report, Reischauer summarized the CBO conclusion by saying that, "although the evidence that welfare increases out-of-wedlock births is mixed, several recent studies have found positive effects of higher welfare benefits on such births."[19]

Unfortunately, at the time of the National Press Club event to counter Charles Murray's claims we couldn't get anyone in the press to quote the study or Reischauer's cover letter. On the other hand, despite the best efforts of the social scientists, there was only modest media coverage of the entire episode. Moreover, two of the most prominent articles, one by Jennifer Dixon of the Associated Press and the other by Cheryl Wetzstein of the *Washington Times*, were wonderfully balanced—despite the fact that they didn't use our CBO study.[20] Wetzstein's article quoted Murray, Rector, and Bennett and devoted as much space to the rebuttals as to the social scientists. The Dixon article quoted both Murray and Rector and concluded with the following quote by North Carolina Senator Lauch Faircloth: "I think these so-called academics should spend more time in the real world and less time in campus offices if they truly want to understand how welfare causes illegitimacy."[21]

The article in the *Washington Post* was also balanced. The author of the *Post* article, Barbara Vobejda, was always fair in her many welfare stories. She often called Ways and Means to get the Republican side of whatever she was working on and then faithfully reported our perspective—without, of course, implying that the Republican view was necessarily the correct one. But at least we got our views out to the public. On this occasion, she used a good quote from Talent in which he held that the current system was cruel to children and that Republican reforms would be "much fairer to kids and poor kids [because it would not] subject them to neighborhoods of crime and drug use, where they are trapped in a cycle of dependency."[22] She ended the article by quoting an unnamed "Republican congressional aide" who said that cutting benefits to young mothers would have a "downside" but that it was the only "real solution" to the problem of illegitimacy.

Thus the social science ploy against Murray and Republican policy was at best only modestly successful. The upshot of this remarkable episode was that Democrats were strengthened in their belief that cutting off teen mothers and their babies was indeed akin to Jonathan Swift's modest proposal and that Republicans were strengthened in their conviction that Murray was right, that professors were anti-Republican, and that the left was blind to, as Robert Rector was quoted in the *Washington Times*, "common sense, theory, and empirical evidence."[23] Here, in the view of Republicans, was a prime example of the left rallying to protect the failed welfare state.

And now Sander Levin was attempting to do precisely what the social science gang recommended: kill the policy of ending benefits for unwed teen moms. But after lively debate, Republicans defeated the Levin amendment on yet another straight party-line vote. This was the first public occasion on which the Republican commitment to Murray Light was tested. All eight Republicans on the subcommittee, at least four of whom were widely regarded as moderates (Shaw, Dave Camp of Michigan, Phil English of Pennsylvania, and Nancy Johnson of Connecticut), strongly supported Murray Light.[24] Again, largely because of our work on the Contract with America bill, the Republicans who had worked the most on welfare policy were solidly in support of a truly radical policy. If some future historian wants to find the exact moment when it became clear that the congressional ground was shifting beneath the nation's welfare programs, and that Republicans had the discipline needed to enact sweeping changes that would alter the topography of welfare programs, she would be justified in choosing the Ways and Means subcommittee markup in general and the unanimous Republican vote to defend Murray Light in particular.

Despite the serious time pressure, despite occasional sharp and tense exchanges such as occurred during the Levin amendment on Murray Light, and despite the members spending nearly twenty-four hours confined with each other over a three-day period, the tone of the markup was usually respectful and even occasionally friendly. During the debate on the child protection block grant on day two of the markup, Rangel offered a complex amendment addressing the safety of children in foster care. Under a few egregious circumstances, such as death of a child in foster care, Rangel wanted the state to be subjected to a review by the secretary of Health and Human Services. The state would also be required to submit a corrective action plan to the secretary explaining how officials were taking actions to ensure child safety. Although Republicans did not want to support an amendment that subjected both the state and the secretary of HHS to such general and unspecified responsibilities in regrettable situations that occur around 1,300 times each year,[25] Republicans were entirely sympathetic with the intent of Rangel's amendment.

Jim McCrery of Louisiana, promising to work with Rangel to craft a bipartisan amendment, asked him to withdraw the amendment, which Rangel did while reserving the right to bring it back for full consideration. McCrery and Rangel then went into the subcommittee conference room directly behind the hearing room and tried for an hour or so to work out a compromise. They failed, so Rangel reintroduced his amendment, which was defeated on another straight party-line vote. But then during a recess to vote on the House floor, McCrery consulted further with Rangel. When the members returned, McCrery offered an amendment that required states to report all deaths among children in foster care in their annual data report to HHS and required the secretary to transmit copies of the report to Congress. The amendment was accepted by unanimous consent. Although the McCrery amendment did not give Rangel everything he wanted, it moved the subcommittee bill in his direction. As I watched the proceedings from the witness table, and heard about the McCrery-Rangel discussions in our back room, it was clear to me that our members were making a sincere effort to accommodate Rangel's concerns and that Rangel and his Democratic colleagues acknowledged and perhaps even appreciated our efforts. Such efforts are crucial to the maintenance of comity during a markup.

Another positive exchange occurred on the second day of the markup. Realizing that Stark was late for a vote, Levin sought recognition and began to ask the chairman's indulgence in not moving ahead with a vote until Stark could make it to the hearing room. Shaw deadpanned that if Levin would talk slower and Stark would walk faster, there would be no problem with Stark making the vote. Of course, everyone laughed. Then both Kennelly and Levin made long and clearly sincere comments on how fair Shaw had been throughout the markup. As Levin was finishing his encomium, Stark walked into the room and cast his vote, to laughter all around.

But there were also some bitter exchanges. Near the beginning of the second day, Jim Nussle of Iowa made a long statement directed at the Clinton administration after Wendell Primus, seated at the witness table as he had been on the first day, criticized our child protection block grant. The essence of Nussle's harsh words about the administration was that the president and the Department of Health and Human Services had had two years to reform welfare and had not done so. Now the administration was consistently taking shots at the Republican bill, even as Wendell had been doing (albeit in a most respectful manner) from the witness table.

Rangel took strong exception to Nussle's comment. He said the administration had a perfect right to criticize the Republican bill and that, besides, Wendell was a professional staff member of the Department of Health and Human Services and members of Congress had no right to go after him as Nussle had done. In fact, he continued, Nussle's remarks were outrageous and contemptuous. Nussle shot back that Rangel had no business talking about our treatment of Democrats when he had given the press statements that Republicans were worse than Nazis because of their welfare reform bill. Suddenly, as both Rangel and Nussle raised their voices, three or four other members tried to speak up. In the midst of this growing disorder, Shaw pounded the gavel on the table and told everyone to be quiet, saying that he was the chairman and he was not going to allow such personal exchanges. Such language would not, he said, help the subcommittee do its important business. At that, Rangel immediately apologized and Nussle no longer tried to get time to speak. Shaw then quickly moved to the next amendment, and an even more serious clash was averted.

This exchange, however, was mild compared with the fireworks that took place at the end of the markup. After Camp moved that the bill be reported favorably to the full committee and the motion was accepted on a straight party-line vote, Shaw recognized Ford for a closing statement. Ford then launched into a severe condemnation of the Republican bill. He said the bill was mean-spirited, short-sighted, and cruel. He said the bill punished children for sins committed by their parents. Even worse, the bill used the nation's children as guinea pigs and crash-test dummies. But worst of all, the bill destroyed hope, the one thing that the poor could not do without. Ford showed considerable emotion as he read his prepared text.

He had barely finished when Shaw let loose. At that point, I had known Shaw quite well for six years and was to work closely with him for another four years. My own experience, confirmed by the opinions of everyone who knew him, was that Shaw was one of the nicest and most respected members of Congress. But this was the maddest I had ever or would ever see him. He told Ford that he was so disappointed that at the end of such a fine markup, during which members had conducted themselves so admirably, that Ford would make such an extraordinarily partisan statement. He had, he continued, restrained himself throughout the markup, as Democrats criticized our bill as mean-spirited and hard on children, and had refrained from pointing out that Democrats had been in charge for forty years as poor children and indeed entire neighborhoods had gone down the tubes. It was Democrats who had created and then jealously guarded a bankrupt system that hurt children. Even after their party leader, President Clinton, had promised to end welfare as we know it, Democrats in Congress, including those on the Ways and Means Committee, had refused to lift a finger to help people get off welfare and into jobs. And now, without providing a bill of their own, they simply sat on the sidelines and attacked the Republican bill.

Shaw then looked directly at Ford and told him that no Republican was mean-spirited and that to talk like that was to question their commitment to the well-being of the nation's children. In fact, to do so was mean-spirited on Ford's part. He then told Ford that he had, with his partisan statement, broken the comity that had prevailed during the markup. Moreover, Shaw predicted—and in this he was correct in the long run—a majority of Democrats would end up voting for a bill very much like the one the subcommittee had marked up and that their own president would sign it.

The moment Shaw finished, Camp moved to adjourn. Levin immediately protested, stating that Shaw had promised Democrats that they could all make closing statements. Shaw, still seething, snapped back that he had made no promises. But almost immediately, Shaw reconsidered, said that he had given his word, and asked Camp to withdraw his motion to adjourn. At this point, most or perhaps all of the Republicans were disgusted and wanted to simply walk out of the room. As Camp said, the bill was passed and there was no reason for Republicans to sit and listen to Democrats berate them. Even so, Shaw insisted that he had given his word and he again asked Camp if he would withdraw his motion to adjourn. Camp did so, and every Democrat made a closing statement. And Republicans, like all politicians with a chance to speak for the record, also made closing statements.

No other Democrat made a statement even close to the stem-winder given by Ford. In fact, although he made it clear that he strongly opposed the Republican bill, Rangel made another eloquent statement about how fair Shaw had been and how smoothly and soundly he had steered the subcommittee through the shark-infested waters of welfare reform. Perhaps because of Rangel's generous and graceful statement, when all the closing statements were over Shaw looked over at Ford and told him he didn't like his statement but that they were still friends. With that, everyone laughed and the subcommittee—amazingly—adjourned on an upbeat note.

The most important outcome of the markup, other than the fact that our bill had passed its first hurdle, was that Republicans on the subcommittee had gotten welfare reform off on the right foot. Regrettably, the bill emerged from subcommittee on a straight party-line vote, so Shaw's hopes for a bipartisan bill were dashed, at least temporarily. But if pushing the bill through the House was going to take Republican unity, the subcommittee had certainly demonstrated almost total discipline on partisan votes. Votes had been taken twenty-one times, and one vote had been taken on final passage of the bill. Republicans had won all of these, which meant that on no amendment did two or more Republicans support the Democrats' position (there were eight Republicans and five Democrats on the subcommittee). In fact, across all twenty-two instances, Democrats had received only 3 Republican votes in support of their amendments and 1 abstention. Given a maximum of eight Republicans voting with the chairman, there were a possible 176 votes for the party position. Of these 176, 172 (98 percent) had been consistent with the party position. Of course, lobbying would now increase and votes might be harder to predict, but subcommittee Republicans had shown themselves to be a partisan voting machine. It was a good indication of things to come.

A formidable number of tasks had to be completed before the markup in the full committee, which was to begin on February 28, less than two weeks away. We immediately put out a press release with a long quote from Shaw announcing that the Subcommittee on Human Resources had become the first congressional panel to pass welfare reform.[26] Under committee rules, we had to write a formal report to Chairman Archer about the markup and its results.[27] The report contained an overview of our eight days of hearings, a brief statement of the purpose of the legislation, and an analysis of every provision in the subcommittee bill. The subcommittee report was accompanied by a report from CBO that analyzed the cost of every provision in the bill. Thus by the time the full committee markup began on February 28, members could have a thorough explanation of the subcommittee bill and an estimate of the cost of every provision. It is worth noting here that these reports, although expensive to produce in both human and capital resources, are a vital part of the legislative process. Members of Congress cannot make good decisions unless they know exactly what every bill entails and how much enacted bills will cost. Although good and abundant information does not guarantee good decisions, good decisions are unlikely without good information.

There were twenty-one Republicans and fifteen Democrats on the full committee, so we could lose 3 Republican votes on Democratic amendments and still produce an 18-to-18 tie vote, which would defeat the amendment. Of course, when all the amending was done, we could lose only 2 votes on final passage of our bill because the tie that would result if three Republicans voted for the Democratic position would doom the bill. In previous Congresses many Republicans would not have supported our tough and controversial policies, such as Murray Light, but under the new regime of a Republican majority with its rapidly emerging party discipline, we were fairly confident that we could defeat all the Democratic amendments. We had no doubt going into the subcommittee markup that the members would be with Chairman Shaw on every difficult vote, but we knew much less about Republicans on the full committee. I was determined that we use the two weeks between the subcommittee and the committee markup to talk with the staff of all committee members who were not on the subcommittee to make sure we could count on everyone's support. We also had a meeting with all Republican staffers to go over the provisions in the subcommittee bill and to ask that we be informed if members had troubles with any of the provisions. My watchword was, Woe to the staff director who takes his chairman into an unanticipated losing vote.

Perhaps the most important activity we pursued during this period was strengthening the work requirement that Democrats had hailed as too weak. Both Shaw and Archer wanted stronger provisions before we introduced Archer's bill to the full committee. Behind the scenes, Shaw talked with Jim Talent and I talked with Robert Rector on several occasions. We all agreed on a much stronger work requirement, one that carefully defined work, specified the number of hours a recipient had to work to count toward meeting the requirement, and phased in a standard that required states to have 50 percent of their caseload in the workforce by 2003. In addition, Rector, who had recently visited a work program in Sheboygan, Wisconsin, where the rolls were declining precipitously, suggested that we include what came to be called a caseload reduction credit. Under this procedure, states would enjoy a credit against their work requirement if they produced a net reduction in their caseload. Thus if a state reduced its caseload by 10 percent, a 50 percent work requirement would be dropped to 40 percent. The purpose of this procedure was to provide an incentive for states to help recipients find work and leave the rolls.

After several discussions, mostly on the phone, we agreed that Talent or his colleague Tim Hutchinson would introduce an amendment in the Education Committee to place these stronger work requirements in that committee's bill and that we include a similar or identical set of requirements in the bill introduced by Chairman Archer as his mark. Both parts of this plan were successfully executed.[28] From this point forward, House Republicans were completely united on the details of the work requirement.

During the period between markups, we also continued to work on the child support title of the bill. Every provision had to be acceptable to both Shaw and Archer. But the chairs of the Human Resources Subcommittee and the Committee on Ways and Means are not going to pore over fifty or sixty pages of legislative language or markup documents, check with all their members, consider the pros and cons of the hundred or so specific policies that would make up the child support package, and then make a rational and informed choice about each policy. If the chairs don't decide after a thorough examination of each provision of the Republican bill, who does? A key to understanding how laws are typically written is that the staff members who work for the chair of the committee make many independent decisions after briefing the chair and making recommendations on the major provisions that should be in the bill. After many years of working with Shaw, I had detailed knowledge of what he wanted. On any major issue about which I had doubts, I simply called Shaw or set up a meeting so he could decide. But this happened rarely. Mostly, I decided what to include, in consultation with Shaw's legislative director and Phil. In addition, Matt had been on Shaw's staff and knew him even better than I did, so I often consulted with Matt. Under most circumstances, and our welfare reform bill was no exception, by the time the bill is ready for markup, two or three members of the committee staff, often a member or two of the chair's personal staff, staff of other members of the committee, and in the case of big bills, leadership staff, have reviewed the bill with varying levels of detail.

Given the time pressures, we were fortunate to have a bill that we could use as a base to draft the Shaw-Archer child support provision. This bill had an interesting pedigree. In 1988 Congress had enacted a host of child support amendments that had originated in our subcommittee. As part of these amendments, Congress had called for a bipartisan commission to make recommendations about how to further improve the child support program. Congress often calls for a commission when it doesn't know what action to take to solve a problem or when all potential courses of action are too politically difficult to enact into law. But commissions are often a bust. It is part of Washington lore that commission reports languish on library shelves gathering dust.[29]

But the U.S. Commission on Interstate Child Support was a rare exception.[30] Under the capable leadership of Margaret Haynes, in its 1992 report the commission issued well over a hundred recommendations. Three factors were instrumental in the impact the commission report was to have. First, members of Congress called for the report because they really did want to write legislation that would improve child support, especially interstate child support (enforcing orders across state lines when the custodial parent and child lived in one state and the noncustodial parent in another), which was widely viewed as the biggest problem faced by child support officials. Second, members of the commission represented a wide array of interests and views. When the commission reached near agreement on a set of serious recommendations (all but one member supporting), it was a clear sign to policymakers that there was a great deal of consensus about the next steps in child support enforcement. Third, several members of the commission—including three members of Congress, an elected state official, two judges, child support officials, advocates, and lawyers in private practice—had substantial contacts with members of Congress or their staffs. These contacts could greatly facilitate the translation of recommendations into legislative action and provide lobbying on behalf of any bill that contained the commission's recommendations. Indeed, the fact that a U.S. senator (Bill Bradley of New Jersey) and two members of the U.S. House of Representatives (Kennelly and Marge Roukema, a Republican from New Jersey) were members of the commission virtually guaranteed that its recommendations would get serious attention in Congress.

The recommendations emphasized establishing an integrated and automated data system that linked all states and that provided quick access to information on all parents who lived apart from their children; establishing a system of income withholding across state lines that provided access directly from the state that was seeking child support payments to the source of the noncustodial parent's income; requiring all states to enact identical laws on interstate enforcement; and requiring every state to create a system of voluntary paternity establishment. Not surprisingly, these recommendations were well received in Washington and by child support administrators and child advocates both in Washington and around the nation. Almost immediately, the bipartisan Congressional Caucus on Women's Issues began converting the report's recommendations into legislative language. On June 24, 1993, Roukema, along with twenty-two bipartisan cosponsors, introduced HR 1600, the Interstate Child Support Enforcement Act. The bill was referred to five House committees, because its provisions were so sweeping that its subject matter touched on the jurisdiction of the Armed Services Committee, the Banking Committee, the Education Committee, the Judiciary Committee, and the Ways and Means Committee.

Although the Roukema bill had been written in cooperation with members of the Caucus on Women's Issues, a number of important recommendations from the commission did not make it into the bill. In addition, several technical provisions were not drafted properly. Thus when it became apparent that welfare reform would be a major item on the congressional agenda, Nancy Ebb of the Children's Defense Fund and Elisabeth Donahue of the National Women's Law Center, both lawyers with expertise in child support law and legislative drafting, worked with the staff of members of the House, including Johnson, Roukema, Kennelly, and Connie Morella of Maryland to perfect the bill. Although not directly involved in the drafting, the Clinton administration played a key role. David Ellwood of the Department of Health and Human Services, and Paul Legler, a Clinton political appointee at HHS and an expert on child support, had already drafted almost all of the most important reforms; they were part of the Clinton welfare reform legislation introduced in June 1994. In developing the Clinton child support bill, Legler had met with state child support officials on many occasions during 1992 and 1993 and had incorporated their ideas. More important, meeting with state officials and following much of their advice meant that this important group was strongly in support of the administration bill.[31] Ebb and Donahue consulted frequently with Legler as they drafted the new Women's Caucus bill, using the Clinton bill as a template.

This pedigree for the bill we were using as our base text would not have been comforting to a lot of Republicans. But it gets worse. Late one night, as I was working on the notoriously complex distribution provisions,[32] I just could not fully understand either the rules already in effect or the specific changes that Shaw and senior Republicans, joined by nearly all Democrats, wanted to make to ensure that mothers and children received more of the money collected by the child support program and government receive less. This was one of those moments, and there were entirely too many as we wrote our sweeping reforms, in which I was keenly aware that precise drafting was necessary and I was on the edge of my somewhat limited capabilities in deciding exactly how the drafting should proceed.

Unfortunately, the person best suited to help with drafting these provisions worked for the Children's Defense Fund (CDF), the mortal enemy of all that is Republican. But it was late and mistakes on the distribution rules would be disastrous. So I called Nancy Ebb of CDF and made a deal with her. If she would agree to wear sunglasses and sneak through the back door of the Rayburn House Office Building late at night, she could have the grand privilege of helping me write the distribution rules. She readily accepted, and I now must confess that a major portion of the child support distribution rules that reside in the statute developed under Republican control were written by a lawyer employed by the Children's Defense Fund. Nancy and I could only hope that neither Archer nor Marion Wright Edelman would ever find out. That's why we took a solemn pledge to keep it a secret forever. I hope I can count on Nancy to live up to our pledge.

And it still gets worse. As if the major contributions made by Ellwood, Legler, Donahue, and Ebb—all Democrats—were not enough, an equally important source of help with the child support provisions was Marilyn Smith of the child support enforcement program in Massachusetts, another Democrat. I had known Smith for many years through my work with the National Child Support Enforcement Association (NCSEA), the professional association of child support officials, scholars, advocates, private sector professionals, and others interested in child support. Smith, a past president of NCSEA, seemed to know everything about child support and everyone of consequence in the field. She served as a middle woman, talking with officials all over the nation and then working with me to provide both broad ideas for reforms and, in many cases, specific legislative language.

Given this unusual background of the bill, I thought it was essential that, before the markup, we meet with all the Republicans on the full committee and review the child support program itself as well as our reforms, in case some of our members didn't like what we were doing. I also knew that several of the child support provisions in the bill were inconsistent with Republican political philosophy. It was a great irony that, in the midst of welfare reform legislation that was sending power and authority back to states, both the child support program itself and our reforms of the program imposed all sorts of mandates on states. Federal statutes stipulated, often in great detail, policies that states had to have in place to locate absent fathers, establish paternity if necessary, establish a support order, collect money from fathers, and divide the money up among the mother and children, the state government, and the federal government. In addition, states were mandated to have elaborate computer systems as well as systems for reporting data to the federal government. These requirements were backed by financial penalties if states were out of compliance with federal rules. Thus Ways and Means had jurisdiction over one of the most prescriptive and tough federal programs, and our plan would make it even more prescriptive and tough. There was a lot for Republicans not to like.

The meeting in Chairman Archer's office—Room H-208 of the U.S. Capitol— on February 23 began at five o'clock in the afternoon. Nearly all the members were present, exhausted though they might have been from nearly two months of Republican rule and from what had already been a long day for most of them. Room H-208 has always been one of my favorite rooms in the Capitol. The long, narrow room is almost completely filled by a massive conference table covered with a rich, blue felt cloth. It was surrounded by twenty or so upholstered armchairs around the table and lined up against both long walls, with a few on either side of the double door that led into the hallway. One of the most remarkable features of the room is the painting surrounding the glass chandelier above the conference table. Finished sometime around 1910, the painting is composed of four panels, each reflecting a military theme: a shield, arrows, a revolver, crossed swords. During various bipartisan bargaining sessions conducted underneath this painting, I often wondered how the painter had been so prescient. I later discovered a more pedestrian explanation for the military theme. The room had been under control of the House Committee on Military Affairs from 1869, shortly after the south wing of the Capitol was completed, until Ways and Means secured control of the room in 1908. Still, even after the Ways and Means takeover and, indeed, on this very day, the occupants of the room were often engaged in wars—built on words rather than swords.[33]

I had been in H-208 on many occasions, because it had been the site of negotiating sessions over the years between Ways and Means Republicans and Democrats and between negotiators in the final stages of cutting deals between the House and Senate. But today I didn't notice any of the features of H-208 I so admired because I was, like the maiden tied to the log headed toward the buzz saw, about to be ripped.

I sat in the middle of one side of the table, Archer was in his normal seat at the fireplace end of the table opposite the entrance, and Shaw was seated to Archer's left. The other members were crowded around the table, and a few sat in the outside ring of chairs. Phil and one or two other staffers were there as well. Archer started the meeting by simply saying we were there to review the child support program and discuss the amendments Chairman Shaw had written. Shaw then made a brief statement about how important the child support program was and mentioned that we had been working on reform provisions for nearly two years. He pointed out very calmly that some of the provisions were controversial but that politically we had to have strong child support provisions, especially in view of the fact that we were requiring poor mothers to bear such a heavy burden by replacing AFDC with a program that required work and imposed a time limit on receiving benefits. It followed that fathers had to do their part to support the children.

As I began to explain the current program, members paid careful attention and asked several questions. This was a part of being staff director that I relished. It was a lot like teaching a graduate seminar, except that the students were members of Congress who were leading the charge to enact the most far-reaching changes in the nation's welfare programs in a generation. My enjoyment was short-lived. When I explained the enforcement mechanisms already in the law, such as the tax intercept in which a father's tax return could be seized to pay overdue child support, members began to object. As we considered all the ways the state program could separate fathers from their money, members got hotter and hotter. When I explained one of the most popular reforms in our bill, mandatory revocation of drivers' licenses, members got even hotter. "How's the guy supposed to get to work?" was a common refrain. Finally, when I told them that we were also going to require states to revoke hunting and fishing licenses, the room exploded. Shoot them at dawn if you like, but don't touch their hunting licenses! Several of the members absolutely refused to support suspension of either drivers' licenses or hunting and fishing licenses. Johnson and Jennifer Dunn of Washington attempted to rescue the provision by pointing out that fathers could avoid losing these licenses by simply paying child support. When they didn't pay child support, the mothers and children suffered, often being forced to live in poverty and to go on welfare. Should a guy be able to go fishing when he doesn't support his kids? Besides, research showed clearly that fathers were much better off financially than mothers following a divorce or separation,[34] and the records of the child support program showed that millions of fathers were not paying child support. Congress and the states had no choice but to tighten the screws.

But Johnson and Dunn and Shaw, as they argued for our amendments, were up against gut reactions to these measures that were deeply inconsistent with the Republican philosophy of limited government. How could Republicans propose to prevent a guy from driving his car to his favorite fishing hole? At one point, after Johnson had made an aggressive and even moving case for revoking hunting and fishing licenses, one of the members told her he was getting "sick to my stomach" listening to a Republican talk about expanding government power in that way. Johnson, as usual, just ignored the male beast and went right on mounting her eloquent defense of the reforms. She had been under attack by fellow Republicans throughout her career for her support of abortion rights. She wasn't about to knuckle under on child support policy to placate a male defending fishing licenses.

Archer and Shaw were moderating influences during the meeting, but the members were still on the verge of mutiny. At one point, as I visualized the problems that would ensue if members refused to support the reforms—let alone if they decided to try to weaken the child support program as it already existed—I myself was getting a little hot. This is an exceptionally foolish condition for a congressional staffer. I had personally witnessed—and knew about more—situations in which staffers had engaged in heated arguments with members. Mostly, they didn't turn out too well for the staffer. But equally important, a staffer simply cannot do his job if he argues with members. The House of Representatives is actually the House of Arguments, and there are plenty of members to do the arguing. When members get into arguments like the explosive one on child support in which I was now trapped like a rat in a maze, the proper role of staff is to either be quiet or offer facts that might clarify the debate. In some situations, like the one in which I now found myself, following this principle means taking lots of abuse from members.

But sleep deprivation works wonders for courage—or destroys judgment. Thus as members attacked the drivers' license provision, I told them that they could remove this provision as well as others from the markup bill if they wanted to. But if they did, Democrats would offer amendments during the markup to restore whatever had been removed, and both their Republican colleagues and Democrats would offer amendments on the floor to restore any removed provision that had not been added in committee. The amendments would pass easily on the floor, if not in committee, and the members who were now attacking the provisions behind closed doors would vote to support them in public.

Fortunately, I made the statement calmly. Then, before any member could attack me, Shaw jumped in and said virtually the same thing. He said that even these controversial provisions would be supported by nearly every Democrat and by an overwhelming majority of our Republican colleagues if they were offered as amendments on the House floor. Shaw's ploy worked, and members began to calm down, at least a little. After the meeting had been under way for over an hour, Archer, probably growing tired of the debate and worried about the fraying nerves of his members, asked Jennifer Dunn to head a task force that would work with Shaw on our child support amendments. And with that, our pleasant and educational session came to an end.

The Dunn task force met twice and made a few modifications in our bill, including the removal of the drivers' license provision. Democrats did in fact try to add it back to the bill during the Ways and Means markup, but the amendment was defeated on a 17-to-17 vote, with one member absent and one member voting "present." As predicted, the amendment was offered again on the House floor and passed overwhelmingly. Every Republican member of the committee, showing the discipline that held even when members wanted to vote against the chairman, voted in favor of adding the drivers' license provision.[35] I'll bet that at least one of them had a stomachache as he cast his vote in favor of the despised provision.

The five days between our child support seminar and the full committee markup were a riotous blur, consisting of preparing markup documents; consulting with Shaw and others on the child support bill; reviewing drafts of our bill and then rushing to Legislative Counsel to discuss and revise the drafts; advising Ari Fleischer on the chairman's opening statement; meeting with staff of both Republicans and Democrats on the full committee; keeping Debra Colton (the lead welfare staffer for committee Democrats) informed about the child support drafting; and meeting or talking on the phone with leadership staff, committee members, representatives from the Clinton administration, and hordes of outside advocates and lobbyists intent on influencing the chairman's mark. Archer wanted some changes in the subcommittee bill, all of which were summarized in a five-page document we prepared to hand out at the markup.[36] In fact, this was the last document I completed before getting at least two hours of sleep early in the morning of the day of the markup.

The Ways and Means Committee was called to order by Chairman Archer at five minutes after eleven in the morning of February 28, with every member present and Room 1100 of Longworth jammed with welfare wonks, advocates, program administrators, lobbyists for various causes, congressional staff, and press.[37] Over the four days between February 28 and March 3, the committee would be in session for thirty-seven hours and forty-six minutes, not counting brief breaks to vote or gobble down a sandwich. The 1,264-page, double-spaced transcript of the markup, located in the main Ways and Means office in Room 1102 of Longworth, occupies four volumes.[38] As markups go, a long one.

Archer's opening statement, written primarily by Ari with some input from Phil and me, was a powerful partisan statement. He opened by saying, "Today marks the beginning of the end of a failed welfare state." He said his markup bill was based on three principles: work, personal responsibility, and state control, each of which he explained in some detail. After a little more than five minutes of strong language condemning current welfare programs and praising the Republican reforms, he concluded that Republicans would revolutionize welfare; "when we are done, we will create a better America."

He then turned to the business at hand, telling the committee that he was prepared to work as long as necessary to finish the markup before the weekend was over. This ploy, of course, was the same as the one Shaw had used at the subcommittee level to focus the attention of members on the business at hand and especially to keep the Democrats from being dilatory. It works wonders to schedule a markup so that it ends on Friday, as both Shaw and Archer had done. In that way, if extra days are required, members must invest their weekend.

Given, first, the number of partisan and outspoken Democrats on the full committee (including, at minimum, the three senior Democrats—Sam Gibbons, Charles Rangel, and Pete Stark—plus Harold Ford, Robert Matsui, Sander Levin, Jim McDermott, and John Lewis) and, second, the radical bill we were bringing before the committee, I was anticipating a protracted and bitter markup. But the first day, lasting over six and a half hours, went by with surprisingly little conflict. Democrats continued their highly negative characterization of the bill, calling it "cruel," "mean," "vicious," and worse, but Republicans did not rise to the bait. Chairman Archer scrupulously followed the rules and intervened whenever trouble seemed to be brewing.[39]

One factor that prevented outbreaks of bitter dispute, as during the subcommittee markup, was the humor and friendly banter members brought to the occasion. At one point, Gerald Kleczka of Wisconsin introduced an amendment that was criticized by his Democratic colleague Jim McDermott. In his criticism, McDermott referred to the amendment of "my good friend." Then, as he began his response to McDermott's criticism, Kleczka referred to the comments of "my ex good friend," an opening that drew hearty laughter both from members and the audience. On the third day of the markup, McDermott was offering an amendment when he noticed that most of the members were absent from the hearing room. He claimed that there was a boycott of his remarks. Archer agreed, saying that no one else was present. But Nussle was present and spoke up, saying, "Hey, come on, I'm here," whereupon Archer observed that McDermott had a huge audience after all. McDermott, not the most popular member among Republicans, responded that "his friends" were gathering. On the last day of the markup, Richard Neal of Massachusetts observed that he was pleased that in drafting the child support provisions in the bill, Chairman Archer had listened to him and Bill Weld, the governor of Neal's state, and included several of their recommendations. As soon as these words had left Neal's mouth, Bill Thomas got Archer's attention and strongly recommended, to peals of laughter, that the chairman carefully reexamine that section of the bill.

One of the issues that aggravated Democrats the most at the beginning of the markup was that the child support title of the bill was still being written. However, we were able to somewhat offset this unfortunate fact by sharing draft copies of the child support title as we moved toward a final bill. Indeed, the entire child support process was remarkably bipartisan. By the time the child support markup document was ready late on March 1, the second day of the markup, we had shared several drafts with Democrats, so anyone who was seriously interested could have followed the bill's development and even had a good shot at participating in writing the bill.

The child support markup document was distributed to the committee early in the morning on March 2. The committee completed the amending process on the first four titles of the bill on that day (the third day of the markup). Given not only the near certainty of many amendments to the child support title of the bill but also the remaining debate on the Democrats' substitute bill plus the vote on final passage of the Republican bill, Archer decided not to wait until the fourth day to conduct the walk-through on our new child support title. After talking with Rangel to be sure that Democrats did not object, Archer adjourned the committee and asked members to return at seven-thirty that evening to conduct the child support walk-through, which went smoothly.

When the committee reassembled at a little after nine in the morning of March 3, nine amendments were offered to the child support title. All were debated in the friendliest possible fashion. Three of them were withdrawn after debate; two were accepted by unanimous consent; one was voted down by voice vote; and three Democratic amendments were defeated by recorded vote.[40] Two of the amendments by Democrats were strongly opposed by Archer. The first, as predicted in our friendly little Republican meeting in Archer's office less than a week before, was to add the requirement that states have laws allowing child support officials to suspend various licenses, including drivers', hunting, and fishing licenses. Three Republicans broke ranks and voted with the Democrats, but the amendment still failed on a tie vote. The second would have given child support officials access to records of the Internal Revenue Service (IRS). Every Republican, and probably most Democrats, knew that Archer was wildly opposed to any expansion of IRS authority. Thus every Republican and two Democrats joined Archer in defeating the amendment.

The most important outcome of the full committee markup, like the outcome of the subcommittee markup, was that Republicans provided almost total support for their bill and for their chairman. Democrats offered more than thirty amendments to Archer's mark. Only one of them passed by recorded vote; 629 of 646 Republican votes (97 percent) were consistent with the chairman's position on the Democratic amendments and final passage of the bill. Every feature of the new block grant program—including repeal of the AFDC program, the end of entitlement cash benefits, mandatory sanctions, and strong work requirements—had been attacked by Democratic amendments. All of these amendments were spurned, most by unanimous Republican opposition. Similarly, no Republican votes were lost on Democratic amendments to weaken the Murray Light provision that would deny cash benefits from the block grant to unwed mothers under age eighteen, arguably the most controversial and tough provision in the entire bill, nor on the sweeping changes in the SSI program for children, nor on any of the other controversial provisions in the bill. On the final vote, every Republican, joined by Democrat Gerald Kleczka, voted in favor of the slightly amended chairman's mark.

At the conclusion of the markup, immediately following the vote on final passage of the Republican bill, Democrats had a surprise for us. It had long been committee practice, originated by the Democrats, that both the markup document and the amendments offered during the markup would be written in plain English. This practice, referred to as a "conceptual" markup, was thought to be easier for everyone to understand because the language was not as convoluted and difficult as legislative text. After the markup, Republican and Democratic staffers would work with legislative counsel to prepare a legislative text based on the "conceptual" markup document and the amendments that had passed during the markup. Staffers and any interested members would review the legislative text to be certain it was faithful to the conceptual markup. Despite this long-standing tradition, under clause 1 of Rule 16 of House Rules, any member had the right to request that "every motion be reduced to writing," which, given the context, clearly meant legislative text.

I suppose that at some point I had heard about this rule, but if so I certainly did not remember it. Thus when McDermott interrupted the final vote and asked Archer, "What are we voting on?" I thought nothing of it. But then he demanded, as a point of order, that the entire bill be reduced to legislative text. That got my attention. He can't do that, was my first thought. When I looked up and saw a grim-faced Chris Smith, I knew something was wrong. I learned later that Phil had called the House parliamentarians and received confirmation that McDermott's demand to see statutory language was certainly within the House Rules, if not the spirit of the committee's traditions. He also learned something in that call that would change Ways and Means markups for years to come. Immediately after Chairman Archer recessed the committee, McDermott approached the chairman and Phil on the dais. He volunteered in a "gee whiz," hand-waving sort of way that he didn't intend anything mischievous or sinister—that the thought had just come to him toward the end that members hadn't had a chance to read the complete text of this important legislation.

After he walked away, Phil privately informed Chairman Archer that he had just been misinformed (Phil might have used a stronger word) by McDermott. The parliamentarians had told Phil minutes earlier that McDermott and his staff had contacted them the day before to explore how he could take the surprise action he did. By "protesting too much," McDermott unwittingly caused Chairman Archer reluctantly to conclude that the mutual trust that conceptual markups depended on no longer existed. Since that day, the Ways and Means Committee has abandoned plain English conceptual markups. This change is not very helpful to the minority because it is cumbersome and time-consuming to reduce every amendment to legislative text. Given that the minority has a much greater interest in amendments than the majority, the burden of McDermott's ploy fell primarily on his Democratic colleagues.

My own reaction to McDermott's ploy was, So what? We have to write the legislative text before we can report the bill to the House anyway. The only effect of McDermott's silly ploy would be to delay the final vote on the bill. After some parliamentary skirmishing, in which tempers flared on both sides, Thomas moved that the committee instruct Chairman Archer to introduce a bill containing the legislation just passed by the committee. In other words, our side had folded and agreed to provide legislative text before a final vote to send the bill to the House. Under House rules, we did not have a choice.

After a voice vote, Archer recessed the committee at the call of the chair. Five days later, on March 8, the committee had a regularly scheduled markup of two Medicare bills. That morning, after working late into the night, we completed the legislative text of the welfare reform bill and introduced it as a regular bill in the House. The bill was given the inauspicious number HR 1157.[41] After committee action on the two Medicare bills on March 8, Archer laid HR 1157 before the committee, an immediate vote was taken, and the bill was reported to the House on a vote of 22 to 11, with Kleczka again joining the Republicans.

The most radical welfare reform bill in history had passed easily through the Ways and Means Committee with all of its major provisions intact and was now headed for a showdown on the floor of the U.S. House of Representatives. Because Republicans were united, Democrats could do nothing to stop us. The rules of the House ensured that, as long as Republicans could keep their votes together, the welfare reform bill would soon move a giant step closer to enactment. But a big and bloody fight on the House floor remained in the way.

## CHAPTER EIGHT

# The Battle
# in the House,
# Part III: The Floor

Stand on the floor of the United States House of Representatives and you are in the midst of the world's greatest institution of democratic debate and decisionmaking. The essence of democracy is majority rule, and Republicans intended to rule the House floor. By now, less than three months into the Republican takeover of the House, Republicans had established control over the floor of the House of Representatives and thereby greatly increased the odds that we could move our welfare reform bill another crucial step toward becoming law. The component parts of the growing bill had burst forth from the House committees with major welfare jurisdiction. In each case, Republicans had maintained near-perfect voting discipline at the committee level, providing the welfare reform bill with much greater mass and velocity than it had enjoyed when it was a mere item on the agenda of an obscure political party struggling to gain power.

Staff members from the three committees with primary jurisdiction over welfare—Ways and Means, Education, and Agriculture—had been meeting with leadership staff since early January, planning how to resolve areas in which committees shared jurisdiction and, more important, figuring out how we could bring the bills together to yield a single megabill.[1] If HR 4 (which Clay Shaw, the chairman of the Human Resources Subcommittee, and Jim Talent of Missouri introduced in early January at the beginning of the 104th Congress) was a major bill, it was modest compared with the bill on which we were now working. On the morning of March 13, I had the great pleasure of retrieving from legislative counsel the text of our joint bill, the product of three months of cooperative labor among our three committees and the leadership, and delivering it to the box on the House floor where bills are officially submitted.[2] The prime authors of the bill, which was given the designation HR 1214, were the chairmen of the three primary sponsoring committees, Bill Archer of Ways and Means, Bill Goodling of Education, and Pat Roberts of Agriculture. Having rammed the respective parts of the bill through our committees, and having melded the work product of the three committees into a single coherent bill, we were now ready for the next major step in creating our revolution: passing the bill on the House floor.

For major legislation, there is no way to the floor of the House except through the Rules Committee.[3] Perhaps the greatest difference between the House and Senate is that the Senate has no committee with powers comparable to those of the House Rules Committee, a failing that produces entire mountain ranges of rhetoric. The controls on debate in the Senate are so loose that everyone gets to say anything they want to say and to say it as many times as they want to say it. By contrast, the floor of the House is almost always a model of organization on which action is strongly governed by tradition and bills are guided by a rule that covers every aspect of debate for the matter at hand—thankfully including the amount of time allotted to both parties. A typical speech on the House floor lasts two or three minutes, the approximate time it takes a Senator to clear his throat.

In the abstract, there is a straightforward series of events leading to passage or defeat of a bill in the House. The bill comes out of a committee of jurisdiction, such as Ways and Means, and is taken up by the Rules Committee. The Rules Committee, meeting in its tiny room on the third floor of the Capitol Building, conducts a hearing and gives members of both parties an opportunity to propose amendments and to defend their amendments in testimony before the committee. Usually, the chairman of the committee that produced the bill will testify first and make a recommendation on the type of rule his committee would prefer. Committees of jurisdiction often prefer a closed rule, in which the bill they have marked up comes to the floor without any amendments being allowed. In this way, their pristine work product will not be marred by the amendments that members of either party who are not on the committee might dream up.

But in the first year or two of the Republican majority, the Rules Committee generally did not favor closed rules, primarily because a sense of fairness to Democrats often pervaded Rules Committee proceedings.[4] Gerald Solomon of New York and his powerful chief of staff Donald Wolfensberger were exceptionally fair-minded and tried to be fairer with Democrats than Democrats had been with us when we were in the minority. This sense of fairness pushed Chairman Solomon and his committee to allow Democrats a chance to change most bills through the amendment process. In nearly every vote on the House floor a simple majority wins; thus the majority party should be able to defeat amendments that alter the essential features of its bill. Under Chairman Solomon, most Republicans on the Rules Committee had a sense that a bold and confident majority party would practice good sportsmanship, allowing the minority party the opportunity to present and defend amendments that could change the bill. A united majority prevails, and there is very little the minority can do. But the minority will squeal less if they at least have a shot at changing the bill through the amendment process, especially if some of their amendments pass and become part of the bill. Majority party members of the Rules Committee knew that if they didn't allow the minority at least a few amendments, the minority would refuse to cooperate on other legislative matters and could employ parliamentary tactics to disrupt floor proceedings.

Besides amendments offered by individual members that affect specific provisions in the bill, the minority party often has two additional opportunities to change the majority's bill. On issues of significance to the leadership of both parties, the minority often has its own bill. In the case of welfare reform, the Democrats selected Nathan Deal, a conservative Democrat from Georgia, to head a group of moderates to fashion a bill that would unite Democrats.[5] There is a saying in the House that you can't fight something with nothing; if the minority is going to have any chance of defeating the majority, the first goal of the minority leadership is to keep their ranks united. To do so, especially on a popular issue like welfare reform, it is necessary to have a bill that appeals to as many members of the minority party as possible. Without a bill of their own, members of the minority may support the majority bill, in part because they have nothing else to support.

As Republicans knew all too well, being in the minority tends to sharpen the mind. Now suddenly House Democrats were being led on welfare reform by Nathan Deal, a man who would soon become a Republican himself. The bill that Deal and his moderate Democratic colleagues produced was one of the most surprising Democratic bills ever introduced in the House of Representatives, and every Democrat, including the liberals who hated President Clinton's bill, would vote for the Deal substitute, despite the fact that it was similar to the president's bill.

When the minority rouses itself to produce a bill that is endorsed by their leadership and members, it would be a great injustice if the majority enacted a rule that failed to allow the minority's bill to be considered on the House floor. Shaw was firmly committed to allowing Democrats to introduce the Deal bill and to lobbying his Republican colleagues as often and aggressively as necessary to make sure Deal's bill was defeated. In addition, we knew that Patsy Mink of Hawaii, a long-time member of the House and a steady voice for liberals, was also drafting a bill.[6] Her bill, of course, would represent a truly liberal welfare reform bill, more liberal than current law and more liberal than President Clinton would support. Shaw wanted the Rules Committee to allow both Democratic bills to come to the floor for votes. This action would mean that there were, in addition to whatever amendments were approved by the Rules Committee, three complete bills on the floor: the Republican bill, the Deal moderate Democratic bill, and the Mink liberal Democratic bill. Each bill would be debated and voted on separately. The rule could be fashioned so that, if more than one of the bills received a majority of the votes, the bill with the most votes would win.

In addition to the substitute bill (or in this case, two substitutes), the minority is given the right to offer something called the motion to recommit. The motion comes in two flavors: the simple motion to recommit and the motion to recommit with instruction. If approved by the House, the former has the effect of killing the bill. The latter, however, amounts to the last opportunity for the minority to amend the bill because they can instruct the committee from which the bill originated in how to amend the bill. If adopted by the House, the chair of the committee with jurisdiction immediately stands up and reports back the bill as changed by the instruction. The changed bill would then be subject to a vote on final passage.[7] If the rule allows the minority a motion to recommit with instructions, the minority can be very artful in fashioning its motion. Perhaps the best strategy for the minority is to focus the motion on the single issue on which the majority party has the most difficulty holding its votes. In the case of welfare reform, for example, the Democrats moved to recommit the bill to Ways and Means and to instruct the committee to include a provision requiring that all savings from the bill (around $60 billion over five years) be devoted to deficit reduction. Any Republican who voted against this motion would be subject in her next election to one of the Democrats' favorite gambits, namely, that she took money from the poor to give to the rich.

All of these issues were swirling about as the Rules Committee required members of the House to submit their amendments. After submitting the amendment, the sponsoring member then usually appears before the committee at a hearing devoted specifically to considering the rule. In the case of amendments in the nature of a substitute, the entire substitute bill is presented to the Rules Committee, and the leader of the minority party or his designee appears before the Rules Committee hearing to defend the substitute bill.

Once the Rules Committee has conducted its hearing, the chairman drafts a rule to place before the members of the committee. At this point, the rule is similar to any bill considered by a committee of jurisdiction, and the meeting of the Rules Committee is a markup. Thus members have a debate about the proposed rule, and then the rule is open for amendment. The typical course of events in the meeting is for the minority to try to expand the rule and make more time for debate and more floor amendments in order.[8] If the majority is united, it will be able to beat back the minority amendments and protect the rule as written by the chair.

If they are wise, the Rules Committee chairman and his staff consult widely in drafting the rule. The most important consultation is with the majority leadership. Indeed, the Rules Committee is a vital part of the Speaker's control of the House. When and whether bills come to the floor, the types of amendments (if any) permitted, and the rules of debate are the guts of the day-to-day operation of the House. If the Speaker is to impose his will and agenda on the House, he must have great influence over the actions of the Rules Committee. Gingrich did. He generally did not intervene in the Rules Committee process until something went awry, but his staff kept a close eye on the Rules Committee. Let some trouble start brewing, and Gingrich would take whatever action was necessary to produce a rule that suited the interests of House Republicans, as Gingrich, in consultation with the rest of the leadership, saw those interests.

The Rules Committee received 159 requests from members to amend the welfare bill, 100 from Democrats and 59 from Republicans. It took twelve single-spaced pages just to present a brief summary of the 159 amendments. To discuss these amendments, review floor strategy, and make tentative recommendations to Chairman Solomon about which amendments should be allowed to come to the floor for votes, Republican staffers from Ways and Means, Agriculture, Education, Rules, and leadership met at ten-thirty in the morning on March 15 in the Rules Committee's hearing room. Phil Moseley, Ari Fleischer, and I represented Ways and Means. Although Archer wanted a relatively closed rule, Shaw was willing to err on the side of openness. He didn't want to overdo it and wind up losing an important vote on the floor, but he welcomed amendments that would allow Democrats to feel that they were having an impact in shaping the bill. To this point, the Ways and Means parts of the bill had had very little Democratic input, nor had the sections of the bill from the other committees. But Shaw was still hoping for a bipartisan bill, and he thought many Democrats would be reluctant to vote against a welfare reform bill on the House floor. So within reason Shaw wanted the Rules Committee to allow several Democratic amendments, including both the Deal and Mink substitutes and the motion to recommit with instructions.

The meeting on March 15 was fascinating. Although I had been working in Congress for nearly a decade, I had never participated in a meeting that would have a considerable impact on a House rule. The lead staffers for the Rules Committee were Don Wolfensberger, who had been a congressional staffer for more than twenty years and was a trusted lieutenant of Chairman Solomon, and Dan Keniry, an exceptionally smart and talented young staffer who soon moved on to bigger and better jobs. There was much less disagreement in the meeting than I had anticipated. Wolfensberger made it clear that Chairman Solomon wanted to have a relatively open rule, a position that Shaw supported completely.[9] As it turned out, no one argued for a closed rule, so the question became how many amendments and which ones should be allowed. After some discussion, we agreed that not more than 20 or so of the 159 amendments should be allowed to come to the floor for debate and votes. We immediately agreed that both the Deal and Mink substitute bills would be made in order, as Shaw had hoped.

There were a few amendments that Shaw and other members of our subcommittee believed had to be allowed on the floor. The first and perhaps most important was the child support amendment on drivers' licenses. If we were to hold Republicans together we had to be certain that female Republicans were satisfied with the final bill. Most Republican women were happy with or at least willing to accept the strong work requirements and even most of the illegitimacy provisions. But if they were going to support strong work requirements on mothers, they wanted to be certain that the child support requirements for fathers were tough. Although many Republicans on Ways and Means objected to the license provision, as I had discovered during that explosive meeting in Archer's Capitol Hill office in February, Archer nonetheless allowed us to support it in the Rules Committee staff meeting because there was a real possibility that we could lose Republican votes if the amendment were not included.

Shaw also wanted an amendment that would increase funding for child care. Thus the second amendment we wanted to be made in order would allow Nancy Johnson of Ways and Means, along with three other Republican women members (Deborah Pryce of Ohio, Jennifer Dunn of Washington, and Enid Waldholtz of Utah) to increase the annual child care authorization by an additional $750 million over five years to nearly $2.1 billion. After extensive discussion, there was agreement that both the amendments wanted by Shaw should be made in order on the floor.

The next day, March 16, the Rules Committee held their hearing on the rule for welfare reform.[10] The fifty-five witnesses took more than six hours to argue for their amendments. The hearing produced two surprises. First, nearly all the presentations and discussions were constructive. Although Joe Moakley of Massachusetts, the crusty senior Democrat on the Rules Committee, got things off to a bad start by claiming that the Republican bill had been cooked up "behind closed doors" and that it would hurt children and fail to promote work, the testimony and discussion that followed were almost free of invective and were sincere on both sides. Even Maxine Waters, a black Democrat from California who was normally a bitter foe of Republicans and who hated the Republican bill, was reasonable in arguing for her two amendments, one to pay $1,000 to anyone on Aid to Families with Dependent Children (AFDC) who graduated from high school and the other to require noncustodial parents to participate in supervised visits with their children.

The second surprise was provided by Richard Gephardt of Missouri, the leader of the Democratic forces in the House. Gephardt told the committee that Democrats "would be happy" if the rule simply allowed the Democratic alternative bill to be considered on the floor. To this day, I have no idea why Gephardt made such a statement. As the hundred Democratic amendments and the stream of Democrats coming to testify showed, Democrats wanted a lot more than a single substitute bill. Gephardt's testimony might have been inaccurate, but it proved a windfall for Chairman Solomon, because when the floor debate began on March 21 and Democrats complained that the rule was not fair to them, Solomon pointed out that the rule gave Democrats far more than their leader had requested.

The Rules Committee issued two rules to structure and govern the welfare reform debate. Because the rule was not quite ready, on March 21 the Rules Committee brought a kind of preliminary rule to the floor that provided only for general debate. Ways and Means had two hours; the Education and Agriculture Committees each had an hour and a half. Later in the day, the Rules Committee met, debated the rule that would govern amendments to the bill, and voted on the final rule, which would come to the House floor the next day for debate and a vote.

The bill the rule made in order was HR 1214, the bill I had thrown in the hopper on March 13. After hours of staff negotiations, with lots of input from members, the bill was organized into eight titles that encompassed all the provisions of the bills the three committees had worked such long hours to produce. The products molded into the eight titles of the new bill included the provisions on the welfare and work program as well as many of the illegitimacy provisions from Ways and Means and from Education; the child protection block grant from Ways and Means; the child care block grant from Ways and Means and from Education and the child nutrition block grant from Education; the provisions on noncitizens from Ways and Means with a considerable assist in drafting from the Judiciary Committee;[11] the Food Stamp reforms from the Agriculture Committee; the reforms from Ways and Means of the Supplemental Security Income (SSI) programs for drug addicts and alcoholics and for children; the child support enforcement reforms from Ways and Means; and a miscellaneous title with a few minor provisions.[12]

The floor debate on the first rule, which simply allowed general debate on the bill, began at about two-thirty in the afternoon of March 21. Chairman Solomon officially opened one of the most consequential, searching, and nasty debates in the history of the House of Representatives. As usual, one hour was allowed to debate the rule, with Solomon controlling the thirty minutes allotted to Republicans and Anthony Beilenson of California, a senior Democrat on the Rules Committee, the thirty minutes allotted to Democrats.

The rule debate foreshadowed things to come, as Democrats unveiled many of their major arguments while making harsh attacks on the Republican bill. The most dramatic moment occurred when Cardiss Collins, a black Democrat from Illinois, took the floor. In the course of her withering criticism of the bill, she declared that if Attila the Hun were alive, he would support the bill because, as she put it, the bill was "the most callous, coldhearted, and mean-spirited attack on this country's children that I have ever seen in my life."[13] She then went on to preview many of the primary arguments that Democrats would make against the bill. Not only was the bill cruel to children but in addition there were not enough jobs for these workers; those jobs that were available paid low wages and therefore guaranteed a life in poverty; ending the entitlement to cash benefits would put children at risk of deep poverty; and reforming the school lunch and Special Supplemental Food Program for Women, Infants, and Children (WIC) carried the risk of leaving children hungry.

Shaw had stayed on the floor for the entire rule debate precisely to respond to this kind of rhetoric. In closing debate on the rule, Shaw immediately took up the Attila the Hun accusation as well as the accusation that the Republican bill was cruel to children. In a calm and reasoned manner, he claimed that there was a "resounding silence in this Hall" from Democrats on the flaws of the current system. He argued that welfare "as we know it" is now the "cruelest system" and that, despite their campaign promises, Clinton and the Democrats had failed to change the system. So now Republicans and Democrats must work together to radically change the "cruelest system." He closed by imploring all members to "break the chains of slavery that we have created with welfare" and "work together for a better America."[14] As always, even in the face of claims that his bill was cruel to children, Shaw offered calm and reasoned argument to create bipartisan support for the bill.

After all debate time on the first rule had expired, the rule was accepted "without objection," which meant that neither a voice vote nor a roll call vote was necessary. The House then moved immediately into the five hours of general debate, beginning with the two hours of debate controlled by the Ways and Means Committee (one hour by Republicans and one hour by Democrats). The debate opened with Archer controlling the time for Republicans, meaning that he could speak himself or allow others of his choosing to speak. Sam Gibbons, the senior Democrat on Ways and Means, controlled time for Democrats.

Archer's opening statement was a review of the arguments for our bill. He began by claiming that "the Republican welfare revolution is at hand."[15] He went on to argue that we were replacing the "failed welfare state," which had spent $5.3 trillion since 1965 on a host of programs that failed to reduce poverty. After years of "endless campaign rhetoric" that failed to "end welfare as we know it" (a little shot at President Clinton), Republicans were now offering a bill that put adults on welfare to work, featured a broad attack on illegitimacy, and saved money to help balance the budget. Archer's speech was workmanlike and effective in summarizing the case against the old AFDC program and for our sweeping reforms. Best of all, it was short. Archer would have made a lousy senator.

Gibbons, opening debate for the Democrats, recognized Harold Ford. Ford's was a somewhat rambling speech, but it was another good overview of the arguments Democrats would use against the Republican bill. Although Democrats had specific criticisms against every major portion of the bill, they used six primary arguments as a general condemnation of the bill's centerpiece, the repeal of the AFDC program, along with its entitlement to cash benefits, and the creation of a new welfare program that emphasized work. Specifically, Democrats charged that the bill was weak on work, punished children, took from the poor to give to the rich, failed to provide enough education and training, failed to provide enough child care, and failed to lift families out of poverty, even if they went to work.[16]

These are all worthy arguments, and there is at least a grain of truth in each of them. But upon careful examination, all have major weaknesses. The irony of Democrats arguing that the Republican bill was weak on work was not lost on Republicans. As we have seen, one of the more remarkable aspects of the debate after Republicans assumed control of the House and Senate was that Democrats suddenly seemed to love work. By contrast, during the most recent welfare reform debate, the 1987–88 debate that led to passage of the Family Support Act, House Democrats had done everything possible to avoid the work requirements Republicans fought so hard to achieve. In the end, the 1988 Family Support Act had no work requirement that applied to single parents on welfare. But now we were back, insisting on strong work requirements, and suddenly many Democrats seemed to be with us.

How could the same House Democrats who had strongly opposed work seven years earlier now accuse Republicans, who were proposing the toughest work requirements ever, of being "weak on work"? One factor, of course, is that their president had made work requirements a major part of his presidential campaign and had then kept work in the spotlight by appointing a high-level task force to write a welfare reform bill that emphasized mandatory work. The glacial progress of the task force was regularly reported in the media, especially in the *New York Times,* sometimes on the front page.[17] Single-handedly, Clinton had overcome his party's opposition to work and laid the base for a plausible case that many Democrats believed in mandatory work. A second factor was that, with Republicans now in the majority in both Houses and intent on requiring work, it was a foregone conclusion that whatever bill passed would have strong work requirements. Given that work requirements were a certainty, many Democrats who had previously been suspicious of work decided that perhaps a work requirement was not so bad after all. A third factor was that work requirements were strongly supported by the American public.[18] Knowing that their new position would be in line with public opinion, it was much easier for Democrats to discover their hidden desire to support work than it would have been if the public had opposed mandatory work.

Given their turnabout on work requirements, it would be possible to accuse Democrats of hypocrisy. But based on my observation of their arguments during both the 1987–88 debate on the Family Support Act and the 1995–96 debate, I think the most reasonable explanation is that Democrats had believed in work all along but that two factors masked this belief: the Democratic affinity for compassion led them to emphasize education and training before work and their commitment to labor unions caused them to worry about displacing regular workers. The vital role in the transformation of Democrats on work requirements was played by President Clinton. Clinton deserves immense credit for leading Democrats to a position that previously was considered right of center on mandatory work and that shattered one of the major barriers to congressional passage of true welfare reform.[19]

And finally, as much as I hate to admit our mistakes, the Democrats' argument about the weakness of the Republican work requirement was partially correct. It was almost fully correct when it had been employed against the bill we presented to the Ways and Means Subcommittee a month earlier. Our close relationship with Republican governors had caused us to write that first bill with truly weak work requirements. But the Education Committee, which had not participated as directly as Ways and Means in negotiations with the governors, had a much stronger work requirement in their bill, and Chairman Archer insisted that we strengthen the work requirement in the bill we brought to full committee. Now in preparation for floor debate, Democrats had endorsed the Deal substitute, which contained a work requirement that was much stronger than the work requirements in previous bills written by Democrats. So now we were involved in an escalation of work requirements, with Democrats and Republicans trying to outdo each other. Most of us considered this to be a pretty good situation.

In the end, and contrary to the Democrats' rhetoric, the bill we brought to the floor had much stronger work requirements than the Deal substitute. The Republican bill phased in its work requirement until states were required to have 50 percent of their caseload in the labor force by 2003; not to be outdone, the Deal substitute required 52 percent of caseload to be working by 2003. Similarly, there were only slight differences between the two bills in the number of hours recipients were required to work each week to qualify as fulfilling the work requirement.[20] Against these similarities, however, the Deal work requirement suffered from a number of serious flaws. First, it was not clear that welfare participants would actually be required to work until they had been on the rolls for five years. Second, the participation requirements gave credit to welfare leavers, the policy favored by governors that we strongly opposed because it gutted the work requirement. Third, Deal had lots of exemptions from the work requirement, not least the provision that anyone engaged in education or training was exempt. Fourth, states could not deny cash to recipients for failing to work unless the recipient had received at least two years of education, training, or services. In view of these pretty substantial holes in the Deal work requirement, it was difficult to take the Democrats seriously when they criticized our bill as being weak on work.

The second Democratic argument against the Republican bill was that it was "extreme," "harsh," "cruel," "abusive," and "mean-spirited" and that it "attacked children," "lashed out at children," and "punished children." This type of rhetoric was taken up, although at a lower volume and with much less frequency, in the Senate. Senator Daniel Patrick Moynihan of New York, one of the bill's severest critics, said the bill would end the nation's commitment to poor children, claiming that children would be sleeping on grates—the Republican version of the Great Society—in the nation's major cities and that their little bodies would freeze at night.[21]

Nor was the claim that the bill would hurt children confined to members of Congress. In an editorial on February 14 as House Committees were preparing to mark up the welfare reform bill, USA Today said the bill used "slash-and-burn tactics" and that children would pay a "catastrophic" price if the bill passed.[22] Anthony Lewis, writing in the New York Times in January, said that Gingrich had "crawled out of a sewer" and that Republican welfare reforms were "punitive" and would throw children into orphanages.[23] The New York Times featured editorials by Bob Herbert. My favorite, "Inflicting Pain on Children," claimed that Republicans were conducting a "jihad" against the poor and that our welfare legislation "makes war on the kids of this country to pay for the capital gains tax cut," that our budget cuts were "loathsome," and that our policies were designed to "deliberately inflict harm" on children and the poor.[24] The Washington Post columnist Dorothy Gilliam called the language used by Republicans on the House floor "venomous" and wondered if the reaction to Republican arguments by black Democrats "resembled the way Jewish people felt in Germany when the anti-Semitic rhetoric escalated and long-held legal rights were being eroded."[25]

Although most of the charges were general and seemed to apply to the entire bill, it is possible to identify specific provisions in the bill that, under a reasonable accounting, could increase the number of destitute children. Perhaps the most obvious were the provisions designed to reduce the number of poor children receiving SSI. The charges against these provisions were that they deprived disabled children of cash benefits and Medicaid coverage, a change that if true surely made them worse off.[26] But this claim begs the question. Republicans were arguing that many children on SSI were not disabled under any reasonable definition of disability. Following the Supreme Court's Zebley decision, and through the use of a test called the Individualized Functional Assessment, children who merely behaved in age-inappropriate ways were found to be disabled and were awarded the SSI cash benefit and Medicaid.[27] Thus many poor children who acted out or who had a learning disability were given a guaranteed cash income and health insurance.

The simple question arises: Should the federal government award cash and health insurance coverage to poor children who don't read well or who act out in school? Even the General Accounting Office (now the Government Accountability Office), in official testimony and reports, held that such children were not truly disabled. Moreover, even if these children were dropped from SSI, nearly all of them would qualify for AFDC (or whatever new cash welfare program Congress enacted in place of AFDC), which would result in both a cash benefit and Medicaid coverage. In most states the AFDC benefit was less than the SSI benefit by around $120 a month, so some families would experience financial loss.[28] However, because most of their children were in the Food Stamp program, the lower AFDC benefit would result in a higher Food Stamp benefit, reducing this $120 loss by about a third, to $80. The income loss, in short, was modest, and all the children would retain Medicaid coverage. At the very least, most of the rhetoric about the horrors of the Republican SSI reforms were overblown. Further, the Democrats own proposals included similar SSI reforms.

Another specific children's benefit that Republicans were trying to change was the child protection program that provided states with federal dollars to help abused and neglected children. The federal child protection program guaranteed payments to states for poor children based on the administrative costs of their system, certain training costs, and state costs for out-of-home placements in either foster homes or institutions (on average, the federal government paid a little over half of placement costs). The Republican proposal was to give the states almost all the money that the Congressional Budget Office (CBO) projected would be given to states over the five years between 1996 and 2000, but the amount of money would be fixed each year in a block grant. The justification for this proposal was that it would overcome what most analysts regarded as a major flaw in federal law, which directed the bulk of federal dollars to subsidizing care only after abused and neglected children had been removed from their families, thereby prohibiting the use of this source of federal funds for prevention or treatment programs that might help keep families together or move children more quickly toward adoption. The major argument that critics advanced to oppose the child protection block grant was that if states had a sudden increase in their child protection caseload they would be forced to live with the fixed number of federal dollars guaranteed under the proposed Republican policy. Moreover, as in the case of all block grants, unless the funding included an annual inflation adjustment, the value of the block grant would wither away over the years.

There is no question that this proposal entailed risk to children. The child protection caseload had surged in the early 1990s,[29] due in large part, according to many experts, to the crack cocaine epidemic that swept the nation in those years. Opponents argued that caseloads could increase more than anticipated by CBO in making the cost estimates for future years and that states would, if the rolls swelled, receive fewer federal dollars than they would have received under the open-ended entitlement the block grant replaced.

Because of opposition in the Senate, especially from Republican Senator John Chafee of Rhode Island, the entire child protection proposal was eventually dropped from the bill, and the open-ended entitlement funds from the federal government continued uninterrupted. Looking back from the present, then, we can determine whether the concern that caseloads would actually increase more than predicted by the budget projection experts at CBO was accurate. As it turned out, caseloads actually increased less than predicted by CBO. It follows that states would have received more money under the block grant proposed by Republicans than states did in fact receive under the open-ended entitlement. If we compare the amount that the CBO estimated in 1995 that the states would receive in the entitlement child protection programs between 1996 and 2000 under the Republican proposal with the amount states actually received, the difference is nearly $1.5 billion over the five years. In other words, if the block grant had been passed as proposed by Republicans in HR 4, states would have received nearly $1.5 billion more to help abused and neglected children than they actually received under the open-ended entitlements.[30] But this outcome could not have been predicted with certainty, so it is clear that the Republican proposal for a block grant did entail some additional risk for children, incurred to increase state flexibility in using federal dollars to provide the most effective help for abused and neglected children and their families. Increased risk? Yes. Mean and cruel? No, especially because the Republican proposal would have given states both more flexibility and more money.

In addition to these specific instances of risk to children, a similar risk was posed by converting the open-ended AFDC funding to capped, block grant funding. As with the child protection block grant, this approach had the advantage of giving states flexibility in use of federal dollars and a financial incentive to help mothers leave welfare, but these advantages were again accompanied by ending the individual entitlement of the AFDC program. Senator Moynihan believed that this was the single most objectionable feature of the bill.[31]

Nor was ending the entitlement the only change in federal policy on cash welfare that could pose a hazard to children. The time limit meant that most families could stay on welfare for a maximum of five years. Before this change, nearly 70 percent of families on the rolls at any given time would eventually be on the rolls for five years or more (counting repeat spells).[32] Unless welfare reform convinced families to look for work rather than staying on welfare year after year, literally millions of families could be expected to hit the time limit and involuntarily lose the cash benefit. Similarly, the sanctions that were a vital part of the work requirements meant that some families would have their cash benefit reduced and that some, depending on state policy, would lose their cash benefit altogether. Clearly, both of these policies increased the risk that more children would be financially destitute than under the AFDC program and its entitlement principle.

It is impossible to avoid the conclusion that the Republican bill did increase the risk that children could lose some benefits. But the point of the bill was to require, and where necessary force, parents to become self-sufficient and leave the welfare rolls after a temporary stay. Republicans believed that pursuing this goal justified subjecting families to additional risk, especially in view of the fact that other American families face the same risk. In the final analysis, Republicans were willing to increase the risk of destitution to force the welfare system, and individuals participating in the system, to change their behavior and to struggle harder than in the past to achieve independence. Most Republicans, certainly including Archer and Shaw and perhaps every other member of the Ways and Means Committee, believed the measures that increased the risk to children were the only way to jolt the system into something more consistent with American values. Republicans were determined to put truth into the famous aphorism that War on Poverty programs were a "hand up, not a handout."[33]

The most likely outcome of the changes in AFDC would be to increase both the number of families leaving welfare for low-wage jobs as well as the number of families losing welfare because of the time limits or the sanctions. Because of the Earned Income Tax Credit (EITC, which by 1996 was worth a maximum of around $3,600 a year), expanded child care, and expanded Medicaid coverage, nearly all the families leaving welfare for low-wage work would be financially better off than if they had remained on welfare.[34] By contrast, the time limit and the sanctions, if implemented aggressively by states, would increase the number of nonworking mothers who lost their welfare benefits. A demanding welfare system like the one we were proposing would increase independence but might also increase destitution. It seemed impossible to determine an acceptable ratio of the number of destitute families compared with the number of families achieving independence through work, but it was certain that Republicans were willing to tolerate a higher ratio than Democrats. In my own view, the hard calculus of Republican work policy was not mean or cruel, but it was tough.

The third major Democratic argument against the bill was one of their classic arguments against Republican policy. This argument, affectionately known to Republicans as the "class warfare" ploy, held that Republicans were stealing from the poor to give to the rich. As one Democrat claimed during floor debate, Republicans stood for "reverse Robin Hood."[35] The typical Republican reaction to the accusation of engaging in class warfare was the same as Reagan's response to President Carter's criticism of Republicans during on the 1980 presidential debates: "There you go again."[36] A major tenet of Republican philosophy is that people own their earnings and government is privileged to get any of the people's hard-earned money. Taken together with the preference for smaller government, lower taxes are the heart of the Republican agenda. Thus, as the presidency of George W. Bush shows so well, Republicans are likely to enact tax cuts whenever they have the votes. Given the Republicans' long-standing commitment to both welfare reform and tax cuts, it was all but inevitable that both would be included in legislation if Republicans took over Congress.

Of course, it was not inevitable that welfare reform would reduce government spending. Indeed, every major reform bill enacted by Democrats over the years increased federal spending. But Republicans thought that the nation suffered from too much rather than too little welfare. Many of the reforms Republicans believed would improve American government and American society resulted in less welfare spending. It is possible, based on sound arguments, to disagree with reducing the number of children receiving SSI, terminating SSI for drug addicts and alcoholics, terminating most welfare programs for noncitizens, and reducing the Food Stamp program, but these policies did save money and thereby reduced the need for taxes in the long run. Even so, because the savings were scored against a baseline that was increasing rapidly, the effect of our bill was not to actually lower spending on the major programs affected by the legislation but to reduce the rate of growth. Even after all of our reforms, CBO estimated that spending on the affected social programs would grow from $168 billion in 1996 to $239 billion in 2000.[37] Only in Washington can spending growth of this magnitude be called a cut, let alone mean and cruel.

Another of the major arguments in the Democratic assault on the bill was that it did not provide enough money for education and training. In the Democratic worldview, mothers should be offered education or training before being required to work and certainly before having their benefits terminated because they had reached a time limit. Democrats resisted policy that, in effect, forced poor mothers into low-wage jobs, the only ones for which they could qualify without additional education and training. But Republicans countered that research had shown that providing education and training was not notably successful in leading to employment or increased earnings.[38] Far better to emphasize getting mothers into a job and emphasize the "soft skills" of coming to work every day, arriving on time, complying with supervision, getting along with co-workers, and being friendly and helpful to customers. The best way to learn these skills, argued Republicans, was to actually hold a job. In the end, the bill was about work, not education.

Yet another argument used by Democrats and closely related to the debate on education and training was that, even if poor mothers found work, they would

not be able to escape poverty. Most of the mothers on welfare had little education and little work experience, the two major factors that create value in the
labor market. Thus they would be confined to low-wage jobs and condemned to
a life of poverty. Republicans strongly disagreed with this claim. In the first place,
based simply on the values that Republicans brought to the debate, if a given family had exactly the same amount of money on welfare as it did working, the family should choose work because self-reliance is the American way while welfare
dependency for the able-bodied is shameful. Second, Republicans argued that the
claim that low-wage jobs would confine welfare mothers to poverty was false.
Matt Weidinger and I prepared simple charts for Shaw and members of the committee to show that low-wage work would always improve the financial condition of families dependent on welfare, if they had two or fewer children (as nearly
75 percent of AFDC families did).[39]

Consider the math. The welfare package in 1996 in the median state consisted of a maximum AFDC annual cash benefit of about $4,700 and a Food
Stamp benefit of around $3,700, for a total cash plus near-cash income of around
$8,400.[40] The family would also receive Medicaid coverage. Thus it was a math-
ematical fact that the mother could not escape poverty if her only source of
income was welfare, even if the cash value of her Food Stamp benefit is counted
(the poverty level for a mother and two children in 1996 was about $12,300). The
only way a mother on welfare could escape poverty was to work part-time or
cheat by hiding other sources of income.[41] By contrast, if the mother went to
work at a minimum wage job and worked year-round, full-time, she would
receive wages of a little less than $11,000. In addition, with two children (in
1996), she would receive around $3,600 from the EITC and would be eligible for
about $2,000 in Food Stamps, bringing the family's total income to around
$16,600. In most cases, child care would be covered, the mother would not owe
any federal income taxes, and her Social Security taxes would be about $850
(and she would be earning credit toward Social Security retirement benefits and
Medicare coverage).[42] Some mothers also would qualify for the child tax credit,
which was then under consideration in Congress and would be enacted in 1997.[43]
Further, the mother would receive at least one year of Medicaid coverage after the
family left welfare, and the children would be covered as long as the family had
low income. Clearly, in most circumstances the mother and children would be
better off in low-wage work than on welfare.

The Democrats' argument about low-wage jobs was misleading in a second
respect. Not only would most families on welfare improve their financial status
by working at low-wage jobs, but many if not most of them would escape poverty
as well. The poverty level for a mother and two children in 1995 was $12,278. The
family with income of $16,600 would be well above the poverty level if all their
income were counted. The income argument definitely favored reform, but

Democrats continued to criticize the bill on the grounds that low-wage work would increase destitution.

Democrats countered the Republican claims about work and income with another of their major arguments against the bill; namely, that it did not provide enough support for working families. By support, Democrats meant child care, transportation, health insurance, and cash supplements—in general, anything that facilitated work by low-income families or supplemented their income. The most frequent charge by Democrats was that the bill did not provide enough money for child care. In addition, under AFDC law, mothers on welfare who were required to work or train, and mothers who left welfare for employment, were guaranteed child care (for up to one year in the case of mothers leaving welfare for employment). The Republican plan was to end these entitlements, fold several child care programs into the child care block grant, increase the amount of federal money available to states, require state matching payments to further increase the total amount of money available for child care, and then let states decide which low- and moderate-income families would receive child care support. Republicans pointed out that states would have significantly more money for child care under the child care block grant and that, if they used work to reduce their welfare rolls, they could use the savings to pay for additional child care.

Republicans also responded to the Democrats' criticism of the lack of help for working families by pointing to growth over the previous decade in programs that provided assistance to poor and low-income working families. The record of creating or expanding these programs really was quite impressive and even appeared to represent something like a long-term strategy by Congress to provide growing levels of support outside the cash welfare program to families willing to work their way off welfare or to avoid welfare altogether by working in low-wage jobs. The EITC had been created in 1975 and then expanded in 1986, 1990, and 1993. By 1996 it was worth a maximum of $3,600 to a working family with two or more children.[44] Similarly, Medicaid coverage had been expanded on many occasions since the mid-1980s, and its linkage to receipt of cash welfare was almost completely cut.[45] As a result, millions of children in low-income working families were eligible for generous taxpayer-paid benefits even after they left welfare, including Medicaid coverage. Combined with the increases in child care funding, the federal government had led the way to creating a variety of programs that provided very solid help to low-income working families. These programs meant that even minimum-wage work would make a family financially better off than welfare alone.[46]

In addition to these reasonable arguments against the Republican bill, Democrats employed a level of invective and near-hysteria against the bill that created real anger and bitterness between the two parties. The debate was like a two-layer cake, with a solid foundation of rational debate, sometimes based on appeal to actual evidence, concerning the most fundamental questions about the type of welfare system the nation should have. This foundational layer, however, was covered by a second layer of negative rhetoric and nastiness. Going beyond even Ford's intemperate attack at the conclusion of the Ways and Means subcommittee markup in February, the bitterest denunciation of Republicans during general debate on the floor was made by another member of the Ways and Means Committee, John Lewis of Georgia. With a distinguished background in the civil rights movement, Lewis was one of the most honored and respected members of the House.[47] Shaw, a fellow southerner, had the highest respect for Lewis because of his bravery under fire during the civil rights struggle. Thus Lewis's denunciation of Republicans and their bill was all the more upsetting to Shaw.

Lewis opened his remarks by saying that the bill was "mean-spirited," "cruel," "wrong," and "downright low-down." The bill was "angry" and "devoid of compassion and feeling." Worse, the bill "takes money out of the pockets of the disabled," "takes heat from the homes of the poor," and "takes food out of the mouths of children." Lewis then warmed to his main point: German Protestant theologian Martin Niemoller, describing Nazi Germany before World War II, said when they came for the Communists, he didn't speak up, when they came for the Jews, the trade unionists, or the Catholics, he didn't speak up. Then they came for the Protestants, but by then "no one was left to speak up." Lewis urged his colleagues, "Read the proposal. Read the small print. Read the Republican contract. They are coming for the children. They are coming for the poor. They are coming for the sick, the elderly, and the disabled. This is the Contract with America."[48]

When Lewis finished, Shaw, following House tradition by addressing Lewis as "the gentleman from Georgia," said, "there is no one in this House that I have more respect for than you," but to compare Republicans to Nazis is "an absolute outrage." Shaw was surprised, he said, "that anybody with your distinguished background would dare to do such a horrible thing." Shaw, visibly upset, sat down, allowing the Democrats to speak next. Visitors in the House gallery, who had probably come to the House expecting a quiet and somewhat boring discussion, got into the spirit of the moment by cheering and applauding both Lewis and Shaw, whereupon John Linder of Georgia, who was serving in the Speaker's chair, admonished the audience not to make any sounds or he would clear the gallery. Gibbons, who was controlling the debate for Democrats, stood up, took the microphone, looked over at Shaw and, red-faced, said: "Sometimes the truth hurts."[49]

Following the general debate on March 21, which ended just before ten o'clock at night, the House took no further action on the bill. Rather, the real action had been taking place in the Rules Committee, which had been meeting during the floor debate to make final decisions about which amendments would come to the floor for debate and for voting on the House floor. The nature of amendments in the Rules Committee is almost exclusively to try to add (or occasionally drop) amendments from the list of amendments made in order by the rule the chairman places before the committee. Thus all the amendments made by Democrats were attempts to add amendments that their Democratic colleagues had submitted to the Rules Committee but that had not been allowed to come to the floor by the chairman's bill.

In the end, the chairman's rule was accepted on a vote that was nearly along party lines, typical of Rules Committee action on a big and partisan bill like welfare reform. Republicans liked the bill; Democrats didn't. The ones who liked the bill voted for the rule; the ones who didn't, voted against it. But the former had the majority, so the rule was adopted. What could be simpler?

Thus the Rules Committee joined Ways and Means, Education, and Agriculture in exhibiting exceptional voting discipline. The Rules Committee had nine Republicans and four Democrats. One of the Republicans had to go out of town at the last minute because of an emergency, leaving eight Republicans present during the critical meeting to approve the final rule. Not only were none of the twenty Democratic amendments approved but Republicans voted against their chairman on only three amendments. There were 4 Republican votes supporting these three Democratic amendments. After the twenty Democratic amendments, the vote on final passage was 7 to 5, with one Republican voting against the chairman. Thus of the 176 Republican votes on the twenty amendments and on final passage of the rule, 171 (97 percent) were in favor of the party position. With discipline like this, Republicans were able to bring the bill to the floor with exactly the amendments favored by the leadership and the chairmen of the committees of jurisdiction, the rule more or less that staff had worked out in our meeting of March 15. Again, this is precisely the way the system was designed to work when the majority can maintain its votes. The rule approved by the committee made thirty-one amendments in order, five of them from Democrats. In addition, the rule made in order both of the Democratic substitute bills, one from Deal and one from Mink. Democrats were also given the right to offer the motion to recommit with or without instructions.

One hour was allowed for debate of the rule itself, followed by a vote on the rule. If the rule was adopted, up to thirty minutes of debate was allowed on each amendment, an hour on each of the substitutes, and ten minutes on the motion to recommit. If all this time is summed—the debate on the rule plus debate on all the amendments, the motion to recommit, plus the one hour on the first rule and the five hours of general debate that had already taken place—the total is around twenty-four hours. Debate would, of course, have to be interrupted from time to time to allow votes on the various amendments. To save floor time and wear and tear on the members, who had to walk a block or two from the House Office Buildings to the Capitol for every vote, the rule allowed Archer to approach the authors of the various amendments and combine several of the Republican amendments into an en bloc amendment that would be debated and voted on as one amendment. As it turned out, ten Republicans agreed to have their amendment included in the en bloc amendment, thereby substantially reducing the number of separate amendments.

On March 22 the House opened for business at ten in the morning.[50] After a few opening one-minute speeches, the welfare reform debate immediately got off to an ugly start. Cardiss Collins, for example, said that this bill, the most important that members would address during the entire session of Congress, "cuts, slashes, and eliminates federal programs."[51] Similarly, Harold Volkmer of Missouri interrupted a speech about the merits of the bill by Jim Talent to observe that, like the Catholic bishops and several prominent Republicans, he was afraid the provision eliminating cash benefits for unmarried mothers under age eighteen would increase abortion rates.[52] As he put it, he didn't think "killing" children was a good way to reduce the welfare rolls. After similar comments by several Democrats, a Jewish Republican member from Pennsylvania rose to criticize the previous day's speech by John Lewis comparing Republicans to Nazis. Jon Fox said that, "as a member of Congress" and "an individual of the Jewish faith," he was compelled to observe that any attempt to "equate" the Republican bill to "Nazi Germany and the atrocities of the Third Reich exceeds the bounds of propriety and is simply untrue."[53] As soon as Fox finished, the member controlling time for Democrats recognized Lewis, who proceeded to repeat everything he had said the previous day, concluding with, "I say it again today . . . for the Record."

Following a few procedural votes, the House got down to the business of considering the amendments themselves. First up was the all-important rule that would make the amendments in order, including the Democrats' two substitute bills and the motion to recommit, and that would govern the time allotted for debate. By tradition, Solomon as chairman of the Rules Committee had the right to introduce and defend the rule. As soon as Solomon began talking, it became apparent that his immediate concern was to justify his rule by comparing it with previous rules governing welfare debates. Solomon compared his rule with the rule made in order by Democrats during the big welfare reform debate of 1987–88. Under that rule, only two amendments and the motion to recommit were made in order. Republicans could present a substitute bill, and Democrats had an en bloc amendment. By contrast, Solomon's rule made thirty-one amendments in order; these included five from Democrats plus the two Democratic substitute bills plus the motion to recommit. Thus Solomon's rule on welfare reform allowed much more input from Democrats than Democrats had allowed Republicans in the last major welfare reform battle.

The debate on the rule was especially vigorous because there are no clear guidelines about what is fair. From the perspective of how Democrats had run the House, the Republican rule seemed fair. But if fairness is defined as allowing the light of the democratic process to force the majority party to subject each of its controversial provisions to a floor vote, the rule fell short. Even so, there is no doubt that Republicans were strongly united behind the rule. It made the important Republican amendments in order and avoided most of the difficult votes on amendments that Democrats had requested but were denied. Many Republicans would have been only too glad to support an even tougher rule, one that gave Democrats even fewer opportunities to amend our bill.

As the rule debate was completed and debate on the amendments began, the first amendment was a "technical" amendment sponsored by Archer. On a big bill, technical amendments that make a list of truly technical changes in the bill—such as corrections of citations in the statutes—are not usual. But often the temptation to stick a substantive amendment onto a technical amendment is too much for the majority to resist. In this case, the Budget Committee had inadvertently put a provision in the bill that, in effect, locked all the savings away for deficit reduction. But our leadership wanted to use the savings for tax reduction. Thus the provision had to come out of the bill. The provisions removing the restriction on use of savings was therefore placed in the "technical amendment." Democrats objected strongly to this provision. Most Republicans agreed with the intent of the amendment but were critical of the Budget Committee for shaping the bill in such a way that such an amendment was necessary. But being in a disciplined majority covers a multitude of sins, including bad planning. Democrats may have won the debate, but in due course we won the vote by 228 to 205, with only one Republican (Connie Morella of Maryland) and no Democrats crossing party lines.

Archer's second amendment was the en bloc amendment containing eleven Republican amendments (Archer's and ten others) approved by the Rules Committee. Collapsing eleven amendments into one reduced the potential debate time on the amendments from five hours and thirty minutes to thirty minutes. The Democrats had a fit. George Miller of California leaped to his feet to make a parliamentary inquiry and began quizzing the chairman about how many amendments had been folded into the en bloc amendment and how much time was allowed for debate. Ford joined the fray, asking that the time for debate be increased to one hour. Under the rules of the House, the time allotted by the rule could only be expanded by unanimous consent, meaning that if no one on the floor at that moment raised an objection, the time allotment could be changed.

But Archer pointed out that the rule had been passed by the House, that the rule gave him the authority to assemble many amendments into an en bloc amendment, and that the amendments he had accepted in the en bloc amendment were "relatively noncontroversial." Therefore, he said he "must object," thereby killing Ford's request for more time. Gibbons, who was controlling time for Democrats, popped right up and asked unanimous consent that an hour and thirty minutes be allotted for the debate. The chair denied this request because a similar request had just failed to attract unanimous consent. Then Gibbons stated that no one even knew what the amendments were, that the big en bloc amendment had arrived on the floor as "a bolt out of the blue," and that the pittance of time allowed amounted to a gag order. Yet again he asked for unanimous consent for more time, now requesting fifty-nine minutes. Republicans immediately objected, so he asked for fifty-eight minutes. Another objection produced a request for fifty-seven minutes, then fifty-six minutes. Finally, the chair pointedly told Gibbons that he had "made his point."

After more skirmishing, the chair tried to get the debate back on track by recognizing Archer. But before Archer could speak, Gibbons, obviously still quite stirred up, requested fifty-seven minutes and forty-nine seconds for debate. The chair again recognized Archer, but Gibbons repeated his time request. Continuing to ignore Gibbons, the chair again recognized Archer, who quickly summarized the en bloc amendment and then recognized Jennifer Dunn of Washington, who summarized her part of the en bloc amendment.

Following Dunn, the chair had no choice except to recognize Gibbons because he controlled the time for Democrats. Gibbons launched into a statement about the unfairness and even arrogance of the way Republicans conducted House business. Then, during a caustic talk by Joe Kennedy of Massachusetts, John LaFalce, a New York Democrat, offered the motion to adjourn. This motion, which was certain to be defeated, would nonetheless disrupt the floor, because Democrats could call for a recorded vote, thereby bringing all the members to the floor and wasting thirty minutes or so. Such tactics are all the minority has when it knows the majority has the votes to enact their legislation.

After Republicans had defeated the motion to adjourn, the chairman of the House followed regular procedure by announcing the vote count. The moment he finished, Gibbons looked over at Republicans still milling about on their side of the House chamber and yelled, "You all sit down and shut up. Sit down and shut up." The chairman, clearly taken aback, asked that the House be in order. Whereupon Gibbon observed that that was exactly what he was trying to do and, just to show he meant business, yelled again for Republicans to "sit down and shut up."[54]

Now the chairman informed Gibbons that he was "entirely out of order." Gibbons' energetic response was that he had control of the time. At this point, Archer decided that it would be a good idea to throw the Democrats a bone by granting more time for the en bloc amendment after all. So Archer asked for unanimous consent to extend the time for an additional thirty minutes, and the chairman asked if there were objections. Gibbons took the floor and gave another impassioned speech about how he had never seen such abuse of the rights of the minority and how mean the Republican bill was. As soon as he said the bill was "mean to children," Republicans began to boo him, whereupon he looked over at the Republicans and said, "Boo if you want to. Make asses out of yourselves [before] the American people."

The chairman gave Gibbons another little talk about how the chair had let him go somewhat far afield with his parliamentary inquiry. After more squabbling, Gibbons observed, "I think I have established the point, Mr. Chairman, that we are proceeding on a cruel bill in an unusual manner." With that, he sat down, the chairman recognized Archer, and Archer turned the floor over to Henry Hyde from Illinois to explain his amendment. For the moment at least, the fireworks had subsided.

Hyde was concerned that, given the intense pressure to reduce nonmarital births, states might use some of the money from the block grant to pay for abortions. In the view of pro-life conservatives, there are few crimes more heinous than public funding of abortions. Hyde's amendment, which would prohibit use of block grant funds for "medical procedures," was part of Archer's en bloc amendment. Given the concern among strongly antiabortion Republicans that some of the anti-illegitimacy policies might encourage abortions, Archer and Shaw (both of whom had voted against abortion rights throughout their careers) welcomed the Hyde amendment and directed Matt and me to work with Hyde in fashioning his language. A legal review of terminology, conducted at our request by the Congressional Research Service, showed that "medical services" included abortion but not most types of birth control.[55] We wanted to outlaw the former while allowing states to use the funds for the latter if they so wished. Republican moderates, and a number of conservatives as well, strongly favored the use of birth control by older women and by women, including teenagers, who had already had a baby. So we arranged for Hyde and Jim Greenwood, a former social worker and a leading moderate Republican voice in the House, to come to the floor for a colloquy, in which members conduct a discussion to clarify some issue. The key exchange in the colloquy was Greenwood asking Hyde if his amendment was intended to rule out "family planning services." Hyde said that his intent was to rule out abortions but without "interfering with access to pregnancy-related services."[56] This brief exchange united all factions of the Republican Party, and the amendment passed easily.

The Hyde amendment and related amendments offered by Jim Bunn of Oregon and Chris Smith of New Jersey show the other side of the illegitimacy debate Republicans had been having among themselves ever since Shaw and Talent clashed throughout the summer and fall of 1994 over the Contract with America bill. Resolution of the conflict about how far to go on illegitimacy had resulted in exceptionally strong provisions, including the Murray Light provision outlawing cash welfare for babies born to unwed mothers under age eighteen and the family cap, prohibiting states from using federal dollars to raise family cash benefits when mothers on welfare had another baby. But now the wing of the Republican Party devoted to vigilance on abortion expressed a concern that teenage girls and mothers already on welfare might abort their fetuses if deprived of a major means of support. This difficult balancing feat—of stirring in enough antiabortion measures to keep our right flank intact while retaining strong anti-illegitimacy provisions—was and continued to be one of the greatest threats to our bill, far greater than the antics of Sam Gibbons.

The final amendment to the block grant program was offered by Chris Smith, along with Hyde, perhaps the leading antiabortion fighter in the House. Smith's amendment would make available vouchers for diapers and formula, but not cash, for additional children born to mothers already on welfare. During the debate, an especially extreme speech against the Republican bill was made by William Clay of Missouri. He observed that Republicans seemed to get upset "every time somebody mentions Nazi Germany in relation to what they want to do to poor people in this country." But, he went on, "Hitler had a minister of propaganda that said, 'Tell a lie, tell it big enough, tell it often enough, and it will become the truth.' That's what Republicans are doing by saying they are trying to help the poor. They are telling the biggest lie in the world." Then he added, "I say they ought to be ashamed, and they ought to go back into history and look and see if [what they are doing] is close to what Adolph Hitler did to people in that country. Let me say, if their level of frustration is such that they think that all of the problems of this country depend on what is happening in welfare, and if this [their welfare reform bill] does not work, if their frustration stays there, what is next? Castration? Sterilization? After that—I hate to say what is next."[57]

After a series of votes on the Archer amendment, the Hyde amendment, the Smith amendment, and two additional amendments, all of which were won by Republicans, the House at last appeared to be running smoothly, with an emphasis on reasoned debate and at least somewhat cordial relations. It helped that Gibbons was no longer controlling time for Democrats. So the block grant and all its provisions, including the work requirement and the anti-illegitimacy measures, had survived the amendment process largely intact, although the Smith and Bunn amendments had weakened both the Murray Light and the family cap provisions. Ironically, both were Republican amendments. After considering two more amendments, the House adjourned at nine o'clock, leaving eight amendments, the two Democratic substitutes, the motion to recommit, and final passage of the Republican bill still to go.

On the morning of March 23 the House opened for business at ten o'clock. After one-minute speeches and other minor business, the House moved into the welfare debate at a few minutes before eleven. The session began with an amendment by Johnson to add money to the child care block grant and an amendment

by Marge Roukema to require states to enter into competitive bidding for purchase of infant formula for the WIC program, a procedure that had been shown
to save money and that was strongly endorsed in writing by the Federal Trade
Commission.[58] These bipartisan amendments were accepted by voice vote. Thus
in sharp contrast with the raucous opening day, this day opened with over an
hour of measured, reasoned, and calm debate—and even bipartisan agreement.

By around six o'clock in the evening, the House had considered all the individual amendments and turned to the surprising bill, HR 982, the Democrats'
substitute bill. Nathan Deal and his colleagues Charlie Stenholm of Texas, John
Tanner of Tennessee, Blanch Lincoln of Arkansas, and other moderate Democrats, as well as their staffs, had sacrificed many hours of sleep to put together
such a massive bill in such a short time. Ironically, many provisions in the Deal
bill were similar to those in our bill, including extending Medicaid coverage for
moms leaving welfare, banning housing benefits for teens having babies, requiring teens to stay in school, and requiring legally binding affidavits of support for
certain noncitizens. Other provisions closely tracked Republican policy except for
a key word or concept that made all the difference, such as replacing a "ban on
benefits" with an "option to ban benefits." Before the Republican takeover of
Congress, the Deal substitute would have been considered so radical that very few
Democrats would have supported it. If Clinton had introduced a bill somewhat
to the left of the Deal substitute, at least half the Democrats and most Republicans would have supported it. But after the Republican takeover of Congress, we
moved the terms of debate on welfare so far to the right so rapidly that Democrats supported a radical bill like Deal's as their last, best chance of stopping our
bill. They hoped to use the bad to defeat the terrible.

Our goal during the Deal debate was simple: defeat the Deal substitute without alienating any of the moderate Democrats who might vote for our bill. Thus
we urged all our members to make substantive criticisms of the Deal substitute
but without saying anything negative about either the bill or its authors. Both at
the staff level and the member level, we admired Deal and his colleagues, especially Stenholm, for their moderate views and for their achievement in writing
such a fine bill in such a short period. Shaw and I had often worked with Stenholm (and his colleague Tom Carper, before he left the House to become governor, then senator, of Delaware) and his staff over the years, both on welfare and
on child care. Working together, we managed to have a substantial influence on
both the 1988 Family Support Act and on the 1990 child care reforms. For Shaw
and several other senior Republicans like Mike Castle, Dave Camp, and Nancy
Johnson, the debate on the Deal substitute was not unlike a mild dispute among
friends. It is also notable that the Democrats who authored the Deal substitute
made almost no negative comments about the Republican bill. Rather, they
focused on substance throughout the floor debate.

Archer's opening speech began by noting that the Deal bill meant that Democrats were now saying, "'Me too,' on this vital issue," but that their bill still had serious flaws.[59] As arguably the major antitax Republican in the House, Archer's first argument against the Deal bill was that it would raise the taxes of over 2 million Americans, because Deal had restructured the Dependent Care Tax Credit, a tax program that helped families pay for child care. Deal wanted to use the money to finance his bill, a move that many Democrats supported because the credit currently helped mostly middle- and upper-income families. Moreover, Archer pointed to the fact that the Deal substitute spent more money not only than the Republican bill (which saved around $60 billion) but also than current law. Thus, he observed, the bill followed the traditional Democratic approach of reforming welfare by spending more money. And since the bill also raised taxes, it was consistent with the general Democratic approach to governing: tax and spend. This argument, of course, was red meat for Republicans. In about two minutes, Archer framed the Deal substitute in such a way that most Republicans would vote against it.

Deal should have immediately refuted Archer's powerful speech, especially because Deal's opening statement did not review the strengths of his bill or defend it against the attacks that Republicans were certain to make. But when Archer sat down, Deal recognized Marcy Kaptur of Ohio, who simply asked to revise and extend her remarks and then placed a long and tedious statement in the record that had little or nothing to do with the Deal substitute.[60] Next, Deal recognized Jane Harman of California, who likewise simply asked to revise and extend her remarks and then placed a statement in the written record. At this point, no one, not even Deal himself, had offered a single argument in support of the Deal bill. His own opening speech had been too general to recount the strengths of the bill. Each of the next several speakers simply made a one-sentence statement and placed their full statement in the record, which of course could have no influence on the floor debate. So far, the debate had done little more than strengthen Republicans in the validity of their arguments against the bill.

The debate on the Deal bill ended with no member of the Democratic leadership giving a strong statement of support. It was met with either complete silence or tepid support from senior Democrats on Ways and Means and with complete silence from old-bull senior Democrats, many of whom were former chairmen of the important committees with welfare jurisdiction. It seemed pretty apparent to all of us that they planned to hold their nose and vote for Deal, but they couldn't bring themselves to publicly state their reasons for support. The bill was defeated 228 to 205. Connie Morella was the only Republican who supported Deal. In less than a month, Deal followed the old aphorism, If you can't beat them, join them, by becoming a Republican.

Having overcome perhaps the biggest threat to our bill, and with the hour approaching eight o'clock, the House adjourned. By eleven the next morning (March 24), we were back on the floor. Within a few more hours, it would be over. After one hour of debate on the Mink substitute (HR 1250) and the vote, Gibbons would offer the motion to recommit. Assuming that the Gibbons motion was defeated, the House would then move immediately to the vote on final passage of our bill. If we could avoid any dilatory tactics by the Democrats, HR 4's fate should be determined by two o'clock.

The Mink debate was marred by unfortunate comments made by two Republican speakers. John Mica of Florida came to the floor to make a speech about alligators! He began by informing the House that the nature reserves in which many Florida alligators live have signs that read, "Do not feed the alligators." He then went on to point out that, if left alone, alligators can "fend for themselves" but that too much food from humans can create "dependency." Although "people are not alligators," like the humans who would feed the alligators, the nation's welfare system has created dependency.[61] Before Mica was finished, Democrats began to hiss and boo his comparison of welfare mothers with alligators. Later during the debate on the Mink bill, Republican Barbara Cubin of Wyoming was recognized to speak. She opened by saying, "In view of the fact that the alligator analogy was hissed and booed, I thought I should bring up another story that is near and dear to my state."[62] She then made the same type of comparison except in this case the animals were wolves. Democrats, of course, hissed and booed again.

A moment's reflection would reveal that Democrats would be likely to take strong exception to welfare families being compared to alligators and wolves. Especially in the midst of a highly partisan and rancorous debate like the one in which we were engaged, provocative comparisons like these are ill-advised. Thomas Foglietta from Pennsylvania, responding to Mica's alligator analogy, said that the comparison was "horrible" and that he was trying to overcome his "emotion" at hearing such a dehumanizing comparison made by the "very wealthy" gentleman from Miami.[63] Moments later, Barney Frank of Massachusetts argued vehemently that the fact that no Republicans objected to the "degrading analogy" of humans to alligators showed that all the Republican talk about their concern for children was not serious.

That the Mink substitute would be voted down was a foregone conclusion, but the magnitude of the vote, 336 to 96, was surprising to most of us. Perhaps it was merely another sign of how far the welfare reform debate had shifted to the right, but fewer than half the Democrats voted for the Mink bill. As I watched members cast their votes, I thought about the long tradition that Mink represented. This tradition had, against all odds and even against public opinion, constructed a system of welfare based on the entitlement concept. In addition to the earned entitlements to cash payments and health insurance in old age and disability—

policies that enjoyed overwhelming support from the American public—liberals had created entitlement programs to provide the poor with cash, Food Stamps and other nutrition benefits, health insurance, and other benefits. But in their determination to help the poor avoid destitution, liberals had created a safety net that demanded very little from those who needed help. It was all protection and no reciprocity. The Mink bill represented the last gasp of this tradition, and every one of the no votes now being recorded, many by highly respected members of the Democratic Party, was another yes vote for a new system based on personal responsibility and reciprocity. In a resounding victory for change, more than 70 percent of members of the U.S. House of Representatives voted against the Mink bill.

After the Mink debate ended mercifully at a little before one o'clock in the afternoon on March 24, the House shifted its parliamentary status, "rising" from the committee status it uses for debate and amendment to the more formal "Whole House on the State of the Union." Jim Kolbe of Arizona, who had worked with Shaw and Santorum in the early days of formulating our bill, was sitting in for the Speaker. Kolbe read the words that signaled a final vote. When he finished, appropriately enough, Sam Gibbons sought recognition from the speaker: "Mr. Speaker, I offer a motion to recommit."[64]

"Is the gentleman opposed to the bill?" inquired Kolbe in accord with House procedure but in complete and utter ignorance of the debate that had been taking place for four days. I resisted the temptation to yell out, "Somewhat."

Gibbons was satisfied with, "I certainly am," whereupon the clerk of the House read out the instructions that accompanied the motion to recommit. It simply required the bill to be returned to Ways and Means for the purpose of adding a requirement that all the savings from the bill be used for deficit reduction. The beauty of this motion, of course, was that it put Republicans in the position of seeming to vote against deficit reduction. But we had anticipated this motion, and the whip organization, under the leadership of Tom DeLay, had prepared Republicans to make this difficult no vote. With huge pressure on members of both parties because of the central importance of welfare reform, Gibbons's motion was defeated 228 to 205 on a nearly party-line vote. The vote on final passage was another highly partisan vote, 234 to 199, with only five Republicans voting against the bill and only nine Democrats voting for it.

This vote was a long way from the bipartisan vote on welfare reform that Clay Shaw had predicted on the last day of our subcommittee markup. All of us were disappointed that the debate had been so partisan, even "bordering on hysterical," as Archer labeled it. But we were elated that the bill had passed the House with only five Republicans voting no. Yet again, Republican discipline had been the key to controlling the House floor. And best of all, once a bill passes the House, its chances of becoming law are high. So now it was on to the Senate, a body that was much more moderate than the House and a body in which the rules gave Democrats a much greater chance to substantially reduce or even block our revolutionary welfare reform legislation.

But there was plenty of time to worry about the Senate. I was headed for the George Washington Parkway and a celebratory glass of wine with my wife. My memory of that night is somewhat imperfect: I might have had more than one glass of wine.

## CHAPTER NINE

# The Senate Joins the Revolution

After the frenzied activity between the congressional elections of November 1994 and passage of the House bill on March 24, 1995, our welfare reform cabal in the House spent six anxious months watching the Senate produce a welfare reform bill of its own. As an editorial in the *Washington Times* in July 1995 pointed out, by mid-summer the House had passed thirty-one bills related to the Contract with America, but only three had become law.[1] The author held that the Senate was the "graveyard" of our magnificent House legislation. If the House was a sleek cigarette boat knifing through the political waters of the nation's capital, the Senate was a stately ocean liner ponderously navigating through the same obstacle-laden waters.

Although the pace of Senate proceedings was frustrating to House revolutionaries, in hindsight it seems clear that the Senate's role of playing Hamlet to our Hotspur shows yet again a major advantage of the nation's bicameral legislative process. Given House rules, we could and did enact a highly partisan bill, with little input or support from Democrats. But in the Senate, where the rights of the minority, even a minority of one, are built into both tradition and rules, the legislative process usually moves at a more leisurely pace and usually involves input and support from the minority party. In the case of welfare reform, the result was a bipartisan bill that contained many features of the House bill, including most of the most controversial.

Several unique factors were bound to have a major influence on what happened to the House bill upon entering the Senate crapshoot. Perhaps the most important of these was the fact that Bob Dole, the Senate majority leader, wanted to be president. By the time the House bill passed in March 1995, it was only twenty months until the presidential election of 1996. Most pundits believed that Dole was the leading candidate for the Republican nomination, but there was plenty of competition.[2] The competition that had the greatest impact on Senate proceedings was that between Dole and the tough, influential, and effective Senator Phil Gramm from Texas. Although Gramm was not the chair of any committee or a member of the Senate Republican leadership, he nonetheless was able to exert considerable influence on the proceedings.[3]

Gramm's influence was multiplied by a growing band of conservative Republican senators who agreed with Gramm on several of the major welfare reform issues. Although the Senate was not as conservative as the House, it was becoming more conservative with each election, not least because House conservatives were being elected to the Senate with regularity. In the 1994 elections, Republicans seized eight Senate seats from Democrats, six by replacing retiring incumbents and two by defeating incumbents. Of these eight new Republican senators, five (John Kyl of Arizona, Spencer Abraham of Michigan, James Inhofe of Oklahoma, Rick Santorum of Pennsylvania, and Fred Thompson of Tennessee) were generally considered to be conservative. Only Olympia Snowe of Maine, Mike DeWine of Ohio, and William Frist of Tennessee were considered to be moderates, although Frist would soon be bitten by the presidential bug, the venom of which causes Republicans to move to the right. In addition to these eight who took seats previously occupied by Democrats, three new Republicans replaced Republican incumbents who retired. All three of these new senators—Rod Grams of Minnesota, John Ashcroft of Missouri, and Craig Thomas of Wyoming—were conservative. Thus of the eleven new Republican senators, eight ranged between conservative and very conservative. These eight moved the political center of gravity in the Senate considerably to the right. As a result, Senator Gramm, who teamed up with Lauch Faircloth of North Carolina as the leader of conservative forces on welfare reform, had plenty of support for the conservative positions he fought to include in the Senate bill. Roughly speaking, Gramm and Faircloth played the role in the Senate played by Jim Talent and Tim Hutchinson in the House. But as events would soon show, they were leading a Republican Party in the Senate that would not support some of the strong provisions already enacted with almost universal Republican support in the House.

Another important factor that shaped Senate debate was the serious ethical problem that afflicted Bob Packwood, chairman of the Finance Committee.[4] Under normal circumstances, Packwood would have had the inside track to leadership of welfare reform in the Senate. As chairman of the Finance Committee, which enjoys roughly the same jurisdiction as Ways and Means in the House, he had the opportunity and responsibility of writing the first Senate bill. Compare Packwood's position with that of Clay Shaw and Bill Archer in the House. Because of their exemplary leadership and ability to forge powerful alliances with the leadership and members of other committees, Shaw and Archer, the lead

Ways and Means Republicans on welfare reform, were able to shape the House welfare reform bill, both when it was under the jurisdiction of their committee and as it moved through other House committees to the floor. Packwood had a better than even chance to do the same thing in the Senate. But Packwood was not as prepared as Shaw and Archer, nor was he as personally committed to reforming welfare programs. But far more important, by the spring of 1995 he was under serious charges that he had violated Senate ethics by making unwanted amorous advances toward female Senate aides, lobbyists, and even a reporter.[5] Understandably, he was distracted as he launched his unsuccessful fight against these charges in the Senate Ethics Committee, among his colleagues and constituencies, and in the nation's media. By March it was clear that his ability to lead Republican forces on welfare reform in the Senate was eroded. This leadership void was filled by Dole, and to a surprising degree, by Rick Santorum. At the risk of stretching credulity, Packwood's difficulties, although embarrassing to Republicans and the cause of some temporary uncertainty in the way welfare reform was handled in the Senate, helped ensure that a bill would pass by giving Dole a free hand during the critical stages of Senate passage. After a long fight to save his career, Packwood resigned from the Senate on September 7, 1995.

By this time, Dole had seized the reins and was well along in developing a bill. Many conservatives were leery about Dole's leadership, not only because they regarded Dole himself as too moderate on social issues but even more because they regarded his competent but controversial chief of staff Sheila Burke as downright liberal. Despite being a former Democrat, Burke was joined at the hip with Dole and had great influence on him. She was certainly not a conservative, and my own experience working directly with her led me to believe that she was not convinced that all the welfare reform proposals pushed by the House and by the Rector-Faircloth-Gramm forces were necessarily good for children, families, or the nation. I knew other Republicans staffers and even members who felt the same way, but none of them had the authority and power that Burke had. But then, very few staffers have ever had the authority and power that Burke wielded in Dole's name.

Especially in the halcyon days of 1995, conservatives were not likely to give Burke or Dole any slack just because she was the most powerful and effective staffer on the Hill while Dole efficiently ran the Republican Party in the Senate and might soon be the president of the United States. On the contrary, a number of important conservatives made exceptionally critical comments about Burke. One of the first public attacks was authored by conservative columnist Robert Novak in late June 1995, by which time it was clear that the Packwood bill was dead and that Dole would probably have to step in. In his syndicated column, which appears in the *Washington Post* and many other leading newspapers, Novak recounted the bill of particulars against Burke, especially that she had kept negotiations open on the despised Clinton health bill long after conserva-tives thought they had killed it; offended members of conservative groups by arrogantly dismissing their arguments; was the leading staff moderate in the Senate who typically wielded more power than some of the senators themselves; had employed stealth and speed to help get Packwood's moderate welfare reform bill out of the Finance Committee; and above all was far too moderate on the marriage and illegitimacy issues that conservatives wanted to make a vital part of welfare reform.[6] On July 7 John Fund, an editorial page writer for the *Wall Street Journal,* wrote an opinion piece about Burke's transgressions.[7] Fund quoted the noted conservative operative Paul Weyrich, who claimed that Burke formed groups of moderate Senate staffers to water down "good conservative ideas" before they came to the floor. Weyrich was especially concerned that, if elected president, the seventy-three-year-old Dole would make Burke his chief of staff and that her power would then be enormous.

Over the next month, at least four additional articles in prominent newspa-pers and a national weekly explored the fight between conservatives and Burke.[8] This remarkable coverage of Republican dirty laundry reached maximum over-drive with a cover story in the *New York Times Magazine* written by welfare reporter Jason DeParle. The long article, which won the Janet Cooke Award from conservative MediaWatch as one of the most misleading news stories of 1995, featured Burke on the cover with red horns sprouting from her head, a not-too-subtle symbol of the claim that conservatives were demonizing her. The headline and subhead to the article neatly summarized its argument: "Sheila Burke Is the Militant Feminist Commie Peacenik Who's Telling Bob Dole What to Think. Well, No. She's Just the Senator's Moderate Chief of Staff, the Latest Victim of the Conservative Attack Machine."[9]

Regardless of whether conservatives were actually conducting a vendetta against her as DeParle claimed, three facts were clear: Burke, like Dole himself, was more moderate than the conservative senators led by Gramm and Faircloth and the influential conservative groups that lobbied constantly on welfare reform; Burke was the most powerful staffer on the Hill; and in both 1995 and 1996 she displayed immense skill and patience in helping Dole steer the welfare reform bill through the Senate, achieving a huge bipartisan vote on both occa-sions. For this last achievement, she deserves everlasting acclaim. But the fight over her influence was still a major distraction for the welfare reform campaign—and many conservatives argue vehemently to this day that, with inside help from Santorum, Faircloth, and Gramm, conservatives managed to overcome Burke's attempts to sterilize the strong work standards and illegitimacy provisions in the House bill.

Yet another influence on the Senate debate was that the entire left-of-center apparatus in the nation's capital, including Democratic senators and interest groups that lobbied for children and for expanded public spending, was recovering from the shock of the 1994 elections and was more effective than it had been during the House battle. Democratic senators were more sophisticated than their House colleagues in fighting the Republican onslaught. They seemed to realize that Democrats were now in the minority and that their own president might well agree with Republicans on welfare reform. As a result, from the beginning they were looking to cut a deal. To do so, they had to accept many of the primary components of the new definition of welfare reform: the end of entitlement, mandatory work, time limits, sanctions, limits on welfare for noncitizens, changes in the disability program for children, a new emphasis on promoting abstinence and marriage, and so forth. One result of the major involvement of Senate Democrats was that the final bill signed into law had a somewhat more moderate cast than it otherwise might have had.

A potentially influential force in the Senate proceedings failed to show up. I refer to Senator Daniel Patrick Moynihan. Both because he was the senior Democrat on the Finance Committee, which had major jurisdiction over welfare programs, and because he was a certified, if somewhat quirky, expert on welfare programs, not just among elected officials but among scholars as well, it would have been reasonable to expect him to play a leading role in finding compromises between those wild-eyed Republicans and Democrats.[10] In addition, in Paul Offner he had arguably the best staffer on welfare issues on Capitol Hill.[11] But amazingly, his single role was to criticize the welfare reform politics of his Republican colleagues and his president.[12] His only idea for legislation was to expand the discredited 1988 Family Support Act, a proposal that was dead from the beginning, not least because it was so pedestrian. Even his Democratic colleagues were dismissive of this nonproposal. Throughout the debate, Moynihan stood on the sidelines throwing boulders at the politicians who were trying to find solutions to the very social problem he had been the first public figure to identify.

If Moynihan stood on the sidelines, Republican governors were not only in the game but continued their aggressive and sophisticated attempts to carry the ball. Although House Republicans had been working closely with the Republican governors for well over a year, we did not give them everything they wanted. As the story of passing the bill in the House shows so clearly, enacting major legislation always involves the delicate task of balancing competing interests. Dating from even before the colorful conference in Williamsburg in November 1994, the governors had worked the inside track in the competition for shaping the bill. Newt Gingrich, Haley Barbour, and Don Fierce had helped bring the governors into the planning, and Shaw had served almost as their point man inside the House. But the interests of House Republicans often clashed with those of the governors, especially over the strength of the work requirements, federal spending cuts, illegitimacy provisions, provisions on noncitizens, and a number of other important provisions. The governors got a lot out of the House process, but of course they wanted more. The moment the House bill passed, Republican governors shifted their attention to the Senate, where, led again by Governor John Engler of Michigan, they became a potent force trying to influence the Senate debate.

The legislative struggle that resulted from this brew can be conveniently divided into two phases. In the first phase, running roughly from early February until early June, hearings were held by several committees and, as in the House, three committees (Finance, Labor and Human Resources, and Agriculture) held markups.[13] By any measure, the broadest and most sweeping parts of the Senate bill were those under the jurisdiction of Packwood's Finance Committee. Packwood introduced his bill and pushed it through committee, whereupon it promptly floundered for lack of support, bringing the first phase of Senate consideration of welfare reform to an abrupt halt. Dole initiated the second phase of the Senate debate by seizing control of the process. He introduced his own bill in August and worked with all factions from both parties to modify his bill and drive it through the Senate by mid-September, achieving a bipartisan compromise in the process.

During the first phase, committees held hearings while members and staff worked on writing legislation and preparing for markups and floor debate. Senate committees, including Finance, Labor and Human Resources, Agriculture, Judiciary, Governmental Affairs, and Indian Affairs, held seventeen hearings on some aspect of welfare reform.[14] One hearing stands out. On March 27, the Finance Committee had its last of eight hearings. As anyone who regularly attends Senate hearings knows, most hearings have one or perhaps two members in attendance; but eleven members were present at some time during this hearing. Probably the major reason for such high attendance was not only that welfare reform was a huge issue that was being thoroughly covered by the media but also that one of the witnesses was Charles Murray. The hearing opened with testimony from five members: Faircloth, Santorum, Nancy Kassebaum of Kansas, Tom Harkin of Iowa, and Hank Brown of Colorado. After members of the Finance Committee asked a few questions of their Senate colleagues, Chairman Packwood informed them, a little abruptly, that he had "to ask that we terminate this so we can get to our next panel."[15] The panel that Packwood was anxious to get to consisted of Richard Nathan of the State University of New York and Charles Murray.

Murray was fascinating. Speaking extemporaneously, he emphasized the following: the primary welfare problem was that too many babies were being born to unmarried parents; illegitimacy will only be reduced if there is radical change in the current system, such as the end of cash benefits for young unmarried mothers; states must have much greater flexibility because then some states will try truly radical reforms that might work to reduce illegitimacy; and the choice is not between being harsh to children or nice to children—no alternative, including current law, will be nice to children.

On this last point, Murray was relentless. He said that he felt "contempt" for those who criticized his "harsh" proposals to end welfare and pretended that there is any alternative that, at least in the short run, would be good for children. He went further: promoting the nurturing of children and diminishing their suffering must ultimately depend on a wise answer to this question: How can government policy in a free society make it as likely as possible that children will be born to two mature adults committed to their care? A Senate debate over welfare legislation that avoids that question or tries to pretend that it is not central has failed.[16]

So here was Charles Murray, author of *Losing Ground* and *The Bell Curve*, two of the most notorious conservative books of the second half of the twentieth century, sitting before several Democratic senators, including Daniel Patrick Moynihan, the greatest expert on social issues ever to serve in either house of Congress, and none of them even asked him a difficult question.[17] Murray had come to testify in support of ending welfare benefits for young, never-married mothers, a version of which had already been adopted by House Republicans and a policy that was deeply despised by many liberals, including scholars, pundits, and members of both houses of Congress. Moreover, Murray did not sugarcoat his drastic solution of cutting off benefits; he called his reasoning "brutal calculation" and said that anyone who didn't admit that there was no good choice for illegitimate children, only bad choices, received his "contempt."[18] In effect, by this statement he labeled many of the Democrats and even a few of the Republicans seated before him as deserving of contempt. Still, they treated him like a choirboy.

And with this missed opportunity to closely question the author of a radical policy proposal that was having immense influence in the House and Senate, the Senate ended the hearings phase of its legislative process and prepared for markups. Senate committees do not allow people who are not members or staff of the committee to examine the transcript of their markup sessions. Thus I was not able to analyze exactly what happened during the Finance Committee markup. But based on media reports and committee votes, it is clear that both the Finance markup as well as markups in other committees went smoothly. The Labor and Human Resources Committee played an important role in welfare reform because it had jurisdiction over the child care program. After conducting two hearings on child care, its members met on May 26 and reported out their child care bill on a unanimous recorded vote. In sharp contrast with the sweeping House provisions on child care, the Senate bill did not attempt to rationalize child care programs by collapsing all the programs under Aid to Families with Dependent Children (AFDC) and the Child Care and Development block grant into one big block grant. Indeed, as we were to discover when the House-Senate conference got under way in the fall, the Senate Finance Committee and the Labor and Human Resources Committee were horrified to think of combining their respective child care programs, which would require one of them to give up jurisdiction. Rather, both committees simply left their jurisdiction over child care intact, with the Child Care and Development block grant remaining at Labor and Human Resources and the AFDC-associated child care programs remaining with Finance. Labor and Human Resources softened the federal regulations somewhat but not enough to lose Senator Edward Kennedy's vote.[19]

The Finance Committee markup on May 27 and 28 was somewhat more contentious than the Labor and Human Resources Committee markup. Still, in comparison with the Ways and Means markups, the Finance Committee's was a picnic. The composition of the Finance Committee was eleven Republicans and nine Democrats, so losing two votes on amendments sponsored by Democrats and only one vote on final passage of the chairman's bill meant that Republicans could not prevail if the Democrats were unified.

Like House Republicans, Senate Republicans knew that their strength was in unity.[20] Republicans stuck together on nearly every big vote, though some were tepid about Packwood's bill.[21] The committee considered sixteen amendments plus final passage to favorably report the bill to the Senate. Of the sixteen amendments, all but two were offered by Democrats. The Democratic amendments included three substitute bills offered by Moynihan, Kent Conrad of North Dakota, and Carol Moseley-Braun of Illinois. Each of these would have completely replaced the Packwood bill with a Democratic bill, thereby probably killing welfare reform. All three were defeated by a vote of 12 to 8, with Democrat Max Baucus joining the united Republicans to produce the 3-vote margin of victory. In addition to these amendments were three modest amendments that, in the scheme of things, had little impact on the bill. Two of them (one by Moynihan on a detail of how SSI payments should be handled and one by Baucus on raising from 10 percent to 15 percent the share of the caseload that could be exempt from the time limit) were offered by Democrats. Republicans accepted both amendments without recorded votes. The committee also accepted without recorded vote an amendment by Alfonse D'Amato of New York on uses of the loan fund for states that ran short on money to pay welfare benefits during a recession.

Like the voting on the three substitute amendments, and unlike the three amendments of minor importance, voting on most of the remaining amendments was partisan.[22] On three amendments, only one Republican voted against the chairman.[23] Thus, counting 16 of the 17 votes (including the vote on final passage in which united Republicans were once again joined by Baucus), Republicans cast their votes 173 of 176 times for the Packwood position, for a cumulative

score of 98 percent for party discipline. This record was in every way comparable with the House, showing that even in the Senate Republicans were almost
always voting the party line.

The one exception to this pattern was, not surprisingly, a vote on illegitimacy.
Perhaps the most conservative Republican on the committee was Don Nickles of
Oklahoma. Nickles, like Gramm and Faircloth, believed that the Republican bill
should have strong illegitimacy provisions. Thus he introduced an amendment
to add the family cap (no increase in benefits if a mother already on welfare had
a baby) to Packwood's bill. On this vote, only seven Republicans (Dole, D'Amato, William Roth, Charles Grassley, Orrin Hatch, Larry Pressler, and Frank
Murkowski) joined Nickles. John Chafee and Alan Simpson, two of the more
moderate Republicans left in the Senate, stuck with their chairman and voted no.
Because Packwood's position was supported by all of the Democrats, the Nickles amendment on the family cap was defeated, leaving intact Chairman Packwood's decision to ignore the conservatives' demand for tough illegitimacy
provisions. Even so, this unusual vote reflected the disarray among Senate Republicans on the illegitimacy issue and served as early warning that Senate Republicans, like House Republicans, would be plagued by this issue.

As Senate committees reported their welfare reform legislation—and as it
became increasingly apparent that the Packwood bill divided Senate Republicans
into various factions on the illegitimacy provisions, on the formula for distributing welfare dollars among the states, on child care money, and on a host of
other provisions—Dole seized control of the deteriorating situation and developed a new bill. Given his presidential ambitions, Dole was more or less forced
to accept the leadership of this high-risk legislative fight. Welfare reform was
one of the most important and popular items on the Republicans' legislative
agenda. If the Senate failed to produce a bill, or if it produced a moderate bill,
Dole would receive much of the blame, thereby jeopardizing his standing as a
presidential candidate, especially among conservatives.

The immediate cause of the Senate problem was that the Packwood bill was
dead. Mirroring in several respects Republicans in the House, Republicans in the
Senate had to balance their moderate and conservative forces fighting both for
strong illegitimacy provisions—including the family cap and Murray Light (ending cash welfare for unmarried mothers under age eighteen)—and for stronger
work requirements, with stiff penalties for individuals who did not comply. Faircloth and Gramm provided effective leadership for the conservatives, who were
insisting on a fundamental overhaul of the Packwood bill. Unlike Archer and
Shaw in the House, who had worked cooperatively and for the most part harmo-
niously with the illegitimacy forces (Shaw had five or six cheeks and used them
all)—and indeed who believed strongly in the illegitimacy provisions themselves
and fought for them in committee markups and on the floor—Packwood

ignored the powerful illegitimacy forces. The only vote on which he lost most Republicans on his committee was the Nickles amendment to put the family cap in the committee's bill. And once the bill emerged from committee, at least a dozen Republican senators were vocal in their opposition. But Packwood continued to ignore the gathering storm on his right. No matter what Packwood personally thought about the illegitimacy provisions, he should have been able to recognize that the Republican forces supporting these provisions were just too powerful to ignore. This mistake on Packwood's part had tough consequences; his bill died an untimely death, and Senate Republicans faced a running battle among themselves over illegitimacy.

Nor was concern about the illegitimacy provisions, or lack of them, the only problem with the bill. In analyzing the Packwood bill, it quickly becomes apparent that, yet again, the radicalization of the welfare reform debate had moved the political center of gravity far to the right, bypassing proposals that would have been considered conservative even a year earlier. Imagine a bill that ended the cash entitlement, replaced AFDC with a block grant, created a five-year time limit, and imposed a work requirement on states. And beyond these huge reforms of cash welfare, imagine that the bill also virtually eliminated the Supplemental Security Income (SSI) program for most noncitizens, ended SSI for drug addicts and alcoholics, reduced SSI benefits for children, and sweepingly reformed the child support enforcement program. But by May 1995, even a bill this conservative was unacceptable to many Republicans. Significant opposition immediately materialized against the bill because it ignored illegitimacy and retained the failed JOBS program. In addition, the Packwood bill was short on savings: it saved less than $39 billion over seven years as compared with savings of nearly $80 billion in the House bill.[24] Robert Rector of the Heritage Foundation wrote a devastating critique of Packwood's bill, and even Wisconsin Governor Tommy Thompson wrote a letter to Senator Faircloth criticizing Packwood's weak work requirements.[25]

Part of the blame for such a politically inept bill goes to the Republican governors, with the exception of Thompson.[26] Once again they were deeply involved in trying to dominate the bill writing process, just as they had tried to do in the House. The governors encouraged Packwood in his already strong tendencies to write a more moderate bill. Although I don't know Packwood's thinking, it is nonetheless clear that on almost every critical issue—including work requirements, illegitimacy provisions, and total savings—he stiffed those on his right and sided with the governors. Packwood's lack of political acumen came to a head in mid-June in a series of closed-door meetings.[27] Faircloth was especially blunt during these meetings, saying he would not support any Senate bill that did not have strong illegitimacy provisions, including—or even especially—Murray Light.[28] Faircloth was also caustic about the governors, creating a tense situation in a Republican caucus meeting on June 14 by criticizing the Republican leaders for allowing Governor Engler to even attend a meeting that Faircloth claimed was for the benefit of Senate Republicans. As Faircloth put it to Robert Pear of the *New York Times*, "I find it most unusual for a governor to lecture us at a meeting called for senators to talk among themselves."[29] Nor was Faircloth alone in his demand for stronger provisions on illegitimacy. Faircloth estimated that at least fifteen Republican senators would vote against the bill if these provisions were not included.

As the Senate backroom debate proceeded, and the fights among the various factions spilled out into the press, additional problems began to emerge. At first exclusively within the Republican caucus but then bursting into public view, the Senate engaged in a major fight over the formula for distributing block grant funds among the states. As the magnitude of the fight grew, the probability that the Senate would pass a bill in our lifetime shrank. Formula fights are so unsatisfying because there is often no reasonable basis on which money can be divided among the states.[30]

We had been fortunate in the House when the formula issue had come up. From beginning to end, we had held firmly (even desperately) to the status quo. After lots of discussion with members and with governors, we did insert a provision that slightly improved the status quo and bought off the critics—temporarily, as the Senate debate was now showing. Specifically, we included $100 million a year in the block grant to compensate states with high population growth.[31] This modification preserved the status quo in that no state lost any money; the $100 million was "extra" money and did not reduce the amount of money going to any state, thereby avoiding the shootout that would occur if any state lost money.

Within three weeks after the Packwood bill emerged from committee, it was clear that it could not pass with its status-quo formula.[32] The solution, of course, was to add more money, which was the solution the House had employed to a limited degree ($100 million a year for the population growth fund). In the end, after lots of fighting, Kay Bailey Hutchinson of Texas organized a group of senators to support adding nearly $900 million over four years (1997 through 2000) to the bill and distributing the money to twenty poor states, Texas (surprise!) prominent among them.[33] Dole included the Hutchinson provision in his bill in early August, and a nearly identical provision was in the final bill passed by Congress in 1996. Thus it cost Republicans more than $1 billion over five years, and a convoluted provision in their bill, to rescue themselves from the formula bog.

At least equal to the threat against the bill posed by the formula fight was the fight between Republican conservatives and moderates over several contentious issues. Between early June, after the Packwood bill emerged from committee, and passage of the Dole bill on September 19, a complex brew of forces pulled the bill to the left, to the right, and then back toward the center, as the balance of forces changed almost daily. While Dole and his staff were developing their bill, word leaked out about its contents, something that always happens because negotiations usually involve lots of parties, all of whom try to use the media (and rumors) to their advantage. Thus it quickly became known that Dole was reluctant to include either the family cap or Murray Light in his bill. Meanwhile, on June 5 the city council of Washington, D.C., one of the most liberal cities in America, approved legislation adopting the family cap.[34] Imagine the target the Dole bill made, as conservatives charged that it was to the left of a welfare reform bill passed by the city council of Washington.[35] Something had to give.

Throughout the summer of 1995, Dole and his staff negotiated with three distinct groups: Republican conservatives led by Gramm and Faircloth; Republican moderates, including John Chafee of Rhode Island, DeWine, and Snowe; and Senate Democrats, led by Tom Daschle of South Dakota. Meanwhile, the president kept stirring the pot as he gave speeches on how bad the House bill was and how the Senate had a chance to moderate the House bill and produce bipartisan legislation that he could sign. All of these forces fought for public attention as they tried to get their respective provisions into the Dole bill. Roughly speaking, conservatives wanted stronger work requirements, more savings, the family cap, and Murray Light; Republican moderates wanted to keep the family cap and Murray Light out of Dole's bill while putting in more money for child care, some sort of guarantee that families would get child care before being required to work, and a strong requirement that states continue to spend their own money on welfare (called the maintenance-of-effort, or MOE, requirement); Democrats wanted everything the Republican moderates wanted plus legislative language that came close to maintaining the entitlement to cash welfare and loopholes in the five-year time limit.

For once, Clinton and the Democrats on the Hill seemed to be on the same page. After a Clinton attack on the House bill delivered during a speech to the National Governors Association in Baltimore on June 5, Senate Democrats introduced their own bill on June 8, a bill that Donna Shalala and Clinton praised as a bill that the president could sign.[36] Wisely, Democrats introduced their bill at a day care center in Washington, thereby emphasizing the point that they intended to strike a balance between strong work requirements and help for mothers—such as ample and guaranteed day care funding—who did the right thing by leaving welfare for work. Their bill included a repeal of the old JOBS program, decent work requirements, and a time limit. But the work requirement had loopholes (just like the work requirement in Packwood's bill), generous and expensive provisions for child care and Medicaid health insurance and only a modification of the cash entitlement rather than an outright repeal. Once again, as if more evidence were needed, the Senate Democratic bill showed how far to the right things had moved. Like Packwood's bill, their bill would have been considered radical a year earlier but now was considerably to the left of the House bill. Although the bill did not satisfy all Senate Democrats, the Democratic leadership had met with every one of its members in formulating the bill. As a result, like the House Democratic bill authored by Nathan Deal, the Senate Democratic bill would probably win support from almost every Democrat when it came to the Senate floor.[37]

The Democrats' bill, combined with their near unity, placed Senate Democrats squarely in the middle of the action. By June it was apparent that Senate Democrats were more united than they had been in years and that they could constitute a formidable opposition against the Republican bill if it moved too far to the right. Even worse from Dole's point of view, there was always a threat that Republican moderates—and on some issues there could be fifteen or more Republican moderates—could join forces with united Democrats (perhaps minus Moynihan) and create a center-left coalition that would control a majority of votes on welfare reform. In such a case, the possibility of producing anything like the House bill would be zero. When the voting actually started, it became evident that Senate Republicans were not a unified machine like House Republicans had been. Democrats and moderate Republicans joined together on the Senate floor to kill a number of provisions considered vital by conservatives.

After Democrats introduced their bill on June 8 and the Finance Committee issued its report containing the hopeless Packwood bill on June 9, members of the Senate, President Clinton and members of his administration, the nation's editorial pages, and public intellectuals of all stripes spent nearly two months sniping at each other. Through the sniping, it seemed clear that Senate Republicans were badly divided into several factions. On June 14 freshman Senator Santorum, although describing himself as the "most impetuous" member of the Senate, told Judith Havemann of the *Washington Post* that Senate Republicans needed to slow down to "avoid 100 fights" on the Senate floor.[38] Robert Rector said the differences between the Dole bill and the bill conservatives wanted were "pretty profound."[39] Governor Engler came to town and pronounced that the Senate Republican bill was "all screwed up."[40] All this and more played out against Moynihan's demonization of the Republican bill. On June 17 Moynihan came up with one of his punchiest characterizations yet: the Republican bill was now "an act of unprecedented social vindictiveness."[41]

Santorum's role in the Senate debate was nothing short of amazing. Although he was not on the Finance Committee and was in the first year of his first term, both of which qualified him for only a marginal role in the proceedings, Chairman Packwood had heard about his work on welfare reform in the House and asked him to join a small advisory group that was helping Packwood craft his bill.

Not surprisingly, Santorum's drive and expertise soon became evident to everyone involved behind the scenes, including Packwood, Dole, Sheila, and other senior staffers. As a result, he was given more and more responsibility. By the time action started in earnest on the Senate floor in September, Dole asked Santorum to help manage the floor debate and to participate in negotiations behind the scenes. Santorum and his crack legislative director, Mike Hershey, worked directly with other senators and senior staffers as the Dole bill was written and then modified repeatedly, as compromise after compromise was achieved. Santorum himself, in a role that was somewhat unusual for a senator, often met late into the night with Sheila and others as the Republican bill was perfected. That Santorum was able to play such a powerful role in the Senate's work on welfare reform is a testament to his knowledge and his ability to work with both Republican and Democratic senators who greatly outranked him. A skeptic might also conclude that Santorum was able to play such a prominent role because so few Republican senators knew much about welfare.

Despite all the public furor, and the obvious lack of unity among Republicans as the summer wore on, Dole, with considerable help from Santorum, was working hard behind the scenes to bring his Republican colleagues together and to do so in a way that would moderate the House bill and thereby make it possible for him to pass a bipartisan bill in the Senate. Unfortunately, Dole got off to a bad start with the first bill he introduced in early August. Even after all the complaints about weak work requirements, weak illegitimacy provisions, the divisive formula, and other provisions, Dole's first bill was strikingly similar to the Packwood bill. Before Dole even introduced his bill, the Gramm-Faircloth forces inside the Senate and the conservative groups outside the Senate began severely criticizing it. Gramm and Faircloth issued a statement listing eight problems with the Dole bill, with a lack of illegitimacy provisions being the most serious, and Andrea Sheldon of the Traditional Value Coalition labeled the bill "Dole-Clinton."[42] Meanwhile, Dole could hear attacks from the left for being, as the president put it, "unduly harsh."[43]

Despite the complaints from every side, Dole held a press conference on August 4 announcing completion of his bill, introduced the bill on August 5 during a rare Saturday session of the Senate, and opened debate on August 7, the following Monday. On the previous day, Gramm had appeared on the CBS news program *Face the Nation* and, although not quite threatening to vote against the bill, strongly criticized it for having virtually no illegitimacy provisions and for being weak on work.[44] Dole had modified the goals statement for the block grant that would replace AFDC to include illegitimacy reduction, but the illegitimacy forces were after much more than a mere goal statement. Similarly, Dole retained the old JOBS program, which was by now anathema to nearly all Republicans except the most moderate, and then compounded the problem of weak work requirements by failing to include strong penalties on individuals who did not participate in their state's work program.

Dole's plan was to allow general debate on welfare reform on August 7 and then begin amendments on August 8, allowing the rest of the week for amendments and completion of the bill before adjourning the Senate for its annual August break. But it was quickly evident that, whatever his strategy, none of the three primary factions—conservatives, Republican moderates, and Democrats—was satisfied with the bill. After several hours of debate on August 7 and 8, Dole decided to pull his bill, Daschle concurred, and both leaders agreed to negotiate with their members and come back at the end of the week with revised and strengthened bills.[45]

Dole and Daschle did in fact introduce revised bills on Friday, August 11.[46] The Dole bill, which now included new provisions that went a long way toward satisfying both conservatives and moderates, was a brilliant piece of legislative engineering. Dole had greatly expanded the bill by including Food Stamp provisions and provisions on child nutrition from the Agriculture Committee. He also expanded the provisions barring welfare for noncitizens and added reforms on education and training programs from the Labor and Human Resources Committee and even reforms of public housing. This vast expansion of the bill directly addressed the complaint from conservatives and from House Republicans that Dole's original bill was too limited in its scope for reforming the welfare state. Now the Dole bill was as broad as the House bill, even broader in some respects, although many of its provisions were more moderate. Even better for conservatives, the bill now saved more than $60 billion, a considerable jump from less than $40 billion in the first bill.

Also in response to conservatives, Dole made several changes in the work requirements. He dropped the detested JOBS program and put all his work requirements in the section of the bill (Title I) that laid out the specifics of the block grant. He included a section requiring states to impose financial penalties on parents who refused to cooperate with the state work program, using language nearly identical to that in the House bill. The continued existence of the JOBS program and the lack of strong individual penalties had been the major complaints from conservatives about the work provisions in Dole's original bill, both of which he fixed.

In perhaps his greatest move in the direction of conservatives, Dole agreed to include several of the illegitimacy provisions for which conservatives had been fighting so hard. He first placed a provision in the state plan section of his bill (the section that required states to have a written plan to qualify for block grant funds and to specify how they would deal with several specific issues requiring states to spell out the actions they would take to reduce nonmarital births).[47] In addition to this state plan requirement, Dole also included an entirely new section in his bill, "Promoting Responsible Parenting."[48] The section began with a long list of findings that, in effect, said that Congress believed that marriage was the foundation of society and that illegitimate births were anathema. Lots of statistics were included to document these claims. These congressional "findings" had been written by Robert Rector and were strongly supported by Gramm and Faircloth as well as by conservative groups outside Congress. More significant than the findings, which were symbolically important but did not require any action, the new section also contained somewhat softened versions of the two provisions that had been at the top of the conservative agenda, the family cap and Murray Light. In both cases, Dole put them in his bill as state options, meaning that states could adopt either or both of them if they wanted to.

A final gift to conservatives was the so-called charitable choice provision, sponsored by Senator Ashcroft. Under this truly radical reform, churches and other faith-based organizations would be able to compete with government and private-sector companies in contracting with states to run all or part of the new welfare program. The Ashcroft language included a provision, detested by liberals, that allowed religious organizations running programs with government dollars to require their employees to "adhere to [the religious organization's] tenets and teachings." According to most liberals and many moderates, this provision violated the underlying principle, central to civil rights law, banning discrimination against individuals who fall into any of several ethnic, national, or racial categories, including religious belief. Many also believed it violated the First Amendment bar against establishing religion. In another provision that caused great consternation among liberals—and again, even some moderate Republicans—Ashcroft allowed religious groups to provide government-supported services in their churches or other facilities without removing "religious art, icons, scripture, or other symbols."[49] Taken together, this package of six or seven new provisions constituted a substantial inducement for conservatives to support the bill. Not surprisingly, nearly all of them did. Even with all these new measures, however, Senator Faircloth was still not satisfied and threatened to oppose the bill, arguing that illegitimacy was the demographic equivalent of the plague and that he would not support a bill that did not have a mandatory family cap and a Murray Light provision.

If Dole moved his bill to the right to capture conservative support, he also included provisions that moved the bill in the direction favored by moderates and Democrats. Responding to the pleas of moderates such as Kassebaum, Chafee, Snowe, Pete Domenici of New Mexico, William Cohen of Maine, Arlen Specter of Pennsylvania, and Jim Jeffords of Vermont, Dole inserted language requiring states to maintain a specified and substantial level of state spending on welfare programs (or MOE provision), added new money for child care, and for good measure threw in an option that allowed states to exempt mothers with infants under twelve months of age from the work requirement. These compromises, which addressed the most pressing demands of the moderates, had been previously agreed to by Republican governors, who wrote a letter of support to Dole on August 8.[50] Having worked with the governors extensively in writing the House bill, I realized that Dole had persuaded them to endorse in writing provisions I knew they opposed. Clearly, Republicans continued to profit from the partnership between Republican governors and Republican leaders in the Capitol forged by Haley Barbour and Don Fierce at Williamsburg.

Although Dole did not solve all his problems with these maneuvers, taken together they brought his bill to a point at which all sides had to at least give serious consideration to supporting the bill. Virtually every issue that had been mentioned by the contending factions was addressed by one or more of the new provisions. No faction got everything it wanted, but Dole showed that he was attentive to their concerns and gave them at least something high on their list.

In introducing his new and expanded bill on August 11, the day before the annual August recess began, Dole promised to renew the welfare debate on the second day after Congress returned in September. Both Dole and Daschle, in exchanges on the floor, agreed that the two days of general debate on August 6 and 7 had been constructive, that both of them had improved their bills with the changes introduced on August 11, and that they would have a good chance of passing a bill within a week or so of the time the Senate returned in September. One of Daschle's comments was especially propitious for the prospects of welfare reform in the Senate. A surprising addition to his bill was a requirement that mothers work after six months, rather than two years, on welfare. He said that Senator Carl Levin of Michigan, brother of Sander Levin, the Democrat on the Ways and Means Committee who had been such a voluble opponent of the House bill, had insisted on earlier work by mothers on welfare in order to "move people into a workforce at the earliest possible moment."[51] It would be difficult to find a clearer symbol of the stark difference in approach taken by House Democrats and Senate Democrats than this change in Daschle's bill, made on the grounds that a senior Democrat in the Senate wanted mothers to work sooner.

Daschle's talk on the Senate floor, however, was not without pointed criticism of Dole's bill, even as amended. None of Daschle's criticisms was a surprise: he wanted still more money for child care, an even stronger guarantee that mothers with preschool children would actually get child care if they went to work, a rise in the minimum wage, and a guarantee that mothers and children leaving welfare would receive Medicaid coverage under most circumstances. These were all familiar criticisms, made in a constructive manner by Daschle, within the context of a clear optimism on Daschle's part that Senate Democrats could work with Republicans to find compromises and pass a good bill. Again, the contrast with the floor statements of senior Democrats in the House could not have been greater.

As promised, Dole did bring the welfare bill back to the Senate floor on September 6, the second day after the end of the August recess, although it still faced daunting obstacles. By fall it was obvious that the first session of the 104th Congress would not end in October or November as is typical for the first session of a Congress.[52] As we will see in due course, Republicans were determined to enact a budget that would change the direction of American government by greatly reducing its size and income. The level of partisanship was by far the greatest I had seen during a decade in the nation's capital, from which it seemed to follow that it would require lots of additional time to pass any legislation, let alone legislation of the magnitude our leadership was planning. Another factor virtually guaranteeing a drawn-out first session of the 104th Congress was that President Clinton's position on the major budget issues, including welfare reform, was unclear and seemed to vacillate almost from day to day.[53] But if he should find the resolution to oppose those Republican revolutionaries and veto any of their big bills, especially the budget bills, deadlock could result. We might find ourselves having Christmas dinner in the Capitol rotunda. Thus there seemed to be plenty of time left for the Senate to take two weeks or more to pass its welfare reform bill and then to convene and complete a House-Senate conference and pass a final bill before the end of the session. As it turned out, there was time enough to pass the bill twice.

After consulting with his members and with Daschle about the floor schedule for the rest of the fall, Dole decided to allow the Senate to take several days to conduct the welfare reform amendment process. Part of his thinking may well have been that the first two days of debate in August had gone well and that the constructive tone and even more constructive action behind the scenes might continue. Further, fifty-two or fifty-three Republicans were on the verge of supporting the new bill he had introduced on August 11. Faircloth seemed determined to stay outside the fold and, indeed, never supported a Republican welfare reform bill other than his own. Nor was it impossible to imagine that at least a handful of Democrats would support Dole's bill on final passage, especially if the amendment process allowed Democrats to influence the bill. More than 220 amendments would be introduced during the course of the debate, nearly two-thirds of them by Democrats.

As debate opened on September 6, the substitute that Daschle had introduced on August 11, before the recess, was the first item of business. The debate on the Daschle bill took the rest of the available time on the sixth and carried over to the seventh. If the Daschle substitute passed, then the Daschle amendment would replace the Dole amendment as the underlying bill, and Senate Republicans would have no choice except to abandon welfare reform.

It is impossible not to be impressed by the huge difference between the Senate debate and the House debate. Perhaps the lengthy rhetoric and the stately pace of the Senate are conducive to civility and reasoned debate. Or perhaps tradition makes a difference. Or perhaps representing an entire state rather than a smaller (and possibly gerrymandered) district forces senators to be more moderate. Or perhaps senators, who are generally older and more experienced than members of the House, are just a different species (something that House members have long suspected). Whatever the cause, the Senate floor debate was not marred by references to Nazis, castration, or wolves and alligators. If one had the patience to read many, many hours of debate, or perchance would enjoy reading about how pigs can detect drugs better than dogs, I highly recommend direct exposure to the Senate debate on welfare, conveniently published in just 605 pages of the *Congressional Record*.[54]

The vote on the Daschle substitute on September 7 was a good omen for Republicans. With the stakes so high, every Republican voted against the substitute. In addition, continuing his support of the Republican bill that had started during the Finance Committee markup, Democrat Baucus voted with the Republicans. Now it appeared even more likely that Dole would be able to pass his bill.

After defeating Daschle, the Senate turned to the routine business of considering amendments one at a time or occasionally in small batches if both sides agreed that the amendments, sometimes with slight modifications, should be accepted. It took the rest of the day and nearly all of the next just to introduce the amendments, as senators had the right to say a few words about their amendment. The Senate disposed of seven amendments on September 8, four on September 11, thirteen on September 12, another thirteen on the 13th, twenty-six on the 14th, nineteen on the 15th, and two on the 19th. Of these eighty-four amendments, fifty-seven passed and twenty-seven were defeated. Thirty-one of the amendments that passed were sponsored by a Democrat or cosponsored by Democrats and Republicans. As a result, twenty-two of the forty-six Democrats in the Senate had their amendments passed and included in the Dole bill. Many of the Senate's most liberal members (including Kennedy, Barbara Mikulski, Moseley-Braun, Paul Wellstone, John Kerry, Bill Bradley, Patrick Leahy, and Tom Harkin) had their amendments accepted. Even Moynihan cosponsored a successful amendment with his good friend Bob Dole. By the time the Dole bill was enacted, Democrats could certainly not claim that they had been shut out of the process, as House Democrats had complained. Cagey old Bob Dole knew how to build a bipartisan bill. Again, the contrast with House action on welfare reform is striking.[55]

As the Senate tried to work its way through its 220-plus amendments, it was greatly aided by continuous negotiations that took place off the Senate floor. If the sides could reach agreement, and if Dole and Daschle, speaking for their respective parties, endorsed the agreement, the amendment could be brought to the floor and agreed to without a vote, thereby saving time and avoiding public disputes, which could easily turn into fights. This procedure was used for 44 of the 57 amendments that passed. In the case of these 44 amendments, time was saved by avoiding or minimizing debate and by avoiding the twenty minutes or so that would be required for senators to come to the floor for a roll call vote.[56] That the Senate was able to dispose of well over half the amendments considered on the floor by reaching unanimous agreement was another good sign that the Dole bill might receive bipartisan support on final passage.

But as the amendment process unfolded, it became clear that there were still serious splits among Republicans. On Friday, September 8, as senators were introducing amendment after amendment, Dole interrupted the action to announce the lucky few amendments that would be discussed the following Monday and receive a vote on the floor. The amendments and votes had been approved by the Democratic leadership, so there was no objection. Dole then announced that he had several modifications to his underlying bill and, operating under unanimous consent, asked that they be added. At that point, any senator of either party could have challenged Dole and objected to his modifications. But no one did, and the results of his bargaining sessions with both Republicans and Democrats were simply added to the underlying bill without a recorded vote. There were seven major changes, two of which were blockbusters. The most important was that Dole gave yet another victory to the Gramm-Faircloth forces by converting the state option on the family cap to a mandate on every state. This provision, which matched the House provision, was strongly opposed by Democrats and even by a number of Republicans.

I don't know if anyone had an accurate count of the number of Republicans who opposed Dole's mandatory family cap at the moment it was introduced, but it was certainly more than five—which meant that if the Democrats were united, as they almost certainly would be, Dole's mandatory family cap could be killed on the Senate floor. It seems likely that Dole, a man who could count votes in his sleep, realized that a majority opposed his mandatory family cap. He may well have cut the deal with Gramm and Faircloth in full realization that the family cap would be removed by a vote on the Senate floor. But even if the Senate did remove the provision, Dole would still get points from conservatives for trying to enact one of their top priorities. He also included a new provision that would provide a cash bonus to states that reduced their illegitimacy rates, another provision that conservatives had put at the top of their list. As long as these two provisions stayed in the bill, Dole was virtually assured of support from every Senate conservative, probably even Faircloth.

Having moved right with these two provisions, it is hardly surprising that Dole also included two provisions that were important to moderate Republicans and to a large number of Democrats. The most important was an overhaul of his maintenance of effort language. He had included MOE language in his August 11 bill as a bone to moderates. But it soon became apparent that the Dole MOE provision was deceptive. The provision did require states to continue spending at a level that equaled 75 percent of their AFDC expenditures in 1994 on poor and low-income families, but the provision was drafted in such a way that loopholes prevailed. In fact, Dole's provision would allow states to meet its terms simply by continuing to cover Medicaid benefits for the elderly, something they will stop doing at approximately the same time that Michael Moore joins the Republican Party. It might have been possible to write an MOE requirement with less impact on state spending than Dole's, but it would have taken special drafting skills.

But never fear, Bob Greenstein and his knights of the children's roundtable at the Center on Budget and Policy Priorities were all over the Dole MOE provision. Before Congress returned in September and renewed the welfare reform debate, Greenstein's center issued a seven-page brief detailing the rather considerable flaws in Dole's MOE.[57] Soon the *Washington Post* was writing an editorial, based on Greenstein's analysis, arguing that Dole's MOE was a "sham."[58] Both Greenstein and the *Post* were correct, half of which is not surprising. Now in September, as the Senate debate was heating up, Dole could strengthen his MOE provision by eliminating his own loopholes and get credit from the moderates for responding to their wishes. Dole's ability to get two buckets of water from the same well might make someone think he intentionally made his first MOE hopelessly weak.

Dole had a second present for moderates. Child care continued to be a huge issue to both moderate Republicans and Democrats. Thus Dole included a provision that exempted mothers with children under six years old from state sanctions if they could not find satisfactory child care. This was a hole big enough to drive a truck through, especially because Dole allowed states to define what satisfactory child care meant. In addition to these two provisions for moderates, Dole reined in Ashcroft's charitable choice language somewhat by clarifying that none of the funds given to religious organizations could be used to pay for "sectarian worship or instruction." In addition, he increased the number of states that would receive additional block grant funds under the Hutchinson formula provision and included a cash bonus for states that helped families leave and stay off welfare, that collected child support for families on welfare, and that reduced the average length of stays on welfare.

In short, Dole's package of changes on September 8 had something for just about everybody. But of course there was still plenty to argue about. No argument was more divisive or involved more passion on both sides than child care. Over the years, Democrats had repeatedly used child care and early childhood programs as a weapon against Republicans. Democrats like Kennedy and Christopher Dodd and many others wanted more money for Head Start, more money for child care, and strong federal child care regulations that applied to all or nearly all child care facilities in the nation. These had all been major issues in the welfare reform legislation of 1988 and in the child care debate that lasted nearly four years and led to creation of the Child Care and Development block grant in 1990.[59] Now once again Kennedy and Dodd were bringing an amendment to the floor with the primary purpose of increasing child care funding, in this case by around $6 billion.[60] The debate on the amendment lasted longer than the debate for any other amendment, occupying more than thirty pages in the *Congressional Record*.[61] The arguments on both sides were entirely familiar from previous debates. Democrats wanted more money because they believed it was wrong for government to require mothers on welfare to work unless government also guaranteed child care. They argued that because the Dole bill set work requirements that would eventually include 50 percent of every state's welfare caseload, Republicans had an obligation to provide plenty of money for child care. They also held that the care should be of high quality because poor children needed such care to boost their development during the preschool years.

Republicans countered that there was plenty of money for day care in the Child Care and Development block grant and that states could also use money from their welfare block grant to pay for care. Extra money would be available in the welfare block grant, according to Republican reasoning, as the caseload began to decline due to the work requirements. Republicans also pointed out that in the JOBS program only around 20–30 percent of participating families even used child care paid for by government.[62] Thus not all the parents required to work under the new legislation would need government money for child care.

Kennedy also complained that, despite the greatly heightened need for child care, Republicans wanted to end three child care programs created as part of the JOBS program in the 1988 welfare reform law. He said that this callous action by Republicans was "outrageous" and that Republicans were perpetrating "fraud."[63] As a result of the inadequate provision for child care, Kennedy labeled the Dole bill the "Home Alone" bill, citing the title of a popular movie in which a child was inadvertently left at home by his parents when they went on vacation. Kennedy also placed letters and other testimony supporting his amendment in the *Congressional Record*, including letters from Catholic Charities, the National Council of State Legislatures, the Parent-Teachers Association, and others. A string of senior Democrats came to the floor to argue strongly for the Kennedy-Dodd amendment, yet another sign of how important child care was to Democrats.

Despite this unified front and aggressive strategy by Democrats, Republicans lost only two of their members on the vote on the Dodd-Kennedy amendment (Jim Jeffords of Vermont and Ben Nighthorse Campbell of Colorado; the former would soon become an Independent; the latter had switched from the Democratic Party after Republicans took over the Senate in 1995). By a final vote of 50 to 48 (Gramm and Alan Simpson of Wyoming, both Republicans who would have voted with Dole, were absent), this $6 billion threat to Republican unity was defeated.[64] But the child care debate was far from over and would yet require extensive and clever bargaining by Dole before the vote on final passage of his bill could be taken.

By contrast with their impressive unity on the child care amendment, Republicans fell apart on the big illegitimacy amendments. Ironically, the three most important and devastating of the illegitimacy amendments for Republican voting discipline were all sponsored by Republicans. It will be recalled that Dole had put versions of both the family cap and Murray Light in his August 11 bill. However, hoping to split the difference between moderate and conservative Republicans, he made both provisions a state option, meaning that states could adopt either or both provisions but were under no requirement to do so. This approach seemed like the best thing for Dole to do. He could tell his moderates that, given the flexibility that states had because of the block grant format, just stating in the legislation that they could adopt the family cap or Murray Light actually gave them no additional requirements or even authority. To placate conservatives, he could point out that a stronger version of the illegitimacy provisions could not survive on the floor. If it came to a vote, every Democrat and at least fifteen Republicans would vote against any version of the two provisions that required states to adopt them. Even so, as we have seen, in his September 8 amendment, Dole tried to ensure that Gramm and other conservatives supported his bill by making the family cap (but not Murray Light) a state mandate.

Both provisions caused consternation among Democrats and moderate Republicans. Though common sense showed that Dole's provisions were, if anything, already too far right for the Senate, Faircloth was determined to push Dole's version of Murray Light even further right. Preferring to go down to noble defeat rather than take half a loaf, he brought to the floor two versions of an amendment to strengthen the state option on Murray Light. Realizing that many Republicans were reluctant to require every state to adopt the radical Murray Light policy, Dole drafted his most important amendment so that it would require states to adopt Murray Light but would also allow them to pass a law opting out of the requirement if they wished. In the full option offered by the Dole bill, states would have to take action to adopt Murray Light, but under Faircloth's opt-out version they would have to take an action to rid themselves of Murray Light.

The debate on Faircloth's amendment was lively and, for the most part, informative. Faircloth opened debate with the best argument in support of his amendment; namely, that "you get more of what you pay for."[65] One of the most basic principles of economics—that people respond to financial incentives in predictable fashion—was open to various empirical tests when applied to welfare and illegitimate births. If it were true, then states that paid more money in welfare benefits should have higher illegitimacy rates. But as Moynihan pointed out during the floor debate, the relationship between state benefit levels and illegitimacy rates was inverse: the higher the benefit, the lower the illegitimacy rate.[66] The economic dictum of incentives shaping behavior, then, was not persuasive to very many senators. Faircloth also argued that there was an issue of fairness involved in the policy of paying mothers who had illegitimate children. Lots of low-income Americans saved their money and planned for babies and did not go on welfare to support their children. In fact, some of them paid taxes, which in turn were used to support other parents who did not adequately support their children. No one rebutted this point. How could they?

Grassley, who followed Faircloth's opening speech, probably spoke for a lot of Republicans when he said that he agreed with everything Faircloth said except his policy conclusion: yes, illegitimate births were a scourge; yes, the morals of some young people—and perhaps their communities as well—were something less than traditional; and yes, something had to be done. But who should do it? Not the federal government, said Grassley.[67] It followed for Grassley that Congress should leave it up to the states to adopt Murray Light and other policies to fight illegitimacy. His position was that the principle of federalism, so vital to Republican thinking about block grants, trumped the admittedly attractive solution of having a federal requirement that states cut off welfare benefits for young mothers who had illegitimate children. Of course, he strongly supported federal work requirements backed by tough penalties on states that did not comply with federal standards, so federalism evidently did not completely dominate his approach to making policy decisions. Members of Congress live by the notion that a little inconsistency is not all bad. But so do the rest of us.

When Senator Gramm's turn to speak came, he utterly rejected the major arguments that financial incentives were not a major cause of illegitimacy and that not enough was known to take action. He simply asserted, as he had probably done a thousand times in private conversations and speeches, that incentives are a fundamental principle of economics, that both research and experience show that incentives change behavior, and that paying young mothers to have babies outside marriage by giving them cash and other benefits was an ill-advised policy and should be stopped. His faith in incentives was untroubled by the fact that states with high benefits had lower nonmarital birth rates; he relied instead on the studies summarized by Robert Rector, which—like the CBO study requested by Ways and Means[68]—found a correlation between welfare and illegitimacy.[69] Having reasserted his firm belief that giving welfare money to young moms had lured them into having illegitimate babies, he had a ready answer for

Moynihan's claim that knowledge was inadequate as a basis for action. If giving the mothers money caused them to have babies, taking the money away would cause them to stop. Case closed. Support Faircloth.

But his Republican colleagues did not follow his advice. Only twenty-three of fifty-four Republicans supported the amendment, with a majority of thirty-one voting against. Those voting against were joined by all but one Democrat (Robert Byrd of West Virginia), yielding a final tally of seventy-six against and only twenty-four in favor of Murray Light.[70] Democrats maintained tight discipline, while Republicans were badly split. So now, in the first direct test of whether Senate Republicans agreed with the tough illegitimacy provisions being pushed by conservatives inside and outside Congress, it was revealed that the majority of Republicans were simply not willing to adopt a policy that would deny cash benefits to young welfare mothers. As if to prove that they meant their vote, when Faircloth brought a slightly different version of his amendment to the floor, it was also defeated, and this time only seventeen Republicans voted for the amendment.[71] Thus eighty-three senators, including thirty-eight Republicans, voted against Murray Light, most of them twice.

Nor were these amazing votes the only evidence that most Senate Republicans were not willing to adopt tough policies to fight illegitimacy. Pete Domenici, one of the most respected Republicans in the Senate, was firmly opposed to the family cap. On its face, the family cap is a much milder version of reducing welfare benefits than Murray Light because it simply denies additional money for an additional birth (about $64 a month in many states)[72] but allows the family to continue receiving its current cash welfare benefit. By contrast, Murray Light denies the mother and child the entire cash benefit.

The debate on the Domenici amendment was fascinating on a variety of fronts.[73] Domenici opened with a brief and straightforward statement, making one argument: on matters as controversial as the family cap, states should decide for themselves. He repeated Governor Engler's line about conservative strings on the block grant being no better than liberal strings on AFDC. Although he stated explicitly that he considered illegitimacy a crisis and that he believed federal funds should not be used to subsidize illegitimacy, he nonetheless thought the family cap should be entirely a state decision.

Democratic Senator Bill Bradley from New Jersey spoke next and, after a brief warm-up, came to the crux of the issue. His home state of New Jersey had already implemented the family cap, and Rutgers University had been studying whether it reduced births and whether it had any impacts on abortion rates.[74] Though the experimental part of the research was deeply flawed because of implementation problems, reliable state records showed that in the year after implementing the family cap, births to mothers on welfare declined by around 1,500. However, the overall New Jersey birth rate had also declined, casting doubt on whether the fall in welfare births was actually caused by the family cap. It might have been caused primarily by the factor or factors that led to a general decline in births among all New Jersey families.

Because the New Jersey experiment was flawed, all conclusions were suspect. Bradley argued that, even if some of the 1,500 decline in births were attributable to the family cap, the policy was still not justified because all 6,000 families on welfare that had babies had been subject to the family cap's financial penalty. "Is the tradeoff of 6,000 children denied benefits worth the 1,500 hypothetical children whose mothers thought twice before becoming pregnant, or, on the other hand, who had abortions?" Bradley asked. "I do not know," he answered. "We should not mandate something when we do not know what we are doing."[75]

Although Bradley ducked the answer to his question, the question is brilliantly stated. Indeed, it captures the entire sweep of the ferocious argument Republicans had been having among themselves since the Bennett-Kemp-Weber forces bushwhacked the Santorum-DeLay welfare reform work group in the spring of 1993. The dark calculus of every version of the Murray provisions was that federal policy would deliberately visit pain on mothers who behaved badly by having illegitimate births. Necessarily, this policy also took money away from their babies. But in the long run, as Murray had forcefully told the Finance Committee only five months earlier, nonmarital births needed to be "immediately, tangibly punishing" if policy had any hope of influencing the behavior of these young women in getting pregnant.[76] Pain was precisely the point of both the family cap and Murray Light. Murray's answer to Bradley's question, as well as the answer of Faircloth, Gramm, and the conservatives outside Congress (even if they were reluctant to say it publicly), was that preventing 1,500 births was indeed worth the modest penalty imposed on the 6,000 families that had their cash benefit reduced.

Dole then rose to defend his provision. He made a valuable contribution to the debate by stating flatly that he supported the family cap. Given Dole's career as a distinctly moderate Republican—and perhaps even, like Richard Nixon, a kind of protoliberal in matters of domestic policy—his position on the family cap was surprising. His first reason for supporting it was probably the most important. He had been, he stated somewhat plaintively, working to "get enough people on board to pass a very strong welfare reform bill."[77] The implication of this statement was that he had placed the family cap in his bill because he couldn't get support from fifteen or so Senate conservatives without either the family cap or Murray Light, and the family cap was the less objectionable of the two. Besides, he said, his bill softened the family cap by allowing states to give the families vouchers rather than cash. He didn't say, but could have, that he was one of the members of Congress most responsible for starting the Food Stamp program, and Food Stamps had shown that poor families can make very good use of vouchers. So the families weren't losing much in his version of the family cap.

Moreover, states could spend their own money if they believed strongly that mothers on welfare should continue to receive the cash increment when they have another baby. Dole closed his speech with a heartfelt statement of what he hoped the family cap would accomplish: "It seems to many of us the time has come when these families must face more directly whether they are ready to care for the children they bring into the world. That is the reason for the family cap. So somebody has to make some decision out there—the families themselves, the parents, the mother. We believe the family cap will certainly encourage someone to make that decision and that if you continue cash payments, there is no restraint at all."[78]

Phil Gramm, as one of the two primary senators defending the family cap, also rose to oppose the Domenici amendment. Among other arguments, Gramm dismissed out of hand Domenici's argument that the federal government should not impose strings on the states, pointing out that the amendment would require states to spend a minimum amount of state money on their cash welfare program (the MOE provision). Gramm did not call Domenici a hypocrite but did say that he had trouble taking Domenici's "argument about States' rights seriously" when Domenici was sponsoring such a forceful amendment dictating state budget appropriations.[79]

The vote was a shocker. Only thirty-four Republicans voted against removing the family cap from Dole's bill. Again, Democrats were unified (this time even Byrd voted with his party), and the final vote was 66 to remove the cap and 34 to retain it. If the vote on Murray Light was a disappointment for the conservative forces fighting for strong illegitimacy provisions, the vote on the family cap was a disaster. The defeat of the family cap, combined with the defeat of Faircloth's two attempts to put versions of Murray Light into Dole's bill, meant that conservatives might not support the bill on final passage. Once again, the illegitimacy provisions were proving to be the biggest threat to Republican welfare reform. Now there was serious doubt that the bill would even get off the Senate floor.

In addition to a major win for Democrats and moderate Republicans in the Senate, these votes on the Faircloth and Domenici amendments represented a hard-fought and all-too-rare victory for the child advocacy groups. The premier groups, including the Center on Budget and Policy Priorities, the Center for Law and Social Policy, Catholic Charities USA, and the Children's Defense Fund, had achieved no important victories in the House because of House rules giving control to the majority and the air-tight Republican unity. But in the Senate, where the rules gave more power to the minority, where there was still a host of moderate Republicans, and where Republican unity was noticeably looser than in the House, the advocacy groups had a lot more to work with. In addition, the advocacy groups had now had nearly a year to recover from the shocking elections of 1994 and to get themselves organized. Now at last they could taste victory on these very important amendments in the Senate. It was not clear yet that these victories on Murray Light and the family cap would be permanent because so much of the legislative battle still lay ahead. But as it turned out, they had dealt a fatal blow to both provisions, at least in their strong version as federal mandates on the states. The Faircloth-Talent-Rector forces continued to fight the good fight, but for once Republicans had been defeated and the defeat stuck. It was a moment for advocates to savor, especially since they were to have so few.

Moments like this, when it is clear that an irresistible force is heading toward an immovable object, occur often in legislative battles. Based on the Domenici vote, it was difficult to imagine that the bill produced by a House-Senate conference would have the family cap. But it was even more difficult to imagine that Talent and Hutchinson and a large number of conservatives, joined in this case by some moderates, in the House and in the powerful private conservative groups would accept a bill without the family cap. Perhaps we could somehow placate Jim Talent and get him to work with the forces outside Congress, especially Rector and the conservative groups, to accept a bill without the family cap. Shaw and I were greatly concerned by this turn of events, but our attitude was that we should start trying to think of legislative gifts we could give to Talent and Rector to compensate them for losing the family cap.

For his part, Dole did not have time to worry about losing a vote on the family cap. He was still in the midst of one of the toughest legislative battles of his career. He had maneuvered brilliantly to transform his ugly ducking of a bill into a handsome, full-grown duck. Then he simultaneously moved both left and right—a neat trick, that—with his amendments. But he did not yet have a swan.

Furthermore, the debate was taking a great deal of floor time. The Senate had finished fewer than half the appropriation bills, and everyone knew by now that Republicans were writing a reconciliation bill that contained the biggest spending cuts in American history. Legislation of this magnitude would require many days of floor debate in the Senate. So in addition to all his concerns about holding his party together on welfare and doing everything possible to cut a deal with Democrats, Dole must have been greatly concerned about time. When the Senate opened for business on Wednesday, September 13, seven days of debate and voting on welfare (including the two days in August) had already taken place, but more than 180 amendments remained to be considered. Although the debate on the Domenici family cap amendment had taken place on the twelfth, the vote was scheduled for the thirteenth, as was the debate and vote on Faircloth's Murray Light amendment. Even after announcing the improvement of his MOE provision as part of the sweeping amendment of September 8, his moderates were still not satisfied. Thus Dole had been forced to further strengthen his MOE language and increase the required minimum state spending to 80 percent in order to keep his moderates from supporting an amendment by John Breaux of Louisiana that would require a 90 percent MOE, thereby alienating the governors. Dole's third modification in MOE language also had to be handled on the thirteenth.

Given all these time-consuming maneuvers, as the end of the legislative day on September 13 approached, the Senate had still disposed of only 37 of the 220-plus amendments. Anticipating that the debate could bog down, Dole had filed a cloture petition on Monday, September 11, thereby placing Democrats on notice that he might call for a vote to end the debate. He told the Democrats that he hoped not to use cloture but that he wanted some alternatives in case they employed delaying tactics. Now on the thirteenth, as his concern about time mounted and as the Senate moved steadily toward the mandatory debating time of thirty hours between filing the cloture petition and calling for the cloture vote to stop debate, Dole decided to raise the stakes. He went to the floor and said that he had been trying to reach agreement with Democrats on several major issues and that indeed he had already made many important changes in his bill that addressed their concerns. He pointedly reminded everyone that he had already filed cloture and that, if the debate continued to drag, he would call for the cloture vote. If he couldn't get the necessary sixty votes to win cloture and proceed with Senate passage of welfare reform, he would pull the bill from the floor and put it in the reconciliation bill.[80] In the elevated language of congressional debate, Dole's talk is known as a threat. He also cleared the schedule so that the Senate could work on welfare reform virtually the entire day of September 14.

When his negotiations with Democrats on the night of the thirteenth and the morning of the fourteenth produced little, Dole upped the ante again. On September 14, after the Senate had debated twenty amendments and voted on several of them, Dole again came to the floor to remind his colleagues of the possibility of cloture and reconciliation. In fact, this time he stated flatly that his negotiations with Democrats were stalled and that he was planning to call for cloture within an hour.[81]

Perhaps as a result of his threats, combined with the cajoling that was undoubtedly going on behind the scenes, within two hours Dole was able to come to the floor to announce that an agreement appeared to be near. He said that Daschle had given him a list of "six or seven" items and that he had moved toward Daschle on every item. The items included more money for child care, a strong MOE, dropping Kassebaum's job training block grant from the bill, a $1 billion contingency fund for states experiencing economic problems, an increase in the hardship exemption on the time limit from 15 percent to 20 percent, and the $20 million for research being requested by Moynihan. Dole was so pleased with the progress they were now making that he revoked his threat to call for a cloture vote, noting however that some big amendments were pending and that he was still working on a final agreement, especially on child care, so that there was still a possibility that he would be forced to shut down debate. The talk was classic Dole: give a little but simultaneously use the threat of cloture to keep up the pressure to reach final agreement.

Following Dole's pep talk, the Senate returned to methodically debating and voting on amendments. Several were of great importance to an overall compromise. Jeffords had proposed an amendment to repeal the illegitimacy bonus that Dole had worked out with conservatives. Given the major losses by conservatives on the family cap and Murray Light, a loss on the illegitimacy bonus would probably have been the final straw for as many as fifteen of the Senate conservatives. Dole took the unusual step of coming to the floor and speaking powerfully against Jeffords, asking both Democrats and Republicans to carefully consider their vote, because if the amendment were passed and the illegitimacy bonus dropped from the bill, welfare reform would be dead. Despite his pleading, ten Republicans voted in favor of the Jeffords amendment. But amazingly enough, nineteen Democrats voted against the amendment, sending it to defeat on a most unusual vote of 37 to 63. More surprising still was that several liberal Democrats, including Kerry, Levin, Graham, John Rockefeller of West Virginia, and Barbara Boxer of California, voted with Republicans to produce Dole's victory. Daschle himself, perhaps realizing the stakes, also voted to defeat the amendment. At the time, watching nervously from the House, I thought that this vote was the best sign yet that Dole was headed toward a big bipartisan vote. I cannot repeat what several House Republicans said about Jeffords and various of his relatives.

As events proceeded on the Senate floor on September 14, negotiations between small groups of members about individual amendments and between Dole and Daschle on an overall compromise picked up steam. Within a few hours, Dole, like a fisherman returning home with his bounteous catch, appeared on the Senate floor to announce that agreements had been reached on twelve amendments and that both sides were willing to approve them without recorded or voice votes. He also noted that the Senate had "made a lot of progress in the last hour" and that several senators were at that moment in productive discussion about "certain aspects of the bill." In order to allow these negotiations to proceed, he asked that no recorded votes be taken, whereupon he left the floor and returned to the negotiations.[82]

Senator Kennedy chose this moment to come to the floor and deliver a provocative speech about Republican intransigence on child care. He said the 104th Congress (meaning Republicans) had made a big deal of all federal laws applying to members of Congress as well as the public, but members of the Senate had made sure that they have a high-quality child care center available to them and their staffs—and now they were denying the same benefit to poor mothers trying to leave welfare.[83] Kennedy even seemed to imply that child care at the Senate child care center was free for senators and their staffs. As soon as Kennedy finished, Santorum took strong exception to his speech, arguing forcefully that the Senate child care center was not free and that the Republican bill had billions of dollars for child care.[84] Moreover, the majority leader was bargaining at that very moment to provide even more money for child care. As Santorum was delivering this heated speech, Kennedy asked him twice if he would yield, whereupon Santorum snapped back that he would not yield and went right on talking. When he finished he yielded to Dole, who had returned to the floor, so Kennedy did not have an opportunity to respond immediately.

Dole himself might have been a little heated about Kennedy's talk, coming as it did when Dole was in the midst of bargaining with Daschle, Dodd, and probably Kennedy's staff about child care. Whatever the cause, Dole seemed to be fed up with the entire situation: the days of debate, the difficulty of finding agreement with Democrats, the fighting among Republicans, and perhaps the Jeffords amendment. In any case, he came to the floor and announced that he intended to "finish this bill today one way or the other, even if there is not going to be a welfare bill." Dole then said that he had been unsuccessfully negotiating on child care for several hours with Dodd and had made a good offer of an additional $3 billion in child care funding. Dodd interrupted him and denied that Dole had made such an offer. Dole fired back that he had made the offer more than an hour previously. Wisely, Dodd said that he would be "glad to look at that." Then Dodd said to Dole that they knew each other well and that Dole knew he would not lie; Dodd simply never heard the offer. Now Dole, perhaps responding to Dodd's sincerity, seized the situation and said, yet again, that he had made a series of good faith compromises on every matter of concern to Democrats. Given that child care was the last major barrier to an overall compromise, and there seemed now to be a possibility that $3 billion over five years could be the key to a compromise, they should make one more try and see if a deal could be reached at last.

After a brief remark by Dodd, Daschle appeared to suggest that they suspend the debate and review the situation, just as Dole had suggested. "I thought we had exhausted all possibilities," he said. And then added: "But maybe not." At this point, Dole, Daschle, Santorum, Dodd, and perhaps others, accompanied as always by staff, left the floor to see if they could cut a deal. Dole returned to the floor shortly to report that they did indeed "have the framework of an agreement." Daschle agreed, and both he and Dole urged other members to come to the floor with their amendments because they intended to reduce their compromise to writing and finish all amendments by midnight. Upon questioning by Breaux, both leaders said that it was possible they would have to allow more time the next day for amendments but that they should try to finish before midnight (leaving about six hours to continue the amendment process).

The Senate then turned back to the routine amendment process. Over the next several hours, nine more amendments were debated and votes taken. Five were accepted on both sides without a vote, and four received a recorded vote. After the fourth recorded vote, Dole again appeared on the floor to report the results of the ongoing negotiations. First, he asked unanimous consent to endorse an agreement that only twelve of the remaining amendments be considered on the floor, meaning that all the rest would be dropped.[85] Second, because midnight was approaching and many members wanted to go home, Dole said the debate would continue on any of the amendments that were part of the agreement but that the votes on all these amendments would be taken at nine-thirty the following morning (September 15). After votes on the amendments had been completed the next day, he and Daschle would present their compromise agreement and forty minutes of debate (equally divided between Republicans and Democrats) would be permitted. After the debate, he and Daschle would each be permitted to introduce one additional amendment, after which the vote on final passage of the frequently amended Dole bill would be taken. Dole also said that he had accepted a Bradley amendment on categorical eligibility for benefits under the new block grant by mistake and that he would ask for a vote on dropping that amendment.[86] Daschle, while endorsing Dole's explanation of the agreement, asked for a slight modification, which Dole immediately granted.

The Senate met as planned the next morning and proceeded to work its way through the amendments that were part of the compromise. After all of these amendments had been considered, Daschle took advantage of his right to offer an amendment by proposing that states be allowed to use money from the block grant to offer noncash assistance to families that had used up their five years of eligibility for cash welfare.[87] After lively debate, the amendment was defeated on a straight party-line vote of 44 to 48 (with eight senators absent).

Dole then noted that all the amendments except one had been completed. The one that had not was a Gramm amendment to reduce the number of personnel in the Department of Health and Human Services, for which a motion to table had previously been defeated on a 49-to-49 vote. So the Senate would vote on that amendment later. Dole then introduced his substitute, which contained all the various amendments and agreements achieved during the seven days of floor debate in September, including those reached the previous day in extended negotiations with Daschle, Dodd, and others. Dole also announced that the two sides had agreed to several additional amendments, none of great importance, that would be passed by unanimous consent. Finally, he announced the schedule for votes on the Gramm amendment and then final passage of the Senate welfare reform bill on September 19.

On September 19, after passing the Gramm amendment on a 50-to-49 vote, with Baucus providing the winning vote, the Senate quickly agreed to the bipartisan substitute on a spectacular vote of 87 to 12, with eleven of the twelve no votes coming from Republicans. Most of the negative votes by Republicans were cast by conservatives, implying that they were still disappointed that the family cap and Murray Light were omitted from the final bill.

Now all that remained was the vote on final passage. But first, numerous senators had to be given the opportunity to explain their position. After an hour or two of talk, the vote on final passage was another triumph for the forces fighting to reform welfare. The Senate approved Dole's bill by a vote of 87 to 12, with eleven, mostly liberal, Democrats joining Lauch Faircloth as the only negative votes.

The Republican vision of welfare reform had taken another giant step forward—but Republicans now faced the daunting challenge of finding a compromise between the House and Senate bills.

## CHAPTER TEN

# Budget Issues
# Trump
# Welfare Reform

A House-Senate conference committee is policymaking at its rawest and is the most intense and dramatic occasion in the federal policymaking process. Both houses have passed a bill. In nearly every case, the House and Senate bills differ, often substantially. The goal of the majority party in the conference committee is to produce a single bill that can attract a majority of votes in both houses. The goal of the minority party is usually to either get their provisions into the final bill or to defeat the entire bill. Once the conference committee has completed its work, the resulting bill is introduced in the House and Senate and, with no amendments permitted, a final vote taken.[1] Members working on the committee, especially those in the majority party, usually believe that a final bill is possible, even probable. Thus they are usually committed to taking whatever actions and spending whatever time is necessary to bring the conference committee to a successful conclusion. To do so, they know they may be forced to give up some provisions they like or to accept some they don't in order to reach a compromise. The major theme of every conference committee is compromise, often between members of the same political party.

As with every other stage of the legislative process in the House, the conference committee is designed so that a majority can work its will. The majority party in each House, often in negotiation with the minority, decides how many members will represent the majority and minority parties on the committee. If the bill in question is important, and especially if there are many committees with jurisdiction over parts of the bill—as was most assuredly the case with welfare reform—the conference committee could have thirty or more members. The conference committee on welfare reform had forty-four members: fourteen Republicans and eleven Democrats from the House, eleven Republicans and eight Democrats from the Senate.

The most important fact to grasp about the workings of a conference committee is that on every provision there are only two votes, one for the House and one for the Senate, and both votes must be yes on all provisions before the conference committee can complete its work. If the House and Senate cannot reach agreement on every provision, even the most obscure, the bill cannot be brought back to the respective bodies for a final vote. It is in determining the votes within the House and Senate delegations that the fun begins. Getting to yes on every specific provision and on the entire bill requires a simple majority of conferees in each house. Thus if one party holds a majority in both houses and if the majority party can control all its votes, it can always determine the outcome of the conference. Individual members of the majority party can bring a conference committee to a standstill and can then extract outrageous concessions for their votes; of course, they might never serve on another conference committee.

As the welfare reform conference loomed following Senate passage of the welfare reform bill, Clay Shaw and I assessed the House and Senate Republican delegations with a wary eye. We were confident that House Republicans would stick together, but we were less certain about the Senate. The Senate has two parties and a hundred emperors. Of the hundred emperors, fifty-four were Republicans; of the fifty-four Republicans, eleven were on the conference committee. Getting these eleven to agree to a final bill, especially one that would be as conservative as the House demanded, would be as difficult as herding cats.[2] We were prepared to compromise, but there were lots of lines in the sand, not least those involving the illegitimacy provisions, especially Murray Light and the family cap. Of course, as we were about to find out, lines in the sand don't last long in a storm.

The conference officially opened on October 24, seven months after the House passed its bill and about one month after the Senate passed its bill. Following Senate passage, both parties in both houses selected their conferees and their leaders. The House leader was Bill Archer by virtue of his position as chairman of the Ways and Means Committee, with its vast jurisdiction over provisions in the bill. The lead Democrat was Sam Gibbons, the ranking member of Ways and Means. In addition to Archer, the House Republican delegation included Bill Goodling, the chairman of the Education Committee, and Pat Roberts, the chairman of the Agriculture Committee. Thus as would be expected, the chairs of all three committees with major jurisdiction over the bill were on the conference committee. In addition, both Shaw and Jim Talent, House members with perhaps the most expertise on the issues and responsible for much of the House bill, were selected to the House delegation.

On the Senate side, the delegation was led by Archer's counterpart, William Roth, chairman of the Finance Committee. He was joined by Richard Lugar, chairman of the Agriculture Committee, and Nancy Kassebaum, chairman of the Labor and Human Resources Committee. Bob Dole, with his presidential aspirations intact, was also on the Senate delegation. The Senate delegation also included John Chafee, who was a powerful but distinctly moderate member of the Finance Committee. We expected him to play a vital role in the conference proceedings, and he didn't disappoint us. The Senate Democratic delegation was led by Daniel Patrick Moynihan, who was still constantly on the verge of apoplexy about the bill.

It might be expected that the House-Senate conference would be the scene of titanic battles between the parties, given the presence of Moynihan and Gibbons. But there are two reasons this expectation would turn out to be false. First, Republicans planned and conducted the conference under the assumption that no Democrat in either House would sign the conference report. House Republicans intended to move the Senate bill to the right. Our assumption going into the conference was that we would move it far enough to the right that Senate Democrats would jump ship. As always, Shaw hoped to work in a bipartisan fashion, but the Senate bill had pushed Democrats as far to the right as they were likely to go. A second reason we did not have partisan clashes during the conference was that all of the important business of the welfare conference was conducted by Republicans in private. The meetings were not open to either the public or Democrats. Routinely, Republicans in each body would develop their position on each issue by either reading documents or working individually with their staffs, who would then work with other Republican staff members to develop the bargaining position of the respective bodies. Members talked with each other directly during the process, and occasionally there would be meetings of the members, both within the House and Senate and between the two bodies. We examine some of these meetings in greater detail below.

To clarify the issues in the conference and to serve as a kind of scorecard, we prepared an elaborate document that summarized and compared every issue in both the House and Senate bills.[3] This document, which consisted of three bound volumes, was a masterpiece: I kept looking for a laudatory review in the *New York Review of Books*. One reason the document was so good was that we had lots of time to work on it. Between March, when the House bill was enacted, and September, when the Senate bill finally passed, we laid out the entire document and then wrote everything except the explanation of the Senate provisions. Thus when the Senate enacted its bill, we simply reorganized the document somewhat to account for the differences in structure of the House and Senate bills and then completed the sections explaining the Senate provisions.

Some idea of the magnitude of the task before the conferees can be gained by reviewing the conference comparison document. The volumes' 752 pages compared the specific provisions in the two bills; provisions and subparts of provisions numbered 1,142. Perhaps 90 percent of these provisions differed at least a little between the two bills. The remaining provisions were identical (or had only minor differences in wording) in the two bills, so conferees could simply accept these as resolved at the beginning of the conference. Some provisions were very similar, and resolving the difference involved only minor changes in one or both bills. The number of hours a week welfare recipients were required to work, for example, was nearly the same in the two bills. But many of the differences were broad and significant. Before the conference could conclude, all the provisions had to be identical and had to be written in legislative language, including the definition of work and the provisions on illegitimacy.

I was somewhat amazed that the Senate had followed the House bill to the degree it did. There were whole titles in the House bill that, at the outset, we had reason to doubt would even be addressed by the Senate bill. These included the Supplemental Security Income (SSI) provisions on children, the noncitizen provisions, the block grant on child protection, the child nutrition block grant, and the deep cuts in the Food Stamp program. Surprisingly, most of these provisions were included in the Senate bill. Yet there were still several major differences between the two bills. The political center of the Republican Party in the House and Senate differed by several degrees. We were no longer the moderate party of Bob Dole, especially after the ferocious seventy-three-member freshman class of 1994 pulled the average conservative quotient of the House even further to the right.[4] The Senate Republican Party was also moving to the right, in part because conservative members of the House like Santorum ran for and won Senate seats. Bob Dole, the esteemed leader of Senate Republicans, who had once been referred to by Newt Gingrich as the "tax collector for the welfare state,"[5] was not generally considered a conservative, and Sheila Burke, his capable and powerful chief of staff, was a former Democrat who served as a bête noire for conservatives.

The Dole-Burke team was determined to take the White House away from Bill Clinton in the 1996 election, a goal that presented both advantages and disadvantages for welfare reform. The major advantage was that, because the new Republican Party was considerably to the right of Dole's political persona, he had to adopt conservative positions on conference issues if he wanted to remain competitive within the Republican Party. As a result, he supported many of the radical provisions in the House bill. Due in large part to Dole's genius as a legislative strategist he was able to get a much more conservative bill through the Senate than leaders in the House thought possible at the beginning of our journey. The primary disadvantage of Dole's desire to run for president was that it soon became evident that he trailed Clinton by a wide margin. One of the issues on which Clinton was vulnerable was welfare reform. After promising to "end welfare as we know it," Clinton had not passed his own bill and was soon to veto two welfare reform bills sent to him by Republicans. Dole's campaign officials did not want to give Clinton a third opportunity to sign a welfare reform bill and thereby negate the one issue on which Clinton was vulnerable.

But this problem did not emerge for another six months. In the meantime, we needed Dole to help us find a solid compromise bill that included most of the radical features of the House bill. Although differences between the House and Senate bills abounded, several stood out.[6] In considering the resolution of these differences, it is important to keep in mind that Republicans believed they had to demonstrate to the public (not to mention themselves) that they could govern effectively. This powerful consideration motivated all members, including the moderates who would have to move further right on many of these issues if we were to achieve a conference agreement.

Among the most difficult issues were those related to illegitimacy, especially the family cap (no additional money for babies born to mothers who were already on welfare) and Murray Light (no cash welfare for unmarried mothers under age eighteen or their babies). Both, of course, had gone down to ignominious defeat on the Senate floor.[7] The vote on Murray Light was especially surprising because a majority of Republicans and all but one Democrat voted against the provision. Nonetheless, the House leadership had made firm commitments to the conservative groups, led by the Christian Coalition, that at least the family cap would be a part of the conference agreement.

Another important difference was that the Senate bill had the maintenance-of-effort (MOE) provision that required states to continue spending a specified amount of money on benefits and services for low-income families while the House bill left it completely up to states to decide how much money to spend. Democrats and many Republicans did not trust states to keep up their level of spending on cash welfare. Under the Aid to Families with Dependent Children (AFDC) program, the federal government spent about $16 billion annually and states spent about $14 billion. If AFDC were converted to a block grant with flat funding, how much, if anything, would states be required to spend? The fear was that many states, especially the poorer states—all of which already had low benefits ($150 a month was not unusual)—might spend less by deliberately reducing their benefit levels. More likely, states would save money by spending the same amount year after year and allowing inflation to eat away at the size of the welfare benefit, as indeed many of them had been doing since 1970.[8] The House's agreement with governors that states could decide for themselves how much to spend on benefits and services for low-income families reflected the philosophy, prominent in many of our policies, that states knew best. State governors themselves believed that they were in the best position to know both the needs of the poor in their state and their state budget. These two factors, the governors argued, should determine spending on the poor, not rules imposed from Washington.

The major argument against state flexibility was that the poor had little power in the typical state legislature. Public education, higher education, highways, state police, and business interests all had substantial power in most states, power with which the poor and children often could not compete. The interests of the poor were fairly well represented in Washington because Democrats considered help for the poor one of their vital missions as a political party. Thus according to most Democrats and more than a few Republicans in Washington, the new law should include the MOE language.

The Senate bill required states to spend on their cash welfare and welfare-to-work program from their own funds at least 80 percent of the amount they had spent under AFDC and their work program in 1994. Although stronger than the House provision, even this provision expired in just four years, after which, unless Congress took action, states would have no MOE requirement. The Senate bill contained a similar requirement on state spending in the child care block grant. Nor was the MOE requirement the only difference between the two bodies over money. The approach to distributing funds among the states also differed.[9] On this issue, the normal partisan lines between Republicans and Democrats are largely irrelevant. When it comes to taking federal dollars, it's every state for itself, except when poor states band together to fight rich states. Another frequent grouping is rapidly growing states versus states with relatively stagnant or even declining populations. Both of these factors were in play in dividing up funds in the welfare and child care block grants.

The claims of poor states were especially compelling. In deciding how to divide up the money in the cash welfare block grant, the House had started, as Congress usually does, with the status quo. Consider first the amount of money available. The House had decided to give states most of the money from the old AFDC program, both the benefits and administration parts, as well as from the Emergency Assistance program that gave states over $3 billion in 1995 to help destitute children during emergencies such as natural disasters, loss of housing, and loss of electricity or home heating.[10] In addition, the $1 billion from the JOBS program was included in the block grant. The total amount of money available in the pot, composed of most but not all of the funds from AFDC, Emergency Assistance, and JOBS, was around $15.4 billion.[11]

To divide up this pot, the House followed the reasonable principle that states should get approximately what they received before welfare reform. Since data for state spending were not yet available for 1995, the House offered states two alternatives: states could either receive the average amount they had received in all three programs during the 1992–94 period or receive the amount they received in 1994. Providing the option of the average of 1992–94 was a nod in the direction of states like Wisconsin, which had been running aggressive welfare-to-work programs and had thereby managed to reduce their caseload. The Senate approach to dividing up the money differed in several ways from the House approach, including more money ($16.8 billion) in the block grant. All but seven states (Kentucky, Louisiana, Maine, Mississippi, Nebraska, Oklahoma, and Wyoming) received more money under the Senate bill than under the House bill. Resolving the differences between the House and Senate formulas would open the entire question of formulas, with potentially disastrous consequences in lost time and energy.

House-Senate differences in child care seemed almost as difficult.[12] Although the Senate went part way toward the House in creating a simplified child care block grant, major differences remained in the way the two bills structured federal child care funds for states as well as in the type and amount of funding. The House bill had ended seven child care programs and put all the money into one block grant. The issue of committee jurisdiction was solved by placing jurisdiction of the expanded block grant under the Education Committee. By contrast, the Senate had maintained separate jurisdiction for the Finance Committee and the Education and Labor Committee by creating two major sources of funding for child care. Like the House, the Senate ended the three child care programs that had been associated with the old AFDC program, but rather than put these funds in the child care block grant the Senate placed them in the new cash welfare block grant that would replace AFDC, so the money would still be under jurisdiction of the Finance Committee. These funds, although they were in the welfare block grant, could be used only for child care. Unlike the House, the Senate designated the child care funds as a state entitlement, meaning that the money did not have to undergo the rigors of the annual appropriations process. The Senate also reauthorized the existing child care block grant and repealed two additional programs (for a total of five).

The Senate bill also contained several innovative provisions that were very appealing to conservatives and, if judged by the philosophical views of most Republicans, good policy. The first of these, originated by Senator Gramm, would limit the number of employees at the Department of Health and Human Services (HHS). In the context of anti-Washington rhetoric that had been a major element of the surprising Republican electoral victory less than a year earlier, there was no way to keep this provision out of the final bill. Behind the scenes, we encouraged the Clinton political appointees in senior executive positions at HHS, some of whom wanted to pass welfare reform, to figure out a way to accommodate an amendment at least similar to Gramm's. As we will see, they did, reducing the number of positions at HHS and in a way that was administratively feasible.

The second innovative program was called abstinence education. For more than a decade, there had been a debate between conservatives and liberals in Washington about the relative roles of abstinence and family planning, especially condom use, in reducing the nation's exploding illegitimacy rate.[13] Conservatives wanted to create a major role for abstinence, particularly in the case of adolescents still in middle school and high school. Conservatives also wanted to be certain that youngsters learned that sexually transmitted diseases (STDs) were rampant and that condoms did not provide foolproof protection against either STDs or pregnancy.[14] Thus with Robert Rector of Heritage again playing the lead role, the Senate provided $75 million a year to divide among the states, roughly in proportion to their population, to be spent on programs for adolescents that had as their exclusive purpose the promotion of abstinence. Programs that advertised the importance of abstinence in billboard commercials or in the media as well as education courses in the schools or other community organizations could be funded under this provision. The statute contained an eight-point definition of abstinence and made it illegal to advocate the use of family planning with abstinence education funds.[15] House Republicans accepted the Senate provisions on abstinence virtually without debate.

Another original provision in the Senate bill would allow religious organizations to compete for funds from the new Temporary Assistance for Needy Families (TANF) block grant and other programs. The provision had been designed in part by Carl Esbeck, a law professor at the University of Missouri, and aggressively and effectively sponsored by Republican Senator John Ashcroft of Missouri, with capable assistance from a member of his staff named Annie Billings. The intent of what came to be called the charitable choice provision was to allow religious organizations to compete with other organizations for grants to provide services in the specified programs while retaining their religious identity. Based on conversations with Shaw and Johnson, and on many conversations with other members and staff, I felt that the House would support charitable choice, albeit with some modifications. It followed that the welfare reform bill would have yet another controversial provision for Democrats and liberals to attack. I doubted, however, that President Clinton would publicly fight charitable choice, and in the end he was the Democrat who really mattered.

Another of the more controversial provisions, this one originating in the House bill, was the radical change in SSI for disabled children. The Senate, to our great surprise, agreed to expel drug addicts and alcoholics from SSI. This reform was in itself an important and badly needed change in the program. But equally to our surprise, the Senate agreed to abandon use of the comparable severity test and the Individualized Functional Assessment in the SSI program for children. In combination, these two provisions had allowed tens of thousands of children with very mild disabilities to qualify for SSI. The Senate also agreed that disability be defined as requiring "marked and severe functional limitations." In addition, the House and Senate agreed to eliminate from the statute the concept of maladaptive behavior, which allowed children who were destructive to themselves, others, animals, or physical objects to qualify for benefits. Another important, though less controversial, feature of the reforms was that all children would have to be retested using the criteria for the adult SSI program before they could continue receiving benefits after reaching age eighteen. Previously, nearly all children in the childhood program more or less "graduated" into the adult program. Overall, the Congressional Budget Office (CBO) estimated that the version of these reforms adopted in final legislation would result in more than 20 percent of the more than 1 million children on SSI losing their benefits.[16]

Achieving similar far-reaching reforms of the child protection programs seemed all but impossible. Whereas the Senate had signaled its willingness to deal on SSI by accepting major parts of the House bill and creating viable alternatives for the parts it did not accept, the Senate simply rejected the House's child protection block grant. Nancy Johnson, whose moderate views on most issues were widely respected by both Democrats and Republicans, had been introducing legislation since the early 1990s that would convert the child protection programs into a block grant.[17] Johnson's proposal gave states great flexibility in deciding how to use their child protection dollars. But Senator Chafee was strongly opposed to the proposal.

Similarly, the Senate's position on the child nutrition block grant did not permit optimism about a compromise with the House. The powerful and determined Senator Richard Lugar, chairman of the Senate Agriculture Committee, was an implacable foe of the House's child nutrition block grant. Like Chafee, Lugar could single-handedly prevent the conference from adopting something he didn't like. Ways and Means Republicans, under Shaw's leadership and girded by the determination of our members to place passage of a bill above most specific provisions, were willing to drop our child protection block grant if the Senate was unwilling to compromise. By contrast, Republicans on the Education Committee were much less willing to compromise with Senator Lugar. This difference held the bill up for two frustrating months. But in the end, like the child protection block grant, the child nutrition block grant died in the House-Senate conference.

A final major difference between the House and Senate was a blockbuster provision that, depending on its resolution, could by itself bring a Clinton veto of the entire bill. The Earned Income Tax Credit (EITC) was a program normally prized by Republicans and had been praised even by Ronald Reagan as a program that promoted work.[18] By 1996 the EITC provided up to $3,600 in cash to working parents with two children (and up to $2,100 to those with one child). Initiated in 1975 as a way to encourage work and to offset the effects of Social Security taxes on low-income workers with children, the EITC had been expanded under Reagan in 1986, Bush in 1990, and Clinton in 1993. By 1996 the credit put around $29 billion in the pocketbooks of some 19.5 million poor and low-income working families, making it the second largest means-tested program after Medicaid.[19]

Although neither the House nor the Senate welfare reform bills contained major EITC reforms when they were passed initially, welfare reform was about to be caught up in the larger battle to balance the budget, which was in full rage by the fall of 1995. In this context of extreme efforts by Republicans to find savings to balance the federal budget, welfare reform could become the vehicle for cuts in the EITC. In the view of many conservatives, the EITC was welfare pure and simple. It was money taken from productive workers whose earnings were high enough to require payment of income taxes and given to less-productive workers, most of whom had earnings so low they did not pay income taxes.[20] Shaw's response was that the EITC was nonetheless different from welfare because the recipient must work in order to receive the benefit.

However, during the welfare reform and budget debates of 1995 and 1996, many Republicans were under the sway of two other prominent tenets of their philosophy. The first was the pressure to balance the budget. The second was that, newly in charge on Capitol Hill, Republicans were determined to produce results for their major constituency, middle- and high-income taxpayers. In such a moment, tax cuts for the families paying income taxes were clearly more important to Republicans than work supplements for poor and low-income workers. Of the major players at the committee level in the two bodies—Archer and Shaw in the House and Roth and Don Nickles in the Senate—only Shaw was likely to resolve the conflicting calculus of cash EITC payments in favor of low-income workers. By the time the House-Senate conference met in the fall of 1995, it was clear that the Republican budget-balancing bills were going to cut the EITC. The only question remaining was by how much.

Although we conducted only occasional and glancing negotiations with the administration, Secretary Donna Shalala had sent a powerful nineteen-page letter to conferees detailing the administration's criticisms of the Republican bills.[21] By our count, the letter raised fourteen major issues and seventy-four lesser issues that the secretary claimed were problems with the Republican bill. My colleague Matt Weidinger and I read the letter several times. Both of us came to the conclusion that, in contrast with the tone of the letter and the way it had been reported in the media, the secretary's criticisms actually showed how close the administration was to our position on most issues. Thus we proposed to Shaw that we prepare an analysis that we could release to the press showing that, despite the administration's protests about our bills, in reality the two sides were much closer together than one might think. He agreed, and Matt and I began to work on the document for an hour or two each day.

When finished, the document contained numerous surprises for anyone who read it carefully. It was twenty-three pages long, including a two-page table listing the eighty-eight issues raised in the secretary's letter, classified according to whether the two sides were in complete agreement, substantial agreement, or no agreement. By our count, of the fourteen major issues, we were in complete agreement on seven and substantial agreement on the other seven, including child support enforcement, maintaining the safety net, adequate resources for child care, and state option on the Murray Light provision. This in itself was news: that there was not even one major issue on which the president and Republicans had substantial differences. On the seventy-four issues of moderate importance, we were in complete agreement on forty-six (62 percent) and in substantial agreement on another fifteen (20 percent). If all eighty-eight major and moderate issues were combined, we had agreement or near agreement on seventy-five (85 percent).[22]

Reporters and others in the press could review the document and see how reasonable our positions were, something that not every member of the press was portraying very accurately. Cheryl Wetzstein wrote a favorable article about the study in the *Washington Times*, stating flatly that we had already compromised with the administration and reached "complete" or "substantial" agreement on eighty-five of the eighty-eight items raised by Shalala in her letter.[23] Barbara Vobejda, writing in the *Washington Post*, cited our study in a way that raised doubts about claims by an administration spokeswoman that our bill was loaded with cuts in children's programs. In particular, Vobejda pointed out that our study showed that we agreed with the administration on "85 percent of the issues" identified by Shalala in her letter.[24] Republican initiatives did not often get this kind of favorable treatment in the *Washington Post*.

Differences between Republicans and the Clinton administration were to be expected, though they might have been less dramatic than most people thought. But we couldn't have any differences with the Senate if we were to produce a final bill. To discuss these differences and their resolution, Phil Moseley and I managed to get a meeting with Sheila Burke in the late afternoon in mid-October. By that time we had completed the conference documents, with considerable help from Sheila and her staff as well as the staff of the Finance Committee. In a little less than two hours, we went through all the titles that were under jurisdiction of the Ways and Means and Finance Committees. Sheila warned us about several areas in which Dole would not be able to hold Republican votes if the House insisted on such provisions as Murray Light, the family cap, the child protection block grant, and the SSI block grant for moderately disabled children. The meeting was extremely productive for us because it was our first opportunity to hear from an experienced and savvy Senate insider exactly how things were stacking up in the Senate. Although she gave ample indication during the meeting that she was troubled by some of the House provisions, she nonetheless promised to help us schedule meetings between our members and Senate conferees.

By the time the welfare reform conference had its first and last public meeting on October 24, negotiations between House and Senate Republicans were well under way at the staff level. The main business of the welfare conference took place in two subconferences. One dealt with cash welfare, child care, SSI, child protection, and most of the noncitizen provisions. Members and staff involved in the negotiations over these issues came from the Ways and Means Committee and the Education Committee in the House and from the Finance Committee and the Education Committee in the Senate. A separate subconference dealt with the Food Stamp and child nutrition programs. Food Stamps were handled by the Agriculture Committees in both Houses, while the child nutrition programs were under jurisdiction of the Education Committee in the House and the Agriculture Committee in the Senate. As often happens in conferences, both the staff and members of the two conferences met separately and established their own rules and procedures for conducting negotiations.

But in both cases, solving most of the minor and moderate differences between the two bills fell to staff. The day-to-day procedures here are always somewhat cumbersome because staff must be sure that their members, especially the chairman, approve of all compromises. To make negotiations easier and less time consuming, conferences operate with the understanding that staff agreements are never final until approved by members. In our case, Shaw and I talked often by phone and met regularly in person. As conference negotiations heated up in November and December, we met at least weekly, usually with formal agendas to discuss issues in detail. Especially in the early stages of the negotiations when all the issues were open except the few that were identical in the two bills, we operated with the benefit of formal written offers exchanged with the Senate. Three days after the Senate passed its bill on September 19, we had sent a draft of the conference comparison document to the Senate. After some modest changes, the three-volume document had been printed and distributed to conferees, and Republican staffers from the House and Senate began to meet and talk on the phone about specific compromises. Most of the initial discussions were among members and staff within the House and within the Senate in order to develop their offers and to consider offers from the other body.

Our subconference got off to a quick start because the House presented its first offer on October 18, only a week after conferees had been named. This offer covered the cash welfare block grant, SSI for addicts and for children, child support, noncitizens, reduction in government positions, housing, and the provisions in the miscellaneous title of the bill. About 420 specific provisions, across all these titles of the bill, had to be resolved by our conferees. As is typical of negotiations at this stage, this offer did not contain any proposed compromises on the major items that divided the House and Senate, but the offer served nonetheless to clear away much of the underbrush that surrounded the big issues. Consider just the title on the TANF block grant. The conference document identified 149 specific provisions that composed the cash welfare block grant in the two bills. Our reading of the two bills, which was augmented by discussions with the Congressional Research Service and a few telephone conversations with Senate staffers, led us to conclude that 25 of the 149 provisions were either identical or nearly so. These 25 issues we labeled as "Agreed" on the offer form. On another 28 provisions, there were either minor differences between the two bills or our members liked the Senate provision as much as or more than the House's comparable provision. In these cases, we offered for the House to "Recede," meaning that we would drop our own provision in favor of the Senate provision. On 18 items, none of them major, we made compromise offers. In most of these cases, our offer would incorporate aspects of both the House and Senate provisions.

A good example of our approach to offering compromises was our offer on the illegitimacy bonus that would provide a cash payment to the five states that achieved the greatest decline in their illegitimacy rate. Thankfully, the Senate had followed the House and included the bonus provision in its bill, so the biggest issue—whether there should be an illegitimacy bonus at all—was resolved. Only details were in question, the most important of them being how the bonus would be calculated and the language to be used to ensure that the bonus did not provide an incentive for abortions. Our members preferred the House provision on the former and the Senate provision on the latter, so our offer was to simply follow the House bill on calculating the bonus and the Senate bill on abortion avoidance (abortion was referred to somewhat artfully in the bill as "induced pregnancy terminations"). Soon enough we would come to issues that could not be solved so cleanly, but the art of compromise thrives on momentum. Shoot the fish in the barrel first, was our motto.

The first time our members met with members of the Senate was especially memorable. After two or three weeks of attempts by the House to set up meetings between our members and senators on the Finance Committee, Sheila took pity on us and helped set up meetings with several Finance Committee members on the evening of November 16, nearly two months after the Senate had passed its bill. Jim McCrery, Dave Camp, and I met with Senator Chafee and his chief staff member for social issues, Laurie Rubiner, to discuss both the reforms of the SSI program for children and the equally fundamental reforms of the child protection programs proposed by the House. At the same time, Shaw and other conferees met with Chairman Roth and others to discuss the TANF block grant. The meeting with Chafee and Laurie was held in Dole's Senate office, the scene of many subsequent meetings between House and Senate negotiators.

The majority leader's office in the Senate consists of four major rooms, connected to six or more offices occupied by the majority leader's staff, one of which was the ornate and grand office occupied by Sheila. The main entrance to the majority leader's offices is immediately off the north hallway leading from the rotunda on the second floor of the Senate side of the Capitol Building. Leaving the hallway perhaps thirty paces from the rotunda, one enters a small reception room just big enough to accommodate two desks, which during Dole's reign were usually occupied by personable young women who answered the phone and greeted guests. The first room in the inner sanctum is about the size of a public school classroom, with a fireplace on one wall, another reception desk, and several elegant chairs and couches. Three or four end tables and coffee tables are scattered around the room, one or more of which often held a huge and breathtaking bouquet of flowers. The floor was covered with a rich beige carpet which, along with the twenty-one-foot ceilings, makes the room seem even larger than it is. On the left wall at either end of the room as you enter are doors that lead to a second room, in one case through a small pantry. The second room, long and narrow, is much smaller than the first. This room contains another large fireplace and a large rectangular table that can comfortably accommodate ten chairs. Several arm chairs are located around the conference table, with additional arm chairs located against the walls. This room leads directly into the majority leader's office, another beautiful room, with a chandelier, plush chairs, a large couch, a desk the approximate size of an sports-utility vehicle, and another conference table with several chairs.

The middle room was often used as a meeting place for members and staff who were dealing with issues of direct interest to the majority leader. No less than five or six times during the course of House-Senate negotiations on the welfare and reconciliation bills, we had meetings around that big table in the middle room. One of those occasions was the night of our meeting with Senator Chafee and Laurie Rubiner. The senator sat with his back to the fireplace; Laurie was next to him on his left. Jim McCrery, Dave Camp, and I sat directly across the table from them. As we engaged in discussion about the two sets of provisions, McCrery would generally open with comments about why a given approach had been taken and why the senator should agree to our approach. If the senator had already rejected a proposed approach, McCrery would typically offer some compromise version of the original proposal. As he explained the original provisions and suggested possible compromises, his comments would be immediately followed by Laurie whispering in the senator's ear. It is not unusual for House or Senate members to consult with their staff during discussions of this type, but Laurie whispered in Senator Chafee's ear after every comment made by McCrery and often while he was still speaking. Finally, McCrery told her that it was very distracting for him to talk to the senator while his staff member was whispering in his ear.

It soon became apparent that we would make very little if any progress on the child protection block grant. The senator laid out the same case against the block grant that the administration and child advocates were making. The major argument, never stated quite so baldly, was that rule number one in the liberal playbook is to never give up an open-ended entitlement. The federal programs that support foster care and adoption provide states with as much money as they need and can match with state funds to provide a home placement, to pay the administrative costs of removing children from their biological family, and to pay for training social workers and others involved in foster care and adoption. The problem is that this money can only be spent on out-of-home placement even though the system was starved for money for treatment and prevention. Our proposal would give states a block grant with capped spending and allow states to spend all the money as they saw fit.[25] Senator Chafee was clear and strong in his complete rejection of this approach because it required the state to give up its source of open-ended funding. Leaving abused and neglected children at risk because of a shortage of money was not something Senator Chafee would support. The senator was very pleasant and never raised his voice, but there was no doubt in my mind that he would not change his position. Senator Chafee was somewhat more accommodating about SSI for children. He and Laurie recognized that the program requirements were so loose that many children with mild disabilities were gaining admission to the program. They were willing to change definitions, to change procedures, and to administer more reviews of children already on the program, but Senator Chafee was firmly against converting a major part of the program to a block grant. Again, he liked the open-ended entitlement and was opposed to any proposal that would result in limiting this basic structural feature of the program. His major concern, in short, was identical to his major concern with the child protection block grant: he would not support ending an open-ended entitlement program for children.

The discussion between principals had been productive and cordial. I had never met Senator Chafee before, although we were to do a great deal of work with him over the next five years. He had a reputation for being a great gentleman, for possessing extensive knowledge of the social programs under the Finance Committee's jurisdiction, and for holding somewhat liberal views on programs for children. Our sometimes intense discussions of child protection and SSI confirmed all of these judgments. We were, of course, somewhat disappointed with the outcome of the meeting. But with big issues at stake on AFDC, mandatory work, noncitizens, child care, charitable choice, Food Stamps, child nutrition, and many other less sweeping issues, we were glad to get clarification on child protection and SSI. I was virtually certain that our child protection block grant was cooked, with Senator Chafee serving as the chief chef and Laurie Rubiner as the chef's capable assistant.[26] As for SSI, we had lost the block grant but still retained the constellation of provisions designed to keep mildly disabled children off the rolls and to remove those already on the rolls. In my view, these provisions had always been easier to defend than the block grant. Now we had to work with the Finance Committee staff and Laurie to develop final language on restricting admission to the SSI rolls.

As Republican welfare conferees worked their way through the thicket of conference issues, they became the victims of a major external event. Like Jonah, they were swallowed by a whale and could no longer steer. In more prosaic terms, our welfare reform bill got swallowed by the whalelike budget reconciliation bill. And what, you might wonder, is reconciliation? In 1974 Congress passed legislation establishing a formal budget process and creating the CBO.[27] Along with the Congressional Research Service and the Government Accountability Office (known as the General Accounting Office until 2004), CBO is among the most reliable and respected institutions in our nation's capital dealing with public policy.[28] These agencies were created by Congress to give its members and staff information about budget and policy issues. CBO is an organization of immensely competent professionals who are apolitical and who study the budget and selected policy issues, estimate the cost of legislation, keep track of the federal budget and deficit, and publish reliable reports on budget and policy issues.

In the abstract, the basic elements of the budget process and reconciliation are simple. First, by early February of each year, the president presents his proposed budget for the next fiscal year, which begins a little less than eight months later, on October 1. Then in March or April all House committees and all Senate committees report their "views and estimates" of the budget for programs under their jurisdiction to their respective Budget Committee. Working with the leadership, the Budget Committees assemble these views and estimates into their respective versions of the congressional budget resolution for the next fiscal year. Each resolution specifies the amount of spending by major budget category such as defense, income maintenance, foreign affairs, and health, as well as the level of federal revenues and debt for the year. Next, the House and Senate each vote on their respective budgets. As with most legislation, the House budget and Senate budget are usually different. Thus the next step in the budget process is for the leadership in the House and Senate to appoint members from the Budget Committee in each branch to a House-Senate conference committee to work out the differences. This budget conference operates like any other House-Senate conference, which means that the majority party in each body has more conferees than the minority party. If the majority party can control all its votes, it will always prevail. The compromise budget is then introduced in both bodies, and votes are taken.[29] Unlike other legislation, the congressional budget resolution does not require approval by the president. There is no necessary relationship between the president's budget and the congressional budget, though if Congress and the presidency are controlled by the same party, the two budgets are often close cousins.

In years when the leadership of the majority party decides to reduce the deficit, the Budget Committees assume an even more central and powerful role. Now the Budget Committees, after receiving the views and estimates from each committee in their respective body, instruct the other committees to achieve certain levels of savings in their budget submissions. The Ways and Means Committee, which is the source of all tax legislation (under Article 1, section 7 of the U.S.

Constitution, all tax bills must originate in the House), may receive instructions on raising or reducing revenues as well as making spending cuts. The committees of each house then write and pass by committee vote the legislation necessary to meet the targets specified by the Budget Committees. If they do not, the Budget Committees have the power to write the legislation themselves. The Budget Committees then combine all these actions into one big bill, called a reconciliation bill. Reconciliation bills are often over a thousand pages long.

Reconciliation assumed immense importance as Republicans assembled their budget resolution for fiscal year 1996 because Republicans were determined to cut spending to balance the budget. Balancing the budget is the legislative equivalent of eating spinach and, normally, is of little interest to the public. But after well over a decade of fighting on Capitol Hill over ways to balance the budget as well as the budget antics of Ross Perot during the 1992 elections, the public was aroused and Republicans were truly determined to achieve a balanced budget.[30] On the scale of Republican values, only smaller government, national defense, tax cuts, and federalism are in the same lofty category as budget balancing. Hoping to have their cake and eat it too, Republicans decided they could maximize all five of these top priorities by increasing defense spending, cutting taxes, and cutting domestic spending. Cutting spending would in turn reduce the size of government, or at least moderate the growth of nondefense spending. But just to be sure, Republicans decided to end a cabinet agency (Commerce) and a host of programs.[31]

The intensity of Republican determination to balance the budget, as well as the method of pursuing it, was like being in a hurricane. In retrospect, I think a little equanimity would have served us well, but there was precious little balance on either side.[32] Republicans were fueled in large part by the huge freshman class of seventy-three members who considered themselves revolutionaries. As many of them said, they came to Washington to change things. The number-one item on their agenda was balancing the budget by reducing the size and scope of government (except for defense). Perhaps the one trait on which they most resembled revolutionaries was their resistance to compromise, especially on the issue of a balanced budget achieved by spending cuts.[33]

After squabbles and internal fights too numerous to count, some of which will be related in due course, the reconciliation bills assembled by the House and Senate Budget Committees in 1995 were each nearly 2,000 pages long. I seriously doubt that either was ever read in its entirety by any single person. As the Budget Committees assembled their bills, it became evident that nothing like the Republican reconciliation bills had ever been seen in the nation's capital. Over the seven years between 1996 and 2002, the House bill would cut Medicare by $270 billion, nondefense appropriations by $200 billion, and Medicaid by $170 billion. The welfare provisions would save a little more than $80 billion (including EITC cuts). These unprecedented cuts, when added to still other cuts and interest savings on the debt, totaled over $900 billion. This enormous sum, by far the biggest spending cut ever passed by either house of Congress, left room for Republicans to balance the budget and still cut taxes by about $245 billion over seven years.[34] These amazing numbers represented the fruition of traditional and fundamental Republican goals.

President Clinton and congressional Democrats differed in their response to the Republican reconciliation bill. Although congressional Democrats could not deny the importance of balancing the budget—to do so would have been political suicide—they simply said no to the Republican plan, relying on Clinton to veto the bill.[35] The president, a self-styled new Democrat who had proven himself to be a full-fledged deficit hawk by forcing Democrats in the House and Senate to pass a remarkable budget-balancing bill in 1993, was having none of the head-in-the-sand mentality of most congressional Democrats. Although Clinton had listened to his brethren on the Hill in 1994 when senior Democrats advised him not to push his welfare reform bill, he was not going to wait for Hill Democrats this time. Ironically, as the Republican reconciliation bill came into focus, Clinton's position was the classic stance taken by congressional Republicans when they were in the minority: me too, but less.

In other words, Clinton chose to agree with the goal of balancing the budget but not by making the deep spending cuts made by Republicans. Even so, the president horrified congressional Democrats in June 1995 by unveiling a skeleton plan to balance the budget within ten years. Apparently listening to his political adviser Dick Morris, among other senior advisers like Leon Panetta, Robert Rubin, and Alice Rivlin, Clinton met Republicans on their own ground and arrived on the battlefield with an outline for a balanced budget of his own. Sure it may have lacked detail, taken ten years to reach balance, and contained a soft number or two, but it was an amazing budget nonetheless. Moreover, although Republicans conveniently overlooked this historical fact, Clinton's place in the balanced budget Hall of Fame had already been secured by his fighting for the Balanced Budget Act of 1993 (without getting any support from Republicans). Now the battle was truly joined. In any other year, the welfare fight would have been the leading story for several months in the media. But the importance of welfare reform was overshadowed by the huge stakes in the budget battle. The president and congressional Republicans were engaged in a fundamental battle over the future of federal taxes and federal spending. The rhetoric on both sides and in the media knew no limits. As one reporter put it in an excellent analysis of the developing budget fight, the battle was over nothing less than the shape of the federal government for years to come.[36]

I thought then and still believe that Republican budget policy took the high road. We were explicit about balancing the budget and came up with policies designed to reach balance (and in retrospect, it is clear that they would have achieved balance even before the planned date of 2002). The public could see Republicans making the hard decisions needed to achieve a balanced budget, including decisions, such as deep cuts in Medicare and Medicaid, that carried enormous political risks. Through a combination of confidence, hubris, and revolutionary fervor, Republicans smashed ahead with their reconciliation bill in both houses. The leadership, especially Budget Committee Chairman John Kasich and his staff, did an effective job of coordinating the work of the House committees to produce the reconciliation bill. Kasich brought the bill to the House floor on October 26. As planned, welfare reform was included in the reconciliation bill.

Despite its more than $900 billion in cuts, including those in Medicare, only ten Republicans voted against the bill. With Gingrich in the lead, Dick Armey planning floor strategy, and Tom DeLay whipping members to vote the party line, Republicans continued their discipline on the House floor. With a margin of only 25 votes, even with no support from Democrats, we could lose 12 Republican votes and still pass bills. In the case of the reconciliation bill, four Democrats voted in favor and only ten Republicans voted against it, thereby producing a 24-vote margin of victory (227 to 203). Under Bob Dole's leadership, as well as that of Pete Domenici, who chaired the Budget Committee, and Domenici's almost legendary chief of staff Bill Hoagland, the Senate passed its reconciliation bill two days later, on October 28. William Cohen of Maine, who was later to serve in the Clinton administration, was the only Republican to vote against the bill. All forty-six Senate Democrats voted against it.

Suddenly, as if fighting a historic budget battle and a welfare reform battle were not enough, two new and highly contentious issues took center stage in mid-November. The government was about to run out of the authority both to borrow and to spend money. Because in most years the federal government spends more money than it collects in revenues, the U.S. Treasury covers the difference, plus interest on the accumulated deficit from previous years, by issuing interest-bearing bonds. Thus the national debt grows almost every year, requiring Treasury to borrow still more money. To exert some control over the borrowing process, Congress maintains a ceiling on the amount of money Treasury can borrow. From time to time, as the national debt increases, Congress must vote to raise the debt ceiling. Of course, if Congress were to fail to raise the ceiling before Treasury needed to borrow additional funds, the federal government would default on its debt, in all probability setting off a catastrophic chain of events that would constitute an economic meltdown.

Given the economic consequences, normal people would conclude that refusing to raise the debt ceiling when additional borrowing authority is needed is never a real option. Nonetheless, it is tempting for Congress to play legislative chicken with a president they want to compel to approve some vital congressional goal. In the case at hand, such was the fervor of congressional Republicans that they were willing to flirt with default if Clinton refused to reach agreement on the budget—or at least to agree to negotiate based on his acceptance of CBO scoring and a seven-year plan to reach balance. None of this ten-year stuff for Republicans![37] But the president shocked many Republicans, and perhaps a few editorial-page writers, by staring down Republicans in their dangerous game of chicken. On November 13 he vetoed the short-term debt extension bill and several ride-along requirements.

But that's not all. Not only would the federal government soon run out of authority to borrow additional money, but November 13, the day Clinton vetoed the debt ceiling increase, the federal government was in the last day of authority to continue spending money on a host of federal activities and programs for which Congress had not yet passed an appropriations bill for the next fiscal year (never mind that it was money the government didn't have and perhaps now could not even borrow). With Congress and the president locked in a death spiral over the budget, and with only three of thirteen appropriations bills passed to keep the government running, yet another game of legislative chicken was in play. As they had with the bill on borrowing authority, at the last possible minute Republicans sent Clinton a bill to continue spending at the previous year's level (called a continuing resolution) along with a major rider. Again, Republicans thought they were being clever by forcing Clinton to accept a rider as the price of keeping the government open: an increase in the Medicare part B premium.[38] But again, Clinton surprised Republicans. On November 13, the same day he vetoed the bill to extend borrowing authority, he vetoed the continuing resolution.

Because Congress and the president could not agree on a budget, the spending bill was squashed like the pawn that it was. The result was that most government agencies shut down on November 14. Now the media was flooded with stories about families that had traveled a thousand miles to see a national park, only to be turned away at the gate because of the government shutdown; and about struggling government employees trying to make their house payments.[39] A *Washington Post*–ABC survey showed that 46 percent of the public faulted Republicans, with only 27 percent faulting the president.[40] Despite our problems with public opinion, on November 15, the day following the government shutdown, the House-Senate conference to resolve differences between the respective reconciliation bills began to meet. Consider the polluted water in which Congress was now swimming. As a result of Clinton's veto of the debt ceiling bill, the catastrophic prospect of default hung over the government. The polls showed that the public saw Clinton as winning—or at least as less guilty than Republicans. More and more Republicans were beginning to question our direction, the wisdom of our leadership, and the intransigence of many fellow Republicans, especially members of the freshman class.

Meanwhile, we continued to work away at finding agreements on the House-Senate welfare reform legislation. Because Republicans were using reconciliation to balance the budget, it was a foregone conclusion that, if the welfare bill had not passed by the time reconciliation was ready for the floor, a version of the welfare bill would be included in reconciliation. The welfare bill produced savings, and savings were vital to the Republican reconciliation agenda. But Shaw and all the subcommittee Republicans were greatly concerned when welfare was swept up in the reconciliation bill. Not that the prospect of being swallowed by the whale was sudden. We had realized at least since early spring that there would be a big reconciliation bill and that, because reforming welfare saved so much money, it would likely be included if it hadn't passed by then. From our perspective, there were several problems with this approach. We wanted welfare to be separate because we intended to focus the nation's attention on Republicans delivering on Clinton's promise to end welfare as we know it. We were following the Washington adage that wise politicians do not step on their own message.

Another reason for concern with the strategy of feeding welfare reform to the whale was a complex provision in the Senate reconciliation procedure called the Byrd rule. Written by Senator Robert Byrd of West Virginia, the rule was designed to prevent the Senate, and therefore Congress, from loading extraneous provisions on a reconciliation bill.[41] For example, no provision that fails to produce a change in spending or revenues can be included in a reconciliation bill. In addition, no amendments of the Social Security program can be placed in a reconciliation bill. Because of the Byrd rule, many important provisions in the welfare reform bill would be dropped if the bill were included in reconciliation. These included the five-year time limit, the state option to adopt the family cap, the charitable choice provision, and the abstinence education program. Dropping these provisions was strongly opposed by most House and Senate Republicans. But once the welfare reform bill was swallowed by reconciliation, these were potentially dead.

Here was perhaps the most compelling reason for keeping welfare separate from reconciliation or at least for continuing the welfare reform conference so that the welfare bill would be ready for separate submission to the president. Finally, although Shaw never spoke with me about this factor, I think he was always uncomfortable cutting welfare spending in the same bill in which we also cut taxes. Inevitably, the tax cut would apply to the rich as well as the middle class, and since the rich pay more in federal taxes than the middle class, the rich would get a larger fraction of the total tax cut. All this, of course, was fodder for the Democrats' class warfare machine.

Despite all these good reasons to keep welfare separate, it was impossible to avoid being swept up by reconciliation. Thus as a supplement to being included in reconciliation, Shaw and Archer recommended to Newt Gingrich and the rest of the leadership that we initiate and then continue the welfare conference separately from reconciliation and await events to decide whether to include welfare in reconciliation. Nor was it even clear that the reconciliation bill would become law. We had little doubt that the House and Senate would reach agreement, but there was every chance that Clinton would veto the bill (especially after he vetoed both the debt ceiling bill and the spending bill). We took the position, which Shaw began discussing with other members as early as September, that if we did include welfare in reconciliation and if the president vetoed reconciliation, we should immediately pull the welfare bill out of reconciliation and send it to the president separately.

As the welfare reform conferees continued their search for compromises, House and Senate Republicans set to work on resolving the hundreds of differences between their respective reconciliation bills. With skill and daring, Republicans had mounted the strongest assault ever on America's version of the welfare state.[42] I would guess that nearly all the Republicans in the House viewed the battle over reconciliation as the most important event of their political lives (some, especially among the freshmen, would drop the word "political"). Democrats also saw reconciliation as a watershed event and as a direct threat to their mode of governing. Removing $900 billion in federal spending, along with several federal agencies, drove Democrats (and many of the nation's editorial-page writers) to the far edge of political sanity. The entire party had been Gibbonized.

In the middle of this circuslike atmosphere, House and Senate Republicans had to resolve differences between their reconciliation bills. As was the case with welfare reform, the most serious issues were between united House Republicans on one hand and moderate Senate Republicans on the other. Although the House was somewhat dismissive of Dole as an old-fashioned Republican, the fact was that Republican policy, as reflected both in the welfare reform and reconciliation bills, was completely dependent on the political skills of Dole to find the places he could compromise enough to keep Senate moderates on board while retaining the major features of the House reconciliation and welfare reform revolutions. His task was immensely complicated, because the job was not to find the middle. No—we were playing this game further to the right on the political spectrum than at any time in history. Dole's charge was to bring both bills toward the center so that the moderates would support it—but not so far that Senate and House conservatives would reject it. It was a virtual certainty that few or even no Democrats would support the conference report on reconciliation, so Dole could not lose more than three Republican votes on the Senate floor. Given the fifty-four Republicans and forty-six Democrats in the Senate, losing four Republicans would produce a fifty-fifty tie and would allow Vice President Al Gore to cast the deciding vote. It was rumored that the vice president did not support the Republican revolution.

In the process of finding House-Senate agreements on the thousands of pages of legislation in the reconciliation bill, Gingrich and Dole adopted one of the most creative and unusual approaches ever seen in a House-Senate conference. For several days in mid-November they set up a kind of court procedure in which litigants representing the House and Senate on various sections of the reconciliation bill came before "judges" Gingrich and Dole to present their case. Roughly, the procedure was for the numerous subconferences to meet together to resolve differences between the bills. But if they got stuck on particularly difficult issues, they would bring their problems to the Gingrich-Dole court in the Mansfield Room on the Senate side of the Capitol Building. Either staff or members would present the case, with someone from the House presenting the House's case and someone from the Senate the Senate's case. Gingrich and Dole would then confer and immediately issue a recommendation, whereupon the litigants would return to their meeting room and resume the fight. The typical recommendation by the judges—pure Gingrich, as those of us who had been working with him for any period of time knew well—was to suggest a few compromises and then tell the litigants to go in a room, lock the door, and don't come out until they had reached a compromise. If Gingrich had his way, there would be no food or bathroom breaks until the combatants had reached a compromise. One of the greatest talents that Gingrich possessed, and one that I rarely saw recounted in the media, was an uncanny ability to dream up compromises. On many occasions I saw him hear the outlines of a policy conflict and then, within literally seconds, propose several possible compromises.

I had the opportunity to appear before the court myself. By the time of the Mansfield Room sessions on reconciliation, the welfare reform conference had been meeting, especially at the staff level, for over a month, and we had resolved all but a few issues. As we were working out the final compromises on child support, the directors of state child support programs from around the nation became concerned about our proposal on payment distribution. As recounted previously, these are the rules—the very rules that Nancy Ebb of the Children's Defense Fund had come through the back door of the Rayburn Building late at night to help me write—that govern how child support collections are distributed between mothers and government. Our plan was to distribute less to government and more to mothers, many of whom we hoped would soon be leaving welfare for work. An unfortunate effect of this approach was that it was costly for both states and the federal government because, rather than retain a large part of child support payments to reimburse government for providing welfare benefits, most of the money would be given to mothers and children. CBO estimated that by 2002 the new distribution rules would cost the federal government $150 million a year and rising. The new rules would also impose similar but somewhat lower costs on states. To offset at least part of this (and other) increases in state child support costs, we included a provision that provided a federal guarantee that the level of collections states retained would not fall below the level the state retained in 1995.[43]

The directors of the state child support programs, an organized and aggressive bunch of public servants, were worried they might lose money because of these new rules. In some states the money that state government received from collections was poured right back into the child support program. So the directors, assisted by the American Public Welfare Association (now the American Public Human Services Association), lobbied against our provision. They were making a straightforward choice between more money for mothers and children on the one hand and more money for government on the other. After clever lobbying, Senator Grassley sided with child support directors and against House Republicans. With Senator Packwood now out of the picture, Grassley was the third-ranking Republican on the Finance Committee. Grassley took the interesting step of bringing Jim Hennessey, the child support director in his home state of Iowa, who was a friend of mine and exceptionally knowledgeable about the child support program, into the Mansfield Room for the event. The setting was almost like a formal college debate.

I opened by explaining the current distribution policy and the change the House wanted to make. I emphasized that the goal of our policy was to shore up the mothers' income after she left welfare for employment. I concluded by saying that Republicans should give the money, paid by fathers after all, to mothers and children and not to government. Hennessey followed and, as I expected, argued that this policy change, so desirable on its face, would have the effect of reducing funds for the child support program in many states. So in trying to help low-income working mothers, we would put a much larger group of mothers at risk of less effective child support enforcement. Besides, he said wisely, Republicans were giving states more and more authority over welfare programs, so why were we forcing this child support decision on them? Gingrich's response was immediate and predictable: Go back to your negotiating table and find a way to split the difference. So we did. Moms wound up with approximately half the money; states and the federal government retained the other half. It was a good solution because there were strong arguments on both sides.

After three days of the Mansfield Room discussions, House and Senate Republicans reached agreement on all the major issues in reconciliation. The few issues still unresolved regarding welfare reform were simply dropped from the bill. In addition, about thirty items were dropped because of the Byrd rule, including the five-year time limit, the family cap, and the bonus for states that reduced their illegitimacy rates.[44] The huge reconciliation conference report, one of the most radical pieces of legislation ever supported by a majority party in Congress, was brought to the floor of both the House and Senate on November 17, four days after President Clinton had vetoed the debt ceiling and continuing resolution bills and three days after the government had closed down. It was in this atmosphere of exceptional hostility between Republicans and Democrats in Congress and between congressional Republicans and the president—which would only intensify in the days and weeks ahead—that Republicans passed their reconciliation conference report in both the House and Senate on nearly party-line votes.

Unfortunately, after the vetoes of November 13, events had begun to assume a logic of their own. As often happens in great political battles, neither side was in full control of events. The wisest, most insightful, and most willful strategists cannot control either the actions of their opponents or the circumstances within which their political fight is taking place. As was now becoming clear, not even Gingrich and Dole, both great leaders by almost any measure, could control their own forces. Just how much external events would control us was now becoming more apparent. The closing of the government following Clinton's November 13 vetoes should have been interpreted by Republicans as a sign that we were losing control of events. The issue now was who would be seen by the media and the public as responsible for the government shutdown. Clinton and the entire White House message machinery began heaping abuse on Republicans. Their goal was to portray Clinton as protecting the poor and the elderly and the environment from those mean Republicans, the same folks who were willing to close down the government. Of course, neither House nor Senate Republicans took this abuse without fighting back. The media was covering reconciliation as almost a sporting event. To do so, they had to report on both sides, and neither Gingrich nor Dole had any trouble having his every word covered in the papers and on the evening news. The real issue was which of the three old white guys the American public saw as most credible.

Game and set went to Clinton. Gingrich was too mercurial and had made several media blunders, none worse than his complaining about being snubbed by the president on Air Force One returning from Israeli Prime Minister Rabin's funeral in November.[45] The White House produced a photograph of Gingrich and Clinton talking on Air Force One, which made Gingrich look even worse. Gingrich's approval numbers in the polls were falling, making him no match for Clinton in the public relations battle now unfolding.[46] Though Gingrich was a fascinating figure, as events were demonstrating, he didn't wear well. In a more rational world, Dole could have been a match for Clinton. He was a war hero, had served in the Senate for nearly thirty years, and was capable of great wit and brevity in summarizing his views. Plus he was one Republican the press really liked. But Dole was overshadowed by Gingrich, who got much more press attention. Moreover, Dole was somewhat tainted because almost everyone assumed he would be the Republicans' next presidential candidate, so everything he said had a certain political overtone. Finally, some Republicans simply miscalculated; they didn't think the public would care much about shutting down the government. They were wrong.

For anyone who might want to demarcate the rise and fall of the Republican revolution, I would say that the battle over the budget that resulted in closing the government, and especially the compelling public opinion polls that seemed to indicate that Americans did not want their various government activities and facilities closed down, was the high-water mark of the Republican campaign against big government. Although most Republicans did not realize their predicament yet, in retrospect it is possible to conclude that the loss of this battle over the size of government in November and December of 1995 showed that reducing government, at least on the scale attempted by Republicans in 1995, did not enjoy widespread public support. Clinton, suddenly a lion in winter standing up to those wild Republicans, saw his poll numbers rise, as Republicans came to be blamed for closing down the government. If this was a chess game, Republicans could be accused of thinking only one move ahead. We sent Clinton big bills that he wouldn't dare to veto. He vetoed them anyway. Then what?

On November 15, just two days after the Clinton vetoes and one day after the first government shutdown began, House Republicans attempted to stop the bleeding by passing a new continuing resolution that had only one rider. Rather than the increase in Medicare premiums originally demanded as the price for keeping the government open, Republicans now were asking simply that Clinton commit himself and his administration to achieving a balanced budget within seven years under CBO scoring. The president immediately made it clear that he would not accept this provision, even if it meant keeping the government closed. As Mike McCurry, the president's press secretary, told the press, if the president accepted the seven-year budget, he would be forced to accept the deep spending cuts necessary to get there, including cuts in Medicare, which the president had repeatedly said were unacceptable.[47] After his vetoes of November 13, lots of Republicans believed him. The Republican strategy of forcing Clinton to make a public commitment to a seven-year balanced budget under CBO scoring as the price for a continuing resolution was nonnegotiable in the House. Given the ferocity of the freshman class, few believed that Republicans would retreat from this minimum goal. It appeared that a long deadlock was possible, even probable.

But on November 19, Leon Panetta surprised everyone by presenting an administration offer to congressional Republicans. The offer was essentially that the president would commit to a seven-year budget as Republicans demanded but that the deal was valid only if Congress agreed that the final budget would protect Medicare, Medicaid, education, and the environment and did not contain more than modest cuts in the EITC. This language, after some reworking by both sides, formed the basis of an agreement, and the president signed the continuing resolution later that day, reopening the government after a closure of five days. The agreement was only good until December 15 at midnight, at which time the government would close again unless a budget deal was reached or the continuing resolution was extended. As soon as the government was reopened, the president and his staff disagreed with what Republicans thought the agreement said. The disagreement about the meaning of their hurried and ambiguous agreement added to the atmosphere of hostility between Congress and the president. Republicans emphasized that the president had agreed to balance the budget within seven years under CBO scoring; the White House emphasized that the president only had to agree to such a budget if a host of programs were protected.

The next day, November 20, Leon Panetta went on the *Today Show* and said that the administration had agreed to balance the budget in "seven or eight years." Republicans had a fit over the expansion of the deal to eight years. To make matters worse, there was every indication that the president would veto the reconciliation bill that Congress had sent him after it passed both houses on November 17. On December 6, the president made it official by sending Congress a formal veto.[48] Now the president had vetoed everything on the Republican agenda: the budget, the reconciliation bill, the continuing resolution, the debt ceiling, and welfare reform (which was in the reconciliation bill). But perhaps welfare reform could be revived, thereby at least keeping the Republican revolution on life support.

## CHAPTER ELEVEN

# Clinton Vetoes
# Welfare Reform,
# Again

With our leadership casting about for a strategy, Clay Shaw and others renewed the call to complete the welfare reform conference and send Clinton the welfare reform bill separately. In addition, with the budget battle virtually drowning out the welfare reform struggle, Shaw and Bill Archer were both determined to do everything possible to keep welfare alive and get as much press coverage as possible. Among numerous other activities, we met with the Catholic bishops who had been such critics of our bill; released our report and held a press conference on Secretary Donna Shalala's letter to welfare conferees criticizing our bill; and held a hearing on welfare success stories.[1]

The meeting with the bishops was one of the most interesting but least productive activities we conducted during this period. Shaw, a devout Catholic, had long been bothered by the very strong, almost virulent opposition to our bill by groups associated with the Catholic Church.[2] Their opposition to our bill was based on a long history of social thought by American Catholic bishops. In 1986 the bishops had issued a lengthy report on social justice that was clearly incompatible with the direction of scholarly and political thinking about social policy.[3] Consider, for example, *The New Consensus,* which ironically was written primarily by Michael Novak, one of the world's leading Catholic intellectuals and a trusted adviser to the Vatican and Pope John Paul II for many years.[4] It will be recalled from an earlier chapter that in this report Novak and his impressive bipartisan group of scholars and administrators urged that welfare reform aim to increase personal responsibility by creating mandatory work requirements and even time limits. Both the 1986 bishops' statement and many documents and letters released by Catholic organizations during the 1995 congressional debate specifically opposed these policies and called instead for more spending on the poor.

In March 1995 the Catholic Conference issued a statement, "Moral Principles and Policy Priorities for Welfare Reform." Like the 1986 report, this report was full of sweeping rhetoric: "Our purpose is . . . to share our principles and experience in hopes they will help lift up the moral dimensions and human consequences of [the welfare reform] debate." The statement called for reform that, among other things, was based on "respect for human life and human dignity" and on "the principles of subsidiarity and solidarity." And, of course, the Catholic Church's views and recommendations "take on special urgency when a fifth of our children are growing up poor in the richest nation on earth."[5] The paper then goes on to specifically oppose both Murray Light and the family cap. In less than a page, the paper says three times that these policies "will" or "are likely" to increase abortions, despite the fact that there was no good evidence to support this claim. Further, the statement specifically supported continuing the entitlement nature of cash welfare, opposed both sanctions and time limits, and rejected any reductions in benefits for immigrants. Rather, the Catholic Conference recommended more spending on a family tax credit, education, training, infant nutrition, work programs, and child support enforcement. The Catholic Conference would replace tough love based on reciprocal expectations backed by sanctions with policies based on squishy admonitions such as "enhancing the lives and dignity of poor children and their families."[6]

In November the bishops released a public statement condemning Republicans (without, of course, using the term Republican) for adopting such rigid policies aimed at reforming welfare and balancing the federal budget. In their lead paragraph, they contrasted the "powerful message of moral courage and consistency" displayed by Pope John Paul II (who "in driving rain and bright sunshine, in Cathedrals and ballparks" called on Americans to "stand up for human life and human dignity") with the current behavior of American leaders, who were "considering measures which will hurt the very people our Holy Father called on us to defend" and had rendered the nation's government "inoperable, paralyzed by partisan struggles and ideological stalemate." The bishops went on to express these same sentiments to every member of the House and Senate in a letter signed by Roger Cardinal Mahony, the archbishop of Los Angeles, and Bishop John H. Ricard of Baltimore. After excoriating the welfare bill and the budget cuts for harming the "weakest members of our society," undermining the "national safety net," and "embracing dangerous policy which will encourage abortion, target legal immigrants unfairly and retreat from the nation's commitment to protect poor children," they recommended that Congress "reject this fatally flawed legislation." If Congress failed to reject it, then they urged the president to veto it.[7]

As our bill worked its way through Congress, we continued to encounter direct opposition of this type from the bishops as well as from Catholic Charities USA, an arm of the American Catholic Church that provides services to the poor. Catholic Charities and their chief representative, Sharon Daly, lobbied aggressively against our bill. During the House floor debate on March 22, Charlie Rangel of the Ways and Means Committee publicly referred to Cardinal O'Connor of New York, who had expressed concern about the negative effect of the Republican bill on children, according to Rangel.[8] So strong was the opposition of Catholic leaders to the family cap that they joined forces with both Democrats and a few pro-life Republicans in trying to defeat it on the House floor. During this period, Daly was a frequent presence on Capitol Hill working against the bill, often in cooperation with left-of-center organizations like the Children's Defense Fund.

In November 1995, I noticed in something that came across my desk that Catholic bishops from across the nation would be in Washington in early December for their annual meeting. I asked Shaw if he would like to meet with a few of the bishops to discuss their position on welfare reform. Shaw immediately agreed, and I called Sharon Daly and asked if one or more of the bishops would be willing to meet with Shaw. She soon called back and said that a small contingent of bishops would be happy to meet with him. A meeting was set for December 4 in Shaw's office with Bishops John Ricard of Maryland, William Skylstad of Seattle, and Joseph Sullivan of New York. Daly was out of town that day and could not attend the meeting.

When the bishops arrived on the fourth they were immediately ushered into Shaw's office. After exchanging some small talk, Shaw got down to business by giving a ten-minute overview of his subcommittee's five years of work on welfare reform. He especially emphasized how he had personally come to the conclusion that welfare had to be based on reciprocal responsibility and an emphasis on work. He did not duck the tough parts of our bill; rather, he emphasized how important it was to create a system that included sanctions for able-bodied adults who did not meet program requirements by making a sincere effort to work. Previous reforms, like those in 1988, had always meant more benefits but only marginal (and then largely ineffective) increases in personal responsibility.[9] This time, he vowed, it would be different. Although a system like this could have some short-term negative impacts on the financial well-being of some families, in the long run more families and children would be better off if a demanding welfare system conveyed the message that adults had to work. Several times during his summary Shaw used the term "tough love" to refer to the type of welfare program we wanted states to implement. He also emphasized that, because of expansions in the Earned Income Tax Credit (EITC), Medicaid health insurance, and funds for child care, families would be much better off financially even in low-wage work than they were on welfare. Our goal, he concluded, must be to get young mothers, by use of strong measures if necessary, to join the workforce and create a better future for themselves and their children.

When he finished, each of the bishops responded. Bishop Skylstad emphasized that his knowledge about the poor was based on direct involvement with poor people through Catholic churches and missions. He also mentioned the church's historic commitment to the poor and the historical and philosophical underpinning of Catholic doctrine on helping the poor, with repeated reference to the 1986 paper written by the bishops. He concluded by informing us that the bishops were strongly united in opposition to our bill. Bishop Ricard added that the Republican bill would fail because there were too few jobs, especially in the inner city, and even the available jobs paid too little to support a family. He also said, although in a pleasant way, that our bill "tears down" because it cuts spending on programs for the poor, something the Catholic Church strongly opposed. Bishop Sullivan, reflecting Bishop Skylstad's emphasis on knowledge gained through direct work with the poor, told us about his experiences trying to help the poor in New York City. Ironically, he told us he was "trying to change behavior" and without much success, precisely the reason Shaw had offered for basing the reformed welfare system on tough love. Although he agreed that not having a job was very "corrosive" to the poor, he claimed that New York City had lost nearly 1 million jobs and that he knew well-educated former seminarians who couldn't find work. How then could we expect uneducated poor mothers to find work?[10]

During the discussion that followed, the bishops expressed their strong opposition to the family cap, which they feared would increase abortion rates. They also expressed the strongest possible opposition to our immigrant provisions and devoted a great deal of attention to the spending cuts in the Republican bill. At one point, one of the bishops argued that we should "fix" the problems with child care and unemployment before we strengthened work requirements. Otherwise, he argued, families would be subjected to too much risk. After more give and take, Shaw ended the meeting by declaring, somewhat incongruously, that we were "all going to work together."

Despite Shaw's closing injunction, the meeting showed clearly that important and influential Catholic organizations would continue opposing our bill with every resource at their command. As I said my farewells to the bishops, I reflected on how glad I was that one of the founding principles of American government was the separation of church and state. I didn't mind that they disagreed with us. Lots of very smart Democrats, beginning with the incomparable Senator Daniel Patrick Moynihan, disagreed with us at least as strongly as the bishops. Indeed, Moynihan often invoked the bishops in his speeches about the terrible effects of the Republican bill on the poor. But the bishops were not used to the give and take of political arguments on matters that bordered so closely on church doctrine. If they could have their way, they would simply ignore our arguments and the poll data—and even the electoral data—and change the nation's welfare programs in the direction of more generosity and fewer expectations of improved behavior through sanctions. Walk softly and carry a big carrot was their philosophy. But Shaw had more votes.

During this period we also attempted to keep welfare reform in the spotlight by holding a hearing on December 6 to show that welfare reform was already a success in a few states, from which it followed that passing national reform would dramatically spread these successes across the entire nation. To portray the successes that states were already having, we invited officials from four states—three with Republican governors (Michigan, Massachusetts, and Wisconsin) and one with a Democratic governor (Delaware)—and mothers who had left welfare for work in three of these four states. We also invited a distinguished researcher to testify about research on recent welfare-to-work programs and an official from a local project, called New Hope, being conducted in Milwaukee.

The hearing went off smoothly. The drop in caseloads in all four states had been remarkable; the most interesting example was the experience of Fond du Lac County, Wisconsin. The director of welfare for Fond du Lac, Edward Schilling, presented testimony about his program and its impact on the caseload. The program was a new welfare reform demonstration, approved by the state legislature, that was being tried in two counties. In many respects, this program was similar to the programs that would be required of every state if Shaw's bill were enacted: it included time limits, a family cap, and mandatory work. After just nine months under the new program, the Fond du Lac caseload had fallen by nearly 40 percent. The three mothers who had left welfare were also impressive. They were especially clear that they were pleased to be earning money rather than collecting welfare payments. Under questioning by both Republicans and Democrats, the mothers held firmly to their view that they were better off working than they had been on welfare. One of the mothers stated flatly that it was bad to stay home and collect benefits because "you do not get a chance to improve the skills you do have."[11] The longer you stay home, she said, the harder it is to find a job.

The New Hope project, organized primarily by a liberal community group in Milwaukee and supported by liberal foundations, offered participants a bargain: if they would work at least thirty hours a week, they would be guaranteed a wage supplement, child care, and health coverage. After initial coaching in how to find a job, participants looked for a job for a maximum of eight weeks. If they did not find work, they could participate in a community work experience program. We wanted testimony on the New Hope project because it showed that there were programs founded and conducted by politicians and practitioners who were clearly left of center and yet expected adults to work and made all their benefits contingent on work. By 1995 the idea that work was the key to individual responsibility and self-sufficiency was no longer advanced only by those wild Republicans and moderate Democrats like Bill Clinton.[12]

Meanwhile, the welfare conference was bogged down by one remaining issue, the school lunch block grant. House Republicans had already been battered in the media for their "cruel" cuts in food programs for poor kids.[13] Now the powerful and widely respected Senator Richard Lugar from Indiana took an immediate dislike to the block grant. I think at the beginning of the conference many of us thought that we could just run over Lugar, who was chairman of the Senate Agriculture Committee. We should have known better. As Morton Kondracke pointed out in a perceptive editorial about the school lunch dispute, Lugar's credentials as a powerful conservative were in fine order, and he stated his reason for opposing the block grant in the clearest possible way: removing the school lunch entitlement would "damage the social safety net."[14] Besides, Lugar believed that the only reason the House converted school lunch to a block grant was to save money to balance the budget. As he told Elizabeth Shogren of the *Los Angeles Times*, "There is no reason school lunches need to be part of welfare reform. They were simply an add-on by those looking for more money."[15] The governors sent Lugar a letter urging him to agree to the block grant; Bill Goodling offered him several compromises; Newt Gingrich and Bob Dole met with him; even Shaw got into the act, uncharacteristically telling *Congress Daily* that "I've never seen this side of [Lugar]. I think it's very disappointing."[16] But Lugar wouldn't budge. As the conservative pundit William Kristol observed, if Republicans intended to be a serious governing party, the idea that their most important bill other than reconciliation could be held up over a school lunch dispute among themselves was "fairly ridiculous."[17]

Fortunately, the Senate conference delegation was composed of eleven Republicans and eight Democrats. Thus Senate Republicans could lose one vote and still have a 10-to-9 majority for passage. In order for Lugar's boycott to work, then, one other member of the Senate Republican delegation had to support him. That member, not surprisingly, was Jim Jeffords, who was so moderate that he was later to leave the Republican Party and join the Democratic caucus in the Senate.[18] Goodling and many others lavished a lot of attention on Jeffords, trying to persuade him to sign the conference report, but Jeffords stuck with Lugar. Then, on the night of December 20, Goodling offered to leave the school lunch statute intact, as Lugar and Jeffords wanted, and to simply add a provision that would allow up to seven states to receive their money as a block grant. In addition, to placate Senate moderates and help persuade Jeffords to sign, Dole convinced the House to sweeten the pot by providing an additional $6 billion for spending on child care, child protection, child nutrition, and a contingency fund for states suffering an economic downturn. On this basis, Jeffords agreed to sign the conference report.

When I heard about the deal, I was elated. The House passed the conference report the next day (December 21) on a vote of 245 to 178, with seventeen Democrats supporting the bill, the most yet. Following House passage of the bill, Archer and Shaw sponsored a press conference with governors John Engler, Tommy Thompson, and Mike Leavitt of Utah to emphasize the decisive House action on the conference report and to pressure the Senate to pass the bill and Clinton to sign it. Held in the handsome and cozy Ways and Means Room H-137 on the first floor of the Capitol Building, the press conference was well attended, with all the members and governors speaking with obvious emotion. As part of the press conference, the governors released a letter to the president, signed by every Republican governor, urging him to sign the welfare reform bill.[19] Clinton was now publicly promising to veto the bill, but there was still doubt about the Senate vote. Nor was the governors' letter as effective as it would have been if even one or two Democratic governors had signed. Without signatures from Democratic governors, the letter could not be expected to put much pressure on Clinton to sign the bill. Both the *New York Times* and the *Washington Post* wrote strong editorials against the bill, urging the president to kill it with a veto.[20]

Moderate Republicans were the biggest obstacle to Senate passage. On December 20, the day Goodling and Dole convinced Jeffords to sign the conference report, Arlen Specter, William Cohen, Olympia Snowe, John Chafee, and Jeffords sent a letter to Dole complaining about several provisions in the conference report. In addition to spending cuts in several programs they considered to be too deep, they claimed that "millions of women and children" would lose Medicaid, that more than 300,000 children would lose Supplemental Security Income (SSI) coverage, that some child protection programs would be converted to a block grant, that more money was needed for child care, and that the provisions eliminating most noncitizens from welfare programs were excessive.

Matt Weidinger and I heard immediately about the letter and obtained a copy from staff members of the Finance Committee. We then, after talking with Shaw, wrote a point-by-point response to the senators' letter and had it hand-carried to all five of them over Shaw's and Bill Archer's signatures on the morning of December 22, the day of the vote on the conference report in the Senate.[21] We pointed out that, at every stage of negotiations, total spending cuts in the bill had been reduced, ultimately falling from about $91 billion in the original House bill to around $60 billion (the EITC cuts were not included) in the conference report, on which they were about to vote. We then presented counterarguments for their concerns, showing in each case how the House had moved in their direction during the House-Senate conference. We also pointed out that the $18 billion in child care in the conference agreement was more money for child care than in any previous bill, including the Senate bill they all had supported in September. Like so many other actions taken as a major vote approaches, we had no idea whether our arguments registered with any of the five Senators or their staffs, but all five supported the conference report, which passed the Senate on a vote of 52 to 47.

Confirming our prediction that Senate Democrats would reject the conference report, Max Baucus was the only Democrat who voted for the bill. Ben Nighthorse Campbell of Colorado and Mark Hatfield of Oregon were the only Republicans voting against the bill.

Now with the welfare reform bill awaiting the president's decision about whether to veto, attention was once again focused on the budget impasse. According to Ann Devroy and Eric Pianin of the *Washington Post*, Clinton had come a long way toward the Republicans before he vetoed the reconciliation bill on December 6.[22] Indeed, on December 7 the White House released a plan to balance the budget in seven years but under Office of Management and Budget (OMB) rather than Congressional Budget Office (CBO) scoring.[23] The president, according to his document, was prepared to agree to $98 billion in Medicare cuts, $54 billion in Medicaid cuts, $46 billion in welfare and EITC cuts, and several other spending cuts. Despite the fact that all these cuts were substantially below the cuts in the Republican bill, Clinton was able to reach balance in seven years because he used OMB scoring, which allowed him to spend nearly $350 billion more than Republicans were able to spend under CBO scoring. Whether OMB or CBO scoring was used, then, was more than a mere detail. Besides mirroring the cuts sponsored by Republicans, Clinton was willing to include tax cuts. Again, however, his agenda followed the "me too, but less" principle. His tax cuts totaled only about $100 billion, compared with Republican cuts of more than $250 billion. In addition, his tax cuts did not include a capital gains reduction, a great favorite among Republicans and especially Chairman Archer, but a tax cut that was anathema to most Democrats.[24]

Although Republicans consistently belittled the Clinton cuts in both spending and taxes, they were remarkable, even shocking, by almost any measure except the cuts the Republicans were pushing. Some consideration must be given to the fact that Clinton was after all a Democrat. Shortly after his inauguration in 1993 he released a booklet outlining his plans for domestic spending over the next four years. "We have heard the trumpets," announces the booklet's inscription, and the trumpets were a call to wild spending.[25] Clinton's plan called for nearly $112 billion in increased spending over four years on seventy-eight initiatives in transportation, the environment, rural development, energy, community development, technology development, housing, lifelong learning, rewarding work, justice, health care (not including his subsequent proposal to create national health insurance), and tax incentives. But now, less than three years later, when confronted by the Republicans' balanced budget, Clinton was proposing cuts that totaled more than $525 billion over seven years, including substantial cuts in the government health insurance programs that, a year earlier, he had been proposing to make universal at a cost of billions.[26] The man knew how to change his mind. I have no hesitation in concluding that no other Democratic president of the twentieth century would have even considered cuts of the magnitude that Clinton was willing to support during the Republican budget revolution of 1995–96.

As the deadline approached on the temporary continuing resolution that had reopened the government on November 19, CBO published its new baseline, which showed a jump in revenues of around $135 billion over seven years.[27] The result, of course, was that Republicans could reduce their spending cuts by $135 billion, which they promptly offered to do by distributing the new revenue among Medicare, Medicaid, and the EITC. But Clinton still refused to budge from OMB scoring, which gave him even more money. Thus despite a flurry of activity on December 14 and 15 to reach a bargain before the continuing resolution expired at midnight on December 15, no deal was reached, and the government closed for the second time.[28] A few more of the appropriations bills had passed by then, meaning that more government agencies had a budget than on the occasion of the first government shutdown a month earlier. Nonetheless, closing the government the second time caused 280,000 federal workers to go on layoff just ten days before Christmas—and millions of Americans to go without government services.

Now the media was again full of stories about the consequences of the layoff. This time the stories had even more edge because Christmas was approaching.[29] As during the previous shutdown, there were sporadic attempts to find a break-through in the negotiations. On December 20, for example, Gingrich and Dole wanted to pass another short-term continuing resolution (called a CR) and to restart budget talks, even without a firm commitment from Clinton to agree to the seven-year balance under CBO scoring. House Republicans promptly rebelled because it looked like Republicans were again being outmaneuvered by the president. While Dole, who had said on the Senate floor that he expected the House to pass the resolution, was left to stew, House Republicans refused to pass the resolution and then promptly went home for Christmas.[30] Tom DeLay, the Republican whip, seemed to mock both the president and Dole—and perhaps even Gingrich—as he quipped, "Read my lips. No CR."[31]

For the next few days, Clinton and the Republican leadership spent most of their time sniping at each other. With the government in midst of what would become the longest shutdown in history, and with the Republican agenda lying in tatters, Gingrich continued to have lousy ratings in the polls. But surprisingly, there was at least modest recognition among the public and the press that Republicans were trying to achieve important and difficult goals. According to a CBS/New York Times poll conducted between December 9 and 11, Democrats opposed the Republican plan to cut Medicare by a margin of 80 to 10, but independents opposed it by the much smaller margin of 52 to 31, and Republicans continued their strong support by a margin of 63 to 26.[32] Although Republicans did not have the support of a majority of the public, considering the fiasco taking place in Washington and the president's rising popularity, these poll numbers were far from being a disaster.

Moreover, two of the nation's most perceptive and respected editorial writers painted a picture of the Washington standoff that I personally found reassuring. Robert Samuelson, whose column regularly appeared in the *Washington Post* and *Newsweek*, wrote on December 27 that Republicans were setting the agenda in the nation's capital.[33] When Clinton introduced his budget in January 1995, he showed no intention of trying to reach balance. By contrast, Samuelson wrote, in less than a year the government was closed and all of Washington was in turmoil over the Republican attempt to balance the federal budget. Similarly, Clinton had no intention of passing welfare reform. His bill was not a factor in the debate, having been denied by congressional Democrats when it finally made an appearance in late 1994. But again, the Republicans' sweeping version of welfare reform had passed both Houses, and Clinton was backed into a corner. Samuelson even went so far as to blame the government shutdown on Clinton, primarily because Clinton kept saying he would produce a balanced budget but had not done so. Samuelson did fault Gingrich for being such a distraction, and he made the compelling criticism that Republicans were trying to do too much. Rather than both cut taxes and balance the budget, Republicans should have stuck with balancing the budget and left tax cuts for another day, as the Charlie Stenholm group had done in the House. Despite this criticism, it was good to remind the nation that Republicans were setting the agenda, and that the agenda was difficult.

A second editorial, this one by David Broder, the dean of Washington editorial writers, was more critical of Republicans but, nonetheless, was a fair assessment of the seriousness of purpose and skill shown by Republicans. He argued that Republicans believed Reagan had ended the threat from communism but had failed to bring federal spending under control. However, the new Republican majority pursued this vital tenet of Republican philosophy in "deadly earnest" and with a "strength and skill" not anticipated by the Democrats on Capitol Hill nor by the president. By contrast, congressional Democrats "waver[ed] ineffectually" and fought no more than rearguard battles to protect existing programs, while their president "triangulated" in accord with the instructions of his political guru Dick Morris and changed his position on the budget "quarterly, monthly, and in the end almost daily."[34]

As the two sides flailed about, unofficial contacts between administration officials and congressional Republican leaders continued. Then early in the week of December 17, Gingrich and Dole agreed to four days of budget talks that would begin on Friday, December 27, almost two weeks after the second government shutdown began. On that Friday afternoon, I was at the headquarters of the Republican National Committee (RNC), located behind the Cannon House Office Building, for a meeting on welfare reform. Just before the meeting began, an assistant stuck her head in the room and told me I had a phone call. It was Phil Moseley, chief of staff for Ways and Means. He told me to leave immediately and come to his office. Within three or four minutes I had dashed the two blocks from the RNC to Phil's office in the Northeast corner of the Longworth House Office Building.

With little ceremony, Phil told me that direct negotiations between the president and Republican leaders had started that afternoon at the White House. It quickly developed that both sides wanted selected staff members to be present. The House leadership wanted Chip Kahn, the superb Ways and Means staffer on health issues, and me to come immediately to the White House. While I ran out to jump in a cab, Karen Humbel, our office coordinator, called in my birth date and Social Security number to the White House so I could clear White House security. Upon arriving, I was directed to the Roosevelt Room to await further word. The Roosevelt Room, just a few steps from the Cabinet Room and the Oval Office, is dominated by a large table that seats about twenty people. Tastefully but not elaborately decorated, the room also has several couches, chairs, end tables, and floor lamps against the walls on three sides of the room. The fourth side features a large fireplace, on the mantle of which is the Nobel Peace Prize that President Roosevelt won in 1906 for his role in negotiating the Treaty of Portsmouth (New Hampshire), which ended the Russo-Japanese War.

When I arrived, the room was full of Republican and Democratic staffers, primarily from Capitol Hill but also a few White House and other administration staffers. They were milling around, trying to figure out what was going on and what their roles might be. After about two hours of waiting in almost complete ignorance of what was going on, Ken Apfel, a senior political appointee in Clinton's Office of Management and Budget, entered the room and told us they were ending talks for the day but would begin again in the morning and meet through the weekend. They were working on a schedule and would let us know what issues would be discussed at what time. We peppered him with questions about format, staff responsibility, how long the meetings would last, who would be present, and so forth, most of which he could not answer. It was clear, however, that Ken was involved in planning the meetings, so he was in a hurry to leave to meet with other White House staffers to complete the plans. I returned to Longworth to talk with Phil and await word from our leadership about tomorrow's sessions.

Sometime after eight that evening we heard from the leadership that the sessions would resume in the morning and that the welfare session, which would also include a discussion of the Earned Income Tax Credit, would begin at about eleven o'clock. One Republican staffer and one Democratic staffer were to initiate the discussion by outlining the position of their respective parties. Lindy Paull, the staff director of the Finance Committee in the Senate, would be the lead

Republican staffer for the Senate; I would be the lead staffer for the House; and Ken Apfel would represent the administration. I would give the initial briefing on welfare, and when the welfare discussion was complete, Lindy would give the initial briefing on the EITC.

Arriving at the White House at around ten o'clock, I again waited in the Roosevelt Room, this time for about an hour. When at last I entered the Cabinet Room, I was somewhat overwhelmed, for seated around the large conference table was a roster of the nation's most powerful political figures. President Clinton sat on one side of the table, in the middle, with his back to the Rose Garden; Senator Dole was on his left and Speaker Gingrich on his right. Dick Armey and John Kasich completed the president's side of the table. The other side of the table was solidly Democratic: Vice President Gore, Dick Gephardt from the House, Tom Daschle from the Senate, Alice Rivlin from OMB, and several other prominent administration officials. Senior staffers from the administration and Republican and Democratic staffers from both the House and Senate sat behind their principals on either side of the table. Lindy and I were ushered to our seats at the end of the table on the president and Gingrich's left, where we joined Ken Apfel.

After some small talk, I gave a brief overview of the Republican welfare reform bill, mentioning the block grant, work rules, sanctions, time limits, and costs. I also briefly mentioned our noncitizen provisions and their justification as well as our policies on child care, child support enforcement, and SSI for children. As soon as I finished my six- or seven-minute overview, the president initiated the discussion by talking about the importance of maintaining state spending. Although I had not mentioned state matching money (the so-called maintenance of effort by states) in my overview, the president obviously knew that going into the conference the House had not required states to continue the level of welfare spending that was required under current law. But we had compromised with the Senate and required states to continue spending at least 75 percent of their 1994 spending level.

The president wanted to make sure that this level of spending was maintained. His approach to emphasizing the importance of state matching funds was to tell about his experiences fighting for spending on social programs in the Arkansas legislature. He argued that highways, schools, and many other interests clamoring for money at the state level are inevitably more powerful than the relatively small number of elected officials fighting for social spending, especially on children's programs. And of all the social programs, it was a given that welfare was the least popular in nearly every state. Unless federal law required that states put up a specific amount of money as a condition of receiving federal assistance, state spending on welfare under the block grant would be very likely to decline.

Gingrich joined in the discussion and essentially agreed with the president that without federal rules for state spending, welfare spending in many states would be likely to decline. I kept thinking that the session would have been livelier if Governor Engler had been there; he would have given twenty reasons why states should be given the flexibility to decide for themselves how much to spend on welfare—as well as on highways—without federal interference. He would say that if a given state cut spending, that was the right decision for that state. But no one was in the Cabinet Room to fight against a state spending requirement on that day. I certainly was not prepared to argue that the states would ensure adequate spending on the poor.

Upon leaving the Cabinet Room, my first thought was that I had just participated in the highest-level welfare seminar in American history. Even after hours of arguing about welfare as a professor in graduate policy classes, in professional conferences attended primarily by scholars, and in congressional policy battles, it never occurred to me that I would one day participate in a welfare discussion with the president of the United States, the vice president of the United States, the heads of OMB and several cabinet agencies, and the Republican and Democratic leadership of both Houses. Except for the president and Gingrich—and of course the staffers, all of whom were brilliant—the quality of debate was about average. But the stakes were slightly higher. And let's not forget the exhilaration. It was fun and exciting to argue recondite points about welfare with this august group. At one point I must have gotten a little too excited. After I had finished making a point about the importance of sanctions in the Republican work program, Lindy, who was seated to my immediate left, leaned over and said, "Ron, you shouldn't interrupt the president."

But exhilaration and manners aside, my second thought, and the one that has persisted ever since, was, What was the point? We were in the midst of the longest government shutdown in history, with legislation that had passed Congress and needed only the president's signature to fundamentally alter the course of the federal government, and we were scoring debating points on welfare. Granted, Gingrich and the president seemed to be thoroughly enjoying themselves, and Lindy and I had a good time too; but it was a lot like playing our fiddles while Rome burned.

Nor did anything much come of the meetings. According to Ann Devroy, an enterprising reporter for the *Washington Post* who talked with participants in all the Cabinet Room sessions, the seminar was in session on Friday, Saturday, and Sunday a total of thirteen hours and covered, in addition to welfare and the EITC, health, taxes, and several other issues. She quoted a participating Republican staffer as saying, "When all is said and done, a lot was said and nothing was done."[35] I wish I had said that.

During the night of January 9, with the government closed because of a blizzard, Clinton announced his veto of the welfare reform bill that Congress had sent him on December 22. Now welfare, the debt ceiling, two continuing resolutions, and reconciliation—some of the most important legislation produced by Congress in decades—had been vetoed. Our agenda had been smashed. The Republican revolution was floundering.

## CHAPTER TWELVE

# The Governors
# Revive the
# Revolution

What a letdown. From the beginning of negotiations on the Contract with America welfare reform bill in May 1994, through White House negotiations that included the strange but exciting Cabinet Room seminar, and through the president's vetoes, our subcommittee and its chairman and staff had been in a constant state of action, often bordering on frenzy. But when President Clinton vetoed the welfare reform bill for the second time on January 9, 1996, it was undeniable that the bill had been deeply wounded, perhaps fatally. Most of us who had worked so hard on the bill had allowed ourselves to believe that Clinton would sign it. We gave him two chances, and he turned down both of them. Now most of us were down. Our bill had blazed a trail from obscurity to the front pages of every major newspaper in the country and had gained universal recognition as an earthquake that would change the foundations of American social policy. That its radical nature had been somewhat obscured by the even larger and more consequential budget bill by which it had been swallowed in no way diminished the importance and potential impact of what we were trying to do. Now, after all this, was the end at hand?

My greatest regret was that the chance to deeply reform welfare comes perhaps once in a generation. Attempts to reform welfare in the Nixon, Carter, and even Reagan administrations had failed, although the Family Support Act of 1988 under Reagan provided at least a start on conservative welfare reform built around work. If our bill had now joined that parade of failure, it would likely be many years or even decades before an opening for fundamental reform appeared again. Republicans had majorities in both the House and Senate. The White House was occupied by a Democratic president who had promised to reform welfare and whose reelection might be influenced by whether he actually signed a bill into law. Nearly every governor from both parties supported reform. And most important, the public was supportive, especially on the issue of work, not welfare.

After a few good nights' sleep and, equally important, after a kind of psychological separation from the exciting and all-consuming final stages of the budget and welfare negotiations with the White House, I came to my senses and realized that the game was not over, not even close. In politics, there's always another chance. Matt Weidinger and I began to talk about the possibilities, and Matt quickly generated a list of twelve bills that we could use to revive the welfare reform debate. These included HR 4 as it was passed in December, the coalition bill that had been written by a small group of House Republicans and Democrats, the Clinton bill, Nathan Deal's Democratic bill, an à la carte bill with selected provisions from various bills, and the Senate bill that passed on such a huge vote and seemed to be endorsed by the president. Matt, as he often did, had a little fun by inventing strategies for moving whatever bill we selected through the House in case our leadership did not support sending another bill to Clinton. Some of his strategies were guaranteed to help the two of us enter another line of work:

—Rambo strategy: drop bill and file discharge petition to get the bill on the floor.

—Committee conspiracy strategy: Bill Archer and Clay Shaw organize House Republicans to force floor action upon the leadership.

—Chinese water torture strategy: move the bill through the House one section at a time.

—Almost treason strategy: negotiate with Senate moderates and have them introduce the bill first.

—Total betrayal strategy: negotiate with the White House.

—Extremist strategy: negotiate with Pat Buchanan.

—Utter stupidity strategy: negotiate with Ross Perot.

Of the several interesting possibilities on our list, by late January most Republicans seemed to think that sending Clinton the Senate bill was the best option. Shaw and others on the subcommittee favored this strategy, in part because they didn't want anyone to think we were out of ideas or that we had given up. Matt and I wrote an editorial for Shaw that appeared in the "Outlook" section of the *Washington Post* arguing for the Senate strategy.[1] On January 29 two opinion pieces appeared in the press that signaled widespread appreciation of the Senate strategy. Morton Kondracke, a respected columnist for *Roll Call*, wrote a column that perfectly reflected Shaw's thinking.[2] Clinton had outfoxed us on the budget, according to Kondracke. But all was not lost. Republicans could put Clinton in a bind by sending him the Senate bill that he had praised lavishly in September. The Senate bill had most of the essential elements that Republicans wanted in welfare reform. Wisely, Kondracke argued that achieving welfare reform would salvage a major part of the Republican revolution and show voters that Republicans were capable of compromise.

Robert Novak, the Darth Vader of conservative reporting in the nation's capital, wrote a similar column in the *Washington Post* the same day.[3] He argued that sending Clinton the Senate bill would present him with an "excruciating dilemma." Novak had talked with Shaw and Jim Bunning, who was also on Ways and Means, both of whom strongly supported the Senate bill strategy. He had also talked with Jimmy Hayes, a member from Louisiana who had recently deserted the Democrats and joined the Republican Party. Hayes, who was to play an important role in convincing Republicans to send Clinton another bill, told Novak that if Clinton signed our welfare reform bill, the Democratic Party would explode, because liberals hated our reforms. Novak got in his usual dig by framing the article as a chance, perhaps the last, for the Republican leadership to get up off the floor in their boxing match with Clinton.

But there was a major problem with the strategy of sending Clinton the Senate bill. Robert Pear, a top welfare reporter for the *New York Times,* saw the problem. In an article only one day after the Kondracke and Novak editorials, Pear reported on all the Republican maneuvering to find the perfect strategy.[4] But Pear, probably suspecting that many conservatives would not favor the Senate bill because it did not have either the family cap or Murray Light, called Jim Talent and asked what he thought of the Senate bill. Talent responded just as Pear had probably anticipated: he didn't like the Senate bill because it was weak on illegitimacy, the most important issue to Talent, as well as work. No doubt Robert Rector of the Heritage Foundation had been busy behind the scenes. I had already talked with Rector several times about the Senate bill and had come to believe that the Senate bill strategy would not work. Seeing Talent's views in the *New York Times* simply confirmed my view that the Senate strategy was fatally flawed but that it was still useful for keeping welfare reform alive until we thought of something better.

As Republicans mulled over the Senate strategy, a deus ex machina appeared in the form of the nation's governors. The National Governors Association (NGA) meets every winter in the nation's capital. With Tommy Thompson as their chairman and John Engler as a lead governor on welfare reform, along with Democrat Tom Carper of Delaware, it was no surprise that the governors would attempt to revive the welfare debate. Gerry Miller, Engler's welfare director, and LeAnne Redick, his Washington representative on social issues, had been telling me that Engler was determined to get a bipartisan agreement among the nation's governors on both a welfare reform bill and a Medicaid block grant by the time of the NGA's winter meeting. A bipartisan agreement among the governors would bring welfare reform back to life in grand style.

When Gerry called me on February 6 and told me they had a bipartisan agreement on both welfare reform and Medicaid reform, I was both surprised and elated. He and I had two phone conversations, and then I ran down to the Marriott on Pennsylvania Avenue to meet with him. Gerry was extremely excited, telling me that we should now be able to parlay this bipartisan agreement, which had been adopted unanimously by the governors, into a bill that Clinton would simply have to sign.[5] How could Clinton refuse a bill that was endorsed by every Democratic governor? Of course, added Gerry, Congress would have to pass the bill exactly as the governors had constructed it. Fat chance.

After I returned from meeting with Gerry and hurriedly briefed Shaw, we participated in a conference call organized by the governors involving several Republican governors, Newt Gingrich, Tom Bliley (chairman of the House Commerce Committee, the committee that would draft the House version of the governors' Medicaid reforms), Bill Roth (chairman of the Senate Finance Committee), Haley Barbour (chairman of the Republican Party), Pat Roberts (chairman of the House Agriculture Committee), and assorted staff members. Optimism pervaded the phone call. Engler described the negotiations between Republican and Democratic governors, which had been ongoing for several months and were capped by a three-hour session the previous day (February 5). He then said he would describe the bipartisan agreement in plain language (Gerry had given us the written version), and it would be up to Congress to draft the proposals—to put "the meat on the bones," as Chairman Bliley put it.

In our talk before the call I had informed Shaw that the bill was a good start but that we could not possibly accept it exactly as proposed. So after Engler's description and the easy optimism that had built up in the first ten minutes of the phone conversation, Shaw, after congratulating the governors for "breathing life" into welfare reform, sounded a note of caution. He said the proposal needed to be studied carefully and that all the factions inside and outside Congress had to be consulted. He could already see problems with the Talent-Faircloth-Rector group. Roth immediately endorsed the need for caution and for consultation. Gingrich then said he didn't want to agree to anything in general terms. He wanted House and Senate staff to study the proposal and determine whether it was solid and could be used as a basis to unite all the factions of our party. Gingrich was about to get on a plane to attend a dinner in California in honor of Ronald Reagan. He hoped to conduct a press conference while in California to endorse the governors' proposal. Shaw said that "endorse" was too strong. Gingrich then clarified his intent, saying that the press conference would emphasize the fact that the governors had "relighted the process" after Clinton's attempts to kill welfare reform.[6]

We all agreed that the next few days were vital to building momentum behind the governors' proposals. Barbour asked Gingrich if he would call Ed Fuelner, president of the Heritage Foundation, and ask him if he could persuade Rector to keep quiet for a few days. Gingrich said he would try, but I couldn't see how anyone who knew Rector or Heritage could think the Heritage hierarchy would try to muzzle him—or that if they did that he would submit. There was no force known to man or God that could keep Rector from trashing the governors' bill and in the most derisive terms. But on Gingrich's promise to accomplish the impossible, the conference call ended and the analysis of the governors' proposal began.

The written version of the proposal, titled simply "Welfare Reform," had a little note at the end stating: "Any changes in the above recommendations would nullify this endorsement." So we were back at Williamsburg. No surprise, given that the real desire of the governors was and had been to write the welfare reform bill themselves. But any bill the governors wrote would not make it out of Ways and Means or any other House committee. There was no deal that could be unanimously approved by Democratic and Republican governors that the House would accept. There would have to be changes, that was a given. No matter what the governors or Gingrich or Dole might propose, Shaw and Archer controlled the drafting and would not accept any bill that would not keep our various factions united.

The governors' deal was spelled out in four double-spaced pages that covered Aid to Families with Dependent Children (AFDC) and the work program, child protection, Supplemental Security Income (SSI) for children, the Food Stamp program, school nutrition, and the Earned Income Tax Credit (EITC). The governors also had a separate document, equally short, outlining their Medicaid reforms. The welfare reform proposal contained a statement that the governors took no position on cutting welfare benefits for noncitizens (apparently they were so divided on this issue that they could not achieve a consensus position). Of great significance, the proposal seemed to assume the vetoed bill as the base and simply proposed changes in that bill. In other words, the governors began with the bill written by House and Senate Republicans and then made changes in that bill to create a new bill. I do not know if the Democratic governors realized what a gift they were giving congressional Republicans, but our general approach would be to simply graft the proposals we accepted from the governors onto the bill that Clinton had vetoed, in the same way we had created the bill for the Contract with America by grafting changes onto HR 3500. Literally hundreds of our provisions would remain untouched. Shaw and I agreed that this alone made the governors' proposal attractive.

After being briefed by Gerry Miller, reading the written document, and hearing Governor Engler's summary over the phone, I was surprised by how little they were asking for. Only nine of the specific proposals amounted to anything serious. The most important provisions included providing $4 billion more in child care entitlement funds; loosening the work requirement, especially by counting each family that leaves the rolls as fulfilling the work requirement;

weakening the family cap by converting it to a state opt-in provision rather than an opt-out (meaning that states would need to take action to adopt the family cap rather than take action to get out of the family cap); dropping or drastically modifying the Food Stamp block grant; limiting savings in the EITC to $10 billion; and requiring state programs to ensure "fair and equal treatment" of all recipients.

Because the proposal converted the family cap from an opt-out to an opt-in provision and watered down the work standards, lots of conservatives would reject the bill out of hand, not least Rector. He and I both had a busy night February 6. At two in the morning, February 7, Rector faxed a two-page critique of the governors' proposal, titled "Problems with the Governors' Welfare Proposal," to his thousand closest friends.[7] Rector had a dozen criticisms and recommendations. As usual, rather than merely criticize the specific provisions in the governors' proposal, he went on the offensive by adding new demands for any new bill that he would support. The first demand on his list was that the leadership "publicly identify reducing illegitimacy [as] the key goal in welfare reform." Given the very weak illegitimacy provisions in the governors' proposal, if adopted this recommendation would quickly put the leadership at odds with the governors. Rector also demanded additional funds for abstinence education and a set-aside of "$300 million per year for states to devise their own programs to reduce illegitimacy without increasing abortion."

He wisely condemned one of the provisions in the governors' proposal to reduce work requirements. Specifically, the governors' proposal to count every family that left the rolls as meeting the work requirement was a policy that would completely gut the work requirement.[8] As we have seen, nearly 60 percent of the family heads on welfare left the rolls every year even without a strong work requirement.[9] But most of them come back, and many others join for the first time. Thus a state could actually see over half of its caseload leave the rolls in a given year and still experience a net increase during the year because of mothers who return and new mothers who join for the first time. Unfortunately, understanding this point required knowledge of a fact (that a substantial fraction of the caseload left the rolls every year) and a process (that caseload size is the net result of the number of families joining and leaving the rolls). I had many conversations with governors and members of Congress in which I was all but certain that they didn't understand why the governors' proposal was so flawed. But Clay Shaw understood the problem, and I was confident that he would never accept this proposal as part of our bill.

With the exception that I never wavered from the view that work requirements (not illegitimacy) should be our lead message, I agreed with every point in Rector's critique and calculated that we could get House and Senate Republicans to accept all of them except perhaps the ones that required more spending. Best of all, we could meet many of Rector's demands, which were fully predictable and most of which our members would have supported even without Rector's importuning, and still meet most of the governors' proposals. Of course, with these modifications, the governors would have a fit—and their proposal might no longer be bipartisan. Even so, there was nothing on Rector's list that had not been in one or both of the vetoed bills, which the Republican governors had supported. So at least there was the potential to give the governors a major part of what they wanted, keep Rector and the conservative groups satisfied, and keep our coalition together. Achieving these goals simultaneously was a lot like threading a needle, but then big legislative achievements always represent many threaded needles.

Matt and I did our own analysis of the governors' proposal. Finished early in the morning of February 7, our analysis identified five major and ten less important issues that posed problems ranging from serious to modest.[10] Of the five major issues, two were on Rector's list: gutting the work requirements and weakening the family cap. The other three on our list were the governors' proposal to virtually kill the child protection block grant, which would dramatically scale back a reform that Ways and Means Republicans had been fighting for since 1992—but which we had regarded as a long shot since learning of Senator Chafee's opposition; a set of expensive changes in the contingency fund that would give states more money during recessions; and overall spending. On this last point, we estimated (after so many iterations of the bill, Matt and I were getting pretty good at doing our own cost estimates) that the $60 billion in savings for the vetoed bill would be reduced to between $45 billion and $50 billion for the governors' bill, a reduction that John Kasich and the leadership would probably not accept, at least not at the outset of the debate. Matt and I, and Shaw upon hearing our analysis, were buoyed by our conclusions. It appeared that a new bill would save less money than the vetoed bills, but who cares about money when revolutionary policy is the product, especially in the context of saving $50 billion rather than $60 billion?

The governors' proposal also included fundamental changes in Medicaid. Although most politicians and the public think that poor Americans, especially children, should have health coverage, the Medicaid program designed to provide health coverage to the poor probably would win a poll as the program that governors hated most. In some states, Medicaid was the second biggest item in the state budget (after elementary and secondary education).[11] By 1995 the cost of the program was $156 billion, $67 billion of which was paid by states. Worse, the program was growing wildly. In the three years beginning in 1990, Medicaid had grown by 18, 26, and 29 percent, respectively, zooming from $72 billion to $132 billion in the process.[12] An item that is big and growing bigger in a state budget is bound to get the attention of governors, who would then look for ways to control the spending.

The most important Medicaid changes being proposed by governors were to allow states to drop coverage for children over the age of twelve, to allow states to define disability so that they were not necessarily required to cover everyone on the SSI program (which had a federal definition of disability), and to increase family copayments for various services, thereby shifting some costs from government to poor or low-income families. Even more important, because Medicaid would become a block grant with fixed funding, there would have to be a formula for determining how much money each state would receive. As we have seen, formula fights in Congress are always a mess. Events would prove that trying to devise a Medicaid formula that kept enough states satisfied to pass a bill through the House and Senate was an impossible task.

The governors revived welfare reform, and for that I still include them in my prayers every night. But their proposals created plenty of difficulties. Medicaid was the biggest, but there were others, as shown so clearly in our own assessment of the governors' proposal and in Rector's criticisms. Soon enough, working with Rector, Talent and Tim Hutchinson sent a letter to every member of the House criticizing the governors' proposal for roughly the reasons reflected in Rector's February 7 list. And the Dole campaign's opposition, supported by Gingrich, to sending Clinton another bill, continued to be a major barrier. So we jumped into phase two of the welfare reform debate realizing that we had three big hurdles to leap if we wanted to win the race: finding a compromise that steered between the Rector-Talent-Faircloth forces and the governors, finding a way to dump the Medicaid provisions, and overcoming the leadership and the Dole campaign's opposition to giving Clinton a chance to sign another welfare reform bill. From our vantage point in the winter of 1996, the odds of leaping all three hurdles seemed roughly the same as the odds of winning the trifecta at Churchill Downs. But at least there was once again a number in the numerator of the calculation. Besides, it was in our power to grow the numerator.

Shaw and members of our subcommittee were once again optimistic, and our best course was obvious. We would simply begin with the governors' bill and repeat the entire process of enacting legislation, including hearings, markups, floor action, and a House-Senate conference. In short, concentrate on what we did best: investigate, propose, defend, and then enact legislation. Republicans straining themselves once again to convert welfare into a work program was good public relations, a consideration of growing importance as the elections of 1996 approached. Moreover, our party discipline in committees and on the floor was still intact, so we were virtually guaranteed passage in the House. The Senate was always more of a gamble, but it would be hard for all those Democrats who supported welfare reform the first time to switch their vote on the second go-round, especially if it meant abandoning a bill that was endorsed by Democratic governors.

On February 20, two weeks to the day after the governors released their proposal, we conducted our first of four hearings on their bill and other welfare
reform issues.[13] We featured Tommy Thompson and Tom Carper as the lead
witnesses. We also invited John Engler, but his plane encountered bad weather
and had to land in Richmond, where he sat on the ground as we conducted the
hearing. Shaw opened the hearing with a hard-hitting, partisan statement. By
now Shaw had only modest hopes that House Democrats would support the
bill. True, there was likely to be more money for child care, one of the major
demands made by House Democrats during the 1995 debates, but Shaw was not
prepared to offer all the compromises that would be necessary to win over
House Democrats, especially the liberal members of our subcommittee like Pete
Stark and Charlie Rangel. So after profusely thanking the governors for reviving welfare reform, he listed all the horrible conditions that would continue if
welfare reform were not enacted: welfare dependency, centralized control of
welfare from Washington, guaranteed benefits for alcoholics and drug addicts,
billions in spending on benefits for noncitizens, and failure to save taxpayers at
least $50 billion or $60 billion in spending over the next seven years. He then
posed the question, "Who then would block such reforms?" And, of course, he
answered his question: "Extreme liberals who have opposed real welfare reform
all along." He closed by looking at the Democrats seated to his left on the dais
and asking whether they and their president would support reform or continue
to obstruct.

It was then Harold Ford's turn to respond. He opened by thanking the governors for their efforts, although not necessarily the results of their efforts. He
said their bill had many flaws, including reduced spending on the poor because
of the failure to require states to match federal dollars with their own, the imposition of time limits, and the lack of a guarantee of "fair and equitable" treatment
in providing welfare benefits. He then yielded the remainder of his five minutes
to Sander Levin for further criticism of the governors' bill. Levin began by chas-
tising Shaw for making such a partisan opening statement, although he did say
that it was probably a Republican staff member who had authored such an unfortunate fulmination. He then, apparently forgetting in an instant his charge of partisanship against Shaw, proceeded to make a highly partisan critique of the
governors' bill and of Republicans in general. After pointing out that the governors had achieved a bipartisan agreement, he again criticized Republicans for
their repeated failure to do what the governors had done—achieve a bipartisan
bill. Rather, congressional Republicans were still trying to impose "shock ther-
apy" on the welfare system by ending entitlements, imposing block grants, and
imposing time limits, all without consulting with Democrats. Sure, the system
needed change—but only in a way that guaranteed that children would be protected and within a system that had federal standards.

After these opening statements, the governors sounded an upbeat and bipartisan note by reviewing the major features of their bill, including the two provisions that Levin had just criticized. Although it went unremarked at the time, the governors' statements showed why the House could not produce a bipartisan bill; namely, Democrats in the House generally opposed the Republican bill, whereas Democratic governors accepted nearly all the major features of the Republican approach: end of entitlement, block grant, time limit, work requirements. They even seemed willing to remain neutral on noncitizen provisions in order to get a bill.

The most interesting part of the hearing arrived when Pete Stark of California began questioning. He opened with the assertion that it was no wonder the governors had been able to achieve a bipartisan bill; their agreement was based on "greed," as demonstrated by the fact that their proposal called for billions in cutbacks in both federal and state funding, especially on Medicaid.[14] Then he invoked the Catholic Church's opposition to the bill because it amounted to allowing the states to "turn their backs" on children. "It is unconscionable," he said referring to the actions of both the governors and the House Republicans. And then, speaking directly to Thompson: "What do you say to the Catholic Church, Governor?" Thompson, a Catholic himself, shot back: "I say the Catholic Church is wrong, just like you are wrong."[15]

Given the continuing importance of the illegitimacy debate, we decided to follow the hearing featuring the governors and their new proposal with a hearing on illegitimacy on March 12. Testimony was taken from four House members, a panel of experts, a panel of program operators, and witnesses representing prominent liberal and conservative organizations (the Catholic Church, the Urban League, and the Christian Coalition). It seems doubtful that there was any fact or idea about illegitimacy that the fifteen prominent witnesses assembled for this hearing failed to mention. As the testimony showed yet again, Republican policy on Murray Light and the family cap had divided the worlds of researchers, advocates, and members of Congress into two opposing camps: those who believed that welfare was a leading cause of illegitimacy and those who didn't.

As suggested by our hearing on nonmarital births, most arguments for and against most of the policies contained in our welfare reform bill had been heard by members. But the nice thing about Congress is that members seem to thrive on repetition: they seem never to tire of repeating arguments for and against legislative proposals and of hearing others repeat the arguments. We held additional hearings on welfare legislation on May 22 and 23; other House committees with welfare jurisdiction also held hearings. The Finance Committee in the Senate held six hearings on the governors' bill and several other issues of welfare reform and Medicaid.[16] I wouldn't be surprised if a careful study showed that over 90 percent of the testimony on facts and arguments had already been stated at welfare reform hearings in 1995.

Fortunately, hearings are typically the least important part of the legislative process, and after the extensive hearings we had held in 1995, the 1996 hearings were even less important than usual. By contrast, the development of the bill is the most important part of the process. While all the public action in hearings was taking place, we were working behind the scenes to develop the governors' bill. While we wanted our new bill to reflect the governors' proposal, we didn't want it to stray too far from a bill that could pass. We could and would change the bill later, both before and during markups, but we had to keep the governors inside the tent by starting as close to their proposal as we could. We frequently met and talked on the phone with the governors' aides, just as we had the previous year, to develop the new bill. I also talked often with Kathy Tobin, my counterpart on the Senate Finance Committee, and we had several meetings with senior Senate staffers. These meetings kept everyone informed of changes in the bill.

After several discussions with Shaw and from time to time with other members of the subcommittee, the decisions made in our staff meetings would be the policy introduced in the chairman's subcommittee bill; in all likelihood, most of these provisions would remain in the bill during its congressional journey. As always, some of the provisions would be changed, especially when the bill got to the Senate, and in the House-Senate conference as well (if we got that far), but the chairman's bill was the blueprint. By this time, of course, after successfully writing a bill that passed the House and Senate while keeping most elements of our conglomerate happy, our various working groups moved efficiently and without undue conflict. We held at least ten meetings between February and April with our reconstituted House leadership staff group. The major purpose of the leadership staff group, just as in 1995, was to coordinate the work of the committees, primarily Education, Agriculture, and Commerce in addition to Ways and Means.[17] The Commerce Committee joined our group because Commerce had jurisdiction over Medicaid, and Medicaid was to be a major and divisive part of the debate this time around. Given the continuing importance of welfare reform to the balanced budget, a staffer named Roger Mahan from the Budget Committee also attended all our meetings.

Following these procedures, we had a draft bill ready by the week of March 25 while the hearings were still going on. On March 26, we arranged a conference call with Gingrich, Bliley, Roth, Shaw, Governor Mike Leavitt of Utah, Governor Thompson, and a few congressional staffers and staffers representing governors. The plan we had worked out before the phone call was to introduce the bill on Friday, March 29, and to announce the introduction with a big press event featuring both members of Congress and governors. But it developed during the phone call that Medicaid was a big problem and that the Democratic governors and Republican governors were not in agreement. Even the centrist Democrats in the House such as Charlie Stenholm would not touch the Medicaid "agreement" reached by the governors. As often happens, the February agreement among governors had been based on broad principles. But once the Commerce Committee began to translate the broad principles into legislative language, making them highly specific and detailed in the process, fissures—even chasms— developed between Republican and Democratic governors. Thus after lots of phone calls and meetings, the press conference was canceled, and we simply introduced the bill without fanfare.

As was the case in 1995, drafting the legislative provisions for the "real bill" was handled by the respective committees of jurisdiction. Because Ways and Means shared jurisdiction with the Education Committee on both the AFDC work pro- gram and child care, we worked closely with the Education Committee at both the staff and member levels to draft all the provisions that related in any way to work or child care. Similarly, the Food Stamp provisions were drafted exclusively by the Agriculture Committee, the child nutrition provisions by the Education Committee, and the Medicaid provisions by the Commerce Committee. This time around there was never any doubt that we would have a single bill with pro- visions from every committee. We set mid-May as a target date for the commit- tees to finish their respective parts of the bill so we could create a large omnibus bill containing the product from every committee. This bill would be introduced by Bill Archer, Bill Goodling, Pat Roberts, and Tom Bliley, the chairs of the four primary committees of jurisdiction.

Our leadership staff group, as well as the Gingrich leadership group in its own meetings, many of which I attended, spent a lot of time discussing whether the bill would once again be part of a reconciliation bill. If it were, it would tech- nically be a product of the Budget Committee, which would mean that the Bud- get Committee would have to mark up the unified bill introduced by the committees of jurisdiction. As in 1995, the major advantage of moving the bill as part of reconciliation, of course, was that Senate rules did not allow a recon- ciliation bill to be filibustered. The disadvantage was the damnable Byrd rule, which could cause many provisions to be expelled from the bill.

In the end, the welfare reform bill was considered as part of reconciliation. This time, however, Republican leaders wisely decided to avoid a huge reconciliation bill and try to enact two or three smaller reconciliation bills. Welfare would be passed on its own but would nonetheless come from the Budget Committee and be con- sidered part of the reconciliation process. Taxes and other nonwelfare provisions would appear in separate bills. I took this decision to be pretty good evidence that our leadership was learning. Let's fight one battle at a time over well-defined issues rather than conduct a war over the future of Western civilization.

As our various meetings and negotiating sessions resolved many of the issues between Republican governors and House and Senate Republicans, Shaw pressed his subcommittee members and the leadership to move ahead on markups. He and Archer conferred frequently, and both agreed that the sooner we moved to markups the better. During this period Shaw met twice with the subcommittee Republicans, and they remained united in their view that we should make whatever changes in the governors' proposal we had to make to keep House Republicans united and then move ahead as quickly as possible. We were aided in this effort by a growing feeling among House Republicans, and perhaps Senate Republicans as well, that despite all our noises about a Republican revolution, not much had been accomplished.

Throughout the spring, several news articles and editorials in prominent newspapers brought public attention to the view that the Republican Congress was "all talk, no action." On April 2 the conservative columnist James Glassman wrote a very tough editorial in the *Washington Post* arguing that Republicans had nothing to show for their control of Congress: no balanced budget, no tax relief, no welfare reform, no changes in Medicaid or Medicare, no changes in any entitlement program.[18] And Glassman knew how to rub it in: he argued that Republicans had not done what they were elected to do because they had been defeated by Clinton. On May 5, Michael Wines wrote an article in *the New York Times* that was guaranteed to put the fear of God in every Republican heart.[19] First, he cited a *New York Times*–CBS News poll that found that 66 percent of the public disapproved of the way Congress was handling its job. Second, he tied the disapproval precisely to the lack of action by Congress, despite all the promises made in the Contract with America. As if these jabs were not enough, he also contrasted the "blue-moon opportunity" presented to Republicans by their shocking sweep of the 1994 elections with the "stalled" Republican legislative agenda, unpopular leadership, and general disarray after twice closing the government—and all this with only forty-five legislative days remaining in the 104th Congress until the elections of 1996.

But the most galling article was a March 26 editorial by Mickey Kaus, a nationally known and respected liberal who supported welfare reform.[20] Taking off from Moynihan's statement (following Clinton's second veto) that there is nothing quite so exhilarating as being "shot at and missed," Kaus claimed that liberals were "gloating" because Republicans were so stupid. The opportunity to enact historic changes in welfare was wide open, but conservatives were as usual blowing the opportunity with their agenda of foolish and untested provisions to fight illegitimacy. According to Kaus, liberals "love[d]" Rector because he was killing welfare reform over the largely irrelevant family cap. He also slammed Dole, who he claimed was pushing the bill to the right only to force another veto by Clinton, a veto that Dole calculated would help his own campaign for the presidency. Adding insult to injury, Kaus published this provocative editorial in the *Wall Street Journal*, the newspaper most read and admired by Republicans. Kaus called me as he was writing the piece to ask some questions, and I seized the occasion to strongly encourage him to criticize Republicans as unmercifully as possible. I don't remember if I suggested that he publish his piece in the *Wall Street Journal*, but if I didn't I should have.

During this period, Shaw was pushing and pulling on every available string to move the legislative process along. We were simultaneously meeting with the governors at the staff level, talking with governors by phone, meeting with the House Republican leadership, meeting with senior leaders from both the House and Senate, agitating in the House leadership staff group and even Gingrich's leadership group, and talking with and meeting frequently with members and staff from Ways and Means. We had even met with the administration at the staff level three times by late May, but in these meetings Shaw wanted me to behave like the high school prom queen who refused to dance with anyone. Much to our relief, nothing came of the meetings with the administration. Any bill we could have worked out with the administration would have given away too much and would have split our Republican coalition.

Perhaps the most important factor during this period is that almost all Republicans, but especially those in the House, were on the same page. Shaw and I felt that, due to the trust we had built up over the years with the governors, we could introduce a bill that represented a compromise with their February proposal, especially if we promised to continue working toward additional compromises on the few provisions to which the governors objected. Equally important, we were within reach of an agreement on all or nearly all of the major issues with the Senate. Thus we would be able to introduce bills in the House and the Senate that were identical or nearly so. Kathy Tobin, the welfare staffer on the Finance Committee, and I had met and talked on the phone for hours in order to identify provisions we could include that would be consistent with the governors' proposal and yet satisfy Republican members in both the House and Senate.

On May 8 we had the second meeting with Republican members and staff from our subcommittee in three weeks. Shaw and I had met earlier in the day to plan the meeting with members, and as a result, when the members assembled we covered lots of ground in a little over an hour. We reviewed the likely schedule of markups and floor action, reviewed the budget numbers, reviewed the communications plan that Ari Fleischer was developing, reviewed talking points against the Clinton bill, and described all the talks that Shaw had been giving to various House Republican groups. The members themselves raised the dreaded issue of Medicaid, which we had not placed on the agenda. Several members, but especially Dave Camp of Michigan and John Ensign of Nevada, said that it looked increasingly likely that we would have to drop the Medicaid reforms from our bill, a position that Shaw had already adopted without making his position public. Welfare reform combined with Medicaid could easily turn out to be an albatross around our neck if we couldn't avoid the governors' recommendation to move them through Congress as part of a single bill.

As always, the meeting and discussion of all the major issues showed that members of the subcommittee (and their staffs) were well informed, strongly united, and ready to move ahead together. It even appeared that we all agreed that it would be necessary to figure out a way to jettison the Medicaid provisions if we wanted to pass our bill. And we all realized that Dole and our House leadership might well not want to pass the bill and give Clinton another chance to sign a welfare reform bill. After a long discussion with Shaw following the meeting, though, I had no doubt that if the Dole campaign and our leadership tried to block us, we would go above their heads to House Republican members and seek their support to force our leadership to actually pass the bill and send it to Clinton.

By mid-May we were ready to get down to serious business by marking up a bill in the Human Resources Subcommittee. All the committees in the House and Senate were ready to move, but we delayed a week at the request of the Dole campaign. On May 15, Dole announced his resignation from the Senate and his aides wanted time to think though their position on welfare before we moved ahead. In addition, they didn't want us moving on a high-profile issue at the same time he made his big announcement, nor did we want to have our message that Republicans were fighting Democrats to pass welfare reform trampled on by Dole's announcement.

Working at the member and staff levels in both the House and Senate, we planned a series of events to bring attention to the fact that Republicans were again moving on welfare reform, this time with the bipartisan support of governors. On May 21, along with Sheila Burke, we called a staff meeting in Dole's office in the Capitol Building to make final plans to introduce our bills. Ari and I had been working on a big event to introduce the bill with as much fanfare as possible, and Ari in turn had been working with a group of House press secretaries representing both the leadership and House members, as well as with communications staffers from the Senate, to explain and develop the details of the plan. We were recommending that the event to announce the new bill be held in the ornate Mansfield Room on the second floor of the Capitol Building and that Eloise Anderson, the black welfare director from the state of California, preside as the moderator. Thanks to Ari's persuasive abilities and the support of Archer and Shaw, both the House and Senate leadership agreed to this plan. Later, both the House and Senate agreed that the Republican leaders and the chairs of Ways and Means and Finance would speak briefly at the press conference, after being introduced by Eloise. She would then open up the proceedings to questions from the press.

Given the number of actors (and egos) involved, Ari had been working with the press secretaries in both the House and Senate to decide who would speak, for how long, and roughly what each member would say. The kiss of death in a press conference is to have one or two members drone on for ten or fifteen minutes and put everyone to sleep. The goal was to give a few of the leaders an opportunity to talk for just a few minutes, to have them reinforce the major achievements of the bill, especially converting welfare to a work program (as always, Ari had a list of the main messages, boiled down to the fewest possible words, that he gave to everyone), to praise their colleagues and the governors for working hard to produce a good bill, and then to give the press a chance to ask questions. The major message was that Republicans, despite the obstruction of President Clinton, were again delivering on their promises to the American people.

The staff meeting on May 21 in the Senate Majority Leader's office was attended by twenty-five senior staffers from the House and Senate and was very productive. Of the scores of staff meetings I attended during the eighteen months of welfare reform, this one featured more senior staffers from both the House and Senate than any other meeting. Phil and I had prepared the agenda. After Sheila welcomed everyone, I reviewed the issues that had to be settled in order to introduce identical or nearly identical bills in the House and Senate. Five big issues and several smaller ones remained. The major issues were whether a few states would be allowed to have Food Stamp block grants, whether the family cap would be an opt-in or opt-out provision, whether states could count everyone who left the welfare rolls toward fulfilling the participation standards (as recommended by the governors),[21] how to resolve a few technical issues on the state performance bonus, and how to reach the savings target given to us by the Budget Committees. After somewhat lengthy but productive discussion, interrupted occasionally by raucous debate, we decided to recommend to our members that the Food Stamp block grant demonstration be included in the bill. We also resolved the technical issues on the high-performance bonus. The budget requirements were more or less beyond our control. The Budget Committee's target for provisions under the jurisdiction of Ways and Means and Finance (not counting the Food Stamp program or Medicaid) was $26.7 billion over seven years.[22] We estimated that our current draft of the conference report would save well over $25 billion. Thus we were still a little more than $1 billion short. We all agreed that before going to markup, the Ways and Means and Finance Committees would try to find provisions that achieved this last billion in savings but that we would not be able to settle the issue at the staff level.

At this point, the two most contentious issues remained: the family cap and the caseload reduction credit. The Senate wanted to side with the governors on both issues by making the family cap an opt-in provision and by counting everyone who left the rolls toward the work participation rate. The House took the opposite position on both issues. After considerable debate, some of it a little prickly, the inevitable decision was to split the difference: we adopted the House position on not counting welfare leavers and the Senate (and governors') position of making the family cap a state option and not an opt-out. This decision, of course, would not sit well with Talent, Lauch Faircloth, Rector, and lots of conservatives, but we needed to get moving. Even though almost everyone on the House side supported a mandatory family cap, we were willing to live with an opt-in provision as long as we could get moving again.

After this fascinating and productive meeting, I rushed over to Legislative Counsel to get our agreements translated into legislative language and get our bill completed for introduction the next day. Later that day we were able to get both Shaw and Archer, plus Phil, Ari, and a few other Ways and Means senior staffers, together in Archer's office for a thorough review of the events planned for the next day. At this crucial juncture in getting started again, Shaw didn't want any of the Ways and Means players to feel left out of the action.

May 22 was one of the busiest and most stimulating days of the welfare reform saga. We started with what we called a "press seminar" at eight-thirty in the morning in Archer's office in Room H-208 of the Capitol. Eloise, busy with her job as welfare director for California, had to take a red-eye flight to Washington. Along with Archer, Shaw, and Roth, she participated in the press seminar, having just arrived at the Capitol in a cab from Dulles airport. Fred Barnes from the *Weekly Standard*, Cokie Roberts of National Public Radio, and Robert Novak, the syndicated conservative columnist, and a few other prominent reporters attended. Eloise stated flatly, as if it would be obvious to anyone who thought about it, that welfare mothers simply had to work and we needed a system that gave them no other choice. She was eloquent in stating unequivocally, as only she could do, that when Congress and the states got the system right, the mothers would prove themselves capable of work and of supporting their children and that they and their children would be better off financially and in many other ways for doing so. Shaw and Archer both expressed great confidence that we would send Clinton another bill, and Shaw was confident that he would sign it. The meeting went well; we were able to defend our major provisions and our strategy for sending the president another bill.

We left the press seminar at a little before nine-thirty and rushed to the Cannon Caucus Room on the second floor of the Cannon House Office Building for a meeting of the entire House Republican conference. Eloise was the featured speaker. She again gave a rousing statement about how we had to stop coddling welfare mothers and create a system that encouraged, and when necessary forced, mothers to work. She assured the members, just as she had the reporters and editorial writers, that if challenged in this way the mothers would prove themselves. In my years in the House, I attended at least thirty meetings of the Republican conference, but there were only a few occasions on which the members actually paid careful attention to an outside speaker (or even one of their own members).

Normally, the conference was something like a cross between a nightclub in which people talk and occasionally watch the entertainment and a boring public lecture in which people only pretend to listen. When Eloise started speaking, the members were in nightclub mode. But within a minute they were in the palm of her hand. When she finished they gave her a standing ovation. At that moment, Ari and I were pretty pleased that we had fought so hard to invite her as the featured person in all these events.

But she wasn't through yet. We had two more events, and the next was the most important of the day. She was the mistress of ceremonies at the press event in the Mansfield Room for the unveiling of our bill, and we hustled right over there as soon as she finished her rousing conference talk. The room was packed with reporters, congressional staff, lobbyists, advocates, and of course, the featured Republican speakers at the press conference: Shaw, Roth, Archer, and Senator Don Nickles of Oklahoma. As soon as Eloise and I arrived, and she had given a zippy introduction to the events, I dashed over to Legislative Counsel to check on the bill and answer questions about the bill from Jim Grossman, our superb counsel and draftsman. I then went to Room 1100 in the Longworth House Office Building—actually walking—to make sure everything was in order for our hearing, which went off without any problems and provided a forum for us to present our new bill.

The events of May 22 showed that, at least temporarily, the path we were on was a good one. Members and staff were back at work on welfare reform, we had a plan favored by most governors, and we were receiving good press coverage that conveyed the message that Republicans were once again working hard on welfare reform.[23] Shaw and Archer, plus our leadership and many Republican members, especially members of Ways and Means, were energized and were confident that we were once again blazing a path to revolutionary reform of welfare. This time around, I detected a change in the attitude of many staffers and members toward welfare reform. Throughout 1995 Republicans pursued a host of goals, all of which seemed within reach: reduce farm subsidies, get rid of entire cabinet agencies, reform Medicaid and Medicare, reform Congress, increase defense spending, cut taxes, pass a balanced budget amendment to the Constitution, and over and above all else, balance the budget within seven years. This list could be extended, but the point is that Republicans tried to do everything at once. And heading into the fall of 1995, most members, despite a certain level of exhaustion from one of the busiest years in the history of Congress, were exceptionally optimistic. In the context of a rampant syndrome of Masters of the Universe, Republicans thought they could change the world. But the Clinton vetoes of the debt ceiling bill and the spending bill on November 13, the reconciliation bill on December 6 that included welfare reform, and the separate welfare reform bill on January 9 brought at first a pall and then reflection among Republicans, including the hotheads.

As the label "do-nothing Congress" began to appear, members feared that we might lose Congress in the 1996 elections. The prospect of losing Congress caused Republicans to focus on the possible and eschew the grandiose. And now here we were again, taking a step-by-step approach to showing that welfare reform was indeed possible. Welfare was now universally regarded, along with the balanced budget, as the most important item on the agenda of the Republican Party, and we needed to be more balanced in our approach to making sure we used our energy fighting for legislation that could actually become law. Shaw held this view by December, if not before, but the story of welfare reform after the veto of January 9 was the gradual expansion of the view that Republicans should focus squarely on welfare reform as a major issue in its own right and aim to pass a bill the president could sign.

Our subcommittee markup on June 5, about two weeks after the bill had been introduced, did nothing to dissuade us from the view that not only had Republicans become more focused, but Democrats had too.[24] I cannot imagine a greater contrast than that between the two markups, March 1995 and June 1996. The most obvious difference was length. Whereas the 1995 subcommittee markup had lasted three days, the 1996 markup lasted only a little more than seven hours and was completed in one day. A second difference was that Democrats and Republicans were much more civil to each other. There were few barbed exchanges during the markup and plenty of humor, as when Charles Rangel told Shaw that he cared so much for him that he was going to withdraw one of his amendments. A third difference was that Democrats, especially Sander Levin and Ben Cardin, said somewhat nice things about the bill. Both commented on the excellent changes Republicans had made since the last markup. But saying nice things about the changes and supporting the new bill were not the same, as the Democrats soon showed.

Another huge difference between the 1995 and 1996 markups was that this time Democrats offered relatively few amendments. Three of the twelve amendments offered by Democrats were withdrawn so that members of the subcommittee could work together on a bipartisan basis to reach mutual agreement on them. Withdrawing amendments in this fashion is a routine procedure and signals not only that members are willing to cooperate across party lines but also that there is already agreement on some aspect of the amendment. In addition to these three amendments, on which there was at least partial agreement, an amendment by Pete Stark on health and safety regulations and an amendment by Sander Levin on deleting a provision that would have raised the age of eligibility for SSI from sixty-five to sixty-seven were accepted unanimously. Thus on five of the twelve Democratic amendments, there was favorable action by the subcommittee. Six of the seven remaining amendments were defeated by recorded vote; the seventh was defeated by voice vote. Although Republican members maintained their unity by defeating every Democratic amendment opposed by Chairman Shaw—and indeed across all seven amendments only one Republican vote went against the chairman's position—the willingness of the two parties to cooperate in perfecting the bill provided a sharp contrast with the 1995 markup. Despite the constructive action and the comity that characterized the markup, every committee Democrat still voted against the bill.

The full committee markup on June 12 was similar in almost every respect to the subcommittee markup.[25] Compared to the 1995 markup, the 1996 markup was shorter, there were fewer amendments, and the atmosphere was far less charged. Democrats offered only twenty-two amendments. Of these, three were accepted unanimously, three were accepted on voice votes, and one was accepted after modification by voice vote. In addition, Democrats won a recorded vote, with seven Republicans voting yes, on a motion by Cardin to require states to include information in their state plan on education, counseling, and prepregnancy health services offered to young mothers. This was the only subcommittee or full committee vote on a welfare issue that Democrats won in the Ways and Means Committee during the 104th Congress, again signaling how much Republicans were trying to accommodate Democrats whenever they could. Taken together, Democrats managed to change the chairman's markup bill with eight of their amendments. Granted, none of them were major, but Democrats had had zero impact on the chairman's bill in 1995. Moreover, on the Cardin amendment seven Republicans voted against the chairman to help carry the amendment; in 1995 not more than two Republicans had voted against the chairman on any Democratic amendment, and none of their amendments had passed.

Despite the remarkable difference in atmosphere between the 1996 and 1995 markups, and despite the good will, the final vote at full committee was along partisan lines, with the exception of Democrat Gerald Kleczka of Wisconsin, who voted with Republicans as he had in 1995. Thus all the changes that we had made in the bill even before the markups began, and the several Democratic amendments that we accepted during both the subcommittee and full committee markups, did not result in additional support from committee Democrats.[26] The other committees with welfare jurisdiction were just as successful in passing their sections of the bill unscathed. Thus as in 1995 Republicans were once again successful in bringing their complex bill through several committees without losing major votes.

As the House and Senate Committees began to report out their sections of the bill, it became increasingly probable that we would send another bill to President Clinton. With the presidential election approaching, it was possible to think that President Clinton, now very much under the influence of notorious campaign adviser Dick Morris, might sign the bill. We might not be in the catbird seat just yet, but we were flying.

## CHAPTER THIRTEEN

# The Revolution
# Threatened

As the House and Senate committee hearings and markups were creating the ingredients for yet another revolutionary welfare reform bill, serious problems loomed. As could be expected, not the least of these were Democrats and their allies outside Congress. They were not about to watch a New Deal entitlement killed off without a fight. One of the cleverest and most effective weapons created by liberals was developed by Wendell Primus, the former Ways and Means staffer who was then a senior official at the Department of Health and Human Services (HHS). The weapon was a social science study. To understand the full impact of this study, we must go back to the spring of 1995, the first time that liberals like Wendell were beginning to worry that Republicans might actually pass welfare reform and that Clinton might sign their bill.

Occupying a senior position under David Ellwood at HHS, Wendell was determined to do everything he could to defeat the bill. Only two hopes remained: convince Democrats in the Senate to stand united against the bill or convince the president to veto the bill, two hopes that were not independent of each other. To rally Democrats against the bill, Wendell had the idea of using statistical techniques to produce what are called distribution tables. These tables show how a given piece of legislation would affect families at various points in the income distribution. Wendell had used these tables on many previous occasions to show Democrats in the House the financial impact their legislation would have on the rich, on the poor, and on those in between. Typically, the analysis proceeded by simulating the effects of the new rules on family incomes, comparing those outcomes to their incomes under current law. The summary results show whether categories of families, usually sorted into five groups of equal size from poorest to richest, gain or lose income relative to current law. For real Democrats, good legislation took money away from families in upper-income brackets and gave money to families in the middle and lower brackets—or in the case of deficit reduction, harmed people at the bottom the least. During the budget negotiations of 1990, Wendell had teamed with the chairman of the Human Resources Subcommittee of Ways and Means, Tom Downey, and used these tables to help sway the entire House Democratic Caucus not to support a major budget compromise because the tables showed that families in the bottom fifth of income would be hurt by the deal. One result was that the deal was modified so that families at the bottom got more money from the Earned Income Tax Credit.

Always bold in his maneuvering, as the Republican bill ploughed its way inexorably through the House in 1995, Wendell talked to Leon Panetta, director of the Office of Management and Budget, and later the White House Chief of Staff. Wendell had worked closely with Panetta when Panetta was head of the House Budget Committee from 1989 to 1993. After Wendell pitched his proposal for the distributional analysis of the Republican bill, Panetta gave him the go-ahead. So Wendell, after talking with HHS Secretary Donna Shalala, organized a working group with representatives from HHS, the Department of Housing and Urban Development, the Department of Labor, and the Department of the Treasury. The original idea was that Treasury would perform the actual computer modeling work, but officials at Treasury were not very cooperative. After a few weeks Wendell decided to turn to analysts at the Urban Institute and to adjust the analysis to focus primarily on spending on poor families with children.[1] HHS had been funding the Urban Institute for many years, under both Democratic and Republican administrations, to build and maintain a model of the American economy and government programs (the transfer income model, or TRIM) that could simulate the impact of government programs on work, income, poverty, and a host of other variables. Sheila Zedlewski, an economist and highly competent researcher at the Urban Institute, performed the analyses for Wendell and his team.

The results of the modeling predicted that the House Republican bill would cast two million children into poverty, exactly the outcome Wendell had hoped for. Excited by these results, he showed them to Secretary Shalala. She also thought they were potentially useful but urged Wendell to repeat the analysis on the Senate bill because that bill was still pending and was the bill a majority of Senate Democrats seemed on the verge of supporting (the House bill had already passed, but with only nine Democratic votes). Wendell and Zedlewski repeated the analysis on the Senate bill; the results indicated that this bill would cast a mere one million or so children into poverty. The analysis became available to Wendell on Friday, August 4, 1995, just as the Senate was getting ready to take up welfare reform. As this analysis was being completed, President Clinton's staff was writing his weekly Saturday radio address on welfare. Afraid that the president might endorse the Senate Republican bill, Wendell worked at the speed of sound to complete the analysis, interpret the results, and write a two-page memo for the president.

Wendell gave the memo to Secretary Shalala, who took it directly to the president. I was not able to discover whether the president had planned to endorse the Senate bill and changed his mind after seeing Wendell's memo. But whatever the cause, the president used his radio address to argue on behalf of the Senate Democratic bill introduced by Tom Daschle. He did not mention either Wendell's memo or the Urban Institute study.

Even so, Wendell was successful in creating a strong piece of evidence against the Republican bill, but in his zeal to fight those evil Republicans, he had presented the administration with a problem of nuclear dimensions. There was now in existence a credible empirical study—still a closely guarded secret—claiming that both the House and Senate bills would cast a million or more children into poverty.

Bruce Reed, the president's chief domestic adviser, was not pleased, to say the least. In fact there is every reason to believe that Reed, the architect of much of President Clinton's policy on welfare, was livid. The president had promised to end welfare as we know it, and with the election only a little more than a year away, the president might find it advantageous to sign a bill like the Senate Republican bill. Reed even thought that welfare reform would be good for both the country and the Democratic Party. But how could the president sign a bill that his own administration claimed would throw a million or more children into poverty? It is remarkable that a staffer at HHS could create such a difficult situation for an entire administration and even for the president himself. More remarkable still, Wendell did it on purpose, knowing full well that he was putting the administration in great difficulty and at the same time putting his continued employment in jeopardy. Watching Wendell carefully throughout this period, and having known him for many years, I have no doubt that he didn't care a fig about keeping his job. Oh, the nerve of those liberals!

As rumors about the report's existence began to swirl around Washington, the administration committed one of the oldest and silliest mistakes that can be made in Washington: they tried to hide the report. But entire careers in Washington are made out of leaking information just like this. Here's a good rule for politicians to follow (and one that Washington types repeat to each other incessantly): don't write down anything you don't want to read the next day in the *Washington Post*. Wendell, an old pro, did not violate this rule: he wanted the report to appear in the *Post*, the *New York Times*, and anywhere else that a maximum number of people would see it. He would have put the study's results in the Bible if he could— anything to expose as many people as possible to the "fact" that those unconscionable Republicans were tossing at least a million little kids into the purgatory of poverty. Officials at HHS and the White House, however, did violate the rule and were bound to be discovered: there was not only a report, there were also an elaborate statistical analysis of the poverty-inducing effects of the Republican bill and a zippy two-page summary of the analysis. And several people in the administration and at the Urban Institute already knew about the report.

To make matters worse for the administration, Elizabeth Shogren of the *Los Angeles Times*, the same reporter who in January had published the story that caused Clay Shaw to reverse his decision not to use the Contract with America welfare reform bill as the blueprint for his own bill, obtained a copy of the report on October 26, 1995, and immediately wrote a front-page story for the October 27 edition headlined, "Welfare Report Clashes with Clinton, Senate." As might be expected, the lead sentence in the story asserted that the "welfare reform plan approved by the Senate and embraced by President Clinton would push an estimated 1.1 million children into poverty and make conditions worse for those already under the poverty line." She referred to the report as "not released to the public."[2]

Senator Moynihan, who had been hearing rumors about Wendell's analysis and had repeatedly asked the administration for a copy, was by this time in a state of near apoplexy. At the opening meeting of the House-Senate welfare reform conference on October 24, 1995, he had chastised the administration for not releasing the report.[3] Indeed, he said that those involved in suppressing Wendell's report "will take this disgrace to their graves," adding a typical Moynihan flourish: "The children alone are innocent." He then wrote a letter to the Office of Management and Budget (OMB), consigned by eleven of the seventeen other Democrats on the conference committee, asking for "any relevant analysis" of the welfare bills.[4]

With a summary of the report about to be published in the *Los Angeles Times*, with Moynihan constantly complaining in apocalyptic terms about the bill's impacts on child poverty and the administration's dishonesty in not releasing its study confirming this impact, and now with a letter from Moynihan, Gibbons, and other Democrats participating in the House-Senate conference demanding that the administration release the report, the administration decided to come clean and inform Congress and the public about its assessment of the effects of the Senate bill. On October 27, the day Shogren's story appeared in the *Los Angeles Times*, Alice Rivlin, the head of OMB, responded to the Moynihan-Gibbons letter and agreed to conduct a new study of the "impact of this bill on children entering or leaving poverty"[5] and to make the results public within one week. A lengthy story in the *Washington Post* the next day reviewed the essentials of the report's history and declared that the administration's decision to release the report was a "personal victory" for Moynihan. The *Post* story made it clear that the administration, and especially the press office at HHS, had been something less than forthright in handling the report.

Behind the scenes, Rivlin put Ken Apfel, the experienced and effective OMB staffer who would soon play a central role in organizing the Cabinet Room seminar sessions, in charge of the report. Ken was ordered to tell Wendell that if he wrote any more reports or released any more data on child poverty he would be dumped in the Potomac. Not only did Wendell manage to keep himself dry but his report continued to make its mark on the debate. In March 1996, as we were reviving welfare reform following Clinton's vetoes, an extensive analysis of the struggle to pass the bill in 1995 written by Jeff Shear appeared in the *National Journal*.[6] Among other insider information offered by this exceptional piece of journalism, it was revealed that on October 22, 1995, President Clinton and Moynihan had had a "screaming fight" on Air Force One over the welfare reform bill and over Clinton's refusal to lead the fight against it—and perhaps to use Wendell's study to do so. In the end, Clinton did veto the two welfare reform bills Republicans sent him in 1995. It is hard to believe that Wendell's report did not play at least some role in the veto decisions. It is undeniable that the report energized the children's lobby in Washington and was used extensively by Democrats and liberals of all stripes to attack the Republican bill.

In June 1996, as the House and Senate were again working on welfare reform bills that Republicans planned to send to the president, Wendell's report and new versions of his analysis were still very much a part of the discussion. Moreover, the estimate that the Republican bill would throw a million children into poverty was constantly cited by scholars, Democratic politicians, child advocates, and reporters and editorial page writers.

Although the report was a clever device, accompanied by all the trappings of serious social science, it rested on questionable procedures and assumptions.[7] Perhaps the shakiest part of the analysis was that nearly every family on welfare was already in poverty. If in the real world families on welfare are already in poverty, how can welfare reform put them into poverty? No problem. Simply change the definition of poverty. Ironically, conservatives had been arguing for years that the official definition of poverty was flawed because only cash benefits were counted as income while income from noncash welfare, especially Food Stamps and the Earned Income Tax Credits, was ignored. So the Urban Institute, using long-accepted methods for computing alternative definitions of poverty, counted Food Stamps and other welfare benefits and the EITC as income. This approach had the effect, on paper, of removing several million families from poverty, including many on welfare. Their actual circumstances did not change, but more of their government benefits counted as income and therefore they escaped poverty through the miracle of definition.

Once the analysis had these families out of poverty, they could be put back into poverty by losing their welfare benefits. The crucial issue here was what assumption to make about how many mothers would work when they lost their welfare benefits. Mothers near the poverty line who didn't work would not be able to make up for the welfare they lost because of the time limit, sanctions, or the choice to leave welfare, and would therefore fall below the poverty line.[8] Although Zedlewski ran several estimates, the basic analysis assumed that two-thirds of the mothers who lost eligibility as a result of the time limit would find jobs but would be able to work only part time. Working part time virtually ensured poverty. If a higher percentage of mothers worked full time, the increase in poverty based on the Urban Institute's assumptions would be substantially reduced. But the estimates were based on studies of welfare reforms that were much less substantial than those contemplated by the Republican bill. No one knew what would happen if states were required to put half of their caseload into work programs, if they reduced or eliminated the family's cash benefit if the mother didn't cooperate, and if they imposed a five-year time limit (even less than five years in many states); nor was it clear what the effect would be of the cash bonus paid to states that were successful at helping mothers leave welfare. Thus there was ample reason to doubt the conclusion of a million children in poverty because no one knew how many of the mothers would work or how much they would work after the welfare revolution created by the Republican bill.

Wendell's report was not the only action taken by liberals to fight the Republican bill. There may not have been a vast left-wing conspiracy against the welfare bill, but as the spring of 1996 faded into summer, the temperature on the left got higher and higher. As usual, the *New York Times* and the *Washington Post* editorial pages led the way. On no less than six occasions between release of the governors' proposal on February 6 and continued legislative progress on the bills by late June, the two bulwarks of liberal thought in America worked themselves into a frenzy. Typical was the *Washington Post* editorial on June 23. Amazingly, the editors asserted that the Republican bill was "not . . . welfare reform at all."[9] It was nothing more than a way for Republicans to cut spending. That our bill was not welfare reform was, of course, news to us. Aid to Families with Dependent Children (AFDC), the Food Stamp program, Supplemental Security Income (SSI), and Medicaid met every test for defining welfare, especially the test of unearned benefits received on an entitlement basis. Clinton, the editorial continued, was in a welfare squeeze of his own making and was not sending the right signals to Republicans, to his potential allies on the left, or to the public. But he'd better start "to lay the predicate for the veto he will be obliged to cast."[10] So the *Post* provided its own definition of welfare reform, asserted that the Republican bill was mostly outside that definition, declared without evidence that the bill would do "enormous damage," and concluded that the president would be "obliged" to veto the bill. This editorial, like many others in both the *New York Times* and the *Post*, was analysis by assertion, outburst, and accusation.

Another sign of distress on the left was the extraordinary lengths to which organizations associated with the Catholic Church were willing to go to attack the Republican bill. Primarily because its members assert that God exists, believe strongly in tradition, follow firm rules of human behavior, and oppose abortion, the Catholic Church is not normally thought of as a part of the left in American politics. But on social issues, organizations associated with the Catholic Church were a consistent, strong, and even vituperative foe of Republican social policy. After Shaw and I met with the bishops in December 1995, we had hoped that Catholic organizations would show greater understanding of and sympathy for the policies in HR 4. But the bishops and Sharon Daly, the lobbyist for Catholic Charities, if anything only strengthened their actions against the Republican bill.

At two critical points in the revitalized legislative process, senior Catholic officials sent letters to members of the House and Senate urging them to defeat the Republican bill. On June 10, 1996, the Most Reverend William Skylstad, one of the bishops with whom we had met, sent a letter to members of the House as several committees were beginning markups of the new bill. The letter claimed that the bill's family cap would increase the number of abortions, that the spending cuts would destroy the social safety net, and that the noncitizen provisions were punitive and an "unprecedented denial of benefits."[11] However, he was wrong on all counts. To answer these in order: there was no scientific evidence that the family cap would increase abortions (although it was certainly a plausible assumption that more poor mothers might have abortions); CBO projections showed that the safety net would dispense about $4 trillion to low-income Americans in the six years after 1996, an increase of nearly one-third;[12] and traditional federal policy since colonial times had been to deny government welfare benefits to noncitizens and indeed to deport those who became dependent on welfare.[13]

Although there were strong, factual arguments against Skylstad's letter, the tone of the letter was constructive and devoid of invective. Not so the letter from Fr. Fred Kammer, S.J., the president of Catholic Charities, to every member of the Senate. Kammer wrote that the Republican bill "reflects ignorance and prejudice" and was a "sham."[14] He explicitly invoked "Jesus of Nazareth," claiming that the bill should not be supported by "believers." Kammer thereby joined Marian Wright Edelman, of the Children's Defense Fund, in holding that God was on their side and against Republicans.[15] My response was to expand my prayer list to include my own soul and those of all Republicans and also the majority of the American public who supported welfare reform. For good measure, I included President Clinton, just in case he too decided to reject his religious faith and jeopardize his soul by signing the Republican bill.

The academic world, as we have already seen in the unusual letter and Washington press event conducted by a group of seventy-six scholars to attack Charles

Murray and his recommendation to end welfare cold turkey (see chapter 7), was virtually united against the Republican bill. Sophisticated scholars may openly attack a fellow scholar like Murray, but they usually do not trash an entire political party. Then as now a large majority of the professoriate votes Democratic,[16] but their scholarly values require them to analyze policies in a dispassionate fashion, and they tended to be circumspect in criticizing the Republican bill. This was especially the case since the Republican position on so many issues was very close to that of Clinton and the new Democrats, not to mention the American public. Even so, just below the surface, most scholars were liberal and were more or less shocked by the Republican bill. Although their views differed somewhat on individual issues, they tended to oppose ending the entitlement, tended to believe that mandatory work would yield modest results, did not like time limits, strongly opposed reducing or ending the benefits of unwed teen mothers, opposed cutting Food Stamps, and opposed ending benefits for noncitizens.

One of the best examples of this attitude is given by Jason DeParle of the *New York Times* in his 2004 book on welfare reform. DeParle relates that in 1994 David Ellwood shared a copy of the Clinton welfare reform plan with Henry Aaron of Brookings, one of the nation's most distinguished poverty and health policy scholars and a former high-ranking official in the Carter administration. After reading the Clinton plan, Aaron wrote to Ellwood, opening his letter with the claim that conditions prevailing in Washington "threaten disastrously bad welfare legislation with which you will forever be ashamed to have been associated. . . . A feral mood is loose on the Hill. . . . A Republican-conservative-Democratic coalition is likely to send back legislation whose ferocity will confront the administration with a ghastly dilemma. Veto the bill and be labeled as defenders of the welfare status quo or sign a bill that betrays what you . . . stand for."[17] Aaron closed by urging Ellwood to resign, which he did more than a year before the Republican bill had been signed by Clinton.

One of the clearest and most reasoned expressions of scholarly arguments against the Republican bill was a report put out by one of the nation's most respected centrist public policy think tanks, the august Brookings Institution in Washington.[18] Entitled *Looking Before We Leap*, and edited by two noted Brookings scholars, Kent Weaver and William Dickens, the volume was published in late summer of 1995, before Clinton vetoed the first bill. The editors opened the volume by positing three arguments: that social science "can provide important insights regarding the promise, limitations, and risks" associated with specific welfare reform proposals; that both the "degree" and the direction of innovation "should be guided by the information that social science provides"; and that the new reforms should be evaluated carefully.[19] Not surprisingly, the editors asserted that none of these three principles was being observed in the welfare reform debate. The editors did not explore what it means for policy to be "guided by" social science research. There is nothing in the Constitution or the rules of the House or the Senate that stipulates any role for research or other evidence. Rather, policy is based on tradition, values, political philosophy, opinion, party loyalty, and bargaining—along with, at times, evidence from social science. Much of the Republican welfare reform policy was based on values: people should work, young people should not have babies they cannot support, children with mild disabilities should not qualify for costly disability benefits, alcoholics and drug addicts should not be rewarded with cash payments specifically for being addicts, able-bodied foreigners should not be able to come to America to work and then join welfare. As the Brookings volume itself showed, most of the value positions taken by Republicans were supported by the American public.[20]

Scholars such as those writing in the Brookings volume—none of whom were conservative—may have shared some of these values, but like Democrats in Congress they were not willing to support the tough policies being advanced by Republicans. Liberals in Congress, the press, universities, think tanks, and advocacy groups were united against the Republican bill. They were joined by organizations affiliated with the Catholic Church as well as resourceful child advocacy groups in Washington such as the Center for Law and Social Policy. But Republicans were in control of Congress and were united. If Clinton joined forces with congressional Republicans, a revolution in American social policy was a certainty.

Ironically, the biggest obstacle to passing the bill was not opposition from the left. Rather, it was the continuing threat that the Republican coalition might fall apart. In the spring of 1996, the biggest threat to the Republican coalition was Medicaid. I don't think there was a particular moment when Shaw or other Republicans on our subcommittee realized that passing welfare reform would depend on separating it from Medicaid. For me, and perhaps for a number of others, the initial indication that Medicaid would be a big problem was an untimely press conference that several Republican governors, including Tommy Thompson and John Engler, held with Newt Gingrich and other Republican leaders on March 14, 1996. The Republican governors declared that, after long negotiation sessions with a small group of Democratic governors, they had reached a bipartisan agreement on the Medicaid funding formula and other issues. But as the *Los Angeles Times* put it the next day, the announcement was "quickly and unequivocally disavowed" by Democratic governors Robert Miller of Nevada, Roy Romer of Colorado, and Lawton Chiles of Florida, all of whom had been involved in the negotiations with Republican governors. To me this fiasco signaled that Thompson and Engler realized that they were not making progress toward a Medicaid deal with the Democratic governors so they tried to co-opt them by announcing an agreement. But the Democrats didn't fall for this ploy and immediately went public with their objections. The *Los Angeles Times* quoted an aide to one of the Democratic governors: "Only in Washington could a gathering of Republican senators, Republican governors, and the Republican speaker of the House be called bipartisan. It's surreal."[21] Shaw and I always assumed that only if the Democratic governors supported the Medicaid deal would there be a chance that Clinton would sign it. Now it was apparent that the governors were not going to be able to work out a deal on Medicaid. The only possible solution, then, was to deep-six the Medicaid reforms.

But the final decision was above my pay grade and above Shaw's as well. If it had been up to us, we would have separated the two bills as early as March and let them move through Congress on their respective merits. If the Medicaid reform didn't survive, that would be because a majority failed to support it or because the president vetoed it. It made no sense to us to risk a veto of welfare reform in order to try to push Medicaid legislation that did not have the support to survive on its own. What could be clearer? Were our leaders going to take us back to the mistakes of 1995?

When the Medicaid proposals were drafted in May by the House and Senate committees of jurisdiction (the Commerce Committee and the Finance Committee, respectively), coverage for children was reduced. The biggest reform in the governors' proposal was that federal Medicaid payments to each state would be capped at an amount below the level projected by current law. In addition, state matching requirements would be lowered. Under pressure to save money so that Congress could balance the federal budget and governors could balance their state budgets, the committees of jurisdiction, following the governors' lead, proposed reforms that would save both state and federal dollars. But in Medicaid's zero-sum game, if both the federal and state governments saved money, something had to give. In particular, either poor and low-income individuals and families had to pay more, or fewer of them would receive coverage, or both. These proposals were light years from the glory days of the Clinton plan for universal health coverage.

Enter Bob Greenstein. Greenstein's Center on Budget and Policy Priorities was all over the Medicaid reforms. In two brief papers released on May 23 and May 24, 1996, Greenstein's center carefully reviewed and explained the Republican proposals, which included both the governors' original proposals and the additional reforms devised by congressional Republicans, especially Republicans on the Commerce Committee in the House.[22] Center analysts estimated that over ten years Medicaid funding could fall as much as $690 billion below current law projections. Even in Washington, $690 billion seemed like a big number. Once the papers had been released, a classic political struggle ensued. Many Republicans dislike the Center on Budget and Policy Priorities because it is a liberal organization with an agenda of increasing public benefits—or at least protecting those that already exist—for poor and low-income children and families. Greenstein, who won the MacArthur Foundation's genius award, was one of the smartest, hardest-working, wisest, and most politically connected people in Washington. He was a kind of Ralph Nader of poor children and families. In just a little more than a decade he had built a formidable organization, with thirty-six employees and an annual budget approaching $3.5 million.

Greenstein had a formula for success. His goal of foiling Republicans by keeping government spending on the poor at high levels was the same goal as that of a bevy of child advocacy organizations, such as the Children's Defense Fund. But his center differed from child advocacy organizations in that Greenstein did analysis first and then built his lobbying around analysis; most advocates used analysis as a tool to support their predetermined goals. Well funded by a host of left-leaning foundations, Greenstein and his experts, calling on their extensive contacts on Capitol Hill, were almost always able to get legislative proposals as soon as they came off the printer in the Office of Legislative Counsel, subject them to careful analysis, often involving sophisticated computer modeling, and then write a brief explaining the legislation and estimating its effects. Amazingly, they were often able to pull off this mighty feat in less than twenty-four hours. Woe to the Republican who holds a press conference announcing a fine new proposal with gilded numbers and overwrought claims. Greenstein ate these guys for breakfast. His numbers almost always were reliable. Scholars, advocates, reporters, and congressional Democrats trusted Greenstein and his analysts and used both his numbers and his conclusions. I even knew several Republicans (I have promised never to reveal their identity) who trusted Greenstein's analyses and attended carefully to his conclusions. Greenstein's center was the Congressional Budget Office at warp speed.

Now, with these two papers, Republicans had no chance of convincing unbiased observers that our Medicaid reforms saved money without reducing services. Undoubtedly there were good reasons for reforming Medicaid, and a good press adviser could think up justifications for reform that sounded humanitarian. But the major reason that Republicans at the federal level and nearly every state governor, regardless of party, wanted to reform Medicaid was because the program cost too much and the costs were growing wildly.[23] The Republican proposal would have reduced this unsustainable growth, but some of the poor would have less coverage and some would have no health insurance at all. Someday soon policymakers will again be forced to face this trade-off. But in 1996 most Republicans in the House who wanted to reform welfare saw the Medicaid reforms, including controlling costs and saving money, as distinctly secondary to the goal of reforming welfare.[24]

Few doubted that Clinton would veto welfare reform again if the bill we sent him included the Medicaid "poison pill." To avoid this weary outcome, Shaw and other members of the Ways and Means Committee started to work behind the scenes to separate the two bills. Several chapters in this episode are particularly important. The first was an attempt to convince Haley Barbour that he and the Republican National Committee should support passage of a third welfare reform bill. Barbour seemed to be opposed to giving Clinton a third chance to sign a bill because welfare reform, and in particular Clinton's failure to deliver on his campaign promise to "end welfare as we know it," was Dole's best issue in his presidential campaign against Clinton. So way back on January 25, 1996, anticipating that the Dole campaign would oppose sending another bill to the president, Clay Shaw, Dave Camp, a congressman from Louisiana named Jimmy Hayes who had recently switched parties, Ari Fleischer, and I had walked over to Barbour's office at the Republican National Committee headquarters located behind the House office buildings. After some small talk, Shaw set the stage by claiming that House Republicans were growing somewhat concerned that, despite our brilliant start in passing the Contract with America bills through the House and some of them through the Senate, few had been signed into law. After more than a year, the Republican Congress didn't have much to show for all the sound and fury with which we began. Given the popularity of welfare reform with the public, didn't it make sense for Congress to pass it again for the third time and show the nation (not to mention ourselves) that we were not a bunch of rigid ideologues who could not pass legislation the nation wanted? Shaw then argued that sending the bill to Clinton for a third time was a win-win for Republicans: if Clinton refused to sign, we win because Dole's attack on him for not delivering on his campaign promise to "end welfare as we know it" would be strengthened; if he signed, we also win because his signature would split the Democratic Party. Shaw then gave the floor to Jimmy Hayes.

Hayes had a spectacular southern accent and a wit about as big as the Mississippi River. He told Barbour that, as a former Democrat, he knew the thinking of liberals inside out. If Clinton signed the bill, the Democratic Party would implode. Hayes then gave a rendition of the speech Maxine Waters, the fiery black member from California, might give at the Democratic convention. I don't recall the details, but it was folksy, powerful, and funny in equal portions. One comment that he put in Waters's mouth was that Clinton—by signing that vicious, mean, rotten, awful, God-forsaken, Republican welfare reform bill—had signed away the birthright of the Democratic Party and betrayed the nation's poor. Hayes also argued that liberals like Waters would be so upset with Clinton that many of them would refuse to campaign for him or would do so only half-heartedly. With a badly split Democratic Party, Dole would have a much better chance of winning the election. And of course if Clinton didn't sign the bill, Dole's argument that Clinton was standing in the way of welfare reform—the opposite of what he had promised in the last presidential campaign—would be even stronger. It was a friendly, even jocular, meeting, but I left having no idea whether Barbour was convinced that we should pass welfare reform.

Now, more than five months after the Barbour meeting, it appeared that the Dole campaign was moving closer to accepting the inevitable and might not stand in the way of welfare reform. No matter what Barbour or Dole decided, House Republicans were becoming even more certain that we had to pass more legislation in general and welfare reform in particular. An important indication of how Republicans were becoming focused on the welfare reform agenda occurred on June 5 during a meeting of the Ways and Means Committee that Chairman Bill Archer called at Shaw's request. The previous week, in an unexpected move, Gingrich had brought a bill to the floor that would grant a radical waiver to Wisconsin. Clinton had said he would sign the Wisconsin waiver request, but he was now hesitating. So Gingrich, in a move designed purely to embarrass Clinton, brought the waiver to the floor on May 30 and passed it after vigorous debate. Unfortunately, when the Wisconsin waiver bill came to the floor late on Thursday, Shaw was driving to his vacation house in the mountains of North Carolina. When I got Shaw on the phone later that night, he was livid. He couldn't believe that Gingrich and the leadership had decided to bring the Wisconsin waiver to the floor without consulting him. We had been planning to have a meeting of subcommittee members on Wednesday of the following week before the subcommittee markup, but Shaw now wanted me to ask Archer to call a meeting of the entire committee so that he could talk with other members about how the leadership was handling welfare reform.

On June 5, soon after the start of the committee meeting in Archer's Capitol office, Shaw gave a strong, almost emotional, speech about how the leadership was playing games with welfare reform. He called the Wisconsin waiver bill a "trick" and implored members to communicate with other members and the leadership that we should be passing welfare reform and not stepping on our message by fooling around with issues like the Wisconsin waiver. He concluded by saying that he was going to pass the real welfare reform bill out of his subcommittee that day. Shaw had hardly finished when Sam Johnson of Texas, a former prisoner of war in Vietnam and as tough as leather, let loose with a strong condemnation of the leadership in general and Gingrich in particular. He said the leadership was "dragging everyone down," especially by not aggressively supporting welfare reform because they wanted to help Dole. As he concluded his diatribe, he banged his hand on the table and argued, red-faced, that Dole was even behind in Texas and that Republicans should focus their energy on keeping the House, not trying to elect Dole.

Another unexpected event that both reflected the mood of House Republicans and galvanized the determination of Ways and Means Republicans to split welfare reform and Medicaid occurred just before the full committee markup of our new bill on June 12. Room 1100 of the Longworth Building, the Ways and Means hearing room and already the site of several memorable episodes in our story, has a library on the other side of its back wall. The main part of the library is long and narrow and completely filled by a beautiful table about sixteen feet long and covered with green felt. It had been the site of innumerable caucuses among Republicans and Democratic members for as many years as anyone could remember. I was once told by a long-time Ways and Means staffer that the Social Security Act had been signed on that table, a perhaps apocryphal story. However, June 12, 1996, witnessed another in the long line of important caucuses around that imposing table.

As the meeting began, the mood was sober, even somewhat apprehensive. Ever since Clinton vetoed the big budget bill in December and the second welfare reform bill in January, Republicans had been reassessing their strategy; there was growing concern that Gingrich and the leadership had not served the Republican majority very well. Too much strategy, too much PR, too much talk, too much testosterone, too little legislative achievement. After I briefed members on the bill passed by the subcommittee and emphasized the rather modest differences (except for the child care money) with the bill we passed in 1995, members wanted to talk about our plans for the bill once it had cleared full committee. They were especially concerned about whether Archer would ask Gingrich to split our bill from Medicaid.

Jennifer Dunn, who was heading a task force on welfare established by Gingrich to work with the Dole campaign, said she had recently told Gingrich that she thought there was growing sentiment among Republicans to split welfare reform from Medicaid so that a welfare reform bill could be signed. Whereupon, according to Dunn, Gingrich said, "Oh, that's easy. We need to continue supporting the Dole campaign." Gingrich might have meant that we should continue to support the campaign at least in the short run, but that was not what Dunn reported. Jim Bunning, not a person to leave you guessing about his mood, turned bright red and almost shouted that Gingrich didn't care about the Republican majority and that we had to pass welfare reform. I doubt that anyone else present agreed that Gingrich didn't care about the Republican majority in the House, if for no other reason than that, without the majority, he would no longer be Speaker. But I think there was general agreement that we'd better start getting the president's signature on some of our major initiatives or we might no longer have the majority. Not a single person spoke in favor of supporting the Dole campaign.

One outcome of this meeting and the Dunn revelation was that two members of our subcommittee, Dave Camp and John Ensign, took it upon themselves to write to Gingrich and Trent Lott (then the majority leader in the Senate after Dole stepped down to run for president full time) and urge them to separate Medicaid and welfare reform. Fifty-two House Republicans besides Camp and Ensign signed the June 13 letter, whose main argument was that passing welfare reform was "in the best interest of the American people."[25] This was always the best reason for passing welfare reform and was the primary reason many of us believed welfare reform was the most important item on the Republican agenda. Nearly two weeks later, on June 26—prompted in part by many members who said they wanted to sign a letter endorsing the split of welfare reform and Medicaid but had not heard about the June 13 letter in time to sign—Camp and Ensign sent another letter, similar to the first but making two additional arguments. The first, a thinly veiled reference to the lack of legislative achievement after eighteen months of Republican rule, stated flatly that "all the talk in the world about reforming the American welfare state is useless unless our reforms are signed into law." The second struck a more plaintive note, arguing that "we have all worked too hard . . . to risk [welfare reform's] final passage." This letter had ninety-four signatures.

On June 14, the day after the first letter was sent, I had planned a meeting of about twenty House and Senate staffers working on welfare reform in our hearing room. The most important issue, of course, was whether to split welfare reform and Medicaid. The Republican staffers from the House Commerce Committee, Howard Cohen and Eric Berger, arrived just after the meeting started. They had been at Legislative Counsel revising the Medicaid bill. The moment they walked in, I knew they were steamed, probably because they had seen the Camp-Ensign letter. Howard and Eric had barely hit their seats when Howard, looking directly at me, asked if Shaw and Archer were supporting the separation of Medicaid and welfare reform. I told him they were. He and Eric immediately stood up and Howard delivered a pithy statement that had something to do with assholes. As the two of them marched out of the room, I looked at our Senate colleagues and observed that there was still some support in the House for keeping the two bills together.

On June 21, one week after Howard left our meeting in such colorful fashion, the Republican conference met in Room 2123 of the Rayburn Building. Ironically, Room 2123 was the hearing room of the Commerce Committee, the very committee Ways and Means was trying to outflank as we attempted to separate welfare and Medicaid. As always, there were several topics on the conference agenda, but the main item was discussion of Medicaid and welfare, a discussion that Shaw intended to turn into a rehearsal of all the reasons Republicans should split the two bills. As usual, members flowed in and out of the meeting, and many talked in small groups as the meeting proceeded. But Gingrich and Dick Armey were there, as were at least 125 members and perhaps fifteen or twenty staffers.

Shaw, in a measured and reasonable speech lasting about three minutes, opened discussion by presenting a strong case for the split. He said that the Medicaid bill was excellent legislation but that it was ahead of its time (a typical Shaw touch, flattering his opponents while he attempts to defeat them) and was too controversial to pass on its own. Welfare reform was within reach but not if tied to Medicaid. He also made the argument, by now accepted among most Republicans, that despite all the ideas and energy Republicans had brought to the House since their electoral victory in 1994, little had been accomplished. If we wanted to hold onto the House, we'd better pass some legislation, he said, and welfare reform could become the signature achievement of the Republican Congress. Shaw even claimed that welfare reform was the single most important item on the Republican agenda. Chairman Tom Bliley of the Commerce Committee then followed with an equally reasonable speech about the beauties of his committee's Medicaid block grant. He claimed, correctly, that Medicaid was ruining state budgets and that the governors on a bipartisan basis agreed with the block grant approach.

There were several other talks by members from the two committees, but more from Ways and Means than Commerce because we had more members in attendance. As the debate rolled back and forth, a pleasant surprise occurred. Tillie Fowler of Florida, who was not a member of either committee, stood up to make comments.[26] Fowler was a conservative member, especially on defense issues, and was respected for being a thoughtful speaker—and for not favoring the sound of her own voice. She made a very simple argument based on nothing more than experience in her own district. She had no doubt, she said, that her constituents knew about and wanted Congress to pass welfare reform. That able-bodied adults on welfare should work was a popular message in her district. By contrast with the popularity of requiring adults on welfare to work, she said she hardly ever heard anything about Medicaid. She then added that she didn't think that most of her constituents knew the difference between Medicaid and Medicare. Her straightforward conclusion was that Republicans should pass a welfare reform bill that required work because it was so popular.

By the end of the conference it was clear to most of those in attendance, including members of the Commerce Committee, that there was a growing consensus to split the two bills and pass welfare reform. Before the meeting closed, Gingrich got up and said, seeming to imply some sort of conspiracy, that Ways and Means had outorganized Commerce. Implicit in this comment, of course, was Gingrich's conclusion that Ways and Means had won the debate and that most members now believed the bills should be separated.

The question of whether we would split welfare reform and Medicaid had been the focus of media attention for several months. Typical was a headline in the *Congressional Quarterly* in its May 25 issue: "Ignoring Veto Threat, GOP Links Welfare, Medicaid."[27] Both by following developments in the press and by talking constantly with Shaw and with my contacts in the House, the Senate, the Republican National Committee, and the media, I was somewhat informed about developments as they occurred—but only somewhat. We were mired in an intramural fight in which several House and Senate committees, the Republican leadership in both houses, the Republican National Committee, the Dole presidential campaign, and a host of outside interest groups were involved. Even so, that events were moving in our direction was signaled by a headline in the *Congressional Quarterly*'s June 22 issue, less than a month after their article claiming that Republicans would keep welfare reform and Medicaid linked, "GOP May Move to Split Medicaid, Welfare."[28] The article, written by Jeffrey Katz, one of the nation's best welfare reporters (and later a producer at National Public Radio), quoted John Kasich as saying that when the bill emerged from the Budget Committee as part of the Republican reconciliation package, he was not sure whether Medicaid would be included. The Katz article said that Ways and Means Republicans had led the fight to separate the bills, but he did not provide any new information, beyond Kasich's comments, about what was going on behind the scenes.

I heard rumors every day of what Dole, or Gingrich, or Barbour, or Lott, or the conservative groups, or some other center of power was doing to either keep welfare reform and Medicaid together or separate them. But who knew what was really going on? As June wore on, both the rumors and the media stories seemed to show that Republicans were moving steadily toward a split. As early as June 16, even before the meeting of the Republican Conference in which Tillie Fowler spoke in favor of our bill, Dick Armey implied on the Evans and Novak TV program that Republicans might split the two bills. The next day Novak wrote a typically perceptive column about what the split would mean for Republicans. According to Novak, the split showed that House Republicans were taking their fate in their own hands and leaving Bob Dole to look out for his own fate. He quoted Republican Bill Thomas, one of the senior and most powerful members of Ways and Means, as saying, "We have to show that we can govern."[29]

During this entire period, Shaw was encouraging Jimmy Hayes to talk to Republicans about his theory that sending Clinton a good bill would present him with a Hobson's choice of either giving the Dole campaign a good issue or alienating the liberal wing of the Democratic Party. Having watched Hayes present his theory to Haley Barbour, I had no difficulty imagining how impressive it would be to other Republicans. I heard from Ari that one of the many Republicans whom Hayes had regaled was Dick Armey, who almost instantly became a convert. Armey invited Hayes to a leadership meeting on June 12, even before the important meeting of the Republican Conference in the Commerce Committee's hearing room and before the Camp-Ensign letters. Gingrich opened the June 12 meeting with the compelling observation that Clinton would sign a stand-alone welfare bill but would veto a welfare-Medicaid bill. He also told the leadership group that the Dole campaign did not want to give Clinton another chance to sign a welfare reform bill. On this occasion, Hayes added to his Hobson's choice theory the observation that, although the Dole campaign did not want to give Clinton another shot at passing welfare reform, it was committing a double blunder. Not only would the campaign miss a chance to crack apart the Democratic Party, but in the end the story would get out that it was cynically holding up a popular bill to gain an advantage in the presidential race. In short, its strategy of not sending Clinton the welfare reform bill would backfire.

The fight over splitting welfare reform and Medicaid was the single most important struggle as Republicans tried to learn how to govern after assuming the majority in Congress following the historic election of 1994. For all the attention given to the budget deficit and the fights between Republicans and President Clinton over the budget and almost everything else on the agenda, the struggle to extract the welfare reform rabbit from the Medicaid briar patch was the key to Republicans making progress on their reform agenda and to maintaining their congressional majorities. Any historian examining the events I have portrayed and reading contemporaneous media accounts will be forced to admit that it is all but impossible to convey all of the factors that influence a decision of this magnitude. Gingrich and Dole were obviously vital to the final decision, but so were Armey and DeLay. Without them, Gingrich and the rest of the Republican leadership would not have supported a split. But Shaw, Archer, Hayes, Billy Tauzin, and Bunning were important to convincing Armey and DeLay that separation was the best course. For rank and file Republicans, the June 21 meeting of the Republican Conference, and the low-key speech by Tillie Fowler, as well as the two letters from Camp and Ensign, were important. And weaving its way through this complex web of causality was the humorous rendition of the liberal explosion depicted so colorfully by Jimmy Hayes and the constant efforts of Clay Shaw to convince, first Republicans on Ways and Means and then all House Republicans, that we should drop Medicaid and pass welfare reform. These and many other factors led ultimately to the outcome we were so fervently pursuing. On July 10, in a meeting of Gingrich's leadership group, the decision was made to split the bills and send welfare reform as a stand-alone bill to the Senate.[30] Lots of things were now moving in our direction.

But not everything. The Republican governors had been restive ever since the Senate Finance Committee marked up their version of the bill on June 26. In the days following the Finance markup, I talked frequently about the Finance bill with LeAnne Redick and Gerry Miller of Engler's staff as well as other state officials. My general aim was to assure them that we would use the House-Senate conference to change many of the provisions they didn't like in the Senate bill. My assurances seemed to placate them somewhat, but they kept calling and telling me that the governors were getting increasingly upset. So I worked with LeAnne and others to develop a list that we could use to guide Shaw's actions during the House-Senate conference and that LeAnne and Gerry could use with Engler and the other governors to show that we knew their concerns.

Eventually my list included twenty-six items that, for Shaw's use, I divided into three categories by degree of difficulty (easy, medium, hard) in resolving. Most of the items concerned provisions that in some way limited the governors' flexibility. Governors still did not like the maintenance-of-effort requirements on either the welfare block grant or the child care block grant; they wanted us to drop even the modest requirements on child care regulations (most of which had been in the law since 1990); they wanted to reduce Medicaid coverage; they were furious about the stepped-up penalties the Senate bill required them to impose on welfare recipients who did not meet the work requirement and even more upset by the Gramm provision that imposed huge penalties on states that failed to meet the work requirement year after year; and they still demanded to count all families that left welfare against the work requirement. In our view these were serious issues but hardly the deal busters governors were labeling them.

Fearing that the governors were getting too upset over these and similar issues, we set up a conference call involving Gingrich, Lott, Shaw, Archer, Bliley, Bill Roth, and several Republican governors, including Engler. The call took place at five o'clock on July 9, the day before Gingrich's leadership group was scheduled to take up the issue of separating the welfare and Medicaid bills, the discussion of which was another reason for the conference call. The governors were sour, saying they now didn't like either the Medicaid bill or the welfare bill. The welfare provision they seemed to dislike the most was the Gramm penalty provision on states. The call was not a total loss, however, because the governors agreed that separating the welfare reform and Medicaid bills was necessary if we were to move the welfare bill through Congress. Equally important, it was obvious for the first time that Lott believed the bills should be separated. But I knew when the call ended that the governors were not satisfied and that Engler was going to be increasingly difficult to keep happy.

On Sunday, July 14, five days after our conference call with the governors, I got a call at home from LeAnne, who was in Puerto Rico. The governors were in San Juan having their annual summer meeting, and LeAnne wanted me to know how furious they were with the developments on welfare reform. Their anger, she said, was directed mainly against the Finance Committee bill and the Gramm provision. Ari, Shaw, Archer, and I had been working by phone on drafting a response to the president's Saturday radio address on welfare. We had ample opportunity to talk and exchange ideas about how to deal with the governors. LeAnne said that one of the ideas the governors were considering was traveling by private jet to meet with Shaw, who was campaigning in his Ft. Lauderdale district. We changed Shaw's schedule for both Sunday and Monday so he could meet with the governors in Ft. Lauderdale, but that plan was canceled when the governors couldn't get a plane. LeAnne called me at work early Monday morning and told me that the governors were still upset and insisted on seeing Shaw. So LeAnne and I set the meeting for nine-thirty the next morning, Tuesday, July 16, the day before the bill was scheduled for the House floor. Because the annual governors' meeting was still taking place, the governors sent only Governor Leavitt of Utah to represent them at the meeting with Shaw in his Washington office.

Leavitt showed up right on time with LeAnne and one other staffer. Shaw's secretary greeted them and ushered them immediately into Shaw's office, where Shaw and I, plus Shaw's welfare staffer Heather Lank, were waiting. I had already been in Shaw's office for at least half an hour reviewing with him why the governors were so upset. I brought copies of the twenty-six-item list that LeAnne and I had been developing so that we could prepare answers for all the complaints Leavitt was likely to raise.

The meeting got off to a disastrous start. After an exchange of pleasantries, which lasted about five seconds, Leavitt, in a direct and almost heated fashion, told Shaw that he was speaking for all the Republican governors, who were ready to go public in denouncing the bill. Shaw sat quietly looking at Leavitt as he delivered his disquisition. When he finished, Shaw responded in an intense but fully controlled voice. The first thing he said was that Leavitt had gotten the meeting off to the "worst possible start." So we were going to start over and begin with history. Shaw said that he had personally worked with the governors since 1993, that he had carried their water in every hearing and meeting, that we had shared drafts of legislation with them sooner than we did with our own members, and that he had taken every phone call from and accepted every request to meet with governors and to address their meetings in Washington. He had even completely changed his schedule for the last three days so he could accommodate the governors' request for yet another meeting. Given this background, it was too late for governors to desert the process now. No governor was going to go public and denounce the bill we had created together. On the contrary, the purpose of this meeting, as of so many previous meetings with the governors, was to find out exactly what the governors were concerned about and to figure out ways that Shaw could help address these concerns.

Leavitt seemed to be taken aback by the intensity of Shaw's response. He immediately said that Shaw had misinterpreted him, and that he had come to Shaw's office from Puerto Rico specifically to work things out. Leavitt then did a very wise thing—he suggested we talk about the specific issues that concerned the governors. He had come with the list prepared by LeAnne. Because LeAnne and I had been talking so much, our lists were very similar. We worked our way through his list, and Shaw, calling on one of his greatest assets as a lawmaker, showed sympathy for all the concerns raised by Leavitt. On most, as I had repeatedly assured LeAnne, Shaw actually agreed with the governors and on many he felt we could achieve at least part of what the governors wanted during the House-Senate conference. By the time the meeting ended, Leavitt had clearly communicated the governors' concerns about the Finance Committee bill, some of whose provisions (like the maintenance-of-effort requirements) were also in the House bill and were certain to be part of the final legislation. But there seemed little doubt that Leavitt, like the other governors Shaw had dealt with, left with the belief that Shaw would get everything he could for them. Even more notable was the rise of good feelings during the meeting—and it is good feelings that create and maintain a coalition.

Once again, Shaw had made the best of a difficult situation, but we didn't have much time to feel good. Besides, Shaw and I both knew that we had not heard the last from the governors. Neither of us had any doubt that Engler would be a constant presence in Washington until the final bill was passed, and to some extent we welcomed it because our views were so similar to those of the governors. While Governor Leavitt went off to meet with people in the Senate, I dashed to Legislative Counsel to work some more on the bill. We were scheduled to be on the House floor the next day. After meeting with Jim Grossman in the Legislative Counsel's Office to review the bill and make a few more changes, I returned to our Rayburn office and, along with my staffers Matt Weidinger and Cassie Bevan, began writing speeches for the floor debate. LeAnne called about setting up a meeting with Shaw, Johnson, and others to discuss several issues that we had touched on in the meeting that morning. Because the bill could be on the floor the next day and we were trying to get as many issues settled as possible before clearing the bill for the floor, we decided to try to meet that very day.

As it turned out, everyone could meet at three-thirty. This was perfect timing, because Shaw and I had to be at a meeting of the House and Senate leaders at four o'clock to begin discussing the issues we knew would have to be compromised between the House and Senate when we melded the two bills in the House-Senate conference.[31] A tight schedule like this would force everyone to be on time and to have a focused discussion. At the appointed hour, Governors Leavitt and Engler met with Shaw, Johnson, and Mike Castle of Delaware, a former Republican governor, in Nancy Johnson's office. Two items dominated the discussion. On the first, we had earlier agreed to allow governors to transfer funds among the new Temporary Assistance for Needy Families (TANF) block grant that would replace AFDC, the newly expanded child care block grant, and the Title XX block grant that had been in the law since 1981. Democrats, and some Republicans, including Johnson and Castle, had complained that there should be limits to the amount of transferring that states could do. Unlimited transfers would give too much power to the states and would allow them to completely avoid congressional intent in creating the three separate programs. We agreed to place a limit on transfers out of the block grants and to insert language stating that any funds transferred to Title XX were to be spent only on children (or families with children) with incomes under 200 percent of the poverty level.

The second big issue was Medicaid coverage, which continued to plague us even after the Medicaid block grant had been dropped. Johnson was determined that no child would lose Medicaid coverage because of welfare reform. Once she took this position, I never doubted that it or something very close would be in the final bill, and our planning was based on the assumption that we would have to sell broad Medicaid coverage to the governors. Under the Medicaid block grant governors would have been able to reduce coverage. Thus I expected that the governors, having lost the Medicaid block grant, would be determined to fight for looser language that would allow them the "flexibility" to reduce the number of families and the length of time that states would have to provide Medicaid to families leaving welfare. But to my surprise, Engler was willing to cover nearly all families for a year after they left welfare if we would insert a provision that states could deny Medicaid coverage to anyone who refused to work if the state found them a job.[32] Shaw asked Johnson and Castle if they could accept this provision. Both said yes, and we had a deal—assuming that no one in the leadership or on the Commerce Committee had a major problem with it.[33]

Shaw and I left promptly at four to hustle from Johnson's office in the Cannon Building to Archer's office in Room H-208 of the Capitol. Because Chairman Roth somehow did not get the word about the meeting, Shaw and Archer had a good discussion with Senator Don Nickles and Senator Gramm about the upcoming House-Senate conference. Without Roth we could not reach even tentative agreements, but it was nonetheless useful to talk with two of the senators we would be bargaining with in just a few days to produce a final bill. An important outcome of the meeting was that Shaw and I realized how strongly Gramm would push the issue of reducing the number of employees at HHS and how much reducing the number of bureaucrats resonated with other Republicans. So I called my friend Rich Tarplin at HHS, a former top staffer for Senator Christopher Dodd, and asked him for a second time if the administration was worried about the Gramm provision. He said they were. They had been working on language that gave Gramm most of what he wanted but that had enough flexibility so that HHS could live with the provision. I told him to send us their language as soon as possible and I would see if Gramm's staff would accept it.

But now an even more difficult issue than the number of HHS bureaucrats was on the horizon. On major issues in Congress, the main show is usually a fight between the bills offered by the majority and minority parties. But over the years, I often worked with bipartisan groups that disrupted the main show by writing a compromise bipartisan bill that attracted enough votes to cause trouble for the majority. The goal of a bipartisan bill is generally not necessarily to actually win a vote on the floor, although occasionally these centrist groups might be able to pull off this dazzling feat. Rather, the goal is to attract enough votes so that the majority is forced to modify its bill to attract enough centrist votes to retain a majority. Psychology plays a role in this game. Just the threat of a centrist bill will often cause the majority to modify its bill by dropping extreme provisions or by adding moderate provisions favored by the centrists. Just before we conducted our subcommittee markup on June 12, we had learned that Mike Castle, an expert on welfare issues, was working with John Tanner, a moderate Democrat from Tennessee, to write a centrist bill. Like the bill by Nathan Deal before it, Castle-Tanner was modeled on our majority bill but with the edges removed. Shaw and I both regarded Castle-Tanner as a credible threat. But both of us were pleased that the bill was being written by Castle, who we knew would be straight-forward with us throughout the fight. In addition, we had worked often and well with Castle's senior staffers Paul Leonard and Booth Jameson. Both Shaw and I had also worked with Tanner when we were in the minority, especially on welfare and child care issues, and we had a great deal of trust in Tanner and his staff as well.

Not surprisingly, we found out about the bill because Castle had Booth, his main welfare staffer, call me to tell me that Castle intended to work on a bipartisan bill with Tanner. Castle and Tanner hoped to bring their bill to the floor as a substitute for our bill, perhaps with the blessing of the Democratic leadership, unless we modified our bill along the lines they suggested. To discuss Castle's concerns, we met with him for nearly an hour on July 11. The next day Castle sent us a letter outlining the major changes in our bill that were discussed during the meeting, including strengthening the maintenance-of-effort requirement, providing states with an additional $3 billion in guaranteed funding to support their welfare-to-work programs, eliminating the optional Food Stamp block grant, and making several changes that would soften the noncitizen provisions, especially for children. After receiving the letter, Shaw and I were certain that the changes we could offer would not be enough to convince Castle to give up his effort to craft a bipartisan bill. Shaw concluded that the Castle-Tanner bill would become a formidable opponent of our bill but that it would be impossible and unwise to try to kill the bill outright. Our plan was to cut a deal with Castle: we would support his right to bring his bill to the floor as an amendment in the nature of a substitute for our bill if he would speak in favor of our bill and vote for it if we defeated his bill. We also intended to ask him to try to get his supporters to vote for our bill after his had been defeated. This strategy, which we discussed with Castle, was a little risky (what if his bill passed?), but Shaw and I were confident that we would prevail.

Jim Talent was not as confident about this strategy as Shaw and I were. During the two years and more that Shaw and I had been working with Talent as we fought, at first against each other but now side-by-side, to write and enact a strong welfare reform bill, Talent and I had developed a solid working relationship. I kept him well informed of important developments, usually by talking with him at meetings of the Republican Conference or by phone. I also spoke frequently with his welfare staffer, Kiki Kless, and with Robert Rector of the Heritage Foundation, with whom Talent and his staff were working closely. As the floor debate neared and Castle looked for other members to support his bill, Talent became concerned that Castle might be making too much headway and might be trashing our bill, something Castle had promised not to do. At nine in the morning of July 17 the Republican Conference met in Room HC-5 in the basement of the Capitol to make final plans for the impending floor debate on welfare reform. The meeting was actually a kind of pep rally, with at least 150 members in attendance amid a somewhat raucous atmosphere.

During the meeting Talent paced back and forth in a small storage room adjoining Room HC-5; it was possible to talk in the storage room without disrupting the proceedings in HC-5. By leaving the door open, it was also possible to simultaneously keep an eye on the proceedings. I kept going back to talk with Talent, but he was getting more and more upset worrying that Castle was trying to turn Republicans against our bill. At that very moment, Castle was engaged in what looked like intense discussions with two or three members. Shaw had worked very hard to maintain harmony among all the key players; the day on which we were scheduled to begin the final showdown on the floor was not a good time to allow dissension among our forces. So I told Talent I would go over and just ask Castle what he was doing. As soon as I approached Castle, I could tell that he was not even discussing welfare. Rather, he and the other members were discussing a totally unrelated bill. Hustling back to Talent with a big smile on my face, I told him Castle was not even discussing welfare. Talent then made a sincere and moving little speech to the effect that he was an overly suspicious and flawed individual. He concluded by saying, "God isn't finished with me yet." You can get a lot accomplished working with a guy like Talent.

God was not through with any of us yet. As we prepared for the floor debate, we had had a short and routine meeting with Republicans on the Rules Committee on July 16. We recommended that Castle-Tanner be allowed to come to the floor for debate and voting, but the decision on this issue was deferred. Only the Speaker could make a decision of this magnitude. To promote efficient use of available floor time, the Rules Committee decided to conduct two hours of general debate before publishing the final rule. Around four-thirty on July 17, David Hobson of Ohio, who was on both the Appropriations and Budget Committees, came to the floor and asked unanimous consent to once again start a general debate on welfare reform, with the Budget Committee controlling the time. There was no objection (an early sign that Democrats were mellowing on welfare reform), and Kasich was soon recognized to initiate debate. The debate was still partisan and somewhat negative, but it was a taffy pull compared with the previous floor debates.

As the afternoon wore on, Shaw and I met with Gingrich, Chairman Solomon, and several members and staffers from Gingrich's office and the Rules Committee in Solomon's office adjacent to the Rules Committee hearing room on the third floor of the Capitol. The leadership had decided that there would be a relatively simple rule: inserted into the bill would be a Republican amendment to convey our agreements with the governors; a batch of technical changes; and an amendment, sponsored by Kasich, that strengthened work requirements in the Food Stamp program. In addition, as always, Democrats would be given the right to offer a motion to recommit either with or without instructions.[34] Gingrich invited us to the meeting because he wanted to be sure that, if the Castle-Tanner bill were allowed to come to the floor for debate, we would have the votes to keep it from passing. After making his concern clear, and emphasizing again that the leadership wanted a simple rule, he asked us whether we should allow the Castle-Tanner substitute to come to the floor. Shaw and I simultaneously answered yes.[35] After some quizzing by Gingrich about whether we could hold our votes against Castle-Tanner, and assurances from us that we could, he agreed. Now the rule was set, and the meeting was quickly adjourned—although Gingrich still had enough doubt that he later sent a signed letter to every member of the Republican caucus reminding them that Castle-Tanner had to be defeated. The next morning, July 18, Porter Goss of Florida, representing the Rules Committee, appeared on the floor of the House and was recognized by the Speaker to place the rule before the House. After an hour of relatively mild debate, the rule was passed overwhelmingly on a vote of 358 to 54, another welcome sign that Democrats were mellowing.

Following general debate, there was a decorous discussion of the Kasich amendment to require work of able-bodied adults on Food Stamps who had no children. The Kasich amendment was adopted on a vote of 239 to 184, after which the House turned to the Castle-Tanner substitute. Of the many hours of floor debate on welfare reform in 1995 and 1996, the Castle-Tanner debate was the most constructive. There was not a hint of name-calling, and several members gave impressive speeches based exclusively on their analysis of provisions in the bill. In accord with our agreement, both Castle and Tanner focused their remarks on the Shaw bill entirely on provisions they either did not like or considered to be lacking. The mild debate on Castle-Tanner indicated to those of us who had been through the debate in 1995 that much of the fire had gone out of the Democrats and that some of them were now, as Shaw had predicted in that first subcommittee markup back in February 1995, characterizing our bill in terms that would allow them to support it later. Liberal Democrats were realizing that a bill they despised had a good chance of becoming law and could well be signed by their president.

As soon as the allotted hour of debate had expired, the speaker announced a recorded vote. Within a minute or so, Shaw was joined on the floor by Gingrich, Armey, and DeLay, all of whom began lobbying Republicans to stick with Shaw and not support Castle-Tanner. They didn't have to say much. Just seeing the leaders on the floor showed our members how high the stakes were and, after nearly eighteen months of party discipline, they knew unity was the key to legislative success. Once again, Republican discipline was superb: Castle-Tanner got only 168 votes in favor, 258 against. Only nine Republicans voted for the bill, and its fate was sealed when thirty-six Democrats also voted against it.[36] As the vote proceeded, the smile on Shaw's face kept getting bigger and bigger. After one more vote, on which we defeated the motion to recommit by 220 to 203, the House moved to final passage without further debate.

In the beautiful and spare words that have been uttered by the Speaker on thousands of occasions over more than 200 years as the House prepares to take its final vote on a bill: "The question is on the passage of the bill." Republicans responded with a nearly unanimous vote (only four voted no). Thirty Democrats joined us (only nine had supported HR 4 in March 1995, and seventeen had supported the conference report on HR 4 in December). The final vote was 256 to 170.[37] We were making progress with Democrats and moving toward a truly bipartisan revolution in welfare. We had leaped the hurdles put up by Medicaid, the Dole campaign, and the Republican governors, and now at last we were attracting support from more than a handful of Democrats.

The Senate passed its bill five days later, on July 23. The Senate vote was an impressive seventy-four to twenty-four, with nearly twenty Democrats supporting the bill. The Senate also appointed members to the House-Senate conference on July 23; the House followed suit on July 24. Now we were in the home stretch. There was not the slightest doubt in my mind that we would send Clinton another bill. But would he sign it?

## CHAPTER FOURTEEN

# Triumph:
# Clinton Signs

At four-thirty in the afternoon of July 25, 1996—two days after the Senate had passed its bill—House and Senate Republican conferees met in the middle room of Trent Lott's office, around that big rectangular table—the same table where Jim McCrery had asked Senator John Chafee's staffer to stop whispering in his ear. The major purpose of the meeting was for Lott and Newt Gingrich to give the conferees a pep talk about the importance of finishing our work quickly. Lott was there but Gingrich had been detained. Others present were Clay Shaw, Phil Gramm, Orrin Hatch, Jim Talent, Don Nickles, Bill Archer, Nancy Johnson, Jim McCrery, Bill Roth, and Rick Santorum. Gingrich arrived, staying only long enough to give the pep talk about finishing quickly.

John Chafee initiated the discussion, with our list of outstanding issues in hand. It soon became evident that what had been scheduled as essentially a pep talk was turning into a major negotiating session. By around seven in the evening the discussion was still going strong. We broke for about an hour for dinner and then came back and started arguing again.[1] At the stroke of midnight we were just completing discussion on the last issue.

In a meeting full of friendly banter and sharp disagreements, the most memorable exchange occurred between Shaw and Gramm. Widely feared for his verbal skills, his quick wit, and his use of power and influence to deal harshly with those who crossed him, Gramm was a major presence in this meeting—and every meeting I ever sat in with him. He was especially animated in this meeting because he was concerned about a provision he was intent on getting into the final bill. Specifically, he wanted to deny welfare to anyone who had a felony drug conviction. Many, perhaps most, Republicans supported drug provisions of this type.

The instant Gramm finished his spirited explanation and defense of his drug provision, the mild-mannered and gentlemanly Clay Shaw hit the table with his open hand, startling everyone in the room. Seated across from Gramm, he looked directly at him and delivered an impassioned little speech that began with the simple statement, which he virtually shouted, that the bill "is about the future and about hope" and that he would not allow a provision that condemns people for their past behavior in the bill.[2] When Shaw finished, I think most of those present knew he opposed the Gramm provision. For his part, Gramm responded in a very reasonable and calm manner, arguing that something had to be done about drug use by welfare mothers and that the real victims of drugs were the children. My notes are not clear on who said what after the opening salvos, but within a few minutes an agreement was reached to put in the Gramm drug provision as a state option. However, in a nod to the popularity of Gramm's position, the state option that conferees agreed to was making it an opt-out provision rather than an opt-in provision; that is, states that did not want to follow the Gramm provision had to enact a law to exempt themselves, the same approach that Gramm and Faircloth were fighting so hard to get for the family cap.[3]

With the entertainment out of the way, conferees turned to solving the remaining issues, including how much to reduce the Title XX block grant, whether to increase the authority of the secretary of Health and Human Services (HHS) to impose penalties on states that did not meet the work requirements, the specifics of the Medicaid provisions, the amount of funding for a performance bonus, how much to cut the Earned Income Tax Credit (EITC), and a number of other issues. Hanging over the meeting was the understanding that, although the Senate would not agree to the opt-out on the family cap, powerful conservative groups outside Congress were insisting on an opt-out. Clearly, something had to give.

At around ten o'clock, facing the reality that the family cap would in all likelihood be killed by the Byrd rule anyway and that we didn't have time to try to pass the conference report twice in the House (the second time after the family cap had been Byrded to death in the Senate), conferees decided to be silent on the family cap, a decision guaranteed to send Robert Rector of the Heritage Foundation—and many other conservatives—over the cliff. Because Temporary Assistance for Needy Families (TANF) was a block grant and provided states with immense flexibility, any state would be free to adopt the family cap, and eventually about half did.[4] But Rector and others wanted to require every state to adopt the provision or at least to make it an opt-out. The Senate flatly rejected both positions. After some discussion, we decided that Jim Talent should call Rector and inform him of our decision. Talent went off to use the phone in another office, returning about twenty minutes later clutching a piece of paper. As was his wont, Rector had presented a counteroffer: he would support dropping the family cap if we would make abstinence education an entitlement program (that is, provide it with guaranteed funding that did not have to be appropriated each year) and also provide $100 million a year in entitlement funds for the illegitimacy bonus (a bonus that would give cash rewards to states that reduced their illegitimacy rates). I was not surprised that Rector was ready with a counteroffer; his proposals would be supported by a majority of Republicans in the House and were both, in my view, good policy. So we reached a compromise with the Senate on terms that actually improved the conference report.

By midnight all differences between the House and Senate bills had been discussed, and we had proposals or agreements to resolve most of them. We had settled four of the biggest issues by dropping the optional Food Stamps block grant, cutting back on EITC changes so that we would include only changes supported by the president, adopting the House provision allowing noncitizens to receive benefits from education and training programs (as well as the EITC), and dropping the child protection block grant. Shaw had entered the session prepared to adopt all four of these compromises because they did not undermine the work requirement and did not lose much money. It was a shame to lose the child protection block grant, but given Senator Chafee's power and influence, it had been a long shot from the beginning. Besides, it was time to fold on provisions that were too controversial in order to hold the sweeping reforms that remained. Shaw was especially intent on doing everything within reason to make the conference report easier for the president to sign, and all these compromises certainly did just that.

The three issues that seemed likely to continue posing problems were interethnic adoption,[5] which would probably be removed from the conference report by the Byrd rule, language on workers' rights, and the specifics of the Medicaid transition. As often happens with big conference reports, one or more of these issues might be unresolved right up until the night before the final votes, and the lobbying would be spectacular. But driving home in the early morning blackness of the George Washington Parkway, I was as ebullient as a person could be after midnight reflecting on a day's work. As I thought back twenty-one months to that cold and dark early morning journey going the opposite direction on the parkway, I could now see the bright sunlight in the Rose Garden as President Clinton signed our revolution into law. We were headed home.

But we weren't quite there yet. The next several days, including the weekend, were a blur of activity as we drafted the agreements, prepared floor statements, dealt with what seemed like a thousand technical issues for the final conference report, lobbied members of the House at both member and staff levels to ensure they would back our report and to detect any serious opposition to the compromises we were reaching, and talked incessantly with the governors and their staffs in hopes of avoiding any last-minute crises.

As my staff and I pursued all these final activities, so typical for the endgame of major legislation, I got a call from LeAnne Redick, John Engler's staffer in Washington, that Engler was coming to town with Governor Terry Branstad of Iowa to discuss the remaining issues, plus some additional issues that the conferees thought were already resolved. The meeting was set for Monday, July 29, at twelve-forty-five in the House Republican leadership's office in Room H-230 of the Capitol, the Speaker's conference room. The plan was for the governors to meet with the House and Senate leadership to raise the issues that were bothering them and then to review the agreements reached in the long July 25 meeting. In this way, the governors would have a chance to comment on the current status of all the major provisions in the bill. The leadership wanted to have the final conference report on the floor by Wednesday, July 31, if at all possible and wanted no last-minute surprises. Everyone showed up right on time, and after some small talk, substantive discussions were well under way by one o'clock.

Three issues dominated the discussions, one of which was surprising: whether states could keep their waivers once the legislation had been enacted. (Most of these waivers allowed states to establish tougher work requirements than permitted under the Aid to Families with Dependent Children [AFDC] law.) To my knowledge, this issue had barely been mentioned before Engler brought it up during the meeting on July 29. I was caught flat-footed, though the problem was apparent: the Bush and Clinton administrations had granted such waivers to twenty-five states. But if our legislation passed, the work requirements under the new TANF block grant would be tougher than even the relatively strong requirements permitted under the waivers to AFDC law. Thus many governors supported—or at least didn't object to—the strong TANF work requirements because they believed their waivers would allow them to avoid the new requirements for at least a few years (by which time someone else might be governor). The issue now was whether we would permit the waivers to continue. Republican conferees wanted to kill the waivers so that all states would be subject to the tough new TANF requirements. But the governors, arguing that the waivers constituted a promise given by the federal government to allow states to conduct a specific work program for a specific number of years, wanted us to continue the waivers under the new law.[6]

The second issue was also a late arrival. Good evaluations showed that education programs for welfare mothers were at best modestly successful.[7] Republican moderates had joined the governors in convincing us to allow some education, but the House-Senate conference in 1995 had placed a 20 percent cap on use of education and had also prohibited any mother from having her participation in education count as work for more than twelve months.[8] We also required teen mothers to stay in school or lose their benefits. The question now arose whether teen moms counted under the 20 percent cap, which would further restrict how much education states could count as work. Both Talent and Shaw wanted all education under the cap, but the governors didn't, because it limited their flexibility.

Just as the discussion was getting serious, Gingrich and Lott had to leave to meet with the president. Someone pointed out that their priorities were warped: what kind of Republican would leave our hundredth negotiating session on welfare reform merely to meet with the president of the United States, and a Democrat at that? Nonetheless, although President Clinton was once again disrupting our march toward truth and justice in welfare reform, we adjourned a little before two o'clock and agreed to reassemble at five. Amazingly, almost everyone was back by five. Senator Don Nickles joined the group, as did Talent by phone.[9] We immediately reengaged on the education issue. Talent, arguing with Engler over the phone, was adamant about limiting education. Inevitably, someone had a great idea: Why don't we give the governors what they want on waivers and Talent and Shaw what they want on the education cap? Everyone subscribed to this obvious compromise, and both issues were settled.

The third issue, however, could not be settled so easily. Medicaid once again reared its ugly head. Medicaid issues had been afflicting us since the governors announced their "bipartisan" agreement on February 6. The leadership had already decided to jettison the block grant in order to avoid a veto, but now another Medicaid problem took its place, and we had only a day or two at most to solve it. Nearly every Democrat and many Republicans, led by Nancy Johnson in the House and John Chafee in the Senate, wanted to ensure that no children lost Medicaid coverage because of welfare reform. The statute required states to provide Medicaid coverage to every adult and child receiving AFDC. But if we now gave states more flexibility to create a new work-based welfare program with a primary goal, backed by incentives and penalties, of getting adults off welfare and into work, some states might lower their income and resource requirements for TANF and thereby drop families between the higher income and resources cutoff and the new, lower cutoffs. If Medicaid were tied to TANF as it had been to AFDC, these families would also lose their Medicaid. The most straightforward solution was to lock in place the current state income and resources standards for AFDC as the permanent qualifications for Medicaid. The problem with this solution was that it would force states that made their TANF eligibility criteria less generous than their AFDC criteria to compute two eligibilities—one for their new TANF program and another for the old AFDC program—to determine whether the family qualified for Medicaid.

Engler hated this provision. From the first moment it surfaced, he vowed to oppose the conference report if states had to compute two eligibilities. From his perspective, computing two eligibilities was a complete waste of time and money. Now when Engler raised the issue again with Gingrich and Lott, we had had the foresight to make sure that Howard Cohen, our Medicaid guru from the Commerce Committee, was present to help us find a compromise as well as determine the feasibility of compromises that might be proposed. Given our impending date on the House floor, we didn't have time to waste on dead-end "solutions." After lots of discussion, Howard said that he could draft language that would guarantee Medicaid coverage to all or nearly all children who would have been covered under AFDC and do so without requiring two eligibility determinations. At this point, the meeting ended. Howard, joined later by a horde of House and Senate staffers, both Republican and Democratic, went off to Legislative Counsel to begin drafting.

Meanwhile, Matt Weidinger and I, joined by a senior staffer from the Education Committee named D'Arcy Phelps, worked until a little after one o'clock in the morning on the conference report and on a brief document summarizing the report that we could give to members, staff, and the press. Returning at about five-thirty, I started working again on the same materials. When the Legislative Counsel's Office opened at nine o'clock, I started running back and forth between our office in the Rayburn Building and the Legislative Counsel's Office in the Cannon Building to meet with Jim Grossman, who was drafting the conference report.

Sometime around noon, Rich Tarplin, my friend at HHS, called with a long list of technical changes for the report. I told him I didn't have time to read the list myself but would do something about it. More important, I asked, did he have the language we needed to accommodate the Gramm provision on cutting staff at HHS? He did and promised to send it right over. I then called Gene Falk, a welfare expert from the Congressional Research Service, and asked him to review the HHS list and tell me the truly technical changes I should make in the report. Several hours later he called me back with ten or so changes from HHS's list that we should make. Meanwhile we had set up a meeting at Legislative Counsel with Senator Gramm's staff and Jim Grossman. By blending HHS's language on the Gramm provision with Gramm's original language, Jim had already written a new version. After brief discussion, Gramm's staffers accepted the new language with a few minor changes and it was slipped into the final legislation, along with many of HHS's technical changes.

Now another nasty little problem arose. At this point, I began to feel like I was playing that carnival game Whack-a-Mole, in which moles pop out of a dozen or so holes in a board in random order and the player tries to hit them with a club before they drop back into their hole. Every time you hit one, another pops up. Now that pesky Wisconsin waiver was popping up. As if we had not already had enough trouble with the waiver, Governor Tommy Thompson and several members of the Wisconsin delegation were trying to jam the provision into our pristine welfare reform report. The problems were the same as when Gingrich brought the waiver to the House floor in May: it was certain to have a cost, and it was polit-ically unwise. At about four in the afternoon, as I was meeting with Jim Grossman, the Congressional Budget Office (CBO) returned my phone call from earlier in the day and confirmed my suspicion that the waiver would have a cost. However, they would not have an estimate of the cost for another few days. But we had only another few hours to decide whether to put the provision in the report. Because Gingrich wanted to do everything possible to enact the provision, I decided that I would ask him directly whether to include it now that CBO was confirming that it would have a cost and therefore reduce savings from the legislation.

Granted, I was not exactly neutral in this decision. Although I regarded the waiver as good policy and would have strongly supported it under other circum-stances, it had gained prominence only because Gingrich brought it to the floor to embarrass Clinton. If we included it in our report, it could become one more jus-tification for a Clinton veto. I was already worried about the very difficult decision Clinton would soon be required to make. Democrats in the House and Senate would want to know whether he was going to sign the legislation before they cast their vote on the conference report. We were moving so fast that the vote on the conference report would probably be tomorrow, leaving Clinton less than twenty-four hours away from a final decision. I imagined some sort of big meeting, with all his advisers and perhaps some Cabinet members debating the decision. We had already taken so many actions to strengthen the hand of Bruce Reed, Dick Morris, and others who wanted Clinton to sign the legislation that it struck me as crazy to now give an additional argument to Donna Shalala, Robert Reich, and others who would urge Clinton to veto the legislation. I could see Shalala telling the president that Gingrich was giving him one final insult by shoving the Wisconsin waiver in his eye. My goal was to prevent Shalala from having this opportunity.

Now, as I was about to ask Gingrich for a final decision on the Wisconsin waiver, I wanted CBO to give me at least an approximation of the waiver's cost so I could give Gingrich a good reason to kill it. As expected, CBO resisted. So we went through a little game in which I played, "Is it more than x?" and CBO responded "Possibly." Through repeated prompting of this sort, I got enough information out of the analyst that I felt justified in claiming that the waiver could cost as much as a billion dollars over five years. In the immortal words of Everett Dirksen, a billion is real money.

A quick phone call revealed that Gingrich was in a meeting in the Dinosaur Room.[10] I dashed out of Legislative Counsel's Office, ran across Independence Avenue, and entered the Capitol through the south staff entrance, winding up in the Dinosaur Room in a minute and a half, tops. A new world record. And sur-prise, Gingrich had been in a meeting with members who had now gone to the House floor for a vote. He was still sitting at his long conference table talking with Bob Walker, a member from Pennsylvania and one of Gingrich's most trusted advisers. I barged in, interrupted their discussion, quickly summarized the situation, and concluded with the CBO concern that, because the waiver could lead to increased Food Stamp and Medicaid costs, the waiver could reduce our savings by as much as $1 billion over five years. Then I asked, "In or out?" Gingrich never skipped a beat: "Out," he said. And returned to his discussion with Walker. The guy could be decisive. Little did either of us know that he would have to be decisive again before the day was over.

Running back to Legislative Counsel, I broke my recently established world record but nearly got splattered by a black Lincoln Town Car on Independence Avenue. Upon my arrival, I was immediately sorry that I had leaped out of the way of that black Lincoln. Assembled in one of the Legislative Counsel meeting rooms was a bevy of Republican and Democratic staffers continuing the Medicaid argument from the night before. It was now almost five in the afternoon, and they had returned to their marathon bargaining. Howard was yelling at a Democratic staffer, who was apparently on the phone with Andy Schneider, the Democrats' major guru on health issues. Standing just outside the door of the meeting room, I heard Howard yell, "How many times have I told you! No one outside the committee can be involved." Killing two birds with one stone, I stepped inside the door and asked Howard if I could talk with him alone outside the room. He came outside, and I asked him whether they were any closer to acceptable Medicaid language than they had been the night before. He equivocated a little, but within seconds I realized that the Chafee and Johnson staffers—let alone the Democrats—were not satisfied with the Medicaid language.

Howard then went back to his slugfest, and I stepped back into the hallway. As I collected my thoughts, I noticed Dave Camp's office across the hall, which brought to mind the complaint about Medicaid from Governor Engler of Michigan (Camp's state), which brought to mind that Gingrich asked us to find a solution to Medicaid that did not require two eligibility determinations. Which reminded me that, in trying to do just that, we were going against the decision of the House and Senate conferees to adopt the dual-eligibility solution. Somehow these distractions, which buzzed through my mind in a minute or less, led me to a sudden conclusion, which should have been obvious the previous day or at least a few minutes ago when I heard Howard yelling at Democrats: no one would be able to write Medicaid language that would satisfy Johnson, Mike Castle, Chafee, and the Democrats in the time remaining. It followed that we were going to have the dual-eligibility determination, which the governors hated. And from that it followed that we were going to have big trouble with Governor Engler. A decision of this magnitude could only be made by Gingrich. But first I had to make sure that Shaw and Camp would support it.

Now my primary mission was to find Shaw and Camp, brief them on the situation, and with Shaw tell Gingrich that it was our judgment that Howard's drafting would fail and that we were going to revert to the dual-eligibility determination, which would unleash the wrath of the governors. Shaw and Camp would probably both be back in town by now, after returning to their home districts to campaign over the weekend (the elections were now a little more than three months away). In all likelihood, they would be attending the meeting of the Republican Conference, which began at five o'clock in Room HC-5 of the Capitol. Once again, I made the dangerous trip from Cannon to the Capitol, this time actually waiting for the stoplight on Independence Avenue and walking most of the way.

Arriving at HC-5, I immediately encountered Shaw standing by the doorway. We walked to the back of the room and entered the small storage room that adjoins HC-5, the same room in which Talent had told me that God was not yet finished with him. I quickly reviewed the situation for Shaw, concluding with the recommendation that we stiff the governors and adopt the dual-eligibility approach. Whatever we did, I told him, we had to do it fast, or we would not be able to file our report today and have it on the floor tomorrow. Spying Jack Howard, one of Gingrich's top staffers, I summoned him over to ask him where we could find Gingrich. Jack told us that he was in a meeting across the hall in Room HC-3. We went out the back door of the anteroom and found that Gingrich was still in his meeting. Shaw stuck his head in; Gingrich asked him to wait a few minutes.

We retired across the hallway, to Room HC-2, which was vacant. As we engaged in small talk, killing time, an event occurred like no other I had ever experienced in a decade as a congressional aide. A certain Republican member appeared suddenly to inquire about a provision that he and a group of Republicans were trying to get into the conference report. I had not heard about the provision until earlier that day, when a senior House Republican whom I had worked with before explained the provision to me, said Shaw had told him to talk with me, and asked if I could help. I asked if he had a CBO cost estimate, but he did not. So I told him I would talk with CBO and, if the provision was free or of very low cost, clear it with Shaw and stick it in the report. Now this House Republican interested in the provision was questioning me very aggressively about why the provision was not already in the report. I explained to him that we could not put it in the report until we knew more about its cost.

At that point he yelled that I was giving him the runaround and that he was sick of it. As he was speaking, he kept moving closer to me; his nose could not have been more than six inches from mine. At that point, Shaw stepped between us as I took a step back. Shaw told the guy that he needed to calm down. In fact, Shaw told him we'd take care of the problem and to find something else to do besides harass staffers who did not work for him. I had seen a number of incidents like this one, sometimes between staffers and members, sometimes between staffers, and sometimes between members. They were especially likely to occur at the end of a Congress, when everyone had been working sixteen- or eighteen-hour days. For what it's worth, I had already talked with CBO, and they later informed me the provision had no cost. Shaw was tempted to leave this provision out of the report, but we slipped it in, and it is now part of the statutes of the United States.

After about thirty minutes, Gingrich came out of Room HC-2. Shaw and I started to explain the issue to him, but he quickly indicated that he remembered it well from the discussion with Engler on the previous day. So I simply told him that Howard Cohen and his merry band had been at Legislative Counsel for many hours, drafting, and didn't seem to be making much progress. It was time to fold 'em and go with the dual-eligibility policy that Engler didn't like. Gingrich reflected a moment and said to go ahead. Another quick and wise decision, although we would soon discover that Gingrich needed to reinforce this decision one more time before we could put the report—and ourselves—to bed. Within a few minutes, I was back at Legislative Counsel telling Howard that we were going to go ahead with the dual eligibility. We already had a version of this policy drafted, so we just slipped it into the report, and Howard and the others folded their tents. I then called my office and found out that LeAnne had called and wanted to see the new language on Medicaid. I thought about not returning her call. It was already past eight at night, and I could tell her later that I had been too busy to return her call. But we had been working together in good faith for a long time, and not returning her call would be a lousy way to behave. Besides, Engler was so mercurial that if he found out the next day that the dual-eligibility provision was in the final report, he might do something extreme.

When I got LeAnne on the phone, she told me that Engler was attending a black-tie dinner party in Michigan but had left strict orders to call him on his cell phone as soon as she had seen the new Medicaid language and had determined whether states would have to compute dual eligibility. I gave her the bad news. She was, of course, pretty upset. After a few minutes of somewhat unpleasant comments, she said she would call Engler and then call me back at Legislative Counsel. She called back within twenty minutes or so and informed me that Engler was furious and was threatening to call a press conference first thing in the morning and denounce the Republican leadership and the report. What a story that would make: House Republicans taking their final welfare reform legislation to the floor while it was being trashed by Governor Engler, previously one of the bill's most fervid supporters. Not good. I told her I'd call her back in a few minutes.

I immediately called Gingrich's office and wound up with Dan Meyer, Gingrich's capable and completely unflappable chief of staff. Dan was only vaguely aware of the Medicaid problem, but he fully understood the part about Engler calling a press conference and attacking our legislation. He said he'd find Gingrich and call right back. Instead, he found several senior staffers, all of whom worked for members of the Republican leadership, and called me back at Legislative Counsel for a group discussion. I reviewed the situation for everyone and pointed out that we needed to decide something within an hour because under House rules we had to file the conference report before midnight in order to get it on the floor tomorrow. It was already past nine, and we needed some time to copy the report and related documents before we could file. As we talked I had an idea. Let's throw half a billion dollars into the Medicaid provision and say it's money to be divided up among the states for the extra costs they incur computing dual eligibility. I would call LeAnne back, tell her about the new provision, which we would be inserting just for Governor Engler (I planned to tell her we knew Engler could be bought for half a billion), and then see what he would do. In other words, we would initiate a high-stakes game of chicken with the governor. No one had a better idea, so we all agreed that Dan would call Gingrich and see if he was up for a little midnight game of chicken. Dan promised to call me back within a few minutes. As soon as we hung up, I called Shaw and brought him up to date. He liked the idea of giving a little to Engler and the other governors to placate them. No sooner had I hung up than Dan Meyer called back. He had one word for me: "File!"

We filed a little after midnight, on July 31. I regretted missing the deadline; not only would filing late give Democrats another thing to gripe about, but also (my thinking might have been a little frazzled at this point) the Rules Committee would need to waive a point of order against the report because we were filing after midnight (it was in violation of House rules to take legislation to the floor the same day it was filed). With these sorts of exciting thoughts rolling around in my mind, I somehow made it home, set the alarm, slept for a few hours, leaped out of bed at the sound of the alarm, then zoomed back down the George Washington Parkway to begin another big day, perhaps the biggest and most important of all.

Back in my office by around seven in the morning, I started writing floor speeches and making plans for contacting potential speakers. By ten-thirty Matt and I were on the floor with Shaw and a number of members from the Rules Committee and the Budget Committee waiting for the final debate to begin. By a little before eleven o'clock the one-minute speeches, a regular feature of the beginning of House sessions, seemed to be about over. We were next, and the finish line was in sight. Another three hours or so and the final vote would be over. But wait! What is Democrat Lloyd Doggett, the last of the one-minute speakers, doing with a big poster board? To use an exhibit during a one-minute speech requires unanimous consent or a recorded vote. Doggett rose to the podium and asked for unanimous consent to use a chart. Gradually it became clear that Democrats were not ready for the home stretch.[11]

The reason, as we were informed by Republican floor staffers who had talked with their Democratic colleagues, was that President Clinton had not yet told the Democrats whether he planned to sign the legislation. Lots of Democrats were wavering and were likely to do whatever the president was going to do. Above all, many of them did not want to vote against the report if Clinton was going to sign it into law. Thus the Democratic leadership was frantically trying to contact their old friend and former chairman of the Budget Committee Leon Panetta, now the president's chief of staff. But Clinton and a substantial portion of his staff, including Panetta and several Cabinet secretaries, were camped out in the Cabinet Room deep in debate about whether the president should sign.

We were about to enter a period of congressional time-out. Democrats were determined not to allow the debate to begin until they knew what Clinton would do and, in the meantime, would use parliamentary maneuvers to burn time. Unlike most such periods of delay, Republicans were not particularly opposed to going along, at least at the outset. After Doggett asked for unanimous consent to use a chart on the House floor, Harold Volkmer, a Democrat from Missouri, objected to the request and asked for a recorded vote, which would eat up twenty or twenty-five minutes; 386 members voted to allow Doggett to use a chart.[12] Robert Wise, a Democrat from West Virginia, offered a motion to reconsider that vote, whereupon Mike Castle moved to lay that motion on the table. Another recorded vote followed, this time on Castle's motion, resulting in the Wise motion being tabled. The previous vote stood; Doggett could use his chart. Now Volkmer offered the motion to adjourn, which was defeated by yet another recorded vote. At this point, with members growing a little impatient with the waiting and walking back and forth from their House office buildings to the floor, Doggett gave his talk, which happened to be on the topic of terrorism, ostensibly clarifying his argument by use of the chart. Careful observation and study, however, revealed that Doggett's chart was not likely to clarify very much about his speech: it was blank. When Doggett finished, Democrats offered another motion to adjourn. This motion, too, was defeated by recorded vote.

Nearly an hour and a half had been used up by these delays, but the Democrats had more delaying tactics. Their whip, David Bonior from Michigan, offered another motion to adjourn, which was handily defeated by yet another recorded vote (even a majority of Democrats voted against the motions to adjourn, demonstrating that they were simply stalling). Scott McInnis from the Rules Committee gained recognition to offer a procedural motion. In the course of his talk, he mentioned that Joe Moakley of Massachusetts, the senior Democrat on the Rules Committee, had endorsed the rule.

When McInnis finished speaking, Moakley leaped to his feet and said that his support for the rule had been conditional on getting the report by eight o'clock the previous night. Because Democrats didn't get the report until nearly an hour after midnight, he could no longer support the rule. Moakley yielded to Democrat Mike Ward of Kentucky, who also wanted to use a chart. Like Doggett's, Ward's chart was blank. He might even have used the same chart on the grounds that the blank chart Doggett used could be used with speeches on any topic. But no, Democrat Rosa DeLauro of Connecticut objected to these preposterous charts and called for a vote on whether the blank chart should again be allowed to be displayed on the floor of the House. This series of events prompted Dave Weldon, a Republican from Florida, to observe that it seemed a bit much to have recorded votes over blank charts. He asked the Speaker pro tem to rule the vote out of order on the grounds that it was dilatory, a class of actions that are prohibited under paragraph 803, section 10, of Jefferson's Rules of the House. But Lloyd Doggett, so far as I know the inventor of the blank chart, raised a point of order that Weldon was out of order. The Speaker pro tem, evidently siding with Jefferson, blank charts, and delay, denied Weldon by ruling for the vote to proceed, whereupon the House turned to its sixth recorded vote in two hours. The older members were panting by the time they put their card in the slot to vote to allow Ward to use his blank chart.

But before Ward could hold forth on the beauties of nothing, Jim McDermott leaped into the fray by seeking recognition and calling, once again, for a vote to be reconsidered. Steve Largent of Oklahoma, catching the parliamentary ping-pong ball in the manner he previously caught NFL footballs, asked to lay the McDermott motion—if not McDermott himself—on the table. The seventh recorded vote of the House version of a filibuster sustained Largent's motion. Moakley, growing tired of blank charts, decided to reclaim the time he had given to Ward in the first place; he delivered a peppy talk on how those rotten Republicans had filed their report late and were now trying to jam it down the Democrats' collective throat before they had had time to carefully read it. During his talk, he referred to our welfare reform report as "no small potatoes," surely one of the most accurate characterizations of the legislation to be used on the House floor by a Democratic speaker.[13]

These various delaying tactics, of course, were necessitated because Democrats wanted to know what their president was going to do before voting on the report. And at this very moment, the president was trying mightily to make a decision. Consistent with his preference for lots of discussion about big decisions, President Clinton had called together his most trusted advisers for a last major discussion on welfare reform before he decided whether to sign the report into law.[14] Those in attendance included top advisers Bruce Reed, Rahm Emanuel, John Hilley, George Stephanopoulos, Ken Apfel, Mickey Kantor, and Harold Ickes; Leon Panetta; cabinet members Robert Reich, Donna Shalala, Henry Cisneros, and Robert Rubin; and Vice President Al Gore. Clinton told this august group that he was less interested in the politics of the decision than he was in the substance of the legislation. He was confident, and the polls certainly supported him, that he would win reelection no matter what he did about welfare reform.[15] No one present knew what Clinton would do, because Clinton himself did not know. Here was a meeting with the president of United States and a host of gifted advisers struggling to determine what was good for the Clinton administration, for the Democratic Party, for the nation's poor, and for the future of the nation's broken welfare system. The decision was all the more difficult because most Democrats assumed that neither signing nor vetoing seemed likely to advance the interests of all concerned parties. There would be losers, no matter which way the president decided.

Clinton asked Ken Apfel, the highly effective Office of Management and Budget official (and head of the Social Security Administration in Clinton's second term) whose purview included most of the federal welfare and health programs, to provide an overview of the conference agreement that Republicans in the House were at that very moment trying to bring to the House floor for a final vote. When Apfel finished his summary, the advisers began dispensing their advice. With the exception of Mickey Kantor, who had been a legal aid lawyer and therefore had had direct experience working with troubled families of the type that tend to be on welfare, no cabinet official spoke in favor of signing the legislation into law. Kantor said he believed the welfare system was so broken that it was time to try something new. Most of those who opposed the legislation gave some version of it being too harsh on children and families. Panetta was especially intense in attacking the provisions that all but ended welfare for immigrants, and no one rebutted him. In fact, it is likely that everyone in the room—including the few who wanted the president to sign—opposed the immigrant provisions, which they regarded as little more than a Republican attack on the weak to save money.

After an hour or so of discussion, Clinton turned to Bruce Reed, arguably his top adviser on welfare policy, and asked him to review the arguments for signing the legislation. An opportunity like this is what draws many young people to politics, including those like Bruce Reed, who could have chosen distinguished careers in fields with shorter hours and longer bank statements. Whether on the staff of the most junior member of a city council or the president of the United States, policy advisers spend their time preparing for the occasions when they will be asked to explain and justify a specific recommendation on a specific policy. It was the fate of Bruce Reed to have the opportunity to bring all the welfare reform arguments together in an attempt to persuade the president—in front of an audience that was, to say the least, not sympathetic—to sign the most important social legislation in at least half a century.

Reed began by stating flatly that the parts of the legislation that required and supported work, including the new child care funds that Clinton and other Democrats had helped secure, were good. If the legislation passed, the impacts on work were likely to be substantial and the nature of welfare was likely to be revolutionized, exactly the goals that Clinton had been working toward since at least 1992. Reed also pointed out that the child support provisions, many of which looked a lot like they had come from the word processors at HHS, were superb and alone nearly justified signing the reforms. Almost everyone who knew anything about child support agreed that these provisions were certain to improve the child support system. Reed also pointed out that the reforms would give states a huge amount of money and sweeping new flexibility to create tough welfare-to-work programs. The welfare demonstrations that the Clinton administration had promoted showed that states had lots of ideas as well as the administrative capacity to implement good programs and, indeed, that many mothers were already leaving welfare for work. Further, the nightmare scenarios being pushed by critics were just not likely to happen. Despite all the consternation over the time limit, given the now growing pressure from within the nation's welfare bureaucracy for mothers to leave welfare for work, and given the financial inducements provided by the Earned Income Tax Credit and child care funds, few families would still be on the rolls at the five-year time limit. Impacts of the immigrant provisions were likely to be modified by legislation that the administration could sponsor the following year, before the cuts were implemented. Besides, millions of immigrants could and almost certainly would apply for and become citizens, thereby qualifying for welfare benefits on the same basis as other citizens.[16]

Reed then made an argument that must have landed with some force on Clinton. Although pundits tend to be cynical about the promises made by politicians during campaigns, those who work with politicians on a regular basis know that they take their campaign promises seriously and usually do everything they can to hold to them. Clinton had made a highly distinctive, surprising, and popular promise to "end welfare as we know it." Sure, Clinton might get a bill to sign the following year, but it would not be surprising if today's bill were his only chance to deliver on his promise, and it would certainly be the last chance before voters cast their ballot in the 1996 presidential election. Advancing this argument one more crucial step, Reed pointed out that if Clinton did not sign the report now, it might be a long time before he or any other president had a chance to so deeply reform welfare and convert it to a work program. The opportunity to sign revolutionary welfare reform does not come along often. Presidents since Lyndon Johnson had been attempting to do something big and bold about welfare, and all had failed. Now Clinton could be the one to achieve major reform.

Soon, the president ended the meeting by thanking his advisers for giving him such sincere and thoughtful advice. Clinton then retired to the Oval Office with the vice president, Reed, Hilley, and Panetta. After Reed and Panetta had reviewed the arguments yet again, the president asked Vice President Gore what he recommended. Gore equivocated, but the president pushed him. Gore then said that it was the president's responsibility to represent all the people and that some people with no voice, noncitizens prominent among them, would be hurt by the legislation. But on balance, the welfare system was so bad and had already hurt so many people that the president should sign the reforms. After a few more minutes of discussion, Clinton said: "That's it. I'll sign it."

Clinton, who had been dressed in casual clothing all this time because it was supposed to be his day off, immediately went upstairs to his private quarters in the White House, changed clothes, and then appeared in the press briefing room, where he was greeted by an overflow crowd. He gave a rather long statement about his decision and then answered several questions from the press.[17] Meanwhile, his staff notified Democrats in the House so the debate and voting could at long last move ahead.

As the word that Clinton would hold a press conference within minutes to announce his decision shot through the House, first among Democrats and then Republicans, I was running around on the House floor trying to keep up with what the Democrats were going to do next, being sure our speakers were lined up in case the debate ever began, and answering questions from members who wanted to know what was going on. I heard McInnis say that the president would soon have a press conference to announce his decision. So I kept poking my head into the members' lounge just off the House floor, where a television set was located. Within a few minutes President Clinton was on the screen speaking from the White House press briefing room. He said he would sign the bill. Just like that. He's going to sign. Our radical legislation would become the law of the land. He's going to sign, he's going to sign. I kept repeating these words as I returned to the floor, acting like nothing had happened, and began answering questions and figuring out what Democrats would do now. The Democrats had their answer: he's going to sign. Now they were ready to debate. Truly, we were in the home stretch.

On McInnis's resolution to waive the rule that would require a two-thirds vote to permit a vote on a bill that had been filed late, the debate lasted only a few minutes, and neither side used all the time allotted. From there, it was on to an hour's debate on the rule and then recorded votes on the McInnis resolution and the rule. The McInnis resolution carried by a very pleasing vote of 259 to 164. Waiving the two-thirds requirement mattered little, since the rule passed by well over two-thirds anyway. The vote on the rule was 281 to 137, with sixty-one Democrats voting in favor. Now, at last, Shaw's patience was being rewarded with big bipartisan votes, and the president was demonstrating that, with a brief announcement, he could do what we could not do after eighteen months of solid effort: get more than a handful of House Democrats to support welfare reform. Watching the vote on the rule, I assumed the bipartisan vote for the conference report would be even bigger.

Although the vote in favor of the rule was enormous, and one Democrat actually spoke in favor of the rule, the rule debate was as fractious as the debates in 1995. At the time (and I see no reason to alter this judgment now), I saw the heartfelt broadsides against our legislation as the dying echoes of the cash welfare entitlement. Several of the speakers, but especially George Miller of California and Charlie Rangel of New York, also attacked President Clinton for his support of the report. Miller was caustic: "This is a President who, along with the First Lady, have spent much of their public life trying to help children. Now he says he will sign a bill that, for the first time, knowingly, he knowingly, he has been presented the evidence by his own Cabinet, he has been presented the evidence by the Urban Institute and others, that will knowingly put somewhere around 1 million children who are currently not in poverty, into poverty.... That cannot be a proper purpose of the U.S. Congress, and that cannot be a proper endorsement for the President of the United States.... But unfortunately this President has joined the Republicans now in making the children the very victims of the system he said he wanted to reform."[18]

The debate on the report itself was equally hostile, although several Democratic speakers made it clear that they planned to support the report. Many of the same members who had used strong language to criticize the report in 1995 reappeared to do so again. Maxine Waters said the report was "shameful"; to Carolyn Maloney, the report was "dangerous"; John Lewis worked himself into a near frenzy, as he had in 1995, to deliver an exceptionally hostile speech pronouncing the report "mean," "base," and "low-down." Similarly, Nancy Pelosi of California, later the first female Democratic leader of her party in the House, claimed that ignoring the needs of children as we did in our legislation was "to dishonor the God who made them." Despite this harsh rhetoric, by now all too familiar to Republicans, we were amazed and pleased to observe that of the twenty-three Democrats who spoke during the debate on the report, eight announced that they would vote in favor.

As the debate and the House odyssey of welfare reform drew to a close, Clay Shaw took the floor. In what was certainly the most important moment of his political life, Shaw did something I had never seen him do before. He walked over to the Democrats' side of the chamber and spoke from their microphone. Looking out over the hundred or so Democrats listening from their benches—the pews of Democracy—he said,

> I hope [Democrats] will give me their understanding in my [coming over to their side] because I do not do it out of smugness or arrogance. I do it out of coming together. We have heard a lot of name calling, a lot of rhetoric, a lot of sound bites ... all through this debate. We have come down a long road together. It was inevitable that the present welfare system was going to be put behind us.... The degree of the success that we are going

to have now is going to be a victory for the American people, for the poor. It is not going to be victory for one political party. It is time now for us to put our hands out to one another and to come together to solve the problems of the poor.

It was a fine and effective gesture and may well have played a role in what happened next, for after all the speechmaking was over, the vote on final passage was 328 to 101.

In the end, the most radical welfare reform legislation in the nation's history had passed the House by a bigger bipartisan vote than the votes by which Medicaid and Medicare were enacted in 1965.[19] The next day the Senate passed the report on an equally impressive bipartisan vote, of 78 to 21. On August 22, 1996, President Clinton signed the welfare reform report into law and set off a revolution in American social policy.

## CHAPTER FIFTEEN

# Ten Years Later:
# The Triumph
# of Work

It has been ten years since the welfare reform law was signed by President Clinton amid predictions of disaster from the left. Thanks to requirements in the legislation itself that provided millions of dollars for research, to an unprecedented level of research sponsored by foundations, to data reported by states to the federal government, and to national data collected and reported on a routine basis by the Census Bureau, a tremendous volume of information bearing on the effects of the legislation has been produced.[1] Most of this research addressed the Temporary Assistance for Needy Families program and, to a lesser extent, changes in family composition and child care reforms. Much less research has been conducted on the effects of the reforms of welfare programs for noncitizens, of the child support enforcement program, and of the Supplemental Security Income (SSI) programs for drug addicts and children. Even so, there is enough information to say something useful if tentative about all these reforms.

But a caveat is in order. Most social scientists agree that the gold standard of program evaluation is random-assignment studies. Unfortunately, few random-assignment studies of the 1996 legislation were undertaken, so some uncertainty must attach to interpretations of the studies on which I base most of my conclusions. Even so, this abundant and diverse information can be used to discover whether the apocalyptic predictions of the left have come to pass; whether children in poverty have increased by a million; and whether the positive effects envisioned by the right on employment, spending, and child well-being have come true.[2]

The most important reform was the replacement of the old Aid to Families with Dependent Children (AFDC) program with the Temporary Assistance for Needy Families (TANF) program. The research on TANF yields a coherent picture that will almost certainly stand the test of time. With its emphasis on work, time limits, and sanctions against states that did not place a large fraction of their caseload in work programs and against individuals who refused to meet state work requirements, TANF was a historic reversal of the entitlement welfare represented by AFDC. One well-documented outcome of both the new TANF program and the state demonstrations that preceded it is a remarkable and widespread change in local welfare offices. An often overlooked aspect of federal policymaking is that many federal edicts lead to modest or undetectable changes at the state and local level. And yet, as a number of observers, including Richard Nathan, Irene Lurie, and Thomas Gais at the State University of New York at Albany, have shown, changes in local welfare offices have been pervasive.[3]

Consistent with the bureaucrats' penchant for signaling change by changing names, many state and local welfare offices now eschew the word "welfare" in their title, preferring "workforce" office or the office of "self-sufficiency." Even the national association of welfare directors changed its name from the American Public Welfare Association to the American Public Human Services Association. But there's more to the story than changing names. Now when applicants for cash welfare show up at the local office, they are usually told that they need a job and that the new "work" or "self-sufficiency" office will help them prepare for and find one. In some states, applicants must actually look for a job before they can even receive a cash benefit, something that would have been impossible under the AFDC entitlement. Most states also have developed a course, lasting a week or less, to help clients develop a résumé and use phone banks to contact employers. Some programs have clients role-play job interviews; others advise on professional dress and may even provide business attire to help the client make a solid first impression. Most of the courses also review the elements of being a good employee: showing up on time, getting along with co-workers and customers, taking directions. In most states the philosophy of the new programs has been to get mothers a job as quickly as possible, not to provide education or training.

Irene Lurie's study of welfare reform implementation in New York, Texas, Georgia, and Michigan shows dramatic changes in welfare offices. Based on observations of 969 encounters between welfare officials and clients in these four states during 2000, she found that "workers consistently implemented policies designed to discourage families from relying on welfare by mandating employment-related activities. . . . They imposed a work-related mandate on applicants as part of a highly routinized process to determine eligibility for assistance. This mandate was imposed with few exceptions, becoming the embodiment of TANF's provision that welfare is no longer an entitlement."[4]

A major reason the 1996 reforms had such an impact on state practice is that the soil had been well prepared. Beginning with the second Reagan administration, in roughly 1985, and continuing through both the Bush and Clinton administrations, the federal government encouraged states to launch their own welfare reform demonstrations to help welfare families make responsible decisions, especially by making the transition to work. By 1996 nearly every state had mounted its own reforms, most of which were similar in one or more respects to the federal reforms enacted in 1996. Because many states were implementing their own welfare-to-work reforms by 1994, I examine the effects of the 1996 reforms by using as the comparison year 1993, the year before many states began to implement their reform programs. Thus most of the results shown below compare information on welfare use, work, income, and poverty for various years between 1993 and 2000, the year before a recession began—or, to gauge the effects of the recession, between 2000 and 2004.[5]

If the 1996 reforms had their intended effect of reducing welfare dependency, a leading indicator of success would be a declining welfare caseload.[6] TANF administrative data reported by states to the federal government show that caseloads began declining in the spring of 1994 and declined more rapidly after the federal legislation was enacted. Between 1994 and 2004, the caseload declined about 60 percent. The number of families receiving cash welfare is now the lowest it has been since 1969, and the percentage of children on welfare is lower than it has been since 1966.[7] Although it is often reported in the media that cash welfare caseloads increase during economic recessions and decline during recoveries, this claim is mostly false. In the forty-one years between 1953 and 1994, the number of families on AFDC declined in only five.[8] Only once—between 1977 and 1979—did the caseload decline (by about 2 percent) two years in a row. By contrast, 2005 was the eleventh year in a row that the caseload declined. Clearly, we are in a new era of welfare use.[9]

Although caseload decline is an important outcome measure of the 1996 reforms, how families fare after leaving welfare is of great importance. The next reasonable test of welfare reform, then, is whether mothers leaving welfare are working. Again, there is abundant information to answer this question. In fact, three lines of evidence can be aligned to produce a consistent story. The first set of evidence is dozens of welfare-to-work studies conducted since the 1980s. These studies almost uniformly show reductions in caseloads and increases in employment attributable to work requirements, as long as the programs included job search requirements.[10] The second line of evidence comes from more than forty state studies conducted since 1996 of adults who left welfare.[11] On average, these studies show that a little less than 60 percent of the adults leaving welfare were employed at any given moment and that over a period of several months or longer about 70 percent held at least one job (although there is good evidence that the share of leavers who were working declined somewhat since the recession of 2001).[12]

A third line of evidence, and the most definitive, is statistics on adult employment for the nation as a whole.[13] Census evidence shows historic changes in employment (defined as any earnings during the year) by single mothers, especially low-income single mothers. From 1993 to 2000 the portion of single mothers who were employed grew from 58 percent to nearly 75 percent, an increase of almost 30 percent. Even more pertinent to assessing the effects of welfare reform, employment among never-married mothers, most of whom join the welfare ranks within a year or two of giving birth, grew from 44 percent to 66 percent.[14] Before 1996 never-married mothers were the ones most likely to be school dropouts, to go on welfare, and to stay on welfare for a decade or more. Yet their employment over this period grew by 50 percent. Employment changes of this magnitude over such a short period for an entire demographic group are unprecedented in Census Bureau records.

Census Bureau data for female-headed families in the bottom 40 percent of the income distribution for female-headed families (those below about $21,000 in 2000) show that their pattern of income shifted dramatically between 1993 and 2000.[15] Ignoring direct federal and state income taxes and Social Security taxes, Census Bureau information on income can be grouped into four categories: earnings, welfare (cash, Food Stamps, housing, school lunch), other income (including social insurance such as Social Security and child support payments), and the Earned Income Tax Credit (EITC). In 1993 earnings accounted for about 30 percent of the income of low-income, mother-headed families, while welfare payments accounted for nearly 55 percent. By 2000 this pattern had reversed: earnings had leaped by an astounding 136 percent, to constitute nearly 60 percent of income, while welfare income had plummeted by over half, to constitute only about 23 percent of income. As a result of the growth in earnings and legislated expansions of the EITC, income from the EITC more than tripled. Thus with earnings and EITC payments leading the way, the total income of these low-income families increased by about 25 percent over the period (in dollars adjusted for inflation).[16]

The pattern is clear: earnings up, welfare down. This is the very definition of reducing welfare dependency. Most low-income mothers heading families appear to be financially better off, although work expenses and Social Security taxes consume part of their earnings,[17] because the mothers earn more money than they received from welfare. Taxpayers continue making a contribution to these families through the EITC and other work support programs, but the families earn a majority of their income. This explosion of employment and earnings constitutes an enormous achievement for the mothers themselves and for the nation's social policy.

Not surprisingly, the increase in total income of mother-headed families has a substantial impact on poverty rates. Although child poverty dropped during the 1960s, after the early 1970s it gradually drifted upward, primarily because an increasing percentage of American children were being reared in mother-headed families, the family type with the lowest work output and the highest poverty rate.[18] However, between 1994 and 2000, child poverty fell every year and reached levels not seen since 1978. In addition, by 2000 the poverty rate of black children was the lowest it had ever been. The percentage of families in deep poverty, defined as half the poverty level (about $7,000 for a mother and two children in 2000), also declined until 2000, falling about 35 percent during the period.[19]

The fall in poverty was widespread across demographic groups. Daniel Lichter of Cornell University used data from the 1990 and 2000 decennial censuses to examine changes over the decade in child poverty rates for groups defined by race or ethnicity, immigrant generation, and national origin. The results show that poverty declined within nearly all the groups and that the decline was caused by increased employment and earnings of females heading families. The authors conclude that "rapid increases in maternal employment during the 1990s provided a hedge against rising child poverty and a route to economic self-sufficiency for growing shares of single mothers and their children."[20]

A special analysis by the Department of Health and Human Services (HHS) and the Congressional Budget Office provides an even clearer understanding of the impact of work on poverty rates among families headed by poor mothers. The analysis examined the changing impact of earnings and government taxes and transfer payments on poverty during the 1990s. In 1990 the poverty rate among children in households with an unmarried female head before any taxes or government transfers was nearly 50 percent. But in 1999 this poverty rate (which might be thought of as the market poverty rate, because it is computed without regard to government taxes or benefits) fell by 20 percent, to a little over 39 percent. Virtually all this decline in poverty is attributable to increased employment and earnings by mothers during the 1990s.[21]

The analysis then added various combinations of government transfers and taxes to market income among these unmarried mothers. One of the analyses shows that in 1990, before welfare reform, the combination of all government cash and in-kind benefits reduced poverty by about 12 percentage points, from around 49 percent to a little more than 37 percent. Although the market poverty rate in 1999 was 10 percentage points lower than in 1990, government cash and in-kind transfers in 1999 still reduced poverty by nearly 10 percentage points, to a little under 30 percent.

The final step in the analysis was to examine the effect on poverty when income from the EITC was added and federal tax payments were subtracted from income. Not surprisingly, given the relatively low level of work and earnings in 1990, adding the EITC increased income only enough to reduce poverty by about 0.25 percentage point. By contrast, in 1999 adding the EITC to income and subtracting federal taxes reduced the poverty rate by 4.50 percentage points. Based on total income, including both market earnings and all government taxes and transfers, poverty among single mothers and children was therefore 36.8 percent in 1990, compared with 25.1 percent in 1999, a decline of nearly one-third. If the 1999 poverty rate had been the same as the 1990 rate, nearly 4.2 million more single mothers and children would have been poor. The prediction that welfare reform would lead to major increases in child poverty proved flawed.

Promoting child well-being was a major goal of all participants in the 1995–96 welfare reform debate. Republicans argued that increased work by mothers on welfare would lead to positive impacts on children because mothers would be setting an example of personal responsibility, would impose schedules and order on chaotic households, and would increase family income. By contrast, Democrats thought that welfare reform would be disastrous for children. Many Democrats believed that mothers would not be able to find and maintain work, would hit time limits or be hit by sanctions, and would experience serious declines in family income, driving them into destitution. Perhaps the most frequent charge, based on a reputable study by the Urban Institute, was that welfare reform would throw a million children into poverty.[22] There were also predictions that more children would be removed from their parents and placed in the child protection system.

Several types of research evidence are now available to make informed judgments about what predictions have come true. A reasonable place to begin is with broad survey data on the well-being of American children. As we have seen, poverty not only did not increase but actually declined every year between 1994 and 2000, with black child poverty reaching its lowest level ever. Although poverty increased after 2000, it remained well below its 1994 level. So great was the decline in poverty that, as Paul Jargowsky and Isabel Sawhill show, the number of neighborhoods with concentrated poverty fell precipitously, as did the number of neighborhoods classified as underclass because of the concentration of poverty and the high frequency of problems such as school dropout, female-headed families, welfare dependency, and labor force dropout by adult males. The authors conclude that the 1990s were a "remarkable decade in which substantial progress was made."[23]

Besides measures of poverty and underclass neighborhoods, a host of additional measures of child well-being is available. One of the best collections of national indicators is the Child and Youth Well-Being Index (CWI), published annually by Ken Land of Duke University with support from the Foundation for Child Development. The Land index reports twenty-eight key indicators of child well-being; these indicators are based on nationally representative surveys, most of which have been administered annually since 1975. The overall index shows a clear pattern of changes over the past three decades. After a few years of modest changes in no clear direction, in 1982 the index showed a decline in well-being that lasted almost continuously until 1995. Since 1995, the index shows an improvement in well-being in almost every year, more than recovering the ground lost in the 1980s and early 1990s. Using 1975 as the base year, the index descended to about 75 percent of its original level by 1995. Since then, it has increased by about 30 percentage points, to about 5 percent above its 1975 level. The CWI is organized into seven domains, each of which measures an important dimension of child well-being such as economic, health, safety, and emotional and spiritual well-being. Most of these domains reflect the overall CWI pattern of continuous increases since 1995. Only two domains, family economic well-being and health, show declines, the latter because of the huge increases in child obesity. As Land concludes, "Children are faring better in recent years."[24]

A similar conclusion is reached by the Federal Interagency Forum on Child and Family Statistics. This group of senior federal officials, representing several federal agencies that generate statistics on child well-being, publishes an annual report based on twenty-five indicators organized into the four domains of economic security, health, behavioral and social, and education.[25] Of these twenty-five indicators, all but three (obesity, activity limitation, and low birth weight) have improved since the mid-1990s.[26] The forum does not mention welfare reform in its explanations of factors that could account for the deterioration in these three indicators. By contrast, measures that seem to have a likely connection to welfare reform—such as family economic well-being, food security, early childhood care and education, and several measures of youth well-being (drug use, enrollment in school, employment, involvement in violent crime)—all show improvement.

The forum presents many of its indicators separately for various income and ethnic groups. In nearly every case in which indicators are presented in this way, low-income and minority children reflect the pattern of general improvement, often showing even greater improvement than white children and children from wealthier families. Similarly, Donald Hernandez of the State University of New York has studied ethnic differences in the Land index. Compared with the huge differences in the early 1990s between white children and black and Hispanic children, both minority groups closed the gap with whites by about one-third over the last decade, narrowing the gap on six of the seven index domains.[27]

Another feared effect of welfare reform was an increase in the number of children taken from their destitute families by the foster care system.[28] By the mid-1990s, the national foster care caseload had increased every year for fourteen consecutive years, rising from 262,000 in 1982 to 507,000 in 1996. The caseload then increased over the next three years at approximately the same rate as in previous years. Beginning in 2000, for the first time in two decades, the foster care caseload began to decline and has declined every year since then, falling from 567,000 in 1999 to 518,000 in 2004, a fall of almost 10 percent.[29] Similarly, the incidence of child maltreatment of all types has declined in most years since 1993, falling by over 20 percent between 1993 and 1999, before rising somewhat beginning in 2000. However, the rate in 2001 was still well below the rate of the early 1990s.[30]

In addition to these broad indicators of child well-being, there is a growing body of scientific research on the direct effects of welfare reform on children, including gold standard studies based on random assignment. Most of these studies were initiated before the 1996 legislation, but nonetheless examined the effects of work programs similar to those mounted by states both before and after the 1996 reforms. Pamela Morris of MDRC and her colleagues have reviewed the impacts on young children of seven random-assignment demonstrations, including thirteen employment programs in the United States and two in Canada, yielding data on 30,000 low-income children.[31] Morris and her colleagues confined their review to children who were between the ages of two and nine when the programs began (between four and fifteen at the point of final data collection). Five results are notable: positive impacts on school achievement were evident among children whose mothers were in certain work programs; impacts were confined to children age five and under at the beginning of the studies; impacts were confined to work programs that increased family income by providing earnings supplements; impacts faded after three years; and positive impacts on school achievement were related to attendance at center-based child care programs during the preschool years. These results are broadly consistent with the large literature on effects of maternal employment, including the finding that when mothers' work leads to increased family income, young children often show modest improvement on measures of social and intellectual development.[32]

A similar review by Lisa Gennetian of MDRC and her colleagues on the effects of work programs on adolescents complements the Morris review.[33] The Gennetian review is based on pooled data from seventeen random-assignment programs. The nearly 6,600 participating children were between ages ten and sixteen at the beginning of the studies; at the point of final data collection they were between twelve and eighteen. Averaged across all the experiments, mothers participating in work programs, compared with mothers in the control programs, rated their children as performing below average in school. In addition, children in the experimental programs were slightly more likely to repeat a grade and to be enrolled in special education classes. They were not, however, more likely to be expelled from school, to drop out, or to have had (or have fathered) a baby. Data from the individual studies provide some evidence that these effects seemed to be concentrated in adolescents with younger siblings, suggesting that the poor school outcomes might be associated with early assumption of adult responsibilities because working mothers shared parental responsibility with their older children. Similar negative effects of maternal employment on adolescents have been noted by several other researchers and reviewers.[34] Although these effects are modest and were not found in all of the individual studies, there is nonetheless reason for concern. Gennetian and her colleagues call for "more investigation rather than . . . an immediate policy response."[35]

Taken together, the survey and experimental information available on the well-being of poor, low-income, and minority children in the decade following welfare reform does not justify the fears expressed by liberals. As Bruce Reed told President Clinton as the president was deciding whether to sign the welfare reform bill, the predictions of disaster from the left were overblown.[36] With some exceptions, measures of child well-being show that children, and especially poor and minority children, have generally lived under improved conditions and have shown modest gains on indicators of development since 1996. On the other hand, the hopes of conservatives have not been vindicated either. High-quality studies of welfare reform show that preschool children of families participating in welfare-to-work studies may experience modest gains in their development and behavior, but equally good studies show that adolescents experience modest problems in school performance. From the perspective of one decade, it does not seem likely that welfare reform will alleviate the serious lags in development and performance shown by children from poor and minority families. Direct interventions with these children will be necessary if the nation is to close the ability and education gaps between them and more advantaged children.

Although welfare reform is a major cause of the dramatic rise in earnings and the decline in welfare dependency and child poverty, at least two other factors account for the improving financial well-being of mother-headed families. First, the economy of the 1990s was exceptionally strong. By 2000 almost 137 million Americans had jobs, up by more than 16 million since 1993. Before the recession hit in 2001, 64.4 percent of all noninstitutionalized adults in the United States were working, the highest share ever. Not surprisingly, the unemployment rate fell from 6.9 percent in 1993 to 4.0 percent in 2000, the lowest in several decades.[37] Sophisticated statistical studies have been conducted by economists to determine the relative contribution of the economy, of welfare reform, and of other factors to the dramatic rise of work and earnings by low-income mothers heading families.[38] These studies all show that both welfare reform and the booming economy are important, but there is little agreement about the relative contributions of each factor. However, previous economic booms did not lead to either the reduction in welfare rolls or the increase in work by low-income mothers heading families that were seen in the 1990s.[39] Without welfare reform cajoling and where necessary pushing mothers into the economy, a growing economy would have had a more modest effect on the employment and earnings of these mothers, as was in fact the case during all previous economic expansions.

Second, beginning more than a decade before the 1996 reforms, the federal government made existing benefit programs friendlier to low-income working families and created entirely new programs designed to help working families. These actions include expansions of child care, creation of the child tax credit, changes in the standard deduction and the personal exemption in the income tax code, changes in Medicaid, and above all three expansions of the EITC. Two studies by nonpartisan and highly respected congressional agencies—the Congressional Budget Office (CBO) and the Congressional Research Service (CRS)—provide an idea of the magnitude of these changes.

CBO undertook a study to determine whether federal policy changes between 1984 and 1998 had resulted in more support for low-income working families. CBO examined several major programs that help working families, including child care, the EITC, Medicaid, and the child tax credit. Taken together, we can label these and similar programs the nation's work support system, because the programs provide financial and in-kind support to poor and low-income working families. CBO calculated the benefits that would have accrued to low-income working families from the work support system under 1984 law and compared that level of support to the level under 1999 law. Because every work support program examined by CBO had been expanded or created since 1984, the analysis was expected to show an increased commitment by federal policymakers to low-income working families. But it is fair to say that even experts were surprised by the finding that if the work support system had remained as it had been in 1984, working families in 1999 would have received only around $6 billion in government work support benefits. By contrast, the 1999 version of the work support system—that is, the one that actually existed in 1999—provided nearly $52 billion in support to working families. In other words, the expansions in the work support system after 1984 resulted in working families receiving $46 billion more in cash and other benefits than they would have received if Congress and a series of presidents had not expanded the work support programs. It would be difficult to exaggerate the extent to which the nation's social policy to help low-income families has shifted from one that provided most of its benefits to families dependent on welfare to one that provides enormous benefits to working families.[40]

The second study, based on information computed by CRS, strengthens the CBO conclusion. Whereas the CBO study provides an estimate of changes in aggregate federal spending on work support programs, the CRS data can be used to compare the financial work incentive for a typical mother with two children on welfare in a typical state (Pennsylvania) in 1986 and 1997.[41] For years, a major charge against the welfare system was that it posed a substantial disincentive to work because families that accepted jobs could be worse off working than on welfare. A mother and two children in a typical state in 1986 received about $8,970 in cash welfare and Food Stamps (all figures are in constant 1997 dollars). If the mother worked and earned $8,000, her welfare income would fall drastically, to $1,900. She would also pay nearly $1,200 in federal taxes but would gain about $540 from the EITC. Thus for working full-time she would have net income of about $9,275, or about $350 more than if she had stayed on welfare. In addition, both the mother and children would lose their Medicaid coverage, the insurance value of which would be around $3,000, after nine months, and the mother would get very modest if any government help paying for child care. Clearly, a mother who elected to stay on welfare rather than accept a low-wage job in 1986 would be making a financially rational decision. By contrast, because of the broadening of the work support system and changes in welfare laws, by 1997 this same mother with a $10,000-a-year job (roughly equivalent to $8,000 in 1986) would have net income of around $15,350, or $7,550 more than the $7,800 she would have received if she had stayed on welfare. The EITC alone was worth an additional $3,000 in cash, and changes in federal income tax law had removed the mother entirely from paying federal income tax. Further, the mother would have Medicaid coverage for one year, and the children would be covered as long as the mother had low income. Finally, there was much more money available for child care in 1997 than in 1986. All in all, the work support system had made work a more attractive option for welfare mothers in 1997 than in 1986.[42]

The anchor of the work support system is the EITC. Although some conservatives regard the EITC as welfare, it has a critical feature that differentiates it from the normal meaning of welfare. Pure welfare means that a benefit is simply given away to prevent destitution. In most welfare programs, greater destitution is met with more benefits. But in the case of the EITC, only those who earn money get the benefit, and more earnings (up to around $14,000) result in higher EITC benefits. Both the basic qualification for the benefit and its mechanics differ greatly from welfare. In the post–welfare reform world, it seems especially appropriate that by 2004 the federal government spent about twice as much on the EITC (around $34 billion) as on the TANF block grant ($16.5 billion).[43] As Jeff Grogger of the University of Chicago concludes, the EITC is "a particularly important contributor to both the recent decrease in welfare use and the recent increase in employment, labor supply, and earnings."[44]

The positive impacts of the 1996 reforms on income, earnings, and poverty have been pervasive and, in some cases, profound. However, no policy produces all benefits and no costs. Although the 1996 law did not produce the failures predicted by its critics, it nonetheless has created challenges that states and the federal government should address. Five are especially important: economic recessions, the proper functioning of the work support programs that are supposed to help low-income working families, the low hourly wage of welfare-to-work mothers leaving or avoiding welfare, the 10 percent or so of these mothers who live alone with their children and do not have income from cash welfare or employment, and the continuing plight of poor fathers. The five challenges are discussed in detail below.

The first is that a system that depends on mothers leaving welfare for work could be seriously disrupted by economic recessions and the resulting increase in unemployment. If the TANF program is dependent on reducing the welfare rolls by placing more previously dependent adults in jobs and then using the welfare savings to pay for job search programs, child care, and other services aimed at increasing or subsidizing employment, a recession that leads to job loss and to difficulty in finding jobs could throw the TANF program into financial crisis. Most observers, including the policymakers who worked on welfare reform, assumed that under the new work-based system, welfare rolls would decline when the economy was not in recession and would increase when the economy was in recession. If the new system actually worked this way, states would need more money during recessions because they would need to continue or even expand their welfare-to-work program at the same time that more parents were coming onto the welfare rolls. Anticipating this problem, Congress included two provisions in the welfare reform law to help states weather the impact of recessions. Congress established a contingency fund that would give cash to states with high levels of unemployment or high enrollment in the Food Stamp program. To qualify for the contingency fund, states had to spend a considerable amount of their own money, which they probably would not want to do during a recession. In addition, Congress created a $1.7 billion loan fund from which states could borrow, to be repaid with interest.

In 2001, after one of the most robust periods of economic growth in American history, the economy entered a mild recession. Although the contraction of the economy lasted for only one quarter, the recession had a lingering effect on employment.[45] Single mothers experienced reduced employment in each of the years 2001 through 2003 before stabilizing in 2004, while both their earnings and total income fell somewhat. In addition, child poverty increased every year after 2000, rising from 16.2 percent in that year to 17.8 percent in 2004, although it was still more than 20 percent below its 1993 peak.[46] In all likelihood the year 2004 will turn out to be the peak year for child poverty following the 2000 recession. The 20 percent decline in child poverty in 2004 compared with 1993 suggests that the new work-based system keeps poverty relatively low during recessions, at least when they are mild.

Many observers were surprised to find that increased unemployment by low-income mothers following the 2001 recession did not lead to an increase in the welfare rolls. Indeed, the rolls declined, albeit modestly, falling from 2.2 million families in December 2000 to 2.0 million families in December 2004.[47] The new system did not function very well during and following the recession of 2001. This conclusion is supported by an examination of trends in employment, income, and poverty experienced by low-income mothers during the recession. Averaged across the bottom 40 percent of single mothers heading families, earnings fell by nearly $1,900, or 23 percent over the four-year period (2000–04). If mothers whose earnings declined had gone back on welfare, we would expect their income from welfare to rise sharply. But welfare income increased by only $254, or 8 percent. Not surprisingly, total income fell by $1,033, or 7 percent. Mothers and children in the bottom 20 percent of mother-headed families, those below around $13,000 in 2004, were hit even harder by the recession over this three-year period. Their earnings declined by nearly one-third, or $1,150. They lost another $570 because with lower earnings their EITC payments also declined. Welfare did not help these families make up for their loss of earnings and EITC. Surprisingly, the welfare received by these mothers actually declined by $520, or about 14 percent. Across all sources of income, the bottom fifth of earners lost almost 20 percent of their income over the period.[48]

It is unclear why more mothers did not make up for lost earnings by joining the welfare rolls, where they would have been quickly greeted in most states by a welfare-to-work program, which would have helped them get back into the job market, while also giving them a cash welfare benefit. Though many states had financial trouble during this period, the explanation for why more mothers did not go back on the rolls is probably not that states didn't have enough money (many states had reserve funds they were carrying from previous years of surplus TANF, only three states obtained money from the contingency fund after 1996, and no state has used the loan fund established by the 1996 law). Perhaps the explanation for the continuing decline in welfare rolls has more to do with the mothers themselves. Some mothers probably just didn't want to put up with a welfare time limit and sanctions in return for a cash benefit of only about $400 a month in the typical state (and below $250 in eighteen states).[49] Other mothers may have felt that being on welfare was stigmatizing. Some mothers might have believed that welfare was not good for them and their children. Whatever other answers might be forthcoming, it is fair to conclude that the new system of tough, work-oriented welfare backed by the EITC and other work supports is effective when jobs are plentiful but less effective during recessions.

The second challenge for policymakers is to track the various work support programs to be sure they perform as planned. The most important work support programs are the EITC program, the Food Stamp program, Medicaid, and child care.[50] The EITC provides working families with children $34 billion a year, or up to nearly $4,500 a year (in 2004) for each eligible family.[51] Unfortunately, working families pay around $1.75 billion a year to commercial tax preparers and banks to help them complete the EITC forms required by the IRS. These private institutions not only charge for their services but also make high-interest loans to families expecting an EITC payment.[52] Low-income working families can ill afford these losses. A major factor driving families to use tax preparers is that the EITC forms are complex and intimidating. Congress and the administration should simplify the EITC tax form, offer free assistance in completing the form, and make electronic filing easier, perhaps by installing user-friendly computer stations in grocery stores, post offices, or other commercial enterprises in low-income neighborhoods. However, simplifying the forms may be difficult, because if they do not contain enough information about the tax filer, an already serious problem with EITC overpayments and fraud could be exacerbated.[53]

Another problem with the work support system is that many families have difficulty receiving the Food Stamps to which they are entitled. A typical mother leaving welfare earns around $10,000 a year. If she has two children, she would be eligible for about $2,300 in Food Stamps. For a mother with perhaps $14,500 in cash income ($10,000 in earnings plus $4,500 from the EITC), an additional $2,000 in Food Stamps is a very substantial income supplement. Yet studies show that only about half of the eligible mothers actually receive Food Stamps.[54] Some families may refuse Food Stamps because they regard them as welfare. Other families, however, want the benefit and are entitled to receive it.

Although the Food Stamp benefit is paid entirely by the federal government, states administer the program and share administrative costs with the federal government on a fifty-fifty basis. Because of this financing arrangement in which the federal government has substantial exposure, the Department of Agriculture, which administers the program, imposes heavy penalties on states that fail to meet high standards of payment accuracy. The biggest problem states have in meeting these standards is that they must adjust the Food Stamp payment amount in accord with other income received by each family. Unfortunately, earnings of low-income families are volatile, causing states to make errors. In virtually every state, Food Stamp cases with earnings have higher payment error rates than cases without earnings. The Food Stamp program is somewhat out of step with TANF and the new emphasis on work. Short of converting Food Stamps to cash, which would be politically difficult, the best available solutions are administrative. The Bush administration and Congress, working closely with the states, agreed on a series of administrative reforms, which were included in the 2002 farm bill.[55] Among the most important were provisions allowing states to assume that all families leaving TANF were eligible for five months of Food Stamps regardless of changes in income, making beneficiaries reapply less often, accepting reapplications by phone or mail, and instituting a simplified test of asset levels that makes it easier for working families to qualify. It remains to be seen whether these administrative reforms will result in more eligible working families receiving benefits.[56]

The Medicaid program is another essential part of the work support system. Medicaid was enacted during the mid-1960s, a time when work requirements for welfare recipients were nonexistent. At the time, to get Medicaid most people had to be on AFDC, Supplemental Security Income (SSI) after 1974, or other aid programs associated with the Social Security Act. If a mother left welfare, she and her children lost Medicaid. Thus starting in the mid-1980s, Congress enacted a series of reforms to broaden Medicaid coverage and reduce or remove the work disincentive effect of the original program.[57] Medicaid is now provided to children through age eighteen in all households with income under the federal poverty level (about $15,000 for a family of three in 2004), children under age six in households with income of less than 133 percent of the federal poverty level (about $20,000), and infants through age one and pregnant women in households under 185 percent of the poverty level (about $28,000), regardless of their welfare status. These age and income coverages were greatly augmented in 1997 when Congress and President Clinton created the State Child Health Insurance Program (SCHIP), which, combined with Medicaid, now guarantees health insurance to virtually all children living in households under 200 percent of the federal poverty level.[58] In addition, mothers leaving welfare because of increased earnings receive twelve months of Medicaid.[59]

Like the TANF reforms and the expansion of the EITC, these Medicaid reforms show that Congress has been working for years to provide incentives for families to leave and stay off welfare or to avoid welfare in the first place. Not so coincidentally, these reforms have led to dramatic expansion in the number of children with government health insurance. In 1995 about 16.6 million children received Medicaid coverage during the course of the year (the SCHIP program had not yet been created). In 2003, the last year for which data are available, about 24.8 million children had either Medicaid or SCHIP coverage during the course of the year.[60] Thus the 1996 bipartisan decision to ensure that no children lost Medicaid coverage if their family left welfare and the 1997 bipartisan decision to enact the SCHIP program have led to a huge increase in the number of poor and low-income children receiving health insurance.

But even here, improvements are possible. Studies show that some eligible low-income families, including those leaving welfare, do not receive Medicaid, although perhaps half the families leaving welfare for employment have some type of coverage—often minimal—through their job.[61] As is the case with Food Stamps, the primary solutions to the problem of ensuring Medicaid coverage for people leaving welfare (and other low-income families) are probably administrative. States administer the program, and some states have worked to make it easier for families to apply for and maintain their coverage. Florida, for example, reduced its application form to one page, provided for application by telephone, and created printed materials in several languages advertising Medicaid availability. As a result, Medicaid coverage of children, which had fallen after Florida implemented welfare reform, began to rise and by 2000 reached an all-time high.[62] Similar results have been shown for advertising the availability of Medicaid in English and Spanish in California. The aggressive California outreach campaign not only increased Medicaid enrollment but also led to more preventive care, to less need for hospitalization, and probably to cost savings.[63] If more states adopted the aggressive administrative policies of Florida, California, and several other states, more low-income children would receive the Medicaid coverage that Congress intended them to have.

Child care is another important part of the work support system. Few question the success of the 1996 child care reforms in providing states with more money and more flexibility in using the money. Now, the major complaint about child care is that states need more money so they can provide child care subsidies to more families and improve the quality of care.[64] Because of the expanding need for child care, states are using a substantial portion of their TANF funds for child care, a move made possible by the flexibility of the TANF block grant and the unprecedented decline in the welfare rolls. In 2000, for example, states used about $4 billion of their $16.5 billion TANF funds for child care—in addition to the nearly $5 billion available from the federal child care fund and another $2 billion of state matching funds.[65] Given these figures, it is hardly surprising that the combined total of state and federal dollars for child care more than doubled between 1996 and 2002 (although it has been flat since 2002).

In addition to increases in child care spending, the emphasis on vouchers and on states' flexibility to set their own child care regulations (both features of previous federal child care legislation retained in the 1996 reforms) has ensured the continuation of a diverse child care market. Parents using child care funds are purchasing center-based care, informal care by neighborhood providers, and care by relatives.[66] A surprising number of eligible parents do not even claim a government subsidy for child care. In most states, for example, less than 30 percent of the single mothers leaving welfare claim a child care subsidy.[67] Although many child advocates would like to create more center-based care that meets high federal standards such as those followed by the Head Start program, the preservation of parent choice and modest state regulation of care has meant that lots of relatively inexpensive care is used, thereby keeping down the overall costs of welfare reform—and for that matter helping the pocketbooks of all low-income families using child care.

Advocates argue that average child care quality is too low and that better quality care would promote child development.[68] This is a powerful argument, especially when applied to children from poor and minority families, who as a group fare poorly in the public schools. The idea that preschool programs can help children who are behind in their development is attractive and enjoys support from empirical studies. The strength of this evidence is a subject of dispute, but there are only a few studies that use scientific methods and that show lasting impacts.[69] The claims of advocates may be reasonable, but they lack strong supporting evidence from studies showing that the type of center-based care now typically available would produce benefits similar to the well-established long-term benefits of model programs.[70] The certain benefit of low-cost care in facilitating work by low-income families is preferable to the uncertain benefit of strong quality requirements that would boost the average cost of care.

Welfare reform has heightened the conflict between advocates who want high-quality child care and welfare reform program operators and others who want inexpensive child care. For now, advocates have Head Start, which continues to receive increased or steady funding from Congress in most years despite its modest performance in boosting school readiness, and several new programs supported by state funds that offer high-quality preschool programs to many poor children.[71] But as long as states keep their child care regulations modest and as long as a major goal of federal and state welfare policy is to maintain a work support system to help low-income families avoid dependency, there will be strong resistance to universal regulations that would improve the quality of child care but raise average prices. Congress and most states will struggle for the foreseeable future with how to balance the need for inexpensive care to promote work by low-income families with the need to pay for more expensive care of such quality as to help low-income children arrive at the public schools ready to achieve. Stay tuned.

The work support system is vital both to encourage adults to avoid welfare dependency and to help low-income working families provide a better life for themselves and their children. Given the serious problems caused both by the decline in two-parent families and by failed inner-city schools, the nation will have many poorly educated and low-skill individuals, often single mothers, heading families for the foreseeable future. Policymakers, experts, and the American public all agree that welfare is a lousy way to help adults who can qualify only for low-wage jobs. Congress created the work support system to improve the financial well-being of these families. There are nonetheless problems that reduce the effectiveness of the system. Welfare reform, by moving as many as 2 million mothers from welfare to work, has highlighted these flaws. Congress and the states should address them.[72]

A third challenge associated with welfare reform is that many low-income mothers begin their work careers in low-wage jobs ($7 or $8 an hour), with few or no benefits and have trouble advancing into better jobs. From the perspective of the Republicans who supported welfare reform, it is unambiguously better for these mothers to be stuck in low-wage jobs than to be stuck on welfare. But it would be even better if these mothers could be helped to move up the job ladder. It is true that mothers on welfare are below average on most traits valuable to employees, such as education and job experience.[73] But experience shows that many can overcome these deficits, just as they overcame their weak education and work experience to join the workforce in the first place. Although the federal government has spent billions of dollars over the past forty years on education and training programs for poor and low-income young adults with only modest success,[74] the picture may be different now.

One difference now is that work, not welfare, appears to be the first choice of most low-income mothers, both married and single. These mothers know, as they never have in the past, that they must work because cash welfare is not a long-term option. The motivation to try education or training is entirely different for a mother who is in no hurry to leave welfare compared with a mother who is already off welfare and not counting on going back. Of course, this increased motivation is offset to some degree by working mothers' busy schedules and the fact that as their earnings rise, their taxes rise, and once they earn over about $14,000, their EITC payments fall.[75] Even so, there is some evidence that programs offering short-term education or education in combination with work produce both high employment and higher hourly earnings. A program in Portland, Oregon, for example, encouraged caseworkers to identify mothers on welfare who were likely to benefit from short-term training to take the high-school equivalency test.[76] In addition, mothers were encouraged not to take the first job offered but rather to search for a job with higher wages and more benefits. The mothers who participated in this program got significantly better jobs than mothers in a control group. Several states are now experimenting with training programs that work with local employers to identify and design training regimens for jobs actually available in the local economy or that provide incentives for low-income young adults to get postsecondary education.[77] If the results are encouraging, money available from the TANF program and from such programs as the Workforce Investment Act should be redirected to pay for these training programs.[78]

A fourth serious issue raised by welfare reform is that there is good evidence that some mothers at the bottom of the income distribution are floundering. In the past, these troubled parents could stay on welfare for many years. Under the old AFDC program, the average length of spells for adults on the rolls at any given moment was twelve years. It would be naïve to believe that all these welfare-dependent parents were suddenly capable of finding and retaining jobs for $7 or $8 an hour. A demanding welfare system requires at least some minimum level of competence and motivation, and not all parents have these minimum levels.

There are several types of evidence that a number of mothers are in fact floundering. As we have seen, about 60 percent of the mothers who leave welfare are working at any given moment and around 70 percent have held at least one job since leaving welfare.[79] The 40 percent who do not work regularly raise some concern, but the 30 percent who have not worked at all since leaving welfare raise even more serious concern. States frequently use sanctions and thirty-six states have policy that allows them to completely terminate cash benefits for rule infractions. At least one study found that mothers who were sanctioned off the rolls had characteristics that make it less likely they will be able to get and hold a job. More specifically, they are less likely to have a high school degree or job experience and more likely to have substance addictions, mental health problems, or three or more children than other welfare mothers.[80] Also of concern are poor mothers heading families who are financially worse off since welfare reform passed. Kasia Murray and Wendell Primus have analyzed census income data for mothers in the 1993–96 and the 1996–2000 periods and found that mothers in the bottom 10 percent of single earners actually lost income during the period 1996–2000.[81] These findings are placed in a broader context by Rebecca Blank and Robert Schoeni from the National Poverty Center at the University of Michigan. Blank and Schoeni, using data from the Census Bureau's Current Population Survey, compared the change in income between the 1992–95 period (before TANF) and the 1997–2000 period (after TANF). Controlling for factors such as family size and inflation, they plotted income for two groups: all families with children and families with children without both parents present. Blank and Schoeni find that all but the bottom 2 percent of families with children had improved their income in the late 1990s relative to the mid-1990s. Even in the case of children living outside a two-parent family, 92 percent of families improved their income; only the bottom 8 percent declined. Remarkably, for both groups of families, those just below the poverty level had even bigger income gains than families further up the income distribution. Blank and Schoeni note with some surprise that "many poor families have increases in their income of around 30 percent."[82]

Blank and Schoeni explicitly tied their analysis to welfare reform by comparing states with strong cash work incentives (which allowed mothers who went to work to retain relatively more of their welfare benefit) and strong penalty incentives (strict time limits and strong sanctions) and found that both cash and penalty incentives were associated with higher income. The authors conclude that "it is the more lenient states with softer penalties where children's income seems to have grown the least."[83] Although the authors interpret their findings as "good news," their work is similar to Murray's and Primus's in showing that there is a group of mothers at the bottom—in this case about 8 percent of the distribution of female-headed families—that is worse off now than before welfare reform. Similarly, Census Bureau data analyzed by Richard Bavier of the Office of Management and Budget show a disconcerting increase in the number of mothers in the bottom fifth of income for female heads of families who report zero earnings and zero income from cash welfare (ignoring SSI). The number of mothers in this category increased in every year between 2000 and 2004, jumping by 60 percent over the period.[84]

Several other research groups, including Robert Moffitt and Katie Winder at Johns Hopkins; Pamela Loprest, Sheila Zedlewski, and others at the Urban Institute; Sandra Danziger and Sheldon Danziger of the University of Michigan; and Robert G. Wood and Anu Rangarajan at Mathematica Policy Research report similar findings on increased hardship among mothers who leave welfare but do not have earnings. The studies by Wood and Rangarajan and the Danzigers and their colleagues are especially interesting because they both have many years of longitudinal data (data collected on the same subjects over time) on mothers who had been on welfare. Wood and Rangarajan followed a representative group of 2,000 recipients who had received welfare in 1997 or 1998 in New Jersey. Although the group that was off welfare and employed increased from about one-third to one-half over the fifty-four-month follow-up period, the group of greatest concern—those who were off welfare but without a job—was consistently a little more than one quarter of the sample. Of this group, about 60 percent had other sources of income, including SSI, unemployment compensation, a working spouse or partner, or recent employment. Thus the mothers who were the least financially stable constituted about 40 percent of those who were off welfare and unemployed, or around 11 percent of the total sample.

The study conducted by Sandra and Sheldon Danziger and their colleagues at the University of Michigan produced results similar to those in New Jersey. The Michigan study followed a sample of mothers who had received welfare in one county in 1997. The mothers were interviewed five times over the 1997–2003 period. A little over 20 percent of mothers in 1997 got off welfare and worked; by 2003, that figure was nearly 65 percent. The share of mothers who were not working, not receiving welfare, not receiving unemployment compensation, and not living with another earner also, unfortunately, increased—from 1 percent to nearly 9 percent.[85]

All the evidence reviewed above, showing that mothers and children at the bottom of the distribution experience hardship, is based on income data. Surprisingly, consumption data provide a different picture. In studies using two nationally representative data sets, Bruce Meyer and James Sullivan show that the material conditions of low-income mothers, as measured by their consumption, improved somewhat after welfare reform.[86] On the other hand, a large part of the additional consumption in the late 1990s appears to be related to work. More specifically, the mothers spent more on housing, food away from home, and transportation. Additional housing costs could well be explained by the fact that the federal housing programs in which many of these mothers participate charge families 30 percent of their income, with the remainder of the family's rent being paid by the government. If mothers earn additional money, they must pay 30 percent of it on housing: in effect, federal housing policy all by itself imposes a 30 percent tax on increased earnings. Additional spending on food away from home and transportation could also be associated with mothers working and needing to use some of their increased earnings to get to work and to eat out because of time pressures.[87]

Evidence on the well-being of mothers and children can also be gleaned from information on food consumption. Christopher Jencks, one of the major critics of the 1996 reforms, and his colleague Scott Winship conducted extensive analyses on the Food Security Supplement to the Current Population Survey for the years 1995–2001. Based on twenty-eight questions related to food security, Jencks and Winship conclude that single mothers had fewer problems related to food in 2001 than in 1995. Further analysis shows that, although the number of low-income mothers receiving welfare between 1995 and 1999 fell from 58 percent to 29 percent, food-related problems dropped dramatically. The decline in food problems leveled off in the 1999–2001 period, but food problems in 2001 were still substantially below the level of problems reported in 1995. Similarly, based on the Department of Agriculture's definition of food security, the percentage of food-insecure mother-headed families declined from around 31 percent in 1995 to about 27 percent in 1999, as the welfare rolls were declining rapidly. Even during the period following the mild recession of 2001, the percentage of food-insecure families did not increase significantly, remaining below the 1995 level. The authors conclude that "single mothers' material standard of living probably improved more during [the economic expansion of the 1990s] than during earlier ones."[88] In an op-ed piece published in the *Christian Science Monitor*, the authors state flatly that their study of food problems led them to conclude that "welfare reform worked."[89]

Income data thus suggest that there was a group of single mothers, constituting perhaps 10 percent of all single-mother families that had been on welfare, that was worse off following welfare reform. Data based on consumption and on food insecurity tend to offset this conclusion, although even here there is some evidence of problems at the bottom of the distribution. On balance, it seems prudent to conclude that scholars should examine this problem in much greater detail and search for solutions that will help mothers hold jobs. An example of the action that seems called for is provided by a program in Ramsey County, Minnesota. As reported by LaDonna Pavetti and Jacqueline Kauff of Mathematica, officials in Ramsey County were worried that recipients who hit the five-year time limit would be destitute when they left the rolls.[90] County officials instituted a program to provide assistance to TANF recipients as they approached the time limit. The essence of the program was case management. Experienced caseworkers were selected for the program, and the number of cases for which they were responsible was cut from ninety to twenty-five, allowing them to spend more time on each case. The goal of the program was to identify and resolve barriers to employment such as mental health issues, substance abuse, and other problems. Another major goal of the program was to identify and obtain services for clients. An extensive assessment battery helped caseworkers identify clients' special needs. For clients who could not find jobs despite the services and individual attention, supported work programs were available that adapted work to the special needs of these clients. As a last resort, clients who had serious problems even in the supported work program were given help in applying for Supplemental Security Income.

Unfortunately, the Ramsey County program did not include a formal evaluation. Both staff and clients believed the program was successful, but without a solid evaluation it is impossible to know whether the program increased the number of clients receiving services, helped reduce employment barriers, helped children, increased work levels, or saved money. Given the research reviewed above showing an increase in the number of poor mothers with no obvious sources of income, much more needs to be known about the effectiveness of programs like the one in Ramsey County. More public and foundation funds should be devoted to conducting research and demonstration programs to determine how these floundering mothers can be helped. The trick will be to maintain a demanding welfare system that strongly discourages welfare dependency while simultaneously allowing states enough flexibility to identify and help these mothers. Some mothers may never be able to achieve steady employment.[91] Welfare programs should accommodate them.

A fifth challenge not caused but probably aggravated by welfare reform is the continuing plight of low-income, especially black, fathers.[92] Welfare has always been primarily a program for females. The old entitlement welfare system of cash, Food Stamps, and Medicaid was designed primarily to help children and their mothers. Poor males qualify for Food Stamps, but they are generally left out of cash and Medicaid benefits. Moreover, the 1996 reforms virtually ignored males except to pursue them in ever more aggressive ways for child support payments. And how have these young men been doing? Two pieces of data capture the depth of the pit into which many young males, especially black males, have fallen. The booming economy of the 1990s, which reduced unemployment from 7.5 percent to 4.0 percent and which helped to sweep single mothers to their highest employment level ever, did nothing to relieve the dismal employment picture of black males between sixteen and twenty-four years of age. In 1989, nearly 60 percent of these males were employed. Near the end of the boom in 2000, only about 56 percent were employed. By way of contrast, in the same year about 75 percent of single mothers were working, a rate that exceeded that for young black males by nearly 35 percent.[93]

A major problem faced by these young males is the astonishing frequency of their involvement with the justice system: well over 20 percent of young black males are either in jail or on probation. Around 700,000 (12 percent) of the

5.7 million black males between the ages of sixteen and thirty-four are in jail.[94] Another 500,000 or so are on probation for felony crimes. Many more are ex-offenders or offenders who have not yet been arrested and jailed. These figures are given added significance by Harvard's Richard Freeman, who estimates that previous incarceration reduces employment rates by as much as 25 percent.[95] A large survey of employers in Atlanta, Boston, Detroit, and Los Angeles shows that employers would rather hire welfare recipients, the long-term unemployed, or almost any other warm body than an ex-offender.[96] In fact, less than 40 percent of employers would "definitely" or "probably" hire ex-offenders. Nor is the impact on employment confined to the offenders themselves. Employers cannot easily distinguish between black males with and without criminal records. Since background checks are often time-consuming and expensive, employers may try to simply avoid the problem by refusing to hire any black males.

The plight of black males is not of recent origin. Orlando Patterson of Harvard, in his jolting book *Rituals of Blood*, lays out a persuasive historical case that black males still bear the legacy of slavery and, more recently, of being reared in mother-headed families without significant male influence.[97] Patterson's analysis is consistent with that of Daniel Patrick Moynihan, who predicted in 1965 that young men who grow up in broken families would produce chaos in their communities, which Moynihan defined as "crime, violence, unrest, disorder . . . and furious, unrestrained lashing out at the whole social structure."[98]

But what to do? There is now widespread understanding of the facts of inner-city life and of failed families, failed schools, and failed welfare. An encouraging note is that policymakers have increased their attention to this problem in recent years. Both foundations and government are now appropriating funds to implement programs for low-income fathers, including those leaving jail. These programs provide counseling, legal advice, job assistance, and parent training. So far the programs that have been carefully evaluated have shown only modest impacts.[99] But modest impacts are the rule when new ideas and approaches are being attempted. Although there is little room for optimism in the short run, in the longer run better programs are likely to make inroads in helping young males avoid incarceration, secure and retain employment, avoid premarital fatherhood, and form healthy married families. As Orlando Patterson has observed, two low-income parents who marry can greatly improve both their economic standing and their ability to provide a strong rearing environment for their children. Given that the nation has had programs addressed to promoting marriage only in recent years, and that the programs are not yet widespread, there is reason to hope that successful programs of this type may eventually be developed.[100] If so, they hold the potential to have positive impacts on poverty, school failure, delinquency and crime, welfare use, and intergenerational transmission of social problems.

Although a major and controversial part of the welfare reform debate was over family composition, a review of demographic trends and studies since 1996 permits no more than modestly hopeful conclusions.[101] Grave problems still remain. The best news is the continuing and substantial reduction in teen births. Annual data from the National Center for Health Statistics indicate that births to teenagers declined every year after 1991, falling one-third from 62 per thousand to 41 per thousand girls between the ages of fifteen and nineteen. The fact that the decline began in the early 1990s shows that factors other than welfare reform are playing major roles. It is possible, however, that welfare reform is contributing to the continuing decline.[102]

The nonmarital birth rate for women of all ages is not as encouraging, although there may be a little room for optimism because of developments since the mid-1990s, especially among black women. For all women, births outside marriage rose from 10.7 percent in 1970 to 32.6 percent in 1994, a shocking rate of increase of nearly a full percentage point each year for a quarter of a century. However, between 1994 and 2004, the rate of increase fell to less than one-third of a percentage point a year. Unfortunately, the rate of increase in both 2003 and 2004 rose nearly to pre-1994 levels. It will require several more years of data to determine whether nonmarital births are in a long-term stable or slightly downward trend or whether they are once again on the rise.

Trends for blacks are especially hopeful. After rising almost every year after roughly the mid-1950s, the percentage of black births that were nonmarital reached the devastating level of 70.4 percent in 1994. But it fell every year for the next eight years, to 68.2 percent in 2002.[103] Unfortunately, after holding steady at 68.2 in 2003, it rose again to 68.7 in 2004. For whites the percentage of nonmarital births has continued to increase almost every year, although at a slower pace since the mid-1990s. In the fourteen years before 1995, nonmarital births among whites increased by a full percentage point a year, rising to 25.4 percent in 1994, from 11.2 percent in 1980. By contrast, between 1994 and 2004, the rate of increase for whites was cut almost in half, rising to 30.5 percent over nine years. Again, given the timing of the decline among blacks, the timing of the reduced rate of increase among whites, and the overall near stabilization, the role of welfare reform in producing these trends is suggestive. Many other factors are certainly involved, but welfare reform could be playing a part in the decline for blacks and the moderating rate for whites.[104] The increase for all groups in 2004 may represent a one-year anomaly, or it may signal a renewal of the unfortunate rise of illegitimacy in American society.

A few studies tie changes in family composition during the past decade to welfare reform. Gregory Acs and Sandi Nelson of the Urban Institute examined changes in the living arrangements of families with children for the period 1997–99.[105] Based on the National Survey of American Families, their study found that the percentage of single-mother families declined from about 17 percent to 15 percent, while the percentage of children living with cohabiting adults increased from 4.1 to 5.6, and the percentage living with a married couple increased from 61.8 to 62.2.[106] Because the increases in cohabitation and marriage and declines in mother-headed families occurred primarily in adults with low income and high school or less education, the authors concluded that welfare reform is implicated because these are the couples that would be most likely to be affected by welfare policies. Such correlational evidence may be suggestive, as the authors argue, but it is far from definitive. Recent work by Richard Bavier of the federal Office of Management and Budget shows that the fraction of children living with married parents has increased since the mid-1990s and that this change is especially large for blacks, a demographic group highly likely to be involved with welfare.[107] Bavier examines birth cohorts as they age. Children born before 1994 were born to parents who experienced high rates of nonmarital births and low and declining rates of marriage. For birth cohorts beginning in 1994, however, children were slightly less likely to be born to a single mother, and the mothers were slightly more likely to get married in the years immediately following the birth. This trend holds for whites, blacks, and Hispanics, although this hopeful pattern has deteriorated somewhat in recent years.

In addition to the rise in nonmarital births since roughly the 1960s, changes in marriage rates and divorce rates have been unfavorable for women with less education. Black women and women with less education are less likely to marry and more likely to divorce, making marriage rates an important factor in the growing income and wealth inequality in the United States.[108] In addition, research shows that these declines in marriage rates, especially for minorities, have been a disaster for children.[109] It is little wonder, then, that Republicans wrote the goals of the TANF program to place as much emphasis on promoting marriage as on reducing illegitimate births.

Unfortunately, only a few states have adopted marriage promotion as a major goal of their welfare reform programs. Even so, early research on programs that featured mandatory work accompanied by income supplements suggests that some welfare-to-work programs might have an impact on marriage rates. Consider the New Hope program in Milwaukee, a demonstration program initiated in 1994 to test whether providing low-income workers with a guarantee that, if they worked full-time, they would receive health insurance, an income supplement, and if necessary child care. If they couldn't find work, the program provided them with a community service job. Five years after the experiment began, 21 percent of the never-married mothers in the program group were married, compared with only 12 percent among never-married mothers in the group that did not participate in the program. Further analysis of the results indicates that increased income and earnings by the mothers and their partners were associated with an increased likelihood of marriage.[110] Similarly, the Minnesota Family Investment Program (MFIP), which featured a work mandate and an income supplement, also produced a positive result for a particular group of parents. More specifically, three years after initiation of the program, 67 percent of the married parents in the program group were still married, compared with only 48 percent in the control group.[111]

Despite these early successes, a thorough analysis of the best experimental evidence on welfare reform and marriage by Lisa Gennetian and Virginia Knox of MDRC shows that there are few if any reliable effects of welfare reform on marriage.[112] Gennetian and Knox combined the results of fourteen programs evaluated by scientific designs to search for effects of welfare reform on marriage. The authors also conducted a variety of analyses of impacts on subgroups defined by race and ethnicity, age of the mother, age and number of children, prior marital status, and prior education and work experience. The only significant effect they found was for programs (the MFIP reviewed above and Vermont's Welfare Restructuring Project) that allowed welfare recipients to retain part of their welfare benefit when they went to work and did not place a time limit on welfare receipt.[113] However, the effect was small, an increase of a little over 2 percentage points in the marriage rate. Further, when the results for these two programs were combined with those of similar programs, the significant impact on marriage disappeared. The Gennetian and Knox analysis also shows the magnitude of the marriage problem that characterizes poor adults. Averaged across all fourteen programs, the authors found that at the time of follow-up two to four years after the beginning of the programs, about 10 percent of the adults were married, about 10 percent were cohabiting, and 80 percent were not living with a spouse or partner. Gennetian and Knox's stark conclusion that "for the overall sample of single parents, these welfare programs did not affect marriage or cohabitation" seems fully justified.[114]

Taken together, these findings show that most of the measures of family composition, for the first time since the 1960s, are stabilizing or rising at a less rapid rate than before the mid-1990s. If these trends continue, a larger share of American children will be born to married parents and more will live in two-parent, married, or cohabiting families in the future. Given the strong research literature on the benefits for both children and adults of living in married families, a continuation of these trends would mean better school preparation, higher rates of school completion, less delinquency, lower rates of mental health problems, lower poverty rates, and continuing declines in welfare use.[115] However, the trends since 2000 in several measures of family composition are less hopeful than those of the later 1990s, and the evidence that increasing family income through employment of mothers has an impact on marriage is discouraging. At best, the nation may have stopped digging its demographic hole.

Child support reforms have led to solid improvements in the enforcement program. States have aggressively implemented the major child support reforms, including expanded databases, new collection methods, strengthened paternity establishment requirements, and stronger data processing requirements. The immediate outcome is that the nation's child support program has joined the electronic age. It might even be argued that in many states the child support program is the most sophisticated and modern of all government services. Child support collections more than doubled between 1995 and 2004, from $10.8 billion to $21.9 billion.[116] Equally impressive, the paternity establishment requirements in the 1996 law have led to a substantial increase in the number of paternities established for children born outside marriage. More than 1.5 million paternities are now established every year, about a 50 percent increase since the 1996 reforms were implemented. This success is probably due both to the carrot of voluntary paternity establishment programs in hospitals and the stick of requirements on welfare mothers with nonmarital births to provide information on fathers or lose their welfare benefits.[117]

Although the improvements in the child support program are remarkable, the number of low-income mothers who receive child support from fathers—and the amount they receive—is still discouraging. The approximately 2.1 million mothers heading families that have a yearly income of less than $21,000 received an average of only about $675 a year in child support payments in 2000.[118] Almost certainly due to the growing effectiveness of the child support program, this amount was about a 70 percent increase over the 1993 amount.[119] But about three-quarters of these mothers received no child support at all in 2000. Perhaps the most that can be said about the child support program as a work support for mothers is that the mothers who receive payments enjoy a substantial income supplement. Despite great improvement in collections and paternity establishment, child support has not proven to be helpful to most low-income mothers trying to escape welfare.

The effects of the provisions for noncitizens, though controversial, were exactly what Congress intended. Both administrative data from program records and survey data from the Census Bureau show that use of welfare by noncitizens has declined. At the time welfare reform passed in 1996, both the number and percentage of noncitizens on the SSI rolls were rising. Between 1984 and 1995, the number of noncitizens on SSI exploded from 181,100 to more than 785,400, an increase of more than 330 percent. Similarly, as a portion of the total SSI caseload, noncitizens increased from 4.5 percent to more than 12 percent. In the six years between 1995 and 2002 not only did the rapid increase in noncitizen participation in SSI stop but the number and percentage on the rolls actually fell, from more than 785,000 to less than 700,000 (12 percent to somewhat over 10 percent).[120]

Noncitizens' enrollment in both the TANF and Food Stamp programs, which had been increasing before the 1996 reforms, also declined. In the case of TANF, the percentage of recipients who were noncitizens, which had increased from 7 percent in 1989 to 12.3 percent in 1996, declined to 8 percent by 2001. This decline is especially remarkable because, as we have seen, the number of TANF recipients was declining rapidly during this period (by over 40 percent between 1996 and 2001), and yet the number of noncitizens on TANF declined even more rapidly. In the case of the Food Stamp program, noncitizen enrollment, which had risen from 4.4 percent in 1989 to 7.1 percent in 1986, fell to 3.7 percent by 2001.[121]

These results from administrative data are confirmed and expanded by survey information from the Census Bureau. Michael Fix and Jeffrey Passel of the Urban Institute analyzed these data and showed that, between 1994 and 1999, the receipt of the following benefits by noncitizens declined: TANF cash welfare by 60 percent, Food Stamps by 48 percent, and SSI by 32 percent.[122] More recent analysis of Census Bureau data by the CRS not only confirms the Urban Institute results but also extends them through 2001 and shows similar results for the Medicaid program. More specifically, CRS found that between 1995 and 2001, the number of noncitizens on TANF, SSI, Food Stamps, and Medicaid declined by 55 percent, 45 percent, 52 percent, and 22 percent, respectively.[123]

For those who believe that noncitizens should not qualify for welfare, the reforms have been a major success and have saved taxpayers billions of dollars. Nonetheless, the termination of welfare benefits for most noncitizens is among the most controversial provisions in the 1996 law. Few areas of social policy present such a stark example of the importance of values in policy choice as that presented by welfare for noncitizens. Republicans generally believe that welfare raises the issue of dependency, with its associated evils of nonwork and nonmarital births, no matter who receives it. Democrats are more willing to risk dependency as a reasonable price to pay to ensure that destitute mothers and children have guaranteed benefits. In addition to the concern with dependency, Republicans believe that noncitizens should not be eligible for welfare until they become citizens because the basis of immigration policy should be a combination of economic opportunity and the risks necessarily entailed by participating in a market economy. To provide welfare to noncitizens who entered the country precisely to take advantage of economic opportunity is to violate the very basis of the implicit immigration contract. American citizens should not be expected to pay for welfare for adults who came to America to work. Rather, as the 1996 reforms required, immigrants should have private sponsors who are legally bound to provide assistance if immigrants face destitution. By contrast, Democrats believe that the need to ensure a basic level of economic security trumps the implicit immigration contract of self-sufficiency and that noncitizens who work and pay taxes in America should be eligible for all welfare benefits.

The 1996 legislation seems not to have changed the reasoning of either side. Rather, Republicans used their control of Congress to muscle through the termination of welfare benefits for most noncitizens and to return welfare policy for noncitizens to its historic roots. As shown by the data summarized here, Republican policy has had precisely its intended effect. Even so, Democrats are still intent on restoring welfare benefits for noncitizens, especially for children and for workers. Republicans are equally intent on preserving the 1996 prohibitions.[124] Again, stay tuned.

Like the reform of welfare benefits for noncitizens, the termination of SSI and Social Security Disability Insurance (SSDI) benefits for drug addicts and alcoholics has fulfilled its primary goal of ending benefits for a category of recipients judged by Republicans to be unqualified for public benefits. Around 210,000 adult addicts were terminated from these two programs. However, some of those who lost benefits reapplied on the basis of disabling conditions linked with addiction (such as mental health problems). A study by the Lewin Group of Fairfax, Virginia, estimated that because some recipients would have lost their benefits even without the new policy and because, within one year, about 71,000 former addicts had reestablished eligibility based on another disabling condition, the termination policy reduced the SSI and SSDI caseloads by about 103,000 cases.[125] This estimate does not, however, take into account the fact that the number of individuals admitted to SSI and SSDI was growing rapidly at the time the programs were ended. There is little doubt that the savings from the termination policy in SSI and SSDI payments, plus the associated medical coverage of these two programs, is in excess of $1 billion a year.

However, little is known about the other effects of the termination policy. The fact that 71,000 addicts reestablished their eligibility because they had other disabling conditions suggests that many of the truly disabled are continuing to receive their benefits in accord with the purpose of SSI and SSDI. But what about the status of the 103,000 or so who would have continued to receive cash and medical coverage under the old policy but now have lost their benefits? The short answer is that little good information exists to answer this question. The Lewin study produced some anecdotal evidence that many of the former recipients faced hardships. Among the outcomes mentioned in their anecdotal account were a decline in participation in treatment programs, only modest increases in work, loss of housing, and a few cases of suicide. However, without a comparison group, it is impossible to know which of these outcomes can be attributed to the termination policy itself as opposed to the otherwise troubled lives of addicts.

Nonetheless, let us stipulate that there are some negative financial outcomes of the termination policy and that the misery index increased for some portion of these 103,000 addicts who lost their benefits. Does it follow that termination was the wrong policy? Republicans offered and defended the termination policy exclusively on the basis of values: federal policy should not reward addiction by providing a guaranteed annual income and health coverage to adults who become addicted to alcohol or drugs. In the complex calculus of policy deliberation, the principle of not providing benefits to people who do bad things has been strengthened but perhaps at the cost of at least a short-term increase in misery for some people. No major figure on the federal level has taken up the case that the increase in misery is too steep a price to pay to strengthen the principle of avoiding rewards for irresponsible behavior. Until someone does, the SSI and SSDI programs will continue to reflect the emphasis Republicans placed on principle, even at the possible cost of some increase in hardship.

The number of children on SSI has fallen substantially since enactment of the 1996 reforms. Because the rate of children entering SSI was increasing when the reforms were passed, a true estimate of the impact of the reforms requires use of statistical techniques to estimate how the caseload would have changed without the reforms. Fortunately, the Social Security Administration contracted with the Rand Corporation to conduct just such a sophisticated analysis of the impact of the 1996 reforms on the SSI caseload. Rand estimated, based on statistical modeling, that by 2005 the SSI child caseload was reduced by 26 percent, or 310,000 cases, compared to its size without the 1996 reforms. Two of the 1996 reforms—the changes in the admission procedures of the children's program and the reassessment using adult criteria when children reach age eighteen—are shown by the Rand study to have major impacts in reducing the caseload. The reduction in the SSI caseload, including both children and young adults, was calculated to save $21.7 billion over ten years.[126]

As with SSI for addicts, a thorough evaluation of the SSI reforms for children requires attention to the impacts of the reforms on children and families. Rand interviewed a sample of 44 families from four states that had lost their SSI benefits because of the reforms. Rand also conducted special analyses on a large national sample of families on which the Census Bureau has collected extensive information for other purposes. In accord with the laws of chance, the Census Bureau study included about 680 families that had formerly received SSI benefits. The analysis of census data found that loss of SSI was associated with increased work effort by parents, increased reliance on cash welfare, and increased family income. In addition, benefit loss was associated with a small decline in poverty. The family interviews were generally consistent with these results.

Of course, it would be important to learn a lot more about how the families that lost SSI benefits coped with change. The Rand study suggests that families responded appropriately to the loss of SSI benefits: they increased their work and earnings while also getting more money from welfare programs other than SSI. But were the children affected in any way? Was their school performance worse? Did they get sick more often? Did they have more conflicts with parents, teachers, or peers? No one knows. That their families worked more and had more money is a good sign, but hardly definitive. The correct conclusion about the impacts of the SSI reforms for children is that the jury is still out. Even so, the dire effects predicted by critics have not materialized, and in the meantime taxpayers are saving an average of well over $2 billion a year.

Sweeping reforms have produced sweeping effects. The evidence that welfare use has dropped, that work and earnings have increased, and that child poverty has fallen is overwhelming. There is some evidence that welfare reform had important effects on illegitimate births and family composition, child care, child support enforcement, welfare for noncitizens, SSI and SSDI for addicts, and SSI for children, all of which are in line with the expectations of Republicans who developed the reforms. Regardless of what one thinks of these reforms, implementation increased child care for working families, increased child support collections for custodial parents, increased the amount of child support collections, and reduced taxpayer expenditures on welfare for addicts, for children with mild disabilities, and for noncitizens. In each case the reforms have also moved the respective programs closer to achieving the goals for which they were designed. However, little is known about the extent to which children were affected by these very substantial policy changes.

Despite these uncertainties, on balance welfare reform has produced a host of benefits for poor mothers and the nation. The combination of a Democratic president who wanted to change welfare, a band of congressional Republicans who had a host of well-developed ideas on how welfare should be reformed, aggressive Republican governors who supported the reforms, and the sudden seizure of power in both houses of Congress by Republicans created the perfect conditions for passage of historic reforms in 1996.[127] It is not too much to claim that the reform measures fundamentally altered the ground of American social policy from dependency-producing entitlement to an expectation of work.

When welfare reform passed in August 1996 the American economy was in the midst of a historic expansion, which featured both job growth and wage increases, especially at the bottom of the income distribution. In addition, federal and state programs that provide generous support to low-income working families were coming to fruition, and new programs, such as the child tax credit and the State Child Health Insurance Program, were enacted at about the same time as welfare reform. Moreover, most states were already implementing their own welfare reform programs when the federal legislation provided them with the flexibility and funds to go even further in the direction they were already heading. In short, if work were a viable strategy to end welfare dependency, improve family income, and reduce poverty, the time to implement the work strategy could not have been better.

The successes of welfare reform have created their own challenges and cleared the way for new opportunities to emerge. Under the partisan atmosphere that has surrounded federal welfare debates for several decades, it is hardly surprising that awareness and constructive responses to these problems and opportunities are growing at a somewhat stately pace. Republicans and Democrats in Congress are still too busy fighting over some of the 1996 reforms to pay careful attention to the future. When Congress awakes to the new problems and opportunities at hand, as it inevitably will, it seems likely that federal policy will move further toward providing financial and other forms of support for low-income working families while maintaining the strong emphasis on work. And interest by the public and policymakers in raising the percentage of children in two-parent, married families seems to be growing. The coming acts in the drama of welfare reform will be neither peaceful nor cheap. More to the point, they will continue to emphasize the traditional American values of hard work, marriage, and strong families to a much greater extent than in the past. In the end, this new foundation of federal social policymaking is the greatest legacy of the Republican-Clinton welfare reform law of 1996. The nation is now on a new and firmer path to ending dependency, increasing self-reliance, and improving the social and economic status of millions of struggling families.

# The Welfare Reform Law That Reshaped American Social Policy

The purpose of this appendix is to provide a brief review of the major reforms in the 1996 law. Any major provision that appeared in any of the major bills, including provisions that were not enacted as part of the final law and provisions that were enacted as part of legislation other than the 1996 welfare reform law, is discussed here.[1]

## TEMPORARY ASSISTANCE FOR NEEDY FAMILIES

The Aid to Families with Dependent Children (AFDC) program is replaced by the Temporary Assistance for Needy Families (TANF) program. TANF can be characterized as differing from AFDC in three major ways. First, the AFDC legal entitlement to cash for poor families with children is replaced by several requirements intended to break welfare dependency. Government still offers cash to support destitute parents and their children but only for a maximum of five years and only if the parent takes steps to prepare for and find work. TANF is conditioned on personal effort.

Second, under TANF, money is given to states in annual lump sums called block grants. The block grant, which gives $16.5 billion annually to states on a formula basis, allows every state to design its own program tailored to local circumstances and local mores and traditions. State programs must meet four broad goals: to support children from destitute families so they can be raised at home by their parents; to help families achieve independence from welfare through work and marriage; to increase the percentage of children being reared in married, two-parent families; and to reduce the incidence of nonmarital births.

In addition to state flexibility, another advantage of the block grant format is that it provides states with financial incentives to help families leave the welfare rolls. Under the old AFDC program, if states helped a welfare recipient find a job, their cash benefit fell or, in most cases, ended. Because the state split the cost of the benefit with the federal government, as each family left welfare, the federal government reduced the amount of money given to the state. For every person added to the rolls, the federal government gave the state more money. The message from the federal government to the states implicit in AFDC was, we'll give you more money if you expand the welfare rolls and less money if you help recipients leave the rolls.[2] By contrast, because the block grant gives states a fixed number of dollars regardless of how many people are on the rolls, states have great incentive to help people get off the rolls. The money states save because they are providing cash benefits to fewer families can be used to invest in child care, training programs, transportation, earnings supplements, or other measures designed to promote work.

A third component of TANF that differs sharply with AFDC is work requirements. The work requirement embodies several separate but interrelated parts. The most prominent is the percentage standard. Using a percentage calculated by dividing the number of welfare recipients actually working or in a work-related activity by the total number of families receiving the TANF cash benefit (with a few small adjustments), the law now requires states to place 50 percent of their caseload in a work activity. The requirement also specifies that in order to count toward meeting the work requirement, a recipient (with some exceptions) must participate in approved activities for thirty hours a week. Special rules with more hours of required work apply to two-parent families.

The definition of approved activities that count toward the work requirement is another important part of TANF's work requirement. The law allows states to use education and training but only for a maximum of one year for any individual and no more than 30 percent of recipients can count as meeting the work requirement through education. Teenage parents in school count toward the work requirement, subject to the 30 percent cap, as long as they maintain satisfactory attendance in school.

To this stringent set of rules requiring work, Congress allows some exceptions. States can exempt mothers with a child under age one from the work requirement (and are given an incentive to do so by allowing such mothers to be dropped from the denominator in calculating the participation standard); states are allowed to count a mother with a child under age one as working when she participates for only twenty hours a week; and mothers with children under age six cannot be required to work if the mother proves that appropriate child care either is not available "within a reasonable distance" from her home or is too expensive.

The strong work requirement is also mitigated by something called the case-load reduction credit. This credit allows states to reduce the work requirement by 1 percentage point for each percentage point by which the state reduces its caseload below its level in 1995. The logic of this provision is that if states can help recipients find jobs and leave the rolls, states should receive some credit toward fulfilling the work requirement. However, states cannot use changes in policy that simply throw recipients off the rolls to count toward computing the caseload reduction credit.

## ILLEGITIMACY REDUCTION

The two most controversial provisions to reduce nonmarital births that House Republicans included in their original bill were ending the eligibility for cash welfare of unmarried mothers under age eighteen (the Murray Light provision) and ending the practice of increasing the cash benefit of mothers already on welfare who had additional babies (the family cap provision). Both were defeated on the Senate floor, and neither was included in the final bill. However, because of the flexibility offered states by the block grant structure of TANF, any state can adopt either provision. About half the states have adopted the family cap; no state has adopted any version of Murray Light.

Despite the defeat of these two House provisions, many provisions designed to fight illegitimacy are included in the final law. Perhaps the most important are the provisions on establishing paternity. A combination of sticks and carrots, the paternity-establishment provisions require states to do everything possible to establish paternity. Mothers applying for welfare with children whose paternity has not been established are required to give the names and addresses of possible fathers, and the state is required to locate these fathers and use blood tests if necessary to establish paternity. States are required to refuse benefits to mothers who do not cooperate. States are also required to design a program for a hospital-based voluntary paternity establishment. In addition, states are required to ensure that teenage mothers remain in school in order to qualify for TANF benefits and to ensure that teen mothers live either at home, with relatives, or in another adult-supervised setting.

The law also creates a $50-million-a-year grant program called abstinence education. States must use this money to establish programs designed to promote abstinence among students and youth through the public schools and other community facilities. The statute requires that these programs be based on specific messages such as the "expected standard for all school-age children is abstinence from sexual activity outside marriage" and that "abstinence . . . is the only certain way to avoid out-of-wedlock pregnancy, sexually transmitted diseases, and other associated health problems." Abstinence programs also must teach that "sexual activity outside . . . marriage is likely to have harmful psychological and physical effects" and "that bearing children out-of-wedlock is likely to have harmful consequences for the child, the child's parents, and society."[3] States are free to use the money to create and implement their own abstinence programs or to fund groups in the state to sponsor the programs. States could also use the funds to conduct public campaigns to bring broad attention to the importance of sexual abstinence.

Under the illegitimacy reduction bonus, states reducing their rate of illegitimacy in a given year are considered for a $25 million bonus payment from the federal government. The logic of this provision is that states would compete with each other to develop new approaches to reducing illegitimacy rates in order to win the bonus.

## CHILD CARE

Five separate child care programs from previous laws are combined into one block grant and funded at a level of about $4 billion (over six years) more than the spending level of the programs it was replacing.[4] The child care block grant is given two streams of funding. One stream, representing the entitlement programs associated with AFDC that were terminated, is entitlement funding, which increased gradually from about $2.0 billion in 1997 to about $2.7 billion in 2002. The second stream is appropriated funding, of $1 billion a year, which would have to undergo the rigors of the annual appropriations process. As it turned out, the appropriators were generous in many years, and the stream of appropriations soon increased to $2.1 billion.

As with the TANF block grant, the child care block grant requires states to contribute their own funds. States are required to continue spending the amount of their own funds that they spent on child care under the various child care programs related to the old AFDC program in either 1994 or 1995, whichever figure was higher. In addition, states are required to provide matching funds for every dollar of federal entitlement funds above an amount the state was guaranteed under the child care block grant. Totaled across all the states, the guaranteed child care amount is about $1.2 billion. Since the block grant contains $2.7 billion in guaranteed funds, an additional $1.5 billion ($2.7 billion minus $1.2 billion) is distributed among the states. These funds, which are made available to states in proportion to each state's share of children under age thirteen, have to be matched by state dollars or the states do not receive the additional federal funds. The matching rate is the rate at which states had to match federal Medicaid payments in 1995 (between roughly 20 percent for the poorest states and 50 percent for the richest states).

States are required to use 4 percent of the block grant to improve child care quality and to increase parent choice of care. To increase flexibility in the use of block grant funds, states are allowed to transfer up to 30 percent of their TANF funds into the child care block grant (states can also transfer up to one-third of the 30 percent into another block grant called the Social Services Block Grant, which allows states virtually unlimited flexibility in spending on social services). Because the TANF block grant is about $16.5 billion, the transfer mechanism can potentially increase child care funding by around $5 billion (30 percent of $16.5 billion = $4.95 billion) in a given year.

## CHILD SUPPORT ENFORCEMENT

The new law includes a series of administrative procedures that states must follow in their child support program. Under the new-hire database, every employer in the country must report, to a central location in each state, identifying information on every person they hire. With such a system in place, in a few years every state would have the employer's address and the Social Security number of most employees in the entire state. States are also required to maintain a computerized registry of every child support case in the state. Several times a week, the state computer system must automatically match the new-hire data received from employers with the registry of case records. For every new employee with a child support order, a letter must be automatically generated by the computer system and sent to the employer instructing the employer to withhold wages, the amount to be withheld, and the address (usually electronic) to which the withheld money should be sent. When fully implemented, the combination of the new-hire reporting and the case registry means that the guts of the child support system are automated, high speed, almost universal, highly efficient, and difficult for those owing child support to escape.

Because about one-third of all child support cases are interstate (the parent owing child support lives in a different state from the child), addressing these cases with new policies was essential. Under the 1996 reforms, every state must report both its new-hire database and its case registry to the federal government, where data matches similar to those performed at the state level are conducted—except in this case the matches are across states.

States are also required to develop a third automated system to provide access to the records of every financial institution in the state. The financial institutions are required to search their records for financial holdings by individuals owing past-due child support and to report positive findings to the state. To protect financial institutions, the federal law requires states to pass laws giving them immunity for sharing financial information.

In addition to these new automated administrative systems, the 1996 law includes several other mandates on states to establish new mechanisms that increase child support collections. The most controversial of these is the requirement that states have laws that allow them to suspend regular driver's licenses, commercial driver's licenses, and hunting and fishing licenses, in the case of fathers owing overdue child support.

Two other major provisions designed to increase collections are included in the law. Social Security numbers, which serve as the main cog in the procedures for identifying parents who owe child support and in matching their records, are required to be placed in the records of many official state documents, such as marriage licenses, obtained by individuals. A new program is established for denying passports to parents who owe over $5,000 in past-due child support.

Finally, there are major changes in the child support distribution rules. Before 1996 the distribution rules required states to give mothers and children on welfare the first $50 of any child support payment made by fathers. This payment was replaced by a provision that would allow mothers not on welfare to receive more child support money. According to the Congressional Budget Office (CBO), under this new provision mothers and children are to receive around $150 million a year in additional child support payments (above previous law).[5]

A final child support provision provides $10 million a year in entitlement funds, given to states in proportion to the percentage of the nation's single-parent families that live in each state, to support both private and government projects to help fathers have smoother visitation arrangements. Typically, these funds are used to support mediation services and to provide a neutral site for mothers and fathers who have serious conflicts to leave and return children for visits with their father.

## WELFARE FOR NONCITIZENS

For the sake of simplicity, this summary of reforms of welfare for immigrants pertains to the law as amended in 1997, 1998, and 2002.[6] The most important provisions are the outright bars on welfare receipt by noncitizens. The most stringent bar is a permanent ban on receipt of Supplemental Security Income (SSI) for noncitizens entering the country after 1996. The second bar is a prohibition on receipt of Food Stamps, Medicaid, and TANF for five years. However, after noncitizens have been in the United States for five years, states can decide for themselves whether to give them benefits from any or all of these welfare programs. Subsequent legislation lifted the Food Stamp bar for children who are eligible for the benefit if they are legal residents, and for other legal residents after five years.

A second major provision of the noncitizen reforms, enacted as part of the Immigration and Nationality Act of 1996, requires that most noncitizens entering the United States have affidavits of support from someone who agrees to support them if they become destitute.[7] The affidavits of support are legally binding and in effect until either the noncitizen becomes a citizen or meets a work requirement (of forty quarters) that qualifies her for welfare benefits. All family-based and employment-based immigrants must have an affidavit of support. In order to serve as a sponsor, an individual must have an income of at least 125 percent of the poverty level and agree to support the noncitizen. Both government agencies and sponsored noncitizens can sue the sponsor if the sponsor fails to meet the financial obligation established by the affidavit of support.

All the sponsor's income—and if the sponsor is married, the spouse's income as well—is deemed to be available to the noncitizen. Because most new immigrants must have sponsors, and because government has the legal right to sue sponsors for nonsupport, it is clear that sponsors and not taxpayers are intended to assume the financial burden of noncitizens who cannot earn enough to support themselves.

The law also includes several important exceptions to the welfare bans that can be organized into two primary categories. The first category is emergencies. Included here are medical services under emergency circumstances, disaster relief, foster care and adoption services for abused and neglected children, and immunizations and treatment for communicable illnesses. Noncitizens in need are eligible for all these programs. A second category of exceptions might be dubbed the "Horatio Alger" exceptions. Given that self-improvement is one of the most fundamental concepts underlying immigration, noncitizens should be eligible for programs that provide them with education, training, and work supports. Children are eligible for Head Start, child nutrition programs, and benefits under federal education programs; adults are eligible for education and training programs under the Workforce Investment Act, the Higher Education Act, and other education and training programs. In addition, adults are eligible for the Earned Income Tax Credit, which provides an income supplement of up to $4,400 (in 2005) for low-income workers. This is a particularly lucrative benefit for noncitizens because so many of them work for low wages.

## SSI FOR DRUG ADDICTS AND ALCOHOLICS

By 1996 there were about 120,000 SSI and 90,000 Social Security Disability Insurance (SSDI) recipients who qualified for the programs because they were drug addicts or alcoholics.[8] In addition, SSI recipients automatically qualified for Medicaid health insurance while SSDI recipients automatically qualified for Medicare coverage. The welfare reform laws vetoed by President Clinton would have ended alcoholism and drug addiction as conditions that would enable an addict to qualify for SSI or SSDI (and Medicaid or Medicare), thereby terminating the eligibility of nearly 210,000 individuals.[9] When the welfare bill was stalled and its passage was in doubt in 1996, Congress passed the provision ending the SSI eligibility of addicts and alcoholics as part of Public Law 104-121.

## SSI FOR CHILDREN

The two most important reforms of the SSI children's program are a change in the definition of child disability and the termination of an assessment method that was too lenient. The change in definition is that the "comparable severity" standard by which the Social Security Administration (SSA) was required to determine that a disability was comparable to an adult disability was repealed. In its place, the new law substitutes the concept that an impairment must result in "marked and severe" functional limitations in daily living skills such as dressing, using the bathroom, walking, talking, writing, and learning in school. Only if children cannot learn and perform these basic functions are they eligible for SSI. SSA is also barred from using a test called the Individualized Functional Assessment in determining a child's eligibility because this test too often yielded the conclusion that children with minor problems were eligible for SSI payments. According to the General Accounting Office (now the Government Accountability Office), SSA, and CBO, both of these changes result in fewer children qualifying for SSI.[10] The law also requires SSA to review children already receiving SSI benefits within one year using the new eligibility requirements. Another important change is that all children receiving SSI must have their eligibility redetermined using adult eligibility requirements before they can enter the adult program at age eighteen.

## CHILD PROTECTION

Republicans proposed to convert several federal entitlement programs that helped states pay for foster care and adoption into a block grant. The CBO would have been required to estimate how much money each state would receive from the federal government each year for five years under the federal child protection entitlement programs. This sum of money would be given to the states in annual block grants, and states would be authorized to spend this money for virtually any child protection purpose. Thus states would have the flexibility to divide the money as they saw fit on prevention, treatment, maintenance, and administration. After extensive debate, the block grant proposal was killed by the Senate, and the 1996 law contains only two minor reforms of the child protection programs. These reforms allow states to contract for child protection services with for-profit providers (previous law had barred for-profit entities from receiving federal dollars) and extend an existing program that gives states additional funding for creating better computer systems in the child protection program.

## CHARITABLE CHOICE

States are authorized to administer and provide benefits and services under the TANF block grant through contracts with charitable, religious, or private organizations. In addition, TANF services can be provided through vouchers that can be redeemed by charitable, religious, or private organizations.

## CHILD NUTRITION PROGRAMS

The child nutrition entitlement programs under the previous law consisted primarily of the school lunch program, the school breakfast program, the child and adult care food program, and the Special Supplemental Food Program for Women, Infants, and Children (WIC). Taken together, these programs cost about $12 billion in 1995. The House Education Committee tried to collapse many of these programs into two block grants with capped funding. The Family Nutrition Block Grant would have combined five child nutrition programs into a single program; the School-Based Nutrition block grant would have combined the school lunch, school breakfast, and after-school food programs into a single program. Funding of the two block grants would have increased every year but not as much as spending would have increased under the entitlement programs replaced by the block grants. The CBO estimated that the two block grants would save about $11.8 billion over five years. When the House bill arrived in the Senate, Richard Lugar, chairman of the Agriculture Committee, did not approve of the block grants and, after lots of maneuvering, managed to kill them. As a result, the final law contained no child nutrition block grants and only modest reforms of the constituent programs.

Almost all the savings were made in the Child and Adult Food Program. This program provides food subsidies to facilities that provide care to elderly and disabled adults or to children. The major change is to subject the federal subsidies to an income test, through which facilities that enroll primarily low-income families or are run by a low-income operator receive higher subsidies than other facilities.

## FOOD STAMPS

Because Chairman Pat Roberts and many Republicans on the House Agriculture Committee fought against the recommendation by the Republican governors to convert the Food Stamp program into a block grant, the 1996 welfare reform law did not change the structure of the Food Stamp program. Even so, the 1996 law includes more than twenty provisions, nearly all of them included in the original House bill HR 4, which save money: over seven years, savings were about $23 billion, which does not include the nearly $3.7 billion in savings realized by the restrictions on Food Stamps for noncitizens contained elsewhere in the welfare reform law.

Of the $23 billion, nearly $19 billion are accounted for by just five reforms: a work requirement on able-bodied adults who do not have children, which results in many childless adults leaving the Food Stamp rolls; numerous reductions in the rules that govern deductions from income in calculating the Food Stamp benefit (lower deductions yield higher income, which in turn produces lower Food Stamp benefits); less generous treatment of young adults with their own children who live with their parents; a reduction in the maximum Food Stamp benefit a household can receive; and an expansion of the definition of income by counting certain types of energy assistance as income.[11]

## MEDICAID

Medicaid, which provides health coverage for the poor (including nursing home care for the elderly poor) and the disabled, is one of the nation's most rapidly growing social programs. In the five years before 1995, for example, total Medicaid spending grew from $72.5 billion to $156.3 billion, an increase of over 15 percent a year.[12] Under federal law, states paid about 45 percent of these costs as well as of the cost increases. Both Democratic and Republican governors wanted more control over the growth of Medicaid spending. Thus the National Governors Association (NGA), on a bipartisan basis, proposed converting Medicaid to a block grant. But when the committees of jurisdiction in Congress, led by the House Commerce Committee, wrote the actual legislative language for the block grant, Democratic governors immediately complained that the congressional block grant was not consistent with the NGA proposal. So controversial was the Medicaid block grant that Republicans came to believe that the welfare bill could not pass if it included the block grant. Thus the Medicaid block grant was dropped.

Even though the block grant was dropped, three Medicaid provisions are included in the new law. The most important is the continuation of Medicaid coverage for all families that meet the eligibility criteria for the old AFDC program as they existed on July 16, 1996. The purpose of this provision is to prevent states from dropping families from Medicaid by creating stricter eligibility requirements for their new TANF program. Largely to compensate states for having to make separate eligibility computations for TANF and Medicaid, a $500 million pot was established to divide up among the states to pay additional administrative costs over the years 1997–2000. Another provision extends the previous law that required states to maintain transitional Medicaid benefits for one year to families leaving welfare because of increased earnings or increased child support payments.

## INTERETHNIC ADOPTION

One barrier to the adoption of children that both Republican and Democratic policymakers were determined to end was ethnic preferences in placing children. Based on evidence that social workers often delayed placing children in foster care or adoptive homes while trying to locate a foster parent of the same race as the child,[13] in 1994 Congress had passed the Multiethnic Placement Act (Public Law 103-382). Drafted primarily by Senator Howard Metzenbaum of Ohio, the act was written specifically to prevent minority children from languishing in foster care while they awaited adoption by a minority family. Unfortunately, the law contained language that allowed agencies to consider the child's cultural, ethnic, or racial background, which defeated the purpose of the provision. Republicans in the House developed a new provision that repealed the Metzenbaum language and substituted language stating simply that states could not "delay or deny" a foster care or adoption placement on the basis of race, color, or national origin. The new provision, which had the support of Senator Metzenbaum, includes severe financial penalties on any state that violated the new prohibition on delaying or denying placement.[14] Although this provision was a part of the original Shaw welfare reform bill in February 1995, an opportunity occurred to pass it as part of the Small Business Job Protection Act in August 1996 because the act contained a provision expanding the adoption tax credit. This bill was signed into law as Public Law 104-188 on August 20, 1996, two days before the welfare reform legislation became law.

## Data Reporting and Research

The welfare reform legislation contains elaborate and expensive provisions for both state-reported data and research. States are required to report extensive data for both their TANF and child care programs. Congress and the Clinton administration insisted on state reports of important measures that would help the federal government and the public make informed judgments about financial accountability and about whether welfare reform programs were working.

States are required to report fifteen data elements (some of which have more than one part) on each family receiving benefits from the TANF block grant. These elements—which include age, family relationships, employment status of adults, race, education status, and types of welfare assistance received and for how long—must be reported quarterly to the Department of Health and Human Services (HHS). States are also required to report on a sample of closed cases including the reason the family left the caseload. In addition, states must report the amount of money they spend on administration, the amount of state money they spend on needy families, the number of noncustodial parents participating in employment programs, the services provided to families leaving welfare, and the cost of these services. The legislation also requires HHS to summarize this information for Congress in an annual report.[15]

Similarly, states are required to report a basic set of data on their day care program and on day care spending. In this case, the data include, for every family receiving support from the child care block grant, family income by source and the gender, race, and age of children receiving assistance. States also must report information on the types of day care facilities used by families, the cost of care, and the hours used a week. States are also required to report aggregate child care data. This reporting includes the number of child care facilities receiving assistance, the number of payments made by the state through various financing mechanisms (such as vouchers), and the number of children receiving services.

The legislation contains three provisions for funding research and evaluation studies. First, $7 million a year for seven years is given to HHS to conduct a national study of children with confirmed cases of abuse and neglect. If conducted properly, this study can provide the best information available about families involved in the child protection system, the duration and type of intervention provided by the child protection system, and child and family outcomes.

Second, the Census Bureau is given $10 million a year for seven years to reconstitute a sample of families that had participated in a previous study (the Survey of Income and Program Participation) and to continue collecting extensive information on them—including new information on children and their schooling—over a period of years.[16] By comparing the condition of these families and children before and after welfare reform, it would be possible to draw tentative conclusions about improvement or decline in the employment and income of families at the bottom of the income distribution as well as the condition of their children. It might also be possible to draw tentative conclusions about the role of welfare reform and other government programs (such as Food Stamps, Medicaid, the Earned Income Tax Credit, and child care) in maintaining the financial well-being of these families.

Third, HHS received $15 million a year for six years to conduct research and evaluation on welfare reform programs and issues of its choosing. HHS is directed to make use of random-assignment studies wherever possible.

## SOCIAL SERVICES BLOCK GRANT

The legislation reduces the Social Services block grant, which provides states with funds to achieve a wide variety of social goals, by 15 percent, to produce $2.5 billion in savings over the period 1997–2002.

## EARNED INCOME TAX CREDIT

In contrast with the 1995 versions of the welfare reform bill, which contained extensive EITC reforms that would have saved $23 billion over seven years, the law as passed contained three minor EITC changes, agreed to on a bipartisan basis, which saved only $2.9 billion over seven years. These provisions instruct the Internal Revenue Service to disqualify some types of income for the purpose of computing the EITC benefit, change the definition of adjusted gross income (AGI) for phasing out the EITC benefit, and allow the Internal Revenue Service to disqualify certain types of EITC applications.

## SAVINGS

As officially estimated by the CBO, savings in the bill over the seven-year period 1996–2002 are as follows:[17]
—Family Support (TANF): $3.8 billion
—Food Stamps: –$23.3 billion
—Supplemental Security Income: –$22.7 billion
—Medicaid: –$4.1 billion
—Child Nutrition: –$2.9 billion
—Old-Age, Survivors, and Disability Insurance: –$0.1 billion
—Foster Care: $0.2 billion
—Social Services block grant: –$2.5 billion
—Earned Income Tax Credit: –$2.9 billion
—Maternal and Child Health: –$0.2 billion
—Total: –$54.2 billion[18]

# Notes

## CHAPTER ONE

*Note*: An earlier version of this chapter appeared as "Liberal and Conservative Influ-ences on the Welfare Reform Legislation of 1996," in *For Better and For Worse: Welfare Reform and the Well-Being of Children and Families*, edited by Greg J. Duncan and P. Lindsay Chase-Lansdale (New York: Russell Sage, 2001).

1. Peter Rossi, "The Iron Law of Evaluation and Other Metallic Rules," *Research in Social Problems for Public Policy* 4 (1987): 3–20. In an address at the annual conference of the Association for Public Policy Analysis and Management in 2003, Rossi slightly mod-ified his view. He still held that the vast majority of social programs did not produce impacts, but he allowed that since his 1987 paper had been published, high-quality eval-uations of a few social programs had shown impacts. See Peter H. Rossi, "The 'Iron Law of Evaluation' Reconsidered," paper presented at the annual meeting of the Association for Public Policy Analysis and Management, Washington, October 2003.

2. Martin Gilens, *Why Americans Hate Welfare: Race, Media, and the Politics of Antipoverty Policy* (University of Chicago Press, 1999), esp. chap. 8.

3. Sheldon Danziger, Robert Haveman, and Robert Plotnick, "How Income Transfers Affect Work, Savings, and the Income Distribution: A Critical Review," *Journal of Eco-nomic Literature* 19 (1981): 975–1028; Robert Moffitt, "Incentive Effects of the U.S. Wel-fare System: A Review," *Journal of Economic Literature* 30 (1992): 1–61; Robert Moffitt, ed., *Welfare, the Family, and Reproductive Behavior: Research Perspectives* (Washington: National Academy Press, 1998); Joseph A. Pechman and P. Michael Timpane, eds., *Work Incentives and Income Guarantees: The New Jersey Negative Income Tax Experiment* (Brookings, 1975); Department of Health and Human Services, *Overview of the Final Report of the Seattle-Denver Income Maintenance Experiment* (1983); Alice Munnell, ed., *Lessons from the Income Maintenance Experiments* (Brookings, 1987).

4. Lawrence Mead, *The New Politics of Poverty: The Nonworking Poor in America* (New York: Basic Books, 1992); Gilens, *Why Americans Hate Welfare*.

5. Social Security, Medicare, Unemployment Compensation, and the entire range of federal and state social programs are summarized in House Committee on Ways and Means, *2004 Green Book*, sections 1, 2, 4, and app. K.

6. House Committee on Ways and Means, *1996 Green Book*, p. 329.

7. Data in this paragraph from ibid., pp. 50, 17, 134, 135.

8. Alice M. Rivlin and Isabel Sawhill, *Restoring Fiscal Sanity: How to Balance the Bud-get* (Brookings, 2004); Alice M. Rivlin and Isabel Sawhill, *Restoring Fiscal Sanity 2005: Meeting the Challenge* (Brookings, 2005).

9. Gilens, *Why Americans Hate Welfare.*

10. At the request of Clay Shaw, chairman of the House Committee on Ways and Means, CRS gave reports for seven of the eight domains to the Human Resources Subcommittee of the Ways and Means Committee, for which I was the staff director. The eighth report, for employment and training programs, was given to us by the GAO. My staff and I put the reports together in one table and used the table for partisan purposes. CRS and GAO are innocent of all charges of deliberately helping Republicans. See House Committee on Ways and Means, *Summary of Welfare Reforms Made by Public Law 104-19: The Personal Responsibility and Work Opportunity Reconciliation Act and Associated Legislation,* Committee Print 104-15 (1994), p. 4.

11. Vee Burke, *CRS Report for Congress: Cash and Noncash Benefits for Persons with Limited Income: Eligibility Rules, Recipient and Expenditure Data, FY2000–FY2002* (Congressional Research Service, 2003); Robert Rector and William F. Lauber, *America's Failed $5.4 Trillion War on Poverty* (Washington: Heritage Foundation, 1995). The $375 billion used in the text differs from figures used by Burke and by Rector and Lauber because I include different programs. It is notable that the health programs, especially after the 1980s, were among the biggest and were the most rapidly growing.

12. Daniel P. Moynihan, *The Politics of a Guaranteed Income: The Nixon Administration and the Family Assistance Plan* (New York: Vintage, 1973).

13. Sally S. Cohen, *Championing Child Care* (Columbia University Press, 2001), chap. 2; Ron Haskins, "Child Development and Child Care Policy," in *Developmental Psychology and Social Change: Research, History, and Policy,* edited by David B. Pillemer and Sheldon H. White (Cambridge University Press, 2005).

14. Moynihan, *The Politics of a Guaranteed Income.*

15. David Whitman and Laurence E. Lynn Jr., *The President as Policymaker: Jimmy Carter and Welfare Reform* (Temple University Press, 1981).

16. House Committee on Ways and Means, *1991 Green Book,* pp. 656–57. Robert Carleson was a major Reagan adviser on welfare reform who always emphasized the importance of work. He played an important role behind the scenes in lobbying for the 1996 legisation. He died as I was writing the final version of this book. RIP.

17. Judith M. Gueron and Edward Pauly, *From Welfare to Work* (New York: Russell Sage, 1991).

18. Gertrude Himmelfarb, *The Idea of Poverty* (New York: Random House, 1985).

19. Danziger, Haveman, and Plotnick, "How Income Transfers Affect Work, Savings, and the Income Distribution." For a more recent review, see Moffitt, "Incentive Effects of the U.S. Welfare System."

20. Mary Jo Bane and David T. Ellwood, "Slipping Into and Out of Poverty: The Dynamics of Spells," *Journal of Human Resources* 21 (1986): 1–23.

21. House Committee on Ways and Means, *1996 Green Book,* p. 505.

22. Charles Murray, "The Coming White Underclass," *Wall Street Journal,* October 29, 1993, p. A14.

23. David T. Ellwood and Mary Jo Bane, "The Impact of AFDC on Family Structure and Living Arrangements," in *Research in Labor Economics,* vol. 7, edited by R. G. Ehrenberg (Greenwich, Conn.: JAI Press, 1985); Rebecca M. Blank, *It Takes a Nation: A New Agenda for Fighting Poverty* (New York: Russell Sage, 1997), pp. 37–39; Irwin Garfinkel and Sara S. McLanahan, *Single Mothers and Their Children: A New American Dilemma* (Washington: Urban Institute, 1986), pp. 58–59.

24. Ron Haskins, "Does Welfare Encourage Illegitimacy?" *American Enterprise* 7 (1996): 48–49; Charles Murray, "Family Formation," in *The New World of Welfare,* edited by Rebecca Blank and Ron Haskins (Brookings, 2001). Robert Rector of the conservative

Heritage Foundation in Washington, a major actor in the debate that led to the 1996 welfare reform legislation, made a list of the fourteen social science studies that found at least one correlation between a measure of welfare generosity and rates of illegitimacy. The title of his list was simply "Studies of Welfare and Illegitimacy." See *Congressional Record*, daily ed., September 13, 1995, p. S13527.

25. Byron M. Roth, *Prescription for Failure* (New Brunswick, N.J.: Transaction, 1994); Paul Amato, "The Impact of Family Formation Change on the Cognitive, Social, and Emotional Wellbeing of the Next Generation," *Future of Children* 15 (2005): 75–96.

26. Christopher Jencks, *Rethinking Social Policy: Race, Poverty, and the Underclass* (Harvard University Press, 1992), esp. pp. 12–14.

27. Irving Kristol, *Neoconservatism: The Autobiography of an Idea* (New York: Free Press, 1995), pp. 43–45.

28. *Public Papers of the Presidents of the United States: William J. Clinton, 1994*, vol. 2 (Government Printing Office, 1995), p. 1529.

29. Department of Health and Human Services, *Report to Congress on Out-of-Wedlock Childbearing*, PHS 95-1257 (Hyattsville, Md.: National Center for Health Statistics, 1995).

30. Rebecca Maynard, "Paternalism, Teenage Pregnancy Prevention, and Teenage Parent Services," in *The New Paternalism: Supervisory Approaches to Poverty*, edited by Lawrence M. Mead (Brookings, 1997).

31. Daniel Patrick Moynihan, *The Negro Family: The Case for National Action* (Department of Labor, 1965).

32. Christopher Jencks, "The Moynihan Report," *New York Review of Books*, October 14, 1965, pp. 216–18.

33. Lee Rainwater and William L. Yancey, *The Moynihan Report and the Politics of Controversy* (MIT Press, 1967).

34. Stephanie J. Ventura and others, *Nonmarital Childbearing in the United States, 1940–1999* (Hyattsville, Md.: National Center for Health Statistics, 2000).

35. Charles Murray, *Losing Ground: American Social Policy, 1950–1980* (New York: Basic Books, 1984).

36. Murray, "The Coming White Underclass."

37. Lawrence M. Mead, *Beyond Entitlement: The Social Obligations of Citizenship* (New York: Free Press, 1986).

38. Mead, *The New Paternalism*.

39. Himmelfarb, *The Idea of Poverty*.

40. Mead, *The New Politics of Poverty*; Isabel Sawhill and Ron Haskins, *Welfare Reform and the Work Support System*, Policy Brief 17, Welfare Reform & Beyond (Brookings, 2002).

41. For the sake of full disclosure, I am on MDRC's board of directors. I have also been a paid consultant for several other large research companies, including Rand and Mathematica Policy Research.

42. Gueron and Pauly, *From Welfare to Work*; Mead, *The New Paternalism*, esp. chap. 9.

43. Gueron and Pauly, *From Welfare to Work*; Daniel Friedlander and Gary Burtless, *Five Years After: The Long-Term Effects of Welfare-to-Work Programs* (New York: Russell Sage, 1995).

44. Mead, *Beyond Entitlement*, esp. chaps. 6, 7.

45. The AFDC program for two-parent families had previously been optional; but the 1988 welfare reform legislation required all states to adopt at least a modified version of the two-parent program, and twenty-seven states had already adopted it; see House Committee on Ways and Means, *1996 Green Book*, p. 395.

46. In 1989 there were a little more than 192,000 two-parent families on AFDC out of a total caseload of 3.8 million; see House Committee on Ways and Means, *1990 Green Book*, pp. 547, 575.

47. House Committee on Ways and Means, *1996 Green Book*, pp. 386–87.

48. Working Seminar, *A Community of Self-Reliance: The New Consensus on Family and Welfare* (Washington: American Enterprise Institute, 1987).

49. Ibid., p. 100.

50. Ibid., pp. 74–82.

51. Jason DeParle, *American Dream: Three Women, Ten Kids, and a Nation's Drive to End Welfare* (New York: Penguin, 2004).

52. David T. Ellwood, *Poor Support: Poverty in the American Family* (New York: Basic Books, 1989).

53. Laurence E. Lynn Jr., "Ending Welfare Reform as We Know It," *American Prospect* 4 (1993): 83–92; Frances F. Piven, "Was Welfare Reform Worthwhile?" *American Prospect* 7 (1996): 14–15.

54. Irvin Garfinkel and Sara McLanahan proposed in 1986 that, if a number of rather stringent conditions were met, AFDC could be time-limited. See Garfinkel and McLanahan, *Single Mothers and Their Children*, p. 185.

55. A negative tax is defined as a provision of the tax code in which individuals or families that meet a specific set of requirements receive a payment from the government. The normal function of the tax code, to collect money from individuals or families to finance government operations, is reversed, and money is sent from government to individuals, families, or businesses. The most prominent tax provision of this type is the EITC, which provides around $35 billion a year in cash payments to working individuals or families through the normal operation of the tax system. In addition, since 1997 the tax code has contained a provision called the Child Tax Credit, which provides families with a tax credit for each child who can be claimed as a dependent. The credit is now worth $1,000 per child and is partially refundable for low-income families with incomes above $10,500. See House Committee on Ways and Means, *1996 Green Book*, pp. 13–59.

56. In 1993 the EITC provided low-income working families with more than $15 billion. After Clinton's 1993 expansion, the EITC increased rapidly. By 1997 it provided working families with nearly $30 billion. House Committee on Ways and Means, *2004 Green Book*, pp. 13–14.

57. Jencks, *Rethinking Social Policy*, p. 13.

58. Mickey Kaus, *The End of Equality* (New York: Basic Books, 1992), chaps. 7, 8, and 9.

59. Robert Scheer, "Tough Luck: A Yuppie Manifesto: The End of Equality," *Los Angeles Times Book Review*, August 2, 1992, p. 1.

60. Herbert Croly, *The Promise of American Life* (Northeastern University Press, 1989 [Macmillan, 1909]).

61. Mickey Kaus, "The Work Ethic State," *New Republic*, July 7, 1986, pp. 22–33.

62. "Sign It," *New Republic*, August 12, 1996, pp. 7–8. The August 12, 1996, issue of *New Republic* features several articles on the welfare reform bill.

63. Franklin D. Roosevelt, "Annual Message to the Congress (January 4, 1935)," in *The Public Papers and Addresses of Franklin D. Roosevelt with a Special Introduction and Explanatory Notes by President Roosevelt*, vol. 4 (New York: Random House, 1938), pp. 19, 20.

64. Ken Auletta, *The Underclass* (New York: Random House, 1982).

65. House Committee on Ways and Means, *Hearings on the Contract with America: Overview*, Serial 104-20, January 11, 1995, p. 374.

66. Burke, *CRS Report for Congress*; Rector and Lauber, *America's Failed $5.4 Trillion War on Poverty*.

67. Moffitt, "Incentive Effects of the U.S. Welfare System"; House Committee on Ways and Means, *1996 Green Book*, pp. 12–14.

## CHAPTER TWO

1. Both the House and Senate assign a number to each bill introduced by members of their respective bodies. In the House, most bills are referred to by the term *HR* (the abbreviation for House of Representatives) followed by the number of the bill. Bills are assigned numbers consecutively by their date of introduction. The Senate follows the same practice except that the bills are labeled *S* (for Senate) followed by the bill number. At the beginning of a Congress every odd-numbered year, the leadership in the House and Senate often have major bills that it intends to pass during that session. These bills are often ready for introduction at the beginning of the congressional session in January and are assigned low numbers.

2. See the Library of Congress, Thomas databases at http://thomas.loc.gov.

3. Kevin Phillips, *The Politics of Rich and Poor* (New York: Random House, 1990).

4. Wednesday Group, "Moving Ahead: Initiatives for Expanding Opportunity in America," October 1991; William Archer, "Who's the Fairest of Them All? The Truth about the '80s," *Policy Review* 57 (Summer 1991): 67–73.

5. Wednesday Group, "Moving Ahead," p. 8.

6. Robert Rector and William H. Lauber, *America's Failed $5.4 Trillion War on Poverty* (Washington: Heritage Foundation, 1995); Vee Burke, *Cash and Noncash Benefits for Persons with Limited Income: Eligibility Rules, Recipient and Expenditure Data, FY2000–FY2002*, RL30401 (Congressional Research Service, 1999).

7. Later work by Adam Thomas, Isabel Sawhill, and Ron Haskins of the Brookings Institution shows that both work and marriage play a preeminent role in poverty. Specifically, the evidence in these and many other publications shows that increasing work and increasing marriage would have a much bigger effect on reducing poverty than any politically and fiscally feasible expansion of welfare. See Adam Thomas and Isabel Sawhill, "For Richer or for Poorer: Marriage as an Antipoverty Policy," *Journal of Policy Analysis and Management* 21 (2002): 587–99; Ron Haskins and Isabel Sawhill, *Work and Marriage: The Way to End Poverty and Welfare*, Policy Brief 28, Welfare Reform & Beyond (Brookings, 2003).

8. Charles Murray, *Losing Ground: American Social Policy, 1950–1980* (New York: Basic Books, 1984).

9. Paul R. Amato and Bruce Keith, "Consequences of Parental Divorce for Children's Well-Being: A Meta-Analysis," *Psychological Bulletin* 10 (1991): 26–46; Elizabeth Terry-Humen, Jennifer Manlove, and Kristin Moore, *Playing Catch-Up: How Children Born to Teen Mothers Fare* (Washington: National Campaign to Prevent Teen Pregnancy, 2005).

10. James T. Patterson, *America's Struggle against Poverty, 1900–1985* (Harvard University Press, 1986), chap. 11.

11. Mary Jo Bane and David T. Ellwood, "Slipping Into and Out of Poverty: The Dynamics of Spells," *Journal of Human Resources* 21 (1986): 1–23.

12. Charles Murray, "The Coming White Underclass," *Wall Street Journal*, October 29, 1993, p. A14.

13. Daniel Patrick Moynihan, "Family Policy for the Nation," *America* (September 18, 1965), pp. 280–83.

14. Lawrence M. Mead, *The New Politics of Poverty: The Nonworking Poor in America* (New York: Basic Books, 1992), pp. 61–65; Martin Gilens, *Why Americans Hate Welfare: Race, Media, and the Politics of Antipoverty Policy* (University of Chicago Press, 1999).

15. Mead, *The New Politics of Poverty*, chap. 3; Robert Haveman and Lawrence Buron, "Escaping Poverty through Work: The Problem of Low Earnings Capacity in the United States, 1973–1988," *Review of Income and Wealth* 39 (1993): 141–57; Sheldon Danziger,

Robert Haveman, and Robert Plotnick, "How Income Transfers Affect Work, Savings, and the Income Distribution: A Critical Review," *Journal of Economic Literature* 19 (1981): 975–1028; Robert Moffitt, "Incentive Effects of the U.S. Welfare System: A Review," *Journal of Economic Literature* 30 (1992): 1–61; Alice Munnell, ed., *Lessons from the Income Maintenance Experiments* (Brookings, 1987).

16. Ten or more stories in the media were devoted in whole or in part to the Wednesday Group study. These included a flattering editorial by David Broder, who had attended the media seminar we sponsored for selected editors and reporters. Broder's editorial addressed both our report and a mock hearing on tax reform sponsored by the House Republican Conference. His editorial concluded with the line: "What I saw on Capitol Hill suggests that Republicans are ready to govern—if given the chance." See David S. Broder, "Republicans Could Govern," *Washington Post,* October 27, 1991, p. C7; Paul Taylor, "From GOP, a New Look at Poverty," *Washington Post,* October 23, 1991, p. A25.

17. The bill, HR 5501, was "to amend title IV of the Social Security Act to provide welfare families with the education, training, and work experience needed to prepare them to leave welfare within 4 years, and for other purposes."

18. Wednesday Group, "Moving Ahead: How America Can Reduce Poverty through Work," June 1992, p. 4.

19. Jason DeParle, "The Transition: To Aid Those Most in Need, Clinton Wants to Help the Middle Class First," *New York Times,* November 10, 1992, p. A20.

20. HR 6083, Welfare Reform Demonstrations Act of 1992; HR 6110, Community Opportunity Pilot Program Act of 1992; HR 6111, Welfare Employment and Flexibility Amendments of 1992.

21. House Committee on Ways and Means, *1996 Green Book,* p. 467; House Committee on Ways and Means, *1998 Green Book,* table 7-2.

22. Thomas Gabe, *Demographic Trends Affecting Aid to Families with Dependent Children (AFDC) Caseload Growth* (Congressional Research Service, 1992); Congressional Budget Office, *CBO Staff Memorandum: Forecasting AFDC Caseloads, with an Emphasis on Economic Factors* (July 1993).

23. Congressional Budget Office, *Sources of Support for Adolescent Mothers* (September 1990).

24. Hobbs and his capable young assistant Peter Germanis were a formidable team. Hobbs was often out lobbying in the states urging governors to conduct welfare reform demonstrations (or on Capitol Hill urging members of Congress to strengthen work requirements), while Germanis stayed at home in his office in the Old Executive Office Building writing reports on welfare reform; see Office of the President, Domestic Policy Council, *Up from Dependency: A New National Public Assistance Strategy,* 8 vols. (1986). I would argue that the work of Chuck Hobbs during the Reagan and Bush years, with considerable assistance from Howard Rolston at the Department of Health and Human Services (HHS)—who helped states plan their demonstrations and collect data so something about the effects of the demonstrations could be captured and publicized—was the most important factor in the welfare demonstration movement that swept the states right up until the welfare reform bill was passed in 1996. The legal basis for this work in urging states to conduct demonstrations was section 1115 of the Social Security Act, enacted in 1962, which gave the secretary of HHS the authority to waive certain provisions of law in order to allow states to experiment with new welfare reform ideas. The movement started by Hobbs eventually exploded into a host of state welfare reform demonstrations. Between 1992 and 1995, fifty-three waivers in thirty-five states were approved by HHS. By 1996, when the welfare reform bill passed, the Clinton administration alone had approved sixty-one waivers in thirty-eight states. All but ten states had obtained waivers

and had conducted or were still conducting experiments. Of great importance, versions of many of the radical ideas that caused such consternation in Washington during the welfare reform debate in 1995–96 were already in the process of being tested by the states. These included time limits on the maximum benefit duration (twenty-four states), stronger work requirements (thirty-one states), and limiting or eliminating the benefit increase when mothers on welfare had additional children (the family cap; fourteen states). In some respects, the 1996 federal welfare reform bill simply expanded and made mandatory reforms there were already being implemented in many states. Considerable credit must also be given to the Clinton administration for aggressively continuing the Reagan-Bush policy of granting waivers. See Jennifer Neisner, *State Welfare Initiatives*, 94-183 EPW (Congressional Research Service); House Committee on Ways and Means, *1996 Green Book*, pp. 434–35.

25. Lawrence M. Mead, *Government Matters: Welfare Reform in Wisconsin* (Princeton University Press, 2004); Tom Corbett, "Welfare Reform in Wisconsin: The Rhetoric and the Reality," in *The Politics of Welfare Reform*, edited by Donald F. Norris and Lyke Thompson (Thousand Oaks, Calif.: Sage, 1995.)

26. Mead, *Government Matters*, esp. chap. 2.

27. Wayne King, "Senate Sends Florio Welfare Bill That Limits Benefits for Mothers," *New York Times*, January 14, 1992, p. A1; Sherry Stone, "New Jersey's Tough Welfare Law May Set National Trend," *Philadelphia Tribune*, January 24, 1992, p. A2; Rita Giordano, "All Eyes on NJ Welfare Reform," *Newsday*, January 26, 1992, p. 39; Paul Taylor, "Carrots and Sticks of Welfare Reform: Author of Landmark Federal Bill Hears Why States Are Going Their Own Way," *Washington Post*, February 4, 1992, p. A13.

28. Senate Finance Committee, Subcommittee on Social Security and Family Policy, *State Welfare Reform*, Committee Print 102-678 (1992).

## CHAPTER THREE

1. DeParle presents a lively rendition of the president's task force in his superb book about welfare reform and its effects on three mothers and their children in Milwaukee; see *American Dream: Three Women, Ten Kids, and a Nation's Drive to End Welfare* (New York: Viking, 2004). For a sampling of his contemporaneous articles about the task force, see Jason DeParle, "Clinton's Welfare Planners Vow an Open Process," *New York Times*, July 9, 1993, p. A10; Jason DeParle, "Clinton to Weigh Payments to Spur Hiring of the Poor," *New York Times*, November 28, 1993, sec. 1, p. 1; Jason DeParle, "Clinton Welfare Planners Outline Big Goals Financed by Big Saving," *New York Times*, December 3, 1993, p. A1; Jason DeParle, "Change in Welfare Is Likely to Need Big Jobs Program," *New York Times*, January 30, 1994, sec. 1, p. 1; Jason DeParle, "Clinton Considers Taxing Aid to Poor to Pay for Reform," *New York Times*, February 13, 1994, sec. 1, p. 1.

2. William M. Welch, "Clinton Wants to Put Welfare to Work," *USA Today*, November 29, 1993, p. A8.

3. Clay Shaw, "Clinton's Radical Welfare Reform Plan," *Roll Call*, December 7, 1992.

4. House Committee on Ways and Means, Subcommittee on Select Revenue Measures and Subcommittee on Human Resources, *Selected Aspects of Welfare Reform*, Committee Print 103-29 (1993), pp. 22–33; David E. Rosenbaum, "Delay Sought in Law Meant to Trim Welfare Rolls," *New York Times*, May 5, 1993, p. B9.

5. Michael Barone, "Slouching toward Dystopia," *U.S. News & World Report*, December 20, 1993, p. 34; Charles Krauthammer, "Subsidized Illegitimacy," *Washington Post*, November 19, 1993, p. A29; Charles Murray, "The Coming White Underclass," *Wall Street*

*Journal,* October 29, 1993, p. A14; Ben Wattenberg, "Teen Pregnancy Epidemic: Remove the Incentive," *New York Post,* December 9, 1993; George F. Will, "The Tragedy of Illegitimacy," *Washington Post,* October 31, 1993, p. C7; William J. Bennett, "The Best Welfare Reform: End It," *Washington Post,* March 30, 1994, p. A19.

6. Robert J. Samuelson, "Essential to the Debate," *Washington Post,* September 8, 1993, p. A19.

7. Janet Hook, "CQ Roundtable: Rambunctious Bunch: The Class of 1992," *Congressional Quarterly Weekly,* March 28, 1992, p. 842. Santorum was elected to the Senate in 1994 and soon showed that he was still a firebrand; see David S. Cloud, "Class of '94: Santorum Pushing Senate to Be More Like House," *Congressional Quarterly,* October 28, 1995, p. 3255.

8. *Responsibility and Empowerment Support Program Providing Employment, Child Care, and Training Act,* 103 (introduced February 2, 1993).

9. Shaw, "Clinton's Radical Welfare Reform Plan"; Rick Santorum, "From the House GOP, a Welfare Reform Plan that Hits Non-Work, Illegitimacy," *Roll Call,* December 6, 1993, pp. 22, 30.

10. Charles Murray, *Losing Ground: American Social Policy, 1950–1980* (New York: Basic Books, 1984).

11. Elijah Anderson, "Abolish Welfare: And Then What?" *Washington Post,* December 31, 1993, p. A21.

12. In the 103rd Congress (1993–94), the full name of this committee was Committee on Education and the Workforce. When Republicans took control of the House in the 104th Congress (1995–96), they changed the name to Committee on Economic and Education Opportunities. Throughout the book, I refer to this committee as simply the Education Committee.

13. Johnson, speaking of J. Edgar Hoover, quoted in *New York Times,* October 31, 1971.

14. Peter Germanis, "Reducing Welfare Spending" (Washington: Heritage Foundation, 1990).

15. John Tapogna and Julie Isaacs, Congressional Budget Office, Memo to Interested Parties, "Proposed AFDC Transition and Work Program," November 29, 1993.

16. Mary Jo Bane and David T. Ellwood, "Slipping Into and Out of Poverty: The Dynamics of Spells," *Journal of Human Resources* 21 (1986): 1–23.

17. Jeffrey L. Katz, "Clinton's Attention to Welfare Boosts Supporters' Hopes," *Congressional Quarterly,* January 29, 1994, p. 176.

18. Between 1993 and 1996, as the Clinton 1993 expansion of the EITC was phased in, its value for a mother with two children increased spectacularly, from $1,511 to $3,556. See Committee on Ways and Means, *1996 Green Book,* p. 805.

19. The mother would have work expenses, especially child care, which would reduce the financial advantage of work. But Republicans believed that many mothers would have all or part of their child care subsidized by one of numerous federal programs and that, even if the mother only broke even, she still had a responsibility to work rather than become dependent on welfare.

20. Committee on Ways and Means, *1996 Green Book,* app. J.

21. *Welfare and Teenage Pregnancy Reduction Act,* HR 1293, 103 Cong. 1 sess. (sponsored by Jan Meyers); *Parental Responsibility Act,* HR 892, 103 Cong. 1 sess. (sponsored by Gary Franks); *To Amend Title IV of the Social Security Act to Eliminate Disincentives in the Program of Aid to Families with Dependent Children That Prevent Recipients of Such Aid from Working toward Self-Sufficiency,* HR 1007, 103 Cong. 1 sess. (sponsored by Chris Shays); *To Amend Part A of Title IV of the Social Security Act and Title XIX of Such Act to*

*Discourage Persons from Moving to a State to Obtain Greater Amounts of Aid to Families with Dependent Children or Additional Medical Assistance under State Medicaid Plans,* HR 910, 103 Cong. 1 sess. (sponsored by Bill Paxon).

22. Jan Meyers, letter to Henry J. Hyde, July 16, 1993.

23. R. Kent Weaver, *Ending Welfare as We Know It* (Brookings, 2000), chap. 7.

24. In HR 3500 the most important part of the cap provision would have restricted growth in AFDC, SSI, the Food Stamp program, section 8 housing, public housing, and the Earned Income Tax Credit to the previous year's spending, adjusted for inflation, plus 2 percent. Our staff calculations produced an estimate of $25 billion in savings for this provision between 1995 and 1999. See section 702 of HR 3500. The version of the cap put in the Contract with America bill was substantially revised (especially by removing EITC from the cap) but still saved at least $18 billion over five years. See Title III of the version of HR 3500 introduced in January 1995.

25. Rick Santorum, Dear Colleague Letter to House Republicans, October 12, 1993.

26. Memo from Dick Armey, Chair, House Republican Conference, to All House Republicans, "Republican Leadership Alert: Welfare Reform," September 29, 1993.

## CHAPTER FOUR

1. House Committee on Ways and Means, *1996 Green Book,* p. 1309.

2. "Murray Light" refers to a watered-down version of Charles Murray's proposal to completely end welfare benefits. See Charles Murray, *Losing Ground: American Social Policy, 1950–1980* (New York: Basic Books, 1984).

3. Jason DeParle, "Abolishment of Welfare: An Idea Becomes a Cause," *New York Times,* April 22, 1994, p. A14.

4. *Congressional Record,* November 20, 1993, p. S16672.

5. Ronald Brownstein, "GOP Welfare Proposals Becoming More Conservative," *Los Angeles Times,* March 9, 1994, p. A20.

6. Both Senator Tom Harkin of Iowa and Senator Joseph Lieberman of Connecticut introduced welfare reform bills in the spring of 1994 that would have been radical if not shocking before 1994. See *Welfare to Self-Sufficiency Act of 1994,* S 2009 (introduced April 11, 1994; Harkin); and *Welfare Reform through State Innovation Act,* S 1932 (introduced March 15, 1994; Lieberman).

7. Ron Haskins, "House Republican Welfare Reform Bill," memo, April 1994.

8. William J. Bennett, "The Best Welfare Reform: End It," *Washington Post,* March 30, 1994, p. A19; Tom Bethell, "Welfare Wizards," *American Spectator,* June 1994, p. 16.

9. Ronald Reagan, *Public Papers of the Presidents of the United States: Ronald Reagan, 1988–89,* bk. 2, September 3, 1988 (Government Printing Office, 1992).

10. House Committee on Ways and Means, *1996 Green Book,* p. 503.

11. Judith M. Gueron and Edward Pauly, *From Welfare to Work* (New York: Russell Sage, 1991).

12. Tom Bethell, "Welfare as We'll Know It," *National Review,* February 7, 1994, pp. 44–45.

13. Charles Murray, letter to Rick Santorum, October 26, 1993.

14. William J. Bennett, Jack Kemp, and Vin Weber, "House Republican Welfare Reform Bill," Empower America memorandum, April 13, 1994.

15. Total cost would be $6,000 a person multiplied by 50,000 work participants, or $300 million; the federal share under our bill was 75 percent of this total cost, or $225 million.

16. *A Bill to Amend Title IV of the Social Security Act to Provide Welfare Families with the Education, Training, and Work Experience Needed to Prepare Them to Leave Welfare within 4 Years, and for Other Purposes,* HR 5501 (introduced June 25, 1992).

17. Ralph Z. Hallow, "Kemp Urges GOP to Drop Welfare Bill, Fight 'Soft' Reforms," *Washington Times,* April 14, 1994, p. A4.

18. DeParle, "Abolishment of Welfare: An Idea Becomes a Cause."

19. William Bennett, Jack Kemp, and Vin Weber, "Alternative Plan for Welfare Reform," *Washington Times,* April 24, 1994, p. B3.

20. Lauch Faircloth, news release, "Faircloth-Grassley-Brown Welfare Reform Bill," April 28, 1994; Cheryl Wetzstein, "GOP Welfare Bill Cuts off Unwed Mothers under 21," *Washington Times,* April 29, 1994, p. A4; Curt Anderson, "GOP Welfare Reform Bill Would End Aid to Young Unwed Mothers," *Associated Press,* April 28, 1994.

21. Major Garrett, *The Enduring Revolution: How the Contract with America Continues to Shape the Nation* (New York: Crown Forum, 2005); Jonathan Allen, "The Legacy of the Class of '94," *Congressional Quarterly Weekly,* September 4, 2004, pp. 2037–41; David Baumann, "Grading the Class of '94," *National Journal,* May 1, 2004, pp. 1322–35; Ed Gillespie and Bob Schellhas, eds., *Contract with America: The Bold Plan by Rep. Newt Gingrich, Rep. Dick Armey, and House Republicans to Change the Nation* (New York: Times Books, 1994).

22. James G. Gimpel, *Legislating the Revolution: The Contract with America, in Its First 100 Days* (Boston: Allyn and Bacon, 1996), pp. 21–24.

23. Jason DeParle, "Clinton Aides See Problem with Vow to Limit Welfare," *New York Times,* June 21, 1993, p. A1; Jason DeParle, "Clinton Welfare Planners Outline Big Goals Financed by Big Saving," *New York Times,* December 3, 1993, p. A1; Jason DeParle, "From Pledge to Plan: The Campaign to End Welfare—A Special Report: The Clinton Welfare Bill: A Long, Stormy Journey," *New York Times,* July 15, 1994, p. A1.

24. For an exception, see Morton M. Kondracke, "The Inside Story: Behind GOP's Turn to Right on Welfare," *Roll Call,* October 24, 1994, p. 7.

25. R. Kent Weaver, *Ending Welfare as We Know It* (Brookings, 2000), p. 180.

26. The ten bills in the Contract with America were:

—The Fiscal Responsibility Act: A balanced budget and tax limit provision, which included a legislative line-item veto.

—The Taking Back Our Streets Act: An anticrime package that included cuts in social spending from a bill recently passed by the Democratic Congress, funds for prison construction, truth in sentencing provisions, a good faith exclusionary rule exemption, and provisions that strengthened the federal death penalty.

—The Personal Responsibility Act: The welfare reform bill.

—The Family Reinforcement Act: The child support enforcement provisions, mostly from HR 3500, as well as a tax incentive for child adoption, stronger child pornography laws, and a tax credit for families that assisted their dependent elderly members.

—The American Dream Restoration Act: A $500-per-child tax credit, some tax code changes designed to reduce the financial penalty against marriage, and a tax credit that encouraged savings.

—The National Security Restoration Act: A prohibition on placing U.S. troops under United Nations command and selected increases in defense spending.

—The Senior Citizens Fairness Act: An increase in the Social Security earnings limit, repeal of the 1993 tax hike on Social Security benefits, and a tax incentive for purchase of insurance to cover long-term care in old age.

—The Job Creation and Wage Enhancement Act: A series of incentives for small business, a cut in the capital gains tax, a provision on neutral cost recovery, and a strengthening of the Regulatory Flexibility Act.

—The Common Sense Legal Reforms Act: A "loser pays" provision for court costs, limits on punitive damages, and reform of product liability laws aimed at reducing litigation against businesses.

—The Citizen Legislature Act: Two versions of term limits for House members, one limiting service in the House to six years (three terms), the second limiting service to twelve years (six terms).

See Gillespie and Schellhas, *Contract with America*; Republican National Committee, *Contract with America: Briefing Book* (1994); Republican National Committee, *Contract with America: Red Book* (1994).

27. Funding for the Title X program rose from $6 million in 1971 to $288 million in 2005, primarily to provide family planning services to women. See the website of the Office of Family Planning, Office of Public Health, Department of Health and Human Services, http://opa.osophs.dhhs.gov/titlex/ofp.html.

28. The gag rule prohibited medical personnel who were paid with federal funds from telling pregnant women that abortion was an option. The gag rule had been instituted under President Reagan in the Title X program that supported family planning in several thousand health clinics around the nation. President Clinton repealed the gag rule. Thus in 1994, when the gag rule was inserted into the welfare reform bill, it was not a part of the Title X program. Despite the implications of several media reports, the gag rule in the welfare bill only applied to a small block grant created by the welfare bill and not to Title X.

29. Michael Barone and Grant Ujifusa, *The Almanac of American Politics 1996* (Washington: National Journal, 1995), pp. 319–22.

30. Both the House and the Senate Office of Legislative Counsel have a strict rule that only those authorized to work on a particular bill can know anything about the bill or have the right to change it. If I had not called Jim Grossman, the Legislative Counsel lawyer I was working with to write the bill, and authorized Armey's staffer to make a change in our bill, Jim would not have even discussed the bill's contents with anyone from Armey's office, or even with Armey himself.

31. Jonathan Alter and others, "Bracing for the Big One," *Newsweek*, October 10, 1994, p. 27.

32. Tim Curran, "GOP Contract Revives 'Gag Rule,'" *Roll Call*, October 13, 1994.

33. Judy Mann, "The Cost of the Politics of Meanness," *Washington Post*, October 26, 1994, p. B10; "The Gag Rule, Revisited," *New York Times*, October 24, 1994, p. A16. See also sec. 108 of HR 4.

34. Jake Thompson, "Meyers Faces a Challenge on 'Gag Rule,'" *Kansas City Star*, November 4, 1994, p. C1.

35. Tim Curran, "GOP's 'Gag Rule' Goof," *Roll Call*, October 31, 1994.

36. The final text of the welfare reform bill was introduced on the first day of the 104th Congress (January 4, 1995) as HR 4, with Clay Shaw and Jim Talent as its major authors.

37. Jeffrey L. Katz, "Chances for Overhaul in Doubt as Time for Action Dwindles," *Congressional Quarterly*, July 30, 1994, p. 2150; Jason DeParle, "Skirmish on Welfare Plan Highlights the Chasm between Right and Left," *New York Times*, July 31, 1994, p. A22.

## CHAPTER FIVE

1. One program was the Supplemental Security Income program, which provides cash aid to the poor elderly and disabled—two groups that all politicians approach with caution, the former because the elderly are the most formidable voting bloc in the nation and the latter because the disabled arouse great sympathy in the American public.

2. Based on data collected by the Committee on Ways and Means. A version of the study that did not include Medicaid costs can be found in Committee on Ways and Means, *Summary of Welfare Reforms Made by Public Law 104-193, The Personal Responsibility and Work Opportunity Reconciliation Act and Associated Legislation*, WMCP 104-15 (Government Printing Office, November 1996).

3. House Committee on Ways and Means, *1996 Green Book*, p. 1321.

4. Bill Archer, "Abolish the Income Tax," *Washington Post*, August 4, 1995, p. A23.

5. Tim Curran, "GOP's 'Gag Rule' Goof," *Roll Call*, October 31, 1994, p. 1.

6. Jeffrey L. Katz, "Organization: Republicans Dust off Blueprints for Changing House Operations," *Congressional Quarterly Weekly*, November 12, 1994, p. 3220; David S. Cloud, "Gingrich Clears the Path for Republican Advance," *Congressional Quarterly Weekly*, November 19, 1994, p. 3319.

7. Elizabeth Shogren, "Key Republican Retreats on Welfare Reform," *Los Angeles Times*, December 2, 1994, p. A34.

8. Clay E. Shaw, news release, "House Republicans United on Welfare Reform," December 2, 1004.

9. Robert Pear, "G.O.P. Vows to Make Cuts in Spending before Taxes," *New York Times*, December 19, 1994, p. A1.

10. The United States Code (2000 edition) is divided into fifty titles, several thousand tables, and six volumes of appendixes. The entire code, published by the U.S. Government Printing Office, weighs 183 lb., 13 oz.

11. Thomas P. Carr, *Office of Legislative Counsel: Senate*, RS208563 (Congressional Research Service, 2003); Thomas P. Carr, *Office of Legislative Counsel: House* (Congressional Research Service, 2003).

12. To get some notion of the caliber of skill and sheer brainpower in the Office of Legislative Counsel, it is worthwhile to look into the background of the legislative lawyer we worked with the most, Jim Grossman. Jim graduated magna cum laude from Tufts University with a bachelor of science degree. He prepared for his career as perhaps the nation's leading expert on several titles in the Social Security Act by majoring in physics and math. After obtaining a master of arts in philosophy from Tufts, he matriculated to law school at the University of Chicago, one of the finest and most demanding law schools in the country, graduating in 1984. When he had been with Legislative Counsel for a little more than a decade, Jim was invited by the International Labor Organization to travel to the African nation of Namibia to draft their social security act and implementing regulations. Jim wrote all the legislative language for major sections of the welfare reform bill including the work program, the illegitimacy provisions, the cash welfare block grant, the child protection block grant, and child support enforcement.

13. Ironically, six years later Thompson was to become the secretary of Health and Human Services in the administration of George W. Bush. In this new capacity, Thompson personally approved the Bush administration's proposal for reauthorizing the welfare reform bill that would have greatly increased the work requirement and imposed work standards on states that, back when he was governor, Thompson would have labeled "micromanagement."

14. Don Fierce, conversation with author, January 10, 2006. This account is also based on contemporaneous discussions between members of Gingrich's staff and author.

15. Charles Krauthammer, "Welfare Reform: Do It Now," *Washington Post,* November 25, 1994, p. A3.

16. John King, "Governors Hesitant about GOP Welfare Plan; Want More Flexibility," *Associated Press,* November 20, 1994.

17. Rod Dreher and Ralph Z. Hallow, "GOP Governors Fear State Tab for Balanced Budget; Say Mandates Must Be Funded," *Washington Times,* November 21, 1994, p. A1.

18. Richard L. Berke, "GOP Governors Caution Congress on Social Agenda," *New York Times,* November 21, 1994, p. A1.

19. Dan Balz, "GOP Leaders Tell Governors Hard Choices Follow Power," *Washington Post,* November 23, 1994, p. A14.

20. John King, "GOP Leaders Promise Governors More Power, but Warn of Tighter Purse Strings," *Associated Press,* November 22, 1994.

21. This was the provision in the Contract with America bill, section 105. However, the provision was softened in the bill introduced in the 104th Congress by Clay Shaw and all subsequent versions, so that the child became eligible for cash welfare when the mother turned age eighteen. See HR 1157, Title I, section 405.

22. House Committee on Ways and Means, *1994 Green Book,* pp. 340–42.

23. House Committee on Ways and Means, *1996 Green Book,* p. 437.

24. Thomas Edsall, "How to Hawk the Newer Deal; Clinton Talks Right while Walking Left," *Washington Post,* February 21, 1993, p. C1; Thomas Edsall, "The Special Interest Gambit; How Clinton Is Changing the Democratic Discourse," *Washington Post,* January 3, 1993, p. C1; William Raspberry, "When Affirmative Action Ends," *Washington Post,* August 2, 1993, p. A17; Ruth Marcus and Dan Balz, "A Campaign Promise Has Clinton Cornered," *Washington Post,* February 10, 1993, p. A1.

25. Dan Balz and Ann Devroy, "First Days Offer Clinton 'Powerful Lessons,'" *Washington Post,* January 31, 1993, p. A1.

26. Robert D. Novak, "Clinton's Road Not Taken," *Chicago Sun-Times,* December 30, 1993, p. 26; *Congress and the Nation: A Review of Government and Politics, 1993–1996,* vol. 9 (Congressional Quarterly Press, 1998), pp. 513–25; Alissa J. Rubin, "Overhaul Issue Unlikely to Rest in Peace," *Congressional Quarterly,* October 1, 1994, pp. 2797–801; Adam Clymer, Robert Pear, and Robin Toner, "For Health Care, Time Was Killer," *New York Times,* August 29, 1994, p. A1.

27. William Claiborne, "Moynihan Presses Welfare Reform," *Washington Post,* January 10, 1994, p. A6.

28. E. J. Dionne Jr., "Clinton: Avoiding the Elmer Gantry Trap," *Washington Post,* January 25, 1994, p. A19.

29. As promised in the Contract with America, on the first day of the 104th Congress, Republicans made a host of changes to House rules, some of which were bound to have far-reaching consequences. The rules changes included the defunding of nearly forty organizations (generally called caucuses) that had been started by groups of House members to represent particular interests, the termination of three standing committees, a requirement that all laws apply to members of Congress, the termination of proxy voting in committee, a limitation on the terms of committee chairs to six years and the Speaker to eight years, and a reduction of House staff by one-third. One of my favorites, and the most symbolic, was the ending of the practice of delivering buckets of ice to offices every morning when the House was in session, a carryover from the days before air conditioning. See James G. Gimpel, *Legislating the Revolution: The Contract with America and Its First 100 Days* (Boston: Allyn and Bacon, 1996), pp. 38–40.

30. "Relevance, Shmelevance," *Washington Post*, April 21, 1995, p. A26.

### CHAPTER SIX

1. *U.S. Congressional Bibliographies*, compiled at the North Carolina State University Libraries; see www.lib.ncsu.edu/conbibs.

2. Ari Fleischer, *Taking Heat: The President, the Press, and My Years in the White House* (New York: William Morrow, 2005).

3. House Committee on Ways and Means, *Contract with America: Overview*, Serial 104-20, January 5, 10, 11, and 12, 1995.

4. Ibid.; House Committee on Ways and Means, *Contract with America: Welfare Reform*, Serials 104-43, 104-44, January 13, 20, 23, 27, 30, February 2, 1995, 2 vols.; House Committee on Ways and Means, and House Committee on Economic and Educational Opportunities, *Child Care and Child Welfare: Joint Hearing*, Serial 104-14, February 3, 1995; House Committee on Ways and Means, *Child Support Enforcement Provisions Included in Personal Responsibility Act as Part of the CWA*, Serial 104-6, February 6, 1995.

5. Committee on Ways and Means, *Contract with America: Overview*, p. 5.

6. Ibid., p. 6.

7. Ibid., pp. 11, 12.

8. Alvin Toffler, *Future Shock* (New York: Bantam Books, 1970); Alvin Toffler, *The Third Wave* (New York: Bantam Books, 1980).

9. House Committee on Ways and Means, *Contract with America: Overview*, p. 15.

10. In his maiden speech as Speaker of the House, Gingrich had surprised many of his foes by being conciliatory and complimentary about the achievements of the Democratic Party, mentioning in particular Social Security and the civil rights laws. *Congressional Record*, January 4, 1995, 141, pp. H4–H8.

11. House Committee on Ways and Means, *1994 Green Book*, p. 30.

12. House Committee on Ways and Means, *Contract with America: Overview*, p. 24.

13. Hernando DeSoto, *The Other Path: The Invisible Revolution in the Third World* (New York: Harper Collins, 1989).

14. Robert Pear, "White House Says Young Will Suffer under G.O.P. Plan," *New York Times*, December 30, 1994, p. A1; Greg Pierce, "Statistical War Spreads on Costs of Welfare vs. Orphanages," *Washington Times*, December 31, 1994, p. A4; Robert Pear, "The 104th Congress: Welfare; Clinton Has Tough Plan on Refusal to Work," *New York Times*, January 11, 1995, p. A18; Barbara Vobejda, "Republican Welfare Plan Is Termed 'Indefensible': Shalala Contrasts Two Parties' Provisions," *Washington Post*, January 11, 1995, p. A4.

15. Laura Duberstein Lindberg and others, "Age Differences between Minors Who Give Birth and Their Adult Partners," *Family Planning Perspectives* 29 (1997): 61–66; David S. Landry and Jacqueline Darroch Forrest, "How Old Are U.S. Fathers?" *Family Planning Perspectives* 27 (1995): 159–61, 165.

16. House Committee on Ways and Means, *Contract with America: Welfare Reform*, p. 68.

17. Anthony Lewis, "Abroad at Home; Eye of Newt," *New York Times*, November 14, 1994, p. A17; Richard Cohen, "Orphanages: Giving Gingrich the Dickens," *Washington Post*, December 6, 1994, p. A19; Joel Achenbach, "A Return to the Orphan Age," *Washington Post*, December 7, 1994, p. C1; Douglas Jehl, "Clinton Says Orphanages Can't Replace Strong Parents," *New York Times*, December 11, 1994, p. A34.

18. For the following exchange, see House Committee on Ways and Means, *Contract with America: Welfare Reform*, p. 80.

19. "Murray Light" refers to a watered-down version of Charles Murray's proposal to completely end welfare benefits. See Charles Murray, *Losing Ground: American Social Policy, 1950–1980* (New York: Basic Books, 1984).

20. R. Kent Weaver, *Ending Welfare as We Know It* (Brookings, 2000), esp. p. 180.

21. *Congressional Record*, September 6, 1995, p. S12681. An Urban Institute study produced the estimate that 1.1 million children would be thrown into poverty by the Republican bill. See Sheila Zedlewski and others, *Potential Effects of Congressional Welfare Reform Legislation on Family Income* (Washington: Urban Institute, July 1996). It was not this sophisticated Urban Institute study, but rather less sophisticated estimates made by HHS staff that were the basis for Shalala's testimony.

22. House Committee on Ways and Means, *Contract with America: Welfare Reform*, p. 96.

23. Charles Murray, "Family Formation," in *The New World of Welfare*, edited by Rebecca M. Blank and Ron Haskins (Brookings, 2001); Ron Haskins, "Does Welfare Encourage Illegitimacy?" *American Enterprise* 7 (1996): 48–49.

24. The following exchange is from Committee on Ways and Means, *Contract with America: Overview*, p. 97.

25. Ibid.

26. House Committee on Ways and Means, *Hearing: Fatherhood and Welfare Reform*, Serial 105-78, July 30, 1998.

27. The following exchange is from House Committee on Ways and Means, *Contract with America: Overview*, pp. 325–26.

28. "Sticks and Stones," *Washington Times*, June 17, 1997, p. A18; Michele Landis, "Ward Connerly's Newest Whine," *Mother Jones*, May 12, 2000; Deborah Kong, "NAACP Opposes California Initiative to Bar Racial Classifying," *Associated Press*, July 9, 2002; "Ward Connerly's Crusade to Erase Black People," *Black Commentator*, August 14, 2003.

29. House Committee on Ways and Means, *Contract with America: Overview*, p. 345.

30. The following exchange from ibid., 1995, p. 355.

31. Michael Novak and others, *The New Consensus on Family and Welfare* (Washington: American Enterprise Institute, 1987).

32. The following exchange from House Committee on Ways and Means, *Contract with America: Overview*, p. 361.

33. Welfare is not the biggest component of the federal budget, but means-tested benefits (those for which an individual or family must have income below a specified level to qualify) are a major part of government spending. In 1996 the federal government spent $261 billion on means-tested benefits, or nearly 20 percent of the $1.56 trillion in total spending. See House Committee on Ways and Means, *1998 Green Book*, pp. 1352, 1356, 1415; Vee Burke, *Cash and Noncash Benefits for Persons with Limited Income: Eligibility, Rules, Recipient and Expenditure Data, FY 1996–1998* (Washington: Congressional Research Service, 1999), p. 11.

34. Quotations from House Committee on Ways and Means, *Contract with America: Overview*, pp. 371, 372.

35. Bob Herbert, "Scapegoat Time," *New York Times*, November 16, 1994, p. A19; "The Coming Welfare Struggle," *Washington Post*, November 16, 1994, p. A24; Judy Mann, "Let's Refrain from Attacking the Poor," *Washington Post*, November 23, 1994, p. D19; "The G.O.P. Assault on Welfare," *New York Times*, November 25, 1994, p. A36.

36. Republican members of the Subcommittee on Human Resources were E. Clay Shaw Jr. (Florida, chairman), Dave Camp (Michigan), Jim McCrery (Louisiana), Mac Collins (Georgia), Philip S. English (Pennsylvania), Jim Nussle (Iowa), Jennifer Dunn (Washington), and John Ensign (Nevada). Democrats were Harold E. Ford (Tennessee),

Barbara B. Kennelly (Connecticut), Sander M. Levin (Michigan), Charles B. Rangel (New York), and Fortney Pete Stark (California).

37. House Committee on Ways and Means, *Welfare Reform Proposals, Including H.R. 4605, the Work and Responsibility Act of 1994, Part 2, Hearing,* Serial 103-108, August 9, 1994.

38. Robert Rector and William F. Lauber, *America's $5.4 Trillion War on Poverty* (Washington: Heritage Foundation, 1995).

39. Vee Burke, *Cash and Noncash Benefits for Persons with Limited Income: Eligibility, Rules, Recipient and Expenditure Data, FY1994-1996 (98-226)* (Congressional Research Service, 1997).

40. John McCaslin, "Ford Fit," *Washington Times,* August 11, 1994, p. A6.

41. Vanessa Gallman, "Gingrich Forming a Task Force to Counsel Him on Welfare Reform," *Philadelphia Inquirer,* January 31, 1995, p. A6.

42. House Committee on Ways and Means, *Contract with America: Welfare Reform,* p. 173.

43. Ibid.

44. Ibid., p. 174.

45. George F. Will, "Shock and Awe in Iraq," *Newsweek,* April 26, 2004, p. 64.

46. House Committee on Ways and Means, *Contract with America: Welfare Reform,* p. 140.

47. Ibid., p. 142.

48. Ibid., p. 176.

49. Ibid., p. 158.

50. Rebecca Blank is now dean of the Gerald R. Ford School of Public Policy at the University of Michigan.

51. House Committee on Ways and Means, *Contract with America: Welfare Reform,* p. 196.

52. Ibid., p. 198.

53. Ibid., p. 199.

54. James M. Talent, Testimony, House Committee on Ways and Means, *Contract with America: Welfare Reform,* pp. 531–35.

55. Ibid., p. 532.

56. House Committee on Ways and Means, *Child Care and Child Welfare: Joint Hearing.*

57. Ibid., p. 119.

58. Quotations from ibid., p. 123.

## Chapter Seven

1. A good markup document is a thing of beauty. The most basic part of preparing the document is to go through the bill in the order in which provisions appear and identify each unique provision and give it a short but descriptive name. The name of each provision in the bill in the order in which it appears is then placed in the left column, labeled "Item" or "Provision," of the three-column markup document. In the second column is a terse description in plain English of the provision under current law. If no relevant law is being amended, a term such as "No provision" or "No comparable provision" is placed in the second column. The third column, labeled "Subcommittee Bill," is a similarly terse description of the change proposed in the markup bill.

2. See the appendix for an overview of the provisions that appeared in the major bills in the nearly two years of debate.

3. By agreement, in order to save time, many committees allow opening statements only by the senior member of the majority and minority parties or their designated representatives. Other members can place a written statement in the permanent record of the markup.

4. *Constitution, Jefferson's Manual, and Rules of the House of Representatives of the United States*, prepared by Charles W. Johnson, parliamentarian of the House, H. Doc. 107-284 (2003). New editions are published each new Congress.

5. Under House rules, members can offer an amendment to an amendment, but the amendment cannot be further amended by third-degree or higher amendments. Even second-degree amendments, however, can be pursued by the minority as a stalling tactic by simply offering an amendment to every amendment, in effect doubling the time it takes to consider each amendment. The majority can avoid all secondary amendments by the simple device of having the chairman send out his original bill at least forty-eight hours before markup and then a second, somewhat different, bill at least twenty-four hours before markup. At the beginning of the markup session, the chairman offers the original bill and then, using his privilege to offer the first amendment, offers the second bill as an amendment of the first bill. From that point on, all amendments offered during the markup are secondary amendments which cannot be further amended.

6. Murray Light refers to a watered-down version of Charles Murray's proposal to completely end welfare benefits. See Charles Murray, *Losing Ground: American Social Policy, 1950–1980* (New York: Basic Books, 1984).

7. Linda Seebach, "Intangible Benefits," *Baltimore Sun*, February 2, 1994, p. 11A.

8. Under House rules, committees publish records of their hearings, often in volumes of 200 pages or more. Libraries throughout the nation have these volumes. In addition, most congressional hearings since the late 1990s are now available on the website of the U.S. House of Representatives, http://thomas.loc.gov/. However, committee markups are not published in book form. The transcripts are kept in the committee offices, where congressional staff, scholars, and all other users must make an appointment with committee officials to read them. The transcripts cannot be removed from the committee room and cannot be photocopied. Nor can anyone using the documents quote any members or even take handwritten notes on the markup proceedings. Some committees, such as the Finance Committee in the Senate, do not allow outsiders to even see their markup transcripts. The few quotes that appear in this chapter are based on notes I recorded during the markups. I did, however, review the markup transcripts in preparation for writing this chapter by making an appointment with Ways and Means officials to read them, as required under committee rules.

9. John Tapogna and Sheila Dacey, CBO's estimators for the AFDC and work programs, sent a detailed memo on how costs of work requirements were calculated. The memo, sent on June 26, 1995, to "Interested Parties" and entitled "Illustrative Estimates of Training and Child Care Costs Required in the Senate and House Versions of H.R. 4," estimated that each additional participant in a work program cost around $6,720 a year. At this rate, increasing the work requirement by 10 percentage points, assuming a caseload of 5 million, would cost about $3.4 billion.

10. Sheldon Danziger and Bob Greenstein, "Sign-On Statement about Out-of-Wedlock Births," Center on Budget and Policy Priorities memorandum to interested parties, June 21, 1994. The two-page statement refuted the claim, made most famously by Charles Murray, that welfare was a leading cause of illegitimacy. The authors sent the statement, along with a cover memo explaining their project, to numerous social scientists, soliciting their endorsement of the statement. See Sheldon Danziger, news release, "Researchers Dispute Contention That Welfare Is Major Cause of Out-of-Wedlock Births," June 23, 1994.

11. Charles Murray, "The Coming White Underclass," *Wall Street Journal*, October 29, 1993, p. A14.

12. Clarence Page, "Coming Soon: The New Underclass," *Chicago Tribune*, October 31, 1993, p. C3; George F. Will, "Underwriting Family Breakdown," *Washington Post*, November 18, 1993, p. A23; Charles Krauthammer, "Subsidized Illegitimacy," *Washington Post*, November 19, 1993, p. A29; and Peter Steinfels, "Beliefs," *New York Times*, November 27, 1993, p. 9.

13. Danziger and Greenstein, "Sign-On Statement about Out-of-Wedlock Births."

14. Ibid. Italics in original.

15. Barbara Vobejda, "Conservative Welfare Idea Criticized; Bills Would Cut Funds for Unwed Mothers," *Washington Post*, June 24, 1994, p. A18.

16. Cheryl Wetzstein, "Shalala Blasts 'Extremists' Who Call for End to Welfare," *Washington Times*, June 24, 1994, p. A4; William Bennett and Peter Wehner, "Shifting Targets in the Welfare Trenches," *Washington Times*, January 25, 1994, p. A14.

17. Wetzstein, "Shalala Blasts 'Extremists' Who Call for End to Welfare."

18. Jennifer Dixon, "Academic Researchers Challenge Claim That Welfare Subsidizes Illegitimacy," *Associated Press*, June 22, 1994.

19. Robert D. Reischauer, director of the Congressional Budget Office, letter to E. Clay Shaw Jr., House Committee on Ways and Means, September 11, 1992. Reischauer's letter was accompanied by the CBO report, "The Effects of Welfare on Family Structure: A Summary of Recent Research Findings."

20. Dixon, "Academic Researchers Challenge Claim That Welfare Subsidizes Illegitimacy"; Wetzstein, "Shalala Blasts 'Extremists' Who Call for End to Welfare."

21. Dixon, "Academic Researchers Challenge Claim That Welfare Subsidizes Illegitimacy."

22. Vojbeda, "Conservative Welfare Idea Criticized; Bills Would Cut Funds for Unwed Mothers."

23. Wetzstein, "Shalala Blasts 'Extremists' Who Call for End to Welfare."

24. There was some confusion among members on the exact nature of the Murray Light provision. The strong version of the provision made any baby born to an unmarried mother under age eighteen permanently ineligible for cash benefits (other benefits would continue). The weaker version ended the cash benefit only until the mother reached age eighteen, at which time the benefit would be reinstated. The subcommittee version of the bill had the strong provision, but Republican members insisted that it be changed to the weak provision before markup at full committee. All versions of the bill after full committee had the weaker version.

25. House Committee on Ways and Means, *2004 Green Book*, pp. 11–77.

26. Committee on Ways and Means, Subcommittee on Human Resources, news release, "Shaw Issues Statement on Subcommittee Passage of Republican Welfare Reform Bill," February 15, 1995.

27. Subcommittee reports on legislative recommendations to full committees in the House of Representatives are usually not printed. The report, along with an accompanying letter summarizing subcommittee actions and a comparison of the subcommittee bill with present law, a section-by-section analysis of the proposed changes in law, and a justification for each change, were submitted by Shaw to Chairman Archer on February 24, 1995.

28. For details, see *Welfare Transformation Act of 1995: Report Together with Dissenting Views,* H. Rept. 104-81, pt. 1; *Welfare Reform Consolidation Act of 1995: Report Together with Minority and Dissenting Views,* H. Rept. 104-75, pt. 1.

29. Ron Haskins, "Presidential and Congressional Commissions: The Select Panel in

Context," in *Child Health Policy in an Age of Fiscal Austerity: Critiques of the Select Panel Report,* edited by Ron Haskins (Norwood, N.J.: Ablex, 1982).

30. *Supporting Our Children: A Blueprint for Reform* (Commission on Interstate Child Support, 1992).

31. The story of how all these bills were developed, including the bill that eventually passed, is well told in Ruth Gillie Krueger, *Analyzing the Development of the American Child Support System: A Study in Social Policy Development* (San Jose, Calif.: Writers Club Press, 2001).

32. The distribution rules stipulate how money collected from fathers whose children were (or had been) on welfare is to be divided up among the federal government, state government, and the mother and children. A basic rationale of the child support program is that the father owes taxpayers reimbursement for the money they have paid in welfare benefits to support his children. But especially now that mothers were being encouraged to leave welfare and support themselves, Shaw and many others began to call for giving more of the collections to the mother so she could maintain her independence from welfare.

33. Investigating the background of the painting, I was led by several telephone calls to the Office of the Curator in the Office of the Architect of the Capitol. The curator, Barbara Wolanin, told me about both the painting and the history of H-208 and then on January 24, 2006, sent me a two-page summary of the history, "Room H-208: United States Capitol," published by the curator's office.

34. Greg J. Duncan and Saul D. Hoffman, "A Reconsideration of the Economic Consequences of Marital Dissolution," *Demography* 22 (1985): 485–98; Irwin Garfinkel and Sara S. McLanahan, *Single Mothers and Their Children* (Washington: Urban Institute, 1986); Lenore J. Weitzman, *The Divorce Revolution: The Unexpected Social and Economic Consequences for Women and Children in America* (New York: Free Press, 1985), chap. 2; Suzanne Bianchi, Lekha Subaiya, and Joan D. Kahn, "The Gender Gap in the Economic Well-Being of Nonresident Fathers and Custodial Mothers," *Demography* 36 (1999): 195–205.

35. See *Congressional Record,* March 23, 1995, pp. H3634–H3635: Roll Call Vote 265 passed by a 426-to-5 majority.

36. To distinguish the chairman's amendment from all the other markup materials, we printed them on green paper, giving rise to the term "Green Sheets" to refer to the amendment.

37. The members of the Ways and Means Committee were, by party, as follows. *Republicans:* Bill Archer (Tex.), Philip M. Crane (Ill.), William M. Thomas (Calif.), E. Clay Shaw (Fla.), Nancy L. Johnson (Conn.), Jim Bunning (Ky.), Amo Houghton (N.Y.), Wally Herger (Calif.), Jim McCrery (La.), Mel Hancock (Mo.), Dave Camp (Mich), Jim Ramstad (Minn.), Dick Zimmer (N.J.), Jim Nussle (Iowa), Sam Johnson (Tex.), Jennifer B. Dunn (Wash.), Michael A. "Mac" Collins (Ga.), Rob Portman (Ohio), Greg Laughlin (Tex.), Phil English (Pa.), John Ensign (Nev.), Jon Christensen (Neb.). *Democrats:* Sam M. Gibbons (Fla.), Charles B. Rangel (N.Y.), Pete Stark (Calif.), Andrew Jacobs Jr. (Ind.), Harold E. Ford (Tenn.), Robert T. Matsui (Calif.), Barbara B. Kennelly (Conn.), William J. Coyne (Pa.), Sander M. Levin (Mich.), Benjamin L. Cardin (Md.), Jim McDermott (Wash.), Gerald Kleczka (Wis.), John Lewis (Ga.), L. F. Payne (Va.), Richard E. Neal (Mass.).

38. Room 1102 of Longworth is the main office for the majority party of the Ways and Means Committee. It comprises a suite of offices, including the huge and imposing office of the majority staff director, which features views of the Capitol from its north-facing window and the Cannon House Office Building from its bank of windows facing east.

Tucked away in a corner of Room 1102 is a self-contained room that is the home of many volumes giving the legislative history of bills enacted by the committee. In this room can be found two of the most valuable resources for anyone wishing to study the 1995–96 welfare reform battle. First, hidden away in cupboards are three-ring binders that contain the transcripts of the committee markups of welfare reform in both 1995 and 1996. These documents are not public, and special rules apply to their use. Second, on the shelves is a wonderful thirteen-volume set that gives the legislative history of welfare reform. Diane Kirkland, a long-time clerk of the committee under both Democrats and Republicans, took great care in preparing these volumes. She has my undying gratitude.

39. Ironically, an unfortunate scheduling conflict may have diverted the attention of Democrats and thereby somewhat reduced their criticism of the bill itself. On the afternoon of February 28, the first day of the markup, the committee had agreed to allow a delegation from Texas to hold a reception in Room 1100, the hearing room where the markup was being held. Ways and Means also controlled a small room in the Capitol, Room H-137, to which the markup moved at three in the afternoon. Democrats were furious that Republicans had allowed what they referred to as "an Archer constituent" (Archer was from Texas) to displace the committee from its hearing room on such a momentous occasion as the markup of welfare reform. In addition to moving members away from the spacious Room 1100 to the very cramped H-137, another consequence of the switch was that there was no space for an audience in the latter room. Of course, in allowing outside groups to use our hearing room, we were simply following procedures created by Democrats during the many years they were in the majority. Unfortunately, we had promised the room on the day we later learned we needed to conduct the markup. As a result, our historic markup was being held in a cramped room, with no room for an audience, for at least a few hours. After this incident, Archer and our committee staff became much more discriminating in deciding when and how often Room 1100 could be used by outside groups or other committees.

40. *Welfare Transformation Act of 1995: Report Together with Dissenting Views*, H. Rept. 104-81. At the conclusion of the full committee markup, House rules required a report even more elaborate than the report that followed the subcommittee markup. The full committee report opens with a brief essay on the purpose and scope of the legislation, the background and need for the legislation, and a brief legislative history. Every provision is then explained in detail, as in the subcommittee report. The report also presents a terse explanation and the exact vote count for every amendment, a financial report on the cost of the bill and related matters from the CBO, an inflationary impact statement, an extensive analysis of exactly how the statutes would be amended by the bill, and dissenting views offered by Democrats.

41. As Matt and I were completing work on the text of HR 1157, we wanted to give a name to the block grant program that would replace AFDC. Matt made another of his famous lists. After a day or two of discussion, we selected the name Temporary Assistance for Needy Families, or as it came to be called, TANF. The name stuck.

## CHAPTER EIGHT

1. The initial House bill introduced in March 1995 (HR 1214) did not contain major Medicaid provisions. Thus the Commerce Committee, which had jurisdiction over Medicaid, was not involved in our leadership staff group until later in the year.

2. The electronic version of the bill is kept in the legislative counsel's computer, but the bill used by the parliamentarian's office to assign bill numbers is the hard copy delivered

to the box (called the hopper) on the House floor. Later in the day on March 21, the first integrated version of the welfare reform megabill was assigned the number HR 1214.

3. The House has a procedure, called suspension of the rules, that allows a bill to come to the floor without a rule if the leadership of both parties agree. The bill, which is usually not controversial, must receive a two-thirds vote to pass.

4. Since the Republican takeover of Congress in 1995, Republicans have moved forcefully to control both the Rules Committee and the House floor. A paper published on the tenth anniversary of the Republican takeover by Don Wolfensberger, who was the Rules Committee staff director in 1995, showed that, especially after 2000, Republicans severely restricted the power of Democrats to modify bills through the amendment process. Compared with 58 percent open rules in the 1995–96 Congress, the House allowed only 26 percent open rules in the 2003–04 Congress. Similarly, Republicans greatly increased the number of self-executing rules, in which amendments are automatically adopted as part of the rule without the opportunity for a separate vote. Self-executing rules increased from 25 percent in the 1994–95 Congress to 32 percent in the 1997–98 Congress and 27 percent in the 2001–02 Congress. Moreover, the House has made increasing use of suspension of the rules, in which bills are debated for only forty minutes and are not subject to amendment. In the last Democratic-controlled Congress in 1993–94, only 49 percent of all bills were considered under the suspension procedure. After the Republican takeover, suspension increased to 58 percent in 1995–96, to 65 percent in 1997–98, and to 78 percent by 2003–04. Thus the relatively open floor procedures that were customary under Chairman Solomon and Speaker Gingrich in 1995–96 quickly gave way to much more restrictive floor procedures in subsequent Republican-controlled Congresses. See Donald R. Wolfensberger, "A Reality Check on the Republican House Reform Revolution at the Decade Mark" (Washington: Woodrow Wilson International Center for Scholars, 2005).

5. This bill was the *Individual Responsibility Act of 1995*, H.R. 1267, introduced March 21, 1995.

6. This bill was the *Family Stability and Work Act of 1995*, H.R. 1250, introduced March 15, 1995.

7. Gary W. Cox, Chris Den Hartog, and Mathew D. McCubbins, "The Motion to Recommit in the U.S. House of Representatives," in *Process, Party, and Policy Making: Further New Perspectives on the History of Congress*, edited by David Brady and Mathew D. McCubbins (Stanford University Press, forthcoming).

8. The term "made in order" simply means that the rule allows the amendment to come to the floor for debate and voting.

9. *Congressional Record*, March 22, 1995, p. H3436.

10. The following account is from House Committee on Rules, "Hearing on H.R. 4, Personal Responsibility Act of 1995," March 16, 1995; House Committee on Rules, "Hearing on H.R. 1214, Personal Responsibility Act of 1995," March 16, 1995.

11. Cordia Strom and David Lehman from the Judiciary Committee staff helped us write the statutory language for the provisions on noncitizens. Shaw also talked with members of the Judiciary Committee, especially Lamar Smith from Texas, as we developed our policies.

12. The committees with only minor jurisdiction, including Commerce, Judiciary, and Banking, simply submitted letters to the Speaker asserting their jurisdiction over the provision in question and giving their permission to include the provision in the final bill. These letters were then introduced at the beginning of the floor debate and included in the permanent record of the debate. See *Congressional Record*, March 21, 1995, 141, pp. H3353–H3355.

13. Ibid., p. H3348.

14. Ibid., p. H3351.

15. Ibid., p. H3352.

16. Although not a major part of the floor debate, child advocates were greatly concerned about converting the TANF funding structure to a block grant with its frozen funding levels, inequities in funding across states, and its possible lack of mechanisms to ensure that states actually used the financial flexibility to spend money on poor and low-income families with children. See Mark Greenberg, "The Temporary Family Assistance Block Grant: Frozen Funding, Flawed Flexibility" (Washington: Center for Law and Social Policy, 1995).

17. Jason DeParle, "Clinton Aides See Problem with Vow to Limit Welfare," *New York Times*, June 21, 1993, p. A1; Jason DeParle, "Clinton Welfare Planners Outline Big Goals Financed by Big Saving," *New York Times*, December 3, 1993, p. A1; Jason DeParle, "Clinton's Welfare Advisers Urge Plan Stressing a Need to Work for Wages," *New York Times*, March 3, 1994, p. A14; Jason DeParle, "From Pledge to Plan: The Campaign to End Welfare—The Clinton Welfare Bill, a Long, Stormy Journey," *New York Times*, July 15, 1994, p. A1.

18. R. Kent Weaver, *Ending Welfare as We Know It* (Brookings, 2000), esp. p. 184.

19. If Clinton could have dictated the outcome and could ignore costs, the recommendation of his task force suggests that he would have given a public job to anyone on welfare who failed to find a job. But liberal Democrats in Congress refused to even have hearings on the Clinton bill after it was reluctantly introduced in the House by Sam Gibbons (HR 4605) and in the Senate by Tom Daschle (S 2224). See Jeffrey L. Katz, "Chances for Overhaul in Doubt as Time for Action Dwindles," *Congressional Quarterly*, July 30, 1995, p. 2150.

20. About half of the AFDC caseload left welfare every year. If every one of these leavers were counted toward fulfilling the work requirement, states would meet a 50 percent work requirement without doing anything. See House Committee on Ways and Means, *1996 Green Book*, p. 502.

21. *Congressional Record*, September 16, 1995, p. S12681; *Congressional Record*, August 1, 1996, pp. S9328–S9329.

22. "Don't Punish Children in the Name of Welfare Reform," *USA Today*, February 14, 1995, p. 14A.

23. Anthony Lewis, "Abroad at Home: Eye of Newt," *New York Times*, November 14, 1994, p. A17.

24. Bob Herbert, "Inflicting Pain on Children," *New York Times*, February 25, 1995, p. A23.

25. Dorothy Gilliam, "Ugly Ways on the Hill," *Washington Post*, March 25, 1995, p. B1.

26. Consider a family of a mother and two children living in Pennsylvania with one child on SSI. The monthly AFDC benefit for the mother and the nondisabled child would be $330. For the one child on SSI, the family would receive a monthly cash benefit of $313. Combining the AFDC and SSI benefits, the family would have a total income of $643 from the two programs. If the child lost the SSI benefit, the AFDC benefit would increase from $330 to $421 (because the family size for the purposes of computing the AFDC benefit would increase from two to three). Thus the family would lose $222 a month ($643 minus $421). Clearly, having a child on SSI provided a big income boost for families on AFDC. See House Committee on Ways and Means, *1996 Green Book*, pp. 440, 274; House Committee on Ways and Means, Subcommittee on Human Resources, *Hearing on Contract with America*, Serial 104-44, January 27, 1995.

27. *Sullivan* v. *Zebley*, 493 U.S. 521 (1990); House Committee on Ways and Means, *1996 Green Book*, p. 263.

28. House Committee on Ways and Means, *1996 Green Book*, pp. 274, 281, 386–87.

29. Ibid., p. 734.

30. These calculations were made by comparing the 1995 CBO estimates on spending in the Title IV-E programs for each year between 1996 and 2000 with the actual spending totals based on administrative data from the Department of Health and Human Services (spending for 2000 is an HHS estimate because the final administrative data were not yet available). The former can be found in *Welfare Transformation Act of 1995: Report Together with Dissenting Views*, H. Rept. 104-81, pp. 122–23; the latter in House Committee on Ways and Means, "Background Material," p. 648. In these calculations, I ignore the Title IV-B programs and their appropriated funding because the 1995 legislation included, in addition to the block grant, authorization for additional funds of up to $514 million to be distributed among the states.

31. *Congressional Record*, September 16, 1995, pp. S12680–S12685.

32. LaDonna A. Pavetti, "The Dynamics of Welfare and Work: Exploring the Process by Which Women Work Their Way off Welfare," Ph. D. dissertation, Harvard University, 1993.

33. Maurice Isserman and Michael Kazin, *America Divided: The Civil War of the 1960s* (Oxford University Press, 2004), p. 114.

34. Norma B. Coe and others, "Does Work Pay? A Summary of the Work Incentives under TANF," Paper A-28, New Federalism: Issues and Options for States (Washington: Urban Institute, 1998).

35. *Congressional Record*, March 21, 1995, 141, p. H3340.

36. *Public Papers of the Presidents of the United States: Jimmy Carter, 1980–1981*, vol. 3 (Government Printing Office, 1982), p. 2496.

37. These estimates apply to the version of HR 4 passed by the House on March 31, 1995. See June E. O'Neill, director of the Congressional Budget Office, letter to Bill Archer, chairman of the House Committee on Ways and Means, March 31, 1995.

38. David Greenberg and others, "Do Welfare-to-Work Programmes Work for Long?" *Fiscal Studies* 25 (2004): 27–53.

39. House Committee on Ways and Means, *1996 Green Book*, p. 399.

40. Ibid., pp. 437–38.

41. Kathryn Edin and Laura Lein, *Making Ends Meet: How Single Mothers Survive Welfare and Low-Wage Work* (New York: Russell Sage, 1997).

42. The credit could be worth up to $1,000 in 2004 and is partially refundable for mothers earning at least $10,500. House Committee on Ways and Means, *2004 Green Book*, pp. 13–59.

43. House Committee on Ways and Means, *1996 Green Book*, pp. 828–29.

44. Ibid., p. 805.

45. Ibid., pp. 396–97.

46. Gregory Acs and others, "Does Work Pay? An Analysis of the Work Incentives under TANF," Occasional Paper 9, Assessing the New Federalism (Washington: Urban Institute, 1998).

47. John Lewis and Michael D'Orso, *Walking with the Wind: A Memoir of the Movement* (New York: Simon and Schuster, 1998).

48. *Congressional Record*, March 21, 1995, p. H3358.

49. Ibid., p. H3359.

50. *Congressional Record*, March 22, 1995, pp. H3419–H3557.

51. Ibid., p. H3427.

52. Ibid., p. H3430.

53. Ibid., p. H3432.

54. This and the following exchange from ibid., p. H3500.

55. Congressional Research Service, American Law Division, "H.R. 1214, Family Planning Services," memo to House Ways and Means Committee, March 22, 1995.

56. *Congressional Record*, March 22, 1995, p. H3500.

57. Quotations in this paragraph from ibid., p. H3502.

58. Government Accounting Office, Human Resources Division, *Infant Formula: Cost Containment and Competition in the WIC Program*, GAO/HRD 90-122, September 1990.

59. *Congressional Record*, March 23, 1995, p. H3678.

60. In making a speech on the House floor, members usually begin by requesting that they be able to "revise and extend" their remarks. This gives them the right to add to or slightly edit their statement before it appears in the *Congressional Record*. Revisions are limited to technical or grammatical corrections. Extensions are often the text of articles or reports that buttress the member's argument.

61. *Congressional Record*, March 24, 1995, p. H3766.

62. Ibid., p. H3772.

63. Ibid., p. H3770.

64. Ibid., p. H3785.

## CHAPTER NINE

1. "The Welfare Reform Bandwagon," *Washington Times*, July 11, 1995, p. 18. See also Helen Dewar, "Conference Panels Cool GOP Revolution on Hill; New Order Runs into Bulwark of Old Order," *Washington Post*, May 28, 1995, p. A8.

2. Charles Bierbauer and Leon Harris, interview with Charles Cook and others, "Dole Needs to Keep Proving Himself, Analysts Say," *CNN News*, September 15, 1995, transcript 1027-9.

3. Gramm did chair subcommittees of both the Appropriations Committee and the Banking, Housing, and Urban Affairs Committee.

4. Florence Graves and Charles F. Shepard, "Packwood Accused of Sexual Advances: Alleged Behavior Pattern Counter Image," *Washington Post*, November 22, 1992, p. A1; William J. Eaton, "Senate Packwood Hearing Carries into Second Day," *Los Angeles Times*, November 2, 1993, p. 2; David S. Cloud, "Abrupt End to Packwood Drama Leaves Void at Key Moment," *Congressional Quarterly Weekly*, September 9, 1995, p. 2699; Jonathan D. Salant, "Lengthy Process Ends in Quick Resolution," *Congressional Quarterly Weekly*, September 9, 1995, p. 2705; Allan Freedman, "Panel's Weighty Evidence Shows Pattern of Abuse, Report Says," *Congressional Quarterly Weekly*, September 9, 1995, p. 2708.

5. Graves and Shepard, "Packwood Accused of Sexual Advances"; Cheryl Reid, "A Newspaper Confesses: We Missed the Story," *American Journalism Review*, January-February, 1993.

6. Robert Novak, "Dole Aide Clashes with Conservatives," *Chicago Sun-Times*, June 26, 1995, p. 27.

7. John H. Fund, "Bob Dole's Dealmaker," *Wall Street Journal*, July 7, 1995, p. A10.

8. Morton M. Kondracke, "Delighting Dems, GOP Spars over Welfare, Dole Aide," *Roll Call*, July 13, 1995; Kevin Merida and Helen Dewar, "Dole's Chief of Staff Is Magnet for Criticism," *Washington Post*, July 21, 1995, p. A4; Karen Tumulty, "Bring Me the Head of Sheila Burke," *Time*, July 24, 1995, p. 30; and Lloyd Grove, "Sheila Burke, on the Wrong Side of the Right," *Washington Post*, August 11, 1995, p. F1.

9. Jason DeParle, "Sheila Burke Is the Militant Feminist Commie Peacenik Who's Telling Bob Dole What to Think," *New York Times Magazine*, November 12, 1995, p. 32. See also, "Janet Cooke Award: DeParle's Drama of Destruction," *MediaWatch*, December 1995.

10. The Senate Finance Committee, with one major exception, had roughly the same jurisdiction as the House Ways and Means Committee. The exception was that the Finance Committee also had jurisdiction over the Medicaid program.

11. Paul Offner was one of the most accomplished and distinctive people I met in two decades in Washington. He had been elected to the Wisconsin state legislature in 1975, where he was a leading figure in health policy. He also co-chaired a commission that revised the state's civil service laws. After losing a race for lieutenant governor, he moved to Ohio to run that state's Medicaid program. He came to Washington in 1992 to serve as Moynihan's top aide on welfare policy and other social issues. Like Moynihan, he detested both the Clinton and Republican welfare reform bills and, apparently with Moynihan's permission or even encouragement, wrote widely and effectively against them (see "Welfare: Still Dreaming about Reform," *Washington Post*, November 11, 1994, p. A17; "Workfail," *New Republic*, December 28, 1992, pp. 13–15; "Flippers," *New Republic*, February 12, 1996, pp. 10–11). He left Moynihan in 1995 to become the commissioner of health care finance for Washington, D.C. Many of his friends questioned his sanity for taking a big job in the corrupt and ineffective administration of Mayor Marion Barry, but as usual Paul was a resounding success during his four years in the job. Among other accomplishments, he discovered that computer problems had left about 25,000 ineligible people on the Medicaid rolls, saving the District more than $10 million a year. Typically, during his tenure in the Barry administration, he wrote a long piece in the *Washington Post* about why it was so difficult to make the District's government more effective and efficient (see "In the Belly of the D.C. Beast; Why It's Hard to Fix a Government Agency," *Washington Post*, June 29, 1997, p. C1). Among other provocative observations, the article claimed that, "In the District, almost nothing works well. But the good news is that there's a lot to fix, and the District is small enough that you can achieve a lot if you persevere." What a surprise: he drew a public admonishment from Mayor Barry! I'll bet he barely noticed. After leaving the job in 1999, he served with scholarly distinction at Georgetown University and the Urban Institute in Washington. Paul died in 2004 at the age of sixty-one, leaving behind a wife and young daughter. He and I argued about everything and, in the process, formed a bond of trust and respect. Although his scholarly and policy achievements brought him fame, his skills and abilities knew no bounds. Once, when he and his family were having dinner at my home, he casually wandered over to our piano and played ten minutes of the most remarkable music I had ever heard. RIP. See Patricia Sullivan, "Former District Medicaid Director Paul Offner Dies," *Washington Post*, April 22, 2004, p. B6.

12. "America's Welfare Debate," U.S. News Debate Series, *Federal News Service*, June 21, 1995; Ann Devroy, "Budget Remark Continues to Plague Clinton," *Washington Post*, October 26, 1995, p. A10.

13. In 1999 the Labor and Human Resources Committee changed its name to Health, Education, Labor, and Pensions.

14. Counting the number of hearings devoted to welfare reform is somewhat arbitrary because the topic of welfare reform could come up in any hearing on AFDC, SSI, Medicaid, Food Stamps, immigration, and so forth. I tried to include only hearings in which the committee included the term "welfare" or some specific welfare program (for example, Food Stamps) in the title of the hearing. Using this approach, I identified eight hearings in the Finance Committee (forty-two witnesses), five hearings in the Labor and

Human Resources Committee (forty-four witnesses), and one hearing each in the Judiciary (ten witnesses), Government Affairs (ten witnesses), Indian Affairs (nine witnesses), and Agriculture (fourteen witnesses) committees.

15. Senate Committee on Finance, *Welfare Reform Wrap-Up,* Serial 104-137, April 27, 1995, p. 2731.

16. Ibid.

17. Charles Murray, *Losing Ground: American Social Policy, 1950–1980* (New York: Basic Books, 1984); Richard J. Herrnstein and Charles Murray, *The Bell Curve: Intelligence and Class Structure in American Life* (New York: Free Press, 1994).

18. Senate Committee on Finance, *Welfare Reform Wrap-Up,* p. 31.

19. See *Child Care and Development Block Grant Amendments of 1995,* S. Rept. 104-94 (to accompany S. 850), (Government Printing Office, 1995).

20. The close division of votes gave Democrats lots of power during Finance Committee proceedings. As it turned out, Democratic Senator Baucus voted with Republicans on most of the big votes, thereby somewhat offsetting the Democrats' potential influence.

21. Cheryl Wetzstein, "Welfare Measure Excites No One," *Washington Times,* May 25, 1995, p. A16; "Stormy Welfare Markup Ahead," *National Journal's Congress Daily/a.m.,* May 25, 1995, p. 1.

22. Four of these amendments were defeated on straight party-line votes of 11 to 9. All four would have altered crucial parts of the Packwood bill, including a John Breaux amendment requiring states to match federal payments (commonly called a maintenance-of-effort requirement), a John Rockefeller amendment on whether the work requirements and time limits could be waived under some circumstances, another and similar Rockefeller amendment on whether some recipients could be exempt from the time limit if unemployment were high in a given state, and a Moseley-Braun amendment that preserved the cash welfare entitlement. In addition to these party-line votes, Republicans maintained perfect voting discipline on another amendment, this one by Bob Graham to soften cuts in benefits for noncitizens. On this vote, the unanimous Republicans were joined by Baucus and Rockefeller from the Democratic side. Similarly, on an amendment by Moseley-Braun to allow recipients to take court action to try to get their benefits, united Republicans were joined by Mark Pryor, Rockefeller, Breaux, Conrad, and Graham to defeat the amendment.

23. Two of these amendments were offered by Conrad (one to maintain the SSI eligibility of certain recipients and one to provide new money for supervised living facilities for pregnant teenagers), and one was offered by Graham (to change the distribution formula to help poorer states); all three were defeated.

24. The first figure is from Senate Committee on Finance, *Report on the Family Self-Sufficiency Act of 1995,* June 5, 1995, p. 42; the second one is from Vee Burke, *Welfare Reform,* Issue Brief Report 104-96 (Congressional Research Service, 1995).

25. Robert Rector, "Provisions in Packwood Welfare 'Reform'" (Washington: Heritage Foundation, Spring 1995); Tommy G. Thompson, governor of Wisconsin, letter to Lauch Faircloth, U.S. Senate, June 13, 1995.

26. Robert Pear, "Republican Squabble Delays Welfare Debate," *New York Times,* April 28, 1995, p. 19.

27. "Splits in GOP Stall Welfare Bill," *National Journal's Congress Daily/a.m.,* June 15, 1995, p. 1; Hilary Stout, "Senate GOP Leaders Delay Welfare Vote as Party Unity Splinters over the Issue," *Wall Street Journal,* June 15, 1995, p. B4; Judith Havemann and John F. Harris, "Clinton Backs Limit on Welfare Benefits," *Washington Post,* June 15, 1995, p. A1; Jeffrey L. Katz, "GOP Rift Delays Action on Welfare," *Congressional Quarterly,* June 17, 1995, p. 1747.

28. As anyone who watched Faircloth operate over the years would know, he often took very strong positions and then held to them. His threats, in short, were serious.

29. Pear, "Republican Squabble Delays Welfare Debate."

30. Consider the case at hand. Under the AFDC program, two factors determined the number of federal dollars received by a state: the amount of the benefit given to welfare recipients, which was completely under state control, and the percentage of the benefit paid by the federal government, which was inversely proportional to state per capita income. Both factors differed greatly among the states. In 1996 the maximum AFDC benefit for a mother and two children varied from $120 in Mississippi to $636 in Connecticut (considering only the lower forty-eight). This gaping difference was offset somewhat by the fact that the size of the benefit was roughly correlated with state per capita income: poor states got a higher percentage reimbursement rate from the federal government, wealthy states got a lower rate. The highest rate was 78 percent in Mississippi; the lowest rate was fixed in statute at 50 percent (which was received by thirteen wealthy states). This two-factor approach to AFDC financing produced spectacular differences in federal reimbursement levels per poor person across the states. Based on the Congressional Research Service estimates of the amount of money each state would receive under the House block grant and Census Bureau estimates of the number of poor people in each state, Mississippi would receive about $150 a person each year while Connecticut would receive about $630.

31. Each state would receive the proportion of this $100 million that equaled their proportion of growth in national population each year, ignoring states that had declining population (with the proviso that states with declining population did not receive less money); see Welfare Transformation Act of 1995: Report Together with Dissenting Views, H. Rept. 104-81, pt. 1 (Government Printing Office, 1995), p. 13.

32. See Cheryl Wetzstein, "Welfare Reform Has GOP Family Feuding," Washington Times, June 19, 1995, p. A5; Leslie Phillips, "Welfare Reform Entangled in Senate Politics," USA Today, June 21, 1995, p. A6; "Moynihan Issues Sharp Reply to Wisconsin Welfare Complaint," National Journal's Congress Daily/a.m., June 23, 1995, p. 3.

33. Hutchinson's somewhat complex provision funneled money to states that met two criteria: a level of welfare spending per poor person that was lower than the national average and above average population growth. Because this approach missed a few poor states, Hutchinson included a provision that deemed as qualifying for the additional money any state with welfare spending per poor person in 1996 that would be less than 35 percent of the national average.

34. During the debate, council member Linda Cropp, a prominent black Democrat, said: "What welfare has done is to institutionalize slavery. It has kept people at a level of poverty . . . they become complacent and satisfied, and they never reach their full potential." I'm glad no Republican said that. See "Liberalism's Paradigm Lost," Wall Street Journal, June 8, 1995, p. A12.

35. J. Jennings Moss, "Clinton Slams Welfare-Reform Plan," Washington Times, June 7, 1995, p. A4; "Liberalism's Paradigm Lost."

36. Hilary Stout, "Clinton Condemns GOP Welfare Plan but Stops Short of Threatening a Veto," Wall Street Journal, June 7, 1995, p. A2.

37. Cheryl Wetzstein, "Senate Democrats Offer Welfare Plan," Washington Times, June 9, 1995, p. A10; Hilary Stout, "Senate Democrats Unveil Welfare Plan Requiring Work, Pledge to Keep Jobs," Wall Street Journal, June 9, 1995; Robert Pear, "From Democrats, Another Welfare Plan," New York Times, June 9, 1995, p. A21; Judith Havemann, "Democrats Offer Tough Welfare Reform," Washington Post, June 9, 1995, p. A6.

38. Judith Havemann and John F. Harris, "Clinton Backs Limit on Welfare Benefits," *Washington Post*, June 15, 1995, p. A1.

39. Pear, "Republican Squabble Delays Welfare Debate."

40. Leslie Phillips, "Welfare Reform Entangled in Senate Politics," *USA Today*, June 21, 1995, p. A6.

41. Robin Toner, "Moynihan Battles View He Gave up on Welfare Fight," *New York Times*, June 18, 1995, p. 1.

42. Cheryl Wetzstein, "Gramm, Faircloth Scoff at Dole's Welfare Reform," *Washington Times*, August 3, 1995, p. A10; Barbara Vobejda and Judith Havemann, "Conservatives Criticize Dole Welfare Plan," *Washington Post*, August 4, 1995, p. A17; Robert Pear, "Dole Offers Welfare Bill, but Conservatives Reject It," *New York Times*, August 5, 1995, p. 8.

43. Robert Pear, "White House Seeks Areas of Welfare Accord with G.O.P.," *New York Times*, August 6, 1995, p. 24.

44. John H. Cushman, "Rivals Criticize Bill on Welfare Offered by Dole," *New York Times*, August 7, 1995, p. 1.

45. See Robert Pear, "Dole Postpones Further Debate on Welfare Bill," *New York Times*, August 9, 1995, p. 1; Judith Havemann and Helen Dewar, "Senate GOP Postpones Welfare Reform Effort," *Washington Post*, August 9, 1995, p. A1; Nancy E. Roman and Cheryl Wetzstein, "Under Pressure, Dole Delays Welfare Action," *Washington Times*, August 9, 1995, p. A1. Also see *Congressional Record*, August 8, 1995, pp. S11838–S11839.

46. A copy of the first Dole bill can be found in *Congressional Record*, August 5, 1995, pp. S11567–S11601; the second is in *Congressional Record*, August 11, 1995, pp. S12428–S12510. It is notable that the second Dole bill is more than three times longer than the first bill. Daschle's amendments to his bill, also introduced on August 11, can be found in *Congressional Record*, August 11, 1995, pp. S12511–S12522.

47. Section 402 of Title I, section 101, of the bill Dole introduced on August 11, 1995, p. S12431.

48. Section 406 of ibid., p. S12434.

49. See Section 102 of ibid., p. S12438.

50. "Senate GOP Ranks Leery on Welfare Bill Prospects," *National Journal's Congress Daily/a.m.*, August 8, 1995, p. 1; Judith Havemann and Helen Dewar, "Dole Courts Consensus on Welfare," *Washington Post*, August 8, 1995, p. A7; Judith Havemann, "Governors Push Welfare Compromise," *Washington Post*, August 11, 1995, p. A10.

51. *Congressional Record*, August 11, 1995, p. S12512.

52. Each Congress consists of two, one-year sessions. Normally in the first year the Congress adjourns for a Christmas–New Year break in late October or early November. The second year of the session usually ends earlier because every member of the House and one-third of the members of the Senate are running for reelection (except those retiring). All bills carry over from the first to the second session of a Congress; when Congress returns after the Christmas break of the first session, it simply picks up where it left off. But at the end of the second and final year of a Congress, all bills die and must be reintroduced at the beginning of the next Congress.

53. David S. Broder, "Rebels without a Pause," *Washington Post*, December 31, 1995, p. W8.

54. Dole introduced his first bill on August 5 and made a brief statement, which was followed by an even briefer statement by Moynihan (*Congressional Record*, August 5, 1995, pp. S11575–S11602; the text of the bill is included in these pages). The Senate debated the bill on August 7–8 before Dole pulled the bill. He then introduced a revised and expanded bill, again with a brief statement, on August 11; on this occasion, Dole's

statement was followed by an extended comment by Daschle, who also introduced his own bill (*Congressional Record*, August 11, 1995, pp. S12428–S12513). The bill was then further debated on September 6–8, 11–15, and 19, 1995.

55. One of the amendments enacted by the Senate was of great importance to state legislatures. In converting welfare to a block grant and giving states both the money and expanded flexibility for spending it, Congress had inadvertently given great power to the executive branch in six states. In these states, governors could decide how block grant funds could be spent without consulting the state legislature. After the House passed its bill, the National Conference of State Legislatures quickly figured out the problem and asked Republican Senator Hank Brown of Colorado to sponsor an amendment requiring that states enact legislation to decide how TANF dollars should be spent. Brown sponsored the measure, which passed on a vote of 92 to 6, on September 8, and remained part of the bill until it became law in August 1996 (*Congressional Record*, September 8, 1995, pp. S12875–S12876).

56. Perhaps the only thing that is virtually identical in the House and Senate is that each body has a chamber for debate in the Capitol building and that three office buildings are separated from their respective sides of the Capitol by a major public street (Independence Avenue for the House and Constitution Avenue for the Senate). In both bodies, members must cross the street or ride the underground subway from their office in one of the three office buildings to the Capitol to vote. Even hearings, markups, and other important business must be temporarily suspended if there is a vote in either body.

57. Center on Budget and Policy Priorities, "The Dole Maintenance-of-Effort Requirement," August 25, 1995.

58. "Mr. Dole's Bogus Welfare Safeguards," *New York Times*, September 8, 1995, p. 26.

59. For full discussion of these issues, see Ron Haskins, "Child Development and Child Care Policy: Modest Impacts," in *Developmental Psychology and Social Change,* edited by David B. Pillemer and Sheldon H. White (Cambridge University Press, 2005); Sally S. Cohen, *Championing Child Care* (Columbia University Press, 2001).

60. In addition to this $6 billion in new money, Kennedy and Dodd wanted to guarantee a total increase of $11 billion in child care funding by setting aside $5 billion in the new welfare block grant that could be spent by states only on child care.

61. *Congressional Record*, September 11, 1995, pp. S13163–S13196.

62. Gregory Acs, Pamela Loprest, and Tracy Roberts, *Final Synthesis Report of Findings from ASPE "Leavers" Grants* (Washington: Urban Institute, 2001), table 8.5.

63. *Congressional Record*, September 11, 1995, p. S13164.

64. Santorum moved to table the Kennedy-Dodd amendment. A yes vote was a vote to kill the amendment by tabling it; a no vote was a vote in favor of the amendment by denying the amendment to table. Thus the vote was actually 50 yes (against the amendment) and 48 no (in favor of the amendment).

65. *Congressional Record*, September 13, 1995, p. S13508.

66. Ibid., p. S13513.

67. Ibid., pp. S13508–S13510.

68. Robert D. Reischauer, director of the Congressional Budget Office, letter to E. Clay Shaw Jr., House Committee on Ways and Means, September 11, 1992. Reischauer's letter was accompanied by the CBO report, "The Effects of Welfare on Family Structure: A Summary of Recent Research Findings."

69. *Congressional Record*, September 13, 1995, pp. S13527–S13528.

70. Senate Roll Call Vote 419; *Congressional Record*, September 13, 1995, p. S13516.

71. In the second version of Murray Light, Faircloth would have refused cash to

unmarried mothers under eighteen who lived in a household with a mother (the mother of the teenager who had a baby) who was already on welfare.

72. Ted G. Goertzel and Gary S. Young, "New Jersey's Experiment in Welfare Reform," *Public Interest* 125 (1996): 72–80.

73. *Congressional Record*, September 13, 1995, pp. S13486–S13489. The Domenici amendment was number 2573.

74. Though there have been random-assignment studies of the family cap in both Arkansas and New Jersey, as well as a number of other smaller-scale studies, the judgment of most reviewers has been that the studies are so badly flawed that no conclusions about effects are possible. Douglas Besharov of the American Enterprise Institute in Washington and the University of Maryland organized a symposium on the family cap, which included articles by Michael Camasso of Rutgers, who conducted the New Jersey evaluation; Peter Rossi, the noted program evaluator, who concluded that the New Jersey study was seriously flawed; and Glenn Loury of Boston University, who agreed with Rossi. The Loury paper includes a review of all the studies of the family cap then available. The symposium also featured an excellent and balanced review paper of the debate over the family cap by Besharov. Of course, the lack of solid evidence from research did not prevent either side in the congressional debate from drawing strong conclusions that the family cap decreased subsequent births or did not, caused an increase in abortion rates or did not, and contributed importantly to the rotation of the earth or did not. See Douglas J. Besharov and Peter Germanis, eds., *Preventing Subsequent Births to Welfare Mothers* (School of Public Affairs, University of Maryland, 2000).

75. *Congressional Record*, September 13, 1995, p. S13487.

76. Senate Committee on Finance, *Welfare Reform Wrap-Up*, Serial 104-137, April 27, 1995, p. 43.

77. *Congressional Record*, September 13, 1995, p. S13487.

78. Ibid., p. S13488.

79. Ibid.

80. Ibid., pp. S13524–S13525.

81. *Congressional Record*, September 14, 1995, p. S13572.

82. Ibid., pp. S13572–S13573, S13575.

83. As part of the Contract with America, on the first day of the 104th Congress, Republicans passed legislation that "all laws that apply to the rest of the country also apply equally to the Congress"; see Ed Gillespie and Bob Schellhas, eds., *Contract with America: The Bold Plan by Rep. Newt Gingrich, Rep. Dick Armey, and the House Republicans to Change the Nation* (New York: Random House, 1994).

84. For this and the following paragraphs, see *Congressional Record*, September 14, 1995, pp. S13581–S13,582. Kennedy said that "what we have done is afforded the child care program" for senators and staff. However, tuition at the Senate child care center was among the highest in the Washington area.

85. The twelve amendments were 2468 (Simon), 2483 and 2484 (Bingaman), 2486 (Levin-Dole), 2503 and 2505 (Wellstone), 2509 and 2568 (Graham), 2550 (Kohl), 2564 (Kennedy), 2615 and 2617 (Gramm).

86. *Congressional Record*, September 14, 1995, p. S13606.

87. The Daschle amendment was nearly identical to Sam Gibbons's "motion to recommit" in the House.

## CHAPTER TEN

1. If amendments are needed to achieve majority support for the conference committee bill in either house, then the other house must accept the changes by majority vote.

2. In 2005, former member Trent Lott, who was majority leader in the Senate when the deals were cut on both the 1995 and 1996 versions of welfare reform, published a book about his Senate career called, fittingly, *Herding Cats: A Life in Politics* (New York: Harper Collins, 2005).

3. House Ways and Means Committee, "Conference Comparison of H.R. 4: Comprehensive Welfare Reform," 3 vols., October 1995. This document is available in the Ways and Means library in 1102 Longworth House Office Building.

4. David Baumann, "Grading the Class of '94," *National Journal*, May 1, 2004, pp. 1322–35.

5. Helen Dewar, "Republicans Wage Verbal Civil War," *Washington Post*, November 19, 1984, p. A1.

6. George Hager, "Historic Votes Add Momentum as Conferees Start Work," *Congressional Quarterly Weekly*, October 28, 1995, p. 3282; George Hager, "The Budget: Reconciliation Now a Major Tool," *Congressional Quarterly Weekly*, October 28, 1995, p. 3286; George Hager, "The Budget: In the House, GOP Leadership Scores Comfortable Win," *Congressional Quarterly Weekly*, October 28, 1995, p. 3287.

7. The family cap was defeated by an amendment offered by Pete Domenici (Amendment 2575); see *Congressional Record*, September 13, 1995, pp. S13487–S13489. The Murray Light provision was defeated by an amendment offered by Lauch Faircloth (Amendment 2603); see *Congressional Record*, September 13, 1995, pp. S13507–S13516.

8. Ibid., pp. S13375–S13377.

9. Gene Falk, "Family Assistance Grants" (Congressional Research Service, October 30, 1995).

10. House Committee on Ways and Means, *1996 Green Book*, pp. 428–34.

11. House Committee on Ways and Means, *Welfare Transformation Act of 1995*, Serial 104-81, March 15, 1995, p. 108

12. Karen Spar, *Child Care: A Comparison of House and Senate Legislation* (Congressional Research Service, 1995).

13. Ron Haskins and Cassie Statuto Bevan, "Abstinence Education under Welfare Reform," *Children and Youth Services Review* 19 (1997): 465–84.

14. Donna M. Strobino, "The Health and Medical Consequences of Adolescent Sexuality and Pregnancy: A Review of the Literature," in *Risking the Future: Adolescent Sexuality, Pregnancy, and Childbearing*, vol. 2, edited by Sandra L. Hofferth and Cheryl D. Hayes (Washington: National Academy Press, 1987), pp. 93–104.

15. Haskins and Bevan, "Abstinence Education under Welfare Reform."

16. Congressional Budget Office, *Federal Budgetary Implications of the Personal Responsibility and Work Opportunity Reconciliation Act of 1996*, December 1996, p. 18.

17. See, for example, *The State Initiatives in Child Welfare Act of 1992*, H.R. 5316, 102 Cong., 2 sess.

18. Lea Donosky, "Sweeping Tax Overhaul Now the Law," *Chicago Tribune*, October 23, 1986, p. C1.

19. For estimates of spending on social programs in 1996, see House Committee on Ways and Means, *1998 Green Book*, pp. 1420–22; for an estimate of EITC spending in 1996, see House Committee on Ways and Means, *2004 Green Book*, pp. 13–41.

20. Michael D. Tanner, *The Poverty of Welfare: Helping Others in Civil Society* (Washington: Cato Institute, 2003).

21. On December 5, 1995, we sent a copy of the report along with a cover letter from Shaw and Archer to President Clinton, arguing that the conference agreement on most issues were settled "along lines your administration favors," E. Clay Shaw Jr. and Bill Archer, letter to William Clinton, December 5, 1995; Donna Shalala, letter to Newt Gingrich, October 26, 1995.

22. House Committee on Ways and Means, "Comparison of Administration Positions on Welfare Issues Raised by HHS with Final Bill Resulting from House-Senate Conference," December 5, 1995.

23. Cheryl Wetzstein, "House GOP Says It Bent on Welfare: White House Called Inflexible," *Washington Times*, December 6, 1995, p. A8.

24. Barbara Vobejda, "Child Support Collections on the Rise; Tougher Regulations in Welfare Bill Still Pending Would Reduce Problem, Administration and Republicans Agree," *Washington Post*, December 6, 1995, p. A23.

25. A block grant would give states a financial incentive to shorten the time children stay in foster care. Researchers, practitioners, and policymakers agree that states and localities should try to place children in permanent homes. Generally, three ways to achieve permanency are to identify families in danger of losing their children and provide them with preventive services, to provide services to families who had children removed and move children back into their homes more quickly, and to terminate parental rights in appropriate cases and then place children in adoptive homes. There is much less agreement that states are able to effectively pursue any of these three strategies.

26. The House's child protection block grant was killed by the Senate in both 1995 and 1996.

27. Rudolph G. Penner, *Repairing the Congressional Budget Process* (Washington: Urban Institute, 2001); Allen Schick, *The Capacity to Budget* (Washington: Urban Institute, 1990).

28. The Office of Management and Budget (OMB), a creature of the president, is less independent than the CBO but is also a highly respected source of budget projections and analysis. Most administrations tightly control OMB, whose head is a presidential appointee and who is often a close and trusted adviser of the president. By contrast, Republicans and Democrats on the Hill must agree on the head of CBO, and on many occasions the head of CBO has demonstrated her independence from Congress. There are no partisan political appointees at CBO, CRS, or GAO, and though most OMB senior officials are political appointees, the main work at OMB is performed by career public servants, who are nonpartisan. A fifth analytic organization, the Joint Committee on Taxation, produces analyses of the tax code for Congress and provides CBO with estimates of tax provisions. Although its head is a joint appointment by the chairs of the Committee on Ways and Means in the House and the Committee on Finance in the Senate, it manages to stay independent because of the integrity of its career staff.

29. Stanley E. Collender, *The Guide to the Federal Budget, Fiscal Year 1994* (Washington: Urban Institute, 1994).

30. Although balancing the budget and reducing government spending has been a traditional Republican goal, the course of the federal budget during the presidency of George W. Bush has been a disaster. The budget surplus was $127 billion in 2001, the first year of the Bush administration. In 2003 and 2004 the federal budget was in deficit $158 billion and $375 billion, respectively. Part of the deficit was caused by increased spending. Compared with spending increases that averaged 3.3 percent a year in the Clinton years, spending increased by an average of 6.5 percent a year in the first three years of the Bush presidency. Some of the increased deficit can be attributed to the 2001 recession, but most of it is attributable to tax cuts and increases in spending. It would be difficult for a

Republican who served in Congress during the Republican revolution of 1995–96 and the accompanying drive to balance the budget and pass a balanced budget amendment not to be amazed by the profligacy of the Republican president and a Republican Congress. See Congressional Budget Office, *The Budget and Economic Outlook: Fiscal Years 2005–2014* (Government Printing Office, 2004), app. F.

31. Guy Gugliotta, "Rules Committee Gets the Last Word(s) on Budget Bill," *Washington Post*, October 26, 1995, p. A11; John E. Yang and Eric Pianin, "House Approves Bill to Balance Budget," *Washington Post*, October 27, 1995, p. A1.

32. Daniel J. Balz and Ronald Brownstein, *Storming the Gates: Protest Politics and the Republican Revival* (New York: Little, Brown, 1996), chap. 6.

33. David Broder, "Rebels without a Pause," *Washington Post Magazine*, December 31, 1995, p. W8.

34. Elizabeth Drew, *Showdown: The Struggle between the Gingrich Congress and the Clinton White House* (New York: Touchstone, 1997), chap. 23; David E. Rosenbaum, "House and Senate Approve G.O.P.'s 7-Year Budget Plan; President Promises a Veto," *New York Times*, November 18, 1995, p. A1; "Reconciliation: Highlights of Conference Report," *Congressional Quarterly Weekly*, November 18, 1995, p. 3513.

35. A small group of moderate Democrats led by Charlie Stenholm of Texas did propose a compromise: it balanced the budget by making smaller cuts in Medicare, Medicaid, and other social programs and leaving out the Republican tax cut. Republicans ignored this effort. See "A Good Budget Compromise," *Washington Post*, October 24, 1995, p. A16; "An Avoidable Shut-Down," *Washington Post*, November 14, 1995, p. A18; Robert Pear, "Battle over the Budget—The Budget: Once Ignored, a Middle-Ground Budget Advances," *New York Times*, November 19, 1995, p. A1; Martin Olav Sabo and Charles Stenholm, "A Budget for All Americans," *Washington Post*, November 26, 1995, p. C7; Norman J. Ornstein, "Congress Inside Out: Let's Make a Deal—Swift Budget Solution Is Behind Door No. 1," *Roll Call*, December 14, 1995.

36. Adam Clymer, "Battle over the Budget: The Overview," *New York Times*, Nov. 14, 1995, p. A1.

37. Helen Dewar, "Neither Side Has Developed an Exit Strategy," *Washington Post*, November 16, 1995, p. A25.

38. "Battle over the Budget: News Analysis—Real Stakes in Shutdown," *New York Times*, November 14, 1995, p. A1.

39. Elizabeth Kolbert, "Battle over the Budget: The Voters—Along U.S. 30, the Deadlock Spawns Irritation and Fears," *New York Times*, November 17, 1995, p. A1; Kenneth B. Noble, "Battle over the Budget: The Closures—Canyon Becomes Peaceful, Pleasing Nobody," *New York Times*, November 19, 1995, p. 1–20.

40. David Maraniss and John E. Yang, "House GOP Standing Firm on a 7-Year Plan," *Washington Post*, November 15, 1995, p. A1.

41. Robert Keith and Edward Davis, *The Senate's "Byrd Rule" against Extraneous Matter in Reconciliation Bills*, CRS Report for Congress (Congressional Research Service, 1995); Robert Keith, *The Senate's "Byrd Rule" against Extraneous Matter in Reconciliation Bills Updated September 9, 1998* (Congressional Research Service, 1998); *Balanced Budget Reconciliation Act of 1995: Possible Extraneous Provisions*, Senate Bill (Congressional Research Service, Republican Staff, Senate Budget Committee, 1995); David R. Sands, "'Byrd Rule' Puts a Dent in Welfare Bill," *Washington Times*, October 31, 1995, p. A8.

42. Robert J. Samuelson, "R.I.P.: The War on Poverty," *Washington Post*, October 4, 1995, p. A25; George Hager, "Historic Votes Add Momentum as Conferees Start Work," *Congressional Quarterly Weekly*, October 28, 1995, p. 3282.

43. Congressional Budget Office, *Federal Budgetary Implications of the Personal Responsibility and Work Opportunity Reconciliation Act of 1996*, pp. 22–26.

44. David E. Rosenbaum, "An Intricate Procedure Lends a Hand to Welfare Recipients," *Washington Post*, November 1, 1995, p. A19; Alissa J. Rubin, "Reconciliation: Senate's Last-Minute Changes Kept Floor Action Lively," *Congressional Quarterly Weekly*, November 4, 1995, p. 3358.

45. Warren P. Strobel, "Fight Ignited by Flight," *Washington Times*, November 10, 1995, p. A14; Al Kamen, "At the Heart(s) of Clinton-Gingrich Flap," *Washington Post*, November 20, 1995, p. A19.

46. Dan Balz, "Gingrich to Lower His Public Profile: Speaker Plans to Reduce Role as Voice of GOP Revolution," *Washington Post*, December 2, 1995, p. A1; Richard L. Berke, "Clinton's Ratings over 50% in Poll as GOP Declines," *New York Times*, December 14, 1995, p. A1.

47. Eric Pianin, "House Approves New GOP Offer to End Shutdown; Proposal Unacceptable to White House," *Washington Post*, November 16, 1995, p. A1.

48. Ann Devroy and Eric Pianin, "Administration Saw Escape Hatch in GOP Compromise," *Washington Post*, November 21, 1995, p. A1.

## CHAPTER ELEVEN

1. House Committee on Ways and Means, *Hearing before the Subcommittee on Human Resources of the Committee on Ways and Means*, Serial 104-37, December 6, 1995.

2. The Catholic organizations that lobbied most effectively against the bill were the Catholic Conference, which represents the bishops, and the savvy Catholic Charities USA. By using the term "hierarchy" I do not mean to imply that only the hierarchy of the Catholic Church opposed the bill. Catholic organizations that represented the laity, such as the National Council of Catholic Women and the St. Vincent de Paul Society, also opposed the bill. Even so, I think it's a good bet that a majority of lay Catholics, like a majority of other Americans, supported a strong work requirement and time limits.

3. National Conference of Catholic Bishops, *Economic Justice for All: Pastoral Letter on Catholic Social Teaching and the U.S. Economy* (Washington: United Satates Catholic Conference, 1986). See also National Conference of Catholic Bishops, *A Decade after Economic Justice for All: Continuing Principles, Changing Context, New Challenges* (Washington: United States Catholic Conference, 1995).

4. Michael Novak, *The New Consensus on Family and Welfare: A Community of Self-Reliance* (Washington: American Enterprise Institute, 1987).

5. Administrative Board, *Moral Principles and Policy Priorities for Welfare Reform*, Publication 5-011 (Washington: United States Catholic Conference, 1995), p. 2.

6. Ibid., p. 5.

7. Roger Cardinal Mahony and Bishop John H. Ricard, SSJ, United States Catholic Conference, letter to members of Congress, November 14, 1995.

8. *Congressional Record*, March 22, 1995, pp. H3438–H3439.

9. The Family Support Act of 1988 was projected by the Congressional Budget Office to call for a net total of $3.3 billion in spending over five years, primarily on welfare-to-work programs and cash welfare for two-parent families. The bill raised about $3.3 billion to finance the new spending, primarily through increased debt collection by the Internal Revenue Service and fraud prevention in the Dependent Care Tax Credit program. See House Committee on Ways and Means, *General Explanation of the Family Support Act of 1988*, Committee Print 101-13 (1989).

10. Employment in New York City at that moment was in its third year of expansion, eventually rising from 2.70 million in 1992 to 3.16 million in 2000, a rise of about 17 percent. See New York City, Department of City Planning, *2003 Annual Report on Social Indicators,* pp. 7–15.

11. House Committee on Ways and Means, *Hearing before the Subcommittee on Human Resources of the Committee on Ways and Means,* Serial 104-37, December 6, 1995, p. 61.

12. Eventually the New Hope project produced significant impacts on a range of important measures: employment increased, stable employment increased, earnings increased, income increased, poverty declined, and school performance by young children improved; see Aletha C. Huston and others, *New Hope for Families and Children: Five-Year Results of a Program to Reduce Poverty and Reform Welfare* (New York: MDRC, 2003); Greg J. Duncan, Aletha C. Huston, and Thomas S. Weisner, *New Hope: A Policy Success for Working Poor Families and Their Children* (New York: Russell Sage, forthcoming).

13. Sara Rimer, "Where School Lunch Is Food, Not a Policy Issue," *New York Times,* March 7, 1995, p. A1; William Booth, "Schools Fearful that 'Johnny Can't Eat': Congress' School Lunch Debate Worries Some in Rural Mississippi," *Washington Post,* March 7, 1995, p. A1; "Food Stamps in Peril," *New York Times,* March 7, 1995, p. A18; "A Bad Food Stamps Bill," *Washington Post,* March 7, 1995, p. A16.

14. Morton Kondracke, "Lugar Holds up GOP Welfare Bill over School Lunch," *Roll Call,* December 7, 1995.

15. Elizabeth Shogren, "GOP Fight over Food Keeps Welfare Reform off the Table," *Los Angeles Times,* December 16, 1995, p. A17.

16. "Food Fight Cont.: House GOP Members Excoriate Lugar," *National Journal's Congress Daily,* December 18, 1995.

17. Barbara Vobejda, "Food Fight Stalls Final Welfare Pact," *Washington Post,* December 10, 1995, p. A10.

18. "If Mr. Jeffords Jumps," *New York Times,* May 24, 2001, p. A28; "Mr. Jeffords' Decision," *Washington Post,* May 24, 2001, p. A28.

19. House Committee on Ways and Means, news release, "Welfare News Conference," December 21, 1995.

20. Judith Havemann, "President Promises to Veto House-Passed Welfare Bill," *Washington Post,* December 22, 1995, p. A1; Cheryl Wetzstein, "House OKs Welfare Compromise; Margin Too Thin to Be Veto-Proof," *Washington Times,* December 22, 1995, p. A14; Robert Pear, "House Sends Senate an Overhaul of the Welfare System," *New York Times,* December 22, 1995, p. A37; "Welfare, Unreformed," *New York Times,* December 22, 1995, p. A38; "Hard Hearts, Soft Heads," *Washington Post,* December 22, 1995, p. A18.

21. E. Clay Shaw Jr. and Bill Archer, memo to Senators John H. Chafee, Jim Jeffords, Arlen Specter, Bill Cohen, and Olympia Snowe, December 22, 1995.

22. Ann Devroy and Eric Pianin, "Clinton to Submit 7-Year Plan to Spur Talks," *Washington Post,* December 6, 1995, p. A4.

23. Office of the President, news release "The President's Plan to Balance the Budget in Seven Years," December 7, 1995.

24. Republican tax cuts included cuts in capital gains, individual retirement accounts, the marriage penalty, the adoption credit, the automatic minimum tax for corporations, the inheritance tax (which Republicans called the death tax), and the amount of Social Security income subject to taxation; the entire package cost about $245 billion over seven years.

25. Office of the President, *A Vision of Change for America,* February 1993, esp. pp. 41–64.

26. Under OMB scoring, Clinton needed net savings of $465 billion over seven years. Because he wanted $100 billion in tax cuts, he proposed around $525 billion in spending

cuts plus technical adjustments worth $32 billion. See Office of the President, "The President's Plan to Balance the Budget in Seven Years," p. 2.

27. Congressional Budget Office, *The Economic and Budget Outlook: December 1995 Update.*

28. Ann Devroy and Eric Pianin, "Government Shuts Down Again after Talks Collapse," *Washington Post,* December 16, 1995, p. A1.

29. Jerry Gray, "Aides for 2 Sides Renew the Quest for a Budget Deal," *New York Times,* December 28, 1995, p. A1.

30. *Congressional Record,* December 22, 1995, p. S19182.

31. David E. Rosenbaum, "G.O.P. Rebellion Scuttles Accord on Budget Talks," *New York Times,* December 21, 1995, p. A1; Eric Pianin and Ann Devroy, "House Republicans Derail Budget Talks," *Washington Post,* December 21, 1995, p. A1.

32. Thomas B. Edsall, "Polls Bolster Both Sides in Bitter Fight over Balanced Budget," *Washington Post,* December 25, 1995, p. A12.

33. Robert J. Samuelson, "Budget Charade," *Washington Post,* December 27, 1995, p. A19.

34. David S. Broder, "Rebels without a Pause," *Washington Post,* December 31, 1995, p. W8.

35. Ann Devroy, "Top Leaders' Budget Meetings Just a Prelude to Bargaining," *Washington Post,* January 2, 1996, p. A1.

## CHAPTER TWELVE

1. E. Clay Shaw Jr., "Welfare: This Fight Is Not Over," *Washington Post,* February 4, 1996, p. C7.

2. Morton M. Kondracke, "GOP Still Could Force Clinton's Hand on Welfare," *Roll Call,* January 29, 1996, p. 6.

3. Robert D. Novak, "Clinton's Welfare Bluff," *Washington Post,* January 29, 1996, p. A19.

4. Robert Pear, "G.O.P. May Revive a Welfare Plan to Snare Clinton," *New York Times,* January 30, 1996, p. A1.

5. National Governors Association, "Welfare Reform," adopted February 6, 1996.

6. What Gingrich actually said to the press in California was that the House would "certainly" pass another bill, probably in early March, that contained "probably 80 to 90 percent" of what the governors wanted. See Judith Havemann and Barbara Vobejda, "Hill GOP Leaders to Study Governors' Welfare Plan," *Washington Post,* February 8, 1996, p. A8; Newt Gingrich, news release, "Statement from Speaker Newt Gingrich," February 6, 1996.

7. Within a few days, Robert Rector also put out a news release, "Welfare Reform and the Death of Marriage," in which he vigorously attacked the governors for preparing a "coffin" for marriage in America. An expanded version of Rector's critique of the governors' proposal can be found in Robert Rector, "Welfare Reform Fraud Once Again: Examining the NGA Welfare Plan," Backgrounder 1075 (Washington: Heritage Foundation, March 18, 1996).

8. Republicans didn't like this provision, but we did strongly support counting net caseload reduction against the work requirement. Democrats argued that this provision gave states an incentive to throw families off the rolls, which had the effect of counting them as working. We responded by prohibiting states from counting toward the participation rate any cases closed because the state had changed welfare eligibility rules.

9. House Committee on Ways and Means, *1996 Green Book,* p. 502.

10. Memo from the House Committee on Ways and Means, Subcommittee on Human Resources, "Overview and Analysis of Governors' Welfare Reform Proposal," February 7, 1996.

11. National Association of State Budget Officers, *1996 State Expenditure Report*, table 3.

12. House Committee on Ways and Means, *1998 Green Book*, p. 969.

13. House Committee on Ways and Means, *Hearings on the National Governors' Association Welfare Reform Proposal*, Serial 104-48, February 20, 1996; House Committee on Ways and Means, *Hearings on Poverty and Out-of-Wedlock Births*, March 12, 1996; House Committee on Ways and Means, *Hearings on Welfare Reform*, Serial 104-62, May 22–23, 1996.

14. House Committee on Ways and Means, *Hearings on the National Governors' Association Welfare Reform Proposal*, p. 40.

15. Ibid., p. 41.

16. Committee on Ways and Means, *Hearings on Welfare Reform*; Senate Committee on Finance, *Hearings on the Governors' Proposal on Welfare and Medicaid*, Serial 104-791, February 22, 28, 29, 1996; Senate Committee on Finance, *Hearings on Welfare and Medicaid Reform*, Serial 1795, June 13 and 19, 1996. Hearings were also held by the Education, Agriculture, and Commerce Committees in the House and by the Finance, Agriculture, and Education and Labor Committees in the Senate.

17. For simplicity, I again follow the procedure of referring to the House Committee on Economic and Educational Opportunities as the Education Committee.

18. James K. Glassman, "A Credo, Not a Contract," *Washington Post*, April 2, 1996, p. A13.

19. Michael Wines, "Republicans Face Plight that Hurt Democrats in 1994," *New York Times*, May 5, 1996, p. A1.

20. Mickey Kaus, "Preserving Welfare as We Know It," *Wall Street Journal*, March 26, 1996, p. A18.

21. Under some versions of this provision, only those who left welfare for an actual job would count.

22. Roger Mahan to Ron Haskins, memorandum, "Reconciliation Instructions for Welfare Reform," June 4, 1996. This memo confirmed the $26.7 billion estimate Roger had given me on the phone several weeks earlier.

23. Richard Wolf, "Republicans Press Clinton on Medicaid," *USA Today*, May 22, 1996, p. A8; Janet Hook and Ronald Brownstein, "Politics Stand in Way of Workable GOP Welfare Plan," *Los Angeles Times*, May 23, 1996, p. A18; Robert Pear, "G.O.P. Submits New Bill to Revamp Welfare and Medicaid," *New York Times*, May 23, 1996, p. B9; Judith Havemann and Barbara Vojbeda, "GOP Tailors Welfare Package to Clinton's Objections," *Washington Post*, May 23, 1996, p. A6; Jeffrey L. Katz, "Ignoring Veto Threat, GOP Links Welfare, Medicaid," *Congressional Quarterly Weekly*, May 25, 1996, pp. 1465–66.

24. Subcommittee reports are not published. They are sent, along with a cover letter from the subcommittee chairman, to the full committee. Once the full committee completes its markup, under House rules it must issue a report on the bill that usually includes its legislative history, a summary of votes on the bill and amendments in full committee, an explanation of every provision, and a CBO estimate of its costs. Full committee reports are publicly available and many are on line. For the subcommittee report, see E. Clay Shaw Jr., letter to Bill Archer, Committee on Ways and Means, June 10, 1995.

25. *Report on the Welfare and Medicaid Reform Act of 1996*, H. Rept. 104-651 (to accompany HR 3734) (Government Printing Office, 1996). The Budget Committee report contains the reports of the Agriculture, Commerce, Education, and Ways and Means Committees; the Ways and Means section is on pp. 1085–1938.

26. Democrats on the Ways and Means Committee, in their minority views, explained why they refused to support the bill: the bill was "still too tough on kids and families," it deprived at least 1 million children and 2 million parents of health insurance, it punished

children for the mistakes of their parents, and it denied benefits to legal immigrants. See ibid., pp. 2037–50.

## CHAPTER THIRTEEN

1. The federal government is known for its revolving door between both the legislative and administrative branches and the scores of lobbying businesses that populate the District of Columbia and the Maryland and Virginia suburbs. There is a lesser-known revolving door, involving scholars who circulate among government, universities, and think tanks. Many of the scholars know each other and maintain their relationships by appearing in or attending various forums—speeches, panel discussions, conferences—that occur almost daily in the nation's capital. Wendell Primus, an economist who worked for the Ways and Means Committee, the Clinton administration, the Center on Budget and Policy Priorities, and House Democratic leader Nancy Pelosi, is well known to scholars of social programs who occupy positions in Washington think tanks, especially those who are not members of the conservative brotherhood. Thus it was natural for Wendell to call on Urban Institute researchers to produce the analysis of the Republican bill's impacts. Their analysis was not a plot to subvert the Republican bill, but given this definition of poverty and assumptions about levels of work, the results were inevitable.

2. Elizabeth Shogren, "Welfare Report Clashes with Clinton, Senate," *Los Angeles Times,* October 27, 1995, p. A1.

3. Daniel Patrick Moynihan, news release, "House-Senate Conference on Welfare Reform, HR 4," October 24, 1995.

4. Daniel Patrick Moynihan and others, letter to Alice Rivlin, Office of Management and Budget, October 26, 1995; see Judith Havemann and Ann Devroy, "Democrats Seek Senate Welfare Plan Study," *Washington Post,* October 27, 1995, p. A7; Judith Havemann and Ann Devroy, "Clinton Agrees to New Welfare Study," *Washington Post,* October 28, 1995, p. A4.

5. Havemann and Devroy, "Clinton Agrees to New Welfare Study"; Matthew Rees, "Clinton's Welfare Deform," *Weekly Standard,* November 20, 1995, p. 19.

6. Jeff Shear, "Looking for a Voice," *National Journal,* March 16, 1996, pp. 591–95.

7. In July 1996 Zedlewski and her colleagues at the Urban Institute published a technical version of the report. The 1996 version used updated data but the same general approach in estimating the Republican bill's impact on family income and poverty. My analysis is based on the 1996 report. See Sheila Zedlewski and others, "Potential Effects of Congressional Welfare Reform Legislation on Family Incomes" (Washington: Urban Institute, July 26, 1996).

8. A substantial share of the more than one million children cast into poverty was attributable to the changes in the SSI program and in the loss of benefits by immigrant children.

9. "Welfare Squeeze," *Washington Post,* June 23, 1996, p. C6.

10. Ibid.

11. Most Reverend William S. Skylstad, bishop of Spokane and chairman of the Domestic Policy Committee of the U.S. Catholic Conference, letter to members of Congress, June 10, 1996.

12. Congressional Budget Office, *Federal Budgetary Implications of the Personal Responsibility and Work Opportunity Reconciliation Act of 1996,* p. 2.

13. House Committee on Ways and Means, *1996 Green Book,* app. J.

14. Fred Kammer, president of Catholic Charities USA, letter to members of U.S. Senate, August 6, 1995.

15. Marian Wright Edelman, "Say No to Welfare Reform," *Washington Post*, November 3, 1995, p. A23.

16. "Professor's Affiliations," *National Journal*, May 21, 2005, p. 1543.

17. Jason DeParle, *American Dream: Three Women, Ten Kids, and a Nation's Drive to End Welfare Reform* (New York: Viking, 2004), p. 116.

18. Talk about biting the hand that feeds you. During the time I wrote this book, I was employed by the Brookings Institution. The following seems to demonstrate that I write without bias.

19. R. Kent Weaver and William T. Dickens, eds., *Looking before We Leap: Social Science and Welfare Reform* (Brookings, 1995), p. 2. Weaver went on to write what is widely considered to be the definitive book about the 1996 welfare reform bill; see R. Kent Weaver, *Ending Welfare as We Know It* (Brookings, 2000).

20. See Weaver and Dickens, *Looking before We Leap*, chap. 6.

21. Edwin Chen, "Bipartisan Bid to Reform Welfare, Medicaid Falters," *Los Angeles Times*, March 15, 1996, p. 1.

22. Cindy Mann, "The Medicaid Restructuring Act of 1996: When Is a Guarantee *Not* a Guarantee?" (Washington: Center on Budget and Policy Priorities, 1996); Richard Kogan, "Federal Caps and State Matching Requirements under the New Republican Medicaid Proposal" (Washington: Center on Budget and Policy Priorities, 1996).

23. Henry J. Aaron and Peter R. Orszag, "The Impact of an Aging Population," in *Restoring Fiscal Sanity: How to Balance the Budget*, edited by Alice M. Rivlin and Isabel Sawhill (Brookings, 2004); Henry J. Aaron and Jack Meyer, "Health," in *Restoring Fiscal Sanity 2005: Meeting the Long-Run Challenge*, edited by Alice M. Rivlin and Isabel Sawhill (Brookings, 2005).

24. Only around 15 percent of Medicaid expenditures were for children on cash welfare. The elderly and the disabled absorbed around 70 percent of Medicaid expenditures in 1994 (the remaining 15 percent was spent on the parents of children on welfare). See House Committee on Ways and Means, *1996 Green Book*, pp. 901–02.

25. Letter from John Ensign and Dave Camp to Newt Gingrich and Trent Lott, June 13, 1996; letter from John Ensign and Dave Camp to Newt Gingrich and Trent Lott, June 26, 1996. See "Lott Leaves Door open to Splitting Medicaid, Welfare," *CongressDaily*, June 18, 1996.

26. When Tillie Fowler died in 2005, the *Washington Post* wrote a lengthy obituary in which Fowler was referred to as a "steel magnolia." See Adam Bernstein, "Florida's Rep. Tillie Fowler Dies; Defense-Minded Republican," *Washington Post*, March 3, 2005, p. B6.

27. Jeffrey L. Katz, "Ignoring Veto Threat, GOP Links Welfare, Medicaid," *Congressional Quarterly*, May 25, 1996, pp. 1465–67.

28. Jeffrey L. Katz, "GOP May Move to Split Medicaid, Welfare," *Congressional Quarterly*, June 22, 1996, p. 1761.

29. Robert D. Novak, "Republicans' Choice," *Washington Post*, June 17, 1996, p. A17.

30. By way of further illustrating the complex set of factors that bear on legislative decisions of this magnitude, after I had written the first draft of this chapter, Trent Lott published his political memoir, *Herding Cats: A Life in Politics* (New York: Regan Books, 2005). Lott takes credit for getting the welfare reform bill enacted and signed by President Clinton (see pp. 135–41). In Lott's telling, he, Dick Morris, and President Clinton formed a "backstairs triad" that saw Morris serving as a go-between to cut deals on legislation pending in Congress in the spring and summer of 1996, including welfare reform. Neither Clay Shaw nor I knew anything about this "backstairs triad," but if we take Lott at his word perhaps he knew that Clinton was going to sign the bill and therefore worked hard to get welfare reform separated from Medicaid. Without doubt, Lott was in all the critical meetings and had the power to heavily influence if not make this decision.

31. Although the bills introduced in the House and Senate on May 22 were nearly identical, both bills had by now been altered by the amendment process in committee, thereby providing several important differences between the bills that would have to be resolved during the House-Senate conference.

32. The language (see section 1931(b)(3) of the Social Security Act) says that Medicaid may be terminated if the adult's cash assistance is terminated "because of refusing to work." The phrase "refusing to work" has been interpreted more broadly than simply referring to a job to cover a range of TANF work rules.

33. The Commerce Committee in the House has jurisdiction over the Medicaid program, but Ways and Means has jurisdiction over two programs—Temporary Assistance for Needy Families and Supplemental Security Income—whose recipients are automatically qualified for Medicaid benefits. The House Parliamentarian has generally held that the qualifications of families receiving Medicaid through these two programs, which are laid out in sections 408(a)(11), 1902(e)(1)(A), and 1931 of the Social Security Act, are under jurisdiction of both the Commerce Committee and the Ways and Means Committee. Thus while Ways and Means had no authority to change the Medicaid program itself, we did share the authority with Commerce to control sections 1902(e)(1)(A) and 1931. Presumably, changing the criteria for eligibility of TANF and SSI recipients for Medicaid would therefore have to be approved by both committees.

34. The motion to recommit is offered on the floor of the House just before the vote on final passage. By tradition, the right to offer the motion is given to the floor leader for the bill in question from the minority party. The motion may be made with or without instructions. The latter is, in effect, a vote to kill the bill if the motion passes. The former means that if the motion is accepted, the bill is returned to the committee that produced it with specific instructions about changes that should be made in the bill. In this case, the chairman of the committee whose provisions are affected by the motion immediately stands and reports back the bill with the change made by the motion to recommit. The House then votes on final passage, a vote that could be affected by the change in the bill initiated by the minority party. Debate on the motion is usually ten minutes, equally divided between those opposing and those supporting the bill, typically the floor managers of the bill from the minority and majority parties.

35. Part of my approach to being staff director of our subcommittee was to take a deferential approach to Chairman Shaw in public and be forthright and persistent in private. But on this occasion, it was so important to honor our commitments to Castle that I blurted out without thinking. Of course, I was not at all surprised that Shaw viewed the situation exactly as I did—why not take a little chance in order to fulfill a bargain with a good colleague? There was no doubt in my mind that if Speaker Gingrich had resisted our recommendation to give Castle a vote on the floor, Shaw would have argued with him. But Gingrich said something like: "Are you sure we can hold our votes?" to which Shaw immediately replied in the affirmative. Gingrich made the bill in order on the floor.

36. *Congressional Record*, July 18, 1996, p. H7976.

37. Ibid., p. H7989, roll call vote 331.

## CHAPTER FOURTEEN

1. For long stretches of time during the two years of the welfare reform debate, like many other married staffers, I had lots of trouble seeing my family, especially my eight-year-old, who was often in bed by the time I got home. Once, when I walked in the door on a Friday night after having not seen him since I put him to bed on Sunday night, he yelled out

to his mother, "Hey, Mom, Ron Haskins is here." So on this night when the negotiations took a break for an hour at seven o'clock, my wife and all three of my children who still lived at home brought dinner, and we ate in the hearing room adjacent to my office.

2. This version of Shaw's comments is based on both my notes from the meeting and from memory.

3. As of 2002 only eight states had no ban on cash welfare or food stamps for individuals with a drug felony conviction. States have many forms of the ban, among them a ban that expires after a few years if the individual is not convicted of another drug felony, a ban that does not apply after individuals have completed their jail sentence, and a ban that does not apply to individuals who have completed treatment. See Gwen Rubenstein, "The State of State Policy on TANF and Addiction" (Washington: Legal Action Center, 2002).

4. By 2004 twenty-four states had adopted some form of the family cap; see Department of Health and Human Services, *Temporary Assistance for Needy Families (TANF): Sixth Annual Report to Congress* (2004), p. 114.

5. This provision, which had a long and torturous history, imposed heavy fines on states that delayed or denied any adoption based on race, color, or national origin (see section 471(a) of the Social Security Act). Previous law had allowed states to consider a child's cultural, ethnic, or racial background in making placement decisions, a practice that was outlawed by our new provision. This new provision was enacted as part of the Small Business Job Protection Act of 1996 on August 1. See House Committee on Ways and Means, *2000 Green Book*, pp. 693–94.

6. The governors' claim that the waivers were a promise by the federal government and that states could count on their waiver for a stipulated period of time was not correct. After 1987 all waivers granted by the Department of Health and Human Services (HHS) contained a standard clause stating that, if there were changes in federal law, HHS and the state would negotiate an agreement on how to proceed. If an agreement could not be reached, HHS reserved the authority to cancel the waiver.

7. Stephen Freedman and Daniel Friedlander, *Early Findings on Program Impacts in Three Sites* (New York: MDRC, 1995).

8. A 20 percent cap meant that not more than 20 percent of the number of individuals necessary to meet the work requirement could do so by being involved in educational activities. The 20 percent included the teenage mothers required by the new law to attend school or lose their benefit. Consider an example. If a state had 200 families on welfare when the work requirement was fully phased in during 2002, 100 (50 percent) would be required to meet the work standard. Not more than 20 of these 100 (20 percent) could do so by participating in educational activities. The 20 percent cap was changed to 30 percent by the Balanced Budget Act of 1997 (PL 105-33).

9. Realizing that, with the governors present, the issue of the education cap and waivers was bound to come up, we had Talent's staff contact him and get him to be available for the five o'clock session by phone from his district in St. Louis.

10. Speaker Gingrich's conference room featured the skull of a Tyrannosaurus Rex on loan from the Smithsonian Institution.

11. *Congressional Record*, July 31, 1996, pp. H9392–H9424.

12. Ibid., pp. H9385–H9388.

13. Ibid., p. H9391.

14. My account is based on an interview with Bruce Reed at the Democratic Leadership Council office on February 2, 2006. Both Ken Apfel, now at the University of Texas, and Jack Lew, now at New York University, who were present at the meeting, agree that the rendition given here is accurate.

15. In June 1995, the Pew Research Center for the People and the Press released a poll showing that the nation preferred Clinton over Dole by a percentage of 54 to 40. Similarly, a CNN–*USA Today*–Gallup poll showed Clinton's lead over Dole growing from 40 to 37 in April 1996 to 50 to 33 in July. See "Bill Clinton's Big Lead and the Electoral College" (Washington: Pew Research Center for the People and the Press, June 5, 1996); CNN–*USA Today*–Gallup polls conducted April 9–10, 1996, and July 18–21, 1996.

16. The petitions that aliens must file to become citizens were already increasing rapidly. From about 560,000 in 1994, they increased to 1 million in 1995, as the national welfare debate created headlines on a regular basis; 1.3 million in 1996, when the bill was passed and signed; and 1.7 million in 1997. The most straightforward explanation of this explosion in petitions is that noncitizens were concerned that they might lose benefits as a result of the 1996 welfare legislation. See House Committee on Ways and Means, *2000 Green Book*, p. 1365.

17. "The Welfare Bill: Text of President Clinton's Announcement on Welfare Legislation," *New York Times*, August 1, 1996, p. A24.

18. This and the quotations that follow are from *Congressional Record*, July 31, 1996, pp. H9395, H9406, H9408, and H9413–15.

19. The creation of Medicaid and Medicare in 1965 was supported by 73 percent of the members of the House and Senate; 77 percent of the House and Senate voted in favor of the 1996 welfare reform legislation. For the Medicaid-Medicare vote, see the Social Security Administration, "Legislative History: Vote Tallies for Passage of Medicare in 1965," at www.ssa.gov/history/tally65.html.

## CHAPTER FIFTEEN

1. In addition to calling for several specific types of research and reports on issues such as reducing teen pregnancy and welfare dependency (see section 413 of the *Personal Responsibility and Work Opportunity Reconciliation Act of 1996*), the welfare reform law contained three pots of money for research: $10 million a year for seven years for the Census Bureau to reconstitute a sample from the Survey of Income and Program Participation (SIPP, an ongoing longitudinal survey, supplying the necessary baseline information) and to supplement SIPP with additional information on children and on several important issues such as nonmarital births and welfare dependency (see section 414 of Title I of the act); $6 million a year for seven years for a longitudinal study of children at risk of child abuse or neglect (see Section 503 of the act); and $15 million a year for seven years for the Department of Health and Human Services (HHS) to conduct studies on the effects of the new law and on issues addressed by the law (see section 413, especially paragraphs (a) and (h) of the act). The Census Bureau study had a problem with attrition and has unfortunately yielded less information than planned. See Laura S. Connelly and Christine Emerson Marston, "Welfare Reform, Earnings, and Income: New Evidence from the Survey of Program Dynamics," *Contemporary Economic Policy* 23 (2005): 493–520. The study by the HHS and several contractors of abuse and neglect has greatly expanded knowledge of what happens to abused and neglected children when they are left with their families, placed in care under state supervision, or returned to their families. Similarly, the decision, made largely by Clay Shaw and Daniel Patrick Moynihan, to give HHS what amounted to an annual $15 million discretionary fund to support research on virtually any issues raised by welfare reform has been vindicated. This $15 million was expanded by $6 million each year by the House and Senate Appropriations Committees as a continuation of funds previously available under section 1110 of the Social Security Act. Research supported by this

$21 million annual fund has yielded hundreds of scholarly papers, some published in the best academic journals, many of which support the conclusions I reach in this chapter. More specifically, HHS used these funds to continue some of the large-scale waiver studies that were ongoing when the bill passed, to augment five of the best state demonstrations to gather detailed information about child outcomes, to commission a synthesis of all the research on welfare reform conducted by the Rand Corporation (see Jeffrey Grogger, Lynn Karoly, and Jacob Alex Klerman, *Consequences of Welfare Reform: A Research Synthesis* [Santa Monica, Calif.: Rand, 2002]), and to conduct two sets of experimental evaluations of state programs designed to test new approaches to improving employment retention and advancement for low-income mothers and helping hard-to-employ families find and retain employment. More recently, the Bush administration has used part of this money to support studies of efforts to promote healthy marriage.

Note: This section is based in part on a personal communication on February 21, 2006, from Howard Rolston, a now-retired senior official at HHS who played a vital role in allocating the department's research dollars. For a critique of the use of these research dollars, see Robert Moffitt and Michele Ver Ploeg, eds., *Evaluating Welfare Reform in an Era of Transition* (Washington: National Academy Press, 2001). In addition to these funds, a study sponsored by the Annie E. Casey Foundation identified about $230 million that five major foundations (the Annie E. Casey Foundation, the Ford Foundation, the Joyce Foundation, the Charles Stewart Mott Foundation, and the David and Lucile Packard Foundation) have invested in research and advocacy involving workforce development. See Janellen Duffy and Ed Hatcher, "Rainmakers or Troublemakers? The Impact of GIST on TANF Reauthorization" (Baltimore: Annie E. Casey Foundation, 2002), p. 16.

2. A problem arises. As this book shows, the bill changed repeatedly as it worked its way through Congress in both 1995 and 1996. Indeed, Clinton and many Democrats argued that the 1996 version of the bill was kinder and gentler than the 1995 version. In addition, in 1997 Congress and President Clinton passed a "technical corrections" bill, which made some important changes in the 1996 law, especially the provisions for noncitizens. The most important change in noncitizen provisions was that noncitizens on Supplemental Security Income (SSI) when the bill passed were exempt from the general SSI ban. It would be possible for someone to argue that the apocalyptic predictions of the left applied to earlier provisions of the bill and not the version signed into law by Clinton. There are two problems with this explanation. First, predictions of disaster from the left were based on computer simulations of the effects of provisions, such as the time limit and sanctions, that were virtually unchanged from the beginning until the end of the debate. Second, many of the dark predictions occurred after the bill passed Congress and before Clinton signed the bill, a period during which the bill did not change at all. For a summary of the final bill, see the appendix.

3. Richard Nathan and Thomas Gais, *Implementing the Personal Responsibility Act of 1996: A First Look* (Rockefeller Institute of Government, State University of New York, 1999); Irene Lurie, *At the Front Lines of the Welfare System: A Perspective on the Decline in Welfare Caseloads* (Rockefeller Institute of Government, State University of New York, 2005).

4. Lurie, *At the Front Lines of the Welfare System*, pp. 231–32.

5. After 120 consecutive months of expansion, the economy suffered a mild downturn that lasted from March until November 2001. See National Bureau of Economic Research, "Business Cycle Expansions and Contractions," available at www.nber.org/cycles.html.

6. Caseload decline is a somewhat flawed indicator because decline can be caused not only by employment but also by states making it more difficult for needy families to stay on or join welfare.

7. Because the population increases every year, data on the number of children or families on AFDC or TANF over time can be misleading. Both the number of children and the percentage of all U.S. children on AFDC or TANF fell dramatically after 1994. The percentage of children on AFDC peaked in 1993 at 14.3 percent. It fell every year thereafter until reaching 5.3 percent in 2002. See House Committee on Ways and Means, *2004 Green Book*, pp. 7–31. By way of comparison, in 1970 the percentage of children on AFDC was 8.8 percent, more than 65 percent higher than in 2002 (see *Annual Statistical Supplement*, Social Security Bulletin 13-11700 [Department of Health and Human Services, 2005], table 9.G1).

8. Department of Health and Human Services, Administration for Children and Families, "Cash Assistance for Needy Families, Aid to Families with Dependent Children (AFDC) and Temporary Assistance to Needy Families (TANF), Average Monthly Families and Recipients for Calendar Years 1936–2001," May 10, 2002, available at www.acf.dhhs.gov/news/stats/3697.htm.

9. House Committee on Ways and Means, *2004 Green Book*, section 7, pp. 27–37; Department of Health and Human Services, *Indicators of Welfare Dependence: Annual Report to Congress, 2003* (Government Printing Office, 2003), appendix A, table TANF 1; for welfare caseloads information, see the Administration for Children and Families, www.acf.hhs.gov/newstat2.shtml.

10. Judith M. Gueron and Edward Pauly, *From Welfare to Work* (New York: Russell Sage, 1991); Grogger, Karoly, and Klerman, *Consequences of Welfare Reform*.

11. House Committee on Ways and Means, *2000 Green Book*, pp. 1471–74, 1500–10. See also Gregory Acs, Pamela Loprest, and Tracy Roberts, *Final Synthesis Report of Findings from ASPE's "Leavers" Grants* (Washington: Urban Institute, 2001), pp. 23–47.

12. Acs, Loprest, and Roberts, *Final Synthesis Report*, chap. 3.

13. See the Bureau of Labor Statistics, http://stats.bls.gov/cps/home.htm, http://stats.bls.gov/cps/home.htm for labor force statistics from the Current Population Survey. All the measures discussed in this section are point-in-time measures.

14. Gary Burtless of the Brookings Institution, unpublished calculations using U.S. Bureau of Labor Statistics data.

15. These figures are from unpublished tables of demographic and economic characteristics of female family heads, distributed by income quintile, that are prepared by Richard Bavier of the Office of Management and Budget using the Census Bureau's Current Population Survey. Bavier makes these tables available to anyone who requests them. All figures are given in 2004 dollars.

16. A study by two other researchers, using longitudinal data from the Survey of Income and Program Participation, shows the same pattern of increased work and earnings and declining poverty among families leaving welfare. See June O'Neill and M. Anne Hill, "Gaining Ground, Moving Up: The Change in the Economic Status of Single Mothers under Welfare Reform," Civic Report 35 (Manhattan Institute Center for Civic Innovation, 2003).

17. Jeffrey Grogger and Lynn A. Karoly, *Welfare Reform: Effects of a Decade of Change* (Harvard University Press, 2005), p. 156.

18. David J. Eggebeen and Daniel T. Lichter, "Race, Family Structure, and Changing Poverty among American Children," *American Sociological Review* 56 (1991): 801–17.

19. Bernadette D. Proctor and Joseph Dalaker, *Poverty in the United States: 2002* (Census Bureau, 2002), table 5; Douglas J. Besharov, ed., *Family and Child Well-Being after Welfare Reform* (New Brunswick, N.J.: Transaction, 2003), figure 4; Bureau of the Census, Poverty and Health Statistics Branch, *Current Population Survey, Annual Social and Economic Supplements*, December 14, 2005, table 3, available at www.census.gov/hhes/www/poverty/histpov/hstpov3.html.

20. Daniel T. Lichter, Zhenchao Qian, and Martha L. Crowley, "Child Poverty among Racial Minorities and Immigrants: Explaining Trends and Differentials," *Social Science Quarterly* 86 supp. (2005): 1037–59; quotation on p. 1037.

21. This analysis retains the same thresholds as the official poverty index (about $13,300 for a family of three in 1990) but uses a broader definition of income than the official measure. House Committee on Ways and Means, *2004 Green Book*, table H-21.

22. Sheila Zedlewski and others, "The Potential Effects of the Budget Reconciliation Bill on Family Incomes" (Washington: Urban Institute, 1995).

23. Paul A. Jargowsky and Isabel V. Sawhill, *The Decline of the Underclass*, policy brief, Center on Children and Families (Brookings, 2006), p. 6.

24. Kenneth Land, *Child and Youth Well-Being Index (CWI), 1975–2004 with Projections for 2005*, available at www.soc.duke.edu/~cwi/. Family economic well-being improved by 13 percent between 1995 and 2000, but then declined slightly. In 2005 it was still 9 percent above its 1995 level.

25. Federal Interagency Forum on Child and Family Statistics, *America's Children: Key National Indicators of Well-Being 2005* (Government Printing Office, 2005).

26. Alcohol use has increased somewhat for twelfth-graders but has declined for eighth- and tenth-graders, see ibid., p. 44.

27. Donald J. Hernandez and Suzanne E. Macartney, "Measuring Social Disparities: A Modified Approach to the Index of Child Well-Being (CWI) for Race-Ethnic, Immigrant-Generation, and Socioeconomic Groups with New Results for Whites, Blacks, and Hispanics," paper prepared for the forum, "Review of the Child Well-Being Index," Brookings Institution, May 10, 2006.

28. House Committee on Ways and Means, *Contract with America: Overview*, Serial 104-20, January 5, 10, 11, and 12, 1995, pp. 58–93.

29. House Committee on Ways and Means, *2004 Green Book*, section 11, table 23; Department of Health and Human Services, Administration for Children and Families, Children's Bureau, "Trends in Foster Care and Adoption, FY2000–FY2004," September 2005, available at www.acf.hhs.gov/programs/cb/stats_research/afcars/trends.htm. But see Jane Walfogel, *The Future of Children Protection* (Harvard University Press, 1998), pp. 130–31.

30. House Committee on Ways and Means, *2004 Green Book*, section 11, figure 1.

31. Pamela Morris, Lisa A. Gennetian, and Greg J. Duncan, "Effects of Welfare and Employment Policies on Young Children: New Findings on Policy Experiments Conducted in the Early 1990s," *Social Policy Report* 19 (2005): 3–22.

32. For reviews of the literature on the effects on children of working mothers, see E. Harvey, "Short-Term and Long-Term Effects of Early Parental Employment on Children of the National Longitudinal Survey of Youth," *Developmental Psychology* 35 (1999): 445–59; Martha J. Zaslow and Carol A. Emig, "When Low-Income Mothers Go to Work: Implications for Children," *Future of Children* 7 (1997): 110–15.

33. Lisa A. Gennetian and others. *How Welfare and Work Policies for Parents Affect Adolescents: A Synthesis of Research* (New York: MDRC, 2002).

34. Greg J. Duncan and P. Lindsay Chase-Lansdale, "Welfare Reform and Children's Well-Being," in *The New World of Welfare*, edited by Rebecca M. Blank and Ron Haskins (Brookings, 2001); Jennifer L. Brooks, Elisabeth C. Hair, and Martha J. Zaslow, "Welfare Reform's Impact on Adolescents: Early Warning Signs" (Washington: Child Trends, 2001).

35. Gennetian and others, *How Welfare and Work Policies for Parents Affect Adolescents*, p. 22.

36. Bruce Reed, interview with Ron Haskins, Democratic Leadership Council office, February 2, 2006.

37. Census Bureau, *Statistical Abstract of the United States, 2004–2005*, p. 371.

38. Rebecca M. Blank, "Declining Caseloads/Increased Work: What Can We Conclude about the Effects of Welfare Reform?" *Economic Policy Review* 7 (2001): 25–36; James P. Ziliak and others, "Accounting for the Decline in AFDC Caseloads: Welfare Reform or the Economy?" *Journal of Human Resources* 35 (2000): 570–86.

39. It is difficult to discern a clear effect of the 1991 recession on the welfare caseload. When the recession hit, the caseload had already grown in five of the previous six years, rising from 3.69 million families in 1985 to 4.38 million families in 1991, during the healthy economy of the 1980s. The caseload continued to increase over the next three years, rising from 4.38 million families in 1991 to 5.05 million in 1994, before its prolonged decline during the welfare reform period. By contrast, as we have seen, the welfare caseload continued to decline throughout and following the recession of 2001. Between 1983 and the peak employment year of 1991, the employment-to-population ratio for never-married mothers rose from 34.5 to 44.0, or by 9.5 percentage points. During the expansion of the 1990s, the comparable ratio rose from 43.4 in 1992 to 65.8 in 2000, an increase of 22.4 percentage points. Clearly a lot more poor mothers went to work during the expansion of the 1990s than the expansion of the 1980s. Employment data are from unpublished calculations by Gary Burtless using Census Bureau data. Caseload information is from the Administration for Children and Families, available at www.acf.hhs.gov/news/stats/newstats2.shtml.

40. Congressional Budget Office, *Policy Changes Affecting Mandatory Spending for Low-Income Families Not Receiving Welfare* (1998).

41. House Committee on Ways and Means *1986 Green Book*, p. 369; House Committee on Ways and Means *1998 Green Book*, p. 408.

42. House Committee on Ways and Means, *1996 Green Book*, section 8, p. 399, table 3.

43. House Committee on Ways and Means, *2004 Green Book*, section 13, table 41; section 7, table 18.

44. Jeffrey Grogger, "The Effects of Time Limits, the EITC, and Other Policy Changes on Welfare Use, Work, and Income among Female-Headed Families," *Review of Economics and Statistics* 85 (2003): 394–408.

45. Gary Burtless, personal communication with Ron Haskins, Brookings Institution, February 21, 2006; Robert Lerman, "How Did the 2001 Recession Affect Single Mothers?" Single Parents Earning Monitor (Washington: Urban Institute, 2005).

46. Carmen DeNavas-Walt, Bernadette Proctor, and Cheryl Lee Hill, *Income, Poverty, and Health Insurance Coverage in the United States: 2004,* Current Population Report P60-229 (Census Bureau, 2005); Joseph Dalaker, *Poverty in the U.S.: 2000,* Current Population Report P60-214, available at www.census.gov/prod/2001pubs/p60-214.pdf.

47. *Annual Statistical Supplement,* Social Security Bulletin 13-11700 (Department of Health and Human Services, 2005), table 9.G1.

48. These income figures are based on cross-sectional data—the same mothers are not observed year after year. Data from tables prepared by Richard Bavier of the Office of Management and Budget. See note 15.

49. House Committee on Ways and Means, *2004 Green Book*, section 7, pp. 36–37.

50. Robert P. Stoker and Laura A. Wilson, *When Work Is Not Enough: State and Federal Policies to Support Needy Workers* (Brookings, 2006).

51. House Committee on Ways and Means, *2004 Green Book*, section 13, pp. 35–41.

52. Alan Berube and others, "The Price of Paying Taxes: How Tax Preparation and Refund Loan Fees Erode the Benefits of the EITC," survey series, Center on Urban and Metropolitan Policy and the Progressive Policy Institute, Brookings Institution, May 2002.

53. Lynnley Browning, "I.R.S. Delays New Scrutiny of Tax Credit for the Poor," *New*

*York Times,* August 7, 2003, p. C6; "Progress on EITC Pre-Certification" (Washington: Center on Budget and Policy Priorities, 2003).

54. For a good example, see Sheila Zedlewski and Amelia Gruber, *Former Welfare Families and the Food Stamp Program: The Exodus Continues,* New Federalism National Survey of America's Families, Series B, no. 33 (Washington: Urban Institute, 2001).

55. "Summary of APHSA Recommendations for Food Stamp Program Reform" (Washington: American Public Human Services Association, 2001).

56. Stacy Dean and Dorothy Rosenbaum, *Implementing New Changes to the Food Stamp Program: A Provision-by-Provision Analysis of the Farm Bill* (Washington: Center on Budget and Policy Priorities, 2003).

57. See House Committee on Ways and Means, *2004 Green Book,* section 15, table 14.

58. Ibid., section 15, pp. 83–98.

59. This provision is found in section 1931(h) of Title XIX of the Social Security Act [42 U.S.C. 13960-1], Sec. 1925 [42 U.S.C. 13961-6].

60. House Committee on Ways and Means, *2004 Green Book,* section 15, p. 44; Leighton Ku, Center on Budget and Policy Priorities, e-mail to Ron Haskins, February 17, 2006.

61. Anna Aizer, "Public Health Insurance, Program Take-Up, and Child Health," Working Paper 12105 (Cambridge, Mass.: National Bureau of Economic Research, 2006).

62. Don Winstead, Testimony before the U.S. House of Representatives, House Committee on Ways and Means, Subcommittee on Human Resources, *Hearing on Health Coverage for Families Leaving Welfare,* May 16, 2000.

63. Aizer, "Public Health Insurance, Program Take-Up, and Child Health."

64. David M. Blau, *The Child Care Problem: An Economic Analysis* (New York: Russell Sage, 2001).

65. *Budget of the U.S. Government, Fiscal Year 2005* (Office of Management and Budget, 2004).

66. *Statistical Abstract of the United States: 2004–2005* (Census Bureau, 2004), p. 363.

67. Acs, Loprest, and Roberts, *Final Synthesis Report of the Findings from ASPE "Leavers" Grants,* table 7.5.

68. Lynn A. Karoly and others, *Investing in Our Children: What We Know and Don't Know about the Costs and Benefits of Early Childhood Interventions* (Santa Monica, Calif.: Rand, 1998); Edward Zigler and Susan Muenchow, *Head Start: The Inside Story of America's Most Successful Educational Experiment* (New York: Basic Books, 1992).

69. Ron Haskins, "Putting Education into Preschools," in *Generational Change: Closing the Test Score Gap,* edited by Paul E. Peterson (Lanham, Md.: Rowman and Littlefield, 2006).

70. Ellen S. Peisner-Feinberg and others, *The Children of the Cost, Quality, and Outcomes Study Go to School* (Chapel Hill, N.C.: Frank Porter Graham Child Development Center, 1999); Gina Adams, Martha Zaslow, and Kathryn Tout, "Child Care for Children in Low-Income Working Families: Trends, Patterns, and Potential Policy Implications for Children's Development," paper prepared for the roundtable, "Children in Low-Income Families," Urban Institute and Child Trends, January 12, 2006.

71. Michael Puma and others, *Head Start Impact Study: First Year Findings* (Department of Health and Human Services, 2005); National Institute for Early Education Research, *The State of Preschool: 2005 State Preschool Yearbook* (Rutgers University Press, 2005).

72. Robert P. Stoker and Laura A. Wilson, *When Work Is Not Enough: State and Federal Policies to Support Needy Workers* (Brookings, 2006); Sheila Zedlewski, "What Strate-

gies Successfully Promote Participation in Work Support Programs: Food Stamps, EITC, Medicaid/SCHIP, the Earned Income Tax Credit, Child Care?" paper prepared for the roundtable, "Next Steps toward a Working Families' Policy Agenda," Urban Institute, May 9–10, 2005.

73. House Committee on Ways and Means, *2004 Green Book*, section 7, pp. 87–91.

74. Robert J. LaLonde, "The Promise of Public Sector-Sponsored Training Programs," *Journal of Economic Perspectives* 9 (1995): 149–68; Harry Holzer, "Can We Improve Retention and Advancement among Low-Income Parents?" Working Families Policies (Washington: Urban Institute, September 2005).

75. For 2003 the maximum credit for a filer with two or more children is $4,204. Filers can claim a payment of 40 percent of their earnings up to $10,510. When their income reaches $13,730, the credit begins to phase out at a rate of about 21 percent of income above $13,730 until the credit reaches zero at about $33,700. House Ways and Means Committee, *2004 Green Book*, section 13, p. 38.

76. The course is commonly called GED, or general educational development. See Gayle Hamilton, *Moving People from Welfare to Work: Lessons from the National Evaluation of Welfare-to-Work Strategies* (Department of Health and Human Services and Department of Education, 2002), available at http://aspe.hhs.gov/hsp/NEWWS/synthesis02/.

77. Judith M. Gueron and Gayle Hamilton, *The Role of Education and Training in Welfare Reform*, Policy Brief 20, Welfare Reform & Beyond (Brookings, 2002); Thomas Brock and Lashawn Richburg-Hayes, *Paying for Persistence: Early Results of a Louisiana Scholarship Program for Low-Income Parents Attending Community College* (New York: MDRC, 2006).

78. Harry J. Holzer and Margy Waller, *The Workforce Investment Act: Reauthorization to Address the "Skills Gap,"* policy research brief, Center on Urban and Metropolitan Policy (Brookings, 2003); Burt S. Barnow and Christopher T. King, "The Workforce Investment Act in Eight States" (Employment and Training Division, Department of Labor, 2005).

79. House Committee on Ways and Means, *2004 Green Book*, pp. L24–L31.

80. Andrew J. Cherlin and others. "Operating within the Rules: Welfare Recipients' Experiences with Sanctions and Case Closings," *Social Services Review* 76 (2002): 387–405. Thirty-six states have a policy that allows them to completely terminate cash benefits for rule infractions. See Department of Health and Human Services, *Temporary Assistance to Needy Families Program (TANF): Fourth Annual Report to Congress,* May 2002, p. 346. But see Jeffrey Grogger and Lynn A. Karoly, *Welfare Reform: Effects of a Decade of Change* (Harvard University Press, 2005), pp. 235–36, who conclude that there are too few studies to draw firm conclusions about the effect of sanctions.

81. Kasia O'Neill Murray and Wendell E. Primus, "Recent Data Trends Show Welfare Reform to Be a Mixed Success: Significant Policy Changes Should Accompany Reauthorization," *Review of Policy Research* 22 (2005): 301–24.

82. Rebecca M. Blank and Robert F. Schoeni, "Changes in the Distribution of Children's Family Income over the 1990s," *American Economic Review* 93 (2003): 304–08.

83. Ibid., pp. 307, 308.

84. These figures are from unpublished tables of demographic and economic characteristics of female family heads, distributed by income quintile, that are prepared by Richard Bavier of the Office of Management and Budget using the Census Bureau's Current Population Survey. All figures are given in 2004 dollars.

85. Robert Moffitt and Katie Winder, "Does It Pay to Move from Welfare to Work? A Comment on Danziger, Heflin, Corcoran, Oltmans, and Wang," *Journal of Policy Analy-*

*sis and Management* 24 (2005): 399–409; Pamela Loprest, "Disconnected Welfare Leavers Face Serious Risks," Report 7, Snapshots of America's Families III (Washington: Urban Institute, 2003); Sandra Danziger, Elizabeth Oltmans Ananat, and Kimberly G. Browning, "Childcare Subsidies and the Transition from Welfare to Work," *Family Relations* 52 (2004): 219–28; Robert G. Wood and Anu Rangarajan, "What's Happening to TANF Leavers Who Are Not Employed?" Issue Brief 6 (Princeton, N.J.: Mathematica Policy Research, 2003).

86. Bruce D. Meyer and James X. Sullivan, *The Well-Being of Single-Mother Families after Welfare Reform,* Policy Brief 33, Welfare Reform & Beyond (Brookings, 2005).

87. Christopher Jencks, Scott Winship, and Joseph Swingle, "Welfare Redux," *American Prospect* 17 (2006): 36–40.

88. Scott Winship and Christopher Jencks, "How Did the Social Policy Changes of the 1990s Affect Material Hardship among Single Mothers? Evidence from the CPS Food Security Supplement," Faculty Research Paper RWP04-027 (Cambridge, Mass.: John F. Kennedy School of Government, 2004), p. 2.

89. Scott Winship and Christopher Jencks, "Welfare Reform Worked: Don't Fix It," *Christian Science Monitor,* July 21, 2004, p. 9.

90. LaDonna Pavetti and Jacqueline Kauff, "When Five Years Is Not Enough: Identifying and Addressing the Needs of Families Nearing the TANF Time Limit in Ramsey County, Minnesota," Lessons from the Field (Princeton, N.J.: Mathematica Policy Research, 2006).

91. Gayle Hamilton and others, *How Effective Are Different Welfare-to-Work Approaches? Five-Year Adult and Child Impacts for Eleven Programs* (New York: MDRC, 2002).

92. Ronald B. Mincy, ed., *Black Males: Left Behind* (Washington: Urban Institute, 2006); Peter Edelman, Harry J. Holzer, and Paul Offner, *Reconnecting Disadvantaged Young Men* (Washington: Urban Institute, 2006).

93. Harry J. Holzer, Paul Offner, and Elaine Sorenson, "Declining Employment among Young Black Less-Educated Men: The Role of Incarceration and Child Support," *Journal of Policy Analysis and Management* 25 (2005): 329–50; Gary Burtless of the Brookings Institution, unpublished calculations using U.S. Bureau of Labor Statistics data.

94. Holzer, Offner, and Sorenson, "Declining Employment among Young Black Less-Educated Men.

95. Richard Freeman, "Why Do So Many Young American Men Commit Crimes and What Might We Do about It?" *Journal of Economic Perspectives* 10 (1996): 25–42.

96. Harry J. Holzer, *What Employers Want: Job Prospects for Less-Educated Workers* (New York: Russell Sage, 1996).

97. Orlando Patterson, *Rituals of Blood: Consequences of Slavery in Two American Centuries* (New York: Basic Books, 1998).

98. Daniel Patrick Moynihan, "A Family Policy for the Nation," *America,* March 1986, p. 227; original published September 18, 1965.

99. Fred Doolittle and Suzanne Lynn, *Working with Low-Income Cases: Lessons for the Child Support Enforcement System from Parents' Fair Share* (New York: MDRC, 1998).

100. Ron Haskins, Sara McLanahan, and Elisabeth Donahue, *The Decline in Marriage: What to Do?* Policy Brief, fall. The Future of Children (Brookings, 2005).

101. For reviews of changes in family composition in recent decades, see David T. Ellwood and Christopher Jencks, "The Spread of Single-Parent Families in the United States since 1960," in *The Future of the Family,* edited by Daniel P. Moynihan, Timothy M. Smeeding, and Lee Rainwater (New York: Russell Sage, 2004); Kay Hymowitz, "Marriage and Casts," *City Journal* 16 (2006): 29–37.

102. Stephanie J. Ventura and others, *Births to Teenagers in the United States, 1940–2000*, Report 10, National Vital Statistics Reports 49 (Hyattsville, Md.: National Center for Health Statistics, 2001); Brady E. Hamilton and others, "Health E-Stats: Preliminary Births for 2004" (Washington: National Center for Health Statistics, 2005), available at www.cdc.gov/nchs/products/pubs/pubd/hestats/prelim_births/prelim_births04.htm.

103. Brady E. Hamilton and others, *Births: Preliminary Data for 2004*, Report 8, National Vital Statistics Reports 54 (Washington: National Center for Health Statistics, 2005).

104. Stephanie J. Ventura and others, *Nonmarital Childbearing in the United States, 1940–99*, Report 16, National Vital Statistics Reports 48 (Hyattsville, Md.: National Center for Health Statistics, 2000); Stephanie J. Ventura and others, *Revised Pregnancy Rates, 1990–97, and New Rates for 1998–99: United States*, Report 7, National Vital Statistics Reports 52 (Hyattsville, Md.: National Center for Health Statistics, 2003).

105. Gregory Acs and Sandi Nelson, *Honey, I'm Home: Changes in Living Arrangements in the Late 1990s*, Report B-38 (Washington: Urban Institute, 2001).

106. Alan Weil and Kenneth Finegold, eds., *Welfare Reform: The Next Act* (Washington: Urban Institute, 2002).

107. Richard Bavier, "Child-Bearing outside Marriage and Child-Raising inside Marriage" (Office of Management and Budget, 2002); Richard Bavier, "Recent Increases in the Share of Young Children with Married Mothers," paper prepared for the National Welfare Reform Evaluation Conference, June 2002.

108. Joshua R. Goldstein and Catherine T. Kenney, "Marriage Delayed or Marriage Forgone? New Cohort Forecasts of First Marriage for U.S. Women," *American Sociological Review* 66 (2001): 506–19; Steven P. Martin, "Growing Evidence for a 'Divorce Divide'? Education and Marital Dissolution Rates in the U.S. since the 1970s" (Department of Sociology, University of Maryland, undated).

109. Sara McLanahan and Gary Sandefur, *Growing up with a Single Parent* (Harvard University Press, 1994); Sara McLanahan, Elisabeth Donahue, and Ron Haskins, *Marriage and Child Wellbeing*, Policy Brief, fall. The Future of Children (Brookings 2005); Ron Haskins and Isabel Sawhill, *Work and Marriage: The Way to End Poverty and Welfare*, Policy Brief 28, Welfare Reform & Beyond (Brookings, 2003).

110. Anna Gassman-Pines and Hirokazu Yoshikawa, "Five-Year Effects of an Anti-Poverty Program on Marriage among Never-Married Mothers," *Journal of Policy Analysis and Management* 25 (2006): 11–30.

111. Cynthia Miller and others, *Reforming Welfare and Rewarding Work: Final Report on the Minnesota Family Investment Program*, vol. 1, *Effect on Adults* (New York: MDRC, 2000); Dave Hage, *Reforming Welfare by Rewarding Work: One State's Successful Experiment* (University of Minnesota Press, 2004).

112. Lisa A. Gennetian and Virginia Knox, "Staying Single: The Effects of Welfare Reform Policies on Marriage and Cohabitation," Working Paper 13 (New York: MDRC, 2003).

113. See Dan Bloom, Mary Farrell, and Barbara Fink, *Welfare Time Limits: State Policies, Implementation, and Effects on Families* (New York: MDRC, 2002).

114. Gennetian and Knox, "Staying Single," p. 14.

115. McLanahan, Donahue, and Haskins, *Marriage and Child Wellbeing*.

116. The statistics in this section are taken from Office of Child Support Enforcement, *Child Support Enforcement* (Government Printing Office, various years).

117. Carmen Solomon-Fears, *The Child Support Enforcement Programs: A Review of the Data*, RL-32875 (Congressional Research Service, 2005).

118. Probably due to the recession, average child support payments received by mothers in the bottom 40 percent of the income distribution did not increase steadily between 2000 and 2004 as they had before 2000. In 2000 the mean child support payment for these mothers was $675 a month; in 2004 it was $674 (both figures in 2004 dollars). All figures are from tables prepared by Richard Bavier of the Office of Management and Budget. See note 15.

119. These data are based on tables prepared by Richard Bavier.

120. The data in this section were taken from House Committee on Ways and Means, *2004 Green Book*, appendix J. See table J-5.

121. Ibid., table J-8.

122. Michael Fix and Jeffrey Passel, *The Scope and Impact of Welfare Reform's Immigrant Provisions* (Washington: Urban Institute, 2002); Michael Fix and Ron Haskins, *Welfare Benefits for Non-Citizens*, Policy Brief 15, Welfare Reform & Beyond (Brookings, 2002).

123. House Committee on Ways and Means, *2004 Green Book*, table J-9.

124. In 2002 legislation reauthorizing farm programs, at President Bush's request, Congress made legal permanent residents who had been in the United States for five years and children of legal permanent residents regardless of how long they had been in the United States eligible for the Food Stamp program. See House Committee on Ways and Means, *2004 Green Book*, pp. 512–15. For information on the 1996 prohibitions, see Fix and Haskins, *Welfare Benefits for Non-Citizens*; Ron Haskins, Mark Greenberg, and Shawn Fremstad, *Federal Policy for Immigrant Children: Room for Common Ground?* Policy Brief, fall. The Future of Children (Brookings, 2004).

125. Lewin Group, *Policy Evaluation of the Effect of Legislation Prohibiting the Payment of Disability Benefits to Individuals Whose Disability Is Based on Drug Addiction and Alcoholism* (Baltimore: Social Security Administration, 1998).

126. Jeannette Rogowski and others, *Final Report for Policy Evaluation of the Effect of the 1996 Welfare Reform Legislation on SSI Benefits for Disabled Children* (Santa Monica, Calif.: Rand, 2002); Jeannette Rogowski and others, *Background Study Design Report for Policy Evaluation of the Effect of the 1996 Welfare Reform Legislation on SSI Benefits for Disabled Children* (Santa Monica, Calif.: Rand, 1998).

127. Ron Haskins, "Comments," in *American Economic Policy in the 1990s*, edited by Jeffrey A. Frankel and Peter R. Orszag (MIT Press, 2002).

## Appendix

1. A thorough summary of all the provisions in the final legislation can be found in House Committee on Ways and Means, *Summary of Welfare Reforms Made by Public Law 104-193, The Personal Responsibility and Work Opportunity Reconciliation Act and Associated Legislation*, WMCP 104-15 (Government Printing Office, 1996).

2. States had to use their own funds to pay part of the cost of AFDC. The amount of state payment varied inversely with the state per capita income but averaged about 45 percent of total AFDC costs. Thus all states had an incentive to hold down AFDC costs.

3. All of these provisions are quoted from Title V, sec. 510, of the *Social Security Act* (42 U.S.C. 701 et seq.).

4. Congressional Budget Office, *Federal Budgetary Implications of the Personal Responsibility and Work Opportunity Reconciliation Act of 1996*, pp. 32–35.

5. Ibid., p. 23.

6. For a review of the 1996 reforms of welfare for noncitizens and subsequent amendments, see House Committee on Ways and Means, *2004 Green Book*, app. J.

7. *Immigration Control and Financial Responsibility Act of 1996*, S. 1664 (introduced April 10, 1996).

8. House Committee on Ways and Means, *1998 Green Book*, p. 304.

9. Of the 209,000 SSI recipients who lost benefits because they had qualified as drug addicts or alcoholics, 71,000 reapplied on the basis of other disabling conditions and had their benefits restored. See Lewin Group, *Policy Evaluation of the Effect of Legislation Prohibiting the Payment of Disability Benefits to Individuals Whose Disability Is Based on Drug Addiction and Alcoholism*, Interim Report (Baltimore, Md.: Social Security Administration, 1998).

10. For example, see Congressional Budget Office, *Federal Budgetary Implications of the Personal Responsibility and Work Opportunity Reconciliation Act of 1996*, pp. 32–35.

11. Joe Richardson and Jean Yavis Jones, *Child Nutrition: Issues in the 104th Congress* IB95047 (Congressional Research Service, 1995); Vee Burke and others, *Welfare Reform: The House-Passed Bill H.R.4*, 95-375 EPW (Congressional Research Service, 1995); Congressional Budget Office, *Federal Budgetary Implications*.

12. House Committee on Ways and Means, *1996 Green Book*, p. 896.

13. Rita Simon, Howard Alstein, and Marygold S. Melli, *The Case for Transracial Adoption* (American University Press, 1994).

14. Howard Metzenbaum, *Testimony before the U.S. House of Representatives, Committee on Ways and Means, Subcommittee on Human Resources, Hearing on Interethnic Adoptions*, September 15, 1998.

15. Health and Human Services, *Temporary Assistance for Needy Families (TANF) Program*, sixth annual report to Congress (2004).

16. Survey of Income and Program Participation is available at www.sipp.census.gov/sipp/sipphome.html; also see Laura S. Connolly and Christine Enerson Marston, "Welfare Reform, Earnings, and Income: New Evidence from the Survey of Program Dynamics," *Contemporary Economic Policy* 23 (2005): 493–512.

17. House Committee on Ways and Means, *Summary of Welfare Reforms Made by Public Law 104-193, The Personal Responsibility and Work Opportunity Reconciliation Act and Associated Legislation*, WMCP 104-15, 104 (Government Printing Office, 1996), p. 137. Programs with savings are noted by a minus sign.

18. Program entries do not sum to total due to rounding.

# Index

WRB indicates "welfare reform bill," and the number following shows that bill's sequence in time, with #1 being the first proposed bill.

Aaron, Henry, 295
Abortion: in general subconference, 239; HR *1214* floor debate, 187–88; HR *3500* rewrite, 76, 78–80; removed from Contract with America, 79
Abraham, Spencer, 195
Abstinence: promotion of, 8; in Senate bill, 233–34; in WRB #3, 316
Academics against WRB #3, 294–96
Acs, Gregory, 355–56
ADC (Aid to Dependent Children). *See* Aid to Families with Dependent Children (AFDC)
AFDC. *See* Aid to Families with Dependent Children (AFDC)
Agriculture Committee (House): jurisdiction over Food Stamps, 279; jurisdiction over welfare, 165; in nutrition subconference, 238; Republican unity, 183
Agriculture Committee (Senate), 199, 238
AIDS Project of East Bay, 127
Aid to Families with Dependent Children (AFDC): ADC described, 4; on childhood disability, 176; CRS spending survey, 127; elimination of, 1; Ellwood's view, 15; Finance Committee jurisdiction, 200; in HR 4, 137, 162; in HR *1214*, 177, 178; in HR *3500* rewrite #2, 96, 97–98; Jencks's view, 15; Kaus's view, 15–16; Meyers's reform bill, 44; MOE provision, 231; in NGA bill, 272; in pre *1970s* welfare, 5; proposed work requirement, 48; replaced by TANF, 332–33; time limits, 27; two-parent family coverage, 12; work requirements, 40. *See also* entries at Child and Children
Allen, George, 93
Amendments-in-order rule, 184–85
American Academy of Pediatrics, 127
American Civil Liberties Union, 35
American Enterprise Institute, 13, 146
American Public Human Services Association, 21, 333. *See also* American Public Welfare Association
American Public Welfare Association, 14, 250, 333
Anderson, Eloise, 282–85
Anti-abortion amendment in HR *1214* floor debate, 187–88
Apfel, Ken: direct budget talks, 264–65; response to the TRIM analysis, 292; Clinton's decision to sign welfare reform bill, 326, 327

Appropriate person rule, 11–12

Appropriations programs in pre-1970s welfare, 5

Archer, Bill: on CBO study, 147; challenging Clinton's welfare task force, 38; on child support enforcement in HR 4, 153, 156; on conference committee, 228; House-Senate conference, 309; HR 4 committee markup, 160; on HR 982, 190; on HR 1214, 166, 172; HR 1214 amendments, 185–87; on maintaining welfare conference work, 247; meeting on Republican leadership, 300; *Meet the Press* appearance, 90; planning HR 4 hearings, 107–11; questioning Shalala, 118–19; on RGA concerns with WRB #3, 306; Rules Committee, 169; selective interest in the Contract with America, 85; Senate counterpart, 195–96; on separating Medicaid from welfare reform, 305; on work requirements, 152–53, 174; WRB #3, 279, 284, 314

Archer amendments to HR 1214, 185–87

Armey, Dick: on budget reconciliation bill, 245; Contract with America, 70, 72, 105; direct budget talks, 265; gag rule in HR 3500 rewrite, 78–80; House Republican Conference, 47; HR 3500 threatened, 63; meeting on Republican leadership, 304; on separating Medicaid from welfare reform, 304; welfare reform vote, 57; WRB #3 House floor debate, 313

Ashcroft, John: charitable choice provision, 209, 214; new conservative senator, 195; on religion's access to public funds, 234

Babbitt, Bruce, 14

Balanced Budget Act of 1993, 244

Bane, Mary Jo: Clinton's welfare task force, 38; HR 4 hearing testimony, 127; welfare research, 6–7, 48–50

Bane and Ellwood study of welfare and work, 6–7

Barbour, Haley: reviving welfare reform, 271; work with RGA, 94, 198, 210; WRB #3 meeting, 299

Barnes, Fred, 284

Barone, Michael, 41

Baucus, Max, 201, 212, 261

Bavier, Richard, 350, 356

Behavior, changing: Catholic bishops' view, 257–58; by cutting benefits to children, 178; Mead's theory, 10; Senate debate, 217; Shalala's HR 4 testimony, 121; Wisconsin welfare reform, 35. *See also* Murray Light; Murray, Charles; Welfare-to-work programs

Behavior, maladaptive, and SSI benefits, 234

Behavioral dysfunction, 13–14, 27

Beilenson, Anthony, 171

*The Bell Curve* (Murray), 200

Bennett, William: HR 4 hearing testimony, 128–29; on illegitimacy, 41; on "moderate" welfare reform, 68–69; on Murray Light, 130, 146; NPC speech episode, 146; opposition to HR 3500, 66; "Real Welfare Reform Bill," 69; on state control of welfare reform, 95; on work requirements, 64

Berger, Eric, 302

Besharov, Doug, 13, 51

Bethell, Tom, 64

Bevan, Cassie, 132, 308

*Beyond Entitlement* (Mead), 10

Billings, Annie, 234

Billmire, Richard, 55

Bipartisan bill, 309–10

Blank, Rebecca, 130–31, 350

Bliley, Tom: reviving welfare reform, 271; on RGA concerns with WRB #3, 306; on separating Medicaid from welfare reform, 303; on WRB #3, 278–79

Block grants: compared in House and Senate bills, 232; conservative welfare reform, 44–45; in HR 4 committee markup, 162; HR 4 hearing testimony, 126; in HR 4 negotiations, 100–02; in HR 4 subcommittee markup, 137, 148–49; in HR 3500 rewrite #2, 83–85, 94, 96; MOE provision, 231; in Packwood bill, 203; Senate fight, 204; state responses, 53, 55–56.

Blum, Barbara, 13

Bonior, David, 325

Boskin, Michael, 125
Boxer, Barbara, 223
Brademas, John, 5
Bradley, Bill, 154, 218–19
Bradley amendment to Dole bill, 212, 225
Bradley and Olin Foundations, 13
Branstad, Terry, 317
Bread for the World, 127
Broder, David, 263
Brookings Institution, 295–96
Brown, Hank, 42, 142, 199
Brownstein, Ron, 63–64
Bryant, Wayne, 34, 36, 61
Budget balancing via EITC, 235–36
Budget reconciliation bill: Clinton administration response, 244; Clinton vetoes debt ceiling and first continuing resolution, 245–46; Clinton vetoes WRB #1, 253; first continuing resolution, 245–46; government shutdown (first), 246–47, 251–53; includes WRB #1, 241–42, 247; passed House and Senate, 245; process, 242; Republican and Democratic bills compared, 243–44. See also Welfare reform bill #1 (WRB #1)
Bunn, Jim, 187
Bunning, Jim: Republican leadership meeting, 301; on reviving the Senate bill, 270; on separating Medicaid from welfare reform, 305
Burke, Sheila: conference committee strategy, 237; conservatives' view, 230; role in Senate welfare reform, 196–97, 207; on WRB #3 introduction, 282–83
Burke, Vee, 127
Buttaro, Karen, 55
Byrd, Robert, 218, 247, 250
Byrd rule in reconciliation, 247, 250, 279

Camp, Dave: in general subconference, 239–41; on HR 982, 189; HR 3500 rewrite, 73; on Medicaid dual eligibility, 321–24; on Murray Light, 148; Santorum-DeLay work group, 46, 65; on separating Medicaid from welfare reform, 301–02, 305; work on WRB #3, 281, 299; on work requirements, 54

Campbell, Ben Nighthorse, 215–16, 261
Canady, Charles, 64
Cardin, Ben, 286–87
Carper, Tom: NGA bill hearings, 276; reviving welfare reform, 270; state welfare reform, 93
Carter, Jimmy, 5
Caseload prediction by CBO, 177
Caseload reduction, 258, 334
Caseload reduction credit, 153, 283–84
Castle, Mike: on HR 982, 189; on RGA concerns with WRB #3, 308–09; Santorum-DeLay work group, 46, 65; stalling the House, 325
Castle-Tanner bill, 310–12
Catholic Charities: HR 4 hearing testimony, 127; on Kennedy-Dodd amendment, 215; rare victories, 220; on welfare reform, 255–56; against WRB #3, 294
Catholic Conference: on illegitimacy in NGA bill, 277; New Jersey welfare reform, 35; on welfare reform, 254–58, 294
Cavnar, Reid, 72
CBO. See Congressional Budget Office
CBPP. See Center on Budget and Policy Priorities
CBS poll during second shutdown, 262–63
Center for Community Change, 127
Center for Law and Social Policy: interest in welfare reform, 21; rare victories, 220; against WRB #3, 296
Center on Budget and Policy Priorities (CBPP): interest in welfare reform, 21; on Medicaid reform, 297–98; on MOE in Dole bill, 214; rare victories, 220
Chafee, John: on child protection, 235, 274; on conference committee, 229; on conference report, 260; on Dole bill, 209; in general subconference, 239–41; on HR 1214 child protection, 177; on illegitimacy in Packwood bill, 202; influence on Dole bill, 205; on Medicaid dual eligibility, 318; WRB #3 House-Senate conference, 314
Chairman's rule, 168–69

Charitable choice provision, 209, 214, 234

Child, children: harshness of HR *1214*, 172, 175–78; harshness of Packwood bill, 200. *See also* Aid to Families with Dependent Children (AFDC)

Child and Youth Well-Being Index (CWI), 337

Child care: block grant in HR *3500* rewrite *#2*, 96, 97–98; compared in House and Senate bills, 233; in Daschle bill, 205; difficulties of welfare reform implementation, 347–48; in Dole bill, 205, 209, 214–16; in the final push, 223–26; in general subconference, 237; HR *4* hearing testimony, 126; in HR *982*, 190; in HR *1214*, 178, 188; increase in Rules Committee, 170; Labor and Human Resources jurisdiction, 200–01; Mondale-Brademas legislation, 5; in Packwood bill, 200; RGA concern, 308–09

Child Care and Development, 200, 215

Child nutrition programs: compared in House and Senate bills, 230; in Dole bill, 208; Food Stamps and block grants, 46–47; in nutrition subconference, 238; in Senate bill, 235

Child protection: compared in House and Senate bills, 230; Democrats' view, 144; in general subconference, 237–38, 240–41; HR *4* hearing testimony, 127; in HR *4* subcommittee markup, 137, 148–49; in HR *1214* floor debate, 176–77; in HR *3500* rewrite *#2*, 96, 97–98; in NGA bill, 272, 274; in Senate bill, 235; in WRB *#3*, 316

Child support enforcement: Commission on Interstate Child Support, 154; in conference committee, 249–50; HR *4* hearing testimony, 126; in HR *4* markups, 137, 153–59, 161–62; in Packwood bill, 203; in Rules Committee, 170; Santorum-DeLay work group, 47–48; Shalala's view, 117; since *1996*, 358; Wisconsin welfare reform, 34

Child Welfare League, 127

Child well-being, 335–40, 343

Childhood disability in HR *1214* floor debate, 175–76

Children's Defense Fund: on child support enforcement in HR *4*, 155–56, 249; HR *4* hearings demonstration, 128; interest in welfare reform, 21; rare victories, 220; against WRB *#3*, 294

Children's Rights Council, 127

Chiles, Lawton, 296–97

Christian Coalition: on illegitimacy in NGA bill, 277; influence on the House bill, 231; interest in welfare reform, 21

*Christian Science Monitor*, 352

Cisneros, Henry, 326

Clay, William, 188

Clinton, Bill, and Clinton administration: on child support, 155; contention with Moynihan on welfare reform, 292; Democratic welfare bills, 81, 116, 236–37; direct budget talks, 263–66; health care reform, 103–04; on House and Senate bills, 236; on HR *4* subcommittee markup, 141; on illegitimacy, 8; on major budget issues, 211; missteps after the *1994* election, 102–04; NGA speech on HR *1214*, 205; prodded by Republicans, 68; response to budget reconciliation bill, 244; signs WRB *#3*, 253; spending plan for first term, 261–62; vetoes entire Republican agenda, 253; vetoes first continuing resolution, 245–46; vetoes WRB *#1*, 253; vetoes WRB *#2*, 266–67; on welfare reform, 14–15, 118, 230; welfare task force, 37–40, 71; Work and Responsibility Act, 81, 116, 236–37; on work requirements, 174

Closed rule, 166

Cloture, use of, 222

Coalition to Stop Welfare Cuts, 127

Cogan, John, 13

Cohen, Howard, 302, 319, 321

Cohen, William, 209, 245, 260

Collins, Cardiss, 171–72, 184

Colton, Debra, 129, 159

Commerce, U.S. Department of, disbanded, 243

Commerce Committee (House): jurisdiction over Medicaid, 271, 278, 279,

297; on separating Medicaid from welfare reform, 302–03

Commission on Interstate Child Support, 154

Committee of jurisdiction, 166, 279

Committee status of the House, 192

Community Legal Services, 127

Compromise, 239, 243

Conceptual markup, 162

Concerned Women for America, 21

Conference committee, 227–28, 229–30. *See also entries at* Welfare reform bill

Congressional Budget Office (CBO): child protection caseload prediction, 177; child support estimate, 249; HR *4* cost survey, 152; HR *3500* cost survey, 66; inception, 242; low-income family support, 341; reconciliation bill scoring, 261; social programs estimate, 179; on SSI, 235; welfare and illegitimacy study, 146–47, 218; on Wisconsin waiver, 320

Congressional Caucus on Women's Issues, 154–55

*Congressional Quarterly*, 304

Congressional Research Service (CRS): on HHS changes in WRB #3, 319; on Hyde amendment, 187; inception, 242; low-income family support, 341–42; on noncitizen benefits, 359; social program count, 5; spending surveys, 84, 127

Congressional staff described, 22–23

Connerly, Ward, 123

Conrad, Kent, 201

Continents analogy, 21

Continuing resolution: deadline, 262; first, vetoed, 245–46; second, counteroffer accepted, 252–53

Contract with America: Archer's view, 85; Armey's view, 70, 72; building Republican unity, 71, 83; divisive issues, 79; Dole's view, 94; HR *4* version, 97; inception, 70; introduced, 110–12; leadership, 105; Lewis's view, 182; O'Beirne's view, 126; as revolution, 104; RGA collaboration, 86; status in July *1995*, 194; *Washington Times's* view, 194

Cook County Public Guardians, 132

Cost of welfare reform, 66

Cost shifting: Hutchinson spending cap, 60; in NGA bill, 275; to states, 85. *See also* Spending cap

Crane, Phil, 118

Crime and welfare, 2

Criminality among low-income fathers, 353–54

Croly, Herbert, 16–17

CRS. *See* Congressional Research Service.

Cubin, Barbara, 191

Cuomo, Mario, 14

Current Population Survey (Census Bureau), 350

Daly, Sharon, 256, 294

D'Amato, Alfonse, 202

Danziger, Sheldon, 6, 145–48

Daschle, Tom, 208, 210–11, 265

Daschle bill: Clinton's support, 290; defeated, 212; final push in the Senate, 224–26; influence on Dole bill, 205; introduced, 208; overview, 205–06; reconciled with Dole bill, 222–26; work requirements, 210. *See also* Senate welfare reform bill

Deal, Nathan, 190

Deal bill (HR *982*): debate, 189–90; Democratic welfare bills, 167–68; reviving welfare reform, 269; in Rules Committee, 170; Shaw's view, 169; work requirements, 174–75

Debt ceiling, Clinton veto, 245

Debt extension, Clinton veto, 246

Deficit reduction, 192, 242–43

DeLauro, Rosa, 326

DeLay, Tom: on budget reconciliation bill, 245; on continuing resolution, 262; Contract with America leadership, 105; on deficit reduction vote, 192; Santorum-DeLay work group, 46; WRB #3 House floor debate, 313. *See also* Santorum-DeLay work group

Democratic Governors Association, 93, 296–98.

Democratic Party: after the *1994* election, 102–04; case against HR *4*, 144; on HR *1214* education and training benefits, 179; on HR *1214* harshness to children, 175–78; on HR *1214* low-wage workers, 179–81; on HR *1214* "reverse Robin Hood" effect, 178–79; on HR *1214* working family support, 181; on HR *1214* work requirements, 173–75; little input to HR *1214*, 169; motivation for welfare, 18; overview of HR *1214* arguments, 172, 173; response to budget reconciliation bill, 244; welfare bills, 167–68, 189–90, 191–92

Democratic unity: compared with Republican unity, 81; lacking between House and governors, 277; in the Senate, 206, 218; welfare bills, 167

Democrats, 136, 229, 236

Demonstrations during HR *4* hearings, 128

DeParle, Jason: on Burke attack, 197; Ellwood-Aaron anecdote, 295; on unwed mothers' predicament, 67; welfare reporter, 38

Dependent Care Tax Credit in HR *982*, 190

Devroy, Ann, 261, 266

DeWine, Mike, 195, 205

DGA. *See* Democratic Governors Association

Dickens, William, 295–96

Dingell, John, 99

Dionne, E. J., 103

Dirksen, Everett, 320

Disability as defined in the Senate, 234

Disability Insurance, 3, 5

Disregard rules, 6, 52

Distribution tables, 288–89

Divorce rates for undereducated women, 356–57

Dixon, Jennifer, 147

Dodd, Christopher: on child care, 215, 224; final push in the Senate, 224–26; Kennedy-Dodd amendment, 215–16

Doggett, Lloyd, 324, 326

Dole, Bob: on budget reconciliation bill, 245; campaign, 251, 299, 301; on conference committee, 228; conservatives' view of, 230; on continuing resolution, 262; on the Contract with America, 94; direct budget talks, 263–66; on family cap, 219; on House-Senate conference, 249; on illegitimacy in Packwood bill, 202; leadership in welfare reform, 196–97; leadership skill, 230, 248–49, 251; majority leader of the Senate, 82; presidential aspirations, 194–95, 230, 282; Republican support waning, 304; on school lunch block grant, 259; on separating Medicaid from welfare reform, 305

Dole bill: amendments, 211–13, 220; block grants, 204; child care, 214–16; Daschle's view, 210–11; development of, 204–05; Faircloth amendment, 220; family cap, 213; final push in the Senate, 224–26; "Home Alone" bill, 215; illegitimacy, 216; inception, 202; initial attacks, 207; MOE, 214; overview of first version, 207–08; overview of second version, 208–10; reconciled with Daschle bill, 222–26. *See also* Senate welfare reform bill

Domenici, Pete, 209, 218

Domenici amendment to Dole bill, 218–22

Donahue, Elisabeth, 155

"Do-nothing Congress," 286

Downey, Tom, 289

Dreier, David, 87

Driver's licenses, revocation for delinquent child support, 158–59, 170

Dual eligibility, Medicaid, 318–19, 321–24

Dunn, Jennifer: on child care increase, 170; HR *4* hearings, 128; on HR *1214* en block amendment, 186; on hunting, fishing licenses and child support, 158–59; Republican leadership meeting, 301; work requirements, 54

Earned Income Tax Credit (EITC): difficulties of welfare reform implementation, 344–45; in direct budget talks, 264–65; effect on poverty, 336–37; in HR *1214*, 178; low-income family support, 342; in NGA bill, 272–73; in Senate bill, 235–36; welfare reform, 15; Wisconsin welfare reform, 34; work and work support, 31–32; working family support, 181; in WRB #3, 316

Ebb, Nancy, 155–56, 249

Economic recession, 343–44

Economic strength and financial well-being, 340–42

Edelman, Marion Wright, 156, 294

Education Committee (House): in general subconference, 238; HR *3500* rewrite #2, 96–97; influence on work requirements, 174; jurisdiction over children's issues, 233, 279; jurisdiction over welfare, 165; in nutrition subconference, 238; Republican unity, 183

Education and Labor Committee (Senate), 233, 238

Education and training benefits: in Dole bill, 208; in HR *1214*, 179; in WRB #3, 317–18

EITC. *See* Earned Income Tax Credit (EITC)

Election, *1994*, 82, 197–98

Ellwood, David, 288; Aaron's welfare reform letter, 295; on child support enforcement in HR *4*, 155; Clinton's welfare task force, 38; on welfare and work, 6–7; welfare research, 15, 48–50

Emanuel, Rahm, 326

Emergency Assistance, 232

EMILY's List, 80

Empower America: on HR *3500*, 66–67, 69; interest in welfare reform, 21, 22; on Murray Light, 146

*The End of Equality* (Kaus), 15–16

Engler, John: on House passage, 260; influence of RGA in the Senate, 199; on Medicaid dual eligibility, 318, 323; Medicaid press conference, 296–97; reviving welfare reform, 270, 271; on RGA concerns with WRB #3, 308–09; Santorum-DeLay work group, 56; on Senate Republican welfare bills, 206; state welfare reform, 60, 93; WRB #3 meeting, 317–19

English, Phil: HR *4* subcommittee markup, 153; language in final markup, 163; on Murray Light, 148; work requirements, 54

Ensign, John, 281, 301–02, 305

Entitlement: benefits history, 3–5; benefits in HR *4* committee markup, 162; described, 27

Esbeck, Carl, 234

Ethnicity and child well-being, 338

Faircloth, Lauch: on Dole bill, 205, 207, 209, 213, 216; on family cap, 209, 284; influence on Senate proceedings, 195, 205, 213; on Murray Light in Dole bill, 216; opposition to HR *3500*, 63; on Packwood bill, 199, 203–04; "Real Welfare Reform Bill," 69; on Republican governors, 203–04; on social scientists, 147

Faircloth amendment to Dole bill, 211, 216–18, 220, 221–22

Faircloth-Rector bill compared with HR *3500*, 63

Falk, Gene, 319

Family Assistance Plan (FAP), 5

Family cap: Blank's view, 131; Catholic Conference view, 255; compared in House and Senate bills, 231, 270; compared with Murray Light, 218; defined, 231; in Dole bill, 205, 213, 216; dropped in House-Senate conference, 250, 270; Faircloth's view, 209, 284; House Republican unity, 61; in HR *4* negotiations, 101; HR *3500* rewrite, 75–76; New Jersey welfare reform, 35; in NGA bill, 273, 274, 277; in Packwood bill, 202; Senate debate, 218–21; in WRB #3, 283–84, 315–16

Family composition since 1996, 355–58. *See also* Illegitimacy

Family Support Act of *1988*: Clinton's work, 116; effect of welfare expansion, 33; evolution of welfare policy, 75; Moynihan's view, 198; O'Beirne's view, 125–26; overview, 11–13; precondition for welfare reform, 18; Primus's view, 40; work requirements, 50–51, 173

Federal Interagency Forum on Child and Family Statistics, 338

Felton, Laurie, 46

Fierce, Don, 94, 198, 210

Finance Committee (Senate): in general subconference, 238; hearings on NGA bill, 277; jurisdiction over child care, 233; jurisdiction over Medicaid, 297; jurisdiction over welfare, 198; Packwood bill, 199–204; welfare reform hearings, 199; WRB #3 markup, 305
Fishing licenses, revocation for delinquent child support, 158–59
Fix, Michael, 359
Flag burning in HR 3500 rewrite #1, 76
Fleischer, Ari: hired, 90–91; HR 4 subcommittee markup, 159; planning HR 4 hearings, 108; Rules Committee, 169; work on WRB #3, 281, 282–83, 299
Flemming, Arthur, 14
Florio, Jim, 34–36
Focus on the Family, 21
Foglietta, Thomas, 191
Fond du Lac County (Wis.) caseload reduction, 258
Food Security Supplement (Census Bureau), 352
Food Stamps: compared in House and Senate bills, 230; described, 4; difficulties of welfare reform implementation, 345; in Dole bill, 208; Dole's role, 219; Kaus's view, 15–16; in NGA bill, 272–73; nutrition block grants, 46–47; in nutrition subconference, 238; in pre-1970s welfare, 5; time limits, 30; work and work support, 31–32; in WRB #3, 283, 316
Ford, Harold: on en block amendment, 185; HR 4 committee markup, 160; HR 4 hearing testimony, 127; HR 4 subcommittee markup, 143, 150–51; HR 1214, 172–73, 185; on Murray Light, 141–42; NGA bill hearings, 276; on orphanages, 145; questioning Murphy, 133; on work requirements, 50
Formula fight in Packwood bill, 204
Foster care system since 1996, 338–39
Foundation for Child Development, 337
Fowler, Tillie, 303, 305
Fox, Jon, 184
Frank, Barney, 191

Franks, Gary, 46, 52, 65
Freeman, Richard, 354
Frist, William, 195
Fuelner, Ed, 271–72
Fund, John, 197

Gag rule, 78–80
Gais, Thomas, 333
GAO. See General Accounting Office (GAO)
Garfinkel, Irwin, 34
Gaston, Brian, 77–78
General Accounting Office (GAO): on childhood disability, 176; inception, 242; social policy spending survey, 84; social program count, 5
General subconference: described, 237–38; first compromise offer, 238–39; first member meeting, 239–41
Gennetian, Lisa, 339–40, 357
Georgia welfare reform, 333
Gephardt, Richard: direct budget talks, 265; in HR 4 hearings, 109, 114–15; in Rules Committee, 170–71
Germanis, Peter, 47
Gibbons, Sam: on conference committee, 228; HR 4 committee markup, 160; HR 4 hearings, 111; HR 1214 floor debate, 185–86; HR 1214 opening statement, 172–73; motion to recommit HR 1214, 192; response to Shaw, 182
Gilens, Martin, 4
Gilliam Dorothy, 175
Gingrich, Newt: authority, 82, 86–88; on budget reconciliation bill, 245; on continuing resolution, 262; Contract with America, 70; direct budget talks, 263–66; on Dole, 230; HR 4 hearings, 108–09; HR 4 opening-day testimony, 111–14; HR 3500 threatened, 63; influence over Rules Committee, 169; on Medicaid dual eligibility, 321–24; Medicaid press conference, 296–97; Medicaid separation from welfare reform, 301–03, 305; meeting on Republican leadership, 300, 304–05; missteps after the 1994 election, 105;

missteps during shutdown, 251; on MOE, 265–66; reviving welfare reform, 271; on school lunch block grant, 259; on state control of welfare reform, 95; Weber-Shaw bill, 30; on Wisconsin waiver, 321; work with RGA, 198, 306; on WRB #1 House-Senate conference, 249; on WRB #3, 278, 306, 313, 314

Glassman, James, 280

Goodling, William: on conference committee, 228; HR 1214 sponsor, 166; HR 3500 rewrite #2, 96; on school lunch block grant, 259; WRB #3, 279

Gore, Al: direct budget talks, 265; Clinton's decision to sign welfare reform bill, 326; on WRB #3, 329

Goss, Porter, 312

Government Accountability Office. See General Accounting Office (GAO)

Government shutdown: advantage, Clinton, 251–53; first time, 246–47, 252–53; second time, 262–67

Governmental Affairs Committee (Senate), 199

Governors. See Democratic Governors Association (DGA); National Governors Association (NGA); Republican Governors Association (RGA)

Gradison, Bill, 24, 30

Graham, Lindsey, 223

Gramm, Phil: amendment to Dole bill, 225; on Dole bill, 205, 207, 209, 213; on family cap, 220; on felony drug convictions, 314–15; on HHS personnel, 233; influence on Senate proceedings, 195; Kennedy-Dodd amendment vote missed, 216; RGA view of penalty provision, 306; on welfare and illegitimacy, 218; WRB #3 House-Senate conference, 309, 314. See also Health and Human Services, U.S. Department of (HHS)

Grams, Rod, 195

Grandy, Fred, 46, 65

Grassley, Charles, 202, 218, 250

Green Book (House Ways and Means Committee), 6

Greenstein, Bob: on Medicaid reform, 297–98; on MOE in Dole bill, 214; on welfare and illegitimacy, 145–48

Greenwood, Jim, 187

Grogger, Jeff, 342

Grossman, Jim, 285, 308, 319

Hallow, Ralph, 67

Harkin, Tom, 199; amendment to Dole bill, 212

Harman, Jane, 190

Hatch, Orrin, 202, 314

Hatfield, Mark, 261

Haveman, Robert, 6, 34

Havemann, Judith, 206

Hayes, Jimmy: on reviving the Senate bill, 270; on separating Medicaid from welfare reform, 304, 305; WRB #3 meeting, 299, 305

Haynes, Margaret, 154

Head Start, 215

Health and Human Services, U.S. Department of (HHS): changes in WRB #3, 319; estimate of loss of benefits, 120–21; personnel cutbacks, 225, 233, 309; on poverty and single mothers, 336–37; Primus's working group, 289

Hearings, defined, 106–07. See also entries at HR 4

Hennessey, Jim, 250

Herbert, Bob, 175

Herger, Wally, 46

Heritage Foundation: on abstinence education, 234; HR 4 hearing testimony, 127; on illegitimacy, 62–63; interest in welfare reform, 21, 22; on Murray Light, 146; on NGA bill, 271–72; on Packwood bill, 203; strategy to right shift Republicans, 69

Hernandez, Donald, 338

Hershey, Mike, 72, 207

Hilley, John, 326

Hoagland, Bill, 245

Hobbs, Chuck, 33–34

Hobson, David, 311

"Home Alone" bill, 215

House bill. See entries at HR 1214

House of Representatives: committee and parliamentary status compared, 192; passed WRB #2, 259–61; passed WRB

#3, 313; process compared with Senate, 166, 194, 212. *See also* Republicans in the House; Rules Committee (House)

Housing and Urban Development, U.S. Department of, 289

Howard, Jack, 96, 97, 322

HR 4: based on HR *3500*, 272; Contract with American version, 97; introduced, 20; process, 21–23, 97–98; on reviving welfare reform, 269; status in January *1995*, 101. *See also entries at* HR *1214*; *subsequent entries*

HR *4* committee hearings, 107–26; Contract with America introduced, 110–12; first day, 109–14; planning, 107–09; second day, 114–22; third day, 122–26

HR *4* committee markup, 160–64; child support enforcement, 161–62; outcome, 162; part of megabill HR *1214*, 165–66

HR *4* subcommittee hearings, 126–33; procedural misstep, 128–30; purposes, 133–34

HR *4* subcommittee markup, 135–60; CBO cost survey, 152; child support enforcement, 153–59; completion, 159–60; Democrats' case against, 144; described, 137; first day, 140–48; markup compared with WRB #3, 286–87; preparation and staff, 138–40; procedures, 137–38; schedule, 140; second day, 148–50; Shaw chairing, 135–36; third day, 150–51; votes, 151; walk-through, 142–43; welfare and illegitimacy, 145–48; work requirements, 152–53; wrap-up, 151–60

HR *982*. *See* Deal bill (HR *982*)

HR *1157*, 163. *See also entries at* HR *4*

HR *1214* (the House bill): amendments summary, 188; Clinton's NGA speech, 205; compared with Clinton administration bill, 236–37; compared with Senate bill, 229–37; described, 171; includes HR *4*, 165–66; three competing bills, 167–68, 189–90, 191–92; TRIM analysis, 289

HR *1214*, Democratic arguments, 173–82; education and training benefits, 179; harshness to children, 175–78; low-wage workers, 179–81; "reverse Robin Hood" effect, 179; working family support, 181; work requirements, 173–75

HR *1214* floor debate, 184–93; amendments-in-order rule, 184–85; anti-abortion amendment, 187–88; child care amendment, 188; Deal bill (HR *982*), 189–90; en block amendment, 185–87; first day, 184–88; Mink bill (HR *1250*), 191–92; motion to adjourn, 186; motion to recommit, 192–93; opening statements, 184; second day, 188–90; technical amendment, 185; third day, 191–93; the vote, 192; vouchers amendment, 188; WIC amendment, 189

HR *1214* in the Rules Committee, 166–72; amendments, 169–70; Archer's opening statement, 172; chairman's rule, 168; Democratic welfare bills, 167; first rule, 171; function and processes, 166–67, 168; Gibbons's opening statement, 172–73; issued HR *1214*, 171; outcome, 183–84

HR *1250*. *See* Mink bill (HR *1250*)

HR *1600*, Interstate Child Support Enforcement Act, 154–55

HR *3500*: described, 65; Empower America memo, 66–67; interim period, 59; threatened from the right, 62–64; was Santorum-DeLay work group bill, 58

HR *3500* rewrite #*1*, 71–81; conservative influence, 76–78; cost, 77; illegitimacy, 74; issues in and out, 75–76; work group members, 72–73

HR *3500* rewrite #*2*: basis for HR *4*, 272; challenges of alteration, 86; overview of needed changes, 83–86; press relations, 88–91; process, 88, 91–93, 97; RGA influence, 94–102

Human Resources Subcommittee (House Ways and Means): Clay Shaw steps down, 41–42; HR *4* first markup, 140–48; influence on welfare reform, 43; WRB #3 markup, 282. *See also* HR *4* subcommittee markup

Humbel, Karen, 264
Hunting licenses, revocation for delinquent child support, 158–59
Hutchinson, Kay Bailey, 204
Hutchinson, Tim: HR *3500* rewrite, 73;
on NGA bill, 275; opposition to HR
*3500*, 64; Santorum-DeLay work
group bill, 56; Senate counterpart,
195; spending cap, 60; on work
requirements in HR *4*, 153. *See also*
Talent-Hutchinson bill
Hyde amendment to HR *1214*, 187–88
Hyde, Henry: on HR *1214* en block
amendment, 187; Hyde amendment,
187–88; Meyers letter, 53; Republican
Policy Committee, 47

Ickes, Harold, 326
Illegitimacy: among blacks, 9; building
unity among House Republicans,
61–62; compared in House and Senate bills, 231; consequences and, 67;
in Dole bill, 208, 216; Empower
America memo, 66; in HR *4*, 100–02,
126, 137; HR *1214* floor debate,
187–88; HR *3500* rewrite *#1*, 74,
75–76; Jeffords amendment, 223;
Murray's view, 10, 199–200; in NGA
bill, 277; in Packwood bill, 202–03; as
political issue, 7; Republican focus,
41; in Rules Committee, 170;
Santorum-DeLay work group, 52; in
the Senate bill, 270; Shalala's view,
117–18; since 1996, 355; Wednesday
Group report, 26; welfare and, 2, 7,
33, 145–48; working mothers and, 18;
work requirements vs., 54; in WRB *#1*
general subconference, 239; WRB *#3*
bonus, 316. *See also* Abstinence; Family composition
Income disregards, 6, 52
Indian Affairs Committee (Senate), 199
Individualized Functional Assessment of
SSI eligibility, 234
Inhofe, James, 195
Insurance principle, 3
Insurance programs in pre-*1970*s welfare,
4–5
Interethnic adoption in WRB *#3*, 316

Interstate Child Support Enforcement
Act, 154–55

Jameson, Booth, 310
Janet Cooke Award, 197
Jargowsky, Paul, 337
Jeffords, Jim: amendment to Senate bill,
223; on conference report, 260; on
Dole bill, 209; on Kennedy-Dodd
amendment, 215–16; in Senate conference committee, 259
Jencks, Christopher, 15, 352
Job Opportunities and Basic Skills Train-
ing Program (JOBS): compared in
House and Senate bills, 232; in Daschle
bill, 205; described, 12; in Dole bill,
208; in HR *3500* rewrite *#2*, 96–97
Johnson, Lyndon, 4
Johnson, Nancy: on charitable choice
provision, 234; on child care increase,
170; on child protection in Senate bill,
235; on child support enforcement in
HR *4*, 155; on HR *982*, 189; HR *3500*
rewrite, 72; on hunting, fishing
licenses and child support, 158; on
Medicaid dual eligibility, 318; on
Murray Light, 148; on RGA concerns
with WRB *#3*, 308–09; Santorum-
DeLay work group, 46, 65; on Shalala,
115; Shaw report, 31; on work
requirements, 54; WRB *#3* House-
Senate conference, 314
Johnson (Nancy) amendment to HR
*1214*, 188
Johnson, Sam, 300
Judiciary Committee (Senate), 199

Kahn, Chip, 264
Kammer, Fr. Fred, S.J., 294
Kantor, Mickey, 326, 327
Kaptur, Marcy, 190
Kasich, John: on budget reconciliation
bill, 245; direct budget talks, 265; on
separating Medicaid from welfare
reform, 304; on spending in NGA bill,
274; WRB *#3* House floor debate, 312
Kassebaum, Nancy: on conference com-
mittee, 228; on Dole bill, 209; on
Packwood bill, 199

Katz, Jeffrey, 304

Kauff, Jacqueline, 352–53

Kaus, Mickey, 15–16, 280–81

Kellogg, Virginia, 122–24

Kemp, Jack: on "moderate" welfare reform, 68–69; on Murray Light, 146; opposition to HR *3500*, 66

Keniry, Dan, 169

Kennedy, Edward: amendment to Dole bill, 212; on child care, 215, 223–24; on Packwood bill, 201

Kennedy, Joe, 186

Kennedy-Dodd amendment to Dole bill, 215–16

Kennelly, Barbara B.: on child support enforcement in HR *4*, 155; Commission on Interstate Child Support, 154; HR *4* subcommittee markup, 143

Kerry, John, 223; amendment to Dole bill, 212

King, John, 95

Kleczka, Gerald: HR *4* committee markup, 160; questioning Kellogg, 124; questioning Shalala, 120; votes with Republicans, 162, 164, 287

Kless, Kiki, 72, 311

Knox, Virginia, 357

Kolbe, Jim, 46, 192

Kondracke, Morton, 259, 269

Krauthammer, Charles, 41, 95

Kristol, William, 259

Kutler, Ed, 24, 142

Kyl, John, 195


Labor and Human Resources Committee (Senate), 199, 200–01

Labor, U.S. Department of, 289

LaFalce, John, 186

Land, Ken, 337–38

Lank, Heather, 307–08

Largent, Steve, 326

Leahy (Patrick) amendment to Dole bill, 212

Leavitt, Mike: on House passage, 260; on RGA concerns with WRB #*3*, 307–09; on state control of welfare reform, 95; on WRB #*3*, 278

Legislation: committees of jurisdiction, 279; development of, 91–93, 153, 278;

nature of, 20–21; path through the House, 166, 168, 192

Legislative hearings, 107

Legler, Paul, 155

Leonard, Paul, 310

Levin, Carl, 210, 223

Levin, Sander M.: on delayed vote, 149; HR *4* markups, 143, 160; NGA bill hearings, 276; questioning Kellogg, 123–24; on welfare and illegitimacy, 145–48; WRB #*3* markup, 286

Lewin Group, 360

Lewis, John: HR *4* committee markup, 160; HR *1214*, 182, 184; on WRB #*3*, 330

Licenses, revocation for delinquent child support, 158–59

Lichter, David, 336

Life after welfare, 334–35

Lincoln, Blanch, 189

Linder, John, 182

Local welfare offices, changes since *1996*, 333

*Looking Before We Leap* (Weaver and Dickens), 295–96

Loprest, Pamela, 351

*Losing Ground* (Murray), 9, 26, 45, 200

Lott, Trent: on RGA concerns with WRB #*3*, 306; on separating Medicaid from welfare reform, 301–02; WRB #*3* House-Senate conference, 314

Loury, Glenn, 13, 129–30

Low-income family issues: fathers since *1996*, 353–54; support, 339–40, 343

Low Income Opportunity Board, 14, 34

Low-wage jobs, 348–49

Low-wage workers in HR *1214*, 179–81

Lugar, Richard: on child nutrition in Senate bill, 235; on conference committee, 228; on school lunch block grant, 259

Lurie, Irene, 333

Lutheran Office of Government Ministries, 35


Mahan, Roger, 46, 278

Mahony, Cardinal Roger, 255

Maintenance of effort (MOE): Clinton's view, 265; compared in House and

Senate bills, 231–33; in Dole bill, 205, 209, 214; Gingrich's view, 265–66

Majority party: amendment process, 166–67; conference committee strategy, 227; in lawmaking, 136–37; procedural misstep, 128–29; Rules Committee strategy, 183; use of legislative hearings, 107, 126

"Make work pay," 15, 31

Maloney, Carolyn, 330

Manpower Demonstration Research Corporation (MDRC): marriage rates since 1996, 357; policy research, 11; on work programs and child well-being, 339–40

Mansfield Room court, 249–50

Mantho, Mary Kay, 96, 98–99

Market forces, governmental influence on, 28

Markup: in the Senate, 200–01; language for, 162–63. See also entries at HR 4 markup

Marriage incentive: conservative rhetoric, 8; New Jersey welfare reform, 35; Santorum-DeLay work group, 47–48, 53; Weber-Shaw bill, 30–31

Marriage rates for undereducated women, 356–57

Mathematica Policy Research, 351, 352–53

Matsui, Robert, 160

McCrery, Jim: on child protection block grants, 148–49; compared with Murphy, 133; general subconference, 239–41; questioning Shalala, 120–22; WRB #3 House-Senate conference, 314

McCurry, Mike, 252

McDermott, Jim: HR 4 committee markup, 160–61; language in final markup, 163; stalling the House, 326

McInnis, Scott, 325

McInnis resolution, 329

McKernan, John, 61

Mead, Larry, 10, 13

MediaWatch, 197

Medicaid: on childhood disability, 176; in Daschle bill, 205; described, 4; difficulties of welfare reform implementa-

tion, 345–47; dual eligibility in WRB #3, 318–19, 321–24; eligibility in Santorum-DeLay work group, 52; in HR 1214, 178; in NGA bill, 272, 274–75; NGA welfare agenda, 270–71; in pre-1970s welfare, 5; RGA concern, 309; separating from welfare reform, 296–305; time limits, 30; working family support, 181; in WRB #3, 278–79, 316, 318–19, 321–24

Medical services, 187

Medicare: described, 3–4; Gingrich's HR 4 hearing testimony, 112; HR 4 markups, 163; in pre-1970s welfare, 5

Meltdown, 322–23

"Me too, but less," 244, 261

Meyer, Bruce, 351–52

Meyer, Dan, 323–24

Meyers, Jan: AFDC reform bill, 44; HR 3500, 62; previous welfare reform bill, 52; Santorum-DeLay work group, 46, 57; state welfare reform, 53

Mica, John, 191

Michel, Bob, 55

Michigan welfare reform, 60, 333

Mikulski, Barbara, 212

Millard, Charles, 80

Miller, George, 185, 330

Miller, Gerry: finance markup, 305; HR 3500 rewrite #2, 96; reviving welfare reform, 270, 272

Miller, Robert, 296–97

Mills, Wilbur, 110

Mink, Patsy, 167

Mink bill (HR 1250): debate, 191–92; Democratic welfare bills, 167–68; in Rules Committee, 170; Shaw's view, 169

Minnesota Family Investment Program, 357

Minority party: amendment process, 166–67; motion to recommit strategy, 168; strategy, 54, 138, 167; strategy in conference committee, 227; use of legislative hearings, 107

Moakley, Joe, 170, 325, 326

MOE. See Maintenance of effort

Moffitt, Robert, 351

Mondale, Walter, 5

Mondale-Brademas child care legislation, 5

Morella, Connie, 155, 185, 190

Morris, Dick: Clinton adviser, 244, 263; influence over Clinton, 287; on WRB #3, 320

Morris, Pamela, 339

Moseley, Phil: after the *1994* election, 85–86; conference committee strategy, 237; markup preparation, 138; planning HR *4* hearings, 107–09; Rules Committee, 169; Santorum-DeLay work group, 45

Moseley-Braun (Carol) amendments: to Dole bill, 212; to Packwood bill, 201

Motion to recommit: described, 168; HR *1214*, 169, 192–93; WRB #3, 312–13

Moynihan, Daniel Patrick: on AFDC block grant, 177; amendment to Dole bill, 212; amendment to Packwood bill, 201; on benefits loss, 120; on Catholic Conference, 257; contention with Clinton on welfare reform, 37, 292; on criminality among low-income fathers, 354; on health care reform, 103; in illegitimacy, 28, 218; on single-parent families, 9; on the TRIM analysis, 291; welfare reform in the Senate, 198, 206; on Wilson, 129; on WRB #1 conference committee, 229

Moynihan amendments: to Dole bill, 212; to Packwood bill, 201

Murkowski, Frank, 202

Murphy, Patrick, 132–33

Murray, Charles: arguments against, 131; Ellwood's and Bane's views, 38; endorsed HR *3500*, 65; on illegitimacy, 7, 26, 41, 62; NPC speech episode, 146; testimony on Packwood bill, 199–200; unwed teen mothers' benefits, 45; on welfare and illegitimacy, 145–46; on welfare dependency, 9–10; on welfare entitlement, 28; Working Seminar member, 13

Murray, Kasia, 350

Murray Light: Blank's view, 131; Catholic Conference view, 255; compared in House and Senate bills, 231, 270;

compared with family cap, 218; defined, 202, 231; in Dole bill, 205, 216; Faircloth's view, 209; fundamental questions, 219; in HR *4*, 101, 162; HR *3500* rewrite, 75–76; Kellogg's view, 122–24; Murphy's view, 132–33; in NGA bill, 277; "Real Welfare Reform Bill," 69; Shalala's view, 120; state responses, 55–56; state welfare reform, 53; unwed teen mothers' benefits, 45; Wilson's and Loury's views, 129–30. *See also* Unwed teen mothers' benefits

Nathan, Richard, 199, 333

National Baptist Convention, *1994*, 8

National Black Women's Health Project, 127

National Child Support Enforcement Association (NCSEA), 156

National Conference of State Legislatures, 21

National Council of State Legislatures, 215

National Family Planning and Reproductive Health Association, 80

National Governors Association (NGA): building unity, 93; Clinton's campaign promise, 37; Clinton speech on HR *1214*, 205; Clinton's work, 116; HR *4* hearing testimony, 126; interest in welfare reform, 21; reviving welfare reform, 270–71; split over Medicaid, 278–79.

National Governors Association bill: hearings, 276–77; overview, 270–71; strategy, 275, 278

National Organization for Women, 35

National Press Club (NPC), 146–47

National Republican Congressional Committee (NRCC), 55, 57

National Survey of American Families, 355–56

National Welfare Rights and Reform Union, 127

National Women's Law Center, 155

Neal, Richard, 161

Nelson, Sandi, 355–56

*The New Consensus* (Novak), 125, 254

New Deal, 85
New Hope project, 258, 356–57
New Jersey Council of Churches, 35
New Jersey welfare reform, 34–35, 61
New paternalism, 34. *See also* Welfare-to-
    work programs
*New Republic*, 16–17
*New York Times*: characterized, 293; on
    HR *1214* harshness to children, 175;
    poll during second shutdown,
    262–63; on welfare reform, 260
New York welfare reform, 333
NGA. *See* National Governors Association
Nickles, Don: amendment to Packwood
    bill, 202; WRB *#3* House-Senate con-
    ference, 309, 314; on WRB *#3* intro-
    duction, 285; WRB *#3* meeting, 318
Niemoller, Martin, 182
Nixon, Richard, 1, 5
Noncitizen welfare benefits: in Dole bill,
    208; in general subconference, 238; in
    HR *4* hearing testimony, 126; in HR *4*
    negotiations, 102; in HR *4* subcom-
    mittee markup, 137; in NGA bill, 272;
    in Packwood bill, 203; Republican
    governors' opposition, 60; in
    Santorum-DeLay work group, 51;
    since *1996*, 358–60; in WRB *#3*, 316
Nonmarital births. *See* Illegitimacy
Novak, Michael: on frugal government,
    124–25; on welfare reform, 254;
    Working Seminar sponsor, 13
Novak, Robert: on Burke, 196–97; on
    reviving the Senate bill, 270; on WRB
    *#3* introduction, 284
NPC. *See* National Press Club
Nussle, Jim, 149–50, 161
Nutrition subconference, 238. *See also*
    General subconference

O'Beirne, Kate: compared with Blank,
    131; HR *4* committee hearings,
    125–26; on welfare and work, 17
Office of Legislative Counsel, 92–93
Office of Management and Budget
    (OMB), 261, 291, 292, 350, 356
Offner, Paul, 198
Okun, Bob, 55
Orphanages, 118–19, 145

Oversight hearings, 106

Packwood, Bob, 195–96
Packwood bill, 199–207; amendments
    summary, 201–02; defeated, 202–03;
    overview, 203
Panetta, Leon: Clinton adviser, 244, 252,
    325; distribution tables, 289; *Today
    Show* appearance, 253; Clinton's deci-
    sion to sign welfare reform bill, 326;
    on WRB *#3*, 327
Parental responsibility: in Dole bill, 209;
    Santorum-DeLay work group, 47–48;
    in Weber-Shaw bill, 30–31
Parent-Teacher's Association, 215
Parliamentary status of the House, 192
Passel, Jeffrey, 359
Paternity establishment: in HR *4* negotia-
    tions, 101; Santorum-DeLay work
    group, 52; Shalala's view, 117–18
Patterson, Orlando, 354
Paull, Lindy, 264–65
Pavetti, LaDonna, 352–53
Paxon, Bill, 46, 52
Pear, Robert, 204, 270
Pelosi, Nancy, 330
Perot, Ross, 243
Phelps, D'Arcy, 319
Phillips, Kevin, 25
Pianin, Eric, 261
Plain English for markups, 162–63
Plotnick, Robert, 6
Politics, politicians: compared with social
    scientists, 49, 130; HR *3500* rewrite,
    73; minority party strategy, 54
*The Politics of Rich and Poor* (Phillips), 25
*Poor Support* (Ellwood), 15
Poverty, 24, 29
Pratt, Margaret, 139–40
Pressler, Larry, 202
Press relations: compared with social sci-
    ences, 91; House Republicans, 89–91;
    HR *4*, 108, 151–52; Medicaid separa-
    tion from welfare reform, 296–97,
    303–04; WRB *#3*, 280–81
Primus, Wendell: on the Family Support
    Act of *1988*, 40; on floundering sin-
    gle mothers, 350; HR *4* subcommit-
    tee markup, 143–44; on Nussle's

comment, 149–50; TRIM analysis, 288–93
Project on the Welfare of Families, 14
Pro-life amendment in HR *1214* floor debate, 187–88
*The Promise of American Life* (Croly), 16
Pryce, Deborah, 170
Public housing in Dole bill, 208
Public policy, bases of, 296

Raines, Franklin, 13
Ramsey County (Minn.), 352–53
Rand Corporation, 361–62
Random-assignment studies, 332, 339–40
Rangarajan, Anu, 351
Rangel, Charlie: on Catholic Conference, 256; on child protection block grants, 148–49; on Clinton's support of WRB #3, 330; Gingrich's response, 113; HR *4* committee markup, 160; HR *4* subcommittee markups, 143, 145, 151; NGA bill hearings, 276; on Nussle's comment, 149–50; procedural misstep, 129; questioning Kellogg, 123, 124; questioning Wilson and Loury, 130; in WRB #3 markup, 286
Reagan, Ronald: attempts at welfare reform, 5; on EITC, 235–36; Low Income Opportunity Board, 14; on work requirements, 64
"Real people" in HR *4* committee hearings, 122
"Real Welfare Reform Bill," 69–70
Reconciliation process, 247, 250, 279
Rector, Robert: on abstinence education, 234; on Castle-Tanner bill, 311; on Dole bill, 209; on family cap, 221, 284, 315; HR *4* hearing testimony, 127; on illegitimacy, 52, 62–63; on Murray Light, 146; on NGA bill, 271–73, 275; NPC speech episode, 146; on Packwood bill, 203; on Senate Republican welfare bills, 206; spending cap in Santorum-DeLay work group bill, 56; on state control of welfare reform, 95–96; on welfare reform, 44; on work requirements in HR *4*, 152–53
Redick, LeAnne: Finance markup, 305;

HR *3500*, 60; on Medicaid dual eligibility, 323; reviving welfare reform, 270; on RGA concerns with WRB #3, 306, 307–08, 317; work on HR *3500* rewrite #2, 96, 98–99; work with Santorum-DeLay work group, 56
Redistribution of income, 4
Reed, Bruce: Clinton adviser, 82; Clinton's welfare task force, 38; on the TRIM analysis, 290; Clinton's decision to sign welfare reform bill, 326; on WRB #3, 320, 327–28
Reich, Robert, 320, 326
Reischauer, Robert, 13, 147
Religion's access to public funds, 209, 234
Republican conference: on separating Medicaid from welfare reform, 302–03, 305; strategy meeting, 311. *See also subsequent Republican entries*
Republican Governors Association: building unity, 60–61; Contract with America, 86; HR *4* demands, 100–02; HR *3500* rewrite #2, 93, 99; influence on Packwood bill, 203–04; influence on Senate proceedings, 198–99; letter to Clinton, 260; on Medicaid reform, 296–97, 298; on school lunch block grant, 259; supporting Dole bill, 210; on welfare reform, 22, 97; Williamsburg meeting, 94–98, 100, 198, 210, 272; on work requirements, 144, 174; work with Santorum-DeLay work group, 55–56; WRB #3 concerns, 305–11; WRB #3 meeting, 317–19
Republican National Committee, 299
Republican Party: *1995* congressional takeover, 18; on balancing the budget, 243; building unity, 54–58; on the CBPP, 297–98; constituency described, 236; early days of majority, 104–05, 166; House minority, 24; internal division, 54–55; learning to govern, 305; on Medicaid reform, 298; on risk to children, 178; on scholars and the media, 146; shift to the right, 43, 69; on taxes, 179; values, 243; on work requirements, 174
Republican Policy Committee, 47

Republican revolution: floundering, 267; House Republicans' view, 280; revival, 285–86

Republicans, 23, 136

Republicans in the House: building unity, 61–62; Contract with America, 83; HR *3500* rewrite #2, 99; on illegitimacy, 68; infighting, 63–64, 86–87; press relations, 89–91; WRB #3 introduction, 284–85

Republicans in the Senate, 63, 68

Republican unity: after the second veto, 274; committee level, 165; compared with Democratic unity, 81; in the conference committee, 228; in the House, 61–62, 183, 311; HR *3500* rewrite #2, 99; on hunting, fishing licenses and child support, 158–59; in lawmaking, 136–37; in the RGA, 60–61; in Rules Committee, 183; in the Senate, 63, 201, 206, 207, 213, 215–16, 218; summary of opposition, 296; welfare reform, 148; work requirements in HR 4, 153; WRB #3, 280–81, 313

"Reverse Robin Hood," 178–79

RGA. *See* Republican Governors Association

Ricard, Bishop John H., 255, 256–57

*Rituals of Blood* (Patterson), 354

Rivlin, Alice: Clinton adviser, 244; direct budget talks, 265; response to the TRIM analysis, 291; Working Seminar member, 13

Roberts, Cokie, 284

Roberts, Pat: on conference committee, 228; HR *1214* sponsor, 166; reviving welfare reform, 271; WRB #3, 279

Rockefeller, John, 223

Romer, Roy, 296–97

Roosevelt, Franklin D.: Social Security Act of *1935*, 3; on welfare and work, 17; on welfare dependency, 142

Rosebud Sioux Tribe, 127

Rossi, Peter, 2

Rostenkowski, Dan, 87, 99

Roth, William: on illegitimacy in Packwood bill, 202; reviving welfare reform, 271; on RGA concerns with

WRB #3, 306; WRB #1 conference committee, 228; WRB #1 general subconference, 239–41; on WRB #3, 278, 284; WRB #3 House-Senate conference, 314

Roukema, Marge, 154–55, 189

Roukema amendment to HR *1214* WIC, 189

Rubin, Robert, 244, 326

Rubiner, Laurie, 239–41

Rules Committee (House): function, 166, 168; WRB #3, 311–13. *See also* HR *1214* in the Rules Committee

Samuels, Leslie, 109

Samuelson, Robert, 41, 263

Santorum, Rick: on child care, 224; final push in the Senate, 224–26; HR *3500* rewrite, 72; joins Ways and Means, 42–43; new conservative senator, 195; on Republican disunity in the Senate, 206; role in Senate welfare reform, 206–07; surprising Senate leadership, 196; testimony on Packwood bill, 199; WRB #3 House-Senate conference, 314

Santorum-DeLay work group, 45–58; bill designated HR *3500*, 58; decisions, 51–54; defending HR *3500*, 64–66; membership, 46; opening agenda, 47–48; pie chart, 48–50; welfare mom chart, 50–51; work requirements, 54; work with Republican governors, 55–56

Sawhill, Isabel, 337

Schilling, Edward, 258

Schneider, Andy, 321

Schneider, Judy, 138–39

Schoeni, Robert, 350

School choice in HR *3500* rewrite #1, 76

School lunch block grant, 259

School prayer, 76, 79

Senate: passed WRB #3, 313; process compared with House, 166, 194, 212; shift to the right, 195; welfare reform passed WRB #2 conference committee, 259–61. *See also* Republicans in the Senate

Senate welfare reform bill (the Senate bill): amendments, 211–13, 214–15; amendment votes, 221–22, 223, 225–26; compared with Clinton administration bill, 236–37; compared with House bill, 229–37; Daschle bill, 205–06, 208, 212; Dole and Daschle reconciliation, 222–26; family cap debate, 218–21; the final push, 224–26; influences, 194–99; markup, 200–01; overview, 199; Packwood bill, 199–204; revived after Clinton's second veto, 269–70; swallowed by budget reconciliation bill, 241–42, 247; TRIM analysis, 289. *See also* Budget reconciliation bill

Service Employees International Union, 127

Seven continents analogy, 21

Shalala, Donna: on Daschle bill, 205; on House and Senate bills, 236; HR *4* hearings, 109, 114, 115–22; on HR *4* subcommittee markup, 141; NPC speech, 146–47; Primus's working group, 289, 290; on Republican welfare reform bill, 254; Clinton's decision to sign welfare reform bill, 326; on WRB #*3*, 320

Shaw, E. Clay, Jr.: Catholic Conference meeting, 254–58; on charitable choice provision, 234; on child support enforcement in HR *4*, 153, 157–59; on Clinton's welfare task force, 39–41; on delayed vote, 149; on Democratic welfare bills, 167–68; on Ford's closing statement, 150–51; HR *4*, 20, 107–09, 135–36; on HR *982*, 189; in HR *1214* rules debate, 172; HR *3500* rewrite #*1*, 73; HR *3500* rewrite #*2*, 96–102; *Los Angeles Times* article, 88–89; leadership in WRB #*3*, 280–81; on maintaining welfare conference work, 247; on Medicaid dual eligibility, 321–24; Medicaid separation from welfare reform, 302–03, 305; report on poverty and legislation, 31–32; Republican leadership meeting, 300; response to Lewis, 182; reviving the Senate bill, 269–70; on RGA concerns

with WRB #*3*, 306–09; Rules Committee, 169; Santorum-DeLay work group, 46; on school lunch block grant, 259; Senate counterpart, 195–96; Ways and Means subcommittees, 41–42; Weber-Shaw bill, 30–31; on welfare and work, 6–7; work requirements, 54, 152–53; work with Republican governors, 198; on WRB #*1* conference committee, 228; WRB #*3*, 278, 280–81, 299; in WRB #*3* final debate, 330–31; WRB #*3* House floor debate, 313; WRB #*3* House-Senate conference, 309–11, 314; on WRB #*3* introduction, 284; in WRB #*3* markup, 287

Shays, Chris, 46, 51, 52

Shear, Jeff, 292

Sheldon, Andrea, 207

Shift to the right: effect on welfare reform, 191–92; Heritage Foundation strategy, 69; problems with Packwood bill, 203; in Republican Party, 230; in the Senate, 195; WRB #*1* conference committee strategy, 229

Shogren, Elizabeth, 88–89, 259, 291

Simpson, Alan, 202, 216

Single mothers. *See* Unwed mothers

Skylstad, Bishop William, 256–57, 294

Smith, Chris, 108, 139, 187; amendment to HR *1214*, 188

Smith, Marilyn, 156

Smith, Scot, 139–40

Snowe, Olympia: on conference report, 260; on Dole bill, 205, 209; new moderate senator, 195

Social policy: CRS-GAO spending survey, 84; pre-*1970*s overview, 2–5

Social sciences, social scientists: compared with politicians, 49, 130; compared with press relations, 91; Faircloth's view, 147; on proper research, 332

Social science study. *See* TRIM analysis

Social Security, 4–5

Social Security Act of *1935*, 2, 3

Social Security Administration, 361–62

Social Security Disability Insurance (SSDI), 360–62

Solomon, Gerald, 166, 184–85

Speaker of the House, 169

Special Supplemental Nutrition (WIC), 47, 172

Specter, Arlen, 209, 260

Spending: CRS-GAO social policy survey, 84; historical overview, 5; in NGA bill, 274; Wednesday Group report, 25–26

Spending cap: in HR *3500*, 66; in HR *3500* rewrite #2, 83, 98; Hutchinson proposal, 57, 60–61; "Real Welfare Reform Bill," 69; Republican governors' opposition, 60–61; Santorum-DeLay work group bill, 56

Staffers, congressional, described, 22–23

Stark, Pete: on child services, 277; HR *4* committee markup, 160; HR *4* subcommittee markup, 143, 145; late for a vote, 149; NGA bill hearings, 276; on Social Security, 113; in WRB #3 markup, 286

State waivers, 300, 317, 319–20

State welfare reform: block grants, 44–45, 84–85; caseload expansion, 32–33; child support enforcement, 156; encouraged since *1985*, 333–34; HR *3500* rewrite, 75–76; Lurie's study, 333; Michigan, 60; New Jersey, 34–35, 61; Santorum-DeLay work group, 53; successes, 258; unwed mothers benefits, 44–45; Wisconsin, 34, 60; Wisconsin waiver, 300, 319–20

Stenholm, Charlie, 189, 278–79

Stephanopoulos, George, 326

Sullivan, Bishop Joseph, 256–57

Sullivan, James, 351–52

Supplemental Security Income (SSI): compared in House and Senate bills, 230; described, 4; in HR *4* hearing testimony, 126; in HR *4* markups, 137, 162; HR *1214* harshness to children, 175–76; in NGA bill, 272, 275; in Packwood bill, 203; in pre-*1970*s welfare, 5; in Senate bill, 234–35; since *1996*, 360–62; in WRB #1 general subconference, 237, 241

Talent, Jim: on Castle-Tanner bill, 310–11; on family cap, 221, 284, 315–16; HR *4*, 20, 152–53; HR *3500* opposition,

62–64; HR *3500* rewrite #1, 72; on Murray Light, 131–32; on NGA bill, 275; NPC speech episode, 146; "Real Welfare Reform Bill," 69; on the Senate bill, 270; Senate counterpart, 195; on work requirements in HR *4*, 152–53; on WRB #1 conference committee, 228; WRB #3 House-Senate conference, 314; WRB #3 meeting, 318

Talent-Hutchinson bill, 77

TANF. *See* Temporary Assistance for Needy Families (TANF)

Tanner, John, 189, 310, 312

Tarplin, Rich, 309, 319

Task Force on Poverty and Welfare, 14

Tauzin, Billy, 305

Tax reform, Gingrich's HR *4* testimony, 112

Technical amendment to HR *1214*, 185

Temporary Assistance for Needy Families (TANF): described, 1; in general subconference, 238–39; research since *1996*, 332–33; RGA concern, 308–09; in Senate bill, 234; in WRB #3, 315

Texas welfare reform, 333

Thomas, Bill, 161, 163, 304

Thomas, Craig, 195

Thompson, Fred, 195

Thompson, Tommy: on child services, 277; on House passage of WRB #2, 260; Medicaid press conference, 296–97; NGA bill hearings, 276; on Packwood bill, 203; reviving welfare reform, 270; Santorum-DeLay work group, 56; state welfare reform, 60, 93, 95; Wisconsin waiver, 319–20; Wisconsin welfare reform, 34, 35; on WRB #3, 278

Time limits: in Daschle bill, 205; dropped in WRB #1 House-Senate conference, 250; early recommendation, 15; in HR *4* negotiations, 102; in HR *4* subcommittee markup, 137; in HR *1214*, 177–78; in Packwood bill, 203; Republican reasoning, 27–30; Shalala's view, 117; Weber-Shaw bill, 30–31; Wednesday Group report, 27

Title XX, 308–09

Tobin, Kathy, 278, 281
*Today Show*, 253
Toffler, Alvin, 112
Traditional Value Coalition, 207
Transfer model income (TRIM) analysis, 288–93
Treasury, U.S. Department of, 289
TRIM analysis. *See* Transfer model income (TRIM) analysis
Turner, Jona, 139

Unemployment Compensation, 3, 5
Unwed mothers: floundering, challenge of welfare reform, 349–53; unemployment rates, 334–35
Unwed teen mothers' benefits: conservative welfare reform, 44–45; House Republicans' view, 61; in HR 4 committee markup, 162; HR *1214* Hyde amendment, 187–88; Murray's view, 199–200; research support, 145–47; state welfare reform, 53. *See also* Murray Light
Urban Institute: on child poverty, 337; on family composition, 355–56; on floundering single mothers, 351; on noncitizen benefits, 359; TRIM analysis, 289–93
Urban League, 277
*USA Today*, 175
U.S. Chamber of Commerce, 21
U.S. Supreme Court, *Zebley* decision on childhood disability, 175

Vobejda, Barbara, 147, 237
Volkmer, Harold, 184, 325
Vouchers amendment in HR *1214* floor debate, 188

Waivers, state, in WRB #3, 317
Waldholtz, Enid, 170
Walker, Bob, 320–21
Walk-through: described, 137–38; HR 4 committee markup, 161; HR 4 subcommittee markup, 142–44
Ward, Mike, 326
War on Poverty, 4, 85
*Washington Post*: characterized, 293; on HR *1214* harshness to children, 175;

on MOE in Dole bill, 214; on NPC speech episode, 146; on reviving the Senate bill, 269–70; on welfare reform, 260; on WRB #3, 293
*Washington Times*, 194
Waters, Maxine: amendments to HR *1214*, 170; Hayes's imitation, 299; on WRB #3, 330
Wattenberg, Ben, 41
Waxman, Henry, 50–51
Ways and Means Committee (House): HR 4 markup, 160–64; HR *3500* rewrite, 77–78; jurisdiction over AFDC and child care, 279; jurisdiction over welfare, 83, 165; Medicaid separation from welfare reform, 298, 302–03; Republican leadership meeting, 300–01; Republican unity, 183; Senate counterpart, 195–96; subcommittees listed, 41; in WRB #1 general subconference, 238
Wealth and consequences of behavior, 29
Weaver, Kent, 295–96
Weber, Vin: Empower America memo, 66–67; on illegitimacy, 62; on "moderate" welfare reform, 68–69; opposition to HR *3500*, 66; Wednesday Group, 24
Weber-Shaw bill, 30–31
Wednesday Group: established, 24; groundwork for welfare reform, 65; on illegitimacy, 62; report, 25–26
Weidinger, Matt: HR 4 subcommittee markup, 153; HR 4 subcommittee markup staff, 139–40; on "medical services," 187; on NGA bill, 274; response to letter to Dole, 260; on reviving welfare reform, 269; WRB #3 floor debate, 308
Weld, William, 93
Weldon, Dave, 326
Welfare: caseload expansion after *1989*, 32–33; compared with low-wage work, 180–81; evolution of policy, 74–75; illegitimacy and, 7, 145–48, 218
Welfare dependency: as behavioral dysfunction, 13–14; illegitimacy and, 7–10; studies and statistics, 6–7; Working Seminar report, 13–14; work programs, 10–13

Welfare mothers, 258. *See also* Unwed mothers; Unwed teen mothers' benefits

Welfare reform: background, 14–19; benefits loss, 120–22; Clinton's view, 118; cost, 39; cost shifting, 60; debate of *1987–88*, 11–12; history, 5–6; influences in the Senate, 194–99; "moderate," 68–69; O'Beirne's view, 126; party unity compared, 81; second HR *3500* committee, 87; shift to the right, 191–92; six enabling conditions, 18–19; state control, 93–98, 100–02; tipping point, 148. *See also entries at HR 3500; entries at* HR *4*; Murray Light; National Governors Association bill; State welfare reform

Welfare reform bill *#1* (WRB *#1*): Clinton veto, 253; government shutdown (first), 246–47, 251–53; swallowed by budget reconciliation, 241–42, 245, 247. *See also* Budget reconciliation bill

Welfare reform bill *#1*, conference, 227–41; composition, 227, 228–29; concurrent with budget reconciliation conference, 247; Democrats excluded, 229, 236; Dole's skill, 247; general subconference, 238–41; Mansfield Room court, 249–50; only public meeting, 237; premeeting strategy, 237; Republican bills and Clinton administration bill compared, 236–38; staff work, 237–38; two subconferences described, 237–38

Welfare reform bill *#2* (WRB *#2*): to Clinton, 261–67; Clinton veto, 266–67; government shutdown (second), 262–67; keeping welfare reform alive, 254; passed House and Senate, 259–61; state-level success, 258

Welfare reform bill *#2*, conference, 254–61; concurrent with budget reconciliation conference, 254; meeting with Catholic bishops, 254–58; school lunch block grant, 259

Welfare reform bill *#3* (WRB *#3*): Clinton signs, 331; committee draft and markups, 279–80; first draft from

NGA bill, 278; House floor debate, 311–13; introduction, 282–83, 284–85; markups, 282, 286 87; part of reconciliation bill, 279; passed House and Senate, 313, 331; press coverage, 280–81; remaining issues, 283–84; reviving the debate, 268–70; separating Medicaid, 296–305; wide-ranging opposition, 293–96

Welfare reform bill *#3*, conference, 305–13, 314–31; the final debate, 329–31; House-Senate conference, 305–11; Medicaid dual eligibility, 321–24; meeting with governors, 317–19; Republican strategy meeting, 314–16; stalling the House, 324–26; technical changes, 319; Clinton's decision to sign welfare reform bill, 326–29; Wisconsin waiver, 319–20

Welfare reform implementation: child support enforcement, 358; child well-being, 335–40; economic recession, 343–44; family composition, 355–58; five challenges summarized, 342–43; low-income family support, 340–42; low-income fathers, 353–54; low-wage jobs, 348–49; noncitizen welfare benefits, 358–60; party views compared, 337; research since *1996*, overview, 332–33; single mothers floundering, 349–53; SSI and SSDI caseloads, 360–62; state-level study, 333; work support programs, 344–48

Welfare research, 2–3, 30

Welfare Restructuring Project (Vt.), 357

Welfare spells, 49

Welfare-to-work programs: affect on marriage rates, 356–57; compared in House and Senate bills, 232; HR *4* hearing testimony, 126; inception of, 10–11; research support, 65; since *1996*, 334–35. *See also* Work requirements

Wellstone (Paul) amendment to Dole bill, 212

Wetzstein, Cheryl, 147, 237

Weyrich, Paul, 197

Whitburn, Gerry, 96

Whitman, Christine Todd, 95

Whole House on the State of the Union, 192

WIC (Women, Infants, and Children), 47, 172, 189

Will, George, 41

Williamsburg meeting of the RGA, 94–98, 100, 198; lasting effects, 210, 272

Wilson, James Q., 128, 129–30

Winder, Katie, 351

Wines, Michael, 280

Winship, Scott, 352

Wisconsin waiver, 300, 319–20

Wisconsin welfare reform, 34, 60

Wise, Robert, 325

Wolf analogy, 191

Wolfensberger, Donald, 166

Wood, Robert G., 351

Work: Kaus's view, 16; low-wage and welfare compared, 180–81; as redemptive, 10–11; welfare and, 2, 6. *See also subsequent entries*

Work and Responsibility Act, 116, 236–37

Workers' rights in WRB #3, 316

Work Experience and Job Training, 34

Work Incentive (WIN), 11–12

Working family support in HR 1214, 181

Working mothers and AFDC, 18. *See also* Murray Light

Working Seminar welfare dependency report, 13–14

Work preparation, 48

Work requirements: AFDC proposal, 40; cost, 48; in Daschle bill, 205, 210; Democrats' view, 144; in Dole bill, 205, 208, 210; Empower America memo, 66; in HR 4 committee markup, 162; in HR 4 negotiations, 100–02; HR 4 strengthened, 152–53; in HR 4 subcommittee markup, 137; HR 1214 floor debate, 173–75; HR 3500 opposition, 64–65; HR 3500 rewrite #1, 75–76; illegitimacy versus, 54; incomes compared, 50; New Hope project, 258; New Jersey welfare reform, 35; in NGA bill, 272–74; in Packwood bill, 203; "Real Welfare Reform Bill," 69; RGA view, 144; in Rules Committee, 170; Santorum-DeLay work group, 47–48, 52; in the Senate bill, 270; two-parent family coverage, 44; Weber-Shaw bill, 30–31. *See also* Welfare-to-work programs

Work support: programs since 1996, 344–48; in Shaw report, 31

Wright, Jim, 102

*Zebley* decision on childhood disability, 175

Zedlewski, Sheila, 289, 293, 351